Justice, Courtesy
and Love

*Theologians and Missionaries
Encountering World Religions,
1846–1914*

Kenneth Cracknell

EPWORTH PRESS

0 7162 0501 7

First published 1995
by Epworth Press
1 Central Buildings Westminster
London SW1H 9NR

Phototypeset by Intype, London and
printed in Great Britain by
Mackays of Chatham, Kent

Justice, Courtesy and Love

For Susan

Contents

Preface

The issues dealt with in this book have occupied me for more than twenty-five years. They concern the relationship of Christian faith to other religious traditions. There is of course a rapidly growing amount of work in this area, and much of it treats the subject with great seriousness and fine theological insight. But often these writings begin in a different place from where I am. For me, as a teacher of Christian theology to potential ministers, priests and pastors of the churches, and therefore as one who must deal with questions of mission, evangelism and witness, the way Christian faith is understood in relation to other faith is neither merely theoretical nor just academic (though it is also properly both). The way the relation of Christianity to other religions is perceived necessarily determines fundamental attitudes in such circles. How important it is to get it right and how disastrous the result of getting it wrong I have learnt from personal experience of missionary activity in Africa, from reflection on my researches into missionary literature and history in India, Japan, China and the Muslim world, and through my involvement in interfaith dialogue in most parts of the world. I need to share something of this life story because it has determined the way in which this book has been written.

In 1962 the Methodist Missionary Society sent me to West Africa to undertake educational and theological work. I was stationed in Eastern Nigeria and worked particularly with the Igbo people, though my colleagues and students in the colleges in which I served came from many other tribal and linguistic backgrounds. But despite the many happy memories, my chief recollection of my years in Africa is tinged with sadness at a theological level. I missed so many opportunities both to learn and to teach in those years because I had not woken from a deep dogmatic slumber. Surrounded by manifestations of godliness and true faith, I could not see what lay under my nose. For I had arrived with a hopelessly inadequate theological framework for the kind of work that I now know could have been done. Like many others, I was convinced that the missionary task was to bring the light of Christ to heathen darkness. The task I thought I had to undertake was primary evangelism leading to conversion. In the traditional Methodist language, I had 'nothing to do except to save souls'.

But deepening experience, including learning the Igbo language, led me to realize that the Igbo and the other peoples of Africa knew much about God before ever a white missionary set foot in their territory. The Igbos knew of both the high God, the transcendent Being, who was called Chukwu, and the immanent form of deity called Chi. Words like 'grace' and 'holy' as well as subtle and fascinating insights into divine-human relations were all already present in Igbo vocabulary. God was everywhere in Igbo thought and speech. But even when I eventually recognized this knowledge of God among the Igbo and other peoples I was still perplexed. Where did it originate? Was it 'original revelation'? Was it to be interpreted as left over from humanity's paradisal state? Could the Igbos along with the other tribes of West Africa be descendants of the ten tribes of the Israelites, dispersed among the nations since the fall of Samaria in 721 BCE? All these ideas were suggested in the writings of some other missionaries about the religions of West African peoples. Such authors believed that the African knowledge of God was genuine, but distorted or corrupted.

But this was hard for me to accept. My own formation had rejected any talk of 'points of contact' and of building upon the religion that already existed among those to whom the missionary went. Barth and Kraemer, I thought, had taught that religion was a purely human work and as such 'the affair of sinful men'. Other respected teachers in the Selly Oak Colleges and elsewhere suggested that the closer their resemblance to Christian faith the more dangerous it was, for had not the most religious people in the house of Israel conspired to put Jesus to death, 'in the name of religion'? Radical displacement of the old by the new was still the most appropriate missiological stance.

Torn between these conflicting points of view and urgently seeking a proper understanding of the significance of West African religion for Christian theology I found, rather to my surprise, that I had the help of missionary predecessors who had travelled the same road and found themselves in a similar quandary. When I started to read books about other religious traditions written by Christian missionaries (rather than textbooks by 'comparative religionists') I discovered that they had frequently addressed the question of the presence of the God and Father of our Lord Jesus Christ in his self-revelation within 'heathen' cultures. Long before I arrived in Africa, and in many cases long before I was even born they had delineated a positive and helpful outline of a theology of religion which was of profound help to me. With a sense of great excitement I abandoned other academic projects and began to read avidly journals and diaries, biographies and autobiographies from those who had gone before me.

At first I read just the works of the immediately preceding generations, and particularly those who had worked in Africa. In the earliest stages of my quest, my understanding of African religion was re-shaped by a range of pioneering works by two missionary scholars within my Methodist tradition, Edwin W. Smith and Geoffrey Parrinder. To these two, the latter of whom became for a time my supervisor at London University, I shall always be indebted.

But my reading led always further back (there are no missiological Melchizedeks, without father or ancestry) and I discovered for the first time the brilliance of the minds and hearts of missionaries in Japan, India and China and other places who tussled with the central questions of the relation of Christian revelation to non-Christian religions almost a hundred years ago. Such writers as Timothy Richard, Thomas Slater and Bernard Lucas unlocked the doors to perceived whole new worlds. Missionaries talked to each other about the theology of religion, and I discovered an inexhaustibly rich series of reports and other documentation which arose out of the frequent international and regional missionary conferences in this period of intense missionary activity. Among this material undoubtedly the most striking was the Report of Commission IV at the World Missionary Conference in Edinburgh in 1910, entitled *The Missionary Message in Relation to Non-Christian Religions*. Here was to be found one of the great turning points in the Christian theology of religions and I read it with astonishment, wondering why nobody had ever brought it to my attention and speculating how it had ever come into existence.

At this point, during my first visit to the Library of the WCC in Geneva in 1978, I found one of the four complete sets, still in existence, of the transcriptions of responses to the far-reaching Questionnaire prepared by the Commission which produced *The Missionary Message*. This Questionnaire had been sent to missionaries all over the world in 1909 and nearly two hundred replies had been received. This material had formed the basis for the Report in 1910 but since then it had lain virtually untouched in the International Missionary Council and later, the WCC archives. My own transcriptions and photocopies of these responses have been constant companions in my reflections ever since. Their authors, long dead, have been a never-ending source of inspiration and encouragement. This material has to be brought to life again, for it represents all that was best about the Christian missionary work of eighty and more years ago and in this respect this book is a labour of love, in order to pay homage to the missionaries of that era.

But I hope it is more than a hagiographical exercise. There are many other good reasons for paying close attention to the positive thinking of previous generations about other religious traditions.

First among these is the need to assess correctly the achievements as well the failures of the missionary movement in the last eighty years. These advances made by theologians and missionaries in the theology of religions and interfaith understanding are not appreciated even by professional missiologists. The first three world missionary conferences, at Edinburgh in 1910, Jerusalem in 1928, and Tambaram (Madras) in 1938 each paid attention to the problems of presenting the Christian gospel in a world where there were many faith traditions, many of which were in the process of renewing themselves. A handful of scholars, notably Jan van Lin of the Netherlands, Carl

Hallencreutz of Sweden, and Wesley Ariarajah of Sri Lanka, using the rich archival material of these conferences, have contributed enormously to our understanding of developments since 1910. There has, however, been no study of the developments that took place before 1910 and this book is, I believe, the first to concentrate on the reasons for the generous and positive attitudes displayed at the World Missionary Conference in Edinburgh.

The second reason for the need of a fresh look at the period covered by this present work arises from attitudes and mind-sets which were present in the WCC when it was founded in 1948, and which had prevailed in its related body, the IMC since the Tambaram Conference in 1938. At Tambaram Hendrik Kraemer had presented the missionary world with the notions of 'biblical realism' and 'radical discontinuity', and had established with massive learning an essentially negative theology of religion. In 1948 the first Assembly of the WCC took place in Amsterdam under the strong leadership of Willem Visser t'Hooft, its first General Secretary. As a disciple of Karl Barth and Hendrik Kraemer, Visser t'Hooft had scant place for inter-religious activity (he was to write a little book entitled *No Other Name*) and for two decades questions about 'other revelation' and 'other spirituality' did not surface in the WCC. The situation in the IMC (which did not join the WCC until 1961) was not dissimilar, and the IMC conferences in this period in Whitby, Ontario (1947), Willingen, Germany (1953), Accra, Ghana (1957-8), and Mexico City (1963) found no difficulty in virtually avoiding the theological issues involved in religious pluralism and interfaith dialogue.

Only at the beginning of the 1970s did the WCC Division of World Mission and Evangelism (as the IMC had now become) return to the issues which were so prominent at Edinburgh in 1910. It did this through the formation in 1971 of the Sub Unit on Dialogue with People of Living Faiths and Ideologies under the leadership of the South Indian theologian Stanley Samartha. Since the late 1970s I have been closely associated with the work of that Sub Unit and know from first hand experience how hard it is to revive the earlier tradition represented by Edinburgh 1910 and still carried by the Jerusalem Conference in 1928. The achievement of the great names associated with the IMC at the beginning of its work in 1912 have been almost forgotten.

Much of the present work is offered therefore as an act of restitution. It is an attempt to give back to the World Council and to the Ecumenical Movement some of its rich but forgotten heritage. The need to recover a more generous outlook towards other world religious traditions is apparent. Both the Sixth Assembly of the WCC at Vancouver (1984) and the Seventh at Canberra (1992) wished to affirm dialogue as a basic attitude. The Vancouver Assembly spoke of 'God's creative work in the seeking for religious truth among people of other faiths'. But ponder here the compromise this form of words represents. It is far from being a confident and hopeful assertion that

God has revealed himself in the other religions, and affirms only a 'seeking for religious truth'. Neither Vancouver nor Canberra was able to speak in the generous and joyful tones of Edinburgh 1910. In this context it appears important to celebrate for the contemporary ecumenical movement that process of exploring and discovery of other religious faith that went hand in hand with the confident expansionism of 'the evangelization of the world in this generation'.

But undergirding the statements of WCC and its member churches should have been the solid and on-going work of Christians involved in inter-faith dialogue at every level and in all parts of the world. This inter-faith encounter ranges from the high-powered multi-lateral dialogues organized on the international scale to the meeting of neighbours across the garden fence of their own homes. In Britain, as elsewhere around the world, local initiatives in 'dialogue in community', between members of the diverse faith traditions represented in the UK, often take place on practical issues, such as schooling and religious education or censorship and religious liberty (the Salman Rushdie affair). These and other issues have raised the consciousness of Christians about religious pluralism to a new level. Often, however, actions of church leaders and individual Christians indicate deep disquiet about such matters as the finality and uniqueness of the Christian revelation. As the Secretary of the Committee for Relations with People of Other Faiths in the British Council of Churches in the 1980s I tried to grapple with some of the re-thinking about biblical interpretation and traditional theology that had to be undertaken if the widespread disquiet in the British churches were not to become disabling and dysfunctional. My own approach is to be found in my book, *Towards a New Relationship: Christians and People of Other Faith* (1986).

But even when the kinds of suggestions made there have been taken on board, another worry has often been expressed, namely that such re-thinking must represent a betrayal of the earlier missionaries and, in the expression commonly used, 'blunt the cutting edge of evangelism'. In response to this fear, I believe that it is important to show that an essentially 'dialogical' attitude, which is consequent upon the affirmation of the faith of the other person, lay at the very heart of the missiological method of the great pioneers. Many of the ideas which appear to have arisen in the 1970s, 1980s and 1990s (and which are therefore to be dismissed in some eyes as 'newfangled') were present in embryo form in the 1970s, 1980s and 1990s. The apparently recent discovery of 'dialogue' has lying behind it the Anglo-American theologians and missionaries treated in the following pages. Contemporary Christians therefore do not betray such people when they struggle today to establish proper inter-faith relationships. I hope these pages will also help make an end to the ill-informed view that 'dialogue' is a modern aberration which represents a loss of self-confidence on the part of modern Christians.

There may be other uses for this book. I could hope, for example, that reading through much of the material brought together here might be useful for historians who have to deal with the role of Christian missionaries in the forming of new nations. Many of these historians have, it often seems, only one conception of the missionary task, which then functions for their work as a misleading stereotype. At the very least I hope this present work may help historians and other scholars not to fall into the trap of thinking that all missionaries had the same aims and goals, the same strategies of church planting, the same attitudes to the culture and religions of the people among whom they worked, the same methods in preaching and educational work. At best it may present a picture rather different from the caricature of the missionaries as the ignorant destroyers of culture and the arrogant supplanters of ancient religious habit and custom. Not a few of the men and women discussed in this book are still remembered in their adopted lands as scholars and linguists, educators and nation-builders. They should be neither despised nor underestimated.

Perhaps, too, professors and students in the area of 'religious studies' may find some correctives to some of the stereotypes which it is occasionally possible for them to harbour when they hear the word 'missionary'. 'Missionary' is not necessarily a synonym of 'evangelist', and 'mission' may mean much more than 'conversionism'. More positively, I hope that many of the stories in this book may act as sources of inspiration and encouragement to Christian students of the other religious traditions of humankind. In many parts of the world, such missionaries were the very first to engage in the scientific study of religion and culture. In most cases their studies have stood the test of time. In this aspect of their work they were the predecessors of contemporary scholars of religion. As we shall see, they brought to the study of religion ideas like justice and fairness, courtesy and empathy, which should be the foundations of the humane science known as the study of religion.

Last, I hope that this book might be a contribution to my own discipline of missiology. It represents my continuing commitment to discovering a better way for Christian witness to go forward. I believe that we must develop a missiology which will more adequately serve Christian communities set amid 'a world of many faiths'. Such a missiology must focus upon the 'new relationship' of creative inter-faith dialogue and mutual witness of people of different faith commitment. Yet this goal will not be achieved without a fresh awareness of the great traditions coming down to the contemporary church from its comparatively recent missionary past. The 'giants in the land' at the beginning of this century need to be rediscovered.

Acknowledgments

This piece of work could not have been accomplished without a great deal of help from my friends. The intellectual debts of which I am conscious are indicated in the notes, but there are countless other ideas and formulations represented in these pages for which I am profoundly grateful. Where they came from I cannot now tell, but I need to say thank you to all my friends and colleagues in the Conference for World Mission at the British Council of Churches, and especially in the BCC Committee for Relations with People of Other Faiths and its two moderators, Bishops David Brown and James Thompson; to my friends and colleagues in the World Council of Churches Commission on World Mission and Evangelization, and especially to the Dialogue Sub Unit, with its two Moderators, Professors Dick Mulder and Diana Eck and its three Directors, Drs Stanley Samartha, John Taylor and Wesley Ariarajah, and lastly to my friends and colleagues in the Cambridge Theological Federation and in Cambridge University. I have kept company, too, with prophets and sages, saints and scholars of many other religious traditions besides the Christian one, and I hope that some of their wisdom and teaching comes through in these pages. The errors, omissions, misstatements and misapprehensions in them are all my own work.

I need also to record my indebtedness to the Librarians and their staffs of many places on both sides of the Atlantic: the Library of Christ's College, Aberdeen; the World Council of Churches Library and Archives in Geneva; the Edinburgh House Library and Archives of the Council of Churches in Britain and Ireland in London; the Resource Room of the Centre for the Study of Christianity in the non-Western World at New College in the University of Edinburgh; the Library of the Selly Oak Colleges, Birmingham; the Libraries of the Cambridge Theological Federation (Ridley Hall, Wesley House, Westcott House, and Westminster College); the Cambridge University Library; the Library of the Cambridge University Faculty of Divinity; the Library of Partnership House, Waterloo Road, London; the Library of the Boston University School of Theology; the Pitts Library of the Candler School of Theology, Emory University, Atlanta; the Woodruff Library of the Interdenominational Theological Center, Atlanta; the Widener Library at Harvard University; the Library of the Episcopal Divinity School, Cambridge, Massachussetts; and the Day Missions Library, at Yale Divinity School, New Haven, Connecticut.

My warmest gratitude goes to my three secretaries who in succession have coped with this complicated text, Myra Macpherson, Cathy Dunn and

Barbara Douglas. Each of them made important and valued suggestions about the work as well as helping with the production of the book. In the last stages of the writing the support of my Graduate Assistant Richard Andrew of Wesley House, Cambridge, has been invaluable. But most of all am I indebted to my wife, Susan White. Her influence is upon every paragraph and every sentence. I hope she will accept the dedication of this book to her.

A Note on Orthography

I have had problems with spelling and punctuation in this work. The earliest quotations come from the seventeenth century, and Milton, for example, was a law unto himself. The eighteenth century saw divergences begin between British English and American English (one language, two orthographies); nineteenth-century habits of punctuation differ seriously from those prevalent today. In addition many of the typescripts and other documents used are deficient in punctuation and accurate grammar. I have tried to keep accurately to the originals in all cases, and have used the expression *sic* very sparingly.

Another problem has been the transliteration of Sanskrit, Arabic, Pali, Japanese, Chinese and many other languages. Throughout this period there were only experiments in orthography, and no agreed standards. A renowned Arabist like Temple Gairdner can refer to *zikr* and to *dhikr*, to *Muhammed* and to *Mohomet*. We find Sanskritists referring to both *mosksha* and *moksa*, to both *cit* and *chit*. In these circumstances I have found it best to stick close to the original in every case, and to assume that the meaning will be clear to those who habitually use Arabic or Sanskrit, or any of the other languages to be found in these pages. Chinese is a special case because of official changes in transliteration since 1914. But people dealing with the period before then who have no Chinese are dependent upon how Chinese words were transliterated by the late nineteenth and twentieth-century missionaries and diplomats. Consequently the older orthography is used throughout this book for Chinese personal and place names and expressions rather than the *Pinyin* style. Thus Peking is written rather than Beijing, Nanking rather than Nanjing, *Tao* rather than *Dao*, *Shang-ti* rather than *Shangdi* and so on. Sinologists, I hope, will be able to make their mental adjustments reasonably easily.

My third problem has to do with the changes which take place in the English language as a result of rapid social developments. Committed as I am to non-exclusive language it has been hard for me to transcribe passages which refer all human beings as 'men' and which talk of the Christian missionary or preacher as 'he'. A different set of necessary mental adjustments have to be made in this case. On the one hand we must remember that the older writers did not mean in every case to be gender-exclusive, but on the other hand these were very male-dominated worlds. For example I have not as yet been able to find the Christian name of Mrs Ferguson Davie, Edinburgh Respondent No. 155. A distinguished physician and surgeon and director of hospitals in Rawal Pindi and Singapore, she is included in the Edinburgh documentation only under her husband's name. I fear that 'he' mostly meant 'he' in the earlier part of this century. The historian can only record the language of the period as accurately as possible and let the reader judge. There is a parallel issue in the use of words like 'native' and 'animist' which are no longer perceived as neutral terms. Again we have to weigh up for ourselves whether such words were being used condescendingly and in a patronizing manner in the quotations which follow. Did 'native' simply mean 'indigenous'? Did 'animism' function purely as a 'scientific' term, for want of any better way of speaking about traditional religion? With such *caveats* readers must judge the transcriptions in these pages.

Abbreviations

ABCFM	American Board of Commissioners for Foreign Missions
ABMU	American Baptist Missionary Union
BMS	Baptist Missionary Society
BCC	British Council of Churches
CEZMS	Church of England Zenana Missionary Society
CLS	Christian Literature Society
CMS	Church Missionary Society
CWME	WCC Commission on World Mission and Evangelism
DWME	WCC Division of World Mission and Evangelism
EDS	Episcopal Divinity School, Cambridge, MA
ETS	Episcopal Theological Seminary, Cambridge, MA
EU	Evangelical Union
IMC	International Missionary Council
IRM	*International Review of Missions*
LMS	London Missionary Society
PECUSA	Protestant Episcopal Church of the United States of America
SBE	*The Sacred Books of the East*
SDK	Society for the Diffusion of Christian and General Knowledge
SPCK	Society for the Propagation of Christian Knowledge
SPG	Society for the Propagation of the Gospel
TEAM	The Evangelical Alliance Mission
UFCS	United Free Church of Scotland
WCC	World Council of Churches
WMMS	Wesleyan Methodist Missionary Society
WMC	World Missionary Conference
YMCA	Young Men's Christian Association

The Early Theology of Religion in the Modern Period

This book tells the story of major shifts in missiological and theological positions in the Protestant missionary movement in the period 1800-1914.[1] These years have been called, famously, 'the Great Century' by the historian Kenneth Scott Latourette.[2] This terminology will suit the purposes of this present work, and help to avoid the use of longer expressions like 'the last years of the nineteenth century and the early years of the twentieth'. The 'great century of Protestant missionary expansion' is our frame of reference. Within it we examine one aspect of missiology: the vital question of the significance of other peoples' religions within the purposes of God. This question came to dominate the thinking of many missionaries and they sought help from home-based theologians who were prepared to take up the issue. As a result of their combined efforts there came to be a sea-change in attitudes towards 'non- Christian religions'.

This shift was signalled to the wider Christian world in *The Missionary Message in Relation to Non-Christian Religions*, the Report of Commission IV of the World Missionary Conference in Edinburgh in 1910. How the Edinburgh consensus on 'justice, courtesy and love' in relation to other religious traditions came to reach so high a level in such a wide-spread manner has hitherto never been fully examined.[3] Reasons for this omission are perhaps obvious. On the one hand such an undertaking demands searching analysis of the views and opinions inherited by individual missionaries before they went to their chosen 'mission fields', and on the other, scrupulous attention to the way in which their new environments altered their perceptions and caused major shifts within their own thinking. The complexity here is made the greater because missionaries, by definition, were not creatures of libraries. None had shelves full of reference books or access to all the recent publications in the field. Very few missionaries were in a position to pen letters to the editors of theological journals. Even fewer thought that their thinking would be of any interest to theologians at home (they were probably correct in this), or would be worthy of their attention (but here they were wrong, as we shall see). To reach an accurate assessment of their theological struggle requires patient attention to their diaries and journals, their speeches at missionary conferences, their correspondence with their home boards, their replies to questionnaires, and, when they are available, their published works.[4] I have tried to give the missionaries, and their theologian companions at home, this patient attention, and hope that they will be enabled to speak afresh through the following pages. To be sure, the missiological issue of the significance of people of other faiths has not gone away.

The 'Great Century' and its Early Missionaries

In terms of overseas mission, nothing like the 'Great Century' had ever happened before in the Protestant world. The Reformers and their immediate successors had by and large stayed at home with the gospel.[5] But in the last decade of the eighteenth century a spiritual revolution, as profound in its effects as the contemporary political revolutions in France and North America, turned the European world view inside out. The Protestants in North America, so freshly emerging from their own vast political change, were seized by similar visions, and joined in with their own sense of an 'errand to the world'.[6] Even the long and impressive missionary record of the Roman Catholic church had seen nothing on so grand a scale as the Anglo-American and continental European 'going into all the world'.[7] Societies and boards of missions proliferated, funds poured in, and missionaries were recruited, trained, and commissioned throughout all the following decades.[8] Just to list the new societies which sprang up in the early days demonstrates a mushrooming of concern for Christian expansion. The Baptist Missionary Society (BMS) was founded in 1792 and the London Missionary Society (LMS) in 1795, followed in 1799 by the Church Missionary Society (CMS). The Wesleyan Methodist Missionary Society (WMMS) was organized in 1813, though Methodist preachers had been at work overseas since 1784. In the United States the first missionary agency was the American Board of Commissioners for Foreign Missions (ABCFM) in 1810. The American Baptist Missionary Union (ABMU) followed in 1814 and the American Methodist Episcopal Missionary Society in 1819. The (Anglican) Protestant Episcopal Church of the USA, and the Presbyterian Church of America set up their Boards in 1821 and 1837, but both Episcopalians and Presbyterians had been at work much earlier than these dates. Missionary bodies in Continental Europe began work in 1797 with the foundation of the Netherlands Missionary Society, followed in 1814 by the foundation of the Basel Evangelical Mission in Switzerland. The Berlin Mission, the first great German society, came into being in 1824. The Danish Missionary Society dates from 1821, the Paris Society for Evangelical Missions from 1822, the Church of Sweden Society from 1835, and the Norwegian Society from

1842. Smaller societies in Edinburgh and Glasgow had been founded in 1796, but their work really began in earnest when the General Assembly of the Church of Scotland decided to take responsibility for foreign missionary work in 1824. In 1843 the newly formed Free Church of Scotland likewise took direct overseas responsibility. The Bible Societies also grew up in this period: the British and Foreign Bible Society was founded in 1804, and the American Bible Society in 1816.[9] Missionary activity overseas was itself part of a new zeal to make the world full of justice and truth.[10]

The theological heritage of Carey and his generation

The missionaries of first part of the Great Century were no more missiological Melchizedeks than their successors.[11] At least five streams of missionary thought had converged to mould William Carey and his generation of missionaries. Each of these currents could be traced back to the Reformation, yet each had undergone great modifications in the course of the seventeenth and eighteenth centuries.

From Europe there had come the massive impulse associated with the rise of Pietism, in which must also be included Moravianism.[12] From the North American continent had come the wave of fresh insight and enthusiasm associated with the Great Awakening, especially as interpreted by Jonathan Edwards. Older than either of these was the missionary theology of classical Puritanism, associated with the names of Richard Sibbes, Richard Baxter and Cotton Mather, which contributed greatly to the eighteenth and nineteenth-century understanding of both Pietism and Revivalism.[13] Anglican patterns of thinking, represented on the one hand by the very earliest attempts to set up missionary societies, and, on the other, by the experiences and reflections of John and Charles Wesley and the early Methodist revival within its English church context, constituted a fourth and a fifth current.[14] All the streams contained within themselves the elements which, for good or ill, were to make up the early nineteenth-century missionary mind-set.[15] We turn immediately to examining how these forces shaped and moulded the first set of Protestant attitudes to other religions in the Great Century.

Six Elements within the Early Theology of Religion

William Carey and his generation represented a new beginning for mission overseas. In their thinking and policy-making he and his contemporaries brought together elements from all the streams of previous Protestant missionary thinking and activity which have just been identified. This new compound we treat as a fresh entity and describe as the early theology of religion among Anglo-Americans in the Great Century. Within this general attitude distinctive elements gave rise to specific concerns about the faith and the fate of non-Christian peoples. Some of these particular concerns sped the missionaries on their way to the ends of the earth. Others were more useful in rallying the supporters of the missionaries. Whether these early theologies of the non-Christian world have any lasting value is not at this moment the question. But to many of their successors, missionaries and supporters alike, the early theology of religion and its distinctive elements represented a great barrier to be crossed. Within the Great Century we discern numerous entrenched positions having to be jettisoned before another set of attitudes, more nearly approximating to the 'justice, courtesy, and love' which this book talks about, could emerge.

Six such elements within the earliest nineteenth-century theologies prevalent in Britain and America can be distinguished. Each of them had its lasting consequences, for none was ever rejected by every single missionary. Each element was, however, modified and re-shaped in the course of the Great Century. Considerable attention to them all is needed in order to see the ways they shaped and fixed attitudes towards non-Christian religions. We shall call them: 1. millennialism (or, as it is often known, post-millennialism); 2. millenarianism (or pre-millennialism), the offshoot and contradiction of millennialism; 3. radical intellectualist anti-idolatry; 4. uncompromising hyper-Calvinism; 5. radical anti-intellectualist revivalism and; 6. intense Biblicism, which was very often combined with an ideal of inflexible and unyielding erudition.

Millennialism

From 1792 to the mid-1830s the founders of the missionary societies on both sides of the Atlantic and those they sent out were all imbued with the hope of the approaching millennium. Basing their thought on texts in Daniel, II Esdras, and the Book of Enoch, which were re-worked in the Book of Revelation ('they shall be priests of God and his Christ and shall reign with Him for the thousand years, Rev. 20.6.), they believed that the world was on the very edge of being converted to Christianity.[16] Like many of their contemporaries they believed a new age for humankind was on the point of inauguration.[17] God was seen as not only redeeming history, in the sense that he would be victorious in the end, but as working within and through history in order to establish his kingdom here on earth. Divine power was being manifested in peoples and nations caught up in current historical events.[18]

Such thinking was in fact a new departure for mainstream Christian theology.[19] To grasp how great this new beginning was we have only to reflect upon the intensely pessimistic message of St Augustine's *The City of God*, and its long and baleful hold on Western thinking.[20] As Augustine conceived them, earth and heaven were irreconcilable. The world was set on its own course for destruction and was the domain of the Devil. Heaven was the sphere of eternity and the rule of God. From the time of Cain and Abel there had been two divisions within the human race, the one, Augustine wrote, consisting 'of those who live by human standards, the other of those who live according to God's will. I also call these two classes two cities, speaking allegorically, one of which is predestined to reign with God for all eternity, the other doomed to undergo eternal punishment with the Devil'.[21] For Augustine it was impossible to think that the 'City of Man' would ever become the 'City of God'. All sense of 'millennium', of a thousand-year reign in which the kingdoms of this world would become 'the kingdoms of our God' (Rev. 11.5) had to be spiritualized or allegorized.[22]

The English poet John Milton (1608-74) mediated these views to the devout in both Britain and America.[23] In the last book of 'sacred epic', *Paradise Lost* (1667), Milton portrayed the Archangel Michael giving Adam and Eve a vision of the way in which world history would unfold as a result of the Fall. The events of the biblical record are rehearsed up to the coming of Jesus into the world. But then, after telling Adam and Eve about the out-pouring of the Holy Spirit and the success of the preaching of the gospel in the New Testament period, Michael showed them the decline and apostasy of the church from the second century onwards:

> Wolves shall succeed for teachers, grievous wolves,
> Who all the sacred mysteries of heaven
> To their own vile advantages shall turn

Then 'heavy persecution shall arise'

> On all who in the worship persevere
> Of spirit and of truth. the rest, far greater part,
> Will deem in outward rites and spurious forms
> Religion satisfied; truth shall retire
> Be struck with slanderous darts...

In all this period scarce indeed will be works of faith, and saints will be few and far between:

> ... so shall the world go on,
> To good malignant, to bad men benign,
> Under her own weight groaning, till the day
> Appeer of respiration to the just,
> And vengeance to the wicked, at the return
> Of him so lately promised to thy aid

The only consolation that Milton could offer Adam and Eve, and of course himself and his contemporaries, was that Christ would return to destroy or 'dissolve'

> Satan, with his perverted world, then raise,
> From the conflagrant mass, purged and refined,
> New heavens, new earth, Ages of endless date
> Founded in righteousness and peace and love,
> To bring forth fruits joy and eternal bliss.' [24]

The first British theologian to repudiate Milton's radical pessimism about this 'perverted world', was his contemporary, the Puritan minister Richard Baxter (1615-91).[25] Milton could still conceive another world to which the saints would be caught up, but Baxter's tough-mindedness and sense of living with a new rationality had no room for any idea of the rapture in which believers would reign in an 'Airy Kingdom' with Christ for a thousand years.[26] Baxter also pondered the meaning for Christian thinking of the discovery and settlement of the 'New World'. He had written a volume called *The Glorious Kingdom of Christ, Described and Clearly Vindicated* (1691), dedicated to Increase Mather, father of Cotton Mather and great uncle of Jonathan Edwards. In this work, Baxter declared that 'a righteous earthly kingdom, the holy utopia of the millennium, has been prophesied on the highest authority'.[27] Equally missing from this work is any expectation of an out-of-this world 'salvation' where 'saints' received their reward and enjoyed their revenge upon those who had persecuted them. The hymn writer Isaac Watts (1674-1748) put Baxter's thoughts into his widely-sung verse:

> Jesus shall reign where'er the sun
> doth his successive journeys run
> His kingdom stretch from shore to shore
> Till moons shall wax and wane no more.

We have just mentioned Cotton Mather (1663-1728) and Jonathan Edwards (1703-1758). Both these New England theologians sensed that the American experience had altered the balance of Western thinking, and had changed the way in which history was to be read. Their intuitions came to expression in two books which were to prove profoundly important to the missionary turn-around at the beginning of the Great Century. Mather's *Magnalia Christi Americana* (1702) was ecclesiastical history transposed into quite another key.[28] The attempt to establish a holy commonwealth in the New World was set by Mather within a providential plan. This began, of course, with the Creation and would terminate with the Last Judgment, before which should come the 'last times'. In this he did not differ from

Augustine. But Mather saw the last times as happening in his own day, beginning with the transformation of historical circumstances in America. 'The tidings which I bring to you are, that there is a revolution and a reformation at the very door, which will be vastly more wonderful than any of the deliverances yet seen by the church of God from the beginning of the world', he had preached in 1696.[29] The 'bigger part' of his congregation would live, he thought, to see it. Indeed the New Jerusalem was already being established in the 'Indian Wilderness'. 'I write the wonders of the Christian religion', he declared, 'flying from the depravations of Europe, to the American stand; and assisted by the Author of that religion, I do... report the wonderful displays of His Infinite Power, Wisdom, Graciousness and Faithfulness, wherewith His Divine Providence has irradiated an Indian Wilderness'.[30] Cotton Mather's 'History' is therefore an invitation to his fellow New Englanders to join in the establishing of the Reign of God on earth. This, he thought, would be 'a Reformation more Glorious, more Heavenly, more Universal faraway than what was in the former century'.[31] This is a far cry from Augustine's and Milton's pessimism about this world's future.

The experience of the religious stirrings in the Thirteen Colonies known as 'the Great Awakening' was to re-inforce the sense of great events unfolding in America.[32] Some forty years after the publication of the *Magnalia Dei Americana*, Jonathan Edwards (1703-58) felt led to argue 'that this work of God's Spirit, that is so extraordinary and wonderful, is the dawning, or at least a prelude, of that glorious work of God, so often foretold in Scripture, which in the progress and issue of it, shall renew the world of mankind'.[33] Edwards argued that

If we consider how long since the things foretold, as what should precede this great event, have been accomplished; and how long this event has been expected by the church of God, and thought to be nigh by the most eminent men of God in the church; and withal consider what the state of things now is, and has for a considerable time been, in the church of God and world of mankind, we can't reasonably think otherwise, than that the beginning of this great work of God must be near.[34]

These words are matched by numerous passages in Edward's *History of the Work of Redemption*, a series of thirty sermons preached in Northampton, Massachussetts in 1739. These form the basis of Edwardsean views of this-worldly salvation and his explicit repudiation of the Augustinian tradition that 'The City of God' could not be and would not be part of this present world. Instead here on this earth there will be 'times of great peace and love' when there shall be universal peace and good understanding among the nations of the world, instead of confusion, wars and bloodshed as has hitherto been from one age to another... Men in their temper and disposition shall be like the lamb of God, the lovely Jesus. The body shall be conformed to the head. And then shall all the world be united in peace and love in one amiable society; all nations, in all parts, on every side of the globe, shall then be knit together in sweet harmony... A communication shall then be upheld between all parts of the world to that end, and the art of navigation that is now improved so much in fear, with covetousness and pride... shall then be consecrated to God, as we read in the sixtieth of Isaiah, fifth verse ['the abundance of the sea shall be converted unto thee'] ninth verse ['surely the isles wait for me, and the ships of Tarshish... to bring thy sons from afar']. And it shall then be a time wherein men will be abundant in expressing their love to one another... [35]

Edwards' missionary treatise *An Humble Attempt to Promote Explicit Agreement and Visible Unity of God's People in Extraordinary Prayer for the Revival of Religion and Advancement of God's Kingdom on Earth* (1748) was based upon this sense that the millennium was very close at hand, 'pursuant to Scripture promises, and Prophecies concerning the Last Time', and that it should be the moment of the gathering of all peoples unto Christ. Like Mather, Edwards believed that this work of God would begin in his native America. "'Tis signified', he wrote in *Some Thoughts Concerning the Revival* (1742),

that it shall begin in some remote part of the world, that the rest of the world have no communication with but by navigation, in Isa. 60.9, Surely the isles shall wait for me, and the ships of Tarshish first, to bring my sons from far. It is exceeding manifest that this chapter is a prophecy of the prosperity of the church, in its most glorious state on earth in the latter days; and I cannot think that anything else can be here intended but America by "the isles that are far off", from whence the firstborn sons of that glorious day shall be brought.[36]

The American historian of missions R. Pierce Beaver has called the *Humble Attempt* the 'most potent means of missionary education and support' on both sides of the Atlantic.[37] Written partly as a response to a 'Concert for Prayer' suggested by some Scottish ministers concerned about missions, the *Humble Attempt* appealed for fervent and constant prayer that Christ would 'advance his spiritual kingdom in the world as he has promised'.[38] Again Edwards was clear that the time was very near 'when the gospel shall universally prevail, and the kingdom of God shall be extended over the whole habitable earth'.[39] This understanding of the imminence of the 'millennium' was determinative for the early Great Century missionary thinkers.[40]

The expectation of the millennial Kingdom is equally marked in most other eighteenth-century writings advocating missionary work. Melvill Horne (1761-1841) declared in his *Letters on Missions, Addressed to the Protestant Ministers of the British Churches* (1794) that 'the night is far spent, and the day is at hand. The latter ends of the world are fallen upon us, and we have more considerations to excite us, if were possible, to more than apostolic labours'.[41] William Carey himself wrote in his *Humble Enquiry* (1792) that in his own day, 'we have the greatest reason to suppose, that the glorious out-pouring of the Spirit, which we expect at last, will be bestowed'.[42] He also argued that the commerce with the East was a fulfilment of the prophesies in Isaiah 60.9. This verse, Carey suggested, implied that in the time of the glorious increase of the church, 'in the latter days', 'commerce shall subserve the spread of the gospel'.[43] Carey was, however, in some disagreement with Jonathan Edwards' *Humble Attempt*. When Edwards had implied that his generation was still awaiting the time when the heathen should be converted, some had latched on to this delay as a reason for caution and inactivity. Carey believed that this delaying tactic was contrary to the evidence: 'this objection comes too late: for the success of the gospel has been very considerable already'. For Carey the millennial hope of an earthly reign of Christ was already in process of fulfilment. The 'heathens' were already being converted.[44]

Anglican evangelical circles were just as alive with eschatological expectation. In his widely read *The Star in the East* (1809), the East India Company chaplain Claudius Buchanan saw the revolutions taking place in France and America as a sign that the time had come for 'diffusing the Light of Revelation'.[45] In Cambridge, England, Charles Simeon told his congregation that 'the great purposes of God were about to be accomplished through the conversion of the nations to the faith of Christ'. One of his hearers responded to this vision, and we find Henry Martyn writing, as he contemplated his task in India: 'yes, it shall be that yonder stream of Ganges shall one day roll through tracts adorned with Christian churches... All things are working together to bring on that day.[46]

The founders of the LMS, too, were overwhelmed by a sense of the approach of the millennial period. Notable for its explicitness about the overthrow of both Roman Catholicism and world religions was a sermon on Isaiah 2. 2-3 preached by the Revd J. Cockin for the LMS, in 1798. It was entitled significantly, 'God's Declared Designs a Motive to Human Endeavours'. 'The Last Days will be distinguished by very remarkable events', Cockin declared, and these 'commotions will very soon end in the total ruin of Popery and Mahometanism. After this it is probable the Gospel will find its way into the East.'[47] The LMS founder and missionary tutor, David

Bogue, kept this momentum going by publishing in 1818 his widely read *Discourses on the Millennium*.[48] Five years later, in 1823, William Miller (an LMS missionary candidate, not to be confused with the founder of the Millerites, or Seventh Day Adventists) wrote to the Directors of the LMS: 'The present day seems to be the commencement of that happy period when the "earth shall be full of the knowledge of God as the waters cover the sea".'[49] In this sentiment Miller was echoing the Serampore Baptists, Carey, Marshman and Ward, who had written in 1808 that the time had now dawned when 'the idols should be cast to the moles and the bats'.[50]

On the other side of the Atlantic, Jonathan Edwards' eschatological thinking had been carried forward by his disciple Samuel Hopkins (1721-1803), particularly through his widely studied *Treatise on the Millennium* (1793).[51] An otherwise dry and remote New England Calvinist, Hopkins was passionate about 'the Days of the Millennium': 'The Spirit of God will be poured out in His glorious fulness, and fill the world with holiness, and salvation, as floods upon the dry ground.'[52] In fact Samuel Hopkins did not believe that the Millennium was just about to begin, calculating rather that it would take place in the twentieth century.[53] Nevertheless he sustained the millennialist thinking in New England in the years following Edwards' death. The American Board of Commissioners for Foreign Missions in Boston came into being in 1810 with the sense that whereas other times 'have been times of preparation, the present age is emphatically the age of action'.[54] The ensuing rhetorical question 'Shall we remain idle in this harvest time of the world?' gained both the appropriate negative response and the corresponding positive action.

Millennialist fervour dominated even the staid General Assemblies of the American Presbyterians in these decades. The 1815 Assembly was moved to pronounce:

> Such mighty plans of benevolence; such wonderful combinations; such a general movement of mankind, in promoting the great cause of human happiness were, surely, never before witnessed! The days of darkness, we fondly hope, are passing away; and the period drawing nigh when the angel bearing the trumpet of the everlasting Gospel, shall carry his holy, life-giving message to every kindred, and people, and nation and tongue.[55]

As we have seen, millennialism was the ground for the founding not only of missionary societies but every kind of voluntary association. If sufficient numbers of people were united truly a new dawn of righteousness for the world would break. At that time, wrote a contemporary, 'Licentiousness and injustice would disappear. Strife and dissension would be wiped out. There would be no more war, famine, oppression, or slavery, neither in the United States nor on the mission fields'.[56]

The millennialist hope survived into the 1840s and '50s before being transmuted into another form of theology. This new thinking still looked for the establishment of the kingdom of God on this earth, but for reasons which followed no biblical scheme, drawing its inspiration from secular ideas of progress and perfectibility.[57] Among the last preachers to appeal to pure biblical millennialism as a missionary motive was Edward Steane, preaching to his fellow Baptists in commemoration of 'The First Fifty Years' of the BMS in 1842.[58] Steane regarded his period in history with incredible optimism. 'All events are manifestly taking one direction. The tide of providence is set in with a strong and steady current... We seem to be standing on the edge of some magnificent disclosure.' Steane felt that the church was waiting for the new page of prophecy to be turned over: 'What the result will be none can question and the Christian need not fear.' He then quoted some lines of verse which are not attributed:

Six thousand years of sorrow have well nigh
Fulfilled their tardy and disastrous course
Over a sinful world; and what remains
Of this tempestuous state of human things
Is merely as the rocking of a sea
Before a calm, that rocks itself to rest.[59]

But Steane was an isolated voice by the mid-nineteenth century. The old millennialist confidence in its biblical form had waned. Nevertheless, hymn writers went on producing hymns with millennial themes long after the dream had faded. An example of this is to be found in the missionary hymn of Alfred Ainger (1841-1919) which is still in wide use even now:

God is working his purpose out, as year succeeds to year
    God is working his purpose out, and the time is drawing near
Nearer and nearer draws the time – the time that shall surely be,
    When the earth shall be filled with the glory of God, as the
        waters cover the sea.[60]

Many of the missionaries at the close of the Great Century found this an exact expression of their deepest hopes even if the idea of a thousand year earthy reign of Christ had been transformed by Victorian ideas of social progress.

Millenarianism

Contemplation of the millennium in the ways inspired by Richard Baxter, Cotton Mather and Jonathan Edwards turned Protestants for a brief period from examining the state of their own souls to seeing visions of the consummation of all history as the kingdoms of this world became the kingdoms of God. Eschatology had ceased, at least for a short while, to concern only the individual's personal destiny in another and other worldly realm. To millennialist thinking belongs the credit of enlarging the horizons of Protestant Evangelicals and making them turn outwards. In the first decades of the Great Century the founders and supporters of missionary societies had been able to look to the ends of the earth with a cheerful optimism because they so profoundly believed that they were absolutely in line with the purposes of God.

But this state of affairs was to change. Millennialist hopefulness was soon to be challenged by other readings of the biblical prophecies. In the secular world things were not quite so hopeful where war and famine oppressed Christian minds. The alternative interpretation of chiliasm began to surface again, in which Christ would return in glory prior to the beginning of his thousand year reign on earth. As part of this coming the final judgment would take place. Condemned souls would depart into hellfire, but the saints would reign with Christ for ever. This scheme, perhaps more familiar than millennialism, is usually known as 'pre-millennialism'. It is however also termed 'millenarianism', and the latter usage is employed in this book.[61]

Speculation about the date of Christ's return or 'Second Advent' (the key millenarian expression) was rife after 1800, with suggestions of the times and seasons of the Parousia ranging from the early 1840s to the late 1860s.[62] The consequences for missionary theology were obvious and immediate. If Christ was coming to reign with the saints within a very few years it followed that the gospel must be preached to all peoples with all possible urgency. Equally pressing was the conversion of the Jews together with the purification of the church.[63]

As we have already hinted, millenarian speculation represented very much more than an obsession with dating the Second Coming. It manifested an acute failure of nerve. The earlier sense of exhilaration and confidence that men and women were on the verge of the 'latter day glory', the time of peace and harmony, had faded. No longer was it bliss to be alive as a new age dawned, for the world was getting worse, not better. The new converts to millenarianism began to abandon confidence in human ability to stem the tide of evil, convert the world to Christianity, or even prevent its own corruption.[64] Millenarian thinking therefore reverted to the older, Augustinian patterns. Souls had to be rescued from the misery of this world. An extractionist salvation was once again in vogue, and with it surfaced the missionary motive of 'saving the heathen from hell fire', which came to predominate in many mid-nineteenth century circles.[65]

This clamant sense of the need to take Christ 'to the heathen' before Christ's physical return was spelt out within various movements of the early part of the Great Century, as, for example, in the teachings of Edward Irving (1792-1834) and the Catholic Apostolic Movement;[66] in the doctrines of J.N. Darby (1800-1882) and his Plymouth Brethren Movement;[67] and in William Miller (1782-1849) and his followers, who were later known as the Seventh Day Adventists.[68] Most millenarian teaching, however, took place within small groupings found throughout the evangelical denominations, both in Britain and America. Anglicans, Lutherans, Baptists, Presbyterians and Congregationalists alike threw up millenarian teachers. Thus in 1849 Horatius Bonar's new *Quarterly Journal of Prophecy* claimed an 'increasing circle of enquirers', especially in Scotland.[69] In the USA a sister periodical, *The Prophetic Times*, declared the common creed of millenarians: '1. That we are living in the last periods of the present dispensation. 2. That Christ will soon appear upon earth, to avenge his elect, and to fulfill his covenant to them and 3. That the expectation of a Millennium of universal righteousness and peace before the return of the Savior, is an unchristian delusion.[70]

The message of millenarianism was also spread in gatherings such as the Niagara Bible Conferences in North America and the Mildmay Park Conferences in London. Many supporters of the mainstream missionary societies took part in these meetings, most notably the Presbyterian leader Arthur Tappan Pierson (1837-1911).[71] In the 1880s and 90s Pierson became the foremost exponent of the doctrine that to engage in evangelization would hasten the return of the Christ. Towards the end of the Great Century, Matthew 24.14 became increasingly used as the dominant missionary text: 'This Gospel of the Kingdom shall be preached in the whole world for a testimony unto all the nations; and then shall the end come.'[72]

As a result of this continuing millenarian fervour a cluster of new missionary societies sprang up in the 1890s motivated almost exclusively by the sense of the imminence of the Lord's Return.[73] Among these were the Regions Beyond Missionary Union, founded in 1878;[74] the Christian and Missionary Alliance, founded in 1887;[75] and the Evangelical Alliance Mission, founded in 1890.[76] We shall see that no missionaries from these societies were asked their opinions about the missionary message in relation to non-Christian religions for the World Missionary Conference in Edinburgh in 1910 and hardly any of them attended it. But many respondents from the mainstream societies and boards showed the influence of millenarianism. This was peculiarly seen in their understanding of other religions because, in David Bosch's words, 'Premillennialists tended to have an even more melancholy view of non Christians than had prevailed among their predecessors.'[77] For this kind of missionary 'Conversion was a crisis experience, a transfer from absolute darkness to absolute light.' 'The millions on their way to perdition should therefore be snatched from the jaws of hell as soon as possible. Missionary motivation shifted gradually from emphasising the depth of

God's love to concentrating on the imminence and the hour of divine judge-ment.'[78]

One ardent missionary adopting the millenarianist position was S.H. Kellogg (1839-1899).[79] Kellogg was a professor in the Presbyterian Western Theological Seminary in Allegheny, Pennsylvania, where he taught mission and world religions. He had served as a missionary to India and had pub-lished a Grammar of the Hindi language. His vigorous and well-informed rebuttal of Buddhism, *The Light of Asia and the Light of the World* (1885) together with a *Handbook of Comparative Religion*, published in 1899, influ-enced many missionaries in the last years of the Great Century to take a hard line against other religions. Kellogg wrote of the 'immeasurable disparity between the best that heathenism can offer and the teachings of the Gospel of Christ'. He claimed as his primary authority for making this judgment 'many years of intercourse with the people of India, and study of their reli-gious works'.[80] But it is clear that his understanding of the imminence of the coming of Christ as Judge is also at work in his assessment of the world's religions. Strict adherence to millenarianism allowed no space to other reli-gious traditions within the purposes of God.

Nowhere could this 'melancholy view' of other religions be more clearly seen than in A. T. Pierson's *The Crisis of Missions* (1886). Here Pierson scof-fed at the liberal idea that there is a 'universal and saving element' running through all religious systems, that there is a 'light of Asia' as well as 'a light of the world'. Such teaching Pierson saw as 'the devil's master-piece of strat-egy to keep the hosts of God within the walls of luxurious indolence'.[81]

Radical intellectualist anti-idolatry

Neither from the side of millennialism nor from that of millenarianism could there be any favourable judgment of other religious systems. Adherents of both positions were equally certain that all religion outside Christ was idola-trous. They remained committed to the 'theological entails' of Augustine, or Calvin or Luther.[82] It is, however, important to see that their radical denial of salvific significance in other religious traditions was attributable not only to their mediaeval and reformation inheritances but to the new rationalism which was becoming prevalent in both Europe and America. Its dominant conviction was that the way to knowledge in every sphere of life lay in rea-son. This position is exemplified in Britain by such figures as Lord Herbert of Cherbury (1583-1648), Robert Boyle (1627-1691), and John Locke (1632-1714), and in America in the next century by Benjamin Franklin (1706-1790) and Thomas Jefferson (1743-1826).

The Bostonian leader Cotton Mather, whom we have already met advocat-ing 'this worldly' eschatology, also stands at the fountain head of this distinc-tive tradition of missionary thought.[83] His achievement here lay in uniting the stream of continental Pietism with this new 'rationalism'. Intending social reform at many levels in New England, on which he wrote prolifically, Mather corresponded with the Pietist social thinker A.G. Francke (1663-1727) in Germany.[84] In Francke's philanthropic activities in Halle Mather saw a model for his own efforts to provide for the social, religious, and intellectual needs of Boston and its neighbouring communities. 'Vital piety and Franckean charity', Mather opined, would unite all the people of God in New England. When and as this happened 'the Papal empire would fall and the Kingdom of God would come'.[85] In his *Advice to the Churches of the Faithful* in 1702, Mather wrote a section entitled, 'A few Sighs for a Distressed Church'. This included 'sighs' for 'The Dispersed Israelites... For the Greek Churches...' and 'For the Nations yet perishing under the Pagan Idolatries and Mohametan impostures'.[86] 'Idolatry' and 'impostures' were to become the characteristic words of eighteenth-century rationalist theology as it turned its attention to other religions.

Jonathan Edwards, as we have seen, became convinced that Mather's sighs were on the verge of being answered. Along with the coming of the millennium, he predicted the downfall of the old religions not so much because they were heathenish but because they were irrational. Edwards' position about other faith traditions was essentially the same as that of Calvin, but to it he added the quality of 'redeemed reason':

> The doctrine of St Paul, concerning the blindness into which the Gentiles fell, is so confirmed by the state of religion in Africa, America, and even China, where, to this day, no advances towards the true religion have been made, that we can no longer be at a loss to judge of the insufficiency of unassisted reason, to dissipate the prejudices of the Heathen world, and to open their eyes to religious truth.[87]

Consequently the 'gods of the nations' were no gods and 'the Gospel' and 'redeemed reason' alike demonstrated that truth.[88] If radical opposition to idolatry arose in Edwards in the first place as a result of his millennialist expectations, he assuredly believed that 'reason' would play the supreme part in the destruction of erroneous belief. When the great outpouring of the Spirit happened the nations would be turned from heresy, from popery, and 'from other false religions'.[89] Then Satan's heathen kingdom would be overthrown and then 'the joyful sound would be heard among them', and, 'the Sun of righteousness shall arise with his glorious light shining on those vast regions of the earth that have been covered with heathenish darkness for many thousand years'. This 'wonderful revival and propagation of religion' would bring 'vast multitudes savingly home to Christ'.[90]

On the European side of the Atlantic, the seventeenth-century ideals embodied in Pietism and the new sense of the powers of rational thought mingled in the founding of the SPCK and the SPG.[91] Thomas Bray (1656-1730), the Anglican clergyman who laid the theoretic base for both societies, was the embodiment of practical benevolence and rational piety.[92] Bray was also deeply Anglican, imbued with the English church-state ideology. He and those who founded the SPG were primarily concerned with the pressing spiritual needs of the British subjects in the American and West Indian colonies. Priests of the Church of England, they thought, were needed everywhere to take pastoral care of the King of England's scattered subjects.

But their ministrations were not necessarily only to be directed to the colonial settlers. In 1710 the SPG fully took upon itself the spiritual welfare of the non-believing world as well. Its Council resolved: '1. That the design of propagating the Gospel in Foreign Parts does chiefly and principally relate to the conversion of heathens and infidels, and that therefore that branch of it ought to be prosecuted preferably to all other' and '2. That in consequence thereof, immediate care be taken to send itinerant missionaries to preach the Gospel among the Six Nations of the Indians according to the primary intentions of the late King William of glorious memory.'[93] But six years previously the Society had considered long and hard how conversion of the heathens should be carried out in the light of those 'rational principles' which were in vogue in their own circles. The missionaries were to 'begin with the Principles of Natural Religion, appealing to their Reason and Conscience; and thence proceed to shew them the Necessity of Revelation, and the Certainty of that contained in the Holy Scriptures, by the plainest and most obvious Arguments'.[94] Terms such as 'heathen and infidels' indicate the mixing of pietism and rationalism, and two years later this mood was captured by Alexander Pope. These verses also show how far the ideas of British imperialism and Western cultural superiority were already apparent in 1712.

> Rise, crown with light, imperial Salem, rise!
> Exalt thy towering head and lift thine eyes!
> See heav'n its sparkling portals wide display,
> And break upon thee in a flood of day.
>
> See barbarous nations at thy gates attend,
> Walk in thy light, and in thy temple bend:
> See thy bright altars thronged with prostrate Kings,
> While every land its joyous tribute brings.[95]

In other, smaller, Anglican societies which were concerned with the mission of the English church overseas, the sense of rational piety also dominated. The New England Company, as refounded by King Charles II in 1661, had as its first Governor Robert Boyle.[96] Besides his scientific work, Boyle had a passionate interest in the spread of the Christian gospel, and served as

Governor for thirty years until his death in 1691. Like the 'rational chemist' and scientist he was, he believed profoundly in the 'reasonableness' of Christianity, and the power of logical argument to defeat 'superstition'. During his lifetime he paid for the translation of the Gospels and the Acts into Turkish and Malay and instigated the translation from Latin of Hugo Grotius' *De Veritate Religionis Christianae*, (1622, ET *The Truth of the Christian Religion*, 1709).[97] In his will Boyle provided not only for the establishment of a society for 'the Conversion and Religious Instruction and Education of Negro Slaves' but also for an annual series of lectures 'to defend the Christian faith', of course by the best reasoning powers.[98]

The pious and benevolent tradition which showed itself in this kind of Anglicanism had immediate consequences in the fight against the African slave trade. One outcome of this 'practical Christianity' was the establishment of the Sierra Leone Company in 1791.[99] Melvill Horne spent fourteen months as Chaplain of the Sierra Leone Company in Freetown and upon his return in 1794 he published his *Letters on Missions Addressed to Protestant Ministers*.[100] This book enshrined a distinctively Anglican approach to missionary activity and needs to be set alongside Carey's *Humble Inquiry* (1792). As a result of his experiences in West Africa, Horne thought it imperative that 'learned missionaries' should engage with ignorance and intellectual delusion. 'Let them remember', he wrote in his *Letters*, 'that in every country, Priests have a strong hold on the sentiments of mankind.' 'If they are not sincere, humble, pious and benevolent, the opposite qualities may be expected to predominate in them', so they needed skilful handling. 'In most, perhaps all systems of Heathenism,' Horne opined, 'there is a large share of *imposture*. As public deceivers, Heathen Priests *must* be bad men.'[101]

Melvill Horne's 'rationalistic' views matched those of his fellow Anglican clergyman, Charles Wesley (1707-88). Wesley's lines about Muhammed expressed accurately the conventional eighteenth-century interpretation of Islam as a great imposture.[102] We can detect in them also the millennialist sense of the impending triumph of the earthly reign of Jesus Christ.

Sun of unclouded Righteousness
  With healing in Thy wings arise,
A sad benighted world to bless
  Which now in sin and error lies,
Wrapt in Egyptian night profound;
  With chains of hellish darkness bound.

The smoke of the infernal cave,
  Which half the Christian world o'erspread
Disperse, Thou heavenly Light, and save
  The souls by that Impostor led,

> That Arab-thief, as Satan bold
>   Who quite destroy'd thy Asian fold.
>
> O might the blood of sprinkling cry
>   For those who spurn the sprinkled blood!
> Assert thy glorious Deity
>   Stretch out thine arm, Thou Triune God!
> The Unitarian fiend expel
>   And chase his doctrine back to hell.
>
> Come Father, Son, and Holy Ghost
>   Thou Three in One and One in Three
> Resume Thine own for ages lost
>   Finish the dire apostasy
> Thine universal claim maintain
>   And Lord of the Creation reign.[103]

Lesser hymn writers also tried their hands at this theme. William Shrubsole, a secretary of the LMS, wrote in 1795:

> Say to the heathen from thy throne
> 'I am Jehovah, God alone!'
> Thy voice their idols shall confound
> And cast their altars to the ground.
>
> Arm of the Lord, Thy power extend
> Let Mahomet's imposture end;
> Break superstition's papal chain
> And the proud scoffer's rage restrain.
>
> Let Zion's time of favour come:
> O bring the tribes of Israel home;
> And let our wondering eyes behold
> Gentiles and Jews in Jesus' fold![104]

In these lines we meet again the characteristically 'rationalist' term 'superstition'. The disparagement of other religious traditions was fundamental not only to hymn writers but also to nearly all theologians and philosophical thinkers in this period.[105] Ralph Wardlaw (1779-1853), another secretary of the LMS, and the author of a *Systematic Theology* (1828) for the use of Scottish Congregationalists, once preached on 'The Contemplation of Heathen Idolatry an Excitement to Missionary Zeal', declaring:

Every view that can be taken of the worship of the idols is a *lie* against the Supreme Majesty. Their number is a lie against his unity; their corporal nature is a lie against his pure invisible spirituality; their confined and local residence, a lie against his omnipresence and immensity; their limited and subdivided departments of operation, a lie against his universal proprietorship and dominion; their follies and weaknesses, a lie against his infinite wisdom; their defects and vices and crimes, a lie against his unsullied purity and perfection.[106]

Wardlaw was clear that idolatry was a violation of reason, and on that count indictable at the Last Judgment. The non-Christian nations will be tried, 'by the light and law of nature and of original revelation; and the ground of their sentence shall be, their wilful forgetfulness and inexcusable ignorance of God, and the perverse violation in their conduct of the suggestions of reason and the dictates of conscience'.[107]

Across the Atlantic Ocean the most eminent missionary theorist of the mid-nineteenth century, Rufus Anderson (1796-1880) interrupted the flow of his argument in his *Foreign Missions, Their Relations and Claims* (1869) for 'self-governing', 'self-supporting' and 'self-propagating churches' (in which he was years ahead of his time), by re-iterating the older Congregationalist sentiments (in which he was years behind):

The gospel is applicable equally to all false religions. Generically considered, there can be but two religions: the one is looking for salvation by grace; the other by works. The principle of evil in all disbelieving men is the same. The refuge of lies in Popery, in Judaism, in Mohammedanism, in Brahminism, Buddhism and in every form of paganism, are wonderfully alike.[108]

For Rufus Anderson, all these were 'great superstitions'.

Yet even from the beginnings of the Great Century there were voices suggesting all was not totally hopeless for people of other religions. While George Burder (1752-1832), preaching at the foundation of the LMS in 1795, was sure that 'heathen superstitions' would lead his audience to exclaim 'How strange, how absurd are their ideas of a Divine Being', he could also speak of the 'broken and mangled fragments of Gospel hope' yet to be found among 'the rubbish of ancient mythology and in the religious rites of the most barbarous nations'.[109] Burder suggested that the custom of sacrifices, even human sacrifices, pointed to glimmerings of Christian understanding in even the South Sea Islanders. This 'shews that the expectation of pardon is by blood. God grant that we may have soon opportunity to improve upon their mistaken traditions and to say, "Behold the Lamb of God which takes away the sin of the world"'.[110] This pattern of arguing from the glimmering to the fulfilment was to be followed by many of Burder's successors as the Great Century unfolded.

Calvinism

The original teaching of John Calvin (1509-64) laid enormous stress on the sovereign and determining will of God.[111] Calvin's massive theological opus was rooted in his sense of the sureness, power and purposiveness of God's saving activity in Christ. This was the one 'foundation for Christian life or 'grounding in Christian piety'.[112] Only God could take the initiative in bringing souls to salvation. Only God could put into effect the good purposes of his perfect will.[113] But such teaching has awkward consequences for missiology if and when it is fully worked out. If God was the single author of salvation and the human will had no part to play in the salvific process then why were so few people on the road to eternal life? Calvin himself taught that

> The covenant of life is not preached equally to all, and among those to whom it is preached, does not always meet with the same reception. This diversity displays the unsearchable depth of the divine judgement, and is without doubt subordinate to God's purpose of eternal election.[114]

Thus it was logical to suppose that God did not intend universal salvation. Some persons were obviously called and others equally obviously not. But why some should be called and some should be damned the human mind was in no position to determine.[115] Human reason was fallible and misleading whenever it tried to work out God's purposes and designs. Through God's revelation alone, as received in Holy Scripture, could human beings discover how God should be glorified and enjoyed for ever.[116]

The doctrines of election and predestination became supremely important for later Calvinists.[117] But, sadly, as the seventeenth and eighteenth centuries wore on the emphasis on God's initiative and sovereign will became 'wooden and rigid'.[118] Developments of this kind are often referred to as 'hyper-Calvinism', and Peter Toon describes the eighteenth-century situation well in his book *The Emergence of Hyper-Calvinism*, particularly in a chapter entitled 'No Offers of Grace'.[119] Resistance to hyper-Calvinism was a key factor within the missionary impulses at the beginning of the Great Century, and the continued wrestling with Calvinistic issues dominated much of the remainder of this period. They turn upon the sentiments expressed in the Westminster Confession and Catechisms of 1647.[120]

The Confession, prepared under the auspices of the Long Parliament from 1643 to 1646, gave form to the five anti-Arminian decisions of the Synod of Dordrecht (or Dort), 1618-9, concerning total depravity, unconditional election, limited atonement, irresistible grace, and the perseverance of the saints.[121] To these tenets it added its own emphasis on 'double predestination' in the scholastic and supralapsarian form taught by Theodore Beza (1519-1605). The Confession's statement reads: 'By the decree of God, for the manifestation of his glory, some men and angels are predestinated unto everlasting life, and others foreordained to everlasting death.'[122] It went on to declare that those whom God had 'predestinated' were chosen, before they were born, out of God's 'mere grace and love, without any foresight of faith or good works, or perseverance in either of them, or any other good thing in the creature, as conditions, or causes moving him thereunto; and all to the praise of his glorious grace'.[123] God's purposes in so electing a part of humanity for salvation could in no way be thwarted. The Divine power was to be manifested in his 'effectual calling' of those 'predestined unto life'. These only, God is pleased, in his appointed and accepted time, effectually to call to salvation.

The key passages for missiological understanding of the non-Christian world, according to this view, are these two:

The rest of mankind, God was pleased, according to the unsearchable counsel of his own will, whereby he extendeth or withholdeth mercy as he pleaseth, for the glory of his sovereign power over all his creatures, to pass by, and to ordain them to dishonour and wrath for their sin, to the praise of his glorious justice.[124]

The actions of 'common grace' will not help them in their plight:

Others not elected, although they may be called by the ministry of the word, and may have some common operations of the Spirit, yet can never truly come unto Christ, and therefore cannot be saved; much less can men not professing the Christian religion be saved in any other way whatsoever, be they ever so diligent to frame their lives according to the light of nature, and the law of that religion they do profess; and to assert that they may, is very pernicious, and to be detested.[125]

The roots of many early missionaries' struggle to do justice to people of other religions lie in this contentious form of Calvinism, with its twin implications, on the one hand, of 'fewness' in the numbers of those who may be saved and, on the other, of 'restrictedness' in the operations of saving grace.[126]

Andrew Fuller of Kettering and William Carey of Leicester were both ministers of the Particular Baptist Church, which adhered strictly to the Westminster Confession, within an intellectual ambience exactly as the Dutch church historian Johannes van den Berg has described it: 'the form of Calvinism which put its stamp upon the preaching was one-sided in its rigidity;

the sovereign character of God's free grace was emphasized at the expense of human responsibility, and man was taught to wait in complete passivity on God.'[127]

Thus Andrew Fuller recorded that in his early years as a Baptist preacher he had been afraid to invite the unconverted to come to Christ lest he might usurp the authority of God.[128] Fuller changed his mind after reading the stories of John Eliot and David Brainerd, and other Puritan missionaries in New England. These, good Calvinists to a man, appeared to have had no difficulty in summoning the unconverted Indians to Christ. By 1785 Fuller had been able to compose his *The Gospel Worthy of All Acceptation*. The title speaks for itself, and the book champions the offer of free grace to all people.

Yet, though *The Gospel Worthy of All Acceptation* was widely read, its arguments did not convince many of Fuller's older Particular Baptist colleagues. In 1785 the twenty-four year old William Carey had suggested at a minister's meeting that there should be a mission overseas. According to the story, J.C. Ryland rebuked Carey with the words, 'Sit down young man; when God wants to convert the heathen, He'll do it without your help or mine.'[129] This famous rebuke became the stimulus which led to Carey's powerful critique of hyper-Calvinism in *The Humble Enquiry into the Obligations of Christians to Use Means for the Conversion of the Heathen*s.[130] This 'using of means' was, in Carey's view, enjoined upon Christians in the Great Commission, Matthew 28.16-20. Carey dealt with the opinions of the Reformers that the Great Commission was binding only upon the Apostles.[131] But Carey also refuted the hyper-Calvinistic view that if the salvation of the heathen was in any way intended (which was doubtful) only God could 'bring them to the gospel, or the gospel to them'.[132]

Carey's *Humble Enquiry* was thus another contribution to the breaking down of the old formidable Calvinism. We must note the missiological dimension to this. Andrew Fuller's views changed through reading the writings of John Eliot and David Brainerd, the great American Puritan missioners to the Native Peoples, who had it seemed had no difficulty in offering the gospel to all comers.[133] William Carey's constant gathering of information about the discoveries of the eighteenth-century explorers, all of which he painstakingly marked on his home-made leather globe, suggested to him that the world view in hyper-Calvinist circles was too small, and so correspondingly was the concept of God.[134]

A similar concern about the logic of world wide mission led to the forming of a new denomination in Scotland in 1843.[135] James Morison, a minister of the United Secession Church, became perplexed about the lack of a philosophical foundation for mission if Presbyterians went on adhering to the Westminster Confession:

If it were not true that Christ died for the heathen, pray what gospel is the missionary to preach when he lands on a foreign shore? Is he to tell them that God loved a few men scattered somewhere or other throughout the world, and therefore, for aught that he could know, there may happen to be some of the favoured ones among them, and for these Christ died?[136]

Morison continued, 'Men need not go to heathen lands with the doctrine of a limited atonement in their creed, or, if they go with it, they must hide it, and preach in a manner practically contradictory to it.'[137] As a result the United Secession Church expelled him in 1841, and he formed 'The Evangelical Union' two years later.[138] No less than two of the pioneers of new religious understanding we look at later in this present work, Andrew Martin Fairbairn (1838-1912) and John Nicol Farquhar (1861-1929), were nurtured in this small and deliberately anti-Calvinist denomination.[139]

To be sure the struggle against hyper-Calvinism was not only based on missiological grounds. Powerful theological currents in the eighteenth and nineteenth centuries were eroding the image of God as Sovereign Will and Supreme Judge. New understandings and ideas about the humanity of Jesus threatened those older systems in which Christ functioned in order to propitiate the wrath of God.[140] Then again, Jesus' own teaching, which the mid-nineteenth century scholars believed themselves to be rediscovering through the developing techniques of 'higher criticism', contributed significantly to the demise of hyper-Calvinism.[141] Jesus appeared now to have taught on the one hand 'the Fatherhood of God' and on the other a new set of social relationships associated with the term 'the Kingdom of Heaven'.[142] This 'discovery', or rediscovery, of a 'kingdom' in which justice and 'brotherhood' and peace were the fundamental ingredients became a cornerstone of late nineteenth-century theology.[143] In Scotland the two great forerunners of this anti-Calvinist revolution were Thomas Erskine of Linlathen (1788-1870), and John McLeod Campbell (1800-72).[144] These men took the Calvinistic doctrine of the atonement away from legalism and placed it firmly in the area of personal relationships. In their teaching God functioned as a 'Father' rather than a 'Judge'.[145] In England the greatest figure was Frederick Denison Maurice (1803-1872) to whose work we devote a section in the next chapter of this book.[146]

Their counterpart on the other side of the Atlantic was Horace Bushnell (1802-76).[147] A contemporary of Erskine, Campbell, and Maurice, Bushnell had as his chief guide Samuel Taylor Coleridge.[148] Bushnell, who was a Congregationalist minister in Connecticut, came to understand God and humanity in terms of the British and German romantic movement.[149] Consequently he was as unwilling as Erskine and Campbell to continue using the thought-world of the law courts in formulating his doctrine of the atonement.[150] His reluctance here was increased by his long-term view of the educational character of the way in which God dealt with humankind, on similar lines to that of G. E. Lessing (1729-81).[151] Bushnell's first influential book, *Views of Christian Nurture* (1847), rooted the growth of the Christian character in upbringing, in both the home and its environing and close-linked 'organic' society.[152]

Bushnell's other emphasis lay upon 'the Eternal Fatherhood of God'. In this Fatherhood Bushnell saw 'one fixed purpose of compassionate love'. God was, for Bushnell, what Christ showed him to be. If Christ, he wrote in his most famous work, *The Vicarious Sacrifice* (1866) 'entered into patience, long suffering and love; burdened in heart for the good of his enemies; taking on His feeling the wants and woes of his enemies', this was and could be no new thought in the mind of God. It was certainly 'no optional superlative goodness taken up by Christ in the year one of the Christian era' for, Bushnell wrote, 'the whole deity is in it from eternity'.[153] Bushnell insisted that Christians must not be left 'to conceive that our blessed Saviour is some other and better side of Deity, a God composing and satisfying God'. On the contrary God was, in Bushnell's view, just such a Being as 'must take our evils upon His feeling and bear the burden of our sin'. Then follow some of Bushnell's most quoted words:

> Nay, there is a cross in God before the wood is seen upon Calvary; hid in God's own virtue itself, struggling on heavily in burdened feeling through all the previous ages, and struggling as heavily now even in the throne of the worlds. This too, exactly, is the cross that our Christ crucified reveals and sets before us.[154]

Bushnell's message was, we know, taken to heart on both sides of the Atlantic, by Congregationalists, Presbyterians, and others of the Reformed traditions.

Robert Rainy, Principal of New College, Edinburgh, addressing the World Presbyterian Alliance in Philadelphia in 1880, spoke significantly of the 'retreat' in modern theology from 'the juridical way of conceiving the divine procedure'. He offered two reasons to account for it. He suggested first that his generation had gained from Horace Bushnell a sense of a 'heightened awareness of the *educational* character of the Creator's dealings with the human race'. In a second suggestion Rainy pointed to 'a "Maurician" concentration on the Fatherhood of God, implying that there were 'certain affections always to be ascribed to him in dealing with His creatures, certain claims which all men have upon Him as His children, and can never cease to have'.[155]

In these words Robert Rainy was speaking not for the theological community alone. This shift was affecting all the Scottish denominations. In the previous year, for example, the United Presbyterian Synod had passed a Declaratory Act which profoundly modified the sense of the Westminster

Confession.[156] The Act insisted that 'while none of us are saved except through the mediation of Christ and by the grace of His Holy Spirit' and that 'while the duty of sending the gospel to the heathen, who are sunk in ignorance, sin and misery is clear and imperative', there had to be some sense of the wideness in God's mercy. It went on:

> while the outward and ordinary means of salvation for those capable of being called by the Word are the ordinances of the Gospel... it is not required to be held that any who die in infancy are lost, or that God may not extend His grace to any who are without the pale of ordinary means, as may seem good in his sight.[157]

In these ways, by the end of the nineteenth century, hyper-Calvinism had been dethroned in Presbyterian and Reformed churches. As early as 1876 the Scottish theologian Andrew Fairbairn commented (in a letter to the Secretary of State for Scotland about the Evangelical Union, the denomination he had chosen to enter as a young man):

> Allow me to say that we agree in every essential point with the theology of the Scotch churches. Our points of difference may be reduced to two. We hold (1) a universal atonement, or the sacrificial death of Christ as a death for all; (2) a conditional election, or election to eternal life through faith. Our differences with the above churches have been grown less every year. Had theological thought been as liberal thirty years ago as it is today, our denomination had never been.[158]

A. L. Drummond and J. Bulloch, the historians of the Scottish Church, comment, 'After three centuries the reign of Calvinism had ended.'[159] Another Scottish church historian, A. C. Cheyne, has described this change of heart and mind as nothing else than 'Victorian Scotland's Religious Revolution'.[160]

But not all the great centres of Calvinist learning capitulated to these challenges, whether theological or missiological. One in the United States which remained a bastion of the high Calvinist views was Princeton Theological Seminary, founded as the College of New Jersey in the days of the Great Awakening.[161] Within the diverging patterns of nineteenth-century American Presbyterianism, Princeton represented the Scottish-Irish heritage. The emigrant Scots and Irish who settled in New Jersey and Pennsylvania in the eighteenth century were much more committed to the Westminster Confession than the New England Congregationalists at Yale and Harvard.[162]

For fifty-six years the Professor of Didactic and Polemic Theology at Princeton was the severe and learned Charles Hodge (1797-1878).[163] From the time of his appointment in 1822 to the time of his death, Hodge insisted upon the duty of humankind to glorify God, on the double decrees of election and reprobation, and on the Bible as the single source of revelation and doctrine. There was no place whatever in Hodge's thinking, spelt out in his three-volume *Systematic Theology* (1871), for genuine religious experience or revelation in other religions. 'Common grace' was sufficient cause of any glimmering of truth within another religion: 'the Holy Spirit is present with every human mind, and enforces, with more or less power, whatever of moral or religious truth the mind may have before it'.[164] To common grace or uncovenanted mercy might be attributed 'all the decorum, order, refinement and virtue existing among men'. But common grace could not save anyone. It was, however, 'sufficient to render men inexcusable for their impenitence and unbelief'.[165]

Hodge was willing enough to discuss Hinduism in his *Systematic Theology* as having an 'interest for Christians and for the religious philosopher which attaches to no other nations'.[166] The Hindus, Hodge opined, 'showed and were doubtless intended to show' what are the legitimate effects of Pantheism: 'that doctrine has had dominant control for millenniums over a highly cultivated and intelligent people, and in their character and state we see its proper fruits'.[167] These could be seen in the 'two leading characteristics of the Hindu worship', cruelty and indecency. Pantheism, Hodge wrote 'denies the distinction between virtue and vice; it recognizes no attribute but power; it deifies evil; it "sanctifies vice"; passion, sensual or malignant is as much a mode of divine manifestation as the most heroic virtue'.[168]

Benjamin Breckinridge Warfield (1851-1921) succeeded Charles Hodge at Princeton as Professor of Didactic and Polemic Theology in 1887. He remained there until his death. Under his leadership the struggle to maintain the older hyper-Calvinism grew even more intense.[169] Warfield's first principle was that Christianity was the one and only 'revealed religion'.[170] 'In the one revealed religion', he wrote in an essay on 'Mysticism and Christianity', first published in 1917, 'God has revealed Himself in acts of special grace.'[171] Chief among these was what Warfield called the 'Open Word':

> Revealed religion comes to man from without; it is imposed upon him by a source superior to his own spirit. The unrevealed religions on the other hand flow from no higher source than the human spirit itself. However much they may differ from themselves in the relative prominence given in each to the functioning of the intellect, sensibility or will, they have this fundamental thing in common. They are all, in other words, natural religions in contradistinction to the one supernatural religion which God has made.[172]

The authority of both Hodge and Warfield ensured that the notion of plenary inspiration of the Westminster Confession itself dominated some missionary circles right to the end of the Great Century.[173] As late as 1914 Presbyterian candidates in the USA for mission work were questioned on its tenets and could be found woefully inadequate.[174]

Few missionaries, therefore, had greater difficulty in the Great Century with their inherited doctrinal standards than those of the Reformed or Calvinist traditions. In the stories which follow this chapter we shall sense the barriers that such men and women had to pass through. Many of them were torn by the need to remain loyal to the doctrinal standard of their forebears and their realisation that these precluded totally any affirmation of the faith of other men and women. In the words of the Westminster Confession such thinking was 'very pernicious, and to be detested'.[175]

Radical anti-intellectualist revivalism

Another force which eroded the old high and dry Calvinist position was Revivalism.[176] This movement would in due course find its fullest expression in the work of Dwight L. Moody (1837-1899) and go on to influence the missionary patterns of last part of the Great Century though the Student Volunteer Movement.[177] Revivalism's earliest manifestations took place, however, at the end of the eighteenth century, and directly challenged hyper-Calvinism in its older form. With so much emphasis being laid in revivalist meetings upon the free decision of the hearers to give themselves to Jesus Christ as their personal Saviour, the Calvinist conception of the 'bondage of the will' was directly challenged. Equally, when the message of the gospel was imparted in the same revivalist meetings on the assumption that everyone was called to respond, doctrines of election and reprobation dwindled into pale shadows of their former selves. But revivalism had another effect upon nineteenth-century Protestant evangelicals and this showed itself in distinctive attitudes to followers of other religious traditions. These attitudes can be traced back to their roots in Pietism, Moravianism, Methodism and the American Awakenings.

The first of these, Pietism, arose from the teaching of Philipp Jakob Spener (1635-1705) and August Hermann Francke (1633-1727) in the Saxon city of Halle.[178] Both Spener and Francke looked for an intense spiritual experience of 'first love' and 'new birth'. Their preaching and teaching emphasized repentance, conversion, and purity of life. In addition Spener, in his *Pia Desideria* (1675), taught the necessity of gathering those most deeply concerned for their own salvation and the salvation of others into groups for mutual edification and encouragement. Societies formed for these purposes became springboards for putting radical ideas into operation. These programmes were in line with Spener's vision of lay people taking the initiative in missionary and social activism rather than formal ecclesiastical councils.[179]

Beyond doubt, the most important missionary development arising from Saxon Pietism was that associated with the name of Count Nikolaus Ludwig von Zinzendorf (1700-1760).[180] Within the Moravian missionary effort Zinzendorf stressed Pietist themes of individual repentance, new birth and sanctification. As a missionary thinker he insisted that there could be no 'group-conversion', and that individuals had to make their own decisions for Christ. Zinzendorf vehemently warned against what he called *Generalheidenbekehrungen*, 'general conversions of the heathens'. Moravian missionaries could therefore aim only to win individual 'souls for the Lamb', never tribes or peoples.[181] In Zinzendorf's thinking there existed 'Candace souls' (Acts 8.27) in every nation.[182] The missionary's task was to find them. 'Civilization' as a motive for mission he utterly repudiated.[183] 'You must take care', he instructed his agents, 'that the heathen does not make any connection with the Europeans and their way of living. You must advise them to let them alone until they can believe that the Creator is his Saviour.' Moravian converts would then form a *diaspora*, a dispersion among the peoples, waiting for the enthronement of the Lamb of God, and were never to be 'Europeanised'.[184]

The influence of Zinzendorf's theology upon John Wesley (1703-91) and the theology of the Methodist movement is well-known.[185] Wesley's understanding of 'heart religion', which he derived largely from Moravian sources, was to be crucial to much nineteenth-century missionary theology.[186] It lay on the one hand in Wesley's commitment to preach the love, rather than the wrath, of God, and on the other hand in his formidable insistence upon evangelical Arminianism rather than the older 'high' or 'hyper' Calvinism.[187] Johannes van den Berg has brilliantly captured the nature of the Wesleyan contribution by entitling his study of the early Great Century missionary motives, *Constrained by Jesu's Love* (1956).[188] This phrase (taken from one of Charles Wesley's hymns) van den Berg sees as expressing precisely the dominating impulse of the founders of the Great Century missionary societies. A love for individuals in need of hope and restitution far outweighed all the other missionary motives which van den Berg found to be at work in this period.[189] Its profound concern for human well-being found expression in the philanthropic enterprise carried out by the Methodists and early evangelicals, of which the campaign for the abolition of slavery was but the chief example. Charles Forman has suggested that the Wesleyan theme 'constrained by Jesus' love' was matched in America by the millennialist Samuel Hopkins' teaching of 'universal disinterested benevolence'. This widespread notion, Forman writes, 'served to break down the acceptance of human suffering and indifference to missions which has been present among some contemporary Calvinists'.[190] As we have already suggested, the missionary motive which centred upon wrath of God and hell as the final destination of the heathen only later came to pre-occupy apologists for evangelical missions (closely connected as it was with millenarianism).

In America the movement known as the 'Great Awakening' established forms of pietistic and revivalistic theology as normative for the new nation. Its effect in determining the nature and character of American history in the nineteenth century is inestimable. Richard Niebuhr for example has called the Great Awakening the moment of 'national conversion'.[191] For our purposes we note once again the influence of Jonathan Edwards in this. When in 1737, as a result of reflection upon what he described as 'the Surprising Work of God in the Conversion of Many Hundred Souls in Northampton and the Neighbouring Towns and Villages of the County of Hampshire, in the Province of the Massachusetts Bay in New-England', Edwards synthesized scriptural objectivity with spiritual experience, he set Protestants thinking in new ways.[192] If older Protestant orthodoxy had emphasized the objective principles set out in the Bible, and had emphasized the 'once-for-all' saving acts of God in the New Testament revelation, the Moravians and the earliest Methodists stressed in their place the *Busskampf*, the struggle to deal with one's personal guilt which led to the inward, subjective experience of the 'new birth'. Edwards combined the two sets of principles, affirming both scripture and experience. His synthesis was convincing for many of his own generation.

Yet this synthesis (achieved by Wesley as well as Edwards) of head religion and heart religion, of theology and faith, of doctrine and experience, was unstable in the extreme.[193] Indeed it began to break down almost as soon as it had been formulated. The immediate cause of the breakdown lay in a second outbreak of religious fervour around the turn of the eighteenth and nineteenth centuries, known as the 'Second Great Awakening'.[194] These spontaneous and populist religious outbursts, often taking the form of 'camp meetings', came to be determinative in moulding mid-century American evangelicalism and its attendant evangelistic activity.[195] The Methodist historian, Albert Outler, has written of the second series of Awakenings as an 'immense and complex upwelling of the Spirit'. The Second Great Awakening, he wrote, 'rescued the Christian cause and defined American Protestantism for the better part of a century'.[196]

It reconquered the Eastern seaboard from the deists; it helped conquer the opening frontiers of the boisterous West. It invented the camp meeting as a new way of getting the gospel to the people. It turned revivalism from an episodic affair to a permanent institution. It relegated the sacraments and Christian nurture to a marginal role and its own theological ethos came to be identified as the distinctive meaning of the word 'evangelical' in America.[197]

In *They Gathered at the River: The Story of the Great Revivalists and their Impact upon Religion in America* (1958), another American writer, Bernard

Weisberger, describes in great detail the new expressions of Pietist, Methodist and Edwardsian teachings within the 'evangelical' denominations and
shows how all these churches came to share the expectation that the 'saved'
would have gone through 'a definite, palpable religious experience'.[198] This
process was well known to both Edwards and Wesley, but their successors
coarsened and over-simplified the way in which they expected it to take
place. Weisberger describes their crude understanding of the 'order of salvation':

> First a man felt a gnawing sense of guilt and wickedness, and then a
> frightening awareness that hell was an entirely just punishment for such a
> wretch as he. Thus, 'broken down before the Lord', the sinner, stripped of
> pride and self-esteem, was ready to throw himself on God's mercy. Now,
> if God had chosen him for salvation, he might read the promises in the
> Bible and feel that they applied to him. He could pass from being 'con-
> victed' of sin and 'anxious' for his soul, to a state described as 'hopeful'.
> Lastly, he might have a climactic emotional experience, some special
> 'baptism of the Spirit', some inward, unmistakable sign that pardon was
> extended and a crown of glory laid up for him in heaven. This was re-
> generation. Without it all men and women, no matter how shining their
> virtues or pious their deeds, were sinners. But the sinner who had this
> experience was 'saved', or 'converted', or 'born again', or 'made a
> Christian', the exact term differing with the time and place.[199]

Protestant revivalism was consequently and consistently 'anti-sacerdotal,
anti-sacramental, anti-intellectualist'.[200] Albert Outler has summarized the
effects of revivalism under three aspects. 'It made', he has written, 'a pejorative distinction between speculative theology and existential faith. It was suspicious of a learned clergy. It regarded conversion as more typically the climax of Christian experience than its initiation. It insisted on personal religion as the only real essence of Christianity.'[201]

For the thousands and thousands of 'born again' believers caught up in
revivalism it had to be extremely doubtful whether their own country-people
in North America or in Europe (for revivalism quickly returned to the home-
lands of the American immigrants) were or could be 'saved'. Most of these
were declared not to be Christians, and therefore among the lost. Clearly, if
revivalist Christians ever thought about it, there could be no hope at all for
the 'Heathen', not just because of their 'Heathenism', but because they had
not experienced 'conversion' and 'second birth', and had therefore no sense
of Jesus as their personal saviour.

Therefore revivalist hymns, like those of Fanny J. Crosby (1820-1915),
sang of the need to

Rescue the perishing, care for the dying
  Snatch them in pity from sin and the grave
Weep o'er the erring one, lift up the fallen
  Tell them of Jesus the mighty to save.[202]

because, in Horatius Bonar's verse:

Men die in darkness at your side
  Without a hope to cheer the tomb;
Take up the torch and wave it wide,
  The torch that lights time's thickest gloom.[203]

This theme could be and would be applied to the needs of the 'lost ones' overseas. So Bonar continued:

Go forth into the world's highway
  Compel the wanderer to come in.

This warm-hearted 'love for souls' became the supreme revivalist motivation for overseas mission and dominated the scene at D.L. Moody's Mount Hermon and Northfield Conventions in the 1870s and 80s. Many of the students who heard Moody preach at these gatherings were so apprehended by the thought of these 'lost ones' and the love Christ had for them, that they formed the Student Volunteer Movement, with the Watchword, 'The Evangelization of the World in this Generation'.[204] In this company was George Sherwood Eddy (1864-1954) who was to become one of the great leaders of the missionary movement in the first half of the twentieth century. In his autobiography, *A Pilgrimage of Ideas: or the Re-education of Sherwood Eddy* (1935), Eddy recalled his original 'missionary purpose' in which 'there was never any thought of harsh dogmatism, of forcing our religion down the throats of unwilling peoples. We held no ideas of a narrow orthodoxy of "perishing millions" who were eternally lost. This I never believed and never preached at home or abroad. But we were swept into the mid-current of enthusiasm in the great world crusade of our day.'[205]

Intense biblicism and inflexible erudition

As and when revivalism took an anti-intellectualist form, it produced an equal and opposite reaction among many Protestant clergy both in America and in Britain. These still held to 'the objective principles set out in the Bible', and they continued to emphasize the 'once-for-all' saving acts of God, as they conceived them. Temperamentally adverse to 'enthusiasm' and 'spiritual excess', such preachers put their trust in strict adherence to biblical

knowledge and the formulations of the Reformed faith set out in the sixteenth and seventeenth centuries. In America, the Awakenings were criticized alike by 'Old Calvinists' and by Lutherans like John L.Nevin. Charles
Hodge remained hostile to revivalism through his long teaching ministry at
Princeton precisely for these reasons.[206]

In Britain one remarkable work which insisted upon exegesis of the
Christian past, rather than on either speculative or experiential religion, was
Isaac Taylor's *The Natural History of Enthusiasm* (1823).[207] Taylor believed
that Christianity was 'exclusively a religion of documents and of interpretation' and that it had therefore had to exclude from 'its precincts the adventurous spirit of innovation.[208] 'True religion', Isaac Taylor wrote,

> was given to mankind in a finished form, and is to be learned, not im-
> proved: and though the most capacious mind is most nobly employed
> while concentrating all its vigour upon the acquirements of this documen-
> tary learning, it is very fruitlessly and very perniciously occupied in
> attempting to give it a single touch of perfectionment.[209]

Theological study was therefore appropriately arduous and unexciting. The
'toils of learned acquisition', Taylor proclaimed, 'indispose the mind to the
wantonness of speculation, and impart to it rather the timidity, the acquiescence, the patience which are proper to the submissive exposition of an
authoritative rule of faith'.[210] Charles Hodge would have agreed. There is a
legend that he once proudly remarked that there had 'never been a new idea
at Princeton'.[211]

Descriptions of the teaching in British and American theological academies
and seminaries at this period confirm Isaac Taylor's views, and suggest why
The Natural History of Enthusiasm had a ready reception, for it was reprinted
more than once. One example chosen at random rounds out the picture of
timidity, acquiescence and submissiveness. Lancashire College in Manchester
in 1851 would have differed little from any other institution of its kind.[212] A
fellow student is here reporting on the training of his friend David Simon,
later Principal of the Congregational Hall in Edinburgh:

> So far as the theological lectures of the College were concerned I am afraid
> that it must be said that their influence on our friend was practically nil.
> Or perhaps it would be truer to say that they created within him a revul-
> sion of feeling against the system of lecturing then in vogue, which con-
> sisted of repeating over again to successive groups of students lectures
> which had never had much contact with reality and had certainly never
> grown beyond their first inception.[213]

Suggestions that Christian truth might be supplemented by other forms of 'revelation' were unintelligible to this caste of mind. 'True religion' had been given to humanity in 'a finished form', and was to be learned not improved. If Christian teaching in the form that Taylor knew it was the 'authoritative rule of faith', all other teaching was spurious and pernicious.

This attitude has been well called by the Australian historian Stuart Piggin 'erudite inflexibility'.[214] Three factors were part of this complex. 'Erudite inflexibility' was bound up with 'a hostile attitude to doubt'. Doubt was a 'moral disease of the soul' not only for Evangelicals but for a wide range of Victorian Christians.[215] Any questioning of what were regarded as revealed Christian truths was viewed as an indication of moral failure. Evangelicals of this period also believed that normative Christianity must involve a 'combative mentality'.[216] Characteristic words include campaigning and aggression and crusade. A third factor was the sense among such Evangelicals that the gospel was simple, straightforward, uncomplicated. Wise stewardship of time meant that it was foolishness to concern oneself with speculation, which after all was both 'false philosophy' and 'foolishness to the Greeks'.[217] In Piggin's view, these characteristics contributed to 'the great confidence of the missionaries, the invincible relentlessness with which they pursued their soteriological purpose and the systematic manner in which they attempted to undermine Hinduism and Islam'.[218] And, of course, the same characteristics of inflexibility and combativeness underlay the attempt to undermine every other religion.

Piggin also comments that a further element in this mind-set was an ineffable sense of superiority. This cultural imperialism had been presaged by Alexander Pope when he wrote of 'barbarous nations' attending at the gates of British imperialism.[219] Such sentiments mushroomed in the early years of the Great Century, never to diminish until the shock of the 1914-18 World War. The beginning of this period had Jane Austen putting into the mouth of one of her heroes the phrase 'Remember that we are English, that we are Christians'.[220] Its third decade was the moment when Thomas Macaulay could affirm with such extraordinary self-assurance that 'a single shelf of a good European library was worth the whole native literature of India and Arabia'.[221] Piggin justly comments, 'Erudite inflexibility must have been a characteristic of many of the well educated missionaries who served in India in our period, not because they were evangelicals, but because they were British.'[222]

Writing in 1894, Guinness Rogers, a Congregational minister and supporter of the L.M.S., commented on these attitudes from his own experience of them. 'The criticism laid upon the Evangelical religion of two generations ago is often too severe, and is strangely oblivious of the service which its representatives rendered to the cause of humanity'. But, he continued, 'it would be idle to deny that its tendency was to become too self-contained, that it lacked insight and breadth of sympathy, that its introspection was often extremely morbid, and its zeal for orthodoxy apt to become a worship of the letter to the injury of the spirit'.[223] In fact as Rogers implies, such inflexibility and self-assurance had been on their way out for some time. It became intolerable to later Great Century thinkers. This kind of Evangelicalism, wrote Rogers, 'finds little tolerance today for some even of its virtues; there is none for its conspicuous defects'.[224]

A hundred years later historians may be more detached and dispassionate, and recognize the great virtues of the first missionary pioneers. In recognizing their courage, zeal, and tenacity in the face of overwhelming odds, we do not need either to affirm or to despise their theology of other religions. Yet there has to be a sharp awareness of the negative elements within the earlier theology. This survey of the elements of millennialism, millenarianism, rationalism, hyper-Calvinism and revivalism together with the intense biblicism, inflexible erudition and cultural superiority has been intended to suggest the background against which a quite different position about the faith of other men and women had to be worked out. To be sure these elements surfaced in different proportions at different times and in different people, but equally certainly when they did come together these ideas often made for a negative and hostile view of other religions. In so far as these ideas were part of the mental furniture of each of the missionaries and theologians we shall survey in these pages, we may measure their achievements in 'justice, courtesy and love' by reflecting upon their individual points of departure.

2

Five Theologians and World Religions

Frederick Denison Maurice

Frederick Denison Maurice (1805-1872) has a claim to be considered the greatest and most influential nineteenth-century Anglican theologian.[1] The American scholars John F. Porter and William F. Wolf attribute Maurice's continuing influence to his being 'not only the greatest Anglican thinker of the nineteenth century, but also one of the clearest examples to be found anywhere of a Christian prophet'.[2] However such claims be assessed, no one can dispute Maurice's overwhelming impact upon the theology of missions in the Great Century. Maurice is the great prophetic thinker of the nineteenth century; the first to plead for justice, courtesy and love when Christians contemplated the meaning of other religions. He had a direct influence on many missionaries, especially in circles where the 'why' questions of mission theology had become unavoidable.[3] But even more apparent is the way in which he shaped the minds of the later nineteenth-century theologians through his disciples, and therefore at second hand. Throughout the rest of this book we shall find men and women of the last half of the Great Century consciously and unconsciously echoing Maurice.

The Kingdom as a present reality

We have seen that the expectation of an earthly reign of Jesus Christ was a fundamental conception in the minds of very many at the beginning of the Great Century.[4] Millennialist expectations had given rise to a theology of religion which was essentially supersessionist. The time had indeed come for idols to be 'cast to moles and bats'. The starting point for Maurice's theology of mission was of one piece with such thinking, though he gave it an entirely original variation. It was this strand in early nineteenth-century thinking, that led Maurice to his first great work *The Kingdom of Christ* (1838).[5]

In this book Maurice set out his central theme of the 'actual presence' of the Kingdom. His version of millennialism was derived from the views held by his first Rector, J.A. Stephenson of Lympsham and from the Scottish lay theologian Thomas Erskine.[6] Like Stephenson and Erskine, Maurice insisted that the Kingdom of Christ was 'that which is *present*', 'that which is *now*'.[7] This reign of God on the earth was to be found in the existence of 'a king- dom, or order, or constitution, which men have been trying to set at nought and deny, but under which they have been living notwithstanding, and which, in the clear sunlight of that day, is shown to be the only one under which they can live'. Such a kingdom was not and could not be, Maurice insisted, a pious or 'fantastical' hope for future bliss, but the presently exist- ing ground of all human reality. Its 'dominion had been asserting itself' and 'making itself felt, for these eighteen centuries'.[8] The Kingdom of Christ of which Maurice spoke and wrote was not, therefore, to be understood as just a kingdom 'over the heart and spirit of man, over that which directly con- nects him with God and the unseen world', but as 'God's sovereignty over all his human relations, his earthly associations, over the policy of rulers, over nature and over art' and this is 'as much the truth now as it ever can be in any future period'.[9] 'The Son of Man claimed it for Himself when He did not abhor the Virgin's womb, when He mingled with the ordinary transac- tions of men, blessing their food, their wine and their marriage feasts.'[10]

> The claim may have been denied at all times; it may be denied especially at the time to which we are looking forward; but the time must assert it, not as something new but as something old; as a government which has actually been in exercise, and the ceasing of which even for a moment would have been followed by dreariness and death throughout the uni- verse.[11]

In this way Maurice aligned himself with, and addressed, the millennialist thinking uppermost in the minds of many of his contemporaries. The princi- ple of the present Kingdom of Christ, he suggested, would not interfere with

> any sound or true apprehensions of our Lord's second coming, but only with a system which has tended to prevent men from acknowledging it; to make them think lightly of their present responsibilities, to give them a fantastic habit of speaking respecting the course of God's providence in the world, as if it signified nothing now, but was only leading to something hereafter; and which is very likely to suggest the thought, that when He has taken the power whose right it is, the Cross will not any longer be the symbol of glory and victory.[12]

Maurice was sure nevertheless that the millennialist and millenarian mind- sets had done 'infinite service' to the church in turning the thoughts of Christians away from 'the expectation of mere personal felicity apart from the establishment of Christ's kingdom; from the notion of heaven which makes us indifferent to the condition of the earth'.[13] The millenialists and the millenarians had been 'one great means of removing the clouds which had hindered us from looking at Christ's Church as a Kingdom', and of delivering Christians from the 'wretched notion of a private selfish Heaven, where compensation shall be made for troubles incurred, and prizes given for duties performed in this lower sphere.' This 'unnatural notion' had clothed itself in the language of scripture and of early Christian thinking, but had severed, in Maurice's view, the 'language from the idea with which it was always impregnated, and connecting it with our low, grovelling, mercantile habits of feeling'. Such thinking had, he said, 'infused itself into our popular teachings and our theological books'.[14]

But Maurice insisted that the millenarians had also done a good deal of mischief. This lay in their substituting the idea of an 'external advent or descent' for the fulfilment of a spiritual redemption, which would be the working out in this world of the goodness and the justice of God. It was, Maurice told his sister Esther, the 'duty and privilege' of Christians 'to believe constantly that Christ the Redeemer of Mankind, who has been manifesting Himself in all ages for the deliverance of the earth from its tyrants and for the assertion of right and truth against wrong and falsehood will be manifested completely for that end.'[15]

The Kingdom of Christ centred on Maurice's vision of the establishment of a 'Spiritual and Universal Kingdom'.[16] Humankind would eventually see the 'hidden hunger' of all previous systems satisfied in the 'Principles, Ordinances and Constitution of the Catholic Church'.[17] Maurice produced a series of 'Hints' to a member of the Society of Friends to show how this satisfaction of hidden hunger might be fulfilled within the existing Christian groupings. *The Kingdom of Christ* concludes with a prayer that all God's enemies might perish. The enemies Maurice had in mind were 'all systems, schools, parties which have hindered men from seeing the largeness, freedom and glory of Thy Kingdom'.[18] Maurice's prayer was that those who loved God should be set free from the 'earthly mists' and be 'as the sun when he goeth forth in his strength'.[19] If, in 1838, 'all previous systems' had meant only the Christian sects, schools and parties, it could only be a matter of time before Maurice would address the 'hidden hunger' and the 'earthly mists' within the 'non-Christian' religious systems of the world.

Maurice's christology

Maurice was entirely clear that nothing could be external to the presence of 'Christ the Redeemer of Mankind manifesting Himself in all ages'. There was not and could not have been any place or time when Christ was not present. In *The Kingdom of Christ*, he wrote that 'the Word of God before He came in the flesh was the light which lightened all men' was a principle as much confirmed 'by the evidence of profane as of sacred history'.[20] But the coming of Christ in the flesh was determinative of the way in which cultures and religious traditions were to be interpreted. They were 'preparations for a clearer day':

> Christ the Living Word, the Universal Light, appeared to men, and showed in his own person what processes He was carrying on in the hearts of all... this manifestation was the signal for the commencement of a new dispensation; sensible emblems were no longer to intercept a man's view of his Lord; national distinctions were to be abolished; men were to be treated as belonging to a higher state than they lost in Adam; they might attain a perfection which did not exist in Adam.[21]

The conviction that Christ is the head of humanity inspired every part of *The Kingdom of Christ*. Christ was the head of all people 'though they neither know or acknowledge him'.[22] God's purpose in creation was all inclusive, and humanity's redemption came not from beliefs or doctrines but from the fact of Christ's headship. 'Man as man' is the child of God and needs only to recognize that he already is such. The Bible was to be seen as a revelation of God, not of religion or theology. The whole of society cohered in Christ. It had its focus and unity in him:

> It was the business of Christ's ministers to proclaim that there could have been no families, no nations, no social impulses, no laws, nothing to resist the selfish and self seeking tendencies in which each of us is conscious in himself and complains of in his neighbours, if here had not been one living centre of the whole body of Humanity, one Head of every man.[23]

In thus proposing that christology should be the starting point of both theology and ethics, Maurice put himself in a position to insist that the gospel had to be heard 'in terms of its universal message'.[24] This view many of his contemporaries understood to be what they called Maurice's 'universalist heresy'. 'Universalism' was then, as now, a term of abuse in circles which prided themselves on scriptural orthodoxy. Maurice's position, however, did not suggest that 'all people would be saved' whether they so willed or no. His view of history turned upon his belief in the 'restoration' or 'restitution' of all things, as in Acts 3.21 and Ephesians 1.10. 'Though I have no faith in man's theory of Universal Restitution,' he wrote, 'I am taught to expect "A restitution of all things, which God who cannot lie has promised since the world began." I am obliged to believe that we are living in a restored order; I am sure that restored order will be carried out by the full triumph of God's loving will.'[25] This position had both missiological causes and missiological consequences.[26] Maurice profoundly believed that if universal salvation were to be denied as a possibility there could be no gospel to proclaim: 'To say that a soul in this world *cannot* be raised out of death is to say that there is no gospel or salvation for human beings at all.'[27] Signs of a 'universal and spiritual society' had to be, and could be, discerned everywhere.

In these ways Maurice modified millennialist hope to such an extent that it became something else, in fact a doctrine of an actually present 'Kingdom of Christ', which was grounded in the incarnation. By so doing he laid the foundations, on the one hand, for a theology of the presence of Christ in other religious traditions, and, on the other, for a missionary theology of completion and fulfilment. These theologies were to be worked out in Maurice's Boyle Lectures of 1845-6, *The Religions of the World and their Relations to Christianity*.[28]

The Boyle Lectures

In his will, made in 1691, Robert Boyle had provided that 'Eight Sermons should be preached each year in London for proving the Christian religion against notorious Infidels, to wit, Atheists, Theists, Pagans, Jews and Mahometans; not descending any lower to any controversies that are among Christians themselves.'[29] Boyle also willed that 'the preacher of these Sermons should be assisting to all companies, and encouraging of them in any undertaking for propagating the Christian Religion to foreign parts'.[30] Maurice was, however, not a missionary thinker in any traditional sense and had no intention of proving the truth of the Christian religion against infidels, notorious or otherwise. Before he could in good conscience take up Boyle's provisions, he had to reinterpret them.[31] There was certainly room for manoeuvre. Boyle had nowhere suggested that his own views of the relation of Christianity to other religions was fixed and final. On the contrary, Maurice suggested, Boyle would have thought that as 'new regions unfolded themselves to European adventure, new facts modifying or changing previous notions respecting the faiths which prevailed in them, might come to light'.[32] Boyle might well have considered that the doubts 'respecting the justice, wisdom, or possibility of bringing other men into our religious fellowship which presented themselves to his contemporaries' might reappear 'in very different shapes, appealing to even opposite feelings and shapes'.[33] Were this to have been so, Maurice surmised, Boyle would have approved Maurice's style of 'proving the Christian religion' in the mid-nineteenth century. Indeed, Boyle would surely have been intrigued by the widespread interest which his Lectureship aroused in the rest of the Victorian period. Maurice's *The Religions of the World and their Relations to Christianity* was reprinted at least six times before 1900. His son and biographer General Frederick Maurice thought they had 'perhaps been the most popular of all his writings'.[34]

As he set the scene in the Lectures, Maurice affirmed his belief that within the previous fifty years 'a prodigious change' had taken place in the views of the educated classes concerning 'Religious Systems'.[35] The predominant idea among philosophers and thinkers during the seventeenth and eighteenth centuries, he suggested, had been that 'religions were essentially the inventions of law-givers and priests'.[36] Then the task of the Christian apologist had been to demonstrate that there existed one exception to this generalization. This was of course Christianity, 'which could not be referred to this origin'.[37] But now, Maurice wrote in 1846, people were beginning to be convinced that if 'Religion had only the devices and tricks of statesmen or priests to rest upon, it could not have stood at all'. These devices and tricks, he asserted, were 'very weak things', which, 'if left to themselves', 'a popular tempest must carry utterly away'.[38] Maurice proposed an alternative view: if these religions had 'lasted a single day, it must have been because they had something better, truer than themselves, to sustain them'.[39]

> This better, truer thing, it seems to be allowed, must be that very faith in men's hearts upon which so many disparaging epithets were cast, and which it was supposed would produce no fruits that were not evil and hurtful. Faith, it is now admitted, has been the most potent instrument of good to the world; has given to it nearly all which it can call precious.[40]

'Faith' was for Maurice an essential ingredient in being human. All religions were in some sense 'legitimate products' of that that faith which is 'so essentially part of man's constitution'.[41] If this were true, Maurice suggested, a different set of challenges then arose to the Christian claims. Increasing knowledge and speculation about the other world religious traditions raised the question of relativism, for many voices suggested that these forms of faith were transitory, adapted as they are to 'particular times and localities':

> Is it not possible that the theology of all alike is something merely accidental, an imperfect theory about our relations to the universe which will in due time give place to some other? Have we not reason to suppose that Christianity, instead of being, as we have been taught, a Revelation, has its root in the heart and intellect of man, as much as any other system... Must we not expect that it too will lose all its mere theological characteristics, and that what at last survives of it will be something of a very general character, some great ideas of the good and the beautiful, some excellent maxims of life, which may very well assimilate, if they be not actually the same, with the essential principles which are contained in all other religions, and which will also, it is hoped, abide for ever?[42]

With these questionings, foreshadowing the controversies which still surround inter-faith relationships, Maurice turned to an extensive survey of Islam, Hinduism, Buddhism and the religions of China, and the ancient religions of Greece, Persia, Rome and the Northern peoples. But analysis of

Maurice's treatment of each these, fascinating as it might have been, has to be omitted here. Maurice's theological understanding of their place and purpose is our sole concern now.

A Christian appraisal of Islam

Maurice's treatment of Islam turned upon the central figure of its great prophet. For most of the thirteen previous centuries Christians had alleged that Muhammad was an impostor and a charlatan, at worst an agent of Satan, at best a plagiarist.[43] More recent views in the West were only just beginning to suggest that Muhammad was a great humanist and statesman.[44] Two years before Maurice published *The Religions of the World* Thomas Carlyle had proclaimed Muhammad as 'the hero as prophet'.[45]

Maurice's judgment was altogether different from that of Carlyle for it pointed to Muhammad as a 'witness for God'.[46] Maurice unhesitatingly affirmed that Muhammad knew himself as nothing other than a witness for God, and that his followers 'received him and honoured him as holding that office'.[47] He described Muhammad's spiritual significance in some of the most generous terms ever used of Islam by a committed Christian thinker. Let us examine these in order of their importance for a Christian theology of religion.

First, Maurice insisted that the great sweeping conquests of Islam in its early centuries should be interpreted as the activity and the presence of God, in that 'they may be regarded as the righteous judgments of God upon guilty nations'.[48] The discovery of what he saw as the real ground of the early Muslim conquests should lead Western people to think of this Islamic invasion 'not wholly as a calamity'.[49] The Muslim armies had come to people for whom 'God was no longer an Absolute Eternal Being' and had said, 'God verily is, and man is his minister, to accomplish his will upon the earth'.[50] Maurice thought that Christians should gladly admit that it was 'a mercy of God that such a witness' should have been given to God's Name, 'when his creatures were ready, practically, to forget it'.[51]

Then Maurice asserted that Islam's very existence gave a new perspective to the nature of religious faith. In an age when some people were beginning to think that the 'theological part of religious systems' was only 'a loose, flimsy drapery for certain maxims of morality, or certain ideas about the nature and spiritual destinies of man', Muslim faith and history had demonstrated that 'all mere maxims, all mere ideas about the nature of man' had 'proved weak and helpless before this proclamation of a living and eternal God'.[52] Christians ought therefore to cherish the theological principle involved here. Islam was a witness against the suggestion that the 'great doctrines which have been embodied in religious systems are the creation of the religious principle in man'. Muslim faith denied that religious truth was the result of 'some outward expression of our feelings or habits of mind'.[53] The message of Muhammad, Maurice insisted

> meant nothing... was nothing except so far as it asserted a being *not* dependent on itself; the ground of man's being; one of whom he was the minister not the creator. The Mahommetan believed that the God whom he worshipped must have revealed Himself – that man could not have discovered him. It was in the power of this belief that he went forth to beat into powder all the gods whom he supposed that man had invented. Take away these characteristics from his faith and it vanishes, with all the doings that are the fruits of it.[54]

The Muslim 'was right when he said there is something in the world which we are not to tolerate, which we are sent into the world to exterminate'.[55] Such a view was consonant with Maurice's own theology and is a straightforward contradiction of Augustinianism and its derivative pre-millenarianism. If Christians suggested in their teaching and preaching that the Kingdom of God was other-worldly and spiritual, they must be prepared to be taught by Muslims 'that every man and every nation exists for the purpose of chasing falsehood and evil out of God's universe'.[56]

Some Christian hints on Hinduism

Maurice's views on Hinduism were no more than a collection of hints, if we may use one of his own expressions. His knowledge of original sources was rudimentary.[57] Secondary sources in his day were also few and limited.[58] The great mid-century interpreters of Hinduism like Monier Williams and Max Müller had as yet published little or nothing and Maurice had to rely on William Jones, Henry Colebrooke, and Horace Hayman Wilson.[59] But even as 'hints', Maurice's ideas were to inspire, both directly and indirectly, a whole generation of missionaries in the latter half of the Great Century. With their first hand and accurate knowledge of Hinduism such missionary thinkers were able to build on Maurice's insights.

Although he was often mistaken in points of detail, Maurice was able to affirm fundamental human aspirations and needs in many aspects of Indian religious traditions. God had not left the Hindu without witness. Maurice made five different points.

First, from a Christian point of view, Hinduism was a 'faith' to be respected and pondered. Maurice wrote: 'the more we think of it, the more fairly we consider its apparent anomalies, the more light we receive respecting it from different and contradictory reports, the more heartily and affectionately we sympathise with the feelings of our fellow men, the more we know of ourselves will awaken in us the more *of reflection and wonder and awe.*'[60]

Second, Christians should recognize that Hinduism was the faith 'not of savages' but of people in whose minds 'respect for learning has occupied all but the highest place'. Indian culture was built upon the principle that 'the seer, the learned man, ought to be at the head that all other people should look up to him'.[61]

Third, Hinduism was evidence for Maurice's hypothesis that there were 'deep truths implied in each of these systems'. This hypothesis, he wrote, 'receives... abundant confirmation from even the hasty glance we have been able to take of Hindooism'.[62]

Fourth, Hinduism bore a special witness that there was 'that in man which demands a Revelation'. At the same time everything about the Hindu system was evidence that there was '*not* that in him which makes the Revelation.'[63]

Fifth, Hinduism asked 'great human questions'. Maurice listed them eloquently. First there were the questions about God 'What do we worship? A dream or a real Being? One wholly removed from us one or related to us? Is he a Preserver or a Destroyer?' Second, there were questions about the significance of death: 'Has death explained its meaning us, or is it still a horrible riddle? Is it still uncertain whether Life or Death is master of the world, or how has the uncertainty been removed?' In third place come the questions about evil: 'What is the evil which I find in myself? Is it myself? Must *I* perish in order that it may perish, or can it be any wise separated from me?' Fourth came questions about the self or the soul in relation to God: 'Can I give up myself and yet live?' 'What are these desires I feel in myself for something, unseen, glorious and perfect? Are they all phantasy, or can they be realized? If they can, by what means? Has He to whom they point made Himself known to me? How am I connected with Him? Must I utterly renounce all the things about me, that I may be absorbed into Him, or is there any way in which I can devote them and myself to Him, and only know Him better by filling my place among them?'[64]

These, he wrote, were the 'great human questions; distance in time and space does not affect them'.[65] If people in the West were not concerned with such issues, Maurice thought, they should realize that they were on their way to losing their dignity as human beings.[66]

The Christian enigma of Buddhism

Maurice knew even less about Buddhism than about Hinduism.[67] He dealt with it, however, as 'by far the most prevailing religion' in the world. Therefore it had to be investigated with the utmost seriousness: 'there had to lie within in a cause for its wide diffusion'; it had 'to express some necessities of man's heart, some necessities of our own'.[68] Westerners had to address 'that which is within the heart of those who hold this faith'.[69]

His own attempts to understand its apparently universal appeal led Maurice to the first of his conclusions about Buddhism. He found its underlying principle to be that 'there is in man, in humanity, a certain Divine Intelligence, which at different times, and in different places, manifests itself more or less completely, and which must have some central manifestation'.[70] This had led in Buddhism to profound feelings of reverence for the human spirit.[71] Second there was in Buddhism a conviction that it is the privilege of the holy man to 'know God', and to 'contemplate the Divinity in His purity'.[72] A third conclusion was that Buddhism recognized that 'a Divine power and wisdom' may dwell 'in human beings and that its dwelling constitutes them heroic spirits, saintly people'.[73] This was Buddhism's 'strange testimony of a Spirit in the human race'. As he searched for a way of understanding the interrelationship of Buddhist and Christian apprehensions of reality, he coined two phrases: 'the Buddhist side of Christianity', and 'Christian Buddhism'.[74] The ideas of complementarity and mutual fulfilment lying behind such phrases are central to Maurice's theology of religion.

These brief summaries enable us to glimpse some of Maurice's own struggle to discern the significance for Christians of three great religious traditions. Though he tried to do scholarly justice to each one, his concern was never primarily that of the student of religion. His first lectures on 'The Religions of the World' were in place only in order that he might take up his central theme, 'Their Relations to Christianity'. This emphasis on 'relationships' makes it possible for a modern interpreter to discern 'Ten Principles' relevant still to discussion of the theology of religion and interfaith dialogue.

Ten principles for Christian relationships with other religions

1. *The phenomenon of religion is always to be understood theologically.* One of the obligations laid upon the Boyle lecturer was to prove the truth of the Christian religion. This was to be done by satisfying 'such objections and difficulties as may be stated, to which good answers have not yet been made'.[75] Maurice was clear that he had been focussing on the objections and difficulties which faced his own contemporaries in *The Religions of the World*. 'In compliance with the directions of Boyle', he wrote, 'I sought for that which seemed to be the most prevailing form of unbelief in our day; and I found it in the tendency to look upon all theology as having its origin in the spiritual nature and facilities of man'.[76]

Maurice sought to challenge such assumptions thoughout *The Religions of the World*. He insisted that God, not human minds, imaginations, or energies, had raised up Islam, Hinduism or Buddhism. Could the proposition that religion was a human construction adequately explain 'any system'? 'Do not *all* demand another ground than the human one?' There would be major consequences, according to Maurice, if such questions were not properly addressed. The first result would be confirmation that the Christian world really had nothing to say to the Muslim or the Hindu or the Buddhist worlds. If Westerners had no more to offer than a humanist view of religion, Maurice insisted that there should be an end to mission and to colonialism alike: 'for mercy's sake let us be silent – the Buddhists are better as they are'.[77] So also would be the Muslims and the Hindus.

So then, if religion was only a human invention, all missionary activity was an exercise in propaganda, making other people into clones of ourselves. Maurice speculated whether mid-Victorian Europeans had not already succumbed to this notion and were not already half acting as though 'we were propagating a system of our own'.[78] 'Has not,' he wondered, 'the impression we have conveyed to the minds of Mahometans and pagans been something of this kind?', so that they might be thought of as saying:

> These Frenchmen, Dutchmen, Spaniards, or Englishmen, acknowledge a certain teacher to whom they attach very high titles. They wish us to acknowledge their teacher instead of those whom we in Arabia, Persia or Hindostan, have been accustomed to honour. In other words, they wish to make us Europeans, to bring us over to their modes and habits of thinking.[79]

In the sentences which follow Maurice showed himself perfectly aware that the best missionaries had never intended this. 'By their language, by their acts...' they brought 'the assurance that there is One who has taken the nature, not of Englishmen, Frenchmen, Spaniards, but of Man; who has entered into man's misery and death; has borne the sins of man; has encountered all his enemies and vanquished them.'[80] This was the 'old proclamation of a divine kingdom', 'the old Gospel' which depended on no philosophical doctrine or theory whatsoever, which shows 'how little we or any human creatures want a theory; what absolute need all creatures have of a Living God who will reveal to us Himself: what relation there is between us and Him; how He works in us to bring us to know his purposes; and to move in accordance with them.'[81]

Only with such a theology could Christians engage in missionary activity without cultural imperialism. More important still was the idea that only with such a theology could Christians see the religions of the world as more than human inventions, and integral to the working out of God's purposes in the world. The phenomenon of religion had to be understood *theologically*.[82]

2. *Christianity is the key to the reconciliation of religions*. Maurice affirmed this principle in the midst of a series of questions summing up attack on the alternative view to the decrying of religions as human inventions, namely in the 'tendency to look upon all theology as having its origin in the spiritual nature and faculties of man'.[83] If this view of 'the explanation of other

systems' was allowed to prevail, it could be used just as well to explain the origin of Christianity. If all religious activity is to be understood in psychological terms, what was specific about Christianity? But Maurice insisted that all religious systems demand another ground than the human one, and went on to ask whether Christianity did not offer the perfect solution to the question as to the nature of this 'higher ground' when it pointed to its own basis in revelation? Does it not actually and consistently refer every human feeling and consciousness to that higher ground? 'Is it not *for this reason*', he asked, 'able to interpret and reconcile the other religions of the world? Does it not in this way present itself to be not a human system but *the* revelation which human beings require?'[84]

The heart of Maurice's theology of religion lies here. Christian faith is not a system but a revelation. Maurice pointed to 'the old Gospel that the Son of God the Deliverer of Man has appeared and will be shown hereafter to be the Lord of the universe'.[85] This 'old Gospel' was in fact 'a proclamation of the eternal Law of the Universe, which wears not out, which grows not old; is not, in any sense whatever, our scheme or theory of the universe, but is sent to confound, to break in pieces our schemes and theories of the universe'.[86] The 'cultured despisers of religion' whom Maurice had so often in mind when he was composing these lectures, would, he said, have achieved much if they had broken down among Christians 'a low and grovelling notion we had formed of our own position and work', if they had convinced Christians 'human systems must indeed perish', and that Christians should recognize that 'what survives must be something of a much higher derivation, of a more permanent character'.[87]

> We owe them the deepest gratitude if they have led us to ask ourselves whether there is any faith, and what kind of faith it is which must belong, not to races but mankind; still more, if they have forced us to the conclusion, that the real test, whether there be such a faith, and whether it has been made known to us, must be action, not argument; that if it exist, it must show that it exists; that if it have power, it must put forth its power.[88]

Christians were not to affirm the theory of Christianity over against other theories. They had, rather, to testify to Revelation. It was this Revelation, rather than any form of Christian ideology, which interpreted and reconciled the other religious traditions.

3. *Creation in the image of God is the basis for evaluating all other religious traditions.* It is apparent from *The Religions of the World* how little Maurice made use of categories like Original Sin or any other aspect of the Fall Doctrine based on Genesis 3. He allowed little or no place to the Devil or to Satanic influence.[89] None of these ideas so widely used in traditional

Christian circles is used by Maurice to account for the existence of religious traditions outside Christianity. This is consistent with the great body of Maurice's theology, which always began with the Creation rather than with the Fall.[90] We have seen already how strongly he believed that the world and humankind had been created in Christ, that Christ is 'the actual head of man'.[91] Since Christ was 'Lord of all before he came in the flesh' there was a divine root in humanity 'whence all that is good in churchmen or in man of the world, in believer or unbeliever, springs'.[92] In *The Religions of the World* an identical sense emerges of the unity of the human race because all people were created in the image of God.

> We turn to the earliest of the Jewish records, and find it declared that God made man in His own image, and gave him dominion over all the other creatures he had formed. Before a word has been said about the difference of one people from another, here is a broad fundamental assertion respecting man as man. Perhaps you will say, 'Yes; but this is set at nought by one which immediately follows it; the fall of Adam is the real, though the creation of man may be the nominal beginning of the history.' As we are examining these records to find what they actually confirm, I consider the simplest, nay, the only honest method, is to take them as beginning where they seem to begin, not to assume a starting point of our own.[93]

Nowhere in the Bible, Maurice insisted, was it ever suggested that the 'constitution of God was nullified, destroyed or even at all affected, by the evil acts of man'.[94] To be sure 'the very first man' forgot that he was made in the image of God and 'denied the law after which he was created'. But that did not change anything in God:

> But neither the first man nor any of his successors could make this degradation or disobedience anything else than an anomaly and a contradiction. The worst man in Scripture is never represented as evil in any other sense than because he fights against the law under which he exists, and of which his very transgression is the continual witness. And therefore in the Bible God is ever represented as addressing himself to the creature whom he had formed as awakening in him by his voice a consciousness of his right condition.[95]

Maurice's conclusion was that all history was marked by God's activity. God had related to humanity always and everywhere as created in the *imago Dei*. The existence of the religious traditions was testimony to this. Maurice's interpretation of other forms of religious faith could not turn upon ideas of sinfulness, fallenness, and the demonic. On the contrary, they all witness to 'an order and a beauty and a power' at work in the world.[96]

4. *All religions are part of human history which itself points to a completion.* For Maurice, the counterpart to the doctrine of creation was a strong teleological sense of history. Maurice wrote of Jewish history that it pointed always to a completion, and 'that completion in a Person'.[97] The witness of the prophetic tradition pointed to a King who should establish righteousness. Individual prophets had declared that 'David and his line were the preparation' for one who would establish a universal kingdom.[98] Maurice believed, as we have seen, that this hope of a universal and restored society had been fulfilled in the Kingdom of Christ, and that this was a 'fatherly kingdom, whose Lord must be a suffering man who is yet the Son of God'.[99] This pattern, which Maurice saw demonstrated in the work and witness of Jesus, would be found implicit in all other cases of religious aspiration. Therefore all religions and all civilizations point to a *telos*, an end or completion.

In this way Maurice was able to write of China's eventual discovery of the meaning of all its history. How right, or so it seemed to Maurice, that Confucius and his followers should have spoken only of what they knew, and did not make the leap of faith into speaking glibly of Divine Fatherhood.[100] Yet how good it would be if then they were to hear of a 'faith which assumed that the ground of all things and all men is a Father, that He has spoken and does speak by His Filial Word to the hearts and spirits of men, so making them wise and separating them from what is base and vain; and that this Filial Word has become flesh and dwelt amongst us?'[101] Would they not see a completion or fulfilment of their aspirations and insights in this? There would surely be immediate consequences. The authority of all earthly fathers would be upheld. The communion of human beings would be grounded in obedience to 'the Spirit of order and harmony'.[102] Maurice wondered if the Chinese would then not think 'that there was some strange adaptation in the one to the other?' What all China had been asking for in all the centuries would now have been disclosed, and Chinese history would set out on a new course. But this would only be possible, in Maurice's view, because the Word had already been present in Chinese history, because God the Word had spoken and does speak to the hearts and spirits of men and women, not only in the Church, but at all times and in all seasons. Maurice's missionary readers saw straightaway that the principle set out here applied just as much to the cultures and civilizations in which they found themselves. The longings of India or Japan were just as much indications of the presence of the divine Word in those lands, and the religious insights and perceptions of their peoples could expect to find completion and fulfilment in the disclosure of the Word become flesh in Jesus Christ.

5. *The insights and testimonies of the religions of the world find responses within the Christian revelation.* Throughout his interpretation of Buddhism Maurice had argued that it had many insights which Christians should recognize and welcome. He wrote, for example, of Buddhist understandings of 'holy men'

who appeared as benefactors in different portions of the globe; 'their foot-steps traced upon earth, yet their home seeming to be somewhere else. What they are is known chiefly by what they have done; their acts are palpable, a mystery hangs about themselves'.[103] Maurice noted that these figures were called Buddhas, (though we should now call them *boddhisattvas*).[104] 'Though they appear in places and times far apart the same wisdom, the same power dwells in them all; they must be the wisdom and power of Buddha, they can belong to no other.'[105] This was reflected in, and could be responded to as one aspect of what Maurice called the 'Buddhism of the Gospel'.[106]

> Even thus do Christians speak of those who in far-off ages, in various lati-tudes, have shed light into the hearts of men, have cheered the poor in the midst of their sore trials with help for the present, hope for the future, have restrained triumphant evil, and laboured that righteousness and truth might flourish. These we hold to be all partakers of the self-same Spirit; in their words and acts they manifest its presence; care not to be great in themselves, but do homage to a mysterious greatness, from which all that seems such in themselves is derived; show that they have their work on earth, their citizenship in the heavens.[107]

When Buddhists thought like this, they were affirming that 'there must be some person, and that a human person, in whom the wisdom resides':

> He need not in his earthly appearance be glorious; he may wear the form of a child; but the Power must be within, and must so reveal itself that men shall see the Divine Priest which is there. Even thus it is the clearest, most invariable proclamation in the Gospel, that each man, in his best, purest state, does but utter some portion of the Divine Mind, does but exhibit some one partial image of the Divine Character.[108]

To be sure, Maurice went on immediately to make the point that Jesus Christ was the 'one perfect Utterance of that Voice'.[109] But this was not merely oversimplification in the interests of apologetics. Maurice was sure that the two religions were not teaching the same doctrine, and that therefore there could be no spurious syncretism. 'The Buddhist starts from the human ground; assumes the existence or possibility of certain qualities and attributes of a divine nature in man; supposes the man in virtue of them to hold inter-course with the Divinity.'[110]

The Christian revelation, however, 'represents all faculties, powers, ener-gies as gifts of the Creator'. If the Buddhists are right there cannot be any-thing to be manifested. If the Christians are, then holy people, holy places, miracles are 'signs of a Presence'.[111] Maurice described the consequences of this in some detail, and showed clearly in the process the grounds of

Christian-Buddhist dialogue. But the suggestion on Maurice's part that Buddhist faith had its counterpart in Christian faith was a pioneering insight. It is still potentially valuable as it avoids the concept that was to grow so prominent at the end of the Great Century, namely that of fulfilment.[112] Buddhism raises perfectly proper questions. The answers which Christianity gives may not necessarily be within the same conceptual frameworks.[113]

The second case was that of Hinduism. In *The Religions of the World* Maurice reflected on the meaning of sacrifice in Indian religion. 'If', he wrote, 'the other portions of the faith of the Hindoos have that which answers to them in ours, their faith in the might and blessing of Sacrifice is one which we are bound with all our hearts to participate.'

If there be any acts of past or present ages on which we can think with delight, which we can be sure had Christ's mark upon them, which have wrought mightily, though in general secretly, for the deliverance of men from idols, here has been the root and spring of them.[114]

But to be so near is yet to be so far. Maurice perceived that it was 'just in this point of deepest sympathy with this ancient people that we arrive at the secret of our opposition':

Upon the question to *whom* the sacrifice should be offered, whether by it we propitiate a Siva, or surrender ourselves in love and trust to Him who cares for us and loves us; whether it is to overcome the reluctance of an enemy, or is the offering of our own reluctant wills to a Father in the name of one who has presented and is ever presenting His own filial and complete sacrifice – upon this issue, let us understand it well, our controversy with Hinduism stands.[115]

The correspondence of the Hindu doctrine of sacrifice with that which answers it in the Christian revelation is obvious. But the difference is radical. The question turned on 'whether we hold a system of opinions or a revelation from God'. Maurice saw the 'differences in our thoughts of God, of the priest, of the sacrifice' as all going back to this primary difference. Nevertheless, both the Buddhist conception of the divine spirit in human beings and the Hindu desire for spiritual oneness with the divine through sacrifice belong to the same realm of discourse. It is for Christians to note that there is 'that in the Revelation' which 'answers' to these and many other aspects of the faith of other men and women.

6. *Christians must never cease to look for all that is good in the world's religious traditions.* In *The Religions of the World* Maurice spoke of the danger that Western or British Christianity might just 'float just upon the surface of our minds, just keeping itself alive by a few phrases and conventions among

the multitude of our pursuits'.[116] If that were to be the case, British imperialism would undoubtedly be bane rather than blessing, for then, only an 'external polish would be communicated to the nations which we rule; their inward condition under our hands will become less strong, less sound than it was before'.[117] Only, he told his contemporaries, if 'our cultivation be of that kind which is truly human, which delights to discern the essential humanity of each nation, to honour it, to sympathise with it shall we understand that which is peculiar in our subjects, or reform that which is corrupt in them'.[118] Maurice's words were not at all heeded, as we well know, and the imperialists frequently forgot the humanity of those whom the British Empire governed.[119] But Maurice, the mid-Victorian prophet of justice and understanding for Hindu, Muslim and Buddhist alike, insisted that Christians had no right to undervalue any good thing which they might find anywhere.

So 'dealing fairly' had to become the basic attitude in understanding other religions. It was vital, Maurice insisted 'to preserve the precious fragments of truth' which may be lodged in other religions.[120] It was fundamental, he argued, that Christians should 'think with delight' on any facts in past or present ages which were indications of desire to do the will of God, 'as indications of God's will, however perverted by man's ignorance and selfishness'.

> When we meet with a fanatical exaltation of spiritual emotions, excitements, ecstasies, we shall be most anxious to assert the reality and universality of spiritual communications to place them on their deepest ground, to show how utterly dreary man's condition would be without them. When we see a fanatical exaltation of human faculties, then most shall we be eager to assert their worth and sacredness; to vindicate them from all aspersions grounded upon the imperfections which attach to them in this world; to maintain that he who refuses them the noblest cultivation despises and blasphemes the Author of them. And that the truths proclaimed by raving sects and idolaters of the intellect may both be preserved, we shall bring them into fellowship. The communication of the Divine Spirit we shall believe to be the only means whereby the Reason, the Heart, the Understanding are enabled to perform their rightful functions, to be vigorous, calm, pure, in harmony with the mind of the Creator, and with all that is truly human.[121]

The other religious traditions had many things in common with the Christian faith, and Maurice was glad to think that this was so, as he wrote: 'I have not disguised from you the Buddhist side of Christianity; I have rejoiced to set it forth, as I rejoiced to set forth the Mahometan and Hindoo sides of it.'[122]

7. *The encounter with other religious systems will help to detect the errors into which 'Christianity as a System' is also prone to fall.* Maurice continually

distinguished between the gospel proclaimed by Jesus and in the early church, and the distortions that have arisen in Christian understanding and practice through the centuries.[123] If the deepest apprehensions of Islam, Hinduism and Buddhism have that which finds an answer to them in the Christian understanding, so too the mistakes and errors of all three have their counterparts in historical Christianity. Thus Maurice wrote, '...the temptations of Jews and Mahometans are our temptations... we carry their practical confusions and divisions in our own bosoms. At every moment we are liable to fall into them.'[124] He wrote a few pages later: 'I showed you we are open to all Mahometan temptations. So we are to all Hindu temptations.' Christians

> may exalt a priestly caste, as if it were to make the rest of men Sudras; we may dwell upon the privilege of holding intercourse with the Divine Being, till we sink into self-worshippers; we may revenge ourselves for this abstract idolatry by plunging into outward idolatry; we may at last bow down before Siva, who we should have known was in all these ways drawing us into his worship, since every act of pride, spiritual, intellectual, sensual, is a mystery of his worship.[125]

Similarly, Maurice reminded his readers that they had seen at least two forms of degraded Buddhism in Christian history. If there had been elements in Buddhism from which Christians might learn, so there were other aspects of Buddhism which were temptations, indeed pitfalls, into which Christians had already fallen. In this second sense Maurice thought it might be 'the idlest of all visions to talk of our converting Buddhists, when, judging from various indications, they are far more likely to convert us'.[126] He continued:

> Assuredly, there are distinct traces of prevalent triumphant Buddhism in the Christian Church in periods gone by. The history of Orders rising up to reform society, to rebuke organised priesthoods for their self-indulgence, coldness, exclusiveness, to assert the rights of the poor, to maintain that every member of Christ's flock has a calling to benefit the rest; beginning thus nobly and then sinking into more intolerable despots than those against whom they protested, self-exalted in their gifts, their knowledge, their ignorance, their poverty; deceiving and being deceived; drawing all reverence to themselves on the score of their humility, holding down the poor in slavery, whom they came to deliver...[127]

The criticism frequently made in the missionary literature about the ignorance and tyrannical behaviour of Buddhist monks, Maurice thought, needed to be tempered by a little knowledge of Christian history. Similarly, what

Maurice thought of as over-exaltation in Buddhism of the mind and the spirit could be matched in Christian phenomena:

> In the history of Mysticism and Quietism, telling how men beginning to seek God with earnest hearts, to denounce the idolatrous notions others had formed of him, to retire into the secret chamber that there might be no hindrance from outward things to the clearness of the vision, to mortify their flesh that it might not stand in their way, went on till their hearts grew puffed up and proud, till they began to boast of wonderful discoveries vouchsafed to them alone, till they became the subjects of all nervous impressions, fantasies, disorders, more sensual than those they charged with being so; how at last they gazed on vacancy, and felt, if they had not honesty to say, 'the vision is gone, we see nothing:' – here we find Christian Buddhism in another manifestation.[128]

To be sure Maurice's commentary could be disputed either as interpretation of Buddhism or as interpretation of Christian history. But the point is clear. The enterprise Christians are to engage in is not the comparison of systems in which Christianity must be always the winner. 'The lessons which these two records supply are not obsolete. Either of these temptations might assault any of us again.'[129] Clearly, Maurice went beyond the idea that comparison must be of like with like. He was not simply against taking the worst of other religious systems and comparing it unfavourably with the best in Christianity. Maurice taught that there may be very serious defects in the morphology of Christianity. The historic shape of Christianity itself may be a system which deserves to pass away. To contemplate distortions within other forms of faith may reveal distortions in forms taken by Christian faith.

8. *The encounter with other religious traditions may offer correctives to Christian theological formulation.* There have been periods in Christian history in which major theological themes were so under-emphasized that they have appeared to be almost totally absent. How they may be rediscovered and re-instated concerns many thinkers today. But how do Christians become aware of what they are missing and overlooking? One of Maurice's most striking insights lay in seeing that other faith traditions could be the catalysts enabling Christians to rediscover doctrines which they might have forgotten, understated or distorted. The Eastern religions and their spiritual teachings were likely, Maurice thought, to challenge Western cultural deformations of the gospel. In *The Religions of the World*, vivid page headings like *Mahomet's Witness for the Gospel*, *Hindoos preaching to Englishmen*, and *The Buddhist Gospel*, made this point.[130]

'Mahomet's Witness for the Gospel'

Maurice thought that the testimony of Islam could and should challenge misguided Christian over-emphases upon the transience and meaninglessness of this present world, together with the Augustinian idea that salvation takes place somewhere else than in this world.[131] In the long course of Christian history, Maurice was quite sure, there had been many voices which suggested that this world is incapable of transformation. Although only heretics ever had suggested that the world's origin lay in an evil Being, Maurice suggested that great numbers of 'orthodox' Christians had acted as if this were true. Therefore

> Those who decided to live pure and holy lives, left the world that they might do so. The sphere of human action was regarded by saints as an ungodly one, and those who moved in it and ruled it showed by their lives that they adopted the opinion. There was no distinct, audible voice, declaring 'The kingdoms of this world are the kingdoms of our God and of His Christ.' The belief silently gained ground, that there was no warrant for such an assertion; that the redemption which our Lord had wrought, whatever it might mean, did not mean this.[132]

But 'Mahomet's witness for the Gospel' contradicted this. Muhammad declared that 'this earth is the possession of the One Lord, the God of Abraham; He claimed it as His when he called out Abraham, and promised that he and his seed should possess a portion of it. The earth is still His. Those who say that He has an equal or rival are liars.'[133]

Maurice could therefore offer a positive interpretation of the extraordinary rise and progress of Islam in its early centuries. If Christians denied the present reign of God by believing in 'the notion that though He might have a reign somewhere else, it was not here,' they destroyed both ordinary morality and all simple trust in God's fatherly rule. Maurice accordingly saw the Muslim conquests in that context, not as 'a testimony against the Gospel but for it; a testimony to one necessary, forgotten portion of it'.[134]

'Hindoos preaching to Englishmen'

Maurice was particularly aware of the malformations in Christian spirituality which had occurred during the period of expansionism which the British had just lived through. The eighteenth and early nineteenth-century adventurers were chiefly concerned with the material rather than the spiritual riches of India. But, asked Maurice, why did they concern themselves so little with these other, more important Indian treasures? So he enquired of 'the Englishman', 'may there not be treasures nearer to you than these Indian treasures, treasures which are yours by clearest title, and yet which you have never reduced into possession?' In Maurice's view, 'Hindooism has been wanted to teach this nation what is very nearly forgetting itself, nearly forcing others to forget, that Christianity is not a dream or a lie.'[135] Thus, just as at the one extreme, Islam might be witness to a this-worldly kingdom,

Hinduism might be, at the other, to a kingdom that is not of this world. Both testimonies were, Maurice argued, correctives to unbalanced Christian formulations.

'The Buddhist Gospel'

By the time he used this expression Maurice had almost reached the end of his account of the world's religious traditions, and the choice he had been setting before his readers had become clear. On the one hand it could be that they looked out upon the world, and were able to 'see a valley covered with the dry bones of different systems'. They could then be told that there was no way in which they could find principle of unity or life in this wilderness. They could choose to think that 'there is no voice which can bid the breath to enter into these bones'.[136] On the other hand they could opt for the possibility that these dry bones could be joined together and unite and find fresh life. If the choice was the first, and there were to be no breath, no voice to speak to the dry bones then the prospects for the future would be, in Maurice's words 'a very mournful one'. But from where would such a voice come? What would make the other possibility a reality?

Maurice thought it would not arise from among Christians as they were presently constituted: 'they too occupy part of this dry valley; they have become dry bones, very dry indeed; clashing always, never uniting'.[137] But the real hope lay elsewhere. At this point, suggested Maurice, 'to check this despondency', along came the Buddhists:

We are but ill provided with a theory, say the Buddhists; we have tried many, and little fruit has come of them. But this we are assured of: you Christians may not have heard it, but there is a quickening, life-giving Spirit which is meant for humanity; which all may possess together; which alone can bring universe our of chaos, unity out of division. Wonderful testimony to be borne from the ends of the earth, from such a medley of strange people, so different in their thoughts, so incoherent in their utterances![138]

It is not necessary to agree with this interpretation of Buddhism or this evaluation of a 'medley' of strange peoples, in order to glimpse Maurice's powerful insight here. Through his study of world religious traditions, he had discovered a 'universal testimony' to spiritual power and life-giving energy. Maurice's theology was equally clear that such a power, which could 'bring us not to some imaginary condition of excellence, but precisely into a true condition', was a reality. The symbol of the true condition for Maurice was Pentecost, which signified that 'we hold this spirit, not as the Buddhists dream by our own right... flowing from no source whence it may be replenished', but from the very nature of Godhead.[139]

9. *Christians are to proceed in their relations with followers of other paths by dialogue and not by polemic.* 'Your business is to urge upon your countrymen the duty of not proving Christianity on paper; but of entering into actual intercourse with Jews, Mussulmans, Hindoos, Buddhists, for the purpose of showing that it is a reality'. Maurice put these words in the mouth of Robert Boyle in the closing pages of his lectures.[140] The expression 'actual intercourse' is very striking, echoed as it is a sentence or two later when Maurice wrote of 'the actual convictions' of these different peoples. Though he could not have used the word dialogue in its modern sense, 'actual intercourse' is a very fair anticipation of its meaning. Astonishingly, Maurice was prescient of a principle which was to find its full expression one hundred and fifty years later.[141] Interfaith dialogue, we affirm today, is not concerned with stereotypes of what it is to be a Muslim, Hindu or Buddhist. It is not a comparing of doctrines learnt out of books. No, dialogue takes place only in concrete circumstances, with 'actual' individuals who have 'actual convictions'. Maurice wrote in one of his most luminous sentences, 'A man will not really be intelligible to you if, instead of listening and sympathizing with him, you determine to classify him'.[142] To classify another person, to assign him or her to an appropriate pigeon hole, renders the other person unintelligible, and prevents any real inter-personal meeting. As Maurice implied here, it is easier to prove many things about human beings and their religious attitudes when one is not actually intimately involved with them.

10. *All Christian theology of religion flows from and feeds back into a theology of Christian mission.* Maurice was far from being an academic theorist, pondering a theology of revelation in other religious traditions in the quiet of his study. Living in his early Victorian world he was caught up along with his contemporaries in the sense of urgency about missionary activity. As a new convert to Anglicanism he became involved with the aims and achievements of the CMS. In later times he was a friend of people like Bishop John William Colenso and his wife in Natal.[143] His reading for the Boyle Lectures made him even more aware that what he was thinking and writing had immense practical implications for overseas missionary activity.

In some concentrated paragraphs in *The Religions of the World*, Maurice offered his own 'hints' concerning the basis and the goals of Christian mission. Here again, Maurice anticipated later missiological insights and controversies. To be sure, Maurice did not use the terminology of later debates. He knew the terms 'discontinuity' and 'displacement' as little as he knew the word 'dialogue'. But we may use the technical language familiar in our time for the convenience of our own discussion.

Indeed, contemporary missiology, when it deals with other religious forms, still finds unavoidable the issues indicated by the terms 'displacement' and 'discontinuity'. On the evidence before us, Maurice cannot be counted among those who think that Christianity supplants, displaces or supersedes all other religious traditions. On the contrary, Maurice insisted in relation to Islam, for example, that it was of the utmost importance to proceed with individual Muslims on the assumption that the Christian message added to, rather than detracted from, their original faith commitment. If what Christians wanted to say to Muslims was heard as setting 'at nought the first conditions of the Mahometan's faith', he was sure that there could be no hope of further conversation.

> Only that which assumes his original faith as its eternal foundation, and which deepens and extends it so that the fact of human life which seems least in accordance with it shall be shown to rest upon it, will carry that Divine stamp which the reason and conscience it awakens will recognise.[144]

In Maurice's view, then, it was necessary for Christians to discover some 'power' which could preserve 'the precious fragments of truth that are lodged within it, forming them into a whole, making them effectual for the blessing of all lands over which it reigns'.[145] In suggesting that there could be a 'transforming mission' in which Islam remained Islam, but with a new sense of its own unity and reality, Maurice came near to articulating the *maieutic*, or 'midwifely' aspect of the task of mission in which the missionary aims to enable Muslims to become better Muslims and not to try to convert them to Christianity.[146]

Maurice also anticipated the discussion of the *missio Dei*, the mission of God, in contemporary missiological circles.[147] Christians, he suggested, are caught up in God's mission, for mission did not belong to the church, and the church is not the subject of mission, but rather, just as much the object of mission as any of the great religious traditions of the world. Thus there is no basis for any feeling of superiority when Christians meet Muslims, Hindus or Buddhists. In *The Religions of the World* Maurice set out his own vision of the *missio Dei*, anticipating the heart of its thinking by a hundred years.

> Christianity... does not say that any particular set of men, calling themselves by the Christian name, are better than others; but it says that God will be true though every man be a liar; that his Kingdom will be established whether we who belong to it care that it should be established, or cut ourselves off from it.[148]

In Maurice's view Christians and Muslims were both caught up in the *missio Dei*. As he had already established, 'It was a mercy of God... that Muslims bore witness to His Name, when his creatures, practically were ready to forget it.'[149] Now, he argued, God was asking both Christians and Muslims to look towards God, as made known in Jesus Christ, 'who has already set up his throne in the highest region of all and calls upon every voluntary creature in his heart and spirit to do Him homage'.[150]

That Maurice should have put his finger upon such major points in 1846 is sufficiently astonishing. Maurice also reflected upon two key moments in the New Testament which still have significant implications for missiology. The first was when St Paul spoke to the philosophers in Athens (Acts 17). After paraphrasing Paul's speech on the Hill of Mars, Maurice commented: 'The language, you see, assumed that the Athenians were in search of God; that they were ignorantly worshipping him; that they had a sense of His being a Father; that they wanted some one living, human image of Him, to supplant those images of Him which they had made for themselves.'[151] The most adequate pattern for Christians, said Maurice, when they approached people of other faith, was established by the way in which Paul spoke to the Greek philosophers in Athens.

> The teaching was adapted to all that was sound and true in the Greek mind; it met whatever wants that mind was conscious of. The Greek asked for one who should exhibit humanity in its perfection; he was told of a Son of Man. He felt that whoever did so exhibit Humanity must be divine. The Son of Man was declared to be the Son of God. He had dreamed of one from whom the highest glory man could conceive must have proceeded. He was told of a Father. He had thought of a divine Presence in every tree and flower. He heard of a Presence still nearer to himself. He was not told that he must cease to believe in powers ruling in the Sun, or Moon, or over any portion of the earth. The Apostles had no commission to declare there might not be such powers, or whether they had actual personality; they were not to deny the existence of kingly men upon the earth, or of saints and angels in the unseen world; only they were to say, This Man is the King of kings and Lord of lords.[152]

The Hill of Mars discourse was clear indication in Maurice's view that how the gospel message is received within a particular culture must be determined by those who hear it rather than those that transmit it. This issue is still contentious in missiological circles.

Maurice's second concern can be found in a discussion of the relationship of Jesus' teaching and ministry to the Law and the Prophets. What, he asked, was the force of the words, 'I come not to destroy but to fulfil' (Matt.5.17)?[153] As far as Maurice was concerned, Jesus had shown himself far from wishing to obliterate 'the principle for which the Jewish nation had testified'. On the contrary, Jesus 'asserted it, established it, expressed it for the first time in all its clearness and fulness'.[154] In and through his teaching, Jesus gathered up 'the very meaning of the old dispensation'. He 'shows us what a truth was involved in every part of it; how every part had been a preparation for the full revelation of this truth'.[155] As a definition of the term 'fulfilment' this was to prove fruitful and we shall see very shortly how Maurice's thinking became a chief source for the use of 'fulfilment' as the basic category for the relationship of the Eastern religious traditions to Christianity.[156]

Conclusion

Maurice's theology of religion was an integral part of his total theological achievement. Because he had come to see creation and history grounded in the eternal truth of God, Maurice interpreted all revelation as the disclosure or manifestation of 'that which is' *eternally*. But without the special revelation of God in historical events, Maurice saw that humankind could, and would, have only a 'consciousness of God'. Without a historical revelation 'the religious feeling or instinct in man' would work freely and independently, dwindling away to groundless speculation or aspiration. It would amount to no more than a child whistling in the dark. In *The Religions of the World*, Maurice demonstrated that 'there is that in man which demands a revelation'. But since there was not 'that in man that makes the revelation', he was committed to the Kingdom revealed and established through the work and witness of Jesus. In the light of that Kingdom he could interpret all other 'revelation' as grounded in the eternal truth revealed in the Kingdom of Christ. It could all begin to make sense.

Scholars and theologians among the missionaries in the last half of the Great Century were to seize upon these ideas. On the one hand they knew they had to find a way of affirming that there was 'revelation' and a true sense of God in other faiths. They could not deny their own experience and the evidence of their own eyes, and Maurice enabled them to interpret these things afresh. He showed them how, since there was only one divine origin for everything, Christ the Divine Word had been present with other men and women throughout history and was the source of goodness and grace in other religious traditions. But on the other hand, the missionaries saw much evidence that the longings and aspirations of other religious traditions were incomplete and unsatisfied. Somehow the separated and uncompleted religious histories of humankind had to be related to the biblical history. Maurice enabled the missionaries to believe that 'all things from the beginning of the world had been advancing towards the revelation of Him in whom heaven and earth are united'. To the degree that they saw revelation or spirituality or goodness in other religious traditions, the missionaries recognized that they needed their sense that God was veritably at work spelt out for them. Because, without exception, these men and women held fast to the central loyalties within Christian faith, to incarnation, cross, resurrection, they needed a theologian to support them who could relate this Christian faith to world cultures and religions. When they took up *The Religions of the World*, such missionaries seem to have known instinctively that they had found the resource they needed.

Brooke Foss Westcott

It was as an expert that he wrote or spoke on Missionary subjects. When Regius Professor of Divinity at Cambridge, he was one of the leaders connected with the Brotherhood of that University at Delhi; as a father he gave no less than four of his own sons to the Society's Missions in India; as a Bishop he encouraged his clergy to listen to the call to engage in the work abroad, and laboured to foster the missionary spirit among the people of his diocese.[157]

These obituary words, written for the records of the SPG in 1901, indicate why Brooke Foss Westcott must be counted among the missionary thinkers of the Great Century. Westcott also contributed to both the theology of religion and the theology of mission in a range of notable sermons and in his last work of systematic theology, *The Gospel of Life*, published in 1892 when he was Bishop of Durham.[158]

Brooke Foss Westcott was born in Birmingham in 1825. He was thus twenty years younger than F.D. Maurice whose work he often echoes or reflects.[159] Unlike Maurice, Westcott does not seem to have passed through a major crisis of faith, although he was not immune as a young man from attacks of doubt.[160] Early in his intellectual life he had determined that the central theme of the Christian faith was to be found in the incarnation, and he taught untiringly that the taking of humanity into God implied the consecration of the entire life of humankind.[161] The roots of this teaching in Alexandrian Platonism were to determine all that he wrote about the meaning and significance of other religious traditions.[162] His admiration for Clement and Origen and all that the Catechetical School in Alexandria represented was equally to shape and mould his theology of mission.

Between 1852 and 1869 Westcott was a schoolmaster at Harrow. During this time his first theological treatise, *The Gospel of the Resurrection: Thoughts on its Relation to Reason and History* (1866), appeared.[163] This book was deemed too 'mystical' by many of his contemporaries, because it pointed to an 'experienced mystery, the mystery of the flesh of Jesus common with ours, yet in Resurrection lifted above our limitations'.[164] The Platonic cast of his mind was immediately made apparent in this work. In 1869 he left Harrow to become a Canon Residentiary of Peterborough Cathedral, and in 1870 was elected Regius Professor of Divinity in Cambridge (while remaining associated with Peterborough until 1883). In both Peterborough and

Cambridge he worked on his commentary *The Gospel According to St John* (1882). Westcott's awareness of other religions is nowhere more clear than in his comments on John 14.6, 'I am the Way, the Truth and the Life'. Only by reprinting them in full is it possible to gain a full sense of what they represented in 1882:

> *the Way* by which the two worlds were united so that men may pass from the one to the other. Comp. Heb. ix 8, x 20, Eph. ii 18. Hence perhaps the Christian faith is spoken of as "the Way", Acts ix 2, xix 9, 23, xxii 4, and xxiv 22. The use of the corresponding word in the Chinese mystical system of Lao-tse is of interest: "In the mysticism of Lao the term [Tao, 'the way', 'the chief way'] is applied to the Supreme Course, the way or passage through which everything enters into life, and at the same time to the highest perfection", Tiele, *Hist. of Rel.*, p. 37.
>
> *the truth* in which is summed up all that is eternal and absolute in the changing phenomena of finite being. Comp. viii,32, i 14,17; I John v.6 in connection with the ch. xiv, 26, Eph. iv,21. For St John's conception of truth see Introduction pp. xliv f. See also Jer. x 10 (Hebr) and Maimonides 'Yad. Hach.' 1.1.
>
> *the life* by which the entire system of being fulfils due continuous purpose answering to the divine will (comp. i3.4), no less than that by which each individual being is able to satisfy its own law of progress and to minister to the whole of which it is a part. Comp. xi 25; Col. iii 4.
>
> It is most instructive to note the two connexions in which Christ reveals himself to be 'the life'. Comp. xi 25, note.
>
> *no man cometh to the Father...* Here for the first time the end of 'the way', even the father is distinctly told.
>
> *but by (through) me.* It is only through Christ that we can, though in God (Acts xvii 28) apprehend God as the Father and so approach the Father. The proposition probably marks the agent (comp. i 3, 10, 17; I John iv.9); but it is possible that Christ may represent himself as his 'door' (x, 1, 9). *It does not follow that everyone that is guided by Christ is directly conscious of his guidance.*[165]

The last sentence was to prove seminal for Anglican thought on the significance of other religions, for the idea that the guidance of Christ need not be 'conscious' functions as undergirding for all 'inclusive' Logos christology when it is used to make sense of the faith of people who are not Christians.[166] But there are other doctrinal notes struck in this passage of commentary which belong, not to Westcott the exegete, but to Westcott the theologian, and required his fuller treatment.

Alongside his labours in textual criticism and translation of the New Testament, Westcott continually published work restating Christian doctrine:

The Historic Faith. Short Lectures on the Apostles' Creed (1883), *The Revelation of the Father* (1884), and *Christus Consummator: Some Aspects of the Work and Person of Christ in Relation to Modern Thought* (1886). Each of these represents an attempt to encourage the voice of 'calm reason' to be heard in the church.[167]

In *Christus Consummator* Westcott was concerned with a central text in the Letter to the Hebrews, which speaks of Christ as the one 'in whom all the treasures of wisdom are hidden'. Accordingly, the key concept in the book is 'fulfilment'. (Westcott's own translation of his Latin title was 'Christ the Fulfiller'.[168]) While Maurice had only just begun to develop the 'fulfilment' theme in relation to other religions, *Christus Consummator* offers a full and seminal treatment of the issues involved.[169] Westcott saw in the teaching of the Letter to the Hebrews an assertion of human destiny fulfilled in Christ in spite of the inroads of sin, because the Creation, not the Fall, was the ground and starting point of Christian theology.[170]

Like Maurice, and in contradistinction to hyper-Calvinism, Westcott believed that humankind had to be understood as bearing the 'image of God':

> We are taught that man received, unalienably as man, a fitness for gaining, through growth and discipline and continuous benediction, union with God... this original capacity of man was the measure of the love of God for his creature. Sin could not increase it; nothing less than personal union with God could fulfil it.[171]

Accordingly Westcott insisted that incarnation had to do with God's original purposes, not 'merely with the restoration of man who had missed his way'. Hence he could refer to the 'Gospel of Creation', however strange and unfamiliar this thought was in his own time. The consequences of teaching the doctrine of the incarnation in relation to the doctrine of creation were, Westcott believed, 'intensely practical'. 'It throws light upon all the broken and chequered sum of human existence. It helps us to understand how the scattered fragments in which man's potential endowments have hitherto been realised, combine to form a whole.'[172]

Westcott set out a vision of how all aspects of human aspiration would be fulfilled in Christ. He had in mind particularly those related to Victorian scientific discoveries, but in addition there was a suggestion that the diversity of religious outlooks would not so much be denied as completed. Even the 'imperfect conclusions of Naturalism' offered 'partial homage to the majestic progress of the divine order' and could be welcomed into this scheme of things. And the 'splendid visions' of Pantheism pointed to 'an end when God shall be all in all'.[173] Then there would be a 'holy unity which shall hereafter crown and fulfil creation as one revelation of Infinite Love, when the

Father's will is accomplished and He has *summed up all things in Christ, the things in the heavens and the things upon earth'*.[174]

This God–centred vision of the place of Christ was incomparably different from the Jesus-centred focus of much late nineteenth-century Christianity, in which Jesus was viewed as a personal Redeemer offering private consolations and individualist spiritual experience. The 'Christus Consolator', Christ as the sympathizer, Westcott did not doubt, was 'an image which touches every heart'. 'But,' he wrote, 'it is not the whole Gospel'.[175]

> Sin, suffering, sorrow are not the ultimate facts of life. These are the work of an enemy; and the work of our God and Saviour lies deeper. The Creation stands behind the Fall, the counsel of the Father's love behind the self-assertion of man's wilfulness. And I believe that if we are to do our work we must learn to think, not only of the redemption of man but also of the accomplishment of the divine purpose for all that God has made. We must learn think of that *summing up of all things in Christ*.[176]

This sense of consummation, of 'Fulfilment in Christ', was the only adequate way of handling theologically the nature and needs of humankind. 'We cannot accept the theory of those who see around them nothing but the signs of unlimited progress towards perfection, or the theory of those who write a sentence of despair over the chequered scenes of life.'[177]

Finally, Westcott brought to his concept of fulfilment a sense of time and space rather different from that of Maurice, whose patterns of thinking were formed before the publication of the *Origin of Species* in 1859. 'We trace back', Westcott wrote, 'till thought fails, the long line of ages through which the earth was prepared to be our dwelling place, but we refuse to accept time as a measure of the soul.'[178] Equally, the future stretched away into unthinkable distances. In the future God would continue to be revealed, as humankind came to understand more of Christ the Fulfiller, 'the Revelation of the Father, made known to us more completely from generation to generation by the Holy Spirit...'[179]

These are important foundations for the Christian theology of religion because it is only possible to speak about other religious traditions positively when Christianity is made to concern the salvation of the whole world, and not just the individual's redemption from sin, suffering and sorrow. Westcott's most important first step in developing his own theology of religion was to go beyond 'Christ the Consoler' to 'Christ the Fulfiller'.

The Gospel of Life[180]

Westcott's interpretation of human activity was dynamic and developmental, and he felt that the student of Christian theology, like the historian and anthropologist, needed to work from observation. 'The religious character of man, no less than his social or intellectual character, is to be sought, not in speculation first, but in the actual observation of the facts of his continuous development.'[181] When the specific nature of this 'religious character of man' was the question, the theologian needed 'to understand the essential ideas of faiths, however strange or even repulsive, in which our fellow men have lived and died'.[182] Westcott believed 'these faiths all show something of what man is, and what man has made of man, though God be not far from each one'.[183] He insisted, as a premise for further discussion, that differing religious traditions bore 'actual historic witness to the reality of some particular phase of religious opinion', and consequently 'we shall in a certain degree approximate towards a true conception of the religion which corresponds with man's nature by a review of the religious strivings of many nations. In their experience lies a witness which cannot be gainsaid.'[184]

The details of the ensuing discussion of what Westcott calls 'the work of the Prae-Christian nations towards the solution to the Problems of Life' and 'the Prae-Christian solution to the Problem of Being' do not concern us now.[185] But his methods remain important. Some of the principles he worked with had been acquired from the work of Max Müller and other pioneers of Comparative Religion.[186] Westcott had a good grasp of those texts of Chinese religion, Hinduism, Buddhism and Zoroastrianism which had already appeared in the *Sacred Books of the East*.[187] But even more important than his sense of the long development of other religions, were to be the insights gained from his own historical researches into the development of Christianity itself.

In *The Gospel of Life* Westcott set out two bases for the interpretation of the meaning of other religions. These were, first, an accurate understanding of the development of religion in the Bible, and second, a reappraisal of the interpretation of Persian and Greek religion by the Alexandrian fathers, particularly Clement and Origen.

A biblical theology of religions

Westcott was the first English theologian to invoke the pattern of Old Testament revelation against religious exclusivism or particularity in respect of other revelation. To be sure, Westcott did not discount the special revelation 'symbolised in the call of Abraham'. But he insisted upon the importance of 'the part fulfilled by heathendom in the training of humanity for Christ', as for instance that the 'services which Persia rendered to the education of the world have descended to us through the influences of the later organisation of the people of Israel'.[188] Equally, he insisted that the contribution of Greek culture 'lives for the simplest Christian in the New Testament', for the 'unconscious labours of the whole Greek race' had prepared 'instruments of precise analysis and exposition' for Christians to use from the first.'[189]

This contribution of nations other than Israel, Westcott argued, was recognized within the Bible itself. 'There are,' he wrote, 'distinct, if scanty, acknowledgements of this world-wide counsel of God even in the Old Testament'.[190] Evidence of this could be seen in the person of Melchizedek, as well as in what Westcott called 'the two most remarkable passages in the book of Deuteronomy, 4.19 and 29.26'. In these passages, he wrote, 'even alien and false worships are presented as part of the divine ordering of humanity', even 'these idolatries had a work to do for Him, an office in the disciplining of men, however little we may be able to understand the scope of its fulfilment'.[191]

But it was within the pages of the New Testament that Westcott discerned most fully the 'conception of a growth of humanity'.[192] When Paul speaks in Galatians 4.4 of the 'fulness of time' (cf. Ephesians 1.10, Titus 1.3, Romans 5.6), Westcott understood this to mean that a whole range of historical circumstances had come together in order for the incarnation to take place and to be understood. This purposeful chain of events illustrated 'the doctrine of the age-long revelation of the Word, who was in the world, and (in another sense) was ever coming into the world which he had made (John 1.9ff.)'.[193] Other verses in the New Testament concerning the position of the non-Christian world in relation to the Christian revelation like Acts 14.17, 17.24 ff., and Romans 1.9 ff. could also be seen in this light. 'The words of the Lord are heard from the beginning to the end. Other sheep I have which are not of this fold (John x.16) – sheep who were not less sheep because they had not recognised their shepherd'.[194]

The theology of religion in Christian tradition

Westcott also looked to specific resources within the early Christian tradition, particularly within the work of Justin Martyr and Clement of Alexandria.[195]

These fathers, and others, particularly men of the Alexandrian school, though they did not rise to the apprehension of the special office of Gentile nations in the divine economy, which a larger view of the relations of our vast human life enables us to do, yet saw clearly there was a work for and of God going on during the apparent isolation of the heathen from the region in which the Spirit revealed Him.[196]

Westcott offers a succinct discussion of Justin's teaching, stressing particularly the sentence: 'a seed of the word is implanted' (or rather 'inborn', *emphuton*) 'in every race of men.' As a result, Westcott emphasised, those who grasped the truth lived 'according to a part of the seminal Word' even as Christians live 'according to the knowledge and contemplation of the whole Word, that is Christ'.[197] Clement's teaching concerning the universal Logos was similarly highlighted, for the 'office which philosophy fulfilled for the Greeks'... 'as a guide to righteousness' was in Westcott's view a work of divine providence.[198]

Two lessons, he thought, would be learnt from this understanding of the Logos. First concerned 'fulfilment'. If Christians were to contemplate the original religious conceptions of humankind, their own understanding of what it is to be religious will be enlarged, 'for if Christianity be as we believe universal, then every genuine expression of human religious thought will enable us to see in the Gospel some corresponding truth which answers to it'.[199] Westcott thought that if we could understand what whole nations and peoples were feeling after, 'we shall have a clue to the discoveries of mysteries for which, we with our limited religious instincts, should not otherwise have sought'.[200]

The second lesson would be learnt by tracing the 'fatal course' within the actual history of the Gentile religions, when they failed to live according to the Word:

> For so much will be clear that in each case the central idea from which they all start, the need of a harmony between man and the world and God, after it had at first found a popular expression through the voice of great teachers, became as time went on, more and more overlaid on the one side by speculation and on the other side by ceremonialism. That which originally found spontaneous acceptance among different races as a religion became universally a philosophy or a ritual.[201]

To this judgment Westcott immediately added words critical of Christian development. 'Something of the same two-fold degeneration may be seen in the history of the Christian faith...'[202] But the church, because it preserved its original records of the revelation, could be open to reformation. It was not Westcott's custom to acknowledge his sources (footnotes in his writings are few and far between), but the echoes of Maurice are unmistakable. Westcott was making his own the thinking that underlay the sixth and seventh principles on pages 50-53 above.

He then offered a programme for scholars in the universities and missionaries in their centres of study.

> I can only hope that some who have the leisure will follow outlines of thought which seem to me to promise to this age a manifestation of Truth fuller in its assurance and more glorious in its promises than men have yet received. We are all placed in a position in which it is fast becoming possible to see that the Gospel is the answer to every religious aspiration and

need of man and men. We must then, if we are to comprehend its scope, strive to hear and to understand every voice of those who have sought God, even if they be only voices of 'children crying in the dark'.[203]

Yet Westcott believed that Lao-Tse and Confucius represented far more than 'children crying in the dark'. They offered humankind unique thoughts, which seemed to Westcott to be 'essential for the interpretation of the Gospel... the solidarity of peoples and, in the end, of mankind, and the continuity of personal life in the family'.[204] A close reading of the limited amount of Chinese literature available to him (which did however include the *Analects*, the *Shu King*, the *Tao-tih King*, the *Li Ki* and the *Book of Mencius*) had suggested to Westcott a number of trains of thought, centring on the theme of 'fulfilment'. 'For there is nothing', he wrote, 'which gave strength to China which does not find a fitting place in the Apostolic doctrine, while the Christian Faith guards against the evils which weakened the Empire.'[205] China's emphasis on tradition and continuity would find 'complete expression in the promise to Abraham and his seed', 'of whom was Christ as concerning the flesh'. Likewise

> The thought of solidarity is hallowed in the conception of the Body of Christ in which Christians are 'members one of another'. The thought of totality is confirmed in the fact that he is heir of all things, through Whom all things are made, and in Whom they are destined to reach their consummation. The thoughts are given to us in the Gospel and they are all quickened by a continuous movement as the revelation of God in men in humanity and in the world is read more intelligently.[206]

Westcott did not, however, think that Christianity already possessed these Chinese 'virtues'. Continuity, solidarity, and 'totality' remain as yet in the future. Thus he suggests that 'the characteristic conceptions of China become a great prophecy, and bear witness to a hope which will not forever be unsatisfied'.[207] This generous and affirmative theology bore its missionary fruit in many Anglicans and Christians of other traditions who came under Westcott's influence and was to play a significant part in the Report of the WMC in 1910.[208]

The practising missionary theologian

In his *Leaders of the Church of England 1828-1944*, David Edwards summed up part of Westcott's achievement as Regius professor in Cambridge with the words: 'He also did all he could to encourage both the new Cambridge Mission to Delhi for dialogue with educated Hindus....'[209] Edwards' anachronistic use of the word 'dialogue' (it did not come into common currency until eighty or ninety years later) in this sentence shows the impression made on a historian by Westcott's approach to the theology of mission. In a time when conversionist attitudes dominated Christian thinking, Westcott had seen a grander vision wherein Christian workers in India became 'Hindoos to the Hindoos'.[210] This was to be worked out through the Cambridge Mission to Delhi.

In 1876 the possibility of establishing an Anglican brotherhood in India had been suggested to Westcott by Thomas Valpy French (1825-1891), a long serving CMS missionary in Lahore.[211] In the following year the Cambridge Brotherhood at Delhi was inaugurated under the leadership of E.H. Bickersteth, a Fellow of Pembroke College, and Westcott took upon himself 'the principal share in giving this direction to the missionary zeal of members of the university', for 'his own large views of missionary work... had determined [the Brotherhood's] aims and spirit'.[212] Entries in his diaries for both his Cambridge and his Durham years show that Westcott was constantly in touch with the work in Delhi and in 1896, his youngest son, Basil Westcott, went to join the Brotherhood. (Basil was to die of cholera after only four years' service, at which time C.F. Andrews felt moved to take his place.[213]) But Westcott had three other sons in the service of the SPG in India: Arthur Westcott in Madras, and George and Foss Westcott in Cawnpore (the modern Kanpur). From their weekly letters Bishop Westcott was well able to engage with the realities of commending the gospel in India.[214] Westcott's insights into mission have therefore much greater value than many of those of the theologians who pronounced on mission from their study armchairs.

Westcott's missionary policies

There are two major statements concerning world mission in the Westcott corpus. Both were originally sermons, one on 'The Call of the English Nation and the English Church' and the other on 'Missions as a Revelation of the Mystery of God'.[215] Published in *The Christian Aspects of Life* in Queen Victoria's Diamond Jubilee year, they show clear signs of belonging within the heyday of imperialism.[216] But where other writers were urging the use of imperial power as God's ancillary to evangelism and of the need to impose Christianity on the subject races, Westcott chose to speak about 'human ministry' to 'the peoples who are placed under our rule'.[217]

Westcott's missionary vision was entirely of a piece with what he had written in *Christus Consummator* and *The Gospel of Life*. Westcott stressed for his listeners (and the readers whom he had mainly in mind) how the nations of the Empire would bring 'the largest possible measure of human experience and powers' to the work of setting forth 'the unsearchable riches' of the Gospel.[218] Westcott believed that there were great nations, China and India especially, who were 'inheritors of ancient and fruitful civilizations, endowed with intellectual powers widely different from our own, which have yet, as we must believe, some characteristic offering to render for the fuller interpretation of the Faith'.[219] He declared that as these nations find in the Gospel 'the strength which they require', they would be able to 'disclose through the experience of life new mysteries in the Incarnation'.[220]

Only when the gifts of every nation have been brought forward, Westcott thought, will 'the splendid imagery' of the last chapter of the Book of Revelation find its fulfilment: 'the nations shall walk amid the light of the City and the "kings of the earth" will bring their glory into it'.[221] When the gospel is fully understood and fully described by every nation and people there would not be, in Westcott's view, merely a 'simple unison', but a 'harmony of thought, feeling and expression', arising out of the 'vast unfolding, uncovering of the truth, deep beyond deep, in different races and peoples'.[222] This was a brand new motive for mission.

> The riches of Christ are commensurate with powers and wants of men. And the full powers of humanity, broken up as it has been into fragments, will not be realised till all the powers of every race have been consecrated. The full treasure of the Gospel will not be realised till every element has been brought into use through the wants of believers.[223]

The gospel had then to be preached in order that the manifold wisdom of God might be disclosed. Gone from Westcott was any sense either that the Kingdom of God had to be extended or the Church to be planted. Absent from Westcott are notions of rescuing 'the heathen' from everlasting torment, and the milleniarist expectation that Christ would return only when the Gospel had been preached to the ends of the earth, prevalent as we have seen, among many of his contemporaries.[224] In Westcott's thinking there could be no anxiety about the outcome of the Christian witness in the world. Echoing Maurice's views about the Kingship of Christ, Westcott affirmed:

> Our part is not to establish this sovereignty, but to proclaim it. Beneath and behind our labour of an hour lies the divine purposes of centuries... that which we permanently work out is a disclosure in time and space of what God has willed.[225]

'Such a faith', Westcott assured his audience, 'takes away our fear'.

Such a faith also created sufficient space for the working out of patient inter-faith dialogue. More immediate eschatological visions have always led to impatience, often to discourtesy, and sometimes even to a disregard for truth. In his second missionary sermon, 'Missions a Revelation of the

Mystery of God', preached in 1895, Westcott showed that had discerned that missionary times had changed.

> Missionary enterprise has now passed beyond the stage of experiment. We have experience of every variety and manner and condition of evangelisation. During this century the whole field of mission – the world – has been laid open. The Sacred Books of all the great religions have been made accessible in trustworthy forms. We feel as never before what is needed. We can see by what thoughts Gentile faiths have prevailed. We can hear and distinguish the manifold cries of various races which they contain. We can trace out with reverent devotion in all the records of human activity the progressive action of the Word, the Son of God, the Maker and Heir of the world in the many phases of its development through time. We can discern the broad outlines of that which we can speak of without presumption as the Divine Plan in the education of the World...[226]

The massive confidence of this statement was reflected in four implicit guidelines that Westcott offered in the rest of the sermon. These, paradoxically, asked for humility and courtesy in the Christian approach to people of different religious backgrounds.

First, Westcott insisted that, 'taught by the Spirit' and with 'patience and tenderness and sympathy', Christians must be able to 'interpret and complete the thoughts of many races', and may be able to 'confirm and satisfy the aspirations of many faiths'.[227] Second, he asked that the English church should give 'freely, as we have not given, of our greatest teachers to India' in order that the Indian people might get beyond the 'sterile theism' of Islam and the 'shadowy vagueness of Hindu philosophy.'[228] Third, he suggested that Christian communities (like the Cambridge Brotherhood in Delhi) had to be established 'in the representative centres of Native life'. These communities should demonstrate 'the free and generous relations of Christian brotherhood'.[229] Above all, Westcott counselled his late Victorian contemporaries to seek 'the spirit of self-repression and self-sacrifice, which gladly accepts a preparatory and transitory function', and 'which rejoices to leave a free course for the unforeseen operation of the Holy Spirit'. This had to be done in order to 'enable peoples widely different from ourselves to bring to God the gifts with which He has endowed them in all their freshness and purity'.[230] This was Westcott's early anticipation of the mission theology known as the *Missio Dei*, that the mission is never human work but a sharing in the divine initiative.[231] As Westcott wrote, all missionary work has its 'origin and strength' in 'the work of the Triune God – Father, Son and Holy Spirit'.[232]

In this way the essentially dialogical constituents of Westcott's theology of mission were demonstrated by these two sermons. Two further quotations, which take up the thought of the *Commentary on the Gospel of St John*, of *Christus Consummator* and *The Gospel of Life*, completed Westcott's message.

In the first of these we see Westcott insisting that two elements had to be held in creative tension by Christian thinkers: on the one side there were the values of other religious traditions and on the other the duty of to bear authentic witness to the uniqueness and the 'novelty' of Christian faith.[233] This tension determined Westcott's vision of justice, love and courtesy in interfaith relationships:

We shall, indeed, always feel and show tender and sympathetic regard for the partial truths, not untaught by the Word 'that lighteth every man', through which great faiths have preserved the life of nations for long ages; but we shall not exaggerate them, and we shall not dissemble our own claims. We have committed to us 'a new thing in the earth', a revelation absolutely unique, essentially different in kind from all other religions.[234]

The second passage speaks of love as the basic constituent of mission activity:

The Unity of love, which we so feel after is that which will, as the Lord has said, lead the world to believe in His Mission. Perhaps it is here that we shall find the true interpretation of the words in which Christ bids the disciple 'take up his cross,' not to bear some trivial vexation, but to die shamefully in the eyes of men, to die to all that keeps Christian apart from Christian – the vainglory of life in its countless forms – so that he may know the fulness of the eternal life which is untroubled by the differences of time.[235]

Meanwhile, Westcott counselled his Christian audience not to 'look anxiously for large results' for results will answer to 'the wise counsel of God'.[236] All that missionaries who came under Westcott's influence could expect was the 'the Christ-like joy of sowers'.[237] Only in the future of God would 'all the treasures of wisdom and knowledge' be brought to light 'through the ministry of the nations'.[238] Against such a theological background concepts like justice, courtesy and love make perfect sense.

Andrew Martin Fairbairn

When A.M. Fairbairn (1838-1912) visited India as the Haskell Lecturer in December and January 1898-9 the impression he made was described by an Indian newspaper reporter in these words:[239]

Here is a Scotch theologian who has devoted his entire life to questions of the gravest import to mankind. It is an impressive sight to see him deliver his message with all the energy, sympathy and earnestness which he can command to an alien people. It is one more illustration of that principle of unity which he traced in all human concerns in the midst of diversity and conflict... We differ from some of his views but we cannot but respect the man with the large heart who has realised the wondrous magic of love and sympathy and the scholar whose moral and intellectual vision is bounded neither by an island nor even by states and empires.[240]

As a lecturer, Fairbairn must have been a striking figure. A man of flowing speech and commanding presence, he was, like many Scottish preachers, full of 'energy and earnestness'. But somewhat surprisingly the anonymous Hindu journalist also chose used the word 'sympathy' to describe Fairbairn's style. His biographer, W.B. Selbie, who had access to other newspaper cuttings from the time of the visit, confirmed that it was Fairbairn's 'sympathy' which left the most abiding impression on his Indian audiences.

Thoughtful Hindus recognised in him one who was something more than the ordinary apologist for the Christian faith. He was that, but they found in him at the same time a student of religions who had some claim to understand their own position, and who had real sympathy with the ideas that underlay it, and with the history and the literature in which it was expressed. They welcomed especially his earnest repudiation of that materialism which to them seemed so characteristic of English thought and life, and his pleas for a more idealist point of view found a ready echo in their hearts. They appreciated the fact that he spoke as one who knew; and his criticisms of their position left no sting because they were based upon principles which they themselves could understand and appreciate. They were profoundly touched by the keen sympathy for them and their fellow-countrymen which the lecturer's whole attitude implied, and which frequently found expression in his words.[241]

In this passage Selbie uses the word 'sympathy' twice, and this immediately raises several questions: How did Fairbairn come to speak 'as one who knew'? How had this late-Victorian divine, president of the International Congregational Union, principal of an Oxford theological college, and author of a range of influential works of philosophical and systematic theology, acquired this extraordinary ability to get alongside Indian intellectuals? What forces had moulded this 'scholar whose moral and intellectual vision was bounded neither by an island nor even by states and empires'?[242]

Early life and ministry

Andrew Martin Fairbairn was born in Inverkeithing in Fife on 4 November, 1838. His family then moved to Dalkeith and later to Edinburgh. In his later teenage years Fairbairn deliberately severed his connection with Presbyterianism, joining the Evangelical Union Church (the denomination of James Morison) and offering for its ministry.[243] After studies at Edinburgh University and in the EU Theological Hall in Glasgow, Fairbairn was ordained a minister of the Evangelical Union Church (now firmly Congregationalist in its polity), and held pastorates in Bathgate, a country town half way between Edinburgh and Glasgow, and then at St Paul Street EU Church in Aberdeen.

In the first of these parishes, Fairbairn worked for twelve years, devoting much of his time to study. Selbie describes a manuscript catalogue of Fairbairn's library at this time: 'It contains the names of nearly 2000 volumes, many of them works in French, German and Dutch. Theology, of course, predominates, but there is an unusual proportion of books on non-Christian religions.' Fairbairn left behind him his notebooks of these years of study. 'Here again', writes Selbie, 'a large proportion of space is given up to Indian, Chinese and Semitic religions, his interest in which led him, even at this early date, to obtain and tabulate information regarding them from every possible source.'[244]

During the Bathgate period, Fairbairn discovered from his reading that he would need to work out his theology in the context of religious plurality. He also realized this would not be done without the aid of German thought. A crisis of faith when he was twenty-seven was another factor which led Fairbairn to Germany to study at the University of Berlin, where the so called 'mediating theologian' Isaac Dorner was the chief attraction. Dorner had won his fame through his attempts to harmonize or mediate between theology and philosophy, using the methods of both Friedrich Schleiermacher and G.W.F. Hegel in defence of the Christian revelation.[245] Through Dorner's influence Andrew Fairbairn recovered his faith and 'returned home to Scotland to re-interpret both God and man in terms of this larger and nobler Christianity'.[246]

This re-interpretation in which the thinking of Schleiermacher and Hegel was to play so large a part began immediately. From the manse in Bathgate Fairbairn published an article in the *Contemporary Review* entitled 'The Genesis and Development of the Idea of God', in which he investigated the conceptions of God manifested in the world religions and compared them with the perfect expression of God in Jesus Christ.[247] He wanted to go more deeply into the study of the religions of India, so he enlisted the help of John and William Muir, both associated with the University of Edinburgh.[248] Through Sir William Muir, Fairbairn made contact with Max Müller.[249]

Selbie cites a letter to Fairbairn from Müller, suggesting that he should take up Sanskrit or Chinese. 'What we want is special work', wrote Müller, 'the general results will come by themselves.'[250]

Fairbairn's next pastoral charge was in Aberdeen; he was minister of St Paul's Street EU Church from 1872-1877. During this period he became much more of an exegetical and apologetical preacher than a student of religions, and attracted an large part of his congregation from the university community.[251] Among them was the future missionary and student of Indian religion, John Nicol Farquhar.[252] But Fairbairn did find time to write articles for the *Contemporary Review* on subjects concerned with the comparative study of religions.[253] He contributed studies on 'The Belief in Immortality: An Essay in the Comparative History of Religious Thought' and 'Race and Religion', and even 'The Primitive Policy of Islam'. These were to be the basis of his first book, *Studies in the Philosophy of Religion and History* (1876). During this time in Aberdeen he frequently corresponded with Dutch and German pioneers of the comparative study of religion, C.P. Tiele, Chantepie de la Saussaye, and Lodewijk Rauwenhoft.[254]

Early contributions to the theology of religion

Fairbairn's *Studies in the Philosophy of Religion and History* consisted of four essays or studies.[255] Detailed analysis of these is not necessary and just one passage can be taken as exemplifying Fairbairn's approach:

> We cannot... accept any hypothesis which would evolve the idea of God from delusions, or dreams, or fears. Shall we trace it, then, to a supernatural source, to a primitive revelation? But a primitive revelation were a mere assumption incapable of proof – capable of most positive disproof. Although often advanced in the supposed interests of religion, the principle it assumes is most irreligious. If man is dependent on an outer revelation for his idea of God, then he must have what Schelling happily termed 'an original Atheism of consciousness'. Religion cannot, in that case, be rooted in the nature of man – must be implanted from without. The theory that would derive man's religion from a revelation is as bad as the theory that would derive it from distempered dreams. Revelation may satisfy or rectify, but cannot create, a religious capacity or instinct....[256]

On the contrary, Fairbairn held that religion was not 'a science or any constructive or reasoned system of thought that can be opposed to it. It is simply spirit expressing in symbol its consciousness of relations higher than physical or social.'[257] Religion was 'a permanent and universal characteristic of man, a normal and necessary product of his nature'.[258] 'He grows into religion but works into theology, *feels* himself into the one, *thinks* himself into the other. He is religious by nature, theological by art. In this sense it can be said, there is only one religion, but there are many theologies...'[259]

Selbie's judgment about Fairbairn's work at this period remains sound: 'If many of its conclusions have now become commonplaces, and others have been altogether abandoned, there is still due to the writer the credit of having stated them when and how he did.'[260] Fairbairn was the first theologian in Britain to use the scientific studies of the new scholars of religion, entering into their labours far more deeply than had Westcott. This Scottish theologian, working as minister of a small denomination, had grasped as had no one else of his period the significance of the existence of other religious paths and ways for Christian dogmatics.

Other important elements in Fairbairn's path-finding work were rooted his early rejection of the attempt to interpret the so-called higher forms of religion by primitive religion. Though he was an evolutionist in principle, he did not allow the ideology of 'evolutionism' to work as a scholarly 'blinker' when he examined the evidence of human religious behaviour. Fairbairn's instinct was that there could be no dogmatic *a prioris* in this area. Neither the positivism of some of the new studies in comparative religions nor the conservatism of traditional theologies could determine the issue. This point was well worth making in 1876, and was not forgotten when David Cairns and his colleagues worked out *The Missionary Message in Relation to Non-Christian Religions* in 1910.[261]

Fairbairn in England

Fairbairn's rapidly growing reputation led to an invitation in 1877 to serve English Congregationalism as Principal of the Airedale College in Bradford, Yorkshire.[262] This had been one of the leading Dissenting Academies, and had become in the course of the nineteenth century a theological college for the Congregational Church. After nine years at Airedale, Fairbairn became the first Principal of Mansfield College, Oxford.[263] In these posts he trained two generations of Congregationalist scholars and opened their eyes to the theological significance of other religions.[264] At Bradford he ensured that the comparative study of religion was part of the syllabus (probably the earliest instance of this).[265] When he become Principal of the new Mansfield College, Fairbairn developed a foundation course for first-year students called 'Theological Encyclopaedia', which led to work on christology, philosophy of religion and comparative religion.[266]

As Principal of Mansfield, Fairbairn became a close friend and neighbour of the ex-missionary James Legge, who had become the first Professor of Chinese in the University.[267] Legge regularly attended Mansfield College Chapel after it was opened, and for eleven years was in constant communication with Fairbairn, especially on matters of the study of religion. It was out of deep knowledge and respect that Fairbairn gave Legge's funeral address in Mansfield College Chapel on 3 December 1897. Some of these words described Fairbairn's own attitudes as well as those of the man he was eulogizing:

> Happily he was sent Eastwards to the oldest of living civilizations, and he studied it with an eye made luminous by love, for if ever a man loved a people, James Legge loved the Chinese, and he could not bear to see them do wrong or to suffer it... He had the insight which comes of the heart even more than of the head into their literature and religion, and he saw that the primary condition of making the West influential in the East was to make the East intelligible to the West.[268]

Fairbairn's personal ideal was to study all religious phenomena with the same 'eye of love'.[269] It was that 'eye of love' which the editor of *The Times of India* discerned when Fairbairn was undertook his experiments in interfaith dialogue in the winter of 1898-9.

Experiments in interfaith dialogue

The Haskell Foundation lectureship had been established to enable Western scholars to visit India where they would expound the philosophical ideas underlying Christianity.[270] Andrew Martin Fairbairn had been appointed the second Haskell lecturer because of his reputation in the comparative study of religion. He sailed for India on the *SS Egypt* in October 1898, and arrived seven weeks later in Bombay. This is Fairbairn's detailed account of his time in Bengal:

> The visit to Calcutta has been a great success so far as the lectures are concerned. The audiences were large... The natives showed immense interest. No such meetings either for numbers or influence have been known in Calcutta. And they were most wonderfully attentive. On the first night I was conscious of a serious conflict of feeling between the men and myself. The natives were restless, and moved uneasily, but I conquered, and while the audiences have grown the attention has deepened. When in the last two lectures I came to deal with Christian beliefs I expected the old disquiet; but it did not return. The men heard with a quiet and patience which even a Christian audience might have envied. One testimony was very remarkable. An orthodox Hindu, registrar of the University, expressed after the fourth lecture his surprise at never having heard the name of Jesus Christ mentioned. After the fifth he said, 'I never thought I could have sat to hear so much of Jesus Christ.' After the sixth, 'I feel that to be a very dangerous man. If he had continued longer, I would either

have had to cease attending or cease to be a Hindu. As it is I have determined to read the New Testament.'[271]

In addition to his public lectures, Fairbairn had many personal conversations with individual Hindus, and these he described in his journal. Here is just one example:

Visited Rajah Bhinga, a very beautiful character; was much impressed with his reverence and spiritual tone. His story was tragic. Had been in ICS, a very distinguished and capable man; but his eldest son committed suicide. The shock so threw him off his balance that he surrendered the world and retired into private contemplation. Has become a genuine recluse, a fine type of the surrender of all things for the sake of the soul. We talked of renunciation of the world in Christianity and Hinduism. He thought our finest characters had been our recluses: this was our point of affinity: he would not allow Hinduism to be without ethical value; if in obedience to it all was surrendered – that was ethical. I was particularly touched by his saying to me as we left, 'I have attained peace, peace, peace,' and he seemed to bless one as only a saint can.[272]

Fairbairn recognized sanctity in people of other faiths and was more than willing to engage with them in conversation about ultimate truth claims.

December 22-26 – Benares... Was visited early by two Hindus more than some. Their names were Lala Baij Nath and Sri Chandra Bose... We talked over the problems of Indian religion: found them profoundly convinced that the Bhagavagita [sic] was the revelation of Indian faith, Christian and more than Christian in its theory of inspiration. Evident that Christianity has caused extraordinary development of interest both in the theory and idea of Incarnation, and in the idea of a Hinduism independent of caste, more ethical and less under the bondage of ceremonial. Both men were anxious to find out why I should hold Christ to be the only Incarnation of God, when they were ready to recognise Him as well as Krishna and Buddha.[273]

This was Fairbairn dealing with central issues of Christian-Hindu dialogue in a conversation 'from one open-hearted man to another'.[274] Recall that the year it took place was 1898.

Fairbairn also met on his tour representatives of what is called the Hindu renaissance.[275] Fairbairn was struck by what appeared to be the distance between the Indian and the expatriate communities, and he noted how few Europeans attended his lectures. He also recorded what he called the 'sordid views of many Englishmen' in India with 'their frank materialism and contempt for all that was not concerned in money-making'.[276] Like Maurice and Westcott, Fairbairn contrasted British and other expatriate attitudes with those of the best members of the Indian community, much to the detriment of the former. Accordingly he interpreted the 'rejuvenscence of the native spirit in religion' in India as a 'reaction against the hard and grinding master-fulness of the British will.'[277]

Reflections on interfaith dialogue and the Christian mission

Fairbairn's considered reflections after his visit to India are to be found in two places. First in the *Contemporary Review*, where he published two detailed accounts of his impressions and conversations during his travels.[278] In two long articles, 'Race and Religion in India' and 'Religion in India', he took up many of the ideas he had jotted down in his Indian journal. His judgments are summed up in the last paragraph of 'Race and Religion in India':

> It is neither by the speculation of the *Vedanta*, nor by the theosophy of the *Bhagavad Gita* that Hinduism will be judged; but by the character of its gods, the worship of its temples, the quality of its priesthood, the social organization and ethical spirit it has made for its people; in other words, its force and behaviour as a religion. On that point no student of history will draw a hasty inference; but if a serious and deliberate inference be possible he ought to draw it without expectancy of fear or favour in either East or West.[279]

This emphasis on religious practice rather than on philosophical specula-tion as the proper ground of the interpretation of other religions was more fully explored in Fairbairn's last large work, *The Philosophy of the Christian Religion* (1902). In the Preface to this book, Fairbairn described how his whole perspective on philosophy had been altered by his Indian travels:

> In India the author suddenly found himself face to face with a religion he had studied in its literature and by the help of interpreters of many minds and tongues, and this contact with reality at once illuminated and per-plexed him. It was not so much that his knowledge was incorrect or false, as that it was mistaken in its emphasis. No religion can be known in its Sacred Books alone, or simply through its speculative thinkers and reli-gious reformers; and of all religions the one we can least interpret is the encyclopaedic aggregation of cults and customs we know as Hinduism.[280]

This change in attitude resulted in numerous questions, which Fairbairn felt he had not dealt with adequately in any of his previous writings.[281] Again there is no space to discuss his analysis at this point. But his conception of religion had indeed changed. As he raised questions like 'What is religion in general?', 'How and why had it arisen?', 'What causes have made religions to differ?', and 'What are the ultimate constituents of religions, – ideas and beliefs, or customs and institutions?'. Fairbairn felt compelled to study 'his own faith in their light'.

> He could not but feel that Christianity stood among the religions which must be historically investigated and philosophically construed; and that no greater injury could be done to it than to claim for it exceptional consideration at the hand of the historical student or philosophical thinker.[282]

> To invoke special pleading for Christian theology not only impuned 'the integrity of the reason which was God's own gift to man', but led also to the conclusion that the human reason discredited so could not be used to 'attest or justify the truth' of Christianity.[283]

> In other words, the philosophy which misreads the origin of religious ideas and the history of any religion will not, and indeed cannot, be just to the Christian; while he who would maintain the Christian must be just and even generous to all the religions created and professed of men.[284]

In *The Philosophy of the Christian Religion*, Fairbairn devoted three full chapters to his own attempt to be 'just and generous' to other religions.[285]

This line of thinking was exactly what fellow Congregationalists, like Slater, Lucas, Hume and Jones, in India and elsewhere, wanted to hear. Even more important for missionaries of whatever denomination was the fact that a leading Western theologian like Fairbairn knew at first hand and had taken seriously the realities of the Hindu and other contexts. Fairbairn's difficulties and discoveries were exactly theirs when they met educated Hindus and tried to speak of Christian faith in a way which their hearers could understand.

Practical suggestions for theological education

As important as the encouragement given to the dialogical missionaries were Fairbairn's reflections on 'The Influence of the Study of Other Religions on Christian Theology' which arose out of his visit to India. Addressing the second International Congregationalist Council in Boston, Massachussetts, in September 1899, Fairbairn spoke of theological education in the light of his experience of the world's religions. This statement is the very first justification for a programme of ministerial formation devised in the light of religious pluralism.[286]

Fairbairn's first proposition for the Congregationalists assembled in Boston was that 'a study of religions which is intended to be an apology for our own, will educate no theologian, conserve and enlarge no theology'.[287] He declared that the student who went 'to other faiths simply to find what is evil in them, in order that he may compare it with the idealised good he professes to find in his own, will come back worse than empty handed'.[288]

Second, Fairbairn suggested to the Council that the comparative study of religion had a 'broadening and, as it were, humanising' effect on the way in which theology was built up. 'Our apologetic has been too critical and defensive, and has suffered from the want of positive and constructive ideas.'[289]

Third, Fairbairn wanted to insist that 'As a comparative science the study of religions may fulfil a direct and immediate apologetic purpose.' It could become 'a finger-post indicating the religion which experience has proved to be in structure and ideal the highest' (by which he meant Christianity of course, but also a Christianity refined and reformed in the light of the lessons from other faith communities). [290]

Above all, Fairbairn proposed that the study of religions had enlarged the entire 'conception of religion, and made evident the unity of its several parts'.[291] Knowledge of other religious traditions, especially the way in which they had been experienced in India, had made it impossible for Christians to go on thinking of theology in isolation from worship and polity, institutions and conduct.

> The thought of a religion is as much expressed in the behaviour as in the speech of its votaries, as much in the customs it sanctions, the laws it enacts, the ritual it observes, the practices it follows, and the social or class distinctions it approves or maintains, as in the creed it subscribes or in the confession of faith it makes. But it is in the interpretation of the highest religious beliefs that the most decisive influence has been exercised. There is a remarkable difference between an idea regarded as a religious belief and as a intellectual conception. The difference relates, not so much to the greater note of conviction which marks the religious belief, as to the greater reality which belongs to it, and the immediacy with which it bears on life.[292]

Not very far away from the hall in Boston where Fairbairn spoke, just across the Charles River in Cambridge, Massachusetts, Wilfred Cantwell Smith was later to spend many years in making clear the distinction between faith and belief.[293] Fairbairn's fertile mind had drawn its own conclusions about the primacy of 'faith' to belief, and then about 'commonalties of faith' rather than differences in beliefs. The memories of encounters like those with Rajah Bhinga, Lala Baij Nath and Chandra Bose deeply affected him. Religion, he wrote, 'has an audacity and vigour of logic quite unknown to philosophy; and this is the more emphasised by its logic being expressed even more in conduct and character, in actions and institutions than in dialectic'.[294]

With so formidable a set of propositions laid before them by so great an expert the Congregationalist theologians at the turn of the century could hardly maintain the inflexible erudition and combative mentality advocated by their predecessors Ralph Wardlaw and Isaac Taylor. By his writings and through his speeches, as well as by his teaching and example, Fairbairn moved theologians within his own denomination and elsewhere in the direction of justice and fairness, courtesy and sympathy as they evaluated other religious traditions. Like his friend and colleague in Oxford, James Legge, Andrew Martin Fairbairn taught them how to discern 'with the eye of love'.

Alexander V.G. Allen

A fourth theologian influential in the circles in which the Edinburgh 1910 missionary correspondents moved was Alexander Viets Griswold Allen (1841-1908).[295] Almost unknown today, Allen's role in missionary theology was that of a foundation layer. Foundations get buried and those who laid them forgotten, but sometimes it is possible to dig away a little and expose what underpinned the massive structures above the surface. In the same way some of Allen's achievement in preparing the way for a new theology of religion needs to be brought to the surface.

What Allen accomplished can be set under two headings: his synthesis of Schleiermacher and Maurice; and his rediscovery of the earlier Greek theology. Allen was the first person on either side of the Atlantic to correlate what Schleiermacher was saying about religion with the theological insight and passion of F.D. Maurice, and then to put them alongside each other in such a way that ministers and missionaries could build upon their insights. Second, like Westcott and Fairbairn in Britain and his American contemporary Charles Cuthbert Hall, Allen highlighted the tradition of Alexandria.[296] As a theologian, Allen was a passionate exponent of Logos christology, offering a reading of Christian thinking emphasizing the Greek Platonic tradition. As a church historian, he was able to demonstrate the constructive relationships between Clement, Origen and others and the intellectual elite of Alexandria. All these insights were important for the 'missionaries among the educated classes' of India, China and Japan.

Allen's remarkable first book was well used in missionary circles. *The Continuity of Christian Thought: A Study of Modern Theology in the Light of its History* was first published in 1884, and republished with a new preface in 1895.[297] Allen wrote a number of other works which were influential in his own time; a study of Jonathan Edwards, the volume on *Christian Institutions* in the International Theological Library, a multi-volumed *Life of Phillips Brooks*, and a fine piece of polemical writing, *Freedom in the Church*.[298] These all breathe a generous spirit matched with intricate scholarship, but only *The Continuity of Christian Thought* had a direct bearing upon the theology of religions and the practice of Christian mission.[299]

Alexander Allen was a New Englander, and lived on the Eastern seaboard all his life except for student days in Kenyon College in Gambier, Ohio, between 1859 and 1864.[300] Born in an Episcopalian parsonage in Otis, Massachusetts, he grew up in Nantucket and Guildford, Vermont. He remained an Anglican all his life but, like others in these pages, Allen had reconstructed the Calvinist-Evangelical creed of his upbringing. This he did through reading S.T. Coleridge and F.W. Robertson of Brighton,[301] and, above all, F.D. Maurice. After training in the seminary at Andover and working as a parish minister at St John's, Lawrence, Massachusetts, Alexander Allen began his forty-year teaching career at the newly-founded Episcopal Theological School (now the Episcopal Divinity School) in Cambridge in 1867. Its campus was deliberately sited only a few blocks from Harvard University, so that the students might have 'the advantage of its library and of its tradition of learning and freedom'.[302] Allen remained Professor of Church History at ETS until his death in 1908.

Allen the teacher

Allen was a gifted teacher. 'In his classroom history became a real presence. Up out of the dead, dull, monotonous past stepped great distinguished things into life... He had the art of doing for us what Augustine said the first reading of Plato did for him; he kindled in one an almost incredible force of desire to know', wrote one of his pupils. Another said, 'His interpretation of the development of the Church, his revelation of what our Church really meant and stood for, why it could afford to be comprehensive in its theology and in its practice, filled me with admiration then and have been sources of inspiration for over fifty years.'[303]

The key to this lay in Allen's constant putting of the question, 'What does it mean?' Allen wrote of himself, 'I am always moving, as it seems to me, underground, beneath institutions and customs and formulas of thought, and trying to get at some deeper meaning.'[304] The deeper meaning was always 'theological', the witness of the presence of God. This sense emerges in Allen's tribute to his friend and senior colleague Elisha J. Mulford.[305] Mulford, author of *The Republic of God*, and a fellow-disciple of F.D. Maurice, had died in 1885. Speaking about Mulford's fundamental principle that God indwelt in the institutions of common life, Allen declared that the 'conception of revelation' was then to be so 'enlarged till it is seen to be a continuous process, which knows no intermission, whose records are to be found in the whole history of humanity, of which the Bible is the eternal symbol, to the interpretation of which it furnishes the key'. The influence of Maurice upon both Mulford and Allen is evident from Allen's words:

> The world in which God indwells, of whose life he is the constant inspiration must already be a redeemed world. It is an actual deliverance which has been accomplished – a deliverance which means that the power of darkness has been broken, that the devil and his angels, the unearthly powers of darkness have no dominion, but only God alone.[306]

For Allen, then, incarnation was the central fact of human history. It could never be seen as a principle of exclusion but, rather, had always to be thought of as bringing about new life for humankind.

> The church is therefore to testify to the life of the indwelling God in nature, in humanity, in history, to the union of the Divine with the human in the incarnation of the Son of God, to the supernatural character of the life of mankind through the presence and operation of the Holy Spirit.[307]

Allen's teaching and his friendship with Mulford led him to develop his ideas and resulted in the 1884 book, *The Continuity of Christian Thought*.

Divine immanence as the principle of continuity

Allen began *The Continuity of Christian Thought* with the proposition that 'the traditional conception of God which has come down to us from the Middle Ages through the Latin church is undergoing a profound transformation'.[308] 'Transcendence' was giving way to 'immanence' as the dominant theological conception. Allen proposed to present 'the outlines of that early Christian theology which was formulated by thinkers in whose minds the divine immanence was the underlying thought in their consciousness of God'.[309] In this story Allen had as his hero Clement of Alexandria, and as his anti-hero, Augustine of Hippo. Of the latter's thinking Allen wrote: 'The Augustinian theology rests upon the transcendence of deity as its controlling principle, and at every point appears as an inferior rendering of the earlier interpretation of the Christian faith.'[310] With his solid erudition always in evidence, Allen set out to prove the case against Latin Christianity.[311] He wanted his readers to establish a sense of continuity with the first exponents of the 'original divine revelation' rather than with what he called 'Latinised' Christianity.[312] He cited in his support the Oxford theologian Henry Scott Holland:

> We have lost much of that rich splendour, that large minded fullness of power, which characterised the great Greek masters of divinity. We have

suffered our faith for so long to accept the pinched and narrow limits of a most unapostolical divinity, that we can hardly persuade people to recall how wide was the sweep of Christian thought in the first centuries, how largely it dealt with these deep problems of spiritual existence and development, which now once more impress upon us the seriousness of the issues amid which our souls are travailing. We have let people forget all that our creed has to say about the unity of creation, or about the evolution of history, or about the universality of the divine action through the Word. We have lost the power of wielding the mighty language with which Athanasius expands the significance of creation and regeneration, of incarnation and sacrifice, and redemption and salvation and glory.[313]

In this Greek theology, wrote Allen, such tenets as original sin and total depravity ('received by the Protestant churches from the Latin church') found no place. So Allen preached discontinuity, as well as continuity. Discontinuity meant dispensing with the original guilt of infants, the absolute requirement of baptism for salvation, and the denial of the freedom of the will. Discontinuity also meant ridding the church of the apparent schism in the divine nature which seemed to require an act of retributive justice, before love could grant forgiveness, and departing from the notion that revelation is confined within a book ('guaranteed either by the inspiration of the letter or by a line of priestly curators in apostolic descent'). Allen also asserted discontinuity with the doctrines of sacramental grace and priestly mediation, and with the concept of election which encouraged the viewing of the church 'as identical with some particular form of ecclesiastical organisation'.[314] All these ideas were irreconcilable with the spirit of Greek theology.[315]

Justin Martyr and Clement of Alexandria

Allen's advocacy set the 'universality of God's action' in Greek theology over against the darker themes of exclusivism in Western and Latin theology. In doing this Allen revealed an explicitly missionary commitment and interest. Allen's chapter on Greek theology is an extended exposition of the two New Testament texts, 'God was in Christ reconciling the world to himself' (II Cor. 5.19, RV) and 'He was the true light, which lightens every man coming into the world' (John 1.9, RV), two verses which were increasingly dominating the minds of missionaries at the turn of the twentieth century.[316] The exposition of the incarnation of the Logos as worked out by Justin Martyr and Clement of Alexandria was particularly germane to missionaries in India, China and Japan.

Allen wrote that Justin represented a whole class of incomers into the Christian church who 'could not but maintain the continuity of their spiritual development'.[317] Missionaries were meeting identical objections throughout

Asia. Like the early church apologists they were continually encountering the objection that Christ had been born a mere one hundred and fifty years previously, while behind the Greek philosophers stood a long line of the most outstanding teachers and thinkers. Many of these philosophers, moreover, had been the same 'schoolmasters' by which the new converts in Christianity had been led to Christ. To answer such objections, wrote Allen, Justin rose 'to the idea of the spiritual essential Christ who is limited by no conditions of time or space'.[318] This spiritual Christ was the Word of which every human race partakes.[319] So, Allen commented

> Justin is the first writer among the ancient Fathers to assert the truth that God has revealed himself to the heathen world as well as to the Jewish people, that he had done so not merely through some subordinate process in external nature, but through his Son, who is the divine reason in every man.[320]

But Justin's thinking in these matters was rudimentary compared with those associated with Alexandria at the end of the second and the beginning of the third century. This great North African seaport was religiously pluralist to an absolute degree. Under such conditions there was likely to be much scepticism and religious confusion. This pluralism had to be resolved by penetrating 'beneath the diversity to some underlying principle of unity'. A principle of unity had to be sought which would do justice to all the elements of truth and spiritual thought wherever they might be found'.[321]

One way of doing this might have been discovered in the attempt to construct a universal religion. Such efforts had been made by Plutarch and by some of the Gnostics and Neo-Platonists.[322] Could not a similar effort be made by Christian philosophers, but now in the light of Christ?

> A secular duty devolved upon the Christian thinkers of Alexandria. They were now forced, if they would address intelligently and successfully the enquiring minds of heathenism, to do justice to the truth in all systems of thought, to interpret their aspirations after the eternal light, to emphasize the value and importance of the divine revelation given in Greek philosophy, and always to keep in view that feature of Christianity upon which rested its claim to be a universal religion.[323]

Many Great Century missionaries in the seaports and cities of the Eastern world would have seen these words as an exact description of their task. Allen portrayed Clement of Alexandria's own experience as a recent convert from a high philosophical tradition as a model for their work of conversion among those of the high religious traditions in India, China and Japan.[324]

Clement presided over the Catechetical School in Alexandria from 190-203 CE. From his writings we discover a learned classical scholar as well as a simple-hearted disciple of Christ.[325] For Clement it was in the 'character of

Christ, not in his miracles or prophecy' that 'the highest evidence of His divine mission to Humanity' lay.[326] But the marrying of reverence for Hellenistic philosophy with simple Christian faith required certain intellectual moves on Clement's part, as Allen suggested:

> We meet in Clement a more emphatic statement than in any other ancient Father of the universality of the preparation of the Old World for the advent of Christ. As a Greek it fell to him to indicate his alliance between the Hellenic philosophy and the new religion. Such an alliance he does not regard as calling for an apology; it is the divine ordering of the world that Greek philosophy should have prepared the way for Christ, and to doubt it would be to undermine the possibility of a revelation, as well as deny the providence of God.[327]

Allen supported this view of Clement by a catena of quotations from the *Stromateis* which 'show how large and free was the conception of the methods of divine revelation'.[328] Clement saw that humanity had its life and being in Christ: 'the whole human race, not any elect portion only, is included as under the operation of grace as well as of law; all human history is unified and consecrated by the visible traces of divine revelation.'[329] Thus, for Allen,

> Since Christ is the indwelling God, His incarnation is not a thing new or strange, an abrupt break in the continuity of man's moral history; it had not been decreed in the divine counsels, in order to avoid some impending catastrophe which suddenly confronted or threatened to disappoint the divine purpose; it was not merely a historical incident by which He came into the world from a distance, and, having done his work, retired from it again.[330]

The pre-existent Christ had not been laid up somewhere out of this world, either in heaven or some other divine realm, but had been at work in the world continuously since its creation. 'He was in the world before He came in the flesh, and was preparing the world for His visible advent. As indwelling Deity He was to a certain extent universally incarnate and the light that lighteth every man, the light shining in the darkness, the light and life of men in every age.'[331]

Allen used the concept of fulfilment to describe the missionary processes which were implied by this conception. These words were to be almost exactly echoed by the Anglican missionary in Japan, Arthur Lloyd.[332] 'Hence,' wrote Allen, 'the prophecies of his advent enter into the organic processes of human history, and in the spiritual life of men may be read the fore-shadowings of Him who was the crown and completion of humanity, the fulfilment of the whole creation.'[333] The thought of Clement of Alexandria became in Allen's hands a potent resource for the theology of religion in the last years of the Great Century.

After this treatment of Clement, Allen pursued his way through Origen and Athanasius. He saw all these Greek Fathers as offering full support to the positions held by F.D. Maurice.[334] Interpreting the doctrine of the Trinity as a fulfilment of Greek as well as Jewish thought, Allen then offered a pattern to early twentieth-century missionary thinkers for 'reconciling' or 'fulfilling' divergent insights in Hinduism or in Islam, in Confucianism or in Mahayana Buddhism. In the following passage the influence of Maurice, and perhaps of Westcott, on Allen's thinking is unmistakable.

But the Christian doctrine of the Trinity could not have triumphed over heathen thought, had it not also been the fulfilment of all that was true in Greek philosophy. In the formula of Father, Son and Holy Spirit, as three distinct and co-equal members in the one divine essence, there was the recognition and reconciliation of the philosophical schools which had divided the ancient world. In the idea of the eternal Father, the oriental mind recognised what it liked to call the profound abyss of being, that which lies at the back of all phenomena, the hidden mystery which lends awe to human minds seeking to know the divine. In the doctrine of the Eternal Son revealing the Father, immanent in nature and humanity as the life and light shining through all created things, the divine reason, in which the human reason shares, was the recognition of the truth after which Plato and Aristotle and the Stoics were struggling, – the tie which binds the creation of God in the closest organic relationship. In the doctrine of the Holy Spirit, the church guarded against any pantheistic confusion of God with the world by upholding the life of the manifested Deity as essentially ethical or spiritual, revealing itself in humanity in its highest form, only in so far as humanity realised its calling, and through the Spirit entered into communion with the Father and the Son.[335]

'The theological renaissance of the nineteenth century'

A broader area of immediate relevance to the search for a theology of religion in the Edinburgh period lay in what Allen perceived as the 'theological renaissance of the nineteenth century'.[336] Allen's extraordinarily great intellectual leap from the fourth century to the nineteenth, omitting almost all the Latin theologians, is in line with his central thesis. The real continuity lay in 'immanence', not in 'transcendence'. Allen discerned significant stirrings of immanentist thought in the sixteenth-century Renaissance and the Reformation, in Quakerism and the Cambridge Platonists. But otherwise, the dominant 'Latinised' theology which made an absolute distinction between transcendence and the created order, had the most deleterious results.[337] The underlying, and in Allen's view, true, continuity of Christian thought seen in Clement and the other Greek theologians could find expression in forms which the high Augustinian traditions found less than orthodox. At the time of the Reformation, for example, the line of continuity found expression in Zwingli, not in Luther or Calvin. Allen adduced this testimony to the possibility of the salvation of the heathen from Huldrich Zwingli:

In the company of the redeemed, you will then see Hercules, Theseus, Socrates, Aristides, Antigonus, Numa, Camillus, the Catos, and the Scipios. In a word, not one good man, one holy spirit, one faithful soul, whom you will not then behold with God.[338]

Allen commented that Zwingli shocked the religious sentiments of the German Reformers 'not only by his clear denial of the Latin view of original sin, but by his conception of the salvability of the heathen'. Zwingli's doctrine of the sacraments seems to have been consonant with the notion that God's presence was a 'real presence' everywhere. When Zwingli suggested that good pagans might be saved apart from the work of Christ, Luther accurately perceived him to be of a different spirit from the other Reformers.[339]

Other bearers of the continuity of Christian thought were the much abused and despised mystics, whichever century they lived in. Allen thought that antipathy to mysticism had had most unhappy consequences. 'The formal Protestantism of the seventeenth century, as represented in its orthodox systems of theology, contained within itself the seeds of its ultimate disillusion. Its very formality aroused protest'. [340] These were 'the protests of humanity against being shut out from the presence of God'. 'The mystics again appear as they had done under somewhat similar circumstances in the age that followed the great system makers of the thirteenth century.'[341] Allen reminded his readers of Arndt and Boehme, Madame Guyon and Fénelon, the Quakers, the Spanish mystic Molinos and of the German Pietists.[342]

Allen had by now arrived in the era of the Protestant missionary movement. In three sentences he gave his own judgment as to why there had been no Protestant missionary movement in the sixteenth and seventeenth centuries.[343]

The absence of the missionary spirit in the Protestant communities is a fact of deep significance. The church was experiencing the gloom which came from the realization that the bridegroom was absent. The sense of melancholy which arose when the disciples felt themselves bereaved by the death of the Master must remain the characteristic of the church's life, until the higher truth should be experienced, that He had risen from the grave, and that His life had become the immanent spirit of life in a redeemed, regenerated world.[344]

This last thought was received with approval by many of Allen's missionary readers, and especially by those who were beginning to look for a new motivation in 'Christ as new life'.[345]

Allen was now in a position to sketch out the steps that were necessary if the immanentist tradition was to be recovered and the nineteenth century were to fulfil its promise of being a time of 'theological renaissance'. These advances centred upon Maurice's (and Athanasius') doctrine of the 'actual redemption of all mankind'.[346] The overthrow of Calvinism had been essential in this process.[347] Equally essential was the recovery of the witness of the Cambridge Platonists, whose 'religious faith and life, their very existence, is in striking contrast with the temper of an age which regarded God as immovably fixed at a distance from the world'.[348]

Allen was aware that many non-theological factors were involved in the nineteenth-century theological renaissance. For example, there was the increasing inability of people to accept faith on the basis of the old authorities, however much 'they might have thought they did or professed to have done'. For such people, faith came with '*a new authentication found in the feelings*'.[349] Allen suggested that it was useless to look to 'awakening' or 'revivalist' movements for any sort of theology which 'advanced the movement of Christian thought'.[350] Rather what had happened in the eighteenth century within evangelical theology was a discovery, or rediscovery, of 'feeling' and 'emotion'.[351] Ideas and concepts were taken up, not because of their intellectual power, but because of their power to appeal strongly to mood and experience.

> If they took up again the discredited doctrine of original sin, holding to it with surprising energy and tenacity, it was not so much, with Augustine or Calvin, as the cornerstone of the system of theology, but because it magnified, by contrast, the value of that work of redemption of which they were conscious as the work of God in the soul – a transformation which no human effort could accomplish.[352]

Against this background, Allen assessed the work of John Wesley. Wesley had found peace with God through trusting in a doctrine of the atonement such as Anselm and Calvin had taught, although it had come to him in Lutheran and Moravian form.[353] Allen wrote that the effect of these beliefs within Wesley's theology 'was to give an almost exclusive prominence to the work and person of Christ. For Wesley, as with the Moravians, Christ takes the supreme place in Christian experience, while, if one may so speak, God is relegated to the background, as if a being from whom Christ had come to deliver us'.[354]

As severe a critic of revivalism as he was of Calvinism, Alexander Allen continued to wield his theological scalpel as he dissected the revivalist trend in Methodism. Recall that at the time in which Allen was writing, large areas of America were experiencing what some of its historians have called the 'Methodist century'.[355] Allen was a close observer of its phenomena, and offered a valid diagnosis of the ambiguities in Methodist theology.[356] Neither Wesley nor his successors had seen into the heart of what was necessary for corporate theological 'renaissance', however clearly they had diagnosed the need for individual spiritual 're-birth'. Allen opined:

> There was something irregular, if not spasmodic or fitful, in the ideas of revival and conversion. There still lurked beneath them the principle of election, even though Wesley intended to reject it. The conception of a redeemed humanity, whose solidarity was in Christ, was still a truth waiting for recognition.[357]

But this truth would have stood no chance whatsoever of entering the consciousness of the nineteenth century had there been no evangelical awakening. Maurice and Schleiermacher alike could only have written because men and women had discovered 'heart-religion'. Allen's judgment is clear: 'without the evangelical awakening, the restoration of a higher theology would not have been possible. Its great service was in illustrating the profound reality of the religious life'.[358]

In this way Allen made the vital connection with the thought of F.D.E. Schleiermacher (1768-1834), whom he called 'the representative theologian of the nineteenth century', and 'the regenerator of theology'.[359]

Schleiermacher, Maurice and the theology of religion

The Continuity of Christian Thought, as we have already suggested, was the first book in which Maurice and Schleiermacher were set alongside each other. This fact alone makes Allen's 1884 book one of the turning points in the theology of mission and theology of religion. It was an extraordinary achievement, and Allen must be given appropriate credit for it.

When Allen wrote in 1884, Schleiermacher had hardly been heard of by the great majority of English-speaking theologians.[360] Why this was so is worth stating. In the first place, it was necessary to be able to read German in order to gain access to his work, and in the second place, those British and American people who had read him often thought him dangerous.[361] Only in 1893, thirteen years after the publication of *The Continuity of Christian Thought*, were the *Reden über die Religion* translated into English as *On Religion: Speeches to its Cultured Despisers*. Schleiermacher's systematic theology, *Christliche Glaube*, had to wait until 1928 to be translated as *The Christian Faith*.[362] The first full study in English of his thought, *Schleiermacher, A Critical and Historical Study*, written by W.B. Selbie, the biographer of A.M. Fairbairn, was not published until 1913.[363] Allen was ahead of his British and American contemporaries in reading and writing about Schleiermacher. Consequently many pages in *The Continuity of the Christian Thought* are merely exposition of the *Reden* which were otherwise quite unknown.

Allen described how 'in the closing year of the eighteenth century' Schleiermacher 'stood up before the German people to advocate personal religion as a relationship to God grounded in the deepest instincts of human nature'. Religion was not a system of dogmas addressed to the intellect. It was not a ritual, nor was it a collection of precepts enjoined upon the will. 'It is the essential primitive action of the human soul, a feeling or sentiment innate in man which unites him with God and with the universal order of things, – it springs from the constitutional endowment of humanity in God's own image'.[364]

As Allen interpreted Schleiermacher, religion included 'the deeper instincts and yearnings of the soul, as they were seen not merely in the individual man, or the local transitory phases of some particular age, but as they were illustrated in the experience of humanity throughout all its history'.[365] On the same page, referring to Schleiermacher's remarkable powers of synthesis, Allen used an image which would come to dominate in the World Missionary Conference Commission IV Report: he spoke of the 'scattered rays of truth' which had 'been illuminating individuals here and there in the long course of human progress'.[366] Schleiermacher's theology had the potential, in Allen's view, to focus or synthesize the scattered rays of human religion.

Schleiermacher was placed by Allen firmly within the German romantic context. Allen saw him building upon the work of Spinoza and German illuminism, as well as upon the insights of Schelling and Lessing. But primarily Schleiermacher was a Platonist: 'Upon Schleiermacher the study of Plato had produced its inevitable effect, releasing him from intellectual servitude, enlarging his mental horizon, stimulating the critical faculty, imparting the desire for the truth at any hazards, love of all that was highest and best, the conviction that the world when rightly viewed was resplendent with the glory of God'.[367] For Allen, Schleiermacher was the first Christian thinker since the days of Greek theology in whose work there is so much of the spirit of Plato that he could postulate 'a God who is with us, and in us and who is allied to humanity by an organic relationship'.[368] With Schleiermacher the incarnation had become again what it had been in Greek theology: 'the actual manifestation of God in the human, the entrance of the divine into humanity itself, so that Jesus of Nazareth became the revelation of God in his absolute glory'.[369]

Schleiermacher thus contradicted two underlying principles of Latin theology by asserting that it was no longer possible to think of Christ as 'one who

has come upon a mission to the world from the distances of space, and then
departed'.[370] Equally, after Schleiermacher's teaching, there had to be an end
'to the sentiment which had prevailed in Christendom since the time when
Augustine wrote his *City of God* that the Kingdom of God was to come in
some other world in the remote future'.[371]

> When Schleiermacher discerned, as by a revelation, in the humble exis-
> tence of the Prophet of Nazareth the unveiled glory of the infinite God the
> thought of ages was reversed. This world was seen as if lit up with the
> light of God: man was introduced even here to the fellowship of saints and
> angels, to the intimate converse of the only begotten Son of God with the
> Father.[372]

Accordingly, Schleiermacher's teachings showed that this world, 'lit up
with the light of God', was an arena of grace: 'that grace, no less than law,
was the dispensation under which all men everywhere were living'.[373]

Schleiermacher saw historical development and educational progress as key
principles for the interpretation of religion. The notion that human life is
essentially an educational process, wrote Allen, was to theology 'what the
doctrine of evolution... has been to science'.[374]

> That it should have lain dormant from the time of Clement of Alexandria,
> by whom it received so full an elaboration as a prominent truth in theolo-
> gy, is a suggestive commentary on the intervening ages of history. The
> belief that humanity as a whole, as well as each individual man, are in this
> world to begin an education under the tutelage of a divine instructor,
> lends sacredness to human life under all its manifestations in every period
> of its development.[375]

Hence there could be 'no distinction between natural and revealed religion', though there could be 'grades in the process of divine revelation',
Allen suggested.[376] At this point in *The Continuity of Christian Thought* came
a series of sentences which anticipate the great controversies of the twentieth
century. Christianity was a 'revealed' religion, but because it corresponded to
the needs and aspirations of 'man as a spiritual being', it was also a natural
religion. The human spirit could not 'be divorced from its relationship with
God'. Since God indwelt in humanity, the mind of man was in 'necessary
and continuous contact with an infinite spirit, by whose inspiration alone'
human beings were 'led to know and receive the truth'. The 'reason or consciousness' was 'divinely gifted with the power to read what God imparts'. It
was 'as vain as it was irrational to attempt to draw the line' between the
human reason 'acting by itself and a divine reason which imparts a revelation'. To do so was 'to separate things that are allied by an inner principle of

fitness, to regard man as separated from, or independent of, the action of God'.[377]

Although few of them had heard the name of Schleiermacher or read his work, his ideas were used repeatedly in the writings of missionary theologians at the end of the Great Century. Someone must have mediated his thinking to them, and I suggest that Alexander Allen was that agent. Indeed there are no other people who could have performed this essential task. This is not to say that the majority of these got Schleiermacher's views directly from Allen. While many missionaries had undoubtedly read *The Continuity of Christian Thought*, or had seen it reviewed, most would not have even heard his name. I do suggest, however, that when they met in missionary conferences and in Synods, on furloughs and study-leaves, or when they travelled together on ocean liners (voyages then took up to six weeks), they had a common interest in solving their major theological problem, namely the existence of the faith of other men and women. Sufficient numbers of them had read *The Continuity of Christian Thought* to spread the seeds of Allen's thinking widely in missionary circles.[378]

Allen's survey of the nineteenth century renaissance of theology went on to take the leading thinkers of the English Romantic movement seriously, affirming the importance of the insights of Coleridge, Wordsworth, Blake, Shelley and Ruskin.[379] F.D. Maurice, Allen thought, belonged within this movement.[380] Here for him lay the essential point of affinity between Schleiermacher and Maurice.

Allen's dependence on Maurice is apparent throughout in *The Continuity of Christian Thought*. In his Preface to the first edition (1884), Allen spoke of how easy it was to appropriate and use ideas 'till by force of repetition they become inseparable from one's own'. 'In this way I have used Neander and Baur, Maurice and Dorner, until it has almost seemed unnecessary to render them the tribute of indebtedness'.[381] In the Preface to the second edition (1895), Maurice was summoned to support the position that Allen took up about Augustine.[382] Undoubtedly Allen had become the outstanding exponent of Maurice's theology in the 'eighties and 'nineties.[383] Recognition of this came *inter alia* in his being asked to write on Maurice in 'The Prophets of the Christian Faith' series in the English journal, *The Outlook*.[384] Two paragraphs from this article effectively summarize Maurice's Trinitarian theology and reflect accurately the message of *Religions of the World*.

For the deep seated and widespread scepticism of the age was assuming that God existed apart from human life, indifferent to human suffering, enforcing obligations and calling for sacrifices with which in Deity there could be no sympathy, for they were alien to the Divine nature. But in the name of God as Father, Son and Holy Ghost, human relationships and duties and obligations of self-sacrifice were taken up, as it were into God, and glorified by His inmost essential life. The Divine became the proto- type of the human; eternal fatherhood and sonship were the pattern from which the human relationship was derived, and not an analogy inferred from the human family. Sacrifice and suffering entered as an integral fac- tor into the Divine life, before it proceeded forth from God as the moral law of the universe. In the incarnation of God in Christ and in the atoning sacrifice on the cross was illustrated the identification of the Divine with human interests.[385]

And again,

So great was the importance which Maurice attached to the doctrine of the triune name that in his book *The Religions of the World* he applied it as a test by which they were to be measured and judged. Confucianism and Mohammedanism could not rise to the truth of the fatherhood of God because they lacked the knowledge of the Son, through whom alone fatherhood could be fully revealed. Brahminism abounded in incarnations of the Divine, but they ended in themselves because knowledge was wanti- ng of the Eternal Father. Buddhism dreamed of an infinite Spirit in which all men shared, but because it did not know the Father and the Son its doctrine of the Spirit was void, as its highest goal was reduced to Nirvana.[386]

Because of Allen's synthesis of Schleiermacher and Maurice, the message of *The Continuity of Christian Thought* had its extraordinary relevance to the missionary activity of the church and to the fundamental question of its rela- tion with other religions. A new theological formulation had become possible, and was in urgent need of proclamation:

The factors of a true theology are now in our possession as they have never been before in all the Church's history, – God, humanity, and nature, bound together in an indissoluble relationship. The preparation begins to be approximately complete for undertaking the result which theology aims to achieve, and which it alone can achieve – the science which shall embrace all knowledge because it sees all things in God. Even now the church holds the key to the situation as the collective body of those who live in the consciousness of a relationship with God in Christ, through the indwelling of an infinite Spirit. [387]

The implications of such ideas were not lost on missionary thinkers. The spirit of Alexander Allen's very last words in *The Continuity of Christian Thought* was their spirit too:

The interest in foreign missions which characterises the Church today, bears witness to the deep-seated conviction that the Incarnate Christ stands in organic relationship to humanity. Notwithstanding the differences which divide the Christian world, it constitutes a ground of hope that the Catholic church, as a whole, has never committed itself to any theory of its existence which can prevent the congregation of faithful men from expanding itself into the fuller life of a redeemed humanity, where the communion of men shall become the communion of saints, and God shall have fulfilled the meaning and the promise of the Incarnation.[388]

Charles Cuthbert Hall

Charles Cuthbert Hall (1852-1908) was President of Union Theological Seminary in New York from 1897 to 1908. He was appointed to that post after a career spent entirely in the pastoral ministry.[389] In his *A History of Union Theological Seminary in New York* (1976), Robert T. Handy describes Hall as the President 'who guided the Seminary into the twentieth century'.[390] All references to Hall by his colleagues and students tell of 'an outgoing person who communicated to others his personal interest in them'. For example the great Baptist preacher, Harry Emerson Fosdick, who had been a student at Union in Hall's time, spoke of him as 'the greatest specialist in personal friendship that I have ever known'. Another former student, Henry Sloane Coffin, who became himself a President of Union, described Hall's personal charm: 'He had that magnetism which gives a room a different feeling because of his presence in it.'[391]

Cuthbert Hall had been ordained as a Presbyterian minister and was pastor of First Presbyterian Church in Brooklyn for twenty years (1877-1897). It was primarily for his fame and skill as a preacher that he was appointed to Union. But he had also been a member of the Board of Directors of the Seminary since the early eighties, and was therefore only too familiar with the biblicist and orthodox Calvinist controversies of the late nineties.[392] These upheavals impinged directly on the Faculty and Board of Directors of Union when Charles Augustus Briggs, Union's most distinguished Old Testament Professor, was arraigned for heresy before the Presbyterian Church court by followers of C. Hodge and B. Warfield for espousing the results of the 'Higher Criticism'. Hall took a clear line in support of Briggs during the latter's trials in 1891-1893.[393]

Hall was, however, primarily concerned with theological education and had already published work on the role of the ministry at the end of the century. In lectures given at the Hartford Seminary in Connecticut in 1895 entitled *Qualifications for Ministerial Power*, Hall had argued that ministry had little to do with theological controversy and much to do with religion as 'profound personal experience'.[394] In addition, he believed that all ministers needed to understand Christianity as 'an affair of world-wide concern'.[395] Laying particular stress on the historical reality of Jesus, and citing Fairbairn's *The Place of Christ in Modern Theology* in his support, Hall went on to declare:

> ...the historicity of Jesus Christ is not more conspicuous in the evolution of modern thought than the advance toward a comprehensive view of His Incarnation as the foundation of a reconstructed humanity, of His Redemption as a redemption of the race, and of His Second Advent as the hope of the Church and as the supreme motive of Christian earnestness. The religion of the Incarnation is producing a reconstruction of socialistic thought, and is now the most profound force at work on the side of purity, equality, and fraternal tenderness among men. The universality of redemption, through Him Who is the propitiation for the whole world, is infusing a new earnestness into evangelization, is disclosing the majestic catholicity of the Christian faith.[396]

As well as being the President of Union, Hall occupied its Chairs of Pastoral Theology (from 1897) and Homiletics (from 1903). From these bases in Union he gave two widely influential series of lectures on behalf of the Haskell Foundation, which had also taken Fairbairn to India in 1897-8.[397] From 1902 the Haskell lectures were known as the 'Barrows Lectures' and were given both in India and in Japan, and Hall travelled to both lands in 1902-3 and again in 1906-7 to deliver his lectures.[398] The books which resulted, *Christian Belief Interpreted by Christian Experience* (1905) and *Christ and the Eastern Soul* (1909), were eagerly welcomed by many missionaries, especially those in India, who felt that their own thinking had been validated by a prominent western theological teacher.[399]

Such missionaries also sensed that Cuthbert Hall had faced up to the realities of grace, sanctity and first-hand knowledge of God which he, like them, discerned in men and women of other faith commitments. This discernment had happened for Hall in just the same way as it had happened for the missionaries, through personal knowledge and encounter. Hall described his return visit to India, as 'a friend returning to his friends'.[400] Hall thought this friendship was 'broad and catholic', indicating that 'hereditary divergences of racial and religious tradition' were not impediments to fellowship. When addressing his audiences he affirmed repeatedly that nothing was further from his thought than controversy. He felt it impossible 'to speak to Indians in an unfriendly or an ungenerous spirit'.[401] Such courtesies were genuine and reciprocated.[402] Hall also wanted to ensure that there should be no manipulation taking place under the guise of politeness. Indeed such manipulation was neither worthy nor necessary. 'I have', he said, 'a settled faith that whatever is true and essential to the fulness of truth must for ever abide under whatever name or religion it has come into being, and whatever is not essential to the truth will, in the end, when it has done its work, be permitted to withdraw and pass away.'[403]

His son and biographer, Basil Douglas Hall, who accompanied the family on both trips to India and Japan, gives many examples of the way in which Hall was received. Auditoria were filled to overflowing; leading citizens of the cities where the lectures were given (Colombo, Calcutta, Allahabad, Lahore, Bombay and Madras) were present in large numbers.[404] One of Charles Cuthbert Hall's own journal entries reads thus: 'But from the outset the spirit of the auditors, as revealed in their countenance and in their demeanor, was so obviously that of friendly readiness to hear what might be spoken, that all other feelings were swept aside, save that of being in the presence of brethren (albeit of other faiths) who, in common with oneself were seekers after God.'[405]

There are, in addition, many independent testimonies from those people of other faiths recorded in B.D. Hall's *Life*. The Muslim poet and leader Sir Muhammed Iqbal asked R.E. Hume more than twenty years after Hall's visit to Lahore, 'Did you by any chance know the greatest lecturer who ever came to Lahore, the late Dr Charles Cuthbert Hall?' Iqbal added, 'Dr Hall remains the most remarkable person I have ever met... he still exercises upon me the charm of his Christian message and Christian personality.'[406] In Calcutta a leading barrister, Satish Chandra Mukerji, concluded that 'The secret of Dr Hall's marvellous success is due to the fact that he has really made a sympathetic and thoughtful study of non-Christian scriptures – *sympathetic*, because he is always willing to admit most gladly when ever he comes across any truth in them; and *thoughtful*, because he never fails to tell them with equal frankness wherein they are inadequate and necessarily require to be supplemented by Christianity.'[407] The oldest Hindu newspaper in India, *The Hindu Patriot* agreed.

> The main reason why Dr Hall has been able to draw the Hindu heart is that he had not interlarded his speeches with ignorant abuse of other religions... More than any other religion Christianity has been commercialized... In the East the Christian races, by pursuing a policy of selfish arrogance, impiety and injustice, made it well-nigh impossible for the Orientals to regard Christianity as a religion. Dr Hall's lectures, instead of lowering Christianity in the eyes of the Orientals, will rather intend to increase their regard for it.[408]

In Japan the impression was much the same. A Sendai newspaper recorded: 'Dr C.C. Hall has come to us almost as a stranger and left us as a friend whose good name will never be forgotten in the community.'[409]

The impression Cuthbert Hall made on the missionaries of India, Japan and the Philippines was equally profound.[410] Evidence for this was the immediate invitation to return and to give another series of lectures. Since Hall had been absent from Union Seminary for no less than fourteen months when he gave the first series, very careful thought had to be given accepting this invitation. With the hope of persuading him, Robert Hume wrote to one of the Board of Directors at Union:

Dr Hall has commended himself to both the Christian and the non-Christian leaders of India as no other man has done, and as perhaps no one else could do... So earnest has been the desire of many Christian leaders of India that Dr Hall should return for added service that it was seriously proposed to send him a general invitation from very many quarters to come and *stay* in India for a period of years. Bishop Lefroy of Lahore, a churchman of High Church proclivities, the Rev. S.S. Allnutt, Head of the Cambridge Mission in Delhi, and other leaders who ecclesiastically and theologically are far apart from Dr Hall, were ready to join in some invitation to Dr Hall to return. Such an invitation could not have been secured for any one else... Since Union Seminary exists for the highest service of the Universal Church, should not the Seminary delight to spare its President for one more short season of service which it is thought he can render as no one else.[411]

Hall's writings about Christianity in its new world-wide context at this period were based on personal knowledge and are shot through with 'justice, courtesy and love'. In the end, four books emerged which bore the marks of these visits in the East: *Christian Belief Interpreted by Christian Experience* (the Barrows Lectures for 1902-3), *The Universal Element in Religion* (the Cole Lectures at Vanderbilt for 1905), *Christ and the Human Soul* (the William Belden Noble Lectures at Harvard in 1906) and *Christ and the Eastern Soul* (the Barrows Lectures for 1906-7).[412] Of these, the second and the fourth are the most valuable for our assessment of Hall's theology of religion and his very early understanding of inter-faith dialogue.

Hall's theological background

Cuthbert Hall worked with theological methods essentially learnt from two foundational thinkers of the Great Century, Samuel Taylor Coleridge and Thomas Erskine of Linlathen.[413] With these men as his masters it is particularly surprising that in all Hall's works there is no reference to Frederick Denison Maurice.[414] But Coleridge and Erskine were sufficient to enable Hall to take off into new theology. From Coleridge he learnt about the validation of truth and the vanity of external authorities. As it seemed to Hall,

'Coleridge put into words the latent yearning of many English hearts for a system of religious thinking, founded more completely upon truth and less dependent on external authority.' To his Indian audience in 1907 Hall quoted Coleridge's *Ode to Dejection*:

> It were a vain endeavour
>   Though I should gaze for ever
> On that green light that lingers in the West,
> I may not hope from outward forms to win
> The passion and the life, whose fountains are within.[415]

Hall commented that such words should be whispered in the ears of all those who would endeavour to satisfy their souls with 'the outward'. From Coleridge, too, Hall derived his sense that:

> unreality was clinging like a mist around the denominational systems; that they were gradually becoming barriers to the advancing knowledge of the truth; that they were undertaking to bind the reason and conscience to fixed moments of the past, and to give an unqualified absoluteness to certain provisional and imperfect interpretations of Christianity, as against the eternal progressiveness of Divine Self-revelation, and the boundless capacity of the human mind to assimilate new aspects of that self-revelation.[416]

In the aftermath of the Briggs heresy trial, Hall was able to concur wholeheartedly with Coleridge's insistence that even orthodoxy must be challenged when it elevated itself above the claims of truth. Particularly apposite was the famous twenty-fifth aphorism in the *Aids to Reflection*: 'He, who begins by loving Christianity better than truth, will proceed by loving his own sect or church better than Christianity, and end in loving himself better than all.'[417]

In *The Confessions of an Inquiring Spirit*, Hall found a summary of Coleridge's views on biblical criticism, together with what Hall called

> an affectionate, pious and wise attempt to place the study of the Written Word on its only sure foundation – a deep sense of God's holiness and truth, and a consequent reverence for that light – the image of Himself – which He has kindled in every one of His rational creatures.[418]

Hall was also much influenced by Thomas Erskine, and frequently quotes from Erskine's *Letters* (1884).[419] In these letters Erskine wrote pithily about those who substituted a belief in the Bible for faith in God, especially in Scotland, where a 'man is considered religious, not because he walks with God in his spirit, but because he acknowledges and maintains the verbal inspiration of the sacred canon'.[420] Hall was particularly struck by Erskine's letter to a Professor Lorimer, where, in Hall's words,

> Mr Erskine makes some additional observations, which are so full of a spirit most needed now, that I cannot forbear to quote them. 'The character of God as a teaching Father who eternally desires and seeks the holiness of His reasonable creatures seems to me the great revelation of the Bible, and the true meaning of Christianity. I am prepared to hear any criticism on the Book, they do not trouble me in the least. I have found a medicine which heals me... a pearl of great price, which when a man has found he needs not that any other should tell him its value... When a person has made this discovery it is of no importance that further testimony be given to this by a doctrine of infallible scripture. Such a person needs no further evidence that this revelation of the character of God is a true revelation; he knows it must be true or his own existence, his own consciousness is a lie.'[421]

Conviction about the inward testimony of the Spirit and the capacity of every soul to receive it had enabled Hall to survive the struggles within American Presbyterianism for a non-literalist understanding of the Bible. The immediate results could be seen in Hall's support of Briggs in the 1891-3 controversies. But there would be more far-reaching consequences, since these ideas from Coleridge and Erskine also helped to forge in Hall a new understanding of God's work in other religions.[422] The pattern here is by now familiar, but familiarity need breed no contempt for any of the theologians or missionaries in this book. These were in each instance hard-won victories.

The gains of biblical criticism

Two aspects of the advances in biblical criticism seem to have seized Hall's imagination. The first was their contribution to ending 'sectarian confession'. In Hall's case, new understanding of the Bible had led to a break with the Westminster Confession.[423] The sectarian confessionalism of this document seemed in Hall's eyes 'to offer a narrower and more shallow foundation for faith than that eternal and sufficient foundation that is laid already in the Living Word and the Written Word of God'.[424] He wrote with some vigour:

> A study of the great sectarian confessions, from this point of view, and even of the so-called Catholic creeds – the Nicene Creed and the Apostles' Creed – shows their inadequacy; an inadequacy growing out of the fact that generally these official deliverances came into existence to controvert certain contemporaneous errors. They were not, and by their framers were

not intended to be – comprehensive instruments. They dealt with matters then in dispute, but left out other fields of truth which, not being under discussion at the time, were silently taken for granted. In illustration of this one may point to the inadequacy of the Westminster Confession of 1643 (sic) in its deliverances on the Person of Christ and on the Christianization of the world. The religious consciousness of later Presbyterianism has demanded and obtained partial recompense for this omission.[425]

Positive gain had also come, as Hall expressed it, from the 'recognition of Revelation as progressive'. 'So long as a standard of Biblical interpretation was maintained by authority whereby coequal religious insight was attributed to all parts of canonical Scripture, the inscrutable nature and perplexing contradictions of certain portions discouraged thoughtful readers.'[426]

But such inscrutable and contradictory material could be now be put into appropriate contexts with the result that:

a light brighter than the sun has poured upon the august fact of Divine self-revelation, showing it to be in its nature and action progressive, evolutionary, cumulative, emerging in the midst of the shadows of paganism, progressing as through the fitful and illusive stages of the dawn, broadening and deepening the current of its outpouring, growing brighter and brighter unto the perfect day; rising at length in full-orbed splendour at the Advent, and giving promise, through the infinite possibilities of the dispensation of the Spirit, of things yet to be that eye hath not seen, nor ear heard, neither have entered into the heart of man.[427]

'Progressive, evolutionary, cumulative'

With the exception of Maurice, for each of the missionaries and missionary theologians we are dealing with, evolution had become 'the determinative category of the age'. Hall was noticeably unblushing in his espousal of 'the progressive, the evolutionary, and the cumulative' as evidence that 'the Divine Spirit is moving mightily' in the affairs of his own times.[428] This view was consonate with the sense of 'upward emergence' which pervaded some missionaries' understanding of the development of religion. Hall couched his conceptions in a preacher's flowing rhetoric:

The Spirit of God is the Spirit of wisdom and counsel and understanding. The spirit of man is the candle of the Lord, a lesser light emerging from the Eternal Light, being of the same substance, partaking of the same qualities. The Spirit of God works through the spirit of man, nourishing the powers of discernment, illuminating the understanding, guiding the judgment. Even so said Christ: 'When the Spirit of Truth is come, He shall guide you into all the truth'. (John 16.13).[429]

Like the other four theologians we are considering, Hall turned to the Christian Platonists of Alexandria for example and guidance. These philosophers, Hall told his Indian audience in 1907, had recalled the 'ideals of a Wisdom, coming out from the abyss of the Unknowable to interpret the secrets of Divine intelligence'. 'Through distant Oriental sources they had entered and filled the Greek consciousness; to find as it seemed their correction and completion in Christ.'[430] Hall cited the image of the burning glass borrowing its power of kindling from the sun which he had found in the *Stromateis* of Clement of Alexandria (6.17,19.), and described how the Alexandrians spoke of Christ as 'the Brightness of the everlasting Light, the unspotted Mirror of the Power of God, the image of his Goodness', and, of course, 'the Word that was in the beginning with God, that came from the Unknowable into the knowable'.[431]

Hall's Spirit/Logos christology was manifestly effective in undergirding his open and dialogical approach to the Indians and the Japanese. It was also in tune with contemporary optimism concerning the human spirit. Hall was quite sure of the 'boundless capacity of the human mind' to assimilate new aspects of the 'Eternal Spirit's' self-revelation.

Hall and the comparative study of religion

Under Hall's leadership, Union Seminary in New York was among the first of the new 'theological universities' to include the study of religions within its main curriculum.[432] Hall's reasons for regarding this as essential to ministerial formation and theological education in general were clear. 'The scientific study of religion', he wrote, 'is one of the most fruitful disciplines of modern scholarship. Religion has been frankly recognized as a universal phenomenon of human life, and an impartial comparison of its modes of expression as a necessary condition of knowledge of the race.'[433]

In 1905 the battle for impartial study of religion was hardly begun, yet Hall felt able to describe the struggle in the past tense. He wrote of 'the distrust' with which the study of comparative religion had been regarded in conservative Christian circles. He commented that 'serious interest in the investigation of non-Christian faiths' had been feared lest it impaired 'the supremacy of the Christian religion':

It was contended that to treat respectfully the religious conceptions of the Far East was to pay tribute to Satan and to rob Christ of His crown. These ominous predictions have not been fulfilled. The study of the philosophy and history of religion, while it has dissolved many prejudices, corrected many misrepresentations and brought to light many admirable facts touching the religious life of races beyond the confines of Christianity, has most clearly shown the point at which the great non-Christian faiths stop short of power for the thoroughgoing transformation of character, which is salvation.[434]

Note Hall's definition of 'salvation' here. The idea of a 'thoroughgoing transformation of character' is a long way from concern for ultimate destiny, with sin and the wages of sin, and with the workings of common and effectual grace as set out by the Westminster Confession and expounded by Charles Hodge and Benjamin Warfield at Princeton. Hall went on to use the language of 'conscience', 'heart', and 'will', as he affirmed the transforming power of the Personality of Jesus Christ. Other religious traditions had 'no World-Saviour to offer':

They are without the vitality that can give life to the soul dead in trespasses and sins. The more attentively we study them, estimating their fitness to minister to the religious needs of man, the more obvious becomes their moral inadequacy. They have their heroes and their saints, their prophets and their sages, but they have no one to take the place of Jesus Christ, the Saviour of the World.[435]

In line with all immanentist thought, Hall saw the comparative study of religions as having already demonstrated 'that the activity of His Spirit is more mysteriously diffused than an earlier age supposed'. Therefore, 'the relations of human souls with God transcend the limits set by theological opinion' as does the 'plan of God for the religious development of the world.'[436]

Hall's period of office at Union Theological Seminary was also the heyday of the new science of the psychology of religion.[437] Hall was among the first theologians to draw, albeit largely uncritically, upon these insights and apply them across the board to the religious development of humankind:

Those many forms and sensations of soul-action can all be grouped under one word: perhaps the noblest word in the whole vocabulary of the finite individual: religion. Professor William James of Harvard University, in the Gifford Lectures on Natural Religion before the University of Edinburgh, has given a broad and helpful, though essentially incomplete, definition of religion: 'Religion shall mean for us the feelings, acts, and experiences of individual men in their solitude, so far as they apprehend themselves to stand in relation to whatever they may consider the divine.' In this form of soul-action we must include under the term religion, interpreting that term broadly and incompletely, not only the witness of consciousness to the concrete deities of polytheism, or to the transcendent deity of Islam, or to the immanent personal presence of Christian monism, or to the impersonal absolute of Higher Hinduism, but also the atheistic idealism of Higher Buddhism and all unformulated conceptions of the spiritual structure of the universe, which bear witness on the negative side to idealistic tendency. Whatever reverential feeling is coupled with the sense of infinity, be it that which seems abstractedly godlike or that which is adored as deity, partakes of the nature of religion.[438]

Out of a desire to understand this wider religious milieu, Hall had made himself as widely read as possible in the Indian religions. As Bishop Charles Brent wrote in his introduction to *Christ and the Eastern Soul*, Hall knew the value of 'the magnificent Vedic hymns' and was 'conversant with the profound philosophy of the Upanishads'.[439] Hall selected from his readings in Indian spirituality (what he himself termed 'the Oriental Consciousness') four elements which he called 'The Contemplative Life; The Presence of the Unseen; Aspiration toward Ultimate Being; The Sanctions of the Past'.[440]

In his studies in Indian Religion Hall clearly relied upon the best Western authorities he could find. One of these was Paul Deussen, Professor of Sanskrit in Kiel University, whom Hall quotes with strong approval:

> Then Deussen concludes with words that express far more clearly and strongly than mine what this entire course of lectures is designed to express: 'The New Testament and the Upanishads, these two noblest products of the religious consciousness of mankind, are found when we sound their deeper meaning to be nowhere in irreconcilable contradiction, but in a manner the most attractive serve to elucidate and complete one another.'[441]

Hall's style of interfaith dialogue

Hall never tried to convey to Indians the impression that he had 'mastered the inner meanings for the East' of these elements in Indian spirituality, but rather that he wanted to discuss them 'with reserve and modesty mingled with reverence and admiration'.[442] His attitude was made clear in the concluding words of his first series of Lectures. He asked forgiveness,

> if in any wise I have presumed upon the right of friendship in speaking thus ingenuously and unguardedly of Elements of Sublimity in the Oriental Consciousness. If I have committed a fault in so doing, the assurance of a generous motive may, perchance, be accepted as an atonement. I have seen many beautiful things in India, wrought by art or conferred by Nature; but nothing so beautiful as these traits of consciousness: the

Contemplative Life, the Presence of the Unseen, Aspiration for Ultimate Being, Reverence for the Sanctions of the Past.[443]

Wherever he could, Hall staked his claims for a universal religious inheritance heritage which belonged to all humanity:

If location is to determine rights of ownership, then that of which I speak to-night belongs to you more nearly and more naturally, than to me; and the fact that I enter into it, and assimilate it, and find this sacred religion of the East, the religion of Christ, the very life of my life, proves only that the world is one family in all its greatest inheritances.[444]

He was, nevertheless, eager to 'argue and persuade', and was as anxious as any of the missionaries that India should make its response to Christ. 'You have', he told his Indian and Japanese audiences, 'a rich inheritance of blessing'. But they had also 'a solemn weight of responsibility'. 'I am moved to quote as I close', he told them, '"Unto whomsoever much is given, of him shall much be required; and to whom men have committed much, of him they will ask the more" (Luke 12.48).'[445]

Cuthbert Hall's gift of friendship was lavishly offered to India and to Japan. His second lecture tour was as much an outpouring of emotional and physical energy as his first, though Hall was now four years older and perhaps more exhausted by the strains of the presidency of Union Seminary. Some unrecognized virus got hold of him in Japan, and though he arrived home safely in New York, he never fully recovered. In the last months of 1907 he had to lay down his duties in the Seminary and in March 1908 he died.[446] He had told his last audience in India:

It may be that never again I shall visit this land. In the course of time I shall pass from the earth into that Unseen, upon which in common we love to meditate. But were I to return from some other world to visit you, my counsel and exhortation would be unchanged: Receive Jesus Christ as the Word – the Logos of the Infinite – Who reveals in sacrifice the heart of God. Honour Him indeed as a Sage, Who comes not to destroy but to fulfil your traditional aspirations. But do more than that: Worship Him as a Saviour who enters the circle of consciousness to make all things new, purging the way the lusts of sin. Then go forth as his prophets and make Him known Eastward and Westward, dedicating your splendid gifts to Him for the world's sake, until His Kingdom come and His Will be done, in earth as it is in Heaven.[447]

Hall's power as preacher comes alive here. Embedded in this paragraph are the central themes of the Great Century; echoes of Bushnell and Erskine,

Maurice and Westcott, Fairbairn and Allen: the rediscovery of Logos christology, the portrayal of Christ as transforming power, and the presentation of
Christian message as one of fulfilment and not destruction. There is even an
echo of millennialism in Hall's last words. But, more than all this, is the
impression of great courtesy and profound love. Hall's essays in presenting
the Christian message to Eastern peoples were valiant attempts to do justice
to all religious traditions.

3

Eight Missionaries and their Theology
of Religion

In this chapter we turn from theologians at home to theologians abroad, six in India and one each in China and Japan; two Anglicans, one Baptist and five Congregationalists; six Britons and two Americans, who were to become central figures in the development of the theology of religion at the end of the Great Century. The title 'theologian' could quite certainly be applied to them all for they were fine scholars and subtle thinkers, but we shall normally refer to them as the 'missionaries' or, occasionally, as the 'missionary theologians'. Our concern with them arises out of their immediate and practical knowledge of the religious traditions and experiential faith of other men and women. Even though they were voracious in their reading and had remarkable academic learning at their disposal, their chief source of information about Hinduism or Buddhism or any other tradition was through personal encounter with living adherents to these traditions. They knew the faith of other men and women at first hand, through friendship and through 'participant observation'. Above all they knew the language of the people they worked among, often so well that they conversed and prayed and even dreamed in it. If the Czech proverb is right in saying that 'as often as you learn a new language, you become a new person', the missionaries we are about to meet were new people, with a new spirituality and a new perception of the world.

Our aim therefore in this chapter is to provide a series of sketches of British and North American missionaries of very different theological backgrounds who were transformed by their meeting with people of other faith. The chief criterion for choosing these eight from among many others is very simple. Each one of them made a decisive contribution to the formulating of *The Missionary Message in Relation to Non-Christian Religions*, that astonishing report from Commission IV at the World Missionary Conference in Edinburgh in 1910.

To be sure, they were not the only ones who influenced the Edinburgh commissioners, as will be shown in chapter four below, and a further two criteria have come into play in selecting the eight missionaries in the following pages. The first of these reflects the quality of their published work in the years up to and around 1910. Although their books now gather dust in the remoter stacks of university and seminary libraries they were significant authors in their day, widely read and discussed in their own missionary circles, where they contributed powerfully to the groundswell of change in attitudes towards other religion. A second measure of judging who should be selected now has had to do with their 'star quality', their ability to influence other missionaries not only through their writings but through their gifts of leadership, their intense personal devotion, their courage and their integrity.

The eight sketches are, I hope, cumulative in their effect. Certainly there are different emphases to be discerned among the eight missionaries, but none of them has been chosen as representing a distinctive point of view. On the contrary, what I hope will emerge is the sense of one common enterprise, and even the birth of one new tradition within Christian theology. In different ways these eight thinkers manifest their indebtedness to Maurice, Westcott and Allen, to Fairbairn and to Hall. What we will see above all is that they learned through these writers to look to the great Greek teachers of the church as their missionary models, both in terms of a theology of religion which stressed immanence rather than transcendence, and by means of that immanence the doctrine of the indwelling Logos or pre-existent Christ, and in terms of a missionary practice which thought of preparation and fulfilment, or of longing and consummation.

The eight missionaries have among them several veterans who, by 1910, had served forty years or more on 'the mission field'. Others of them were much younger men whose chief work was to be done after the World Missionary Conference. The order in which they are dealt with reflects this, and their date of birth is the determinative factor. In each case I have drawn for the rounding out of their views on the theology of religion upon the response which was made to Commission IV of the Edinburgh Conference.

Thomas Ebenezer Slater: 'Justice, Courtesy and Love'

The first of the missionaries in our chronological order is Thomas Ebenezer Slater (1840-1912). He was at once a model of the way of dialogue and a pioneer in the Christian understanding of Hinduism. His most important book, *The Higher Hinduism in Relation to Christianity: Certain Aspects of Hindu Thought from the Christian Standpoint* (1902) is still referred to by scholars of Hindu thought.[1] But his earlier work *The Philosophy of Missions* (1882) establishes him as the earliest missiologist of the modern kind, for its methodology and analyses were at least twenty years ahead of their times, and often feel as though Slater is dealing with twentieth century issues.[2] Among those who discovered his writings in the last years of the Great Century was John

Henry Barrows, a professor of theology at Oberlin College, Ohio, and, as we have seen, one of the protagonists of the World Parliament of Religions in Chicago in 1893.[3] Barrows once wrote of Slater that there was no one better fitted to interpret Christianity to Hindus, and Hinduism to intelligent Christians. 'My own observations and studies have convinced me that the method of sympathetic approach is the only proper method in dealing with the educated non-Christian classes of Asia. By training, experience, and by the cast of his mind, Mr Slater has illustrated the true and wise Christian temper in the approach of the Occidental to the Oriental spirit.'[4]

Thomas Slater went to India with the LMS in 1866 when he was twenty-six, having had a thorough theological education (in the Isaac Taylor mode) in the Congregationalists' academy in Birmingham. His first five years in India were spent on the staff of the Bhowanipur Institution in Calcutta, where J.N. Farquhar would follow him thirty years later.[5] After another three years spent in high school teaching in Madras, Slater was seconded by the LMS to work with young men who had passed through English-medium colleges. Slater had inherited the concerns of Alexander Duff, William Miller and others for special missionary work in India among those educated in the increasing number of schools and colleges in which the English language was the sole medium of instruction.[6] 'They had been taught to read, write in English; their new terms of reference were Christian; in many cases they had turned their backs upon Hinduism as a religion, if not as a social system.'[7] A full-time worker was needed to give his whole attention to this group, the 1874 Madras Missionary Conference had decided.[8] Slater volunteered for the job, and the LMS agreed that he should be given one year to explore methods of working with such young men. He began by visiting young men in their homes.[9] A number of discussion groups including both the students and teachers in and around Madras sprang up. Slater also gave public lectures which in due course were published. The first of these was a book entitled *God Revealed* (1876). Slater was sure that it was pointless to present Christianity as 'an antagonistic Religion among other Religions of the world' and as 'a voice sounding the knell of doom to non-Christian nations'. On the contrary Slater proposed, 'in the firm persuasion that all are *by nature* Christians, to hold it up as that which Hindus would find satisfied and realised the noblest and earliest ideas of their sages, and the truest sentiments and yearnings of their hearts'.[10]

The historian Eric Sharpe has shown that Slater refused to hold anything Hindu in contempt, for, as early as 1876, his view was that if there happened 'to be error, falsehood, evil in what a man calls his religion, it may be owing to ignorance and want of light; and such a man is an object for pity and for help, not for reproach or condemnation'.[11] Consequently Slater formulated a principle: 'The aspect in which I would set Christianity before you is not an aspect of antagonism but of consummation.'[12] This was so unusual a position in 1876 that it aroused instantaneous condemnation from fellow missionaries and Sharpe has discovered in the LMS archives for this time a series of anonymous letters signed 'True Friend of Missions'. In one of these Slater was accused of being a Unitarian. Accordingly, the LMS Directors called upon Slater to give assurances that he still subscribed to the Evangelical Faith. In a twenty-four page response to the Directors, Slater wrote that while his answer remained 'Yes' to this question, his attention was concentrated less on Christianity as a body of doctrine, as on 'Divine Facts and Divine Life in Christianity'.[13] Slater was moving rapidly towards becoming a theologian of faith and experience.

Slater had also become acquainted at that period with Sir Monier Monier Williams, the Bowden Professor of Sanskrit in Oxford since 1861.[14] They had discovered that they had much in common. Slater invoked his name in order to support the position he had taken up. Monier Williams, Slater told the Directors of the LMS 'entirely sympathised with the mental attitude I have sought to take up in relation to the Hindus. He remarked that there was scarcely an idea and a truth in Christianity that did not exist in some form in Hinduism, and he thought the missionaries had as a rule not taken the pains to make themselves acquainted with such things, and in consequence had greatly retarded the spread of Christianity in the country'.[15]

The philosophy of missions

Slater's brush with the LMS Directors obviously put the idea into his head to give an extended exposition of how his mind was changing. His own passionate conviction that the spread of Christianity in India was being retarded by the views represented by the 'True Friend of Missions' needed outlining in full. *The Philosophy of Missions: A Present-Day Plea* (1882) argued that mission should be seen as a task of the whole Church. Putting his finger on the church v. society issue Slater described the missionary enterprise as 'something outside the ordinary organisation of the Church'. In America, however, the 'position of missions in the work of the Church had been better understood', and missions were part of 'regular Church work, instead of being left, as here in Europe, to separate and voluntary societies'.[16]

Against this wider missiological background Slater than showed how his experience of India indicated that 'silent, steady *spiritual* revolution' was taking place.[17] 'Faith in the religious systems of Hinduism and Mohammedanism, and adherence to the social systems of ages, are giving way.'[18] Slater saw this as 'among other things' evidence for Christianity itself: '*The religion of Christ has never received such justification as it has been afforded by the missions of the nineteenth century.*'[19] Slater thought that Christianity's divine origin was demonstrated not only by the facts of its existence and persistence in the world, but by its growth and diffusion among the different races of humankind, and by what he called its 'regenerating power' in all kinds of conditions. Christianity had a special gift in being assimilable in conditions of advancing civilization. He saw this as marking Christianity out as 'the universal religion of the world'.[20]

But nothing of the far-reaching significance of Christianity was understood in the West. 'In the minds of many the simple preaching of the Gospel – "teaching the poor ignorant heathen" the elements of Christian truth – has summed up the duty of the missionary.'[21] This simple preaching affected only one class in the community. It touched 'the mind of any nation only at the point of its weakest and most ignorant individuals'.[22] Slater wanted to set before Western Christians the 'high vocation of the missionary to give to a foreign race a Christian civilisation'.[23] This would be done through permeating 'the national mind with Christian ideas'. 'Hence every open avenue into a nation's life must be entered, every available agency employed, so that points of contact between Christianity and the mind of the people may be multiplied.'[24] The modern missionary therefore had to be 'many-sided', 'a master of many arts' and originator of various schemes for human progress.[25] *The Philosophy of Missions* was thus a protest against missiologies deriving from intellectualist biblicism and anti-intellectualist revivalism. It recaptured some of the older millennialist sense of the broader sweep of God's kingdom in history, and took up some of the old 'civilizing' motives.[26] To the liberally-minded believers in progress of whatever kind in Victorian England, Slater wrote: 'Every friend of culture should be a friend of missions.'[27]

The motives which may have brought him to the mission field in 1866 no longer concerned him. Perhaps, in the light of both Maurice and Fairbairn, he was speaking for his generation, when he wrote:

> The ghastly argument drawn from *the appalling picture of the future misery of the heathen*, which once roused missionary assemblies, has been abandoned. The strongest claims of missions on British Christians used unquestionably to be derived from this source. The most pathetic pleas for the heathen world were those which gathered round the mouth of the bottomless pit into which myriads of unsaved souls were represented as falling. The lurid verse of Montgomery's missionary hymn, 'The heathen perish', which begins with the words, 'See the short course of vain delight', and which to so many presented the great impelling motive for missionary activity, is seldom sung – indeed, it has disappeared from many of the hymn books.[28]

1882 is very early indeed to find a discussion of what could become alternative missionary motives if the threats of hell and damnation were no longer in force. Nevertheless Slater tackled the issue head-on, speaking as though liberal views had won out:

With the loss of this motive, it is asserted, the great inspiration of missions has gone. Ardour and energy have cooled, if the heathen are not perishing, why trouble to rescue them? If they are not rushing into hell, why hasten to them with the tidings of salvation? If they are not condemned already in their state of nature and of sin, why increase their responsibility by giving them the knowledge of the Gospel? If they are in the hands of a just and merciful God, why not leave them there?[29]

Slater lamented the fact that the vast and difficult subject of motivation was not dealt with in missionary meetings.[30] What these should be dealing with, he suggested, was a different set of instigations and impulses which would help Christians obey the Great Commission, Matt. 28.19-20. The cause of world mission was to be firmly based, in his view, on 'the Divine Command and on the whole spirit of the Gospel':

Nowhere are we urged in Scripture to philanthropic efforts among the heathen, on any grounds relating to their final and eternal condition; but because the Gospel *here and now*, is, by virtue of the Saviour's word and work, the right of *all*, and the only regenerating and redeeming force in human society. To stay our helping, healing hand because there may exist conflicting theories as to what may happen in the ages that are to come, would be as great infatuation and as gross a crime as it would be to refrain from stopping a pestilence or a fire, because we are ignorant or doubtful of some of their constituent elements and latent possibilities.[31]

Slater's own view of what the future held for the world was a modified millennialism, in that he believed in 'universal restoration'.[32] The kingdoms of this world were to become the kingdoms of our Lord and his Christ, where Christ should reign for ever and ever, Revelation 11.15. Slater suggested that the 'divine love which agonised on Calvary', which 'ever pleads and redeems rebellious hearts', should lead Christian minds away from 'notions of divine decrees', and establish the doctrine of Divine Paternity. This would logically require the 'revelation of the Father to the children, *through the proclamation of the Gospel*, and the pressing home to each individual heart' of the divine appeal.[33] Slater had read his Erskine, Bushnell, Campbell and Maurice to good effect.

G.E. Lessing was another powerful influence on Slater, who made full use of the idea of the 'education of the human race'.[34] Lessing had spoken of 'the vast, slow wheel which brings mankind nearer to this perfection' which was itself only put in motion 'by smaller, swifter wheels'.[35] In this light Slater thought that the biblical revelation had to be conceived as the supreme 'educator of humanity'. In the scriptural record Slater saw 'the great Father...

training His human family for Himself'.[36] No part of the human race could be left in ignorance of this revelation.

Slater was also profoundly concerned therefore that the gospel should actually be 'good news'. It is hard to imagine that Slater was unaware of the missionary motivation of the Hudson Taylor and the China Inland Mission, or of the growth of millenarianism in other circles, which were to become powerful forces in the seventies and eighties.[37] Nevertheless he chose to write, as it were, hypothetically, when he pointed out the terrible difficulties of holding doctrines of hell and damnation when engaged in Christian missionary work in India:

> If there are those who still believe that the heathen, as heathen, are exposed to endless torment, let them, by all the terrors of such a vision devote themselves to their rescue with the most passionate energy; though we would utter the solemn warning that, in teaching such a doctrine, they are taking away with one hand what they are offering on the other, and weighting the Gospel with an appalling burden which, in the view of the fatalism and pantheism, and idolatries of the East it cannot bear.[38]

No injury should therefore be done in the name of biblicism or revivalism to the gospel of the 'all-embracing love of a heavenly Father, who loveth all men, and hateth nothing that he has made'.[39] It is apparent from these words also that Slater had drunk deep from the well of Maurice.[40] In fact there are many direct borrowings as well as echoes of Maurice's theological formulations in Slater's pages. One passage in *The Philosophy of Missions* could have been written by Maurice, had he lived until 1882:

> We have grasped more clearly the truth that there is 'one God and Father of all, who is over all, and through all, and in all'; one Divine Son who has revealed to men this Father; *one family* on earth and in heaven. And missions are bringing their Father near to those who know not the brotherhood. They represent Him as yearning with an infinite solicitude over every member of his Human family whom in Christ He has redeemed, and whom in Christ He is seeking to recover to His home and heart. They recognise *the brotherhood of men*, the brotherhood of nations; they acknowledge the equality of all souls in the sight of God; the claim of all on the same Divine affection; an equal place for all in the same parental heart. They testify to *the unity of the race in Christ*. They reveal Christ as the organic root and Head of the Human family; the Representative of the race, in whom every tribe is interested, and towards whom every soul stands in vital relation. They declare Him to be the source of all true civilisation, of all social virtues, and of the highest political and national life. They point to Him as 'the light of the world', as the 'Fountain of all the

truth and goodness' that gleamed out in the ancient world, as the fulfiller of all pre-Christian hopes and aspirations, as the 'central truth that reconciles the systems of men', as well as the spiritual 'bond that unites the lives of men', as the explanation of human nature, the justifier of its deepest convictions, the satisfaction of the human heart.[41]

Maurice's Boyle Lectures, *The Religions of the World* (1846) are cited on page 66 of *The Philosophy of Missions*, where Slater was expounding the conception that the 'successful diffusion' of the gospel among the nations is evidence of its divine origin and justifies its divine claims. Maurice had written that it was vital to offer the Christian faith to all the world in order to establish whether Englishmen are 'holding a faith which addresses us as members of a class, or one which addresses us *as men*, which explains the problems of our human life... *which is for men*, here and everywhere'.[42] Slater knew that Maurice's perceptions were wholly accurate. Christianity, wrote Slater, was indeed the embodiment of ideas that lie at the root of all spiritual and intellectual life. In Slater's missiology this was indeed the 'embodiment', or incarnation, for which the world was waiting, and which it was the task of the whole church to take to, and to express in, the world.

Mission as dialogue

Slater's sense of the individual as a person in a total historical and cultural context rather than as a soul to be saved, led to an emphasis on the moral claims laid upon individuals in their social and religious contexts. Thus Slater wrote of the need for 'transforming action upon individuals of new truth' for 'nations are redeemed through the regeneration of the units'.[43] Preaching was appropriate enough for large assemblies on special occasions, but for the regeneration of individuals smaller scale activity, the discussion groups, the one-to-one conversations were much more appropriate. In modern terms, we would call such programmes mission as dialogue rather than mission as proclamation.

Because mission was to be done through personal relationships, rapid and immediate results could not be expected, certainly not in India.[44] Describing LMS and other missions in the sub-continent to his Western audience, Slater explained:

They are wisely worked, to a large extent, on the understanding that *no* great immediate results should be impatiently expected, but that a gradual elevation of the tone of society – effective mainly through the instrumentality of our schools and colleges – the inculcation of a healthy morality and of Christian ideas of excellence in various spheres of life, necessarily contribute to the ultimate triumph of Christianity.[45]

The true criterion of success could not be statistical, counting the numbers of 'converts' but rather, it had to be asked 'How far has Christian teaching told on the systems of the East? How much nearer are *India* and *China* to their conversion?' It followed that 'no branch of missionary work is to be judged from the results which they produce alone, but *as part* of a great effort designed to accomplish vast and glorious issues, reaching far into the future Church and the world'.[46]

Implicit here was a fundamental principle of interfaith dialogue.[47] It is not possible to talk to another person if all the time you are expecting an immediate result of conversion.

But notice also Slater's conviction (also derived from Maurice) that in Christ there is that which answers the needs and aspirations of human hearts. He believed that from the bottom of his heart, and remained a passionate missionary of Jesus Christ, albeit with a new minted theology of religion.

Christ the fulfilment of other religions

Writing more than thirty years before Farquhar's The *Crown of Hinduism* (1913) was published, Slater announced, in lapidary form, the fundamental understanding of the last decades of the Great Century about the other religions within the purposes of God: '*All other religions wait for their fulfilment in Christianity*.'[48] This principle, Slater thought, was perhaps 'the most philosophic of the grounds' on which the claims of mission could be based. 'There is no aspect of our race,' he wrote, 'so deeply affecting and profound as the natural history of the human consciousness, the dim groping of men, through the ages, after God.' The thought may have owed something to the theory of evolution, or to Lessing's educational theories. Slater however justified it from scripture. 'We know that the great Gentile world, though beyond the pale of an historical revelation, has not been outside the sphere of the divine providence ; that "in the generations gone by" He "suffered all the nations to walk in their own ways", yet "left not Himself without witness" (Acts 14.16,17).'[49]

In true Maurician vein Slater asserted that 'These old religions have endured according to the amount of truth they contained, according to the fitness of their doctrines for the special circumstances of their country, race and culture that prevailed'.[50] They testified, unknowingly, to the One who is 'Heir of all the ages and who, in the fulness of time should come to fulfil not only the prophesies of Judaism but as the desire of all nations, and the fulfiller of the "unconscious prophecies of heathenism"'.[51] The thought of Slater's fellow Congregationalist Horace Bushnell was also enlisted here in conjunction with the increasingly prevalent notion of evolution.[52] Bushnell, we have seen, taught that 'the world is governed supernaturally in the interests of Christianity'.[53] Another strong influence on Slater was Schleiermacher, mediated through the writings of his disciple, the church historian

Johann August Wilhelm Neander (1789-1850).[54] Slater cited Neander as declaring that 'Christianity is the end to which all developments of the religious consciousness must tend, and of which, therefore, it cannot do otherwise than offer a prophetic testimony'.

> Thus there dwells an element of prophecy, not merely in revealed religion, unfolding itself beneath the fostering care of the Divine Vintager (John xv), as it struggles onward from Judaism to complete its disclosure in Christianity, but also in religion as it grows wild on the soil of Paganism, which by nature must strive unconsciously to the same end.[55]

Like A.V.G. Allen, Slater united the idea of the religious consciousness, ultimately derived from Schleiermacher, with fundamental conceptions about God and humanity originating in F.D. Maurice.[56] As Slater wrote, 'There is unrest in every religious system apart from Christ. *Apart from Him*, they are fragmentary and fleeting systems, and this is their weakness and their sadness; their capacity of union with Him is their strength and justification.'[57] Then in a passage which is straightforwardly Maurician, Slater spoke of these religions as 'doubtless adapted to the cultivation of the religious *need*; but this need wants *satisfying*. Throughout these ancient systems there is ample evidence of that in man which *demands a revelation, but not that in man which gives* the revelation.'[58] As religious systems, wrote Slater 'they wrought no deliverance, they remain unfulfilled. Their unrealised yearnings, their unsolved problems oppress the mind with the deepest sadness. In the Gospel alone can religious complexities and spiritual instincts be completely satisfied.'[59]

The Philosophy of Missions finished with a rhetorical flourish, and chose a two lines from a hymn not now found in the hymnbooks. The American Episcopalian Arthur Cleveland Coxe expressed the unfulfilled longings of humanity in this verse:

> Far and wide, though all unknowing
> Pants for thee each mortal breast.
>   Human tears for Thee are flowing,
>   Human hearts in Thee would rest.

In these words Slater saw a description of his own missiology, at the heart of which was the conception of 'the necessity of Christ to the spiritual rest and perfection' of humankind.[60]

The Higher Hinduism in Relation to Christianity

The Philosophy of Missions showed Slater in 1882 moving towards a theology of religions which was based upon a Logos christology. 'Our allegiance to

Christ' demanded that 'we affirm nothing good but His'. This meant that missionaries had to 'own the good and true' wherever they were to be found. Such evidence of goodness and truth must be claimed 'for their rightful Author'.[61] These thoughts were to be fully developed in *The Higher Hinduism in Relation to Christianity*, where Slater was equally sure that 'religious truths that have been venerated for ages as the felt facts of man's inner consciousness' were to be claimed 'for the spiritual Christ who was immanent in grace and truth in human thought prior to the Incarnation, the light of every saint and seer who has relieved the darkness of the pagan world'.[62]

Slater believed profoundly that the more the facts of the world religions were known, the more they would be found to bear witness to this 'spiritual Christ'. With A.M. Fairbairn now as his chief mentor, Slater eagerly engaged in the new discipline of comparative study of religion.[63] *The Higher Hinduism* along with *Studies in the Upanishads* (1897), and *Transmigration and Karma* (1898) show Slater to have been an accomplished student of religion in his own right. These three books offered accurate expositions of the Vedanta, but detailed analysis is not relevant now. It is the conclusions of *The Higher Hinduism* which have lasting value for the theology of religion.[64]

In *The Higher Hinduism in Relation to Christianity*, Slater stated that 'the Veda and the Vedanta will ever stand out among "the monumental achievements of the human mind"'.[65] They still had 'noble thoughts' to contribute to the religious system of the world. Long ahead of his time Slater was speaking here of a 'religious system' for the world.[66] Equally ahead of his time, Slater postulated an Indian Christian theology. 'Vedantic thought', he wrote, 'is so thoroughly Indian that the *Indian Christianity* of the future will of necessity take a Vedantic colouring.'

In harmony with the ideas laid out in *The Philosophy of Missions*, Slater reaffirmed in *The Higher Hinduism* that each nation of the world was 'the manifestation of a human want'.[67] He specified the 'demand of the Indian heart' as the need for a fixed, unchangeable foundation on which the soul may rest among the changes of the fleeting world.[68]

This Indian form of Christianity would be the result of interchange or 'dialogue' (though to be sure the latter is not Slater's term) for 'the West has to learn from the East and the East from the West'.[69] It was no accident, but rather a Divine purpose, that had brought the East and the West together. There had consequently to be a proper response from Western Christians to the questions raised by the Vedanta. To the wholeness of Christian theology there had to come its insights into the 'science of the soul', and of the 'omnipenetrativeness and immanence of Deity'.[70]

Just as the religion of Christ triumphed over the religions of Greece and Rome, not by destroying but by absorbing from Greek philosophy and literature, and from Roman jurisprudence and government, all that was good and true, so will it be in India. Christ will yet satisfy the spiritual hunger and thirst to which the great religious ideas of the East only give expression; and India, while retaining and transmitting something of her idealistic and mystic passion and subtle thought... will surely find the enlightening revelation of the Gospel to be in *complete accord* with the best sentiments of her best minds, the true realisation of the visions of her seers, the real fulfilment of the longings of her sages.[71]

T.E. Slater and the World Missionary Conference

Slater had retired to England when he was invited to respond to the Edinburgh Commissioners. He had leisure to write a lengthy memorandum in response to the Edinburgh questionnaire.[72] It represented a distillation of his thinking about other religion in The *Philosophy of Missions* and *The Higher Hinduism in Relation to Christianity*. Slater was quoted substantially on eleven of the fifty-seven pages dealing with Hinduism in *The Missionary Message* (1910).

His Edinburgh Response shared two visions, 'some great apostle and leader, an Origen or an Augustine may any day be raised up who would far outplay all our efforts' and then 'the time must come when the intellectual power, and meditative spirit, and mystical genius of the Brahman will be required for the development and enrichment of the Church'.[73] Taking up suggestions made in the works of Maurice, Westcott, Fairbairn, Allen and Hall, Slater wrote that in the second century, 'the Person of Christ exercised a deep influence on the Oriental mind. He was recognised as the Divine Word – the Logos of the Infinite – Who speaks in Nature and in the heart of man, and Who reveals in sacrifice the very heart of God.'[74] This 'Logos which preceded the teaching of the Christian faith' Slater compared with '*Brahman*, or divine essence' in Indian thought. When the Hindu mind had been renewed by the Spirit of Christ, it would reveal 'the wealth of philosophic truth that underlies the Christian faith and that is opened out especially in the Incarnation: and will transmit to the theology of Christendom something of its idealistic and mystical passion and subtle thought' and explicate a Christ, 'discerned not so much objectively and historically, as inwardly and spiritually'.[75] Pondering on Christ's '*pre-existence* in the bosom of the Eternal', it would 'contemplate Him as "the first born of all creation"; as the implanted or "Spermatic Word" in all men; as the "Light Spiritual" of the world; as the "Reconciler of all things unto Himself"'.[76] Manifestly, the apologetic task was 'to *connect our great message with India's religious past*: and present it, not as something foreign to their thought, but as the true completion of what they themselves have been earnestly searching for'.[77]

Slater suggested a programme for Christian-Hindu discussions which would get to central issues while avoiding 'the old missionary crudities'. It turned upon the Christian proposition that 'God must be *eternally personal* in His nature' over against the Hindu perception that the Ultimate is Impersonal. But it could be observed in the history of religion that 'the Impersonal has ever been becoming the Personal; the Divine ever finding fuller expression, till it reaches its fulness in the Christian Incarnation'.[78] Slater described the Incarnation as taking place 'when God as Son, Who had been impersonally immanent in the world as the Divine Idea or Logos, became personally present and active in its life'.[79] In Hinduism 'an imperson-al conception of the Absolute is at the root of its thought' but that same time the mind of India 'has ever been struggling to realise the personal'.[80]

In affirming that Christ the Logos had always been the 'spiritual light of the world' and 'the source of those truths in other faiths that have nourished the best souls', Slater saw the 'old religions' as testifying 'however unknow-ingly to the "Heir of all the Ages"'.[81] The whole cumulative religious tradi-tion of humankind had been '*waiting for its realisation* in Him who fulfils, not only the prophecies of Judaism, but also "the unconscious prophecies of heathendom"'.[82]

> One has but to trace out the *idea of God* as conceived in the chief religions of the world, to see how single rays of the great truth have illumined dif-ferent minds... The God of Egypt, the Invisible; the God of Persia, the Prince of Light; the God of the Brahman, an Absolute Intelligence – *Sat-Chit-Ananda* – the existent, 'joy-thought'; the God of the Buddhist (if he can be called theistic) an Absolute Calm; the God of the Greeks, the Ineffable; the God of the Romans, the Righteous Lawgiver; and the God of the Muhammedan, an absolute Sovereign;— all may be summed up in the God of the Bible, and even then the Idea would not be complete.[83]

Nevertheless Slater remained convinced that 'apart from Christ, these old religions are fragmentary and decaying systems, and this is their weakness and their sadness; their capacity of union with Him is their strength and jus-tification'.[84]

Thus he remained a convinced Christian missionary. But he represents mission with a new song in its heart. To Thomas Ebenezer Slater this book owes its title, for however much was wrong in the lands to which missionar-ies went and however fragmentary and decaying the religious systems of those countries might have appeared to be, Slater told his contemporaries, 'We shall never gain the non-Christian world until we treat its religions with justice, courtesy and love.[85] No higher ideal could be set before Christians or anyone else ninety years later. Slater was a model for interfaith dialogue, in which all religious traditions must be approached with 'justice, courtesy and love'.

Timothy Richard: The Missionary as Strategist

The Baptist missionary Timothy Richard (1845-1919) worked in China from 1869 to 1916. One of the greatest Welsh missionaries, among all the people sent overseas by the BMS he can be matched only by Carey in originality and vision. Brian Stanley has recently described him as 'an original and controversial thinker without parallel in the Society's history'.[86] Though he was eventually given an honorary LL D by the University of Wales in 1916, long before that Richard had been honoured in China by being made 'Red Button First Grade' of the Mandarinate in 1903, followed by the 'Raising of his Ancestors for Three Generations' to equal rank. In 1907 he had been decorated with the Order of the Double Dragon. Throughout China he was known as 'Li T'i-mo-t'ai'.[87] Yet the scale of his achievements in China has never been recognized in the West. His biographer, the Methodist scholar W.E. Soothill, reflected sadly on Richard's funeral in the Golders Green cemetery in 1919: 'one could not help thinking of the contrast between the present small congregation and the public funeral which would have been his in the land where he was known and revered. Among his own people he was almost a stranger; among the "strangers" of the Far East he was regarded as almost a sage by millions.'[88]

His role as a forerunner of interfaith dialogue and contributor to the theology of religions needs close attention.[89] Not all his visions and theories in this area have stood the test of time. In his own day he was often regarded with grave suspicion as a dreamer and as a heretic. William Soothill offered a clue to the paradoxes in Richard which baffled his own contemporaries when he wrote, 'He was a man of sympathies so broad as to startle men of the narrower persuasion.'[90]

Richard was 'startling' particularly in the generosity of his outlook upon men and women of other faith. He transcended every one of the factors in his upbringing which might have made him closed and narrow-minded. As a product of revivalism, trained in traditions of biblicist erudition and inflexibility, Richard ought to have resembled many of his contemporaries. Why he was so different from them is a matter of speculation.

Born in 1845 in Ffaldybrenin, a small hamlet in Carmarthenshire, West Wales, some fifteen miles from Lampeter, Richard's upbringing was humble but highly literate. His father, a Baptist deacon, was a man of 'broad sympathies, having among his friends Rowland Williams of St David's College, Lampeter.'[91] This may be the first clue to his son's wide outlook. In 1858 the second Welsh Revival caught up the twelve-year-old Richard, and he became an ardent Christian of the revivalist type.[92] He preached his first sermon when he was sixteen. For the few next years he taught as an apprentice schoolmaster, attending the Swansea Normal College in his summer holidays. As soon as he could Richard entered Haverfordwest Baptist College. There he was taught by at least one professor with missionary experience, Dr G.H. Rouse, who later returned to India.[93] Little is known about Timothy Richard's studies at Haverfordwest, but he did win the Hebrew prize. He was also criticized for over-reliance on the theological ideas of Horace Bushnell.[94] Since Richard had never set eyes on any book of Bushnell's, this criticism might well have been taken as a compliment. It certainly indicated a certain cast of mind in Richard and his capacity for original thought. As soon as he finished his theological studies he offered for service in China with the BMS. He arrived in China in February 1870.

Early days in China

Timothy Richard's own record of his life and ministry, *Forty Five Years in China* (1916), gives many instances of an unusual ability to learn from new experiences. Richard himself described them somewhat laconically: 'When catechising my first convert before admitting him into the Church, I asked him "Are not all men sinners in the sight of God?" The man replied in distress "I do not know about other people but I know I am a great sinner"'. Richard continued, 'I was much struck by the sincerity of the answer and the foolishness of the question, and felt that the man was a true Christian in spirit. Never again did I repeat that question.'[95] Richard had the gift of being able to look at all questions with fresh eyes. The vexed issue of Ancestor Worship went on bothering the missionary conferences long after Richard had come to his own conclusion:

During my first year in China a missionary friend came to me in great triumph bearing in his hand the ancestral tablet of one of his native Christians. He told me that as the man had become a Christian he was going to burn his tablet. I remarked, 'When he burns the tablet, I suppose you will at the same time burn your parents' photographs.' This was a new thought to him – the Ancestral Tablet was never burnt.[96]

Richard had been quick to learn that Christians were not the only ones with a religion of grace and personal devotion. Early in his career he went to visit 'a devout man' of whom he had heard, a salt-manufacturer living about eight miles from Chefoo. Richard described the incident:

I took with me some Gospels, a few tracts and a hymn book and he received me with great kindness, and insisting on my having a meal with him whilst we talked of religion. After a time he took me to an inner room, spotlessly clean and said to me, 'This is the place where I worship daily.' On my showing the hymn book to him, he picked out one of the hymns which spoke of the fleeting character of this world and said, 'This hymn is ours.'[97]

Richard reported opening his eyes in astonishment. He had to know what this meant. But his Chinese did not run to getting appropriate answers. Richard went on:

> As this was the first time I had met a man of his stamp, I was dumb and felt that his religious experience was not only much earlier than mine, but possessed a depth which astonished me... I never saw him again, but have always felt that he, if not a Christian, was at least not far from the Kingdom of God. My knowledge of the Chinese language and history of religion was too imperfect at that time to take advantage of that most rare opportunity.[98]

Richard headed the section in his record: 'Visit to a Salt-manufacturer: perhaps a lost Nestorian'.[99] It was in any case, as Richard described it, 'a long happy day together'.[100]

Such incidents happened in Richard's first seven years in China. They set him off into new paths of theological and spiritual exploration. Richard started by re-reading the Gospels. He here discovered for himself 'the Kingdom of God'. Far from the lecture halls of Ritschl and Kaftan in Germany, Richard was exploring for himself first principles of Christian theology based upon the teaching of Jesus. He was spurred on in this by the Wesleyan Methodist missionary David Hill with whom Richard had formed a deep friendship. During the course of their work in famine relief in Shanxi in 1878 they had long discussions about future Protestant missionary activity. Richard remembered one evening when Hill told him of his own discovery that 'instead of emphasizing the Kingdom of God on earth', he had been 'preaching another doctrine, and from that time he had begun to be more scriptural and less theological'.[101] As Richard described it, he had discovered 'a gospel in the New Testament which made Chinese as well as Europeans glad – the Gospel of the Kingdom of God wherein dwelleth righteousness, peace on earth, goodwill to men'. Consequently he declared, 'We had come to China not to condemn but to save; not to destroy but to fulfil; not to sadden but to gladden.'[102]

In Richard's studies one text struck home with particular force: 'In whatsoever city or town you shall enter enquire who is worthy and there abide till you go hence' (Matt. 10.11). These words were to determine Richard's missionary activity. By the 'worthy' he understood 'those of all classes whose character has won the respect of their fellows and who have shown themselves to be aware of and responsive to spiritual issues'.[103] Faithful to such light 'as they have had, they are likely to be faithful to the further and fuller light which is brought to men, until finally they will rejoice in "light of the knowledge of the glory of God in the face of Jesus Christ"'. Seeking out the 'worthy' became his chief aim. He began to question other forms of preaching and teaching, often upsetting his fellow Baptist missionaries who remained wedded to street preaching, tract distribution and work among the very poor.

Forty-five Years in China contains records of many encounters with 'the worthy', including Muslim and Confucianist scholars, Buddhist monks, and Taoist priests. At the same time Richard redoubled his efforts to read Chinese books. During his first two years in China he had studied Legge's translations of the classics. But his new concern for 'the worthy' made him look for 'popular religious books which were used by the devout sects'.[104] Richard's studies brought him 'a vocabulary of religious terms differing in many respects from that adopted in the translation of the Bible'.[105] Having absorbed these new ways of thinking, he was able to prepare 'a catechism in Chinese, avoiding foreign names' and 'adopting our Lord's method of appeal to conscience rather than appealing to an authority the Chinese did not recognise'.[106]

Richard was now firmly set on the path of interfaith dialogue. An encounter in 1884 with a Buddhist bookseller in Nanking surprised and delighted him. Richard asked this man why he had converted from Confucianism. ' "I am surprised", he answered, "that you, being a missionary, should ask that question. Do you not know that Confucianism shirks some of the great questions of life?" "That is true. But does Buddhism answer them?" I asked. "Certainly", he replied, "and I will show you the book which converted me to Buddhism." It was *The Awakening of Faith*.' Richard recorded that 'I sat up until the small hours of the morning reading the book which had converted the Confucianist to Buddhism. At length I called out to Hill who was lying down in the same room, "Listen! This is a Christian book. Though the terms are Buddhist, the thought is Christian".'[107] By 1884, after fourteen years in China, Richard had penetrated deeply into Chinese religious culture.

Second stage: mounting controversy

In the autumn of 1884 Timothy Richard and his wife Mary, a missionary in her own right of Scottish Presbyterian background, returned to Britain for their first leave.[108] Richard's visions for a new style of missionary activity in which he argued that the traditional methods adopted in Africa or the South Seas were inadequate to the high culture and civilization of China were rejected, as 'impossibly expensive'. Richard had also made some theological enemies in China. When he returned to his station in Taiyuan in 1886 he found he was no longer acceptable as a colleague to younger missionaries.[109]

As Richard recalled the matter thirty years later, the issue turned upon a tract which he had published on 'Taoism, acknowledging what was good in it and showing where Christianity had advanced beyond it'.

> This acknowledgement of any good in the native religion was condemned as rank heresy in the opinion of some of my young colleagues, and my method of carrying on mission work was deemed highly unsatisfactory. They desired me to change my theological views and to submit to their guidance. To neither of these proposals would I agree, first because I believed my views to be in harmony with those of the most enlightened ministers at home, and secondly, because I had many years experience in missionary work while they had had none. I insisted therefore on the same liberty of action as they claimed for themselves. Upon this they sent a long letter to the Committee [sc. of the Baptist Missionary Society in London] censuring me both in regard to my theological views and my methods of work.[110]

Brian Stanley gives a differing account from Richard's, based upon the archives of the BMS. Richard's chief opponent was Herbert Dixon, newly come to Taiyuan after previous service in the Congo Mission. The dispute turned not on a tract on Taoism but on Richard's proposed *Course of Study*, intended for Confucianists. Dixon alleged in a letter to the Secretary of the BMS, A.H. Baynes, that Richard's message was 'a conglomerate wherein Science, Heathenism, Roman Catholicism and Christianity are bundled up in a new "Gospel for Nations", and claimed that this missionary approach had been a complete failure'.[111]

He described with horror Richard's use of chanted litanies and his hanging of a large white satin cross, flanked by yellow streamers 'exactly like those used in Buddhist temples' in the Taiyuan chapel. Dixon's final complaint was that Richard had distributed a Chinese guide to enquirers, whose provisions for a pyramidical structure of ecclesiastical offices amounted to 'most barefaced popery'. It was this pamphlet in particular which united Richard's colleagues in opposition; they enclosed an English translation with their collective letter to Baynes, written on 20 April.[112]

Stanley gives a full account of the contents of the pamphlet and it is clear that Richard misremembered the exact details of the controversy. But the memory of the painfulness of the situation lasted to the end of his life. Mary Richard wrote in her diary of 'suffering from persecution for heresy, even dear friends... turning against us'.[113] Richard did remember accurately the next steps in this strife. 'Since my colleagues were in this mood, it was quite clear to me that we could never work harmoniously together. To remain would induce permanent strife which would be fatal to missionary work. I therefore decided to leave Shensi' (Shanxi).[114] In October 1887 the Richards removed to Tientsin (Tianjin).

The controversy went on for two years during which the Richards lived with tension and insecurity.[115] At home the nearly eighty-year-old James Legge was asked to arbitrate.[116] Eventually the Committee of the BMS decided against Richard (18 December 1888). 'While expressing confidence in Richard's fidelity to the central truths of the Gospel, the Committee declared its disapproval of many of his missionary aims and methods...'[117] E.W. Price Evans comments that it is 'as easy as it is unfair to blame the Committee of 1889 [sic], more or less conditioned (as we all are) by the time-spirit and conscious of the responsibility to the home churches and to the whole wide field of the Society's work'.[118] Nevertheless home boards have usually accepted tradition and the prevailing mood of the time uncritically and are not so easily excused for not listening to their missionaries. For Timothy Richard the rejection was decisive. He had to leave the service of the BMS and look for some other way of carrying out his missionary activities.

Richard's large circle of Chinese friends found various openings for him. Eventually, at the invitation of Li Hung Cheng (Li Hongzhang), Viceroy in Tianjan (Tiensin), he became editor of the Tiensin daily paper *Shih Pao* (*Shibao*). 'I wrote', Richard recorded, 'on many subjects bearing on reform in China. I also published many articles showing how the Japanese were rapidly reforming', but what exactly he said and how he said it belongs to another book.[119] Richard was, to be sure, a forerunner in the dialogue where Christians align themselves with all who want to establish some sort of community and harmony among human beings. After Richard had edited the *Shibao* for a year, the possibility opened up of his being appointed General Secretary of the Society for the Diffusion of Christian and General Knowledge. The BMS agreed to support Richard in this work in Shanghai.[120]

A full study of the role of such agencies as the Christian Literature Society of India and the Society for the Diffusion of Christian and General Knowledge in China in interfaith relations is much needed. Many of the forerunners of dialogue and the early pioneers of the theology of religion who are discussed in this book were associated with either the CLS in Madras or with the CLS of China (as the SDK in Shanghai was later called). For our purposes we note that Richard was to build on the principles laid down by his predecessor Alexander Williamson.[121] These were intended to provide for 'the circulation of literature based on Christian principles throughout China, her colonies and dependencies' and, written from a 'Christian standpoint with a knowledge of native modes of thought and adapted to instruct and elevate the people', would particularly influence the 'more intelligent and ruling classes'.[122] Ernst Faber, the great German Sinologist and missionary who had worked with Alexander Williamson, said about his task at the SDK: 'I am engaged in the conversion of the Chinese mind.'[123] In that work Richard now engaged himself with an enormous zest.

Third stage: the height of his powers

So in 1891, aged forty-six, Richard was at last able to use his extraordinary qualifications and wide experience without missionary society trammels and restrictions.[124] Richard worked in four areas. The first was what he was able to accomplish through the SDK (later, the CLS) in Shanghai.[125] Second, he worked unremittingly with the political authorities, the viceroys, the mandarins, and even the Emperor. It was at this period that Richard, together with a Roman Catholic bishop, received the mandarin rank of 'Red Button First Grade', and was appointed as an advisor on Christian Missions to the Throne.[126] Richard constantly sought to use his considerable influence within Chinese reform movements as well as in peace-making and reconciliation. [127] As an integral part of this, Richard was involved in some of the first interfaith conferences which ever took place in China. A third area was his work as an educationalist, particularly as founder and first Chancellor of Shanxi University, which was itself a result of an act of statesmanship.[128] The fourth, and from the point of view of this book the most important, lay in his efforts in evaluating Chinese religion, especially Chinese Buddhism, from the Christian viewpoint.

Christian literature: Conversion by the Million

Richard began his work at the SDK/CLS with the statement that 'the best way of helping China is to give such kind of enlightenment as the Society attempts to give... we cannot even dream of establishing modern schools throughout the Empire... we do not intend to reach all the mandarins in the Empire... but the chief mandarin, together with the High examiners, Educational Inspectors of the counties, Professors of Colleges... might be reached'.[129] In his twenty-five years of service to the CLS, Richard was responsible for 'fifty books on the works of God in order to improve the conditions in China, thirty-seven books on the Laws of God to improve social and international relationships, thirty-three books on the providence of God to improve education, and forty-eight books on the Grace of God to improve religion and character. A total of 168 volumes in all.'[130] One piece of work which connected with his wider theological concerns was a translation of Lessing's *Education of the Human Race*.[131] The title of his 1907 collection, *Conversion by the Million*, indicated his abiding policy after fifteen years. If missionary work were to be properly done, every missionary would have to be grounded in 'comparative religion' and 'the science of missions', instead of being 'generally ignorant' of these. Then instead of having about 'fifty converts as is presently the case', each well trained missionary might have 5,000. 'If a hundred choice men follow this plan, the Chinese Christian leaders could under the blessing of God convert the rest of China in a generation or two.'[132] That would be conversion by the million. Certainly this was too visionary for the missionary societies. But without such a vision missionaries would, in Richard's view, degenerate into 'mere pastors of churches', instead of the founders of churches, colleges and schools, over which local people were in control.[133]

The theologian of religions

The theologian missionaries all worked out their theology of religions with ample first-hand information. Richard's intense involvement with as many forms of Chinese religion as he could discover meant that he could make significant contribution to discussions about Christian interpretation of Confucianism and Taoism, at both popular and classical levels.[134] But of China's three religious traditions Buddhism attracted him most as a Christian theologian. His passionate concern for a proper Christian understanding of Mahayana Buddhism culminated in the publication of *The New Testament of Higher Buddhism* in 1910.[135]

'Higher Buddhism' had in Richard's day become a popular Western term for Mahayana teaching, within which was also found the 'Pure Land' teachings. Within 'higher Buddhism' in the later school the great text was the *Saddharma Pundarika*, or 'Lotus Scripture'. Richard translated this, calling his version, *The Essence of the Lotus Scripture*.[136]

The *Saddharma Pandarika* depicts the exalted Buddha on a Himalayan peak declaring a new vehicle for universal salvation, and in chapter 25 is found a poignant and attractive account of the 'grace' of Avalokitesvara (in the Sanskrit form), or Kwanyin (in Chinese), or Kwannon (the Japanese form).[137] Richard had been among the first to label such teachings within Mahayana Buddhism as 'Gospel' or 'New Testament'.[138] We remember his reactions on being shown *The Awakening of Faith* by his Buddhist bookseller friend in 1884.[139] During his early years with the CLS Richard had been asked to explain why Buddhism had attracted 'so large a number of adherents leading them to build such numerous and beautiful temples in China'.[140] Richard translated *The Awakening of Faith* in support of his answer: its doctrines were, he said, 'one Soul immanent for good in all the universe... one Divine helper of men... individual immortality and growth in the likeness of God... the importance of faith to produce good works... the willingness of the best spirits to make sacrifices for others'.[141]

As a Christian theologian Richard made much of all this.[142] He had, very early on, decided that the doctrines of Mahayana Buddhism and Christianity had common elements as a result of interaction of traders and travellers belonging to these faiths in the markets and caravan stops of the Silk Road. 'These days of excavations', he wrote, 'have brought to light proofs of the extensive traffic in thought and commerce in early days between distant countries'.[143] China had been connected by 'land and sea with the West'. Buddhist pilgrims made great journeys westwards and 'Hindu, Parthian and Nestorian missionaries lived in Loyang, the capital of China a thousand years ago'.[144] These people had much to share in matters of faith and religion. 'About the fifth and sixth centuries BC there arose in China, in India and in Babylon, in Judea and in Greece a large number of prophets and sages who laid more emphasis on ethics than on religious ceremonies paid to a multitude of gods.'[145] In these men and women, Richard wrote, 'we are face to face and side by side with the choicest and most enlightened souls', who were 'striving to obtain a glimpse within the veil into the transcendency of God', and who recognized 'the Divine current of spiritual force which inspires all nations and races with modern Life, Light and Love'.[146]

These phenomena fitted smoothly into Richard's progressive evolutionary understanding of the Kingdom. 'We Christians believe that the kingdoms of this world shall become the kingdoms of our God, and then there will be but One Faith.'[147] The next stage in this evolution would not be 'a monopoly of any one of these competitive religions but a federation of all, on a basis that acknowledges with gratitude all that is best in the past in different parts of the earth as Divine'.[148] The 'highest and permanent elements in all religions' were designed for the deliverance of the human race from poverty and oppression, rebellions and wars, ignorance and superstition and from the disease of selfishness and sin. 'To loose these burdens', says Richard, it was necessary 'to begin the establishment of the Kingdom of God on earth which Jesus Christ commanded his disciples to preach, and this is the one Great Religion of the Future.'[149]

In all this Richard reflected the evolutionary optimism prevalent in some circles at the end of the Great Century. He sought, however, to justify his position from both Bible and the early fathers. During his first eight years as a missionary he had decided that Christ had not come 'to destroy but to fulfil', and he was never to tire of citing Matt. 5.17.[150] Now he devoted all his energy to substantiating this idea. In *The Higher Buddhism* Richard noted that the apostle Paul had quoted Greek poets with approval at Athens and that Justin Martyr and Augustine referred to other religions as being derived from God, but with the proviso that 'Christianity was fuller and more perfect'.[151] Richard also cited John 1.9 and Acts 10.34, together with John 3.16, declaring that 'Since God is the great father of all, and "so loved the world that he gave his only begotten son" to save it, it is incredible that he should leave all outside the Jews and Christians without any knowledge of the *Way of Salvation.*'[152]

But what was the purpose of the Christian mission, if all people were within the range of God's saving activity? Having put the question, 'Why is there further need of sending missionaries to Japan and China when they possess this priceless treasure?' into the minds of his readers, Richard replied: 'For two reasons. First because modern Christianity is the winnowing fan which helps separate the chaff from the wheat: secondly, because Christianity helps to replace atheism by faith in God.'[153] He explained immediately that in Buddhism 'count-less "Buddhas", vague "worlds", endless mythologies, require to be well sifted in order to separate the golden grains from the worthless chaff'.[154] This was the case particularly with Mahayana Buddhism whose doctrines were so mixed with other forms 'that only those who possess the fuller light of Christianity can recognise in them the likeness to true Christianity'.[155]

The man of interfaith dialogue

Richard's theology of religion made it axiomatic 'that the search for truth and goodness was valuable wherever it was found, not only in the Christian church but among non-Christians'.[156] In his *Conversion by the Million* (1907) Richard wrote that God was 'the Saviour as well as the Creator of the world', and that it is God and 'not missionary societies who inspires men to this end.'[157]

> God's first missionaries to India were the ancient sages who taught benevolence, righteousness, propriety, knowledge and faithfulness. God's next band of missionaries were the best from India who taught the New Buddhism of faith in God and salvation of their fellow-men. Instead of finding all the mandarins ministers of unrighteousness, we found many of them as much the ministers of God as any of the missionaries, fully deserving the description given by St Paul.[158]

Accordingly Richard found it appropriate to gather other 'ministers of God' in China in an interfaith conference in Shandong in July 1904. Richard recalled that he and his friend the BMS missionary A.G. Jones 'decided that the time had truly come when we might invite the Chinese leaders of the religious sects to meet the Christians in conference, and discuss measures for the revival of religion in China'.[159] This was the first multi-lateral interfaith conference to be held in China in the modern period. It was taken seriously by the Chinese authorities. The Governor of Shantung (Shandong) sent four representatives and thirty other Shandong officials took part in the gatherings. There were about a hundred leaders of religions other than Christianity present. The meetings took place over a four-day period with social occasions in the evenings. Neither Richard nor Soothill tell anything of the conclusions except that the Christian missionaries be asked to prepare a set of text books on religion for use in Government schools.[160] Nevertheless it was a major step forward in inter-religious relationships in 1904. As Soothill wrote:

> Some ask what good resulted from the conference. I do not know. If nothing resulted but increased kindness and friendliness, the extinguishing of the forces of ill-feeling and *odium theologicum*, the development of mutual respect and even respect for the other man's point of view, that would be the justification for holding such conferences all over China if there were enough Richards and Joneses to go round.[161]

Nevertheless Richard and Jones were not voices crying in a wilderness. Concern for better interfaith relations in China was growing in other circles. In Shanghai the American Presbyterian missionary Gilbert Reid had organized monthly meetings for inter-religious discussion from 1910 onwards at his 'International Institute'.[162] 'Leading Confucianist, Buddhists, Taoists, Mahommedans and Christians were invited to describe the good done by their various religions.'[163] Richard recalled that through these meetings he had come to know the 'Taoist Pope'.[164] On one occasion, Soothill records, Richard was asked by the Taoist leader to lecture on Taoism in his place, telling Richard 'he could do it so much better'.[165] Richard recalled this period when 'some of the devout leaders often used to call at my house and remain late in the evening, discussing religion'.[166] A different kind of venture took place in 1911. Richard recalled that after the 1911 Revolution 'there was a strong public opinion not only that the Government had failed, but that the religions of China had failed also', and as a result a meeting was set up by leading reformers in Shanghai and leaders of many faiths to discuss publicly the contribution of religion to the future of China.[167]

One of the last of the many accounts of encounters with people of other faith described in *Forty Five Years in China* took place in 1914, not long before Richard left China. This brief note captures some of his attitude and achievement.

> Another day I had a visit from the chief Buddhist Abbot, priests and devout laymen. I called their attention to mistakes of the past. Christians had been apt to condemn the devout non-Christians, who in their turn had condemned the Christians. But those who were familiar with one another's scriptures recognised that they had much in common. At the close of my address, a Chinese barrister, in the name of the Buddhists, thanked me for having translated two of their most important scriptures into English and thus having helped to remove misunderstanding.[168]

Richard's views were widely known by the time of the World Missionary Conference in 1910. The Commissioners on 'The Missionary Message in relation to Non-Christian religions' sought his response to their question-naire and Richard wrote a masterly summing up of his position for them.[169] Three central issues emerge from this Response which encapsulate one mis-sionary's contribution to the theology of religion as the Great Century drew to a close.

Richard laid great emphasis on the error of the old missionary theology, distancing himself both from his own missionary past and from the ideas of most of his contemporaries. 'Past views of theology, like past views of sci-ence, are out of date.'[170] But the gospel had not changed, for the true gospel 'of the Grace of God and the sacrifice of Divine love' was eternal and would never grow old: 'only its temporary dressing must be renewed from age to age'.[171]

The chief changes in the temporary dressing of the gospel in his time, Richard thought, were two-fold. The first lay in the doctrine of God. As one answer to the question why was the Christian mission making such slow progress in China, Richard wrote:

> By presenting only the transcendent character of God and in practice ignoring or denying His immanence in human hearts and by presenting God's judicial rather than His Fatherly attitude towards sin, we unneces-sarily create a great intellectual hindrance to the Gospel acceptance.[172]

Richard's second contribution lay in emphasizing 'the Kingdom of God in human hearts as a new birth to immortality'.[173] Such a definition meant a new focus for salvation. For Richard salvation was now to be defined as 'the regeneration of society', through 'the pervading light and love and all the graces of the Holy Spirit'.[174] Such a vision of 'True Christianity', he thought, could alone 'win the head and heart and conscience of all religions and races and tongues, and make them willing to unite in one Universal Kingdom of God, so as to include the best from all to shine forth in a greater glory of religion than was ever known before'. [175]

The rediscovery of the Kingdom of God as the central issue for Christian mission in this world was good news to those on the margins of society. In words of astonishing prescience Richard wrote that if Christians and follow-ers of other religions did not 'harken to the cry of the poor and the oppressed':

> God will call Socialists to listen to it and bid Revolutionists and Nihilists break the oppression. The strength of the revolutionary spirit throughout Asia today, manifested in the universal indignation against oppression and in behalf of the poor and needy, lies in the hearts and minds of men to

bring order out of chaos, and deliverance from the sufferings of the poor and the crimes of their oppressors.[176]

We know how tragically right Richard was in this judgment. After the bitterness of eighty years of strife and civil war, political and cultural revolution, of occupation and counter-occupation, liberation theology is only now finding a voice in China. Elsewhere in South East Asia Christians and Buddhists are beginning to talk together about their shared task in hearing the cries of the poor and dealing with the crimes of their oppressors. As they come together in new forms of interfaith co-operation they might remember Li-T'i-mot'ai who saw a vision of justice a hundred years ago. The words of his first biographer W.E. Soothill sum up Richard's life and witness, and his abiding claim on Christian attention: 'The East he loved, the West he loved, and strove to bind them in bonds of mutual service. Many are his disciples but none has yet risen to take his place.'[177]

Robert Allen Hume: The Interpretation of Indian Religion

An American Congregationalist is our next witness to the profound stirrings taking place in the thinking of many missionaries at this period. Robert Allen Hume (1847-1929) was a second generation ABCFM missionary (having been born in Bombay) who served the Maratha Mission in Ahmednagar for fifty-two years.[178] Of solid New England Congregationalist stock, his writings show an independence of mind and generosity of spirit to match his heritage. His two important books, *Missions from the Modern View* (1905) and *An Interpretation of India's Religious History* (1911) have fine insights into the theology of religion, and the need for justice, courtesy and love in dealing with Indian religious tradition. *Missions from the Modern View* consists of eleven chapters. The first six are missiological lectures originally given in Andover, Chicago, and Bangor.[179] The last three were material from India, which gave, Hume said, 'exact illustrations of how I have given the Christian message to Indians'.[180] *An Interpretation of India's Religious History* was a further series of lectures given in Chicago, Oberlin, Beloit, and other mid-Western and New England colleges and seminaries in 1910.[181] The two lecture series complement each other and can be treated as a single unit. Together they represent thinking arising from more than thirty years of missionary activity.

Robert Hume went to Ahmednagar in North West India in 1874, and worked 'among educated and uneducated Hindus, and Indian Christians, as Evangelist, Editor, Principal of Divinity School, and Administrator'.[182] Ahmednagar Theological Seminary was famous in Hume's day not least because of the presence on its teaching staff of Narayan Vaman Tilak.[183]

Hume was distinguished by his capacity for deep friendships with Indians, a trait which emerges strikingly in his Edinburgh response.[184] He had also the capacity to inspire others with his passion for Indian learning, among whom was his son, Robert Ernest Hume, who became a leading authority on the Upanishads and author of a notable text book on comparative religion.[185]

Charles Cuthbert Hall wrote a characteristic preface to *Missions from the Modern View*, declaring Hume to have summoned 'the Church at home to rise to a higher plane of thought'. Hume's lectures, wrote Hall, 'admirably illustrate the readjustment of ideals and methods that has taken place already in the most intelligent circles of foreign missionary workers. These lectures are a gospel for the West'.[186] Hall called Hume one of 'our foremost missionaries' showing 'how far beyond much of our relatively narrow and provincial thinking' such people have advanced. Hume was part of a world-wide movement which was no longer simply interested in individual converts but had its sights on the Christianizing of India:

> The literatures and religions of the East are studied in the West. The strategic posts of service in India and the Far East are occupied by an increasing number of men whose training, historically, philosophically, socially, qualifies them to see clearly and to handle tactfully the most splendid problem of modern times, the Christianization of the Asiatic consciousness.[187]

These people were not like 'the armchair theorists of the West', without 'first-hand knowledge of the Eastern land, the Eastern atmosphere, the Eastern mind and soul', who were likely to reach fallacious conclusions. In what Hall calls 'the readjustment of missionary ideals and methods', the initiative had to come 'from those whose experience in the field is co-ordinated with broad theoretical training. It is one of many splendid features of modern missionary activity that persons are to be found at important posts of foreign duty who join ripe experience with thoroughgoing culture.'[188] One of these persons was Robert Allen Hume.

God the chief actor in history

Hume's doctrine of God was strongly Trinitarian. He was committed to universality of Christ and for this used a Logos christology.[189] He held self-consciously a 'larger view', immanentist understanding of the operations of the Holy Spirit.[190] 'Modern Christian thought,' he wrote, 'is rightly making the Holy Spirit truly universal in His presence and activity.'

> Christian thought has always emphasized the divinity of the Holy Spirit, but it failed to recognize His omnipresence and His universal activity. In

no respect does the modern doctrine of the immanence of God so largely and so helpfully enrich modern thought and life as in recognition of the omnipresent activity of the Holy Spirit. If the Holy Spirit is truly God, then He is God in the heart of every man trying to make him holy.[191]

This 'larger view' of God and of 'his Spirit's universal activity in the hearts of men' enabled Hume to affirm 'that God has always been the chief actor, even in the religions of non-Christians'.[192] There are many corollaries to such a statement. Most of them overthrow the central themes of the Westminster Confession and discard, explicitly or implicitly, any sense of the wrath of God against sinners, any notion of the cross as propitiation or penal substitution, any conception of limited atonement, and any suggestion of common grace or uncovenanted mercy. The 'eternal attitude' in the heart of God was revealed for Hume in Jesus Christ, and must 'always have been the same before and since the Christ', for Christ alone 'revealed... what God's eternal attitude is'.[193] Hume described God as 'the great sufferer', 'suffering because His children are ignorant of and estranged from Him', and who therefore 'must deny Himself for the good of His erring children'.[194] Horace Bushnell's exposition of *The Vicarious Sacrifice* (1866) had obviously prevailed in the New England Congregationalist circles to which Hume belonged intellectually.[195] He understood the cross therefore as 'expressing God's eternal and infinite pain for sin in man and His readiness to do all that He can to reclaim them'. Consequently God had to be understood as 'ever exerting His divine power in seeking them in order to bring them into harmonious filial life'.[196] All religious activity on the part of human beings is 'response to His call, however feeble and mistaken that response may be'.[197]

Hume ascribed the demise of the doctrine of 'limited atonement' to contact with world religious traditions through the missionary movement. What he called the 'logic of the heart' made the churches appreciate there could be no uncovenanted mercies of God'.[198] Equally the vision of the countless masses of non-Christians going into outer darkness could not continue to be borne or believed. So contact with 'the people of ethnic faiths has been one prominent influence in leading the advanced churches of Christendom to discard the restriction of God's saving love to those who intelligently accept Jesus Christ as Saviour and Lord'.[199] In any case to offer any other motive for missionary work would not only be to dishonour God but increasingly revolt the minds and hearts of many who should be supporting the missionary cause.

Thus he wrote about the effects of preaching limited atonement and predestination to eternal damnation of unbelievers:

Probably no one thing causes more dislike to foreign missions among large numbers of the best Christians in evangelical churches than the supposition that the average missionary believes and teaches to non-Christians that there is no salvation except for those who definitely express their faith in Christ as Saviour. An appeal for support of missions on such a score would doubtless have the opposite effect, and would kill missionary interest in thousands of churches now.[200]

We can see from all this evidence provided by Hume that the doctrines of Coleridge, Erskine, Campbell, Bushnell, Maurice, Westcott, Fairbairn and Allen established themselves in the thinking of 'the best Christians' in the last years of the great century. Hume was able, moreover, to use them constructively in a theology of religion that often sounds as though it might have been written today.

God the Father of all has never left his Indian children

God 'the Father of the spirits of all men' had never been without witnesses in India, in seeking to reveal Himself to His Hindu children.[201] Hume set out in both *Missions from the Modern View* and *An Interpretation of India's Religious History* to demonstrate the witness that had been borne to the Divine Father by Indian saints and sages. 'More protestant reformers', he wrote, 'have appeared in the religious history of India than in the religious history of Israel; perhaps more than in the Christian Church.'[202]

While this statement may seem surprising to some, is it not just what we should expect from such a living, righteous, spiritual, living God, as has been revealed to us in Jesus Christ? The Lord Jesus Christ never implied or said that God the Father of the spirits of all men had through what Jesus himself did or said become different from what He evermore had been and must be. Jesus Christ came to reveal the Father, not to make God a Father.[203]

Gotama the Buddha, the Jain sage Mahavira, Sankara, Ramanuja, Chaitanya and the Sikh Guru Nanak were Hume's heroes, and always he described them as operating under divine inspiration. Just so, Hume interpreted the rise of Buddhism as inspired by God:

In the sixth century BC, doubtless under the influence of the divine Spirit, there arose in India a new religious leader to protest against the two most unsatisfactory features of the religion then prevalent in India. These evils were, first, an unethical ceremonial and sacrificial system, and second, an unethical and depressing intellectualism.[204]

Christians, he wrote, 'have not always considered that the Buddhist revolt against Brahmanism as more or less due to the help of God.'[205] This Hume thought objectionable in that they had no difficulty in seeing Old Testament prophets 'unquestionably inspired of God'. Yet the Buddha had wrought immense good by his teaching, as had Mahavira, the Jain sage:

> We believe that it is the influence of God which makes men more considerate to animals to-day than they once were. Why not believe that it was He who helped the founder of the Jain system to his emphasis on kindness to animals? And why was it not from God that the impulse for a simple and kindly life came to Mahavira?[206]

Among the sages and saints of 'modern Hinduism', Hume pointed to Kumarila, Ramanuja, and Chaitanya. Kumarila taught 'the existence and activity of an all-powerful god' as the cause of the world. 'From whom did this reformer get that conviction of a god at work among men, if not from God Himself?' Hume asked.[207] In a similar case was Ramanuja who taught a modified monism or a qualified idealism. God, whom Ramanuja worshipped as Vishnu, was a personal being. Ramanuja also taught that human soul was real and distinct and that the way of salvation was by faith and trust, or *bhakti*. 'Since', wrote Hume, 'the somewhat allied Christian doctrine of salvation by faith was unquestionably developed in Europe under the influence of God's Spirit, why is it not right to assume that this protestant reform in the Hindu religion was also prompted by God?'[208] Later had come Chaitanya, contemporary with Luther and, like Luther, the leader of a reformation which was a protest against the doctrine of salvation by meritorious deeds and austerities.[209] Hume believed that the *bhakti* movement, and its way of salvation, *bhakti marga*, arose 'under God's influence'.[210]

But many Indian missionaries were suspicious of the close resemblance between *bhakti marga* and the doctrine of salvation by faith. Many urged that the *bhakti* concept had been borrowed from Christian sources. Hume rejected such ideas outright. Firstly because the beginnings of the *bhakti* doctrine could be found in the in the Bhagavad Gita'.[211] But he had also theological reasons for his rejection of the desire to explain away resemblances between Hindu and Christian doctrines. It was he said 'not strange, but natural' that there were 'counterparts to the doctrines of Christianity in the various phases of Hinduism', because 'the divine Spirit who taught these truths to Christians was never inactive toward non-Christians'.[212] It should have caused no surprise that people had guessed at God's grace, even without the revelation of Jesus Christ. Such perceptions 'ought to make God seem very great, very near, and very active in the minds and lives of all men, as the modern Christian view requires us to believe'.[213] Hume rejoiced to discern the pattern of God seeking the human heart everywhere, and to declare God as 'the great Reality in actual relation to every soul'.[214]

The unsatisfactoriness of Hinduism: what went wrong?

But if God had been continuously at work within Indian religion, why was so much of spoilt, corrupted and depraved? Hume asked, 'If we believe that God has always been the chief actor, even in the religions of non-Christians, then why has not the Hindu religion been more satisfactory than the Christian believes it to have been?'[215]

His own answer was succinct. 'Because the Hindu has his full share of the limitations and sins of humanity.'[216] Earlier Hume had defined religion as the 'interpretation in thought and in practice of what God is trying to teach', and therefore, because of human limitations and sins men and women 'only partially, and often very imperfectly' understood what God was trying to teach.[217] In Indian religion recurred a pattern of 'limitation' and 'sin'. 'As we run through an outline of India's history,' he wrote, 'four words will correctly epitomize the characteristics of that history: – progress, arrest, degeneracy, and reform – all four repeated over and over again through millenniums [sic].'[218]

In India there had been so much progress: animism had given place to better religious forms, dualism, pantheism, and then incipient monotheism. Nevertheless, 'Superstition, polytheism, idolatry, formalism, unmeaning ceremonies, immorality', had characterized a large part of Hinduism.[219] Even 'higher Hinduism' had most severe limitations. Hume saw six or seven of these. There was its 'cold intellectualism': 'By its wisdom Hinduism knew not a personal God and rested in an ultimate It, to whom no man can pray, whom no man can love, and in gratitude to whom no man can serve brother men.'[220] There was its 'unregulated imagination': 'The Hindu can believe in the teeth of clear evidence, because the ideals of his imagination seem more conclusive than the evidences of the experience of life.'[221] There was its traditionalism, its lack of altruism and 'the inaction, its unprogressiveness, its 'dull contentment with things as they are, which result from the conception of the world as unreal, and from the Karma doctrine that every man must inevitably be what he is'.[222]

Such factors made Hume think that 'Hinduism is doomed'.[223] But this was not a re-expression of the older missionary dogma. Hume was far from thinking that Hinduism had to be displaced and eradicated. On the contrary he thought that 'God's way of dealing with men and with institutions and religions is not to destroy, but to fulfil.'[224] How did the revelation of the gospel help in that process?

The revelation of God in Jesus Christ

The seventh weakness of Hinduism was its inadequate recognition of the nature of God as 'entering relationships'. The 'supreme characteristic of God which Jesus Christ revealed' in Hume's view was God's need for 'His human children'. God 'so longs for them that He counts no sacrifice or effort too great to bring them all into intimate filial relations with Himself'.[225] Despite God's patient teaching 'by divers portions, in divers manners', India has not yet come into a sense of filial relation to God. This one simple, undeniable, historical fact was 'enough of itself to show that India needs, and must have, the help of the Lord Jesus Christ in order to grow'.[226]

But few human beings have come into a sense of this filial relationship without Jesus Christ. This was the force of the famous verse, 'No one comes to the Father but by Me' (John 14.6). It was necessary to portray the life and ministry of Jesus in India in all its historical concreteness. The sufferings of Christ were the demonstration that God 'must always suffer, when for any reason His human children fail to live up to right relations with Himself'.[227] No doctrine even resembling this existed in Hinduism. In this context Jesus would become India's great Guru, taking up in his teaching all the truth 'which they have thought of God in the past'.[228] Hume was sure that it was 'the religious men and women of India among others whom our Lord had in mind when he said, "Other sheep I have, which are not of this fold: them also I must bring, and they shall hear my voice; and they shall become one flock, one shepherd"'.[229]

Not to destroy but to fulfil

Many years before J.N. Farquhar published *The Crown of Hinduism* (1913) Robert Hume had been thinking about the missiological principle known as 'fulfilment'. Hume could not believe that the Christian response to the richness of Indian tradition was destruction and displacement. The best features of Hinduism were to him, as we have seen, 'the work of the divine Spirit' in which Christians should rejoice. Christians had therefore to understand that every true element in any religion was something which the Christ came to fulfil and not to destroy. The word 'fulfill', as he spelt it, clearly fascinated Hume. 'To "fulfill" means to "fill full",' he wrote, 'that is what Jesus Christ did to the Judaic system. With spiritual principle He filled full the partial and limited views of the earlier prophets of Israel.'[230] Christ was 'the fulfiller of earlier and more partial teachings of God which have been current in His human children in any land and at any time'.[231]

India's preparation for the Christ

'What God has done for and through every other people,' Hume thought, 'He has undoubtedly been doing for the Hindu. As He brings India into contact with the Christ, the Christ will enter into the preparation of the past and will fulfil all of India's best thought and life till every jot and tittle is utilized, and through the Christianized thought and life of India God will enrich the world.'[232] Hume gave many examples of his 'fulfilment theology'. Chief among them was the filling full of India's rudimentary and inadequate understandings of personality in the Divine. The impersonal It had to be transformed into the loving Thou of the God and Father of the Lord Jesus.[233] In Hume's view Indians could not remain satisfied with an impersonal universe. God had spoken to Hindus through their longings for a personal God to whom they could pray. 'Though consistent Hindu speculation makes the ultimate Reality of the universe an impersonal monism, doubtless Hindus long ago did what many Hindus now do, viz.: think and speak as if the ultimate It were a person with a loving, gracious heart.'[234]

Fulfilment would take place in other aspects of Indian thought. One way Hindu thinking had moved towards a personalist understanding of God was in *avatar* theologies. Hume was moved to see them, not merely points of contact with Indian theology, but India's own insights in incarnational theology. In response to Indian insights Hume asked if were not possible that God had 'led the pious Hindu also to believe in God's readiness to empty Himself and take a lowly form in order to help His needy children'?[235]

'Filling full' would happen to Indian asceticism. To be sure Hume feared that 'the modern spirit' was a real threat to the Indian conception of the world and of God. But he thought it 'vital to sustain it' and to ask 'for what has this ascetic phase of Hindu thought and life been preparing itself and how will it find fulfilment?' His answer was forceful: India's ascetic past is 'a marvellous preparation for a deep appreciation of the Christ who reveals God as the great sufferer, the One who must deny Himself for the good of His erring children'.[236]

Hume's missionary activity was therefore carried out, in his own words, 'with ardent desire and expectation' that the spiritual gifts abounding in India should be made available to the whole church. If Indians should 'under the guidance of the universal Spirit, find and accept in the Lord Jesus Christ the fulfiller of their long aspiration and search' they would also be 'inspired by the divine Spirit marvellously to interpret Him to their brethren throughout the world'.[237]

The Christianization of the Indian consciousness

One of Hume's earliest experiences as a missionary in India was meeting Keshab Chundar Sen at a conference in Calcutta in 1883.[238] Hume had invited Sen to speak to the missionary community. Sen spoke to them with his customary frankness that he 'felt absolutely sure that the spirit of Jesus rose from the dead'. But he neither knew nor cared about the physical resurrection. 'He said that Hindus as a whole would never care.'[239] Sen also implied that he did not know or care whether the Lord Jesus was metaphysically divine or not. 'He reverenced and loved and followed Him because He was ethically and spiritually divine'. On these grounds Keshab said that the object of his life was to lead his countrymen to Christ. 'It is the character of Christ, and the ideal quality of His teachings, not His resurrection from the dead, which draws the East toward Him.'[240]

This experience was formative for Hume. In both *Missions from the Modern View* and *An Interpretation of India's Religion*, he returns constantly to these issues. The first effect was a gradual rejection of the emphasis on individual conversion. Like Bernard Lucas, Hume increasingly pondered the 'Christianization' of India.[241] Three factors he saw as enabling an enterprise on this scale. Only in Hume's time had the history of India's religion been fully described showing all the high moments, as well as the disasters of Hinduism and other traditions. Second, there was the 'evolutionary doctrine' of natural selective development, which would have increasing effects in India. Last there was what Hume called 'genetic psychology', a science in its infancy in his period.[242] When Hume put these factors together he saw the religious future of India as 'a full re-expression of the religious spirit' of all sections of Indian spiritual life.[243]

Consequently all aspects of Christian thought and life would have to become 'domesticated in India'. Only then would a new and Indian form of Christianity arise. Both his books suggest ways in which this would work itself out. The keynote of Indian theology would be unity: 'In no country more than India has there been patient effort to find a basis for unity.'[244] The unsatisfactoriness of India's impersonal monism would be transformed by the 'personal monism' taught by Christ: 'That they may all be one; even as Thou, Father art in Me and I in Thee, that they may be also one in Us.'[245] Second, India would through this sense of Christian monism be released from *maya* and unreality.[246] When unity and reality were established, two other major problems of the Hindu tradition would also be addressed and solved through Christian theology. The first was the Hindu longing for 'some manifestation of the great unknown which is near, which is visible, which is approachable, which responds to the appeal of human need. This is the psychological explanation of idolatry, of the deification of the saints, and of belief in incarnations.'[247] Hume suggested that *avatara* theologies in

Hinduism were a preparation for the coming of the perfect incarnation in Jesus.[248]

A fourth aspect of India's Christianization lay with the doctrine of *karma*. Hume called this 'at once intensely logical and intensely unsatisfactory'. Yet, as Hume wrote: 'In this conception, with all its error and unsatisfactoriness, we can see both the influence of a righteous God and the dimness of vision of His Indian children. For the Karma doctrine is India's chief response to conscience.'[249] But the cross of Jesus Christ, properly interpreted, would be the answer what the *karma* doctrine was trying to resolve. After thirty-six years of service in India, Hume wanted to affirm that 'on a large scale, the suffering Christ, more than the teaching Christ, is drawing both the ignorant and the learned, both the degraded and refined, marvellously to Himself, and through Himself to God, and into willing suffering for erring fellow man'.[250] From his wide first-hand knowledge of the leaders of the Indian renaissance Hume declared that as more and more India's best men and women accept Christ's loving power', they will 'prove marvellous interpreters of His character and influence'.[251]

The fulfilment of Western Christianity

Hume believed profoundly that contact with India would change contemporary forms of Christian faith in both America and Europe. He was among the first to distinguish between 'gospel' and 'culture', between Christ and Christianity and to put his finger on the sore spot of Western syncretism:

> As Christianity has developed in the West, it has been a mixture of Christian practices with some non-Christian ideas of the peoples who accepted it. Its leaders are more and more seeking to know its essentials; to recognize at their true worth things that are not fundamental, and to cast out those elements which are inconsistent with the simplicity that is in Christ Jesus. Dogmatism about denominational peculiarities and ecclesiastical arrangements and non-essentials is being counted as at variance with the Christian spirit.[252]

'Contact with ethnic faiths' would 'through comparison and differentiation, help in securing an analysis of the very essence of Christianity'.[253] When the West truly recognized that 'the essentials of the Christian religion are certain spiritual and ethical conceptions of God and of man' there would come a purification of principles and motives.[254] This would lead, Hume thought, to change in at least three areas.

First, Western Christianity needed to become more *spiritual*. 'The Hindu type of religion', wrote Hume, 'is meditative and reflective.' The West needed to copy 'the quiet, thoughtful, meditative type of the East'.[255] Second,

Western Christianity needed to become more *courteous*. 'The principal thing which Orientals dislike in Occidentals is their bluntness in the relations of life.'[256] Like the other missionary theologians, Hume was an advocate of courtesy in inter-religious relationships. He saw the want of courtesy as a fundamental defect in Western Christianity itself. As Christians in the West came into contact with Indians and other Asians, they see 'that the most courteous way of doing things is an important virtue, pleasing to God'.[257]

Western Christianity also needed to become less individualistic, more aware of inter-personal relationships. Hume wrote of the Indian sense 'of the unitedness of men as actual members one of another with reciprocal service-ableness and duties'.[258] He saw the Christian West, in 1911, as only just 'beginning to recognize that society is an inseparable, indissoluble organism of which God is the head, the life, the source, and therefore, that the smallest member of society is actually connected with God and with every other human being'.[259]

A new form of Christianity

Hume refused ultimately to speak of 'Eastern' and 'Western' Christianities, because he saw Christianity itself was a 'growing religion'. He refused to play the foolish game, as it seemed to him, of proving that Christianity was true and other religions false.[260] He had absorbed the message of Alexander Allen and affirmed that 'some phases of thought and life which have seemed to Christians at one time to be absolutely the best, have, after added knowledge and experience, been seen to be not full-orbed apprehension of spiritual truth'.[261] There are echoes of Allen in this next passage:

> When Christianity went into imperial Rome, its type of theology, its mode
> of worship, and especially its ecclesiastical system and methods were un-
> avoidably and thoroughly Romanized. The Christianity which went into
> the Greek world had been Jewish. But a Greek environment developed the
> phases and formative principles of Christ's teachings into that type of
> Christianity which is called the Greek theology and the Greek church; and
> on the whole, Christianity gained thereby. The Roman environment
> brought some gain and some loss to Christianity by creating that type of
> our religion which is called the Latin theology and the Roman Church.[262]

Hume's own experience of Christianity as a growing religion had taught him to watch for two new developments, a result of encountering both Christian and non-Christian Indians. The first would occur in a range of new insights brought into Christian theology as the Indian mind was discipled to Christ. Hume expected them to transform the whole face of Christianity.

If, as we believe, Christianity is the fullest interpretation of universal religion which has yet been made, and if it is a growing religion in which there is room for all fuller knowledge that may come to mankind... then Christianity as now developing and to be developed hereafter, will become the religion of India and of the world.[263]

But more than this, Hume confidently expected those who were not Christians to teach the church truths which lay outside its present experience. Missionaries, he said, needed from 'some non-Christians some truths which those have received'. 'Too often', he continued, 'the Christian enthusiast has not realized that a humble readiness to learn is a Christian virtue needed to qualify him for his task as well as zeal to impart what he has already received.'[264] 'A humble readiness to learn' overthrows all the inflexible erudition and combativeness of the first missionaries of the Great Century. Coupled with the sense pervading all Hume's thinking that God has been at work in every part of the story of the world, Christians may truly learn from people of other faith.

Postscript: Hume and the World Missionary Conference

When Hume wrote to the Commissioners at Edinburgh in 1909 he took the opportunity to reflect on the astonishing changes that had taken place in his thinking since he had arrived in Ahmednagar in 1874. 'I have been a missionary,' he wrote, 'for nearly thirty-five years. I am most grateful to my God that both study and missionary experience have greatly altered both the substance and the form of my convictions as to what constitutes the vital and the most important elements of the Christian gospel'.[265]

He had come to India as a missionary imagining that 'he knew in large measure already nearly the whole of the Christian Gospel, but that gradually he had grown into a much fuller conception of God as the Father of spirits, and of His way of dealing with both His Christian and non-Christian children, of the essential Christ-likeness of His attitude toward every man, and of the effective universality and activity of the Holy Spirit'.[266] These 'larger convictions' had given him greater hope and joy and power in his conversation with Indian people, and made him more patient in sharing what he summed up as the Gospel: 'God is like Jesus Christ.'[267]

Patience could well be read as courtesy; Christ-likeness as love; the honouring of what God had already done in India as justice. Hume made a powerful impression on the Report of Commission IV.[268]

John P. Jones: The 'Broken Lights' are Lights from God

In the strongly flowing currents of positive missionary thought in the last years of the Great Century, John Peter Jones (1847-1916) had a distinctive voice. Born in Wrexham, North Wales, he had migrated with his parents to the American mid-west, where he graduated from the Western Reserve University in Cleveland, Ohio, becoming one of its first DDs in 1895. As a theological teacher of the ABCFM in Madurai, South India, Jones knew both Slater and Hume well, as well as his younger colleague, Bernard Lucas, and his views often coincided with theirs. As a theological teacher, too, he was also passionately concerned about ensuring that coming generations of missionaries and Indian pastors alike were aware of the new thinking represented by Slater and Hume. Jones wrote extensively about India and Hinduism for his home audience in America, and gave the Hyde lectures at the Andover Theological Seminary in 1902, repeating them at Yale and Hartford and elsewhere. These lectures were published as *India's Problem: Krishna or Christ (1903)* and were very widely read in America. In 1908 Jones produced a more general book, *India: Its Life and Thought*. Another set of lectures to theological students at Yale, later given at Bangor, Maine, and Oberlin College in Ohio in 1910, was published as *The Modern Missionary Challenge: A Study of the Present Day Missionary Enterprise*. Jones also contributed to British and American missionary and theological journals, and from this material we can piece together another story of 'dialogical conversion'.[269]

When John P.Jones arrived in South India in 1888 his 'paramount motive' had been extirpate heathen religion. But in 1902 this kind of motivation was no longer valid, he told his audiences of theological students in that year. The Christian missionary movement had changed its views concerning the character and origin of Hinduism. 'Through modern enlightenment and the study of Comparative Religion no man can go out as a missionary, even as I was expected to do less than a quarter of a century ago with a general belief that great religion is entirely of the Devil and is in itself evil and only evil continually.'[270] Jones told the students that 'our thought concerning our fellow men contains elements of truth and justice that our fathers knew nothing of' and that 'the best Christian feeling towards the heathen world today is far more true, righteous, sympathetic'.[271] Jones was positive that his generation knew Hinduism and other non-Christian religions 'better than our fathers did' and were not so anxious to trace all these back to Satanic origin. As he said, 'We are learning the sympathies as well as the antipathies of religions.'[272]

Consequently the missionary task had now transformed itself into the need to 'study appreciation' and to 'consider historic facts', to the end that the 'ethnic and all the non-Christian religions' could be seen to have had their 'uses' in God's world.[273] Jones went as far as to say of such faith traditions that 'some still have their uses'. 'They are the expression of the deepest instincts of the human soul. And they have, especially such a faith as Hinduism, not a few elements of the truth which a missionary should know, no less than he should understand the great evils which enter as part of them.'[274] A year or two later Jones wrote, this time for a predominantly British readership, that 'The day has come when missionaries must study with more seriousness the religion of India, that they may understand its true inwardness and discover its sources of power. Above all, they must be conversant with its highest ideals and understand the relationship of the same to those of their own faith. And they must not forget that they must approach the study with genuine sympathy and appreciation.'[275]

Jones thus believed that the study of Hinduism was crucial for the future of Christian understanding. He wrote:

India is the Mother of religions. No other land has been so prolific in religious thought or has founded faiths which have commanded the allegiance of so large a portion of the human race. While the Aryans of the west have been content to borrow their faith from the Hebrews; Indo-Aryans have produced the most wonderful and mighty ethnic religion (Brahmanism) and also one of the three great missionary religions of the world (Buddhism). A third of the human race today cling with devotion to these two products of the fertility of the mind, and the spirituality of the heart, of India.[276]

From his first hand knowledge, for he appears to have been a great traveller, Jones described the religious communities in India. These include also the Jews in Bombay, Poonah and Cochin. Of Zoroastrianism he wrote that it was 'the purest of ethnic religions. It has preserved its ancient integrity and high tone much better than its sister faith, Brahmanism.'[277] Buddhism he dealt with as an Indian religion, founded by the one teacher who in Jones' view could be placed side by side with Jesus. He wrote of Jesus and Gautama in his 1908 book, *India: Its Life and Thought*, as the 'two most powerful personalities that ever impressed themselves upon the world'.[278] Their lives and teachings would, Jones thought, 'react upon each other with ever increasing power during the coming years'.[279]

More of a systematician than either Slater or Hume, Jones saw the problems which then arose for Christian theology. If it was no longer tenable to believe that Hinduism had arisen 'from below' and had therefore to be 'denounced root and branch as a thing purely Satanic'.[280] Jones enquired what other theories were available. He noted that some older theologies had suggested that the truths of Hinduism had filtered down from some primitive revelation, and that these were the 'relics of a vanishing faith, divinely communicated to some of the earliest members of our race'.[281] Other theories hazarded the view that God had 'directly, from time to time, guided the thoughts and answered the deep yearnings of the soul of the Indo-Aryan'.[282] 'Modern scholarship' was indeed 'practically of one voice' in maintaining that God hath not left himself without witness among the many nations of the earth', even if this witness had 'been comparatively feeble'.[283] But, said Jones, it was nonetheless a revelation, because God had disclosed truth and wisdom to the Indian people. To be sure it appeared inadequate compared with that of Christ ('dim and starlike', he wrote, 'compared with the noon-day brightness of the Sun of Righteousness in the Christian religion'[284]), but revelation it most certainly was.

To believe that there was 'revelation' in other religions could only lead to a quite different missiological and theological approach in India. 'The day has come', he wrote, 'when the Christian must accept and believe that God has been dealing directly with this people through the many centuries of their history, leading them to important truths.'[285] More than any of his colleagues Jones believed there were propositional truths 'embedded in the religion' of India. Whence did such truths emanate? The solution to such questions had to lie in the plain assertion that they originated in God.

Jones allowed readily that India had had its share of evil hearts and worse lives, and in many cases 'the truth of God' had been changed into a lie, and had led to the worshipping of the creature rather than the creator.[286] But notwithstanding such features there was so much of truth and beauty in Hinduism. These were perhaps 'broken lights', Jones allowed, but they were undoubtedly *'light'*. He therefore committed himself wholeheartedly to searching for 'points of contact'.[287] Like Slater, Lucas and Farquhar, Jones believed in the 'fulfilment' by Christianity of Hindu hopes and aspirations and produced his own series of examples of points of contact and ways of fulfilment.

To take one example, Jones saw the Hindu concept of *avatara*, or 'descent', as sharing common ground with the Christian understanding of incarnation. *Avatara* ideas had in his view been insufficiently appreciated by westerners, yet because the *avatara* understanding had been so popular in India for so many centuries, Jones wrote that Christ should be made most welcome there. Because the 'most popular god of the Hindu pantheon (Krishna) is also the leading incarnation of Vishnu', the ground had been prepared for understanding Jesus as the 'incarnation of God'.[288] More aggressively perhaps, he wrote: 'the Christian doctrine of incarnation furnishes, perhaps, the best leverage with which the Christian missionary is to overturn the faith of that people'.[289]

Jones also thought that there were points of contact in the Hindu teachings about sacrifice. He was impressed that words for sacrifice in Sanskrit were more numerous than they were in Hebrew, and pointed to a need for vicarious atonement.[290] He felt too that the 'intense meditativeness' and 'devotional ecstasy' to be found in *yoga* and in asceticism generally was a mark of profound seriousness and depth of spiritual apprehension. This 'spirituality' (Jones used the term) was yet another 'point of contact', for it represented the highest Hindu ideal, that of sharing in 'true heavenly wisdom'.[291] Just assuredly, the doctrine of *karma* pointed toward Christian fulfilment, for teachings centring upon the concept of *karma* represented the most elaborate system of eschatology outside the New Testament.[292] Like the Christian understandings of judgment and the wrath of God, *karma* was, he wrote, 'ethical in its character' and as such its 'fundamental principles' had 'chords which harmonise with those of the Christian doctrine'.[293]

Lastly there was, for Jones, the whole range of *bhakti* devotionalism which summed up as the 'the Doctrine of Faith', for it maintained that through trust in a personal god, salvation could be obtained.[294] This 'basal truth' of *bhakti*, Jones suggested, 'could not fail of arousing within the devout, lofty and stirring emotion'.[295] He affirmed the followers of the *bhakti* movements as people who proclaimed 'the true oneness of the brotherhood of faith among all the devotees of the same god'.[296] So striking was this resemblance within *bhakti* devotion to Christian self-abasement and longing for union with the divine that Jones was inclined to think that its had some Christian provenance lying behind it.[297] Despite all the elements of idolatry and sensuality that, in Jones' view, sometimes contaminated the *bhakti* tradition, it furnished, he thought, 'a common ground of fundamental truth of which Christian missionaries have not yet sufficiently availed themselves in their work for this people'.[298]

Christ: inclusive or exclusive

Like every other missionary of this period, Jones was quite clear that Hinduism was not a way of salvation on a par with Christianity. Chapter three of *India's Problem: Krishna or Christ?* entitled 'Hinduism and Christianity contrasted' was obviously designed to ensure that no one in the West would be tempted to think that there was any real choice. But even so the listing of Hinduism's deficiencies was done courteously and, to the best of Jones' ability, fairly. Most striking here is the clarity with which Jones set out the basic and underlying theological differences. These lay in monotheism and pantheism, in doctrines of creation and redemption, and of sin and regeneration.[299] One doctrine which he highlighted in this compare and contrast exercise was that of God's immanence, and he brought his survey to a close with an idea to which he was to return: 'Hinduism has done some good, doubtless. It has had a mission in the world and that has unquestionably been, partly, in the conservation of the great doctrine of God's immanence at a time when the Western world had largely forgotten it.'[300]

Nevertheless this mission was drawing to a close, and 'the leaven of death and dissolution' was now at work in Hinduism.[301] Immediately apparent to us

now is Jones' uneasy awareness that in asserting that Hinduism was waning
and would eventually vanish he was laying himself open to the familiar
charge, which he in fact levelled at others, of Western arrogance and spiritual
'exclusiveness'. But he could not avoid presenting Christianity as 'the only
way of salvation', standing alone, as he said, brooking no rivalry nor accepting any divided homage.[302] But setting out such a view needed no longer be
done with quite the same sense of combativeness and erudite inflexibility that
had marked the past. Christian faith now was seen to stand in a different
relationship with the religious traditions of humanity and was no longer
'unwilling to acknowledge the truths which are found in other faiths'.[303] Yet,
he continued,

> While it recognises such, it maintains that they are but broken lights of the
> Truth which it presents in all its full-orbed glory. It reveals Christ as the
> fulfilment of the good and pious of all nations, and His revelation as the
> realisation of Truth wherever found.[304]

But this assertion of the exclusive claims of Jesus Christ was distinct from
both earlier and later doctrinaire 'exclusivism' in another, and supremely
important, regard. John P. Jones was also highly critical of Western forms of
Christianity. In his assertion about Christ the fulfiller he was not remotely
suggesting that this implied the finality and exclusiveness of Western
Christianity. On the contrary Jones confidently expected new and better form
of Christianity to arise in India. New patterns of Christian thought, life and
worship had to spring up in the sub-continent to produce an Indian form of
Christianity, and would eventually do so, even if Jones was aware of how
Western it looked at the end of the Great Century.

'Oriental Christian life and character'

> Protestant Christianity has not yet been sufficiently long in India to devel-
> op and foster an Indian type of character of its own. And yet we see it
> rapidly working towards that consummation. A century is too brief a time
> for this purpose. Moreover, native Christian life in that land is too much
> under the dominance and guidance of the West to enjoy a large degree of
> spontaneity; and without spontaneity life is not natural. Nothing could be
> more fatal to the success of the Christian church in India than the idea
> that Indian Christians must be in every respect moulded after the pattern
> of western life and habits. There are so many things which can be adopted
> from Indian culture and civilisation into the new form of faith and obedi-
> ence in India that it would be folly for the missionary to regard these
> things as part of the faith to be supplanted, and to teach that 'western cus-
> toms are inseparable from Christianity and must be accepted by the Orient

with our faith. The Christian of India will always be, and it is well that he should be, differentiated from the Anglo-Saxon Christian.'[305]

The great bare white Congregationalist churches of New England could not be simply transplanted to India, for, as Jones said, 'the inhabitant of India is tropical and poetical in temperament'.[306] 'He beholds things,' Jones continued, 'and appreciates and appropriates spiritual blessings more through the help of forms and ceremonies than does the man of the West.'[307]

A rite appeals to his nature more strongly and lends to him greater facility getting at its underlying truth and antitype than it does to us. Indeed it is his nature to look at Christian truth through the eyes of a poet; and ceremonies consequently convey to him the largest significance and are more revealing of the spirit within.[308]

There had therefore, said Jones, to be a profound distinction between the customs and practices of the sending agencies and the needs and habits of the indigenous communities.

It has been, and, to some extent, continues to be the fault of our Congregational Missions in India that they try to lift the native Christian to those dry, unadorned, simple forms of religious service which indeed satisfy the missionaries, but which ignore the great difference of nature and temperament between themselves and the converts. It should be remembered that in India people think vocally. Even as they must and do read aloud in order to read intelligently, so must they worship aloud in order to worship feelingly and thoughtfully. Hence the wisdom and urgency for them of a ritual and a responsive service.[309]

Along with this went Jones' intense critique of Western aggressiveness. The inflexibility and combativeness in so many previous Great Century missionaries Jones characterized as 'assertion' and 'attack'.[310] Such missionaries, he wrote, 'stand always prepared to fight manfully for [their] convictions and to obtrude them at all points upon friend and foe alike'.[311] But in Indians Jones recognized virtues of quite another kind. The whole culture of the subcontinent prized patience, meekness, gentleness, and endurance above the alleged 'masculine' or active virtues. 'The equally important passive virtues we of the West have much neglected if not despised as weakness.'[312] The Indian Christian would, Jones hoped, 'increasingly illustrate the beauty and potency of the passive virtues, of the spiritual element of endurance and non-resistance. He will show to us that a true and perfected character, a character moulded after that of the Divine Exemplar, must have also, and with equal emphasis the sweet and feminine passive graces of life as an essential element.[313]

Therefore Jones urged that the Western Christian posture in India should be essentially that of one who is a learner as well as a teacher. Only through being prepared to listen could missionaries help forward the encounter between India's ancient civilization and the Christian faith and thus affect, as it had to, 'conceptions of life in the West'.[314]

'The invasion of an Oriental Christian thought'

Together with his South Indian colleagues Thomas Slater and Bernard Lucas, Jones urged the Western church to take to itself elements in Indian religion in order to re-work some basic Christian doctrines. He specified distinctive Indian understandings of the doctrine of the Spirit which should be brought into play to enhance Christian pneumatology. Jones wrote of his belief that quite soon 'the Indian Christian Church will formulate for itself and enunciate to the world an advanced and helpful doctrine of the Holy Ghost beyond anything that the West has enunciated'.[315] As 'the home of an all-prevalent spiritual pantheism', India would give as much emphasis to God's 'immanence as the West has given to His transcendence'.[316] Indian Christians would elaborate and illuminate the sense of God working within us beyond any Western conception.[317] Quite as passionately as his colleagues, Slater, Hume and Lucas, Jones feared the ambitions of missionaries as they set to work to 'occidentalise the native Christian community'.[318] This would happen if they chose to be 'ignorant of, or indifferent to, the grand possibilities of thought and of life which lie in Eastern character and teaching'.[319] In an article in *The East and the West* in 1904, Jones insisted that missionaries were neither to assume 'on the one hand that Hindu ideals are un-Christian, nor on the other, that our Western ideals, both in their emphasis and exclusiveness are the all-in-all of Christian life'.[320] Jones nevertheless was optimistic that many westerners would learn wisdom and enter upon their work with 'less depreciation of things Oriental and with a larger desire to conserve to the utmost Eastern habits of thought and social customs, so long as and so far as, they can be made the vehicles of Christian thought and the channels of Christian life'.[321]

Optimism about India's religious future pervades Jones' writings. In *India: Its Life and Thought* there is a ebullient picture of the 'Progress of Christianity in India'.[322] But Jones' eye was not focussed upon the statistics of the membership of the church. It is a 'sad truth', he wrote in 1908, that the total Indian Protestant community is 'at present only one three-hundredth part of the population'.[323] Yet he saw Christianity rapidly becoming the religion of India much more as a result of India's spiritual and intellectual stirrings than because of traditional missionary propaganda and activity.

India would be converted without the help of the missionaries, since the currents in Indian culture were moving 'in the direction of an enlightened and enlightening religion'.[324] Antagonism to Christianity in India was always in Jones' view hostility to 'adjectival Christianity – the too Western type of our faith'. Rarely was there the same opposition to 'substantival Christianity'.[325] It followed that Christianity could only become 'the universal religion of India' if it was 'dissociated from many Western ideas and practices which seem to us essential even to its very life'.[326] 'When we learn', Jones told his contemporaries, 'to forget our antecedents and prejudices and to study well the Hindu mind and its tendency, then perhaps we shall be prepared to present a Christianity which will commend itself universally to that land'.[327]

Jones and the World Missionary Conference

Like his Indian missionary contemporaries, Slater, Hume, Lucas and Farquhar, Jones stressed in his response to the Edinburgh commissioners the need to 'fulfil' Hinduism: 'the preacher should regard Christianity not as a supplanter of Hinduism or of any other religion, so much as it is a fulfiller of the best that these religions possess.'[328] Jones then moved on to the image that we have seen as dominant in his writings. 'The broken lights of these ethnic faiths are, after all, lights from God, and are a part of that revelation whose full-orbed beauty and illuminating grace is found in Christ and His faith alone.'[329] Even more than his closest colleagues Jones discerned a shape for the Christ who was yet to be, who would take into himself all the lights of the world's religions. Transfiguration, as the 'full-orbed beauty' of the revelation in Christ, lay in the future and was not the present possession of Western Christianity.

If there remained traces of the old aggressive missionary attitudes in his writings, they were there despite of his avowed wish to learn a new style of behaviour. His emphasis on courtesy as a transforming virtue for Western Christians was part of his having fallen in love with India. Justice for the truths of Hinduism as we have seen concerned him deeply. Jones belongs among the forerunners of interfaith dialogue and precursors of a new theology of religion.

Arthur Lloyd: A Ronin for Christ

Arthur Lloyd (1852-1911) is another of the lost heroes of the Great Century's search for theological understanding of other people's religions.[330] His name is hardly known today, and virtually nothing of his achievement is remembered.[331] Yet in the Japanese context he was one of the great pioneers of interfaith dialogue, having been a member of the Council of the Asiatic Society of Japan from 1899 onwards, and was held in great affection and

respect by Buddhist scholars.[332] Lloyd knew the Japanese people intimately
and wrote extensively to interpret Japanese culture to Westerners.[333] At least
one Japanese novel owes its translation into English to him,[334] and he was
among the earliest scholars to research into the burgeoning of modern
Japanese sects.[335] Among European scholars of Japanese life and culture he
was highly respected and he was often cited in studies of Mahayana
Buddhism in the early twentieth century. Passionately wanting his fellow
Christians in Japan to discover the context in which they sought to preach
the Gospel, Lloyd was the first English translator of Amitaba Buddhist sermons concerning grace, faith, and spiritual growth.[336] In the midst of all this
activity Lloyd developed theories of inter-religious relationships of such
compelling interest as to cause Timothy Richard to make the sea voyage to
visit him in Tokyo in 1907.[337] Lloyd's highly original views of the early interactions of Christianity and Buddhism were widely discussed in the missionary, as well as the more academic literature of his period,[338] and as a result he
was asked to speak on Buddhism and inter-religious relationships at the Pan-
Anglican Congress of 1908.[339] But despite this volume of work and achievement he has sunk almost without trace from modern missiological reflection.[340]

The reason why his name is lost to missionary history is, however, not difficult to surmise. There was always a sense about Lloyd that he was not of
the mainstream of missionaries. In the earliest records of the SPG, Lloyd
was mentioned as having 'fostered and extended the educational work of the
Anglican mission', but he had done this by accepting 'the superintendency of
the English branch of the celebrated school of Mr Fuzukawa'.[341] Finally he
left the service of the SPG altogether, and eventually became a professor in
the Imperial University. Lloyd remained deeply committed to Christian mission in Japan and spelt this out for the 1908 Pan Anglican Congress in
London. Here he made a deep impression on Bishop Charles d'Arcy who
was to be responsible for the Japanese religions section of the *Missionary
Message*.[342] D'Arcy welcomed Lloyd's contributions despite his not being regularly employed by any missionary society.

Lloyd began his missionary life in Japan in 1884, at the age of thirty-
two.[343] Like C.F. Andrews, he had started out both as a student of classical
literature and an Anglican clergyman of high church persuasions.[344] He had
been Fellow and Dean of Peterhouse (still occasionally called at this period
St Peter's College) and through his work he was fully in touch with the
growing work of the SPG in Japan. The need of the rapidly developing
Anglican church in Tokyo for competent educationists seems to have been
sufficient cause for Lloyd's missionary commitment.

Non-Roman Catholic missionary activity in Japan in the Great Century
dates from 1859, the year after the conclusion of the Treaty of Amity and
Commerce at Edo.[345] This treaty had provided for the right of residence,

together with freedom to practise Christianity and to erect places of worship in the Treaty ports of Edo, Kobe, Yokohama, Osaka, Niigata and Nagasaki. In the years between 1859 and 1872, called the 'time of promise and preparation', Western missionaries, mainly Americans, had to be content with learning the language and customs of the Japanese. But from 1873 onwards the mission took off surprisingly quickly. For example Tokyo, the ancient capital city, was opened to Western residents. The notorious 'Anti-Foreigner Edict' disappeared from public notice boards and missionaries found a new welcome within Japanese society. Among the new mission boards and societies responding to this transformed situation was the SPG, which found itself working alongside fellow Anglicans from the USA and Canada.

The rapid expansion of the Japanese church was especially marked among the educated classes, and especially affected were members of the Samurai tradition. As a direct consequence of the modernization of Japan large numbers of Samurai found themselves socially and economically dispossessed. The missionaries church discovered that they had access to these people. For example the ABCFM missionary D.C.Greene estimated in 1892 that forty per cent of the total body of Protestant Christians in Japan were of the Samurai class, even though the latter constituted only five per cent of the total population. Among the Christians of Tokyo nearly seventy-five per cent were of this class.[346] It was against this background that Lloyd arrived in Japan in 1884.[347]

Lloyd immediately joined the staff of the Canadian SPG missionary Alexander Croft Shaw in Tokyo. In 1879 Shaw had baptized 130 Japanese and established the school of which Lloyd was to take charge. Shaw had many connections with Japanese intellectuals. One of these, the 'Mr Fukuzawa' already referred to, had already established a college where Shaw had been teaching not religion, but ethics. Lloyd inherited this work. As well as learning Japanese thoroughly, Lloyd gradually gained a great influence among Tokyo students and even started a Japanese student congregation.

But the first phase of his work in Japan was to be cut short because of the ill-health of his first wife. Lloyd left Japan in 1890, and as a result of his link with the Canadian Anglican church became for a brief period a schoolmaster in Toronto. When his wife died Lloyd was free to return to Japan. This time he served with the PECUSA mission, again in Tokyo.[348] Nevertheless, Lloyd found his gifts more appropriately used at the Imperial University. Very soon he became fully employed at the University and at its associated institutions, the Higher Commercial College and the Imperial Naval College. It was at this point that Lloyd set out on what he called his 'evangelical adventure'. Here is his own description of his espousal of the path of a Samurai *ronin* as reported by C.F. D'Arcy.

In the old days of Japan when a Samurai was about to undertake some doubtful enterprise which his clan could not be expected readily to endorse, he would cut himself off from his kinsmen and become a *ronin*. If the *ronin* failed, no shame fell upon the clan. If, however he succeeded, the *ronin* 'returned in triumph to his feudal lord, bringing with him the fruits of his victory'.

Lloyd thought of himself as 'a *ronin* for Christ's sake'. 'If I fail,' he wrote, 'I fail, and the faithful will disown me, though I myself shall hope to be saved "so as by fire". If I succeed, my work will bear its fruit, and the result will be *ad majorem Dei gloriam*'.[349]Like C.F. Andrews a few years later, Lloyd felt that,for the sake of the gospel, he had to sever all official connection with a missionary agency.[350] A little later he wrote to those responsible for *The Missionary Message* (1910): 'For the last six years I have been independent of all ecclesiastical jurisdiction.'[351] But this was no severance from the worshipping life of the church, and even less from Christian discipleship. 'Among the things which I have shed, I have not found it necessary to include any of the articles of the Apostles' or Nicene Creeds, or my belief in Christianity as the Supreme and Perfect Revelation of God to man.'[352] His secular academic appointment as a lecturer in the Imperial University, the Naval Academy and the Higher Commercial School was assured and, happily remarried, he devoted himself to the twin task of studying Japanese Buddhism and of improving Western understanding of Japanese life and culture until his death in 1912.

Wheat among the tares

Lloyd's missiological thinking was both original and far-reaching. It is found in two books: *The Wheat among the Tares: Studies of Buddhism in Japan* (1908), which bore a further sub-title: 'A Collection of Essays and Lectures, giving an Unsystematic Exposition of Certain Missionary Problems of the far East, with a plea for more systematic research', and *The Creed of Half Japan: Historical Sketches of Japanese Buddhism* (1911).

As we have it now, *The Wheat among the Tares* is much shorter volume than he intended. A much larger work was destroyed by a fire at the Yokohama printers.[353] In the work which went up in smoke Lloyd had given a fuller exposition of views expressed at the time of the 1908 Pan-Anglican Congress. This assembly, he wrote, he had seen as an opportunity of 'presenting to the Christian public of England a plea for more diligent and sympathetic study by Missionaries and Mission Associations of the religions of the East, and more especially of the Buddhism of Japan and China'.[354]

Along with his demand for new and accurate study was Lloyd's passionate concern to see the missionary name cleared of the reproach (which, he thought, 'on the whole well merited') of being 'indifferent to, and ignorant of, the religious conditions of the people amongst whom they work in the Name of Christ'.[355] Such reproach was nowhere more clearly merited, he thought, than in Japan. The historian Richard Drummond has described the missionary situation in Japan around the turn of the century:

> A number of the now emerging Japanese Christian leaders were superior in cultural breadth and theological depth to any of the missionaries. The proceedings of the great missionary conference held in Tokyo in 1900, however, show little awareness of this situation. No provision was made for Japanese participation in the conference, and in spite of the undoubted and great devotion of these men, many of whom were the products of the evangelical revivals, particularly among students in England and North America during the late nineteenth century, adequate concern was absent for the problems of relationship between churches and missions in the changing situation.[356]

Even worse, as another historian of the Church in Japan, Charles Igleheart, has noted, there 'was almost no discussion of the content of the Christian message nor of the problems of communicating it to non-Christians'. 'Little reference', Igleheart continues,' was made to the cultural context in which the proclamation had to be made nor of the problems of relationship to Buddhist thought, Confucian ethics or emerging Shinto nationalism.'[357] Working in just that context Lloyd was sure that ignorance would lead to misrepresentation of Japanese religion, which could only lead in turn to alienation by the Japanese from the Christian message. 'It was not on such lines that the great apologists and Writers of the first Christian centuries carried on their work.'[358]

A missionary programme

Lloyd's second chapter in *The Wheat among the Tares*, 'On the Study of Comparative Religion', began with a paraphrase of the Nicene Creed. 'All this,' Lloyd asserted, 'I steadfastly believe and it is to guard against a possible misunderstanding that I write it down here.'[359] Such a strong profession of orthodox faith he obviously thought necessary in view of the material he was about to discuss. Most Christian audiences then, as now, assumed that discussion of comparative religion would only be comparatively religious. But Lloyd had in view eight vital points to make which arose from his own study of religion. At the outset he felt it necessary to ward off misrepresentation and calumny. He was aware, too, that there were those who believed him no longer to be a Christian.[360]

1. The first of Lloyd's eight points turned upon the doctrine of God, and of divine activity among all peoples: 'It is unworthy of the great love and

wisdom of God to suppose that He has confined His revelation of Himself either to the people of the Jews in the days before Christ or to the people called Christian in the days since. God has never left Himself without witness; and to every nation He has given something at least of the Divine Truth.'[361]

2. The prophetic figures in every age had been inspired by God: 'To some individuals... much has been given, and in abundant measure; and these men have stood out amidst their fellows as the great religious teachers of the non-Christian world. There have been many such men: may we not say of them that the Lord and Giver of Life has breathed on them too?'[362]

3. But discrimination is necessary. They did not all stand for the same things; their messages are not always compatible with one another. The records of their teachings have not preserved without additions and corruption. 'None of these has ever said that he died for the sins of man and was declared to be the son of God by the Resurrection from the dead', nor was everything they said inspired, 'and the blind devotion of after ages has enveloped their teachings in a mass of extraneous matter which come neither from them, nor yet from the Holy Spirit of God'.[363]

4. None of these religious figures failed to grasp some aspect of the Divine truth, and all 'precious fragments' needed to be sought out and preserved. 'Still are precious gems of truth, which are all needed for the Crown of Him Whom we worship as the Son of God, Whose kingdom shall have no end in time or in space, or in height, breadth, or depth of Truth, to Whom belong the glory and the wealth of all nations'.[364] There are echoes of Maurice in this passage: the sense of 'consummation' in Christ, the gathering up of what Maurice had termed 'precious fragments'.[365]

5. The new scientific study of religion had to be enlisted as ancillary to this task. Lloyd had no grasp that many of its practitioners might want to see a neutral and dispassionate search for truth in its own right.[366] 'It is the duty,' he wrote, 'of the student of Comparative Religion to search for these gems... to find and gather that precious residuum of Universal Faith which is true for all time and for all men.'[367]

6. Though holding, on the one hand, that the 'precious fragments' of truth were needed for the full-orbed splendour of Christ, Lloyd believed on the other hand in 'religious universals'. 'If Christ, Moses, Confucius, Sakyamuni, Mahomet should have agreed in enunciating a truth, and that truth should have been unanimously accepted by the peoples amongst whom these religious leaders hold spiritual sway, there would be a strong presumption in favour of considering such a truth to be one of the Universals of Religion. A remarkable thing about Christ is that practically all that He said is a "Universal" of this kind.'[368] It was 'only in our age that such a wide range of religious comparison has become possible' Lloyd wrote, 'because the Divine Providence has of late been bringing to light the hidden facts of science and

history in a most remarkable manner. The comparative study of religion was an instrument in the hand of God: 'It is the high privilege of the student of Comparative Religion to be able to assist in this work of the Divine Providence... we, students of a new science, are in a very real fashion fellow workers with God.'[369]

7. But syncretism was not the name of this game. The findings of Comparative Studies of Religion had to be submitted to the judgment of the church: 'It is not the duty of the individual student to form a new religion or establish a new sect.'[370] After the gathering and the sorting it was the duty of the whole church to come to its own judgment. Even so, the final judgment would be eschatological, and not dependent upon what the church decided. In 'the ultimate resort these results will be referred to the Judgment of Him to Whose appearance as a Judge we Christians look forward with reverent joy'.[371]

8. In any case syncretism would not be taking place on the level of ethics or mysticism. His 'religious universals' were doctrinal in form and had more to do with 'Unity-in-Trinity and Trinity-in-Unity, i.e. with the nature of the Godhead and were in that sense 'Universal of the Faith'. 'I find', he wrote, 'unconscious imperfect testimony to them all in the heathen and non-Christian religions with which I am acquainted – in the Amida of the *Sukhavati-Vyuhas*, in the Eternal Sakyamuni of the *Saddharma Pundarika*, in the "Three Bodies of the Buddha". I find a similar correspondence in the teaching of the Confucianists that there are three Eternal Principles, *Teu*, *Ri*, *Ki*, Heavenly Will, Heavenly Reason, Heavenly Energy, and that these three are one.'[372] The Christian Triune God, in Lloyd's view, had not been left without witness to his trinity in unity in other religious traditions.

Lloyd and Amitabha Buddhism

By 1909, nearly twenty-five years of research into Japanese forms of Buddhism had led Lloyd to highly original and idiosyncratic conclusions about the Amida ideal in Buddhism. In this form of faith Lloyd saw traces of early Christian gnostic and Manichean elements. These conclusions he described briefly in *The Wheat and the Tares*, and set out more fully in *The Creed of Half Japan*, as well in articles for *The East and the West* and the *Journal of Asiatic Studies*. Judgment upon the lasting value of Lloyd's theories rests with specialists in the interactions of Mediterranean and Sanskritic cultures in the period between the sixth century before Christ and the first six centuries of the Christian era. In his own setting Lloyd's work was part of his developing theology of other religions.

But attempts to affirm the universality of God's action would have been unacceptable to some of his fellow missionaries. Nevertheless, twenty-five years of detailed study had left him no choice in the matter because, as he wrote in 1909, 'I have learned that God has nowhere left himself without witness, and I am trying to discover that witness here in Japan.'[373] But how was he to convey this sense of God as having been already active in revelation in Japan to fellow missionaries? One way of accounting for the 'wonderful preparation for Christianity' in Japan was to postulate the influence of Christianity itself in a diffused or corrupted form.

None of the Japanese tradition was more challenging in this regard than the redemption story in what Lloyd called 'the doctrine of the saving Vow of Amida'.[374] Amida or Amitabha Buddhism was, he thought, the expression of the highest form of Buddhism.[375] Writing to the Edinburgh commissioners Lloyd suggested it was 'a faith so wonderfully like Christianity' that it was difficult 'to resist the inference that it was in the Divine providence intended as a *Praeparatio Evangelica* for the Gospel in Japan'.[376] Both *The Wheat and the Tares* and *The Creed of Half Japan* sought to demonstrate the way in which some forms of Buddhism had moved towards the idea of salvation by faith in a transcendent Buddha figure. This was Amida or Amitabha Buddha, whom Lloyd described in these words:

Amida without beginning and without end: all love, wisdom, benevolence and power. He is the Father of all the world and all sentient beings. In ages incalculably remote he appeared in various forms among men, all his incarnations being to bring salvation to mankind. In his last incarnation he appeared as the Bhikshu Hozo... and as such he registered a vow that should the Perfect Consummation of the Buddhahood ever be in his power, he would not accept such deliverance unless such deliverance should also mean the salvation of suffering mankind. In fulfilment of that vow he endured much suffering and many agonies, but he triumphed in the end, and the fruit of his labours has been the opening of a Paradise in a Pure Land, into which all may enter who call upon his name with Faith.[377]

As Lloyd wrote about the developed form of Mahayana Buddhism which he saw to be the creed of half the Japanese people, 'It is theological, it recognises man as a sinner, it preaches the Gospel to the Poor, and it has a salvation by Faith in a Saviour who has done everything for the soul'.[378]

Consequently the task he had set before him as 'Christian *ronin*' was to see how Mahayanan hopes and insights might be expressed in Christian terms. This was the great experiment: to see if he could 'conduct Japanese Buddhists through Shinshu theology to Christ'.[379] This process was full of pitfalls, as Lloyd fully recognized, but he was buoyed up by a greater hope:

I would not wish it to be understood that I advocate a fusion of Christianity and the Mahayana into one. But I can see that, if what I have said be true, there may follow a gradual turning of Buddhism towards

Christ in such a way that without abating one jot of respect which all religious men should have for Sakyamuni, there shall be a further recognition of that higher confidence which we shall feel, and in conduct show, for Christ as the fulfiller of all that Sakyamuni taught and revealed, and which rightly belongs to Him as the only being of whom it can be said that he was proved to be the Son of God with power by the Resurrection from the dead.[380]

Two consequences for Christian ethics and spirituality would follow if the process were successful. First and paramount it would help meet the clamant need to develop a Christian style of life in Buddhist lands. Lloyd wrote in *The Creed of Half Japan* that Buddhism needed special preachers. These would have to be people of 'sympathy and patience' who, while proud of being Christians, were 'yet willing for Christ's sake, to be followers of S'akyamuni in all things lawful and honest'.[381] These men and women would be able to say to Buddhists, 'I will walk with you and together we will go to Him to whom you say S'akyamuni Himself bore witness.'[382]

After twenty-five years in Japan Lloyd had lost any sense of need for activism and polemic, let alone for any kind of combativeness or aggression. On the contrary, he wrote, 'Japan will be converted by our being what we are through God's grace, rather than by our doing this or scheming that'.[383] Through life in the East, he had learnt simplicity in faith and practice.[384]

In addition Lloyd, the former high churchman, had discovered that no one group had a 'monopoly of Christian faith or grace, and that a divided Christianity, which is a disobedience to the spirit of Christ's prayer, can never do the greatest things for God'.[385] By the end of his missionary career, Lloyd had changed, by his own description, from being a 'a more or less strait-laced Anglican' into an ecumenical (his word is 'non-descript') Christian, worshipping regularly with Roman Catholics as well as Anglicans.[386] How much he learnt from Roman Catholic missionaries it is impossible for me to determine.

Lloyd's practice in dialogical mission: the Amitabha Christ

In some verses of his own composition which stand at the beginning of *The Wheat and the Tares*, Lloyd addressed Christ as 'the truest Lord, Of boundless Life and Love uncircumscribed', and continued:

Long years Thy shadow, brooding o'er the East,
  Hath told of Peace and Hope for sinful men.
Now turn the Shadow to Reality,
  And bless us as we gather round Thy Feet,
O Amitabha-Christ, Sole Lord of All.[387]

Happily, Lloyd offered his Christian readership in *The Wheat and the Tares* abundant evidence of his style in conversations with his Buddhist friends. Most of the chapters were talks and addresses originally given to Buddhist groups in Tokyo and other cities, which had then been published in the *Japan Mail* or as *Transactions of the Asiatic Society*. They exemplify vividly Lloyd's practice in interfaith dialogue. Extreme courtesy was the keynote in addressing sophisticated Japanese audiences. Yet always there was a challenge to the Japanese to sift the 'wheat from the tares' in both Buddhism and Christianity, and then perhaps to gather at the feet of the 'Amitabha Christ'.

Three of the chapters were originally sermons given to Buddhist congregations and demonstrate Lloyd's profound knowledge of Japanese teachings, enabling him to speak to different Buddhist gatherings on texts from the *Saddharma Pundarika*.[388] Lloyd's dialectic in all three can be seen in the argument of the first of them. First he stated that St Paul's teaching was that in Christ the fullness (*pleroma*) of God dwells; 'there is no need to turn to any one else, for in Christ we have everything'. But then he supposed that his Buddhist listeners would say that the same thought was to be found in the *Saddharma Pundarika*: 'Sakyamuni is the *pleroma*, the *Mandala*. He, begotten before the worlds is the sum-total of the universe.' But, suggested Lloyd, this Sakyamuni was to the Buddhist exactly what Christ was to the Christian.[389] What was to be made of that? Lloyd affirmed for his audience how 'passing strange' it was that these two figures, glorified and exalted Christ of St Paul and the glorified and exalted Sakyamuni of the *Saddharma Pundarika* should appear in the world's religious development at the same time. Anti-dialectical Christians would, he suggested, only cry 'there cannot be two Christs'; anti-dialectical Buddhists would only cry 'There cannot be two Sakyamunis: we can accept your Christ as a partial manifestation, but we cannot find room for two *pleromas* in the Universe.'[390] But in true dialogue another conclusion might be reached along the lines which Lloyd suggested:

> It is, however possible that the two may be found to be intended as the same Divine Person, and my aim... is to try to establish their identity; for I feel sure that if I can do so the world, Christian and Buddhist alike, will be the gainer. It is no longer the fashion to introduce prayers into Sermons; perhaps in these Sermons preached from a writing table and not from a pulpit, I may be allowed to pray that I have may have wisdom, boldness and charity in unfolding, and my readers, patience and forbearance in reading, so that the result of my work may be to edify, not to destroy, to bind together and not to scatter.[391]

'Wisdom, boldness and charity' are counterpoints to the 'justice, courtesy and love' urged by Lloyd's almost exact contemporary T.E. Slater. Lloyd must be commemorated as a pioneer of dialogue and as one whose 'new and perhaps dangerous missionary experiment' opened up new ways for Christians and Buddhists to relate to each other.[392] Notto Thelle, a long-time Norwegian missionary in Japan and now Professor of Missiology in Oslo, has seen in Lloyd a precursor of the Centre for the Study of Japanese Religions in Kyoto run by the National Christian Council of Japan. Thelle has written: 'A true dialogue – including that based on missionary concern – opens itself to spiritual search and does not necessarily yield to the temptation of cheap apologetics.'[393] Lloyd would have agreed, and rejoiced that his vision had not been lost altogether.

Bernard Lucas: The Empire of Christ

'He was a layer of foundations, and it is commonly the fate of foundations to remain hidden.'[394] Eric Sharpe's remark about T.E. Slater, is even more relevant to another LMS thinker, the Englishman Bernard Lucas (1860-1921). His three formidable books, *The Empire of Christ: Being a Study of the Missionary Enterprise in the Light of Modern Missionary Thought* (1908), *Christ for India: A Presentation of the Christian Message to the Religious Thought of India* (1910) and *Our Task in India: Shall We Proselytise Hindus or Evangelise India* (1914)[395] were in truth foundational for the theology of religion and the missionary approach to Hinduism at the end of the Great Century but are now largely forgotten.[396]

Born and educated in Birmingham, Lucas trained for the Congregationalist ministry at Cheshunt College, leaving for India in 1886 aged twenty-six. At Cheshunt he was nurtured in an 'ultra-orthodox and strongly sectarian position'.[397] In India he learned to speak both Telegu and Kanarese fluently and wrote hymns in both languages. Most of his career was spent in Bellary in South India, one of the leading LMS centres. At first he was engaged in direct evangelistic work in the villages, but before long he found it more profitable to engage with educated Hindus, rather on the lines of T.E. Slater.[398] Much later, as the senior LMS missionary in South India, Lucas became one of the leading figures in the early stages of the ecumenical movement in South India, laying foundations in another way, and the Church of South India scheme in 1947 has Lucas in its early background.[399] Similarly the vision that brought into being the United Theological College at Bangalore in 1910 owes much to Lucas, and he was one of its first faculty members. A.T.S. James, one of the historians of the LMS, has written of Lucas' profound love and understanding of India. Lucas, James reckoned, understood Indian life and thought better than any other LMS missionary of this period, for he 'seemed to be able to think Hindu'.[400] Lucas believed that Hinduism was 'fundamentally spiritual' with the result that he pleaded 'for the way of co-operation with all that it best in Hinduism in the building up of Christianity'.[401] A.T.S. James commented in 1923 that 'this line of thought is always open to misconstruction'.[402] Like Timothy Richard in China, Lucas was consistently misunderstood by many of his junior contemporaries.

'The laying of foundations'

The image of foundation-laying was used by Lucas himself. In the first of his books, *The Empire of Christ*, he described the building of the Great Hall in New Delhi in commemoration of Queen Victoria in 1908. It was to be roofed 'with a magnificent dome'. But when Lucas was writing nothing more than the foundation walls could be seen, and as he wrote, 'the earth-filling has covered over much of the work which for months has been going on'. Consequently 'hidden from sight and doomed for ever to remain unseen is an exact counterpart underneath of the wonderful dome which shall one day rise to crown and glorify the edifice'.[403] This image caught precisely the kind of foundations Lucas believed necessary if Christianity were really to take hold of India and develop an appropriate superstructure.

Lucas' message was that despite a hundred years of sacrificial activity there were no such foundations. 'In the contemplation of her missionary work in India the Church has first to realise that in the truest sense of the word the introduction of Christianity into India has yet to take place.'[404] Christianity was still 'exotic' and nowhere was there any 'indigenous Christianity': 'The Indian Church has produced not a single theologian, nor has it given birth to a single heresy.'[405] He continued in this vein:

> When we contrast the first century of Christianity in Europe with the first century of modern missions in India, this statement is deeply significant. The contact of Christian thought with that of Greece was productive of a ferment in both, which had an immense influence in the spread of Christianity in the West. In India we have a philosophical atmosphere as stimulating, and far more permeating than that of Greece when Christianity first came into contact with it; yet while Christianity has profoundly stirred Hindu thought and feeling, Hindu thought has had absolutely no influence on Christian thought.[406]

The reason for this lay in a defective missiology, as Lucas proceeded to show. He was not however scornful of his missionary predecessors. On the contrary, he greatly admired the first stage of European protestant missionary work in India, which set out to win souls for Christ.[407] This aim was, he wrote, 'determined by the theology of those who undertook it, and in that theology the emphasis had been unduly placed upon the individual, to the exclusion of the race to which that individual belonged'.[408] In India the individuals who were most likely to respond to such an appeal were those whom the Hindu systems had made outcastes and 'not worthy of salvation'.[409] The task of Christianizing India had therefore been attempted by means of mass movements within the poorest and the most oppressed groups.

To this task the missionaries gave themselves with an earnestness and devotion worthy of all praise, and their success has added a bright chapter to the history of the Church. When these men heard of the 'failure of Christian missions' they were genuinely astonished, and pointed in triumph to the thousands of their converts. The real fact is, not that Christian missions have failed, for their success has been conspicuous, but that the Church has failed to realise the nature of the task which awaits her.[410]

The practical consequences of moving towards the oppressed groups were everywhere to be seen. Since the converts from these sections of society were never distinctively Hindu, there were very few cases of such new Christians 'seeing in Christianity the fulfilment of Hinduism'.[411] The result had been that 'to a large extent the Indian preacher has been strong in his denunciations of Hindu misconceptions, and weak and deficient in his enunciation of Hindu concepts of truth'.[412]

But twentieth-century missionary thought, said Lucas, was more focussed upon the 'race rather than the individual, life rather than death, on earth rather than heaven'.[413] It had to be able to contemplate 'the regeneration of a great people, and not merely the conversion of the individual'.[414] If it would do this, Christian evangelization would be no longer 'the forlorn hope of plucking a few brands from the burning; it is the building of an empire; into which are incorporated all the kingdoms of the world. The mission of the church is not to destroy but to fulfil the religious aspirations of men.'[415] Lucas repeated this theme again and again in his three missiological works: missionaries were not in India impose a creed, but to evoke a richer faith; 'not to deny but to affirm; not to destroy but to fulfil'.[416]

Lucas was also clear that the new theological thinking at the end of the Great Century, and represented by Fairbairn, Allen and Hall, supported him in these convictions. At the centre of these was the understanding of God's providential dealings with the whole of humanity. 'We have come to recognize that salvation is a much greater and more far reaching purpose on the part of God than our fathers conceived it to be, and that throughout the whole family of man there has been a vast preparation for this great purpose of the ages.'[417] Nowhere was this preparation more clear than India.

The religious preparation of India has been within and not outside the scope of God's providential dealing with the race. The Church however must realise that she must work in truest co-operation with the Spirit, and not in opposition. In the work of redemption the Spirit has preceded the Church in India, and we must follow with due regard to Him who has preceded us.[418]

'Religious India', he wrote, will then 'raise her memorial to the Christ of God, under whose sway and inspiration she will eclipse all her former glory. Other hands will rear and beautify the dome above, but it is ours which must lay deep and strong the foundations of the temple that is yet to be'.[419]

Lucas' 'foundational' theology

Tracing the sources of Lucas' theology is not easy because he chose to write almost entirely without reference to other authors and with very few foot-notes. In all three books there is just one reference to a fellow Indian missionary, namely A.G. Hogg.[420] He also used quotations from the historian Julius Richter as well as Charles Cuthbert Hall on the first pages of *Christ for India* to set the tone of what was to follow.[421] Clearly he was exceedingly well read in the literature that was available to him, and we must try to discern the factors which that formed his foundational theology.

First there is the tradition of Maurice and Fairbairn. From Maurice, Lucas derived his insistence that 'the Fatherhood' in God was no mere metaphor, and expressed, not an attribute of the divine Mind, but 'the revelation of an essential relation between humanity and God'.[422] Only if this were true, Lucas insisted, would India discover that the world was a revelation of the Father.

It is the truth that matter is the medium for manifestation of spirit, that the universe is the expression of mind. The incarnation, when rightly interpreted, is the highest expression of this truth; and the life of Christ is an eternal witness to the fact that the temporal expression is a real, even though limited, revelation of the eternal ideal.[423]

Matching this controlling idea of the Fatherhood of God was what Lucas called the 'altered conception' of humanity prevalent in the last years of the Great Century. Here Lucas is echoing Westcott as well as Maurice. The Westcottian ideas of solidarity with all humanity and of 'Christus Consummator' led on the one hand to considerable alterations in the missionary motive and on the other to equally great changes in the understanding of missionary goals and aims.[424] It was no longer possible, Lucas thought, 'to believe that millions of God's children are passing away into endless torment without a single chance of redemption', still less 'that the Divine Father has limited the revelation of Himself to an infinitesimal section of the race, utterly unmindful of the lot or destiny of the rest'.[425]

As a positive corollary to this disavowal, Lucas insisted that 'we have come to recognize that salvation is a much greater and more far reaching purpose on the part of God than our fathers conceived it to be'.[426] Lucas' own interpretation of salvation turned upon the conception of 'entrance to eternal life' and the needs of 'the famine stricken millions whose existence is a living death'.[427] This conception of salvation, Lucas wrote, 'draws a contrast not between the joys of an imaginary heaven and the miseries of a materialistic hell, but between the fulness of the divine life within the soul of the reconciled son and the emptiness of him in the far country who has not yet come to himself'.[428]

> To the newer, as to the older thought it is the fact 'that God so loved the world, that he gave his only son that we might have life and have it more abundantly,' which constitutes the ground of appeal for foreign missions. The newer thought, however underlines the words 'world', 'life' and 'more abundantly'; it hears more acutely the children's cry for bread, and responds more readily to the reports of famines in distant lands.[429]

Finally, Lucas' theology stressed the importance of the 'personhood' of Jesus for helping India to understand the Christian conception of the 'personhood' of God and the significance of human personality. 'Jesus', he wrote, 'is that supreme revelation both of God and of man for which India has waited long'.[430] It was this rather than 'theological conceptions of Christ, or theories of the atonement and our schemes of salvation' that India was waiting for.[431] They were looking for 'that oneness with God' which came from a 'sympathy with the crucified' and that 'sense of salvation which comes from the pulsation of a bounding religious life'.[432]

The role of the missionary

Besides foundation-laying, Lucas had two other images for the work of the Christian missionary in India. One was the New Testament picture of disciples who responded to the request, 'Sir, we would see Jesus' (John 12.20). Accordingly, in his *Christ for India* (which is in itself well worth examining as an remarkable attempt at apologetics) Lucas attempted to offer India a Christ untrammelled by Western trappings or entailments. He sub-titled the book 'a presentation of the Christian message to the religious thought of India'. Constantly Lucas tried to speak of Jesus and his teaching without interposing Western conceptions and prejudices. Yet Lucas recognized that it was impossible for a Westerner to stand in the Hindu's place. He hoped nevertheless that he could try 'to stand by his side and try to direct his gaze in the right direction. It is not possible to do so, however, as long as one stands in front of him.'[433]

His other potent image was that of missionaries as 'importers of new seed' in which he drew the distinction between lesser and greater tasks in the Christian mission in India. The real work of developing Christian understanding in India belonged entirely to the Indian church. Missionaries must recognize, he wrote, 'that we are, and must ever remain importers of new seed; we are not and can never become Hindu cultivators'.[434]

'Christianity is of the East, Eastern'

A constant theme therefore in Lucas' writing is the need and potentiality of Indian cultivation of Christian theology. Thus in *Christ for India*, Lucas postulated a change in world religious understanding as a result of the encounter of India with Jesus:

His personality has introduced into the world a new standard which modifies the conception of the personality both human and Divine. This has been the history of religious thought in the West and it will be the same in the East. The conception of the Divine and the human which are characteristic of Hindu thought are as inadequate, in the light of the personality of Jesus, as those of the West. His appearance on the horizon of Indian religious thought foreshadows the rise of a New Vedanta in which the old dualism of a noumenal and a phenomenal Brahma are resolved.[435]

Lucas was clear that India had to be left to give 'her own interpretation of the personality of Jesus'.

The West cannot, and ought not to attempt to impose upon India its own distinctively Western interpretation. On the contrary it should anticipate an enrichment of its own religious thought when once the Indian mind has perceived the religious value of His personality and interpreted it in terms of Indian thought.[436]

Lucas' vision anticipated much later twentieth-century thinking about the distinction between religion and religions, gospel and culture, revelation and Christianity. 'Christianity,' Lucas wrote, 'viewed as a system of doctrines is rightly classified as one of many religions.'[437] But, he went on, viewed as 'as the interpretation of the Universal Christ revealed in the presence of Jesus, it is not a religion, but Religion itself'.[438] These words matched his view expressed two years previously that the East had 'yet to give us its interpretation of the Christ' and to 'furnish us with its representation of the Christian life'.[439] Until this had been done the 'revelation' remained incomplete and 'the world's religious thought' had not reached its maturity.[440] Such thinking enabled Lucas to formulate a quite different motivation for mission than that with which he had come to India.

> The Church does not impoverish herself in giving of her best to the world, but enriches herself. In the religious realm the kings of the East have still yet to bring their treasures into her storehouse. Christianity is of the East, Eastern; and in returning to the home of her birth she will renew her strength and re-invigorate the West.[441]

Mission was about spiritual growth and mutual enrichment. Bernard Lucas had moved into a wholly new thought world. We need not wonder that he was often misunderstood by his contemporaries.

J.N. Farquhar: The New Type of Christian Missionary

As far as the theology of religion is concerned the best known of all the missionaries in this chapter is certainly John Nicol Farquhar (1861-1929).[442] He has, not least as a result of the writings and researches of Eric J. Sharpe, a firm place in the history of the study of Indian religion and in the development of the Christian understanding of other religions.[443] For us Farquhar represents yet another Scottish connection in the search for an adequate Christian understanding of the significance of other religious traditions.

Farquhar was educated at the Grammar School and University in Aberdeen where he entered into the great Scottish traditions of logic and philosophy. Only when he was twenty-five did he go south to Oxford. Farquhar's godly parents were members of the small Evangelical Union which we have already met twice in this book.[444] 'I grew up', he wrote later, 'with all the words of the New Testament ringing in my ears.'[445] The evangelical and revivalist atmosphere of the John Street EU church in Aberdeen was responsible for Farquhar's early Christian nurture, but when he was eleven years old Andrew Martin Fairbairn came to the pulpit of another EU church in Aberdeen.[446] This young minister, fresh from his twelve years of intense study in Bathgate, moved for five years in the same circles as the adolescent Farquhar. Fairbairn's passion for the gospel and awareness of other religious traditions was an early influence upon the younger man. Growing up within the Evangelical Union also meant for Farquhar that he never had any personal struggle with the entails of hyper-Calvinism with its strict sense that only an elect few could be saved.[447]

After finishing his classical and philosophical studies at Aberdeen, Farquhar was awarded a exhibitionership at Christ Church, Oxford for the years 1885-9. Again his and Fairbairn's paths crossed. In 1886 the new Mansfield College had been founded to serve Congregationalists and other

Protestant nonconformists. Fairbairn became its first principal and Farquhar regularly worshipped at Mansfield College chapel. Among his fellow worshippers was the venerable James Legge, a fellow Aberdonian and Professor of Chinese in the University.

In addition to Fairbairn's direct guidance Farquhar experienced the indirect influence at Oxford of Max Müller and Monier Monier Williams, the Boden Professor of Sanskrit of his day.[448] Certain high ideals of learning were set before him which he was to honour throughout his life. His evangelical commitment never wavered, however, and by 1890 he felt drawn to offer his services to the LMS. Among those who wrote letters of reference for LMS was Andrew Fairbairn.[449]

Thus it was that in 1890 that Farquhar became an LMS educational missionary. He sailed for India in December that year, arriving in Calcutta in 1891. He spent twelve heroic years (for he did not like teaching) on the staff of Bhowanipur College, including seven years as Principal. There he learned to speak Bengali fluently, as well as continuing his work in Sanskrit literature.

But however valiant his efforts, school-mastering was not Farquhar's metier. With heartfelt relief he found himself appointed in 1903 as National Student Secretary for the Indian YMCA He then began a ministry which took him the length and breadth of the sub-continent. So successful he was in this work that John Mott and others created a post especially for him as 'Literary Secretary of the YMCA of India and Ceylon'.[450] During his twenty years of outstanding service to the Indian YMCA, Farquhar produced no less than seventeen books and brochures, as well as seminal articles in the *Contemporary Review* and the newly founded *International Review of Missions*.[451] Ever a creative thinker, he instigated no less than three series, *The Religious Quest of India*, *The Heritage of India* and *The Religious Life of India*, These were to have significant repercussions in the twenties and thirties, inaugurating as they did another stage in Hindu-Christian understanding.[452] That achievement falls outside the Great Century, and we hope to discuss it in a sequel to the present work. In 1923 Farquhar became Professor of Comparative Religion at Manchester University, where he remained until his death in 1929.

It is, however, his work while he was a younger missionary which concerns us, for Farquhar was an important contributor to the thinking of *The Missionary Message*. By 1910 he was widely known not only as a scholar of Hinduism, but as one who was personally involved in putting 'justice, courtesy and love' into effect in his relationships with Indian people. A glimpse into Farquhar's activities and their reception by Indians comes from a speech given by the Diwan (roughly, 'Prime Minister') of Mysore state in 1907:

The critical spirit in which you have traced the origin and age of the *Gita* and the appreciation you have evinced of the teachings of that great book, show well how well equipped you are for the new field of activity upon which you have entered... You belong to the new type of Christian missionary who have made a critical study of the life and customs of the Indian people, and can readily enter into their feelings and aspirations... We Indians cannot be too grateful to you and other Europeans possessing true insight into Indian character and sympathy with Indian aspirations, for your interpreting our religion and our thought to your fellow-countrymen, thereby bringing a better understanding between the two races.[453]

The Mysore minister of state recognized in Farquhar a scholar able to speak of the 'greatness of Hinduism', for he had many years previously set his face against any undiscriminating denunciation of Hinduism, so much so that in many of his writings he had gone almost to the other extreme. Readers of the Farquhar article in the *Contemporary Review* in 1910 would have gathered a great deal about virtues of Indian traditions and very little about idolatry and superstition.[454] In this as in other writings Farquhar expounded five elements in this greatness: the Hindu conception of God and the world, the Sanskritic organization of society, Hindu asceticism, India's quest for a spiritual faith, and the great variety and pluriformity of the Indian religious tradition.[455]

Yet Farquhar was never able to forsake his orthodox upbringing. He remained to the end of his life a missionary from the evangelical and revivalist tradition. How did he make sense theologically, on the one hand, of the great qualities in Hinduism and, on the other, of the unchanging nature of the redemption in Christ His answer was straightforward and, in his terms, highly reasonable: All things were evolving upwards. The good was becoming progressively better. There was much good in Hinduism and it would evolve into something better.

So far, to be sure, Christianity was the highest point on the evolutionary scale of religion. He wrote in 1903 that 'the belief that Jesus Christ, the Son of God, died for our sins on Calvary, produces a religion which satisfies the modern mind. At the same time it had proved to be 'the fulfilment and goal of all the religions of the world, the crudest as well as the loftiest'.[446] Christianity was the only faith in all the world which was 'purely spiritual and essentially ethical', and which at the same time offered 'historical facts of the largest significance and the mightiest emotional power, which fully satisfy the demand of the human heart for sacrifice and an object of worship more imaginable and comprehensible than the God of the Vedanta'. [457]

The life of the Son of God on earth satisfies at once the instinct that has produced the avatars of Hinduism and the idols of all the earth; for the story of his life in the Gospels appeals to the feelings and the imagination more completely than any mythical incarnation or any idol of stone or wood. And his death on the Cross gives us a sacrifice which satisfies the human desire to make atonement for sin, and thereby explains in a satisfactory manner all the animal and human sacrifices that have ever taken place on this earth of ours.[458]

Farquhar's unwavering evangelical and revivalist Christian faith is apparent from these words.

'Evolution is everything'

Farquhar was entirely comfortable with evolutionary patterns of thought.[459] Since Christianity was the highest form of religion, there would necessarily be a natural evolution on the part of Hinduism into Christianity. All other religion forms could be 'made sense of' in these terms. There was no longer any need to ascribe their origin to dark spiritual forces or to corruption of original revelation. All non-Christian religions were to be seen as stages through which humanity must pass on its way to the highest, which would, to be sure, be a form of protestant Christianity. In 1910 Farquhar told the readership of the *Contemporary Review* that Christianity would be the evolutionary crown of Hinduism'.[460] The New Testament would remain the focus of all revelation. Farquhar suggested it would be the 'central sun in the light of which everything must else must be read and estimated'.[461] But the greater books of Hinduism will form 'a sort of second Old Testament, set like stars around the sun; and the teachings of the old saints will be abundantly used by the Christian sons of India'. Every Hindu belief, rite and institution would then be seen as 'a germ, an adumbration, the full blown flower and reality of which will come with Christ'.[462] This anticipated the well-known, though not always accurately quoted, conclusion to *The Crown of Hinduism* in 1913:

> We have already seen how Christ provides the fulfilment of each of the highest aspirations and aims of Hinduism. A little reflection on the material contained in this chapter will show that every line of light which is visible in the grossest part of the religion reappears in Him set in healthy institutions and spiritual worship. Every true motive which in Hinduism has found expression in unclean, debasing, or unhealthy practices finds in Him fullest exercise in work for the downtrodden, the ignorant, the sick, and the sinful. In Him is focused every ray of light that shines in Hinduism. He is the Crown of the faith of India.[463]

Farquhar and the World Missionary Conference

J.N. Farquhar had already begun thinking about writing his great work *The Crown of Hinduism* when he responded to the Edinburgh World Missionary Conference Questionnaire in 1909 and this fact was well known. Thus the authors of *The Missionary Message* felt that they could allude to Farquhar's already established views when they wrote that among those who saw Hindu theism and philosophy as 'alike fulfilled and superseded by Christianity... Mr Farquhar of Calcutta may be taken as a typical representative'.[464]

But fulfilment is no easy idea, especially when it is coupled with the further notion of supersession.[465] How did Farquhar set out his thinking in his response? 'Religion', he told the Commissioners, 'is one of the essential elements of man's nature, and every religion has its roots in certain elemental instincts deeply embedded in the soul of man.'[466] Ignorance in primitive times has led to some very crude expressions of these religious instincts and 'the long struggle upward' has complicated matters. 'Yet all religions are in a sense valid, as being genuine products of man's religious nature.'[467] Nevertheless there was only one true religion. 'While all religions are human, Farquhar wrote, 'there is only one which satisfies all the religious instincts and yet can be held by modern thinking man. Every religion except Christianity is incredible, either on account of its crude metaphysics or a wild theology or a low ethical system.'[468]

> But if all religions are human, and yet men can in the long run hold only Christianity, clearly it must be, in some sense the climax of the religious development of the world. If all the great religious instincts, which have created the other faiths, find ultimate satisfaction in Christianity, then Christianity stands in a very definite relation to every other religion. It is the fulfilment and crown of each.[469]

First, fulfilment had to begin with conservation. Farquhar was insistent that every really religious element in the life of any people should be preserved. 'The religious convictions and emotions are not to be condemned and destroyed. Religion cannot be killed and then re-introduced.'[470] Second, there would be elements which could be built upon: 'Thus the wise Christian teacher will use every fragment of real morality and religion as a basis for better things.'[471] Third, the fulfilment of Indian religions by Christ would be similar to the fulfilment of Judaism by Christ, 'even if the gap be far greater and the historical connection absent'.[472]

How might these prescriptions be applied to Hinduism? Farquhar suggested that the first area to be assessed for 'fulfilment' is Indian religious history. There were 'remarkable phenomena' which could 'only be interpreted as an age-long yearning for such a faith as Christianity'. Among these remarkable phenomena are the 'unending series of great reformers, each straining after the production of a spiritual religion'; the 'search for a satisfying monotheism'; the 'reaching out for *God with us*'.[473] 'Millions of people shower all the wealth of their rich religious emotions on Rama, Krishna and others like them'. Much in popular Hinduism would find 'fulfilment' in Christ. Farquhar discussed appreciatively the work of Sankara and Ramanuja, together with the Saivite saints of the south and the Bhaktas of the north, yet none of the reformers 'has produced a system able to bring the people under the influence of a spiritual religion'.[474] All had in common a search for a monotheism which would lead to 'faith and love for God (*Bhakti*)' and 'most have also taught that man might enjoy pardon and salvation by God's grace, although such a doctrine runs right in the teeth of *Karma*'.[475] Such ideas underlay and inspired the *Bhagavadgita*, which Farquhar wrote was 'perhaps the greatest piece of literature that Hinduism has produced'.[476]

'Higher Hinduism' was, he declared, 'simply full of preparation for Christ.'[477] 'The Ascetic Ideal' demonstrated that Hindus more than any others knew that 'through much tribulation we must enter the Kingdom of God'; the Vedanta was 'the summit of Hindu thought'; *Yoga* expressed the words of Jesus, 'the pure in heart shall see God'; and the *Bhakti* path showed that 'the truly religious man comes into direct contact with God and lives in joyous love for Him and faith in Him'.[478] But every one of these noble conceptions foundered on the rocks of 'popular Hinduism', with what Farquhar discerned as its three baleful elements of 'idols, animal sacrifice and the priest'.[479] Equally no progress can be made toward the highest religion while the 'world-process' was conceived as 'eternal and repetitive', and while transmigration and *Karma* were held to be axiomatic, the world 'could never be conceived as the outcome of a gracious divine will active for man's good'.[480]

Thus, despite his assertions to the contrary, the tendency of Farquhar's assessment of Indian religion tended to be negative. In respect to the last three criticisms "fulfilment' had to be displacement. There had to be a clean break from the world-denying elements in Hinduism. There had to be a supersession of the root idea of *karma*. Idols, animal sacrifices and priestcraft had also to be abandoned. What distinguished this from later ideas of 'radical discontinuity' was Farquhar's other rooted conviction that only 'a religion which uses to the full' the elemental instincts so clearly manifest in Hinduism will be able to speak to the Indian soul. Such a religion will have to be one which 'transcends them and transmutes them into spiritual realities'.[481] In this way Farquhar affirmed that 'fulfilment' meant that 'searchings' and 'aspirations' of Hinduism would be met in full in Christianity.

For all their concreteness and precise scholarship, Farquhar's writings formed only one contribution among many others within the ferment of ideas at this time. From the missiological point of view they are not as important or as original as those of other writers in this section who felt the issues in a more visceral way. Farquhar had not been trained in theology and he did not feel the same pressure as his colleagues to affirm God's presence with other men and women over against the radical denial of truth in other revelation. To be sure he referred to the Letter to the Hebrews and John's 'significant use' of the Logos, but he uses both as example of how the process of 'fulfil-ment' took place. 'Fulfilment' was so common a concept within this period that we can see people like Slater, Lucas, Jones and Hume using it without Farquhar's scholastic connotations of evolution and supersession. But for all that, Farquhar still deserves to be honoured for his concern with the themes this book is highlighting. In 1910 he wrote an article for *The East and The West* on the training of missionaries in which he affirmed 'the splendid rise of the sense of personal dignity' in Eastern countries, which meant that Western Christians were no longer the sahibs and colonial masters.[482] Westerners, Farquhar suggested, had better wake up to this great new fact. Three new attitudes had to be established as a result. Missionaries had to unlearn 'the unconscious arrogance' which had become a 'race-characteristic' of the West, for the results are 'immeasurably disastrous'.[483] Second, they needed 'the stern discipline of a scientific training' to learn the 'open honest spirit' which marks the *Sacred Books of the East*. 'The harsh, aggressive tone of much missionary literature and lecturing stands in contrast with the work of the great scholars'.[484] Third, a profound study of other people's religion was more necessary than ever, because the missionary 'who had not made that study' would say 'a hundred unintelligent things' which would 'wound his audience without his realising it'.[485] The first of these desiderata is justice; the second is a new birth of courtesy, and the basis of the third is love.

C.F. Andrews: New Visions of Christ

Charles Freer Andrews (1871-1940) arrived in India in 1904, when he was thirty-three years old.[486] March 20, the date he landed at Bombay, he kept as his 'Indian birthday' until the end of his life.[487] From his very first days everything about India had him fascinated and enthralled and he began almost immediately to write in newpapers and journals about Indian affairs, always taking a 'pro-Indian stance'.[488] Justice, courtesy, and love were the keynotes of a ministry in India which ended only with his death in 1940. However, the greater part of his work in interfaith dialogue was accom-plished only after 1914 when he left the service of the SPG and went to live with Rabindranath Tagore, mingling with all kinds of Hindu groups. Through these rich and profound contacts he became in due course the inti-mate friend and adviser of M.K. Gandhi.[489]

Nevertheless Andrews' 'missionary years', as Daniel O'Connor has called them, from 1904-1914 were of fundamental significance in making him the *Dheenobandhu*, 'friend of the poor', and turning him into the Christian prophet and revolutionary thinker that India remembers today.[490] These attitudes and habits of mind arose largely from his work in the theology of religion and his sense of the importance of listening to India. This pioneering work is our chief concern now, since Andrews' influence on Christian missionary thinking and attitudes at the time of the World Missionary Conference was unique. The Hinduism section in *The Missionary Message in Relation to Non-Christian Religions* (1910) referred to Andrews even more often than Slater and Farquhar, giving exceptionally long quotations from Andrews' own words.[491]

The making of Andrews

C.F. Andrews grew up in Birmingham, where his father was an 'Angel', or minister of the Catholic Apostolic Church.[492] Andrews senior was in temperament politically Conservative and staunchly imperialist, and the family belonged to the newly wealthy middle class. Hence it could afford Charlie's relatively expensive education at King Edward VI's School in Birmingham and Pembroke College, Cambridge.

While at Cambridge Andrews made his pilgrimage away from his father's religion into high church Anglicanism, thus breaking with the millenarianism and verbal inspirationalism of his upbringing. His tutor, Charles Herman Prior, was B.F. Westcott's son-in law. and through him Andrews was introduced to the intimate family circle at the Bishop's Place in Durham.[493] Prior helped his pupil through all the vicissitudes of Cambridge religious life, notably the evangelicalism of the Cambridge Intercollegiate Christian Union, and its doctrines of eternal punishment.[494] As Andrews recalled in later life:

> It seemed nothing less than blasphemy to hold such ideas as these about the God of Love whom Christ revealed. What shocked me most of all was that He, the Saviour, was made responsible for the horrible creed of Hell. The Christ who had spoken so tenderly of the Father's care for the fall of a single sparrow, who had said that the very hairs of our heads were all numbered, who had taken little children in their arms and blessed them, was actually supposed to be the author of this monstrous doctrine of eternal torment. [495]

Here a familiar pattern in our studies of the path-finding missionaries has recurred. An open and receptive attitude to other people of faith could not be achieved until hell and eternal loss as motivations for mission had been abandoned or transmuted. In Andrews' case, apparently, this rejection of such views took place before he ever thought of his missionary vocation. Looking in a different direction, he found intellectual foundations for his faith in the teachings of Westcott and the Lux Mundi school.[496] Through his membership of the Westcott family circle Andrews formed a deep friendship with Westcott's youngest son Basil and, under the latter's influence, he was ordained in Southwark Cathedral in June 1897.

Even though B.F. Westcott had left Cambridge just before Andrews arrived, his influence on Andrews was profound and direct. [497] They met each other frequently in vacations and latter Andrews worked in the Durham diocese. From many conversations with Westcott Andrews' concern for India mounted and he became an enthusiast for the Cambridge Mission to Delhi. Andrews recalled from one of these conversations how Westcott placed India 'side by side with Greece' and how he had suggested that 'Indian thinkers would be able to interpret fully the Gospel of St John'.[498] Westcott's son Basil died of cholera in India in 1900 and for Andrews a sense of vocation to the Cambridge Brotherhood in Delhi became irresistible.[499]

St Stephen's College, Delhi, where Andrews arrived in February 1904, was the fulfilment of a dream that there should be 'an Alexandria on the banks of the Jumna'.[500] Maurice, Fairbairn and Allen each shared with Westcott a similar vision of Clement's School at Alexandria as the pattern for Christian missionary activity in the context of the great Eastern religious traditions. They each would have been happy to see how the new buildings at St Stephen's College, in Moghul style, embodied this vision.[501] In these surroundings, Andrews taught English literature and what he called 'Comparative Religion'. S.K. Rudra, the first Indian principal of St Stephen's, was Andrews' teacher in Indian things and guided him into the intellectual life of Old Delhi.[502]

In this city of the great Mughals and the Jama Masjid, Andrews met Muslim scholars like Hakim Amal Khan, Nazir Ahmad. and Zuka Ullah, all of them disciples of Sir Syed Ahmad Khan, 'the Erasmus of Delhi'. [503] There were often 'discussions' in the evenings in the Delhi Public Library which were precisely 'interfaith dialogue' in our contemporary sense. In such gatherings Andrews felt he encountered the presence of God in Sikhs and Hindus as well as in Muslims.[504] Of the Muslim scholar and mathematician Zuka Ullah he wrote much later:

He lived a life of simplicity and comparative poverty, with the consciousness of God's presence ever about him; and he left off during the greater part of his life many of the outward observances which were connected with his Islamic faith. Yet never by any word that passed from his lips in my presence (and we talked freely and intimately about these very things) did I gather that he regarded himself as other than a true Muslim. [505]

Zuka Ullah is the hero of one of the most famous anecdotes in the mythography of interfaith dialogue. 'What is the use of argument and controversy?', my old Mussulman friend once said to me, 'Tell me your beautiful names for God and I will tell you mine.' [506]Andrews met many such people who impressed him by their goodness and with whom he spoke of 'the deep things of religion'. To them he applied the words 'Blessed are the pure in heart, for they shall see God.'[507]

At this period Andrews wrote *North India* (1908) in the 'Handbooks on English Church Extension' series. It has to be said that the rest of the books in this series are conventional histories and no more. Andrews, however, took the opportunity to publicize many of his own views on the national movement and the Indian renaissance. Contemplating the needs of the Indian church, Andrews was eloquent on the need for a change in 'missionary theology'.[508] Christianity would have to stripped bare 'of its present foreign accretions and excrescences', if it was to be made indigenous: 'otherwise it will remain an exotic plant, unacclimatized and sickly, needing the continual support and prop of the West'.[509] The greater part of this revolution was needed in the area of the theology of religion:

> We must believe that God has not left Himself without a witness for the thousands of years among the most religious people in the world. We must believe that holy men of old spoke as they were moved by the Holy Ghost, and we must no longer despise the Holy Ghost by speaking slightingly of their message.[510]

Christians really had to believe that Christ was the light of the world, 'the Divine Word who is the life of men, that He himself has been enlightening every Indian coming into the world'.

> The many millions of yearning human spirits in India have had His spiritual light to guide them, before any missionary came to teach them the true message of the Incarnation. We shall then find, if not an Old Testament, yet, a true *praeparatio evangelica* in the Vedas and Upanishads, in the poetry, and in even in the legends of ancient India, as well as in the traditions of Muhammad, the utterances of the Sufi mystics, the sayings of Kabir, and the verses of the Granth.[511]

This demanded a real change in missionary methods. 'Christ's words, "I came not to destroy but to fulfil", will need to be written on all our work in letters of gold.' If there was anything of 'good report' in Hinduism, or Buddhism or Islam, and Andrews thought there was much in each of them, that needed to be taken account of and not neglected. 'We must no longer', he wrote, 'build up a wholly foreign system which turns Indian Christians into foreigners in their own country.'[512] On the contrary missionaries needed to become Indians to the Indians in order to win the Indians. 'Men and women who come out to work must be trained and disciplined in this spirit, just as they are trained and disciplined in learning the vernacular.'[513]

Another invitation, three years later, to write a textbook about mission and the 'educated Hindu classes' gave him a further opportunity to express openness and sympathy to all renewal movements in India. *The Renaissance in India* (1911) was intended to be another fairly anodyne guide to missionary work for study circles at home. Andrews used it to teach his theology of interfaith relationships and repeated his theme that 'the Eternal Word was the Light of the Buddha and Tulsi Das in their measure, even as He was in so much greater a degree, the Light of the Hebrew Prophets; that Hinduism in its higher religious history was a true *praeparatio evangelica*, even though in its lower forms it has sometimes proved unspeakably degrading'.[514] There was, he declared, in the ancient literature of India, 'much that will be treasured not less but more than before, when India finds in Christ the fulfilment of her religious ideal'.[515]

Always Andrews saw in Christianity the solution to the religious problems of India.

> Theologically the Christian faith contains the supreme and absolute doctrine of the Unity and Transcendence of God, which Islam holds so firmly; at the same time this is combined with the Doctrine of the Divine Immanence and Divine Incarnation which Hinduism has sought to realise with such pathetic yearning.[516]

In 1911 he was still hopeful that the missionary leopard might change his spots by disestablishing the Anglican communion as the state church in India, appointing Indian bishops, and abandoning the Book of Common Prayer, along with its sixteenth-century Rubrics and Articles.[517] Then, and perhaps only then there might be a future and a hope for Christianity in India, for which it would be possible to dream dreams.

> The Indian Church of the future must embrace not only every race in India but also the higher religious instincts of the people. The great heritage of the Indian past must be conserved, and this can only be accomplished by the people themselves. We who have come from the West have been slow to realise that society is an organism which cannot be pulled down and put together again like a machine. Our temptation as missionaries has always been to engage in this destructive work, expecting new life to spring up afterwards.[518]

But the missionary years were drawing swiftly to a close. O'Connor has vividly portrayed Andrews' increasing alienation from the Brotherhood and indeed the whole Anglican establishment in North India, chiefly because of his deepening acquaintance with Rabindranath Tagore and his followers in the Brahmo Samaj, with Munshi Ram (Swami Shraddhanand) and the followers of the Arya Samaj, and from late 1913 with M.K.Gandhi. [519] India was to speak of 'CFA' (Andrews' initials) as standing for 'Christ's faithful Apostle'.[520] But from 1914 this apostolate was not in the service of the institutional mission.

Andrews and the World Missionary Conference

C.F. Andrews accepted the questionnaire from the Edinburgh Commissioners on 'The Missionary Message in Relation to the Non-Christian Religions' with the same alacrity as he showed towards the invitation to write his two handbooks, *North India*, and *The Renaissance in India*. The result was a vivid piece of writing which caught the imagination of the person responsible for drafting the section on Hinduism.[521] Long sections are reprinted *verbatim* in *The Missionary Message*.

Four main themes can be seen in Andrews' Edinburgh response. They concern his christology, his sense of Indian religion as *praeparatio evangelica*, his desire for the shaping of indigenous Indian Christianity, and the transformation of the Western pattern of Christianity because of its encounter with the East.

The 'central standpoint of the Incarnation' determined his view of the church's mission. 'I now look at all human life and history', Andrews wrote, 'from the central standpoint of the Incarnation. I think more of the extension of the Incarnate life in wider and wider reaches of humanity, till all is summed up in Christ Himself.'[522] The resonance here with Westcott's themes, *The Gospel of the Incarnation* and *Christus Consummator* is apparent, but Andrews has also read the Anglican *Lux Mundi* contributors, J.R. Illingworth and R.C. Moberly.[523] 'In the New Testament the Epistle to the Ephesians and the Johannine writings have become more and more luminous and inspiring'. References to both a plentiful in the Response. One of these, which became widely used because of its citation in *The Missionary Message*, affirmed: 'I now find the *anima Christiana* in Guru Nanak, and Tulsi Das, and Kabir (according to St.John 1.9) in a way I never did before and I cannot use the word heathen as I used to do.'[524] Because Andrews' starting point was the incarnation he always repudiated any starting of Christian theology 'primarily from the Death of Christ' or making it 'consequent on the Fall' and regarding therefore 'the saving of individual souls from the punishment due to sin as the one great objective'. These echoes of F.D. Maurice are matched by a more distant one of A.V.G. Allen.[525] Andrews obviously knew himself not to be alone as he repudiated 'Latin theology' which had 'defined and confined the Faith' instead of making it 'more a matter of heart and moral apprehension' than of 'intellect and logical reasoning'.[526]

The second theme was the preparation for the gospel in Indian religion. 'The whole field of Indian theism', he wrote, 'needs working over by missionaries, and its treasures bringing to light. At present it is far too little understood or appreciated.'[527] Andrews believed the Vedanta offered correctives to crude Western theology in the areas of transcendence, individualist ideas of human personality, and in theories of creation, and could lead to a 'more balanced and complete Christian philosophy'. 'In this way', Andrews went on, 'it also may be a true preparation for Christianity as a corrective of the West.[528]

A third area he brought to the attention of the Edinburgh Conference was 'the need to use the best parts of Hindu ritual, festival, religious observance and custom' in order on the one hand to make Christianity indigenous in India, and on the other, to help the West break free from a Christianity which is 'bare and cold and puritanic'. This would be 'more in accordance with the joy in the lilies of the field, and the birds of the air which Christ expressed, – more all embracing, many-sided and in touch with Nature, more catholic.'[529]

Fourth, 'The Christian Practice of the European', wrote Andrews, 'offends at every point and in quite unlooked for directions. His extravagance, his callousness in taking life, his pride and hauteur, his materialism and general irreligion' had led to the widespread Indian conviction that the East had to teach the West not vice versa.[530] Accordingly Andrews perceived that the elements in Hinduism which it had derived from Buddhism and Jainism, 'its tenderness towards sentient life, its meekness and kindliness, and also its passionate spirit of utter self-sacrifice and devotion which it has derived from later Bhakti developments' would form 'a wonderful ethical approach to Christianity along lines which we have hardly travelled far in the West, except as individuals'.[531]

In his Edinburgh Response Andrews referred to his 'simple joy' in his Indian friends. His own courtesy and love overflowed to the point where sometime it overtook his sense of 'justice' in dealing with other aspects of Hinduism. There were those, both missionaries and visitors to India, who spoke of 'Andrewsism' and reported that Hinduism was much more evil than Andrews cared to portray it.[532] Andrews was of course concentrating upon the religion of the educated classes, as well upon the finest elements within Indian thought and culture. It was right that he, as well as other colleagues in India, Slater, Hume, Jones and Lucas, should have focussed their attention here. It is the good in the faith of other men and women that is the Christian 'problem'. Tares can be accounted for, but the wheat is not so easy to explain.[533]

We leave Andrews with some reflections of Daniel O'Connor in *Gospel, Raj, and Swaraj*. Around the time of the Tambaram Conference in 1938, he tells us, Andrews 'unceremoniously dumped' his copy of Hendrik Kraemer's *The Christian Message in a Non-Christian World* into his waste-paper basket. O'Connor continues:

> As we now, towards the end of the twentieth century come out from under the long shadow that conference cast over so much of Christian relations with people of other faiths, it is striking how in fact all the main strands in how we think about mission, as dialogue, evangelization, inculturation and liberation, along with ecumenism, are adumbrated in the thought of C.F. Andrews, as he struggled to come to terms with his Christian identity in the new context of India at the beginning of the twentieth century.[534]

His gift of friendship for Indians lay behind each of these struggles, and made him a towering figure in the search for justice, courtesy and love in inter-religious relationship.

4

The Theology of Religion at the World Missionary Conference 1910

The World Missionary Conference Comes into Being

'Edinburgh 1910' was by no means the first 'world missionary conference'.[1] The first beginnings of the desire on the part of missionaries and home agencies to take counsel from each other may be seen in the 'Missionary Conference' in Liverpool in 1860. Here a number of evangelical groups met for mutual support and edification. Perhaps even to their own surprise, they heard themselves addressed by Lord Shaftesbury as an 'Oecumenical Council'. Yet the gathering in Liverpool was structured in such away that working missionaries could confer together.[2] This was the tradition which the WMC of 1910 revived, after a series of conferences which had the very different aim of raising home support.

Thus in 1878 there had been a 'General Conference on Foreign Missions' in the Mildmay Hall in London in which all sessions were public meetings, and the missionary speakers were chosen for their ability to inspire and enthuse an audience. A pattern of conferences every ten years or so was established by the 'Centenary Conference on Foreign Missions' in 1888, again held in London.[3] Of this gathering Arthur Tappan Pierson wrote enthusiastically, 'This was indeed the grandest ecumenical council ever assembled since the first council in Jerusalem.'[4]

The term 'ecumenical' was used deliberately for the next world gathering in New York. This was the 'Ecumenical Missionary Conference', held from April 21 to May 1, 1900. At the 'century-point', there was the feeling not only that all denominations must come together in the common cause of the 'evangelization of the world', but that also they must form a global plan of campaign. This Conference met at the romantic moment of the earliest days of the twentieth century, and gathered astonishing support. In its daily sessions some 4000 people crowded into Carnegie Hall and in all, between 170,000 and 200,000 people were estimated to have attended its meetings.[5]

With such numbers attending there was no opportunity whatsoever for consultation among missionaries. As a demonstration of the alleged world-

wide 'conquest' of Christianity it was magnificent. As a sober and rational
facing up to the difficulties in the path of world-wide mission it was a complete failure. As a result there was no desire among the missionary participants at all for any follow-up of 'New York 1900'. Indeed the Ecumenical
Conference itself took no action to plan any future conferences or co-operation. As George Robson wrote, 'After the New York Conference of 1900 the
hope of another Missionary Conference after another ten years was enter-
tained by many but for the realisation of this hope no provision had been
made.'[6]

Despite this widespread lack of enthusiasm, Fairley Daly of the Livingstonia mission did approach Robert Speer of the Presbyterian Board in New
York to see if a new beginning could be made. The American-Scottish axis
was formed and Daly and Speer and their friends opted for a conference in
the capital of Scotland in the summer of 1910.[7] This would have a quite different style from New York in 1900. Edinburgh was to be a working conference rather than an opportunity for triumphalist manifestations. John R.
Mott summed up the hopes of Speer, Daly and others in 1906:

> To my mind, the missionary enterprise at the present time would be
> helped by a thoroughly unhurried conference of leaders of the Boards of
> North America and Europe rather than by a great popular convention. I
> feel strongly on this point.[8]

From the time of the first planning meeting in Edinburgh in January 1907
all preparatory work was done on this basis. Gone are grandiloquent expressions like 'General' or 'Ecumenical' in ideas for the title, but the planning
group of the conference nevertheless aimed world-wide. It named 'The
World Missionary Conference'. Its aims were succinct: 'to consider missionary problems in relations to the non-Christian world'. Note the word 'problems. Though this was the era of the slogan 'the evangelization of the world
in this generation', triumphalism formed no part of the framework within
which the preparatory committees worked.[9]

But there was nevertheless a quiet confidence in the minds of the planning
committee that the problems could be overcome. What was to happen between 1914 and 1918 was inconceivable in the years before 1910 and few
doubted the possibility of taking the gospel to every part of the world within
their lifetime. But those who shared in the task of preparing Edinburgh 1910
had a profound awareness of the magnitude of the problems surrounding the
Christian missionary enterprise. No better example of this sense of crisis can
be found than in the writings of the presiding genius of the WMC, the
American Methodist layman, John R. Mott (1865-1955).[10]

Mott's most significant book from this period, *The Decisive Hour of
Christian Missions*, was not published until after the conference, in the latter

part of 1910. It has particular value for us, nevertheless, since it contains the material that Mott collected for Commission I, ('Carrying the Gospel to All the Non-Christian World') between 1908 and 1910. The forceful analyses to be found in *The Decisive Hour* on the nature of the world situation demonstrated Mott's perception that at the end of the Great Century the church was facing a crisis, and that vast forces were ranged against it. Mott's powers of leadership arose from his sense both of the crisis and of the opportunities. Let him describe first of all the crisis.

> Throughout the whole of Asia a ferment is in process... It affects over three-fourths of the human race, including peoples of high intelligence and ancient civilisation... Among innumerable multitudes of the inhabitants of the non-Christian world the forces of youth and age, of radicalism and conservatism, of growth and decay, are seething and struggling for mastery. As we survey the unparalleled situation in these lands, the question is forced on us as to what will be the issue of it all.[11]

Mott indicated that the situation world-wide was fraught with danger, highlighting various perils. In first place was the rise of nationalism. He was convinced that the Japanese victory over the Russians at Mukden in 1905 had been a turning point in this, ensuring that in 'all parts of the non-Christian world, but especially in Asia, this national spirit has been growing, and associated with a spirit of racial pride and antagonism'.[12] This, he predicted, would have immediate consequences in relation to the task of Christian propaganda.

> The awakening of a national spirit in China tends to close the minds and hearts against everything connected with the foreign teacher. Without doubt the officials are indirectly doing much to prevent the people from accepting Christianity. Apparently they cannot free their minds from the conviction that the missionary movement after all is only another form of political activity.[13]

Mott realistically adds that the reason for this was that 'they have had experience in the past of certain forms of Christianity which abundantly explains the strength of this conviction'.[14] He went on to give examples of rising nationalism from India, in the *Swadeshi* movement and the role of the Indian National Congress and again from Africa. 'Nationalism in Egypt', he writes, 'is in most respects a pro-Moslem movement, and therefore intensifies the dislike of the Egyptian towards the foreigner and the Christian'.[15] Mott was equally prescient about the rise of new nationalist movements in southern and western Africa.

There followed a full chapter entitled 'Critical Tendencies and Influences' by which Mott meant, in his own words, 'tendencies, movements and influences... which are not only tending to close those nations against Christianity, but are placing in danger their moral and religious future'.[16] First among these were the 'corrupting influences associated with western civilisation'. What he means by this could be called ideological secularism, 'a materialising of life and a new immorality'.[17] Mott was specific in formulating the challenge to Christianity as laid down by perceptive Africans and Asians:

> You come to us with your religion. You degrade our people with drink. You scorn our religion, in many points like your own, and then you wonder why Christianity makes such slow progress among us. I will tell you. It is because you are not like your Christ.[18]

Mott pointed to the trade in intoxicants and opium carried on by the West, well aware of the 'power and machinery' of imperialism deliberately 'to defraud, to oppress and degrade native races, because of greed'.[19] He diagnosed the spiritual poverty of the West which seemed to go hand in hand with what he called 'the process of modern secular education' and the a-religious and anti-religious nature of exported western ideas.[20] But he also noted the paradox that while everywhere men and women were becoming more secularized, others of their contemporaries were becoming more 'fanatical'. His description of the resurgence of religions in 1910 has striking parallels in today's world.

> The non-Christian religions are recognising their own inadequacy and are accordingly attempting to adapt themselves to new conditions, and are manifesting increased activity, enterprise and aggressiveness. Efforts are being put forth to regain and strengthen their influences over classes which have been slipping away from their grasp and to extend their sway over peoples who have hitherto not been reached by them.[21]

Mott's commentary on the religious situation took note of Buddhism in Burma, Sri Lanka and Japan, Confucianism in China, Hinduism in both traditional and in what he termed 'Neo-Hindu' forms in India, and above all Islam, of which he wrote: 'Of all the non-Christian religions, Mohammedanism exhibits the greatest solidarity and the most activity and aggressiveness, and is conducting a more widespread propaganda at the present time than any other religion save Christianity.'[22] His world-wide survey of Islam included Turkey, India, China, Russia, the East Indies and Africa, both north and south. Mott discerned the significance of 'new religious movements' particularly in China and Japan. 'The growth of these sects is a sign of unrest among the people and their religious longings.'[23]

The Decisive Hour makes it obvious that allegations that the people of Edinburgh were blind to contemporary challenges are misguided. For them the gospel had to be offered in a 'word of conflict' just as much as did their successors in later parts of this violent century. Mott also shows us that he and his contemporaries were far from believing that all other faiths were moribund, just waiting to be replaced by the Christian faith. The question of the significance of the missionary message in relation to the non-Christian religions, therefore, was real and earnest, and Mott made sure that Commission IV would address it head-on. He personally ensured that it would have the best available human resources.[24]

Oldham joins Mott in preparing Commission IV

'The one man who more than any other engineered Edinburgh and supervised its preparatory stages was Joseph Houldsworth Oldham (1874-1969).[25] W.R. Hogg's judgment was shared by all the people present in the WMC. Temple Gairdner described Oldham in action at Edinburgh. Just beneath John Mott, he wrote,

> sat the General Secretary of the Conference, a man strangely contrasted with the Chairman. Small of stature and of unassuming face and mien, he stepped in and out of his place at the table, as one not merely unnoticed, but not meriting notice. The Chairman, though he did not intervene at the discussions, at least gave the closing address and his voice was frequently and authoritatively heard; but the Secretary, from beginning to end never opened his lips, save to give out formal notices. Why was it then that the first time he rose to give out a notice, the whole Conference applauded as though it would never cease? Some did so perhaps because they wished to show their appreciation of a triumph of organisation. But those that knew were aware, that more than any one other, the spirit that was in this very unobtrusive exterior had been at the back of the great Conference, not merely in respect of its organisation and its methods, but also of its ideals, its aspirations and its hopes.[26]

When he was appointed to be the Secretary of the Preparatory Committee at Oxford in 1908, Oldham was just thirty-four years old. Behind him lay his education at Trinity College, Oxford, where he had become a leading member of the Student Christian Movement (along with Temple Gairdner and A.G. Fraser). In 1897 he went to India as General Secretary of the YMCA in Lahore, and there married Fraser's sister Mary, daughter of Sir Andrew Fraser, Lieutenant Governor of Bengal. In 1900 he was invalided home from India with typhoid. On regaining his health he studied theology at New College, Edinburgh and in Halle, where he did some reading under Gustav

Warneck. When he had completed his theological studies he became a Secretary in the Mission Study Council and was responsible for the programmes of the United Free Church of Scotland. In these ways he had become fully conversant with every dimension of the Christian mission: through his marriage relations with Colonial Governments; with the intensely practical issues facing a YMCA worker; with the contrasting aims and methods of Anglo-Saxon and Continental missions through his work with Warneck; and with the issues facing the constituencies at home through his work with the UFCS. Oldham had also acquired powerful theological tools, not least the Kingdom-centred theology of the newly conceived and rapidly growing Student Movement, for which he had written a study book on *The Teaching of Jesus* (1896). Such were his qualifications. How did the Preparatory Commission come to choose him?

We have seen already the immense commitment and influence of the Scots in the preparation of the WMC. Leading members of the Church of Scotland and of the UFCS were appointed to the International Committee. At the last moment, one of these was unable to attend its Oxford meeting in June 1908 and Oldham (as study secretary of the UFCS) went in his place. As that meeting progressed it was clear that they needed to employ a full-time executive officer and 'by a common impulse with one accord', Oldham was elected to the job.[27]

The main task of the Oxford committee meeting was to determine the most pressing questions facing the missionary movement and to select key members for Commissions to work upon them. Eight issues were chosen including the one which concerns us, 'The Missionary Message in Relation to Non- Christian Religions'. As important was the designation of men and women to serve on the Commissions, each of which was to have twenty members with a Chairperson to guide its procedure and have the final decision in all questions that would arise. Furthermore, a Vice Chairperson would be appointed from the opposite side of the Atlantic from that of the Chair. As Robson recorded: 'To select the men and women for these Commissions was a task too important and difficult to be completed at Oxford, but so much progress was made that its completion by means of correspondence was not long delayed.'[28] What George Robson did not record is the delicacy and persuasive powers of Oldham as the new Secretary in finalizing the shape of each of these Commissions.[29]

Cairns is chosen as Chairman of Commission IV

Mott and Oldham were a formidable pair when it came to avoiding the older mistakes of the Great Century about other religions. Neither of them wanted prejudice and propaganda to be the keynotes of Commission IV. They saw the need for a Chairperson and personnel who could guide the thinking of the WMC about the nature of the Christian Gospel and the content of the missionary message. As Mott wrote in the first public announcement of the World Missionary Conference in *The East and The West*, in October 1908:

> The apologetic experiences of missionaries in relation to the non-Christian religions have been so extensive, varied and instructive that to gather them up and make their lessons available will be a service of inestimable worth. The value of this contribution will be greatly enhanced by the fact that the study is to be made by some of the ablest apologetic thinkers and writers upon both sides of the Atlantic.[30]

The choice of Chairperson had fallen upon David Cairns (1862-1946), the Professor of Systematic Theology in Christ's College, Aberdeen. Cairns was neither missionary nor involved in missionary policy making.[31] In this he was a complete contrast to Robert Speer, his Vice-Chairman, the Secretary of the Board of Mission of the Presbyterian Church in the USA. In this capacity Speer had already won the confidence of the missionary movement as we have seen in his taking the initiative for the WMC. The choice of a theologian suggests already that Mott and Oldham were looking for something more than a competent survey of the world's religions. But Cairns was a rather special theologian who had come to the attention of Oldham through their common interests in both SCM and UFCS study programmes. They had shared together in meetings of the Theological Society at New College, Edinburgh.

As in the case of the other theologians already discussed, Cairns had as a student and young minister struggled with Calvinism and modernity, and had come to understand Christianity as the Kingdom of God in conflict against evil. Describing his early searchings, Cairns wrote:

> I needed some ideal and *telos* towards which the whole vast process of Divine Providence was leading mankind, for if what I had earlier learned from Jesus of the Gospels and from such interpreters of Christianity as I had earlier accepted as mine, i.e., from such men as... Kingsley and his master, Maurice, and MacLeod Campbell were true, then human life must be a creation and education of the Family of God that should yet be... This goal I and many of the youth of my generation found in our Lord's teaching of the 'Kingdom of God' ...I began to wish to write about it, for I felt that what had emancipated me could emancipate others also.[32]

In this passage the most significant name is that of F.D. Maurice, the theologian with whom this work began. Cairns gives a full description of how his thought-world was dominated by Maurician thinking:

Maurice, whose big two-volume Life I also read, deeply influenced me and I find that of all the English Church writers of the last century, he is the one who, with all his limitations, still attracts me most. There is a considerable element in his writings which I cannot spiritually use. But there is also, to me at least, more of the spiritual and eternal content of Christian faith in him than in any other of the theologians of England of the last century.[33]

With Maurice, Cairns coupled MacLeod Campbell as the greatest Scottish theologian, by virtue of his book, *The Nature of the Atonement*.[34] Both Maurice and Campbell had led Cairns away from Pauline thinking to the Kingdom teaching of Jesus. 'It seems a very obvious thing to say,' he wrote in later life, 'but it is perhaps necessary to repeat it, that the text of the Gospels is primary... The Gospels have to make their own impression.'[35]

We have Cairns' own account of the impression that the gospel had made on him by the time Oldham had made contact:

My study of the Gospels thus confirmed what I had already learnt from Maurice and MacLeod Campbell... God must be the Universal Father corresponding to the filial call to *all mankind* of the Eternal Son. If it is our highest duty as well as privilege to follow Christ in living the filial life, and if that is true of all human beings, then God must be Father of all. Supposing our nature is either utterly corrupt or subhuman, there can be no such *obligation*. Reality must always underlie obligation. There must be that in us still which is akin to God. A *totally* corrupt being cannot be described as akin to God.[36]

What had emancipated Cairns from his doubt and unbelief as a young man was a sense that God was at work in cosmos and history. He had found an 'ideal and a *telos*' through his Christian faith.[37] Into this pattern now fell missionary literature which he found much more attractive than spiritual or contemplative writings and he described the effect of what he calls 'the aggressive hopefulness of all missionary work' upon a temperament such as his, which 'normally saw how difficult it was for good causes to go forward'.[38] But it also gave him a sense of what the Gospel was doing in the world.[39] The gospel was creating the world-wide church with the result that the church was:

pushing its influence out into all the great pagan and Moslem civilisations, leavening and changing them, creating hospitals, schools and colleges, influencing heathen chiefs and kings, destroying cruel social customs and laws, bringing peace instead of war, and so on. I felt that I had found what I was seeking for, that in the Gospel and in the Church we had the potentiality at least of effecting the enormous change which was necessary to make a real Christendom out of our very faulty, corrupt simulacrum of it.[40]

Cairns was determined to make his fresh understanding of Christianity relevant and intelligible to the student classes of his day. His first large work was *Christianity in the Modern World* (1906) which faithfully represented his addresses given to SCM and similar groups like the one at New College, Edinburgh, in which he first met J.H. Oldham.[41] *Christianity in the Modern World* made Cairns' reputation among his fellow theologians, and ensured that he would be appointed to a theological chair within the UFCS. But his ability to speak to the younger men and women of his day had been noted not only by Oldham but also by Tissington Tatlow, the highly influential General Secretary of the SCM.[42] By virtue of his office Tatlow was a member of the International Committee. Oldham and Tatlow insisted that Cairns took on this task, and Cairns had all the right qualifications for the job.

Aware, as few other theologians at this period, of the religious diversity of humankind and of the challenges this diversity brought to Christian thinking, Cairns also fought his way out of hopeless Augustinianism and scholastic Calvinism into his own version of the 'reign of God from shore to shore'.[43] Through reading F.D. Maurice and MacLeod Campbell and learning personally from Henry Drummond and Wilhelm Herrmann, he was confident that the Kingdom of God was a 'campaign against all the enemies of God and humankind... not only against sin but against disease and pain and death, and with victory lying not only beyond history in another world but also within history and this world.'[44]

The other Commissioners

In the twelve months that followed the meeting of the International Committee in Oxford in the summer of 1908, a set of Commissioners was assembled by Oldham and Mott in consultation with other members.[45] It had been decided that there should be twenty members in each Commission, with members who were based in the home region of the Chairman functioning as the executive or advisory committee in each case. Consequently the choice of the British representatives for Commission IV was a crucial matter. It was they who would have to meet frequently for consultation and discussion. Happily the British Isles were well supplied with people able to make relevant contributions to the high ideals of Mott, Oldham and Cairns. In the event the ones chosen were Henry Chapman of the home committee of the United Methodist Church in Britain, a former missionary in China; Alfred Garvie, the Principal of the Congregationalist New College in London; Richard Glover, a Baptist minister in England who was greatly involved in the affairs of the BMS;[46] Charles Frederick d'Arcy, the Church of Ireland Bishop of Ossory, Ferns and Leighlin; George Owen, the Professor of Chinese at London University; J.E. Padfield of the CMS, a former missionary among the Telegu-speaking peoples of South India; William P. Paterson from Edinburgh University; the one woman member of the Commission, Mrs G.J. Romanes of Pitcalzean in Scotland; and Charles H. Robinson of the SPG and editor of *The East and The West*. These made up the home advisory and executive committee for the Commission.

Only four Americans served on Commission IV, the Vice-Chairman, Robert Speer who was secretary to the Board of Foreign Missions of the Presbyterian Church in the USA;[47] A.B. Leonard, his counterpart in New York for the Board of the Methodist Episcopal Church;[48] E.Y. Mullins, the President of the Southern Baptist Seminary in Louisville, Kentucky;[49] and a New York pastor, Julius B. Remensnyder. In contrast the European continental representation was relatively strong: the Indologist, Wilhelm Dilger from Tubingen;[50] J.W. Gunning of the Dutch Missionary Society;[51] J. Lepsius of the Deutsche Orient Mission in Potsdam;[52] Gottfried Simon of the Rheinische Mission in Bielefeld and his colleague Johannes Warneck, the expert on traditional religion.

Seven members of the Commission need to be singled out. They were to play a more significant role than the rest because of their participation in the writing of *The Missionary Message*.

The Section on Animistic Religions was written by W.P. Paterson and Johannes Warneck. Paterson had become Professor of Divinity at Edinburgh in 1907 after thirteen years as professor in Aberdeen. He had studied in Germany and was a student of religion as well as theology.[53] Warneck was the famous son of a famous father, and had won his own reputation though his seminal work *The Living Forces of the Gospel: Experiences of a Missionary in Animistic Heathendom* (ET 1909).[54]

George Owen was put in charge of Chinese Religions. He had been one of the first wave of London Missionary Society pioneers in China, along with James Legge and Griffith John, becoming the leader of the panel of translators of the Bible into Mandarin, which was completed in 1906. In 1908 he had been appointed Professor of Chinese at King's College, London.[55] Japan was dealt with by the Irish scholar C.F. d'Arcy, the author of *Idealism and Theology* (1899), who was reckoned at the time to be the leading religious thinker of his country.[56] The choice for Islam fell upon another theologian, who like d'Arcy had no prior knowledge of the field to which he was to give his attention. Alfred Garvie was one of A.M. Fairbairn's most distinguished pupils and had substituted for Fairbairn when the latter went to India. Garvie was the author of the standard work on Ritschl at this period.[57] Gottfried Simon, from Sumatra, was asked to provide expert assistance for Garvie.[58] The seventh of David Cairns' closest colleagues was the English scholar of missions, C.H. Robinson, who was entrusted with the section on Hinduism.[59]

The task of the Commission

The meeting in 1908 of the International Committee was not fully reported, but items 4 and 6 of the Minutes indicate that the task of the Commission on the 'Missionary Message in Relation to Non-Christian Religions' had a two-fold thrust. It had first to 'set out the elements in Christianity which have most influenced non-Christians' and, second, 'to set out the Christian Apologetic in relation to (a) Hinduism, (b) Buddhism, (c) Islam and (d) animist religions'.[60] But despite the use of the word apologetic here, the Committee chose to emphasize the 'missionary message' rather than the 'missionary apologetic'. This usage made it possible for David Cairns and his fellow Commissioners to think about the nature of the gospel itself rather than merely to collate the best techniques in presenting the gospel, and Cairns and his colleagues took fully the opportunity to address ultimate religious issues, and indeed to address the complexities of inter-religious encounter.

There are no records of any of the meetings of the Commissioners. Our only evidence of the complexity of their discussions survives through the opening words of the *Missionary Message*. There the Commission said about its remits from the Executive Committee:

> Simple though this task may appear, the endeavour to carry it out reveals how intricate and how comprehensive such an enquiry should be. We have to enquire into the conflict of faith in the non-Christian lands, the influence of that conflict on the mind of the missionary, the effect of the whole upon the theology of the church at home, and the suggestions which it offers for the training of missionaries.[61]

The Questionnaire

The Commissioners felt therefore that it would be necessary to 'ascertain from the body of missionaries' what were the things that were really alive in the other religions and what 'had the power of keeping men back from Christ'.[62] The second aspect of their enquiries would be to find out from missionaries and from people converted to Christianity, what were 'the elements of the Gospel which had the greatest power of appeal' in winning and changing human hearts.[63] Accordingly they worked on a questionnaire to be circulated as widely as possible.[64] We reproduce this in full.

1. Kindly give your name, station, and the Church or Society in connection with which you are working. Name the non-Christian religion or religions with which you have to deal in your missionary work, and say with what classes of the population you yourself come into contact.

2. Can you distinguish among the doctrines and forms of religious observances current among these classes any which are mainly traditional and
formal from others which are taken in earnest and are genuinely prized as
a religious help and consolation?

3. What you consider to be the chief moral, intellectual and social hindrances in the way of a full acceptance of Christianity?

4. Have you found in individuals any dissatisfaction with their own faith on
specific points? If so, give details.

5. What attitude should the Christian preacher take towards the religion of
the people among whom he labours?

6. What are the elements in the said religion or religions which present
points of contact with Christianity and may be regarded as a preparation
for it?

7. Which elements in the Christian Gospel and the Christian life have you
found to possess the greatest power of appeal and which have awakened
the greatest opposition?

8. Have the people among whom you work a practical belief in a personal
immortality and in the existence of a Supreme God?

9. To what extent do questions of 'higher criticism' and other developments
of modern Western thought exert an influence in your part of the mission
field, and what effect do they have on your missionary work?

10. (This question was addressed to foreign missionaries.) Has your experience in missionary labour altered in either form or substance your impression as to what constitute the most important and vital elements in the
Christian Gospel?

11. (This question was addressed to converts to Christianity.) What was it in
Christianity that made special appeal to you? Did the Western form in
which Christianity was presented to you perplex you? What are the distinctively Western elements, as you see them, in the missionary message
as now presented? Was it the sense of sin which enabled you to go
behind the Western forms? If not, what was it? [65]

Along with this extensive questionnaire went an accompanying letter marked
'Strictly Private and Confidential' and signed by David Cairns personally.[66] It
began by assuming that the recipients would already have received some
information about the World Missionary Conference. Cairns set out the purpose of Commission IV as being

...primarily to ascertain the elements in Christianity which are proving most powerful in the winning of non-Christian peoples, the main hindrance to the acceptance of the Faith and the elements in the non-Christian religion which prove specially burdensome or attractive to their adherence.

This was both clear and predictable. But in pleading for their help, because of their 'expert opinions on these matters such as you can give and secure for us would be of altogether incalculable value', Cairns went on to express a view with more radical implications:

It would almost certainly influence deeply the whole future teaching of Apologetics to missionaries and would be certain also to cast a flood of light on almost every department of Theology, Dogmatics, Church History and Interpretation of Scriptures.

It was a broad hint that the Commission had its own agenda, and that for it Cairns would be glad to enlist the support of missionaries.

Assessing the replies

The Edinburgh Conference took place in the days before any kind of duplication processes had been invented, other than the printing press itself. There was no cyclostyling, no photocopying or xeroxing. Instead J.H. Oldham employed a team of typists to transcribe the answers as and when they were received. Consequently there were originally just four copies made of the sets of replies.[67] In addition to the full set of Commission IV responses which went to David Cairns and which is now in the Library of Christ's College, Aberdeen, there are other sets, more or less complete, in the Library of the Ecumenical Centre in Geneva, in the Day Missions Library at Yale Divinity School, and in the former Missionary Research Library at Union Theological Seminary, New York.[68] Each of these libraries has a different classification system for the typescripts of the replies, but happily Oldham's clerks assigned a number to identify each of them. In our analysis below, the number of each reply is cited with the relevant page numbers. Thus T.E. Slater's response will be cited as 229, followed by the appropriate page numbers.

'We believe', Cairns had concluded his letter, 'you will be glad to make this permanent contribution to the cause to which you have given your life, in view of the surpassing importance of the enquiry and the far-reaching results which, with God's assured blessing, will issue from it.' It is clear, from the extent of the replies the Commission received, that the great majority of the missionaries who were approached were delighted to be asked and glad to be taken seriously by those they saw representing their home authorities.[69]

Many and varied were the issues touched upon in their replies. Historians interested in the condition of the Muslim world from Albania (where there were in 1909 outposts of the ABCFM, and of the German Orient Mission) and throughout the Turkish Empire; or in most parts of the British Raj; or in the Indonesian Archipelago will find first-hand and expert observations in the responses from the Islamic mission field. Likewise historians of pre-1914 Africa, of British-Indian relations of the same period, or of the intellectual condition of China and Japan at this crucial era will discover invaluable resources in the replies from each of these areas. Missiologists attempting to give an account of how the gospel message was being contextualized and made at home in other religious traditions will also find vast materials available in these documents. The missionary methods of the late nineteenth and early twentieth century are chiefly responsible for the planting of Christian churches in almost every part of the world. The ways in which Christian faith came to be accepted in such vastly different situations were first worked out by these men and women. As a result of their vision and achievement the churches of Africa, Asia and the Pacific region have taken root and flourished. Everywhere they have enriched the world church by bringing out of their storehouses treasures both old and new. The insight which enabled (and still enables) them to do this has to do with the theology of religion which they also began to explore.

But in these pages the main concern is with the beginnings of inter-religious understanding, and with those who began to work out new patterns of Christian theology which might more adequately reflect the activity of God in the faith of other men and women. The replies which Cairns and his colleagues received represent the very earliest attempts within the missionary movement this century to specify how Christians might conduct themselves in relation to these other great traditions.

Their authors are people who deserve to be rescued from oblivion. More than that, their comments and insights have intrinsic value because they still speak to contemporary Christians locked in the same conflicts about the uniqueness, finality and insurpassability of Christian revelation.[70] Hints and suggestions abound in the responses for contemporary Christians' struggling to understand exclusive faith claims alongside the faith of neighbours who have different loyalties and pray and worship in different ways. The hesitations and stumbling blocks referred to in the responses are still those that face the world-wide Christian community.[71] The following pages may be treated as a raid on their articulateness or a rediscovery of what they discovered, in many cases, more than a hundred years ago.

A sense of an intellectual quest of first magnitude must come through this analysis. As we read these replies we can overhear at only one remove the passionate discussions in hill stations, on ocean liners, in missionary conferences. Cairns and his five colleagues who were responsible for compiling the

Sectional reports were taken aback at the quality of the replies they received. But along with the intellectual quality came a mind-expanding sense of the oneness of the world. Into the office at 100 Princes Street, Edinburgh, where Joseph Oldham's staff worked at the end of 1909 and the beginning of 1910 came envelopes with rare postage stamps and strange postmarks, some indeed from the most isolated post offices on the face of the globe. The romance of all this was not lost on the Commissioners. No more should it be lost on us.

Cairns and his colleagues repeatedly expressed the desire that the whole of the mass of material they received might be published. 'If the correspondence we have received from the five great fields could be made accessible to students in the fulness of its detail, its colour and clarity, we believe that its value would be universally recognised.'[72] But this was out of the question, as the Commissioners acknowledged:

> It would have been a counsel of perfection to have resolved to print the entire correspondence. It seems to us to contain material of the highest importance for the student of Church History, of Biblical Interpretation and of Dogmatics and Apologetics, and we can, further, conceive of no better introduction to the non-Christian religions than is provided by these papers, for students who are contemplating missionary work abroad. It is of course impossible to carry out so extensive a plan.[73]

The Continuation Committee which was responsible for the follow-up after the WMC seriously considered the possibility of publishing the whole of the replies. Probably it was the amount of editing the letters would have required before they could be printed that led the Continuation Committee to advise against the publication of the whole material.[74]

So here for the first time since 1910 an attempt is made to analyse and describe the replies to Commission IV. This material has to be given back to the world ecumenical movement, which for various reasons has almost lost the generosity concerning the other religious traditions of the world represented by Edinburgh 1910.[75] We hope that this extended treatment will be of value to many scholars who might well find immediate access to this material impossible.

The practical experience of encounter and dialogue with people of other faiths runs through these pages. When the mature and sensitive reflections of the missionaries were fused with the theological acumen of the home-based Commissioners one of the great reports of the ecumenical movement was created.[76] *The Missionary Message in Relation to Non-Christian Religions* may, we hope, shine with even greater vividness and clarity when placed more fully against the context of men and women who sought justice, courtesy, and love in their relations with their fellow human beings.

Analysis of Main Responses

The eleven questions formulated by the Commissioners which were sent out to their sample group have been listed in full on pages 191-192. Questions 5, 6, 9 and 10 are now highlighted as those to which the answers are most fruitful in establishing the theologies of religions prevalent among the missionary respondents.

Question 5 was directed specifically at the missionary as 'preacher': 'What attitude should the Christian preacher take toward the religion of the people among whom he labours?'. From the one hundred and fifty-seven recorded answers a set of 'guidelines' can be distilled. These could be seen as principles to be followed in presenting the gospel to followers of other religious paths.

Question 6 was framed rather tendentiously. It asked about 'the elements which might be points of contact' in the religions with which the correspondents were working. With benefit of hindsight we may judge it simplistic to have suggested that there could be such points of contact in the other religions. It begged the question whether other religions were in fact a preparation for Christianity. Even in 1910 this was a controverted issue and the implication did not go unchallenged.[77] But framed in the way it was, question six serves our present purposes well in that it gave respondents the opportunity to write fully about their theology of religion. Some made good use of this opportunity and provided lengthy statements of their position. Others offered comments and stories which served to indicate their presuppositions. Implicit in these responses are convictions about the presence of the Holy Spirit and the Divine Word within the other religious traditions.

Questions 9 and 10 proved equally valuable in eliciting a wealth of responses germane to the themes of Protestant theology of religion at the end of the Great Century. Question 9 asked, it will be remembered, about 'higher criticism' and other developments of modern Western thought, and whether they exerted any influence. Question 10 enquired if 'experience in missionary labour' had altered missionaries' apprehension of the form or substance of the Christian gospel.

We can only wonder that either question was ever put, since neither related directly to the 'how' of missionary work with which Edinburgh 1910 was supposedly concerned.[78] Each of them manifested an anxiety more related to the 'why' of missionary activity in the face of the 'acids of modernity'.[79] Certainly, from the answers to question 9, a vivid picture emerges of the widespread intellectual ferment at the beginning of this century, which was especially apparent in Japan and among Indian educated classes. More to our purpose, however, question 9 gave the missionaries a chance to reflect on the nature of the Divine purpose, as they perceived it, in their particular historical and cultural circumstances. In their answers, they made clear their understanding of the presence and activity of God in the world's religious traditions.

The presence of question 10 in the list is equally significant. It postulated a sharp distinction between 'form' and 'substance' in missionaries' understanding of the Christian gospel. The Commission itself was anxious about questions of Christian identity and essence, and what it called 'the deposit of faith in its essential nature'.[80] Yet its hint (it was no more), that there might have been a problem about the nature and content of the gospel, received short shrift from many respondents. Their tone was of astonishment and exasperation that this issue could ever have been raised. But for others this question gave opportunity to express reflections about theological and spiritual pilgrimages in the presence of the great world religions. Some of these answers read like early contributions to the famous *Christian Century* series, 'How my mind has changed'. Other respondents offered insightful comment about their changes in emphasis in presenting the Christian faith. Many of them believed that changes had to be made in the light of the questions about the gospel message raised by the people among whom they were working.

But these perceptions were by no means all that was elicited as a result of question 10. In some responses a new missiological factor is at work. By 1910 the faith of other men and women was beginning to change the way Christians understood their own attitudes and understandings. We have already met adventurous missionary theorists suggesting that Christianity had to be transposed into another key. Among the respondents are many others who had come to believe that their received Christian traditions were no longer central and determinative. For them Christianity had ceased to be a 'system of dogmas' and had become 'a spirit' and 'a life'. These respondents were already searching for a new spirituality as the basis for interfaith encounter.

'Profound sympathy and deep appreciation'

The first and clearest guideline to emerge from the responses is that other peoples' religious ways are without exception to be treated by Christians with appreciation and respect. In *The Missionary Message* itself, the five separate sections, W.P. Paterson's on 'Animism', George Owen's on 'Chinese Religion', C.F. d'Arcy's on 'Japanese Religions', Alfred Garvie's on 'Islam', and Charles Robinson's on 'Indian Religions', each have a summary conclusion to this effect. Of these the most categorical is Robinson's: 'The replies, one and all, lay emphasis on the necessity that the missionary to Hindus should possess, and not merely assume, *a sympathetic attitude towards India's most ancient religion.*'[81]

There is some evidence to suggest that 'one and all' is overstated. At least half a dozen Indian missionaries had a more negative view. Yet Robinson's exaggeration is pardonable, so overwhelmingly positive are the replies of all the others. Almost as resounding is Bishop C.F. d'Arcy's impression of the response to question 5 from Japan: 'There is perfect agreement of all missionaries who have dealt with this question as to the necessity of sympathy and understanding in relation to the old religions.'[82] This time d'Arcy does not exaggerate; such negative remarks as there are in the Japanese responses do not come in answer to question 5. George Owen's conclusion for the China section was almost identical: 'All the writers agree in saying that the missionary should treat sympathetically those forms in which religious thought and longing present themselves to the Chinese mind.'[83] But traditional religion (called in 1910 'Animism') and Islam presented greater difficulties for the missionaries of that period. Yet Paterson felt he could summarize the views of the respondents on 'animism' in these words: 'The whole attitude of the missionary should be marked by sympathy.'[84] Garvie focussed on the fundamental attitude of the Christian world to Islam, and the need for a new and much more profound knowledge of Islamic faith: 'This knowledge must be accompanied by and have its motive in sympathy.'[85] Nevertheless, neither Paterson nor Garvie was able to report a general and overwhelming response of 'sympathy and appreciation' among missionaries who worked with the 'animists' or Muslims, in quite the same way as it had come from those working among the followers of the great Asian traditions.[86]

The missionaries speak for themselves

What follows now is a catena of quotations in alphabetical order intended to allow the missionary respondents to speak in their own voices. These answers make the same point over and over again but they are set down like this to enable readers to form their own idea of the 'overwhelming impression' which the Commissioners received. (T.E. Slater, R.A. Hume, Timothy Richard, Arthur Lloyd, John Peter Jones, Bernard Lucas, J.N. Farquhar, and C.F. Andrews responded vigorously to question 5 and they should be kept in mind as part of the 'overwhelming impression' received by Cairns and his colleagues.) In each case the individual missionary and his or her background and location is identified, and further information is given in the footnotes. Unless otherwise stated, the Indian missionaries were speaking of Hinduism in one or other of its manifold forms. In China, however, the reference may be to any or all of China's three religions, Confucianism, Taoism and Buddhism. Japanese missionaries were usually referring to one of the Japanese forms of Buddhism, rather than to Shintoism. Missionaries in Africa were usually speaking of traditional religion ('animism') but occasionally of Islam as well. There are also one Chinese and four Indian Christians among the respondents. The smallness of this number represents quite accurately how few Asian Christians there were in Edinburgh. Here now is a representative selection of the positive answers to the question, 'What attitude should the Christian preacher take toward the religion of the people among whom he labours?' The references are to the individual typescripts (see above, page 193).

Samuel Ambat (Basel Mission, Malabar): 'Our attitude... should always be that of benevolence and fairness', willingly acknowledging, 'what is good and noble and divine in their faith and cult' (122, p. 15).[87]

T. Grahame Bailey (Church of Scotland, Wazirabad, the Punjab): '...an attitude of thorough comprehension and knowledge, an attitude of sympathy, admitting all the good in non-Christian religions' (125, p. 3).[88]

W.T. Balmer (WMMS, Sierra Leone): '...sympathetic, striving earnestly to understand the native conception of things' (285, p. 5).[89]

J.R. Bannerjea (YMCA, Calcutta): '...not one of wholesale condemnation but recognition of good elements in their religion' (129, p. 1).[90]

J.W. Bashford (Methodist Episcopal Bishop in Peking): 'A thoroughly friendly and appreciative attitude' (41, p. 2).[91]

James Beattie (Presbyterian Church of England, Amoy): '...open-mindedness and intelligent sympathy... full credit given to the light which the people already possess' (42, p. 7).[92]

Mrs Ferguson Davie (SPG, Rawal Pindi, a medical missionary): 'We have to find out what is good in their religions... For the foreign missionary especially, the teaching should be rather constructive than destructive' (155, pp. 27 and 24).[93]

Jerome Dean Davis (ABCFM, Kyoto): 'We should recognize the truth which is in these religions' (2, p. 5).[94]

John L. Dearing (ABCFM, Yokohama): 'One of sympathy... Never should the preacher in Japan preach against the old religions but rather appreciate all that is good in them...' (8, p. 2).[95]

Agnes de Selincourt (Zenana Bible and Missionary Society, Allahabad): 'An attitude of reverent sympathy' (224, p. 5).[96]

Courtenay H. Fenn (Presbyterian Church of the USA, Peking): 'Study it carefully, *con amore*... commend every element of truth, every high ideal to be found in it' (53, p. 6). [97]

A.G. Fraser (CMS, Kandy): '...one of sympathy' (156, p. 5).[98]

J.C. Garritt (Presbyterian Church of the USA, Nanking): 'Certainly an attitude of sympathy, of willingness to acknowledge the truths that lie mixed with error' (57, p. 4).[99]

F.R. Graves (Protestant Episcopal Church of the USA, Shanghai): '...an attitude of understanding and sympathy' (61, p. 5).[100]

D.C. Greene (ABCFM, Tokyo): 'The missionary, as well as his Japanese associate, is bound to take a sympathetic attitude towards the native religions and judge them, as he would wish Christianity to be judged, by its ideals and not by its imperfect realisation of these ideals' (12, p. 5).[101]

H.G. Grey (CMS, Punjab): 'Our attitude should be one of the greatest sympathy...' (167, p. 3).[102]

Henry Gulliford (WMMS, Mysore): 'Intelligent sympathy... sympathy with the spiritual aspiration... the liveliest sympathy... sympathetic and well-informed criticism will be most helpful. Such criticism should come from a true knowledge of the people' (168a, p. 7).[103]

F.H. Hahn (Gossnerische Mission, North India): 'The preacher should not fight it or despise it in an overbearing spirit, but should look upon it with compassion... recognising what is good in the religion of his people...' (169, p. 5).[104]

William Harris (Presbyterian Church of the USA, Changmai, Thailand): '...at all times thoughtful of the feelings and prejudices of the people among whom he labours. He should frankly appreciate the good and true element in the religion of the people...' (332, p. 4).[105]

R.H.A. Haslam (CMS, Kangra, the Punjab): 'Intelligent... Respectful... Sympathetic... Honesty... There should be a full recognition of any Element of truth in the religion...' (171, pp. 5-6).[106]

Isaac Taylor Headland (Methodist Episcopal, Peking University): '...the attitude of a friend... by being friendly toward it he may get into the heart of the native...' (62, p. 3)[107]

G.F. Herrick (ABCFM, Constantinople): 'Always an attitude of respect, and to its devotees, of profound sympathy' (264, p. 5).[108]

W.E.S. Holland (CMS, Allahabad): 'Generous and delighted in recognition of the good wherever found. No stinginess in acknowledging all of good to be found in Hinduism: no discounting or depreciating it' (177, p. 3).[109]

Franklin E. Hoskins (Presbyterian Church of the USA, Beirut): 'No matter what that faith should be the attitude of the Christian preacher should be one of sympathy, a willingness to recognize and emphasize every point of contact and likeness" (265a, p. 10).[110]

F.P. Joseland (LMS, Amoy): 'The only attitude permissible in these enlightened days is one of *profound sympathy*... sympathy not abuse is to be the keynote of our attitude to all religions' (68, pp. 6-7, emphasis his).[111]

Francis Kingsbury (South India United Church, Pasumalai): '...broad-minded and large-hearted, not only to appreciate but also to welcome truth, no matter where he finds it' (187, p. 4).[112]

John Lazarus (Danish Mission, Madras): '...deep and genuine sympathy' (192, p. 4).[113]

D.G.M. Leith (WMMS, Madras): 'Sympathy towards all that is good in it. The good represents the highest thought of some earnest soul seeking the Light' (193, p. 6).[114]

P.J. Maclagan (Presbyterian Church of England, Swatow): 'In brief, an attitude of sympathetic interpretation' (79, p. 4).[115]

J. Mathers, (LMS, Bangalore): 'He ought to make himself *thoroughly acquainted* with it – its history, and its present content. He ought to respect every manifestation of the religious spirit that is the outcome of a genuine faith, however mistaken that faith may be' (203, p. 28, emphasis his).[116]

D.A. Murray (Presbyterian Church in the USA, Osaka): 'An attitude of respect and appreciation toward the religion of the people... there are many excellencies in these religions... if it were not so they would never have gained such hold upon such large numbers of people' (32, pp. 5-6).[117]

Pandita Ramabai (Mukti Mission): 'The Christian Preacher should gladly recognize what is good and acceptable in the ancestral religions of the people' (21, p. 4).[118]

David B. Schneder (Reformed Church of America. Sendai): 'The attitude which I have been taking toward the old religions is one of respect. In the main they have been elevating' (43a, p. 7).[119]

Arthur H. Smith (ABCFM, Shantung): 'Respectful sympathy, and a study to get at the real attraction of such religion would seem to be important' (94, p. 8).[120]

J. Vale (China Inland Mission, Chengtu): 'Thoroughly sympathetic one' (103, p. 3).[121]

W.G. Walshe (CMS and CLS, Shanghai): '...that of a careful and sympathetic study of the popular religions... He should remember that he is a guest, not a conqueror' (352, p. 8).[122]

C.T. Wang (Chinese YMCA, writing from Connecticut): 'Sympathy for such religion or religions' (104, p. 5).[123]

Andrew Watson (Presbyterian Church of the USA, Cairo): 'The Christian preacher should be willing and ready to acknowledge all that is good in non-

Christian systems, whether on the lines of doctrine or precept... His attitude should always be conciliatory...' (280, p. 5).[124]

George Whitehead (SPG, Burma): 'The missionary should rejoice in every element of truth and goodness that he finds in the religion and the practice of the people with whom he has to deal' (252, p. 6).[125]

S.M. Zwemer (Reformed Church of America, Bahrain): '...the missionary should cultivate sympathy to the highest degree and an appreciation of all the great fundamental truths we hold in connection with the Mohammedans' (283, p. 5).[126]

In this by no means exhaustive A to Z sample of Christian missionaries and four of their Indian and Chinese colleagues we note the constant use of the words 'sympathy', and 'appreciation'. Set against the background of the world-views outlined in the first chapter of this book these forty replies (out of one hundred and eighty seven) are not less than stunning. A sea change has taken place. To be sure most of the comments did go on to speak of truths and insights as mixed with error, or being buried and hidden, or having to be complemented or fulfilled. They remain the views of missionaries, and missionaries want to change people. But entirely missing is the note of condemnation of superstition and idolatry.

There is another point to notice. The question put to missionaries asked about the attitude of the missionary to the religious systems – Buddhism, Hinduism, Confucianism and so on. Later insight has come to question such an emphasis, insisting that inter-religious understanding should focus upon people rather than the systems that they follow.[127] We can see even in 1909-10 many respondents (Gulliford, Harris, Herrick, Murray, Taylor) instinctively couching their replies in terms of people rather than systems. This instinct for the personal rather than the abstract found full articulation in the correspondence and we treat it under the heading 'Identification and Solidarity'.

Identification and solidarity

'The first word of the Gospel' wrote Robert Hume to the Commissioners, 'is the word Brother, never the word Sinner, nor even the word Christ, as is sometimes imagined' (180, p.9). Many other missionaries wanted to express a similar sense of solidarity with those among whom they worked. Wilfred Barbrooke Grubb, known as the 'Livingstone of South America', and the only representative of workers on that continent among all the Edinburgh respondents, particularly condemned the 'prevalent tendency' of the 'white races to sneer at Indians, and almost to deny them the privilege of being man at all' (316, p. 7).[128] Missionaries, he believed, had to 'abstain from any superior aloofness' and impress upon the South American Indian people that the 'hearts of all are the same in the sight of God' (ibid., p. 8). This insight profoundly affected Grubb's strict evangelical theology. He was against condemning 'too rigorously heathen customs and ideas' (ibid., p. 7), and was positively for recognizing 'anything that is good in heathenism' (ibid., p. 6), producing a memorable epigram: 'In order to lighten a dark room, we need not sweep out the darkness, but simply let in the light' (ibid., p. 7). Ferdinand Hahn, of the Gossnerische Mission, wrote of the religion of Oraon or Karukh peoples in North West India as 'the attempt of human beings to grapple with the great questions of our life: whence the evil? whence death? what's to be done to get rid of it, to receive comfort, to secure peace for the hereafter?' (169, p. 4). For Hahn, key adverbs were 'gently' and 'patiently', as he spoke of recognizing the beginning of spiritual life in them: 'The preacher should understand that he has to do with fellow men who are groping in the dark after the light, who are waiting in the dim light of the stars for the rising of the sun, who are struggling to get out of the mire and to set their feet on a rock' (ibid., p. 5).

A similar reply came from Bishop J. E. Robinson, an American Methodist missionary in Bombay.[129] In writing of the need for 'deep sympathy' Robinson referred to the need to 'dwell upon the deep, underlying, common needs of our spiritual nature' rather than to 'inveigh against the wickedness and absurdities of the other religions', for 'these represent the earnest effort and heart struggles of countless multitudes of human beings during many generations to find, to propitiate and please God' (217, pp. 7-8). Robert H. Nassau, with no less than forty-five years experience in Equatorial West Africa, stressed the urgency of a proper attitude towards the people: 'I have known missionaries who have come with only a feeling of hard duty towards degraded fellow-members of the human race. They felt a personal antipathy to colour, dirt, vermin, and ugly faces. Unfortunately they showed their antipathy in their manners' (303, p. 11).[130] Nassau commented: 'They filled a certain niche on the roll of station members; but never had an influence for good. Rather, some of them, by their harsh words or curt manner, brought only evil to the missionary name' (ibid., p. 11).

Strong criticism of such lack of courtesy and sympathy on the part of some missionaries was also voiced by George Lefroy, Anglican Bishop in Lahore.[131] He wrote to the Commissioners of 'a very widespread failure, as it seems to me, on the part of the Missionaries to enter into genuinely brotherly and equal relations with Indian Christians...' (190, p. 21). He told of 'a degree of positive harm done, by want of courtesy and kindliness and tact', and gave this example:

I can think of one or two men, priests in our own communion – perfectly genuine, hearty bluff men – who might very likely do admirable work in one of the Colonies, amongst our own kinsfolk where their want of refinement, breeding and good manners would not be so much noticed – but who for Indians are simply impossible people, outraging the Indian instincts of courtesy and good manners at every moment of their lives and 'widening the gulf' in the most appalling way. For men of this type – be their essential honesty and desire to serve their Lord what it may – *we have no place whatever in India* (ibid., p. 22).

Lefroy sounds here like the upper-class Englishman he in fact was, but his point was and is still valid. Courtesy is of the essence in interfaith dialogue, and by 'courtesy' Lefroy himself meant a genuine warmth of love and personal regard. He set out graphically what he intended:

What I mean was well put by a Missionary in an address to Missionaries given some years ago in Lahore. He said it was very nice to see pictures of Missionaries with their arm, perhaps, around the neck of some convert, or in a brotherly attitude of some kind – but he noticed that it was always the Englishman's arm which was around the Indian's neck, never the converse position, and he could not help longing that we should sometimes see something of that too (ibid., p. 18).

Lefroy thus anticipated that cry of anguish from V.S. Azariah which made so indelible an impression upon the Edinburgh Conference itself.[132]

Fellowship, and solidarity with 'fellow-members of the human race', were absolutes. Virtues like 'winsomeness' (G.P. Taylor, Irish Presbyterian in Bombay);[133] 'friendliness' (Bishop James W. Bashford in Peking), and 'understanding' (Bishop F.H. Graves in Shanghai) are highly rated in the responses. J.H. Wherry, an American Presbyterian in Peking,[134] advised having a 'quiet, eirenic, compassionate' bearing and J.C. Young (United Free Church of Scotland in Aden) a 'respectful' one.[135] Sidney Gulick (ABCFM, in Kyoto) applied this to the missionaries' public behaviour: 'We should show our real and deep respect for the "heathen" religions; we should take off our hats at their shrines – as we expect them to do in our churches' (15, p. 5).[136] All these counsels are summed up in the word 'love'. As Elwood Morris Wherry, an American Presbyterian in Ludhiana, North India, noted: 'It is love that wins', adding: 'Of course controversy is sure to arise, but we strive to keep it within the limits of a friendly and sympathetic discussion' (251, p. 3).[137]

How this was worked out in practice may be seen in the many references to personal friendships in the responses. The Dutch American David B. Schneder in Sendai, Japan, wrote:

Among my personal friends are some Buddhist and Shinto priests. I enjoy these friendships which are profitable and instructive to me. I also attend the funerals of friends that are conducted according to the Buddhist and Shinto ceremonies. I think an attitude of respect and friendliness is good (34a, pp. 7–8).

There is also a great insistence in the responses that meeting the people of other faiths is more important than reading books about their religions. Campbell Moody (Presbyterian Church of England in Formosa) devoted his answer to question 5 almost entirely to the issue of how one should familiarize oneself with the outlook of the people. Reading books, he thought 'goes very little way' (81, p. 5).[138] Similarly, William Shedd (American Presbyterian, Urmia, Persia) made this explicit statement, which anticipated Wilfred Cantwell Smith and the WCC Guidelines by nearly sixty years: 'We meet Moslems and not Islam' (272, p. 15).[139]

'Not to disfigure the image of our neighbour'

Last, we note in the responses many and varied expressions of respect for the spirituality belonging to the different peoples of the world. In 1910 examples of this came mainly from Indian, Chinese and Japanese contexts, but not exclusively so. One example will suffice. Arthur H. Smith, a veteran leader in China, wrote of the Chinese that they are not just as 'impressible by spiritual truth as we Occidentals are but often far more so. Deep religious conviction, strong emotion, and the capacity for high resolve are as real in China as in any country in the world' (94, p. 11).

Dialogue can be recognized as a welcome way of obedience to the commandment of the Decalogue: 'You shall not bear false witness against your neighbour.' Dialogue helps us not to disfigure the image of our neighbours of different faiths.[140]

So stated the WCC *Guidelines* in 1979. But the spirit behind these words had been captured seventy years previously by the American Presbyterian missionary, Courtenay H. Fenn, Professor of Systematic Theology in the North China Union Theological College in Peking. He wrote, as we have seen, that the study of another person's religion was to be done carefully and with love, and that every element of truth and every high ideal in it was to be commended. This had to be done not merely by means of books, but also by 'interviews with its most intelligent devotees' as well as with its ordinary adherents (53, p. 6).

Reverence must be encountered by reverence

The English Methodist missionary, W. Arthur Cornaby, a colleague of Timothy Richard in the CLS in Shanghai, insisted that the 'fullest justice had to be done to Chinese religious thought' (145, p. 19). He went on to stress that 'the ancient writing of China, for which we are indebted to Confucius as "transmitter", contains many a passage on the majesty, righteousness, and goodness of God' (ibid., p. 20).[141]

Other scholar-missionaries made similar points to the Commissioners. 'An unsympathetic student of the Gospels invariably misinterprets them, the same is true of an unsympathetic understanding of other faiths', wrote T.E. Slater in his reply to question 5, (229, p. 51). Campbell Moody in Formosa wrote that as a result of the kind of scholarly and constructive methods he was suggesting, 'sometimes the preacher will commend the teaching of Confucius, and even of Buddha' (81, p. 11).

'As genuine fellow-pilgrims'

The WCC *Guidelines* (1979) were clear that Christians had to assure their partners in dialogue that they come 'not as manipulators but as genuine fellow-pilgrims', to speak with them 'of what God has done in Jesus Christ'.[142] 'Asking a fair judgment', 'comparing the best with the best', 'like with like' and similar themes recur in the Edinburgh Responses. Even more impressive is the presence of suggestions that the Christian revelation had something to discover or rediscover through encountering other forms of faith, elements of truth of 'vital importance', which had to be 'conserved and even emphasized'. We have seen this in the case of John Peter Jones in South India.[143] These stirrings were one aspect of a rising spirit of receptiveness to other people's 'faith', or 'spirituality'. The examples which follow would have carried the assent of many other missionary respondents.

William Shedd provided this statement of the issue:

A sympathetic attitude in religious matters implies first of all a readiness to learn from others truths which we have not apprehended; and I fully believe that in our contact with Orientals we can find something to learn. It implies also a readiness to put the best construction possible in honesty and truth upon the practices and doctrines of the non-Christian religions (272, p. 13).

In contrast to many others among his fellow-missionaries in Muslim lands, Shedd was able to speak of Islam as a 'living faith' and having within it elements of 'genuine faith' (ibid., p. 1).

From North China the Canadian Presbyterian Murdoch Mackenzie was clearly a forerunner of contemporary theories of inter-religious dialogue.[144] Seventy years later a WCC *Guidelines* principle suggested that 'Partners in dialogue should be free to "define themselves" in their own terms.'[145] Mackenzie affirmed a corollary of this: that Christians 'should seek so to state the case for the non-Christian that the latter would gladly accept the statement of it and make it his own' (78, p. 12). The 1979 *Guidelines* continue that this 'is of primary importance since self-serving descriptions of other peoples' faith are one of the roots of prejudice, stereotyping, and condescension'. 'Christianity', wrote Mackenzie seventy years before, should make all its preachers

> sympathetic, patient, ready to learn, willing to put themselves in the place of those whom they address, desirous of knowing the exact truth concerning the particular system met, the precise influence it exerts over its adherents, what in it accounts for their belief in it, what it has stood for which is now to its credit, and how to lead those holding it to firmer standing ground, fuller knowledge, and holier life (ibid., pp. 10-11).

Only a proper attention to the other person would bring this about:

> the missionary may have read Books which inclined him strongly to opposition to the non-Christian religions or *vice versa*. He knows that much in the ordinary religious life of many in the Home lands is not quite in harmony with their Sacred Scriptures. The facts in the Books stand. So does the lack of harmony with these in the life. Every missionary should be of an enquiring turn of mind. Subjects deserving of such an attitude, and imperatively demanding it, are met with continually (ibid., p. 11).

Mackenzie spoke of the element of 'discrimination' in such 'listening': 'Indiscriminate praise or censure, acceptance or rejection, are to be deprecated by calm, candid minds' (ibid., p. 12). 'It has', he wrote, 'been intensely disappointing to me to find some missionaries seemingly ever ready to see good in the non-Christian religions and ready to criticize their own' (ibid., p. 12). Yet this was not his final word, for he added immediately that it had been just as disappointing to 'meet those who can see nothing worthy of attention in those systems' (ibid., p. 13).

Three further testimonies come from India, where, more than in any other region, respondents believed there was something to be learnt from another faith-tradition. There was the strongly held view of the American Methodist, J.H. Messmore in Pauri.[146] He wrote in answer to question 5 that a Christian should not entertain, still less give utterance to, the idea that non-Christian faiths are 'the deliberate invention of evil-minded men'. He went on to say that the missionary

> should always consider that the various creeds and systems are the result of man's search after God – sympathy, consideration, appreciation, and the broadest charity should characterise all his references to other faiths. He should always remember that he himself has no monopoly of the truth, and that there is much valuable truth in all the great non-Christian religions (203, p. 3).

Messmore also affirmed the liberalizing influence which mission work in India could have on the missionary: 'his belief in the vital elements of Christianity grows strong; but he learns that the Jew and Christian are not the only ones to whom messages from God have come' (ibid., p. 4).

The theme 'no monopoly of the truth' was expressed in theoretical and philosophical terms for the Commissioners by A.G. Hogg.[147] In 1910 he was a relatively new professor at the Madras Christian College. When he wrote his response, his important contribution to the critique of 'fulfilment theology' had yet to be worked out. But, in 1910, after just over six years in India, Hogg was clear that 'the missionary has no right to assume that his beliefs are the ultimate truth' (176, p. 19). He showed in two sentences a precise understanding of interfaith dialogue. Reflecting first upon his encounter with faithful Hindus, Hogg asserted that in this situation the missionary's 'attitude will be one of respectful enquiry and even perplexity' (ibid., p. 16). Hogg wrote that 'the missionary will make them feel that he recognizes them as children of God like himself, loved of the Father and blessed by Him in virtue of their trust. Also he will maintain in himself, and allow them to perceive in him, a willingness to learn from them new lessons of faith and life' (ibid.).

Hogg formulated the relationship in these words: the missionary and the Hindu should be regarded 'as equally pilgrims of faith but having much to learn from each other' (ibid., p. 17). Hogg noted that if the missionary's own 'private conviction is that, in respect of beliefs, he has more to teach than to learn, he will at least acknowledge that they have similarly a natural right to suppose their beliefs superior to his own' (ibid., p. 17). But 'at the same time he will not conceal from them that he thinks that they have somewhat to learn from him, and that if they could exchange some of their beliefs for his, their faith in God would thereby win a deeper inspiration and a new fruitfulness for themselves and for others' (ibid., p. 16). Eventually this was to be called, by the 1979 WCC *Guidelines*, 'authentic mutual witness'.[148]

'Authentic mutual witness' and a 'willingness to be candid'

Many others among the respondents agreed with Hogg. While totally committed to sympathy and appreciation, they were deeply concerned about what they saw as indiscriminate praise and acceptance of other religious traditions.

Thus Mrs Ferguson Davie, a medical doctor in North India, was perturbed by what she called 'the present age of broad ideas of free thinking' (155, p.27). Although she had in mind Europeans in India who were not missionaries, she expressed a general concern lest 'the spirit of sympathy' which 'has grown of late years' should go too far: 'One hears such expressions "All religions have a great deal of good in them"; or "all religions are the same at bottom" or "Their religions are best suited for them"' (ibid., p. 26). She had heard people 'read selected extracts from the Koran and pronounce it to be a magnificent book, the fine points being of course those selected', (ibid.). She was sure that missionaries 'have to find out what is good' in other religions, but had also 'to show what is better in Christianity' (ibid., p. 27). The American Methodist Gideon Draper, of Japan, while urging the discovery of 'the best in the beliefs of the people' cautioned against an 'undue adulation': 'There can be no successful compromise with any system of error' (9, p. 2).[149] Duncan Leith, an English Methodist in Madras, wrote that in expressing sympathy to all the good 'one has to be careful to show that it is not an easygoing tolerance that blindly agrees to all'. 'Our words', he adds, 'are sometimes given a wider meaning than we intend' (193, p. 7). These last words would have carried the assent of Copland King, an Australian member of the SPG at work in New Guinea.[150] He commented that if too great a sympathy or appreciation of the old religion is shown, 'the convert will consider that there is no need for him to resign (*sic*) or fight against what exercises such a hold on his teacher' (328, p. 7). Samuel Zwemer, from the Reformed Church in America, who became the first Editor of *The Muslim World* in 1913, urged the cultivation of the highest degree of appreciation and sympathy with Muslims. But, having granted that the Christian should admit 'the excellencies of doctrine and life in Mohammedanism' (283, p. 5), he went on to say that, while there is every reason to avoid giving offence, 'compromise will not win the respect of Moslems' (ibid., p. 5). A fellow American, Henry M. Woods (Presbyterian Church of the USA, Hwaianafu), concurred:[151]

Experience shows that there is nothing more harmful than a compromising spirit which would adapt the Gospel to heathen beliefs, which deals in vague reassuring speeches that there is much good in all, and that a heathen will not go far wrong who follows his own system' (113, p. 8).

Such sentiments, said Woods, are not in line with what he called the 'sincerity of the Gospel' or with 'declaring the whole counsel of God'. Woods adduced in his support of this answer a range of biblical texts from Acts 20.20-27 through. to Galatians 1.8-10 and I Thessalonians 2.4-7 to II Timothy 2.24-26 (ibid., pp. 7-8).

A similar instinct for biblical justification found expression in the joint reply of President Kajinosuke Ibuka and William Imbrie, who wrote from the Meiji Gakuin, the college of American Presbyterian Mission in Tokyo.[152] They used, as did many others, the account of Paul's Areopagus speech in Acts 17. Ibuka and Imbrie interpreted Paul's approach to the Athenians as 'open-minded and tactful'. 'He willingly recognized the truth that men feel after God and they find something of him. The Christian preacher in Japan should take the same attitude towards its non-Christian religions; and with the same willingness' (17/19, p. 6). But Paul was not only open-minded and tactful; he had also been candid: 'He told the same Athenians that they worshipped an unknown God in ignorance.' Adducing other examples of Pauline candour from the correspondence to the churches in Corinth, Galatia, Ephesus, and from the speech before King Agrippa in Acts 26, Ibuka and Imbrie specified: 'The Christian preacher to the Gentiles in Japan should take for his example the Apostle to the Gentiles no less for his candor than his open-mindedness and tact' (ibid.).

William Ambrose Shedd of Persia was a fine exponent of a dialogical approach to mission which involved both listening and speaking. Concerned that his encounters with people of other faith should become the means of authentic witness in which the Christian missionary would 'deliver something new and true' (272, p. 13), Shedd stated: 'In order to do this, he will need to know the points of agreement in order to find as broad a basis as possible for discussion; but his real aim will be to find points of divergence. This purpose is not destructive but constructive. So far as old faiths are true they should of course be confirmed; so far as they are defective... and erroneous' they should be challenged 'in order to secure a hearing for the Gospel'. This had not to be done in a way which would alienate and repel, but simply as a matter of truth and integrity. He added that there was 'much danger of ignoring real differences because they are hidden by superficial resemblances' (ibid., p. 14). Writing a little later of the 'broader question as to the place of the faiths of the world in God's self-revelation and in His redemption of the world' (ibid., p. 15), he made this careful statement of his own faith-commitment:

I believe that Our Lord is in truth the Sun of Righteousness and that the extinguishing of the moon and stars is not required to prepare for his Rising, but on the other hand, the Sun has no need of moon or stars in order to illuminate his Coming. The names of Buddha, Mohammed and many others of less fame may be regarded as worthy of great honour and yet not worthy of comparison with Christ. I would distrust *a priori* judgments based on theological theory, and give the religious leaders and religious systems every right to a fair hearing; but fairness implies readiness to condemn as well as to commend (ibid., p. 16).

Shedd's words take us into an analysis of Christian 'theology of religions'. A theology of religions, negative or positive, is determinative of the way Christians behave towards people of other faiths. But it is not merely read off from texts or traditions within the Christian past. The 'theology of religions' can only be done as and when Christians feel the pressures to interpret the presence of holiness, wisdom, truth, spirituality and justice among those who do not name Jesus as Lord. Otherwise such theology and theologies remain abstractions, with concomitant abstruseness and ultimate irrelevance.

Many religious paths

First we turn to theological views which hinted at 'pluralism', where Christianity is understood as neither excluding nor including all other religious views, but rather as being one religious path among all others. In pluralistic thinking people may be 'saved' through living up to the highest ideals of these religious paths. Pluralism in this sense often carries a further implication that all religious traditions are needed to interpret completely the relationship between the divine and the human. To look for anything like this kind of pluralistic theology in the Edinburgh responses is an unlikely enterprise, like hunting parrots in Norway or polar bears in the Sahara. Missionaries who had been sent in order 'to make Heathens into Christians' were not predisposed to arrive at the conclusion that there were other paths to God than their own.

Yet surprisingly, there are some hints of pluralistic thinking in the responses. To be sure they are hardly more than the beginnings of theologies, underdeveloped in themselves and scarcely noticed by those who first read the replies. Nevertheless hints they were, and it is important to see that the movement which began in missiological circles with some of the speeches at the International Missionary Conference at Jerusalem in 1928, and which continued in the work of W.E. Hocking and the *Laymen's Report* in 1934, had missionary precursors.[153]

One indication of a pluralist tendency is a favourable citation of Max Müller. The CMS missionary Duncan Dixey, at work in the remote North West of India, suggested in his answer to question 5 that 'sympathy' meant 'treating other religions as less perfect revelations'.[154] To support this view, Dixey quoted Müller: 'Other religions are languages in which God has spoken to man and man to God' (329, p. 2). As remarkable are the views of the Welsh Baptist missionary in North India, W.R. James.[155] In answer to question 5, James declared that the attitude missionaries ought to take towards other faiths is 'unquestionably one of great sympathy with those who sincerely believe them and of never yielding hostility to everything that is false' (183, pp. 11-12). This unexceptionable sentiment on James' part was, however, surrounded by a cluster of pluralistic remarks. In describing idol-worship, James asserted that Hindus were not adoring senseless images, but rather expressing a true belief in a 'prayer hearing God': 'I should be sorry to say', he wrote, 'that during the time of ignorance at which God "winks" that he has never heard a petition addressed to an idol' (ibid., p. 2). He thought that Islam, and the new theisms of the Brahmo Samaj and the Arya Samaj did unquestionably 'minister a good deal of spiritual help to those who implicitly accept them, and kindle some amount of hope in the hearts of such' (ibid., pp. 4-5). On the approach of the missionaries to other traditions James commented that they erred 'in the past through indulging too much in denunciation of other faiths', referring the Commissioners to the example of Jesus: 'Our Lord did not tell his disciples when he sent them out into the world to preach to denounce any system. What he told them was to preach the gospel' (ibid., p. 12). In words reminiscent of those of Barbrooke Grubb, James affirmed: 'Darkness cannot be driven out by pounding it with a hammer or sweeping it with a broom' (ibid., p. 12).[156] Then he went on: 'It is rather remarkable that the Bible never calls a religion false. It calls men false prophets, false teachers, false brethren and so on, but never calls any religion false as long as men believe in it, and act up to the light they have' (ibid., p 13). His final question 'While they believe it with all their hearts, can it be false for them?' (ibid., p. 13) comes very close to the famous adage from the phenomenological study of religion, 'the believer is always right'.

These were remarkable opinions to come from missionaries belonging to pronouncedly evangelical societies, and who remained themselves, according to their own testimonies elsewhere in their responses, distinctly evangelical in theological outlook. Quakers, however, were not evangelicals, and might be expected to hold different views. The teaching of the 'Inner Light' lay behind the emphasis on the mystical element in Indian religion in the response of the Society of Friends' missionary from England, Joseph Taylor.[157] Taylor approved of Charles Cuthbert Hall's *Christ and the Eastern Soul*, where 'the mystical elements in Hindu thought' were 'so beautifully brought out' (237, p. 8).

Joseph Taylor was not the only respondent who spoke in praise of the mystical element in the religious encounter, and Duncan Dixey and W.R. James were far from being the only ones to discern God at work in the other religions of humankind. Their affirmations fitted in well with the thrust of the remarks of the greater part of their fellow respondents. Yet these colleagues moved much more in the direction of 'inclusivism' rather than 'pluralism'. We turn then to see how this inclusivism was conceptualized.

We have already seen how Maurice and Westcott, Fairbairn and Allen, and to a lesser extent, Cuthbert Hall had begun to provide different kinds of 'tools' and 'building blocks' for the task of constructing a positive theology of religion. But for the working missionary the task of constructing such theology was never completed. It could only be done in moments of respite from more pressing commitments. It was as a rule attempted in isolation from congenial intellectual company and usually far away from adequate libraries. Often it was theology done literally 'at a 120 degrees'.[158] Yet this task was seen by many as central if the Christian message were to take root in their contexts. The Edinburgh questionnaire opened the gates for a flood of sober and realistic reappraisals of missionary theology.

We have indicated that asking working missionaries about 'Higher Criticism' and other aspects of modern Western thought in question 9 was a stroke of genius. The Commissioners were to be sure interested in the effect that intellectual currents in the West were having upon the recipients of the missionary programme. Did such movements hinder the missionary proclamation? Most respondents read the question like that and answered accordingly. But there were some who read question 9 in conjunction with question 10 and replied with some vigour, affirming the benefits of 'Higher Criticism' and 'modern Western thought'. New movements within theology and philosophy had enabled them to think in news ways about 'revelation', 'spirituality', and 'goodness' among people of other religious traditions.

Evolution the category of the age

The scientific concept of 'evolution' matched 'progressive revelation' as a theological idea which in turn measured up against notions such as 'the education of the human race'. All three conceptions were foundational for the new theories of revelation outside the Christian framework. All the missionaries responding to the Commission, even those with forty years service, had known of evolution from the very beginning of their work (Darwin had published *The Origin of the Species* in 1859). As J.R. Illingworth wrote of the 1880s and 1890s, 'Evolution is in the air. It is the category of the age.'[159] Certainly some of the older missionaries were vehement in their rejection of Darwin and his theories, but many had clearly seized the opportunity offered by this new 'category' to reformulate their ideas about God's working in the religions and cultures they knew well. Far away from the libraries of Oxford, Cambridge, Yale, Harvard, Halle or Tübingen, they addressed the issues which increasingly pre-occupied European and North American theologians.

W.H. Campbell, for example, had worked for twenty-four years with the LMS among the Telegu people of South India.[160] He described his reason for his evaluation of other religious traditions even when they took 'crude' and 'seemingly futile' forms: 'This is due to the acceptance of the evolution idea, and the conviction that behind all evolution there is God' (133, p. 16). Campbell reflected on the theological change which had led to the 'general recognition of life in this world as an education rather than as a period of probation' (ibid.). This he considered had in turn brought about 'a fairer and kindlier estimate of non-Christians and Christian converts', and had 'enabled missionaries to take a more hopeful view of the results of their work' (ibid.). He thought that 'most missionaries' connected with the LMS, 'who have accepted the results of intelligent criticism' recognize in their teaching and preaching 'the fact that there has been a change in theological thought' (ibid.). Among them were Lucas, Slater, and Farquhar, all of them fully committed to evolution as a category for understanding religion.

There was firm acceptance of the implications of 'evolution' in Japan and China. There was, for example, the answer to question nine from Basil Wood, a CMS missionary in Osaka.[161] He wrote that nothing would be quite so calculated 'to stem the alienation of the educated classes from the Christian Faith' in Japan as a frank and humble welcome for 'the revelation of God's mind and will through the study of history and nature', along with which should go a 'willingness to modify older thoughts in the light of newer thoughts' (37, p.8). The American missionary thinker Sidney Lewis Gulick told the Commissioners that 'Our Kumiai Christians (pastors and educated men) are very sensitive to all western discussions of Christianity from a historical and critical standpoint' and thought that they were 'more keen to follow current discussions than the pastors of our home churches' (15, p.6). Clearly approving of the Japanese Christian readiness 'to follow radical teaching', Gulick recommended the Commissioners to read chapter two, 'The Modern Standpoint', in Bernard Lucas' *The Empire of Christ* 'which pleases me much' (ibid., p. 7).[162]

From China there came the views of Frank P. Joseland (LMS, Amoy). With twenty-two years' experience of Chinese work, and with a sharp perception of the preaching of some of his contemporaries, Joseland couched his reply as a warning: 'Personally I fear that if the *scientific attitude of absolute loyalty to Truth* is not made to embrace the Bible and all religious Truth including what we called the "Evangelical Faith", there is bound to be serious trouble in store for the Christian Church in China in the near future (68, p.10, emphasis his).

Arnold Foster, a Cambridge graduate and another LMS missionary, welcomed evolutionary categories when applied to the Old Testament ('the Bible is a record of progressive revelation' (54, p.20).[163] Such views had, he affirmed, 'considerably' modified the method of teaching the Old Testament in China, and helped in the communication of Christian faith itself. For support in this view Foster referred to his Cambridge teachers B.F.Westcott and F.J.A.Hort (ibid., pp.18-19).

One of the few Lutherans to be found within the body of the Edinburgh respondents was F.W. Steinthal.[164] He graduated in theology from Copenhagen in 1886, and had come to India at the age of thirty-five, when he joined the 'College Branch' of the YMCA. His contribution to the Edinburgh Commission took the form of a series of essays. How much these were appreciated by the Commissioners may be seen by their constant quotation within *The Missionary Message*.[165] Concerning theological developments in his day, Steinthal wrote: 'We are all indebted to the modern researches for a truer view, deeper understanding, and clearer insight, not only into many details, but also into the whole life of the Bible' (234, p. 35). He continued:

> The historical development of God's revelations of His dealings with Israel and with individuals, the relation between the subjective receptivity and objective revelation, the historical character of the Biblical facts in their certainty and limitation, God's use of human agencies and means in the psychological and sociological development, all that makes God's revelation a more living and practical reality should be a help in mission work, and no missionary society should withhold this help from the new missionaries in their training institutions at home (ibid.).

Such preparation, Steinthal thought, was not only necessary to help them interpret the Christian scriptures properly but also, in its implications, to enable missionaries 'to respect the old religion' as 'the expression of the highest and divinest in the people's life, the remnant of God's image, the search for the living God' (ibid., p.16).

The work of God in the world's living religions

But evolution was not the only category available to the Edinburgh respondents in the search for a theological understanding of the place and purposes of other religious traditions, even if their early twentieth-century understanding of the processes of evolution and the long-term 'education of the human race' inevitably lay behind their use of more ancient ideas like the universal working of the Logos, or the Divine Wisdom, or the Holy Spirit. Many of them made valiant efforts to disentangle themselves from nineteenth and early twentieth-century thought-forms in order to recapture elements within traditional theologies, whether biblical or patristic.

Such missionaries spoke of God's activity within other religious traditions as the working out of salvific purposes. Figures like Muhammad, Confucius, Gotama and Kabir were prophets sent from God or in other ways agents of the divine activity. The American Methodist pastor T.H. Messmore insisted, for example, that 'Jew and Christian are not the only ones to whom messages from God have come' (203a, p. 4). Consequently 'sympathy, consideration, appreciation, and the broadest charity should characterise all his reference to other faiths' (ibid., p. 3). Many contemporaries shared these views. Colin Campbell Brown, an English Presbyterian in Chainchefu (Chinchew), wrote almost casually that '...Confucius was sent of God' (48, p. 7).[166] Henry T. Hodgkin, in 1909 a medical missionary in Chengtu before he became world leader of Friends' Missions, implied the same idea when he wrote that Christians 'should be most careful not to overthrow the influence of Confucius. His influence is perhaps being lost too rapidly as it is' (64, p. 6).[167] Confucius represented a 'philosophy truly Chinese and an ethic the equal of which is hardly to be found outside those places where the Bible has penetrated' (ibid.). Frank Joseland concurred with Brown and Hodgkin. In his view China's religion had been divinely inspired: 'their sages, Confucius, Lao-tze, Mencius and their successors have borne a noble and praiseworthy part in the Evolution and consolation of the race' (68, p. 3). He made this very strong statement: 'Better far such religions as the Chinese have than none at all. Each of them attempts to satisfy some side of their nature, and each complements the other. Moreover in all there is a *soul* of good' (68, p. 6, emphasis his). Paul Kranz, Timothy Richard's close Lutheran colleague in the CLS in Shanghai, wrote that '*Confucius is our Ally*' against materialism' (69, p. 6, emphasis his).[168] He referred to two booklets he had published in China, *Confucius and Christ, Friends*, and *Christianity the Fulfilment of Confucianism*. These books, he told the Commissioners, had reached their fifth and sixth reprintings (ibid.). Kranz went on to state what was for him a fundamental principle: 'The *God of Confucius and Mencius* is still alive, he has manifested himself more fully in Jesus Christ etc., this is *our message to China*' (ibid., p. 7, emphasis his). Last, there is the opinion of one of the few Chinese church leaders whose views find a place in the Edinburgh material. This was C.T. Wang, of the YMCA Chinese staff, who wrote: 'Great leaders of all other religions must have been sent by God also for certain purposes, some of which we may not be able to account for, but that they were men with a mission from God cannot be denied. They are to be classified among the old prophets of the Jews' (104, p. 5).

Missionaries from Japan were just as forthright in their affirmation that God had been working in Japanese history and tradition before they arrived on the scene. The American Presbyterian D.A. Murray believed himself to be speaking on behalf of 'most missionaries', in saying that they had come, as a result of their experiences, 'to have a different conception of the word "heathen" and of the possibility of God's grace extending more widely than they had previously supposed' (32, p. 13).[169] Sidney Gulick reflected upon the change in his thinking as a result 'of seeing the good and the true and beautiful in the native faiths' (15, pp. 6-7). He wrote of his 'growing feeling that God has been at work in the Orient long before Christian missionaries arrived, and that Christianity is but completing the work begun and carried on for millenniums' (*sic*, ibid., p. 7).

In India, George H. Westcott, Bishop Westcott's second son, who was working with the SPG in Cawnpore (Kanpur) when he wrote his response, offered a theology for these affirmations.[170] This was based mainly on the verse 'God has not left Himself without witness' (Acts 14.17), to which many others also referred directly or by allusion. Westcott built also upon Romans 1.18 and 12.24. Westcott quoted these words from a *Quarterly Paper* of the Cambridge Brotherhood in Delhi:

> The Bible does not lead us to suppose that God left Himself without witness at any time or in any country. We are expressly told that the testimony of nature and conscience to God has been universal, and we cannot doubt that every sincere striving after truth, and in India there have been many such, has met with its reward. (250, p. 23).

Missionaries from other traditions agreed with this line of Anglo-Catholic thinking. Thus Edwin Greaves of the LMS, working in Benares (Veranasi), wrote after twenty-eight years' experience: 'I have learned to accept more fully the fact that God has been operative in the whole of history, and that he has spoken in other ages and in other lands' (166, p. 18).[171] A young American, just at the beginning of his long career in Southern Asia, George Sherwood Eddy, echoed this on the basis of only limited experience in South India: 'my views of God's dealings with mankind have broadened. He is working more than I once realized among all non-Christians, dealing with individuals, preparing communities, guiding nations' (153, pp. 4-5).[172] Paul D. Bergen of the Presbyterian Church of the USA said of the Chinese people 'God has spoken to them through their fathers in divers manners' (43, p. 5).[173]

But the problems remained. How were Christians to speak *theologically* of the status of these non-Christian religious traditions? Did they, or did they not, carry revelation from God that Christians ought to heed? Even more sharply put, the issue was whether Christ was present within the other religions? If this was the case, how exactly could that presence be described and discerned? It was at this point in their search that, with the help of Maurice, Westcott, Fairbairn, Allen and Hall, missionary thinkers rediscovered the Logos doctrine.

The Logos

One respondent who had known F.D. Maurice personally was Arnold Foster of the LMS.[174] The former's understanding of the Logos determined Foster's response: 'the Christian position which recognizes the work of the Logos in every land enlightening all men, has always been held to justify the Christian teacher in looking for traces of the knowledge of God among all races, and in gladly welcoming all such indications as he could find that the soul of man is naturally Christian, (54, p.9). But other thinkers took their usage of the *Logos* directly from the earlier fathers. For example, Paul Kranz in Shanghai said that the Christian preacher 'should recognise the *logos spermatikos* and the *anima naturaliter Christiana'* (69, p.5).

It was in India that Logos patterns of thinking came most easily to the missionaries' minds. W.E.S. Holland (CMS, Allahabad) considered that the Christian should have 'A genuine belief that all of good everywhere is an outshining of the light of the Eternal Word who lighteth every man – and all light followed must tend to lead to Him from whom it came' (177, p. 3). Holland also thought that missionaries should be 'delighted' when they recognized good anywhere, and, as we have seen, that the preacher must have 'no stinginess in acknowledging all of good to be found in Hinduism'. This goodness was to be neither discounted nor depreciated, (ibid., p. 3). Holland's reference to John 1.9 made explicit what others among his contemporaries left unsaid. Writing from the Buddhist context in Burma, George Whitehead cited Clement of Alexandria and unconsciously echoed Maurice, when he declared:.

> Every religion exists by virtue of the truth that is in it, *not* by virtue of its falsehood. I believe that Clement of Alexandria acknowledged Socrates and others as, in a minor way, prophets of God. I should acknowledge Gautama, though he knew not of the existence of God, but he was a most earnest and virtuous man whose sole object in life was to do what he believed to be right, and to spread what he believed to be the truth (252, pp. 6–7).

Another echo of Alexandrian Logos theology sounded from India came from the recently arrived Nicol Macnicol of the UFCS who later became one of the foremost translators of *Bhakti* literature.[175] Writing from Poona (Pune), Macnicol spoke of the firm points of contact between Christianity and Hinduism. These he found particularly in what he called 'the preparation for Christ' in the teaching of Tulsi Das, and in the lyrics of the Maratha saints Tukaram and Dnyaneshwara. Macnicol wrote that 'the Christian doctrines of the divine grace, of the Incarnation and of salvation by faith are by no means foreign and strange to followers of the "bhakti way"' (198, p.18). The religions of India, Macnicol told the Edinburgh Commissioners, were all 'at some time or other a sincere attempt to find God, and to learn his will' and may perhaps be 'still capable of so being used by an earnest spirit'. Consequently the missionary task was to 'look for that in it which is the product of such seeking and which Christianity fulfills...' (ibid.). They had to 'endeavour to make such aspects of the religion of those to whom he speaks stepping-stones to higher things'. He or she should not however encourage non-Christian hearers 'to be content with the fragments of truth which their religion may possess' (ibid., p.14). In echoing the terminology of Clement of Alexandria, Macnicol allied himself with all the other voices who wanted missionary work to do for India what Alexandrian theology did for Hellenism.[176]

Other missionaries were, however, more inclined point to the work of the Holy Spirit to express what Robert Hume in his response called the 'effective universality and activity' of God (180, p.15). Daniel C. Greene of Tokyo wrote, in answer to question 5, that the Christian preacher 'ought not to believe that the Divine Spirit has confined His working to Christian lands, or that the Heavenly Father has failed to respond to the prayer of His children who have been seeking to find Him' (12, p. 5). George Whitehead, whom we have just noticed evoking Clement of Alexandria, preferred nevertheless to use Holy Spirit rather than Logos language. He affirmed that 'all truth and all goodness wheresoever found came through the inspiration of the Holy Spirit, however ignorant a person may be of this source' (252, p. 6).

Further testimony about the work of the Holy Spirit came from Anna M. L. Smith, who had worked among Muslims in Bangalore in South India.[177] She was unusual among missionaries of her day in discerning the presence of the Holy Spirit in the Muslim community and tradition of faith. To be sure, she had her eyes on the people themselves and not on their religious beliefs. Nevertheless she was convinced of their sense of the presence of God.

> I have seen such genuine resignation to the will of God, and patience in suffering among some of the poorest where circumstances made the performance of 'religious duties' impossible, that I felt God has revealed to them something of his love, not through any words of the Koran, or through doctrines of Islam, but through His Spirit (231, pp. 1-2).

The process of fulfilment

Despite this weight of favourable comment about God's working in other religions, the missionaries were adamant about the finality of the Christian gospel. *The Missionary Message* refers to 'the unanimous expression of the absoluteness of the Christian revelation', which was manifest even when the respondents were most 'keenly alive to the necessity of doing the fullest justice to the religions of India'. They insisted on 'conserving the supreme place of Christianity' as that which 'absolutely supersedes Hinduism by absolutely fulfilling all which is noblest in the ancient faiths'.[178] The theology of religion implied or fully spelt out in the Edinburgh correspondence had to be

Christocentric. In relation to Christ they believed all other religions were teleological, and moved to their fulfilment in the Christian revelation.

Various methods of describing how this process of fulfilment would work out were employed by the missionaries. Broadly speaking, the methods were based upon five concepts: the idea of the *paidagogos*, the 'schoolmaster' or 'tutor' to Christ, found first in Paul's Letter to the Galatians;[179] the notion of the *praeparatio evangelica*, first used by Eusebius of Caesarea;[180] and the ideas of completion or fulfilment and then of consummation first used in the Letter to the Ephesians and most recently spelt out by B.F. Westcott in *Christus Consummator*.[181] In addition, the concept of the foreshadowing of 'good things to come', found in the Letter to the Hebrews, gave rise to the use of the notion of 'transfiguration'.[182] These various and complex ideas enabled missionaries to interpret the other traditions of faith as part of God's plan. For them a large part of the sense of wonder at the 'evangelization of the world in this generation' lay in their seeing the religious traditions finding their fulfilment in Christian revelation.

1. The theme of other religious traditions acting as *tutors unto Christ* was infrequently utilized by Edinburgh respondents. But the Methodist thinker, Duncan Leith in Madras, declared that for him missionary work meant endeavouring to discover what aspects of all previous religion and faith 'can be observed to be a tutor to Christ' (193, p. 7). He then added this vigorous comment: 'These aspects have then to be emphasised and compelled to do their tutorial work' (ibid., p. 7).

2. The respondents most often used the *praeparatio evangelica* concept without citing Galatians 3.24-6. James W. Bashford, as a senior American Methodist Bishop, wrote that Confucianism 'has seemed to me often to furnish a divine preparation of the Chinese for Christianity, as the Decalogue furnished a divine preparation of the Jews' (41, p. 2). James Beattie, in Amoy, thought that 'Chinese ethics' were 'largely serviceable to the propagation of the Christian religion and a preparation for it' (42, p. 2).

W.H. Campbell, from South India, stated that Hinduism was a 'preparation for Christianity' and that even its errors should be regarded 'as means being used by the Divine wisdom to lead men to see their need of the truth, while its truths are an anticipation of, and a step towards the realisation of the higher truth revealed by and in Christ' (133, p. 10). From Japan, J. D. Davis affirmed that Confucianism was 'in some measure a preparation for Christianity' (2, p. 3). He added, remarkably, that he saw Tenriko, (one of the new religions of Japan), as 'a preparation for Christianity' but this is perhaps, more because it 'is now incorporating Christian ideas in its teaching' (ibid., p. 3). George Douglas in Manchuria gave a similar testimony in answer to question 11: 'I have learned a deeper respect for the non-Christian faiths and for those who sincerely hold them. They have in a very real sense prepared the way of the Lord' (49, p. 20). Such an attitude had practical consequences for missionary activity: 'In our preaching we never treat Confucius as hostile to Christ. We preach Christianity as the "fulfilling" of the law, Confucian as well as Mosaic' (ibid., p. 8).

Sidney Gulick, in Kyoto, wrote that 'every good teaching in the native faith is a gift of God the Father of all men to that people and is a preparation for the coming of the full revelation in Jesus Christ' (15, pp. 3-4). Paul Kranz, in Shanghai, thought that 'Confucius' *longings for perfect virtue* are *satisfied* by Christ. Thus, Confucius leads to Christ' (69, p. 6). Kranz had an attractive way of offering autobiographical fragments, and he wrote about his own change of mind: 'When I first came to China (1892), I rejoiced if I found a new error or flaw in Confucius' life and his doctrine; but since 1902 I have recognised this to be *wrong*' (ibid., p. 5). This was the year when he went to work with Timothy Richard at the CLS.

Frank P. Joseland also thought that both Confucianism and Buddhism were 'stepping stones to Christianity' (68, p. 7). Listing Confucian and Buddhist virtues, Joseland commented that these had 'provided Christianity with both a terminology and a fuller content to work upon' (ibid., p. 8). From India Henry Whitehead, formerly a member of the Oxford Mission to Calcutta and by 1909 the Bishop of Madras, wrote out of his particular concern for Indian village life.[183] He suggested that even 'in the lowest forms of religion in India there is some element of truth and something that may be regarded as a preparation for Christianity' (201, p. 11). 'At the same time', he commented, 'it is necessary to remember that the main object of the Christian preacher is to bring home to the hearts and consciences of the people the great differences between Christianity and their own religion and not mainly the points of contact between them' (ibid., p. 11).

Henry M. Woods, of the American Southern Presbyterian mission in Hwaianfu, summing up his extensive biblical reflections in his answer to question 5 (largely as we have already seen, about candour and speaking the truth in love), concluded with a forthright affirmation: 'There are many noble thoughts in Confucianism which give a basis for the presentation of Christian Truth... and in Buddhism... and so these religions may be considered as a preparation for God's Truth' (115, pp. 8-9).

The preparation for the fullness of the Christian revelation therefore had to be followed by the 'completion', and not by eradication of the other religious traditions. The missionaries' theology of religion was one of continuity, rather than discontinuity. We turn to the three concepts used by the respondents in their descriptions of how this completion might take place. These centred upon these three words: 'fulfilment', 'transfiguration' and 'consummation'.

3. Most of the missionaries responded to the Commissioners in terms of *fulfilment*, and indeed Edinburgh 1910 was the moment of apotheosis of this idea. As in the case of J.N. Farquhar, the key text and watchword for many

other respondents was Matthew 5.17, 'I have not come to destroy but to fulfil.' Paul D. Bergen, as a professor in the Shantung Union College, described Christianity typically as the 'flower and fulfilment' of China's historic past. 'God has spoken to the Chinese through their fathers in divers manners and now He speaks to them through His Son' (43, p. 5). In his answer to question 11 Bergen added to this, 'I regard Christianity as a fulfilment of much that exists only as a promise in China' (ibid., p. 9). From Japan, Sidney Gulick wrote: 'we should ever insist that Christianity does not come to destroy anything that is good or true in the native faiths but rather to stimulate, to strengthen, and to "fulfil" it – to give it life and real energy' (15, p. 4). The trouble with the old religions was not, he thought, that they were without truth, but rather that the truths they possessed were often so mixed up with folly and superstition that they were as good as lost. Gulick saw Christianity as the source of 'insight, ability to distinguish between truth and error' and also as giving 'the truth a vitality before unsuspected' (ibid., p. 4). In similar vein R.S. Fyffe, an Anglican missionary in Burma, answered question 5 by quoting Matthew 5.17, and commenting that this was 'Christ's attitude where any good is to be found in what went before' (158, p. 12).[184] These words were not as gloomy as they may sound, for he continued: 'In Burma we do not wish to destroy the picturesque if ineffective Pagoda but to plant the cross upon it. We should like to see a Buddhist Christianity growing in Burma, not our Western plant, and bringing forth fruits of meditation and devotion' (ibid., pp. 12-13).

George Douglas in Manchuria gave a high place to Confucianism as a 'law' or 'torah'.[185] He added that Christianity was to be preached as 'the fulfilling of the Law, Confucian as well as Mosaic'. He gave the Commissioners a list of seven Confucian sayings from which it was possible to begin a dialogue about Christian faith: 'Such sayings of their ancient sage, now deified, lead easily to the higher teaching of Jesus Christ' (49, pp. 8-9). Henry Hodgkin, the Quaker, affirmed the continuing power of Confucianism and concluded: 'Our attitude should be similar to that which Christ exhibited to Moses, "I am come not to destroy, but to fulfil"' (64, p. 5).

A host of similar comments are to be found from missionaries in India. O.J. Grainger was the one member of the Disciples of Christ Missions to be consulted for Commission IV.[186] Writing of the religion which surrounded him in Jabbulpore, Grainger insisted that there should be 'no attempt to destroy it', a reference to Matthew 5.17, nor, he continued, 'to build anew on the cleared ground'. Rather, Hinduism should be used 'as a starting point to lead the people up to Christ's revelation' (165, p. 4). Grainger listed four things which needed to be fulfilled in Hinduism: *Bhakti* devotion; *karma*, the idea that sin will be punished; *avataras*, and the idea of sacrifice (we can compare this list with that of John Peter Jones). In Islam Grainger noted opposition to idolatry, monotheism, 'certain common religious traditions', common belief in the Old and New Testaments, and belief in rewards and punishments in the afterlife as matter requiring fulfilment in Christ (ibid., pp. 4-5).

J. Mathers of the LMS in South India, a disciple of, as well as successor to T.E. Slater, wrote in answer to question 5 of the missionary: 'His motto should be Christ's – "I came not to destroy, but to fulfil"; and in the fulfilment, what is needful to disappear will be found to have disappeared' (203, p. 28). In spirit Mathers was an early practitioner of dialogue, as we see from these words:

> what is most needed today is the sympathetic sharing of our spiritual experience with them. The paths of argument, of dialectics, however skilfully conducted, will avail little. The policy of denunciation will avail less. But sympathetic personal intercourse, friendly talks on religion, and the practice, where possible, of common prayer, will bring these men to a life of dependence on and communion with Christ (ibid., p. 29)

To this he added, 'It is this type of work that India needs *imperatively*... and it can only be done by men of intellectual keenness, of spiritual power, and above all of a sympathy that can recognise and appreciate the view point of another' (ibid., emphasis his). A mark of Mathers' own intellectual acumen was his recognition that Christianity in its Western form owed nearly everything to the Greek philosophical framework. That being the case, India would have to be allowed to find its own fulfilment for its religious history.

F.W. Steinthal, the Danish Lutheran Secretary of the YMCA in Calcutta, thought that the missionary attitude must take note of 'the message of Him who came "not to destroy but to fulfil" – not only the religion of the Jews but 'also the truths of Hinduism' (234, p. 18). This fulfilment he saw as the relation of the 'perfect day to the dawn, as the realisation to the longings of the soul' (ibid.). Like his other missionary colleagues, Steinthal specified themes in Hindu religion that could be 'fulfilled'. These included the longing for *mukti* which had 'even in its pantheistic corruption with its denial of human and divine personality the true ring in it of the human soul's cry for an abiding life without the sorrows and sins of selfishness' (ibid., p. 20). Steinthal added in brackets the following phrases: 'He shall save His people from their sins. He who loseth his self shall save it. I live no more.' And 'likewise the idea of *samadhi*, oneness with God', he suggested, 'still has in it the true longing for fellowship with the living God (ibid., p. 20). In brackets here Steinthal added 'my heart panteth after the living God. I and the Father are one'. More simply the Canadian William Alexander Wilson of the Presbyterian Mission in Indore wrote that Christ is for the Hindus 'the fulfilment of their best hopes' (254, p. 12).

Some missionaries who were otherwise wholly committed to the fulfilment concept did express some slight reservations about it. One such was the Methodist 'literature missionary' Henry Gulliford working in Mysore City. In pleading for intelligent sympathy with the spiritual aspirations of other men and women, Gulliford insisted that 'Jesus Christ fulfils in many ways; but we must not be content with trying to show that Christ fulfils Hinduism and Islam as he fulfilled Judaism' (168a, p. 7). To illustrate his point he listed in answer to question 6 many 'points of contact', and commented, 'but I would not in all cases say they were a "preparation" for Christianity' (ibid., p. 7). Such ideas as *bhakti, avatara* and *pravasilla* (expiation) indeed offer positive areas for fulfilment. But Gulliford warned that the great difficulty lay for the preacher in the vernacular vocabularies: 'Every great word he utters, such as God, sin, faith, repentance, incarnation, heaven, hell, all have been pre-empted by pantheism and a false system of thought' (ibid. , p. 9). But even so Gulliford was on the side of the new missionary methods, and not of the earlier generation ('of half a century ago') that 'went in for a "clean sweep"' (ibid., p. 9). After thirty-two years experience as a missionary, Henry Gulliford confidently expected forms of Indian philosophy and theology to arise which would be non-Western and profoundly Christian, however slow this process might be (ibid., p. 13). Gulliford's reservations were to be expounded brilliantly by A.G. Hogg in later writings, notably *Redemption from this World* (1924) and *The Gospel Message to the Hindu* (1947).[187]

4. Other missionaries used a different set of images for the relationship of the old religion with the new. These were based upon light and light's ability to *transfigure*. Thus F.W. Steinthal wrote of 'the perfect day' to describe the relation of Christianity to Hinduism, which he called 'the dawn'. We look now at a series of similar statements from the missionary respondents which use images of shadow and light, or of broken or refracted light compared with brilliance of white light, or of the light of moon and star compared with that of the sun.

Like Steinthal, many respondents mingled fulfilment language with transfiguration imagery. Duncan Leith from Madras, for example, offered an amendment to Matthew 5.17: 'Christ has not come to overthrow Hinduism but to transfigure it' (193, p. 75). Leith's practical counsel was, that the missionary had always to keep the Hindu point of view 'clearly though silently in his mind' in order 'to set forth Jesus Christ' (ibid., p. 7). His own examples were drawn first from the incarnational thought-forms of Vishnaivite Hindus. 'They manifest', he wrote, 'the cry of the human heart for an incarnation. The presence of that cry is an evidence of the preparing Hand of God' (ibid., p. 8). Then he discussed the 'the idea of the Twice-born', which he interpreted to indicate a realization that 'change is regarded as essential in the life of a man, before he can be regarded as attaining the highest possibility of his life' (ibid.). Another feature of Hinduism which is open to transfiguration is the *Bhakti* idea: the 'message of the *Bhagavad Gita* that every activity of life should be performed without attachment' (ibid.). So too are, 'the ideal of the ascetic life – exemplified in the life of the *samyasi*' (*ibid.*) as well as the idea of 'absorption into the supreme as constituting the final goal of human life' (ibid., pp. 8-9). In Leith's view 'The Hindu view is metaphysical rather than ethical, yet it is possible for one to rise to the other' (ibid., p. 9). With the citation of the last phrase and its use of the word 'ethical', we see Leith's main thrust in his 'transfiguration' conception. His conclusion in the response runs as follows: 'Experience has impressed upon me that the vital Gospel for India is to leave aside dogma, go direct to the moral issue, seek the surrender of the life to Jesus as the moral pattern... I am willing to leave all else to be sought out by the individual soul afterwards' (ibid., p. 12). This would indeed be transfiguration.

But the dominant thought of those who wrote about transfiguration lay in the 'shadows' language of Hebrews 10.1. Ibuka and Imbrie of the Meiji Gakuin, the leading Presbyterian College in Tokyo, told the Commissioners of the opinions prevalent among many Japanese pastors:

> Some of them are well read in the Christian literature of the west, and are quite well informed as to the new emphasis which is placed upon the elements of truth contained in the non-Christian religions. There is a conviction among them that the non-Christian religions are not wholly of man. At times they think of them and speak of them as a preparation for Christianity; sometimes comparing them to Judaism, as shadows of the good things to come (17/19, pp. 6-7). [188]

Several missionary respondents wished to adopt the methodology of the Letter to the Hebrews. George Howells, Principal of Serampore College and one of the most learned Baptist missionaries of his day, told the Commissioners that, since 'the Hindu scriptures contain large elements of truth as helpful and as noble as anything in the Old Testament', what he called the 'new Christian apologetic in India' had to proceed along such lines 'as the writer of the Epistle to the Hebrews takes toward the Judaism of the Old Testament' (179, p. 6). [189] An indication of the kind of transfiguration Howells wanted came in these words (deeply impressive to Cairns, as can be seen from the heavy pencil scoring on the Aberdeen typescript):

> In my experience the personality of Christ with its corollary, the Christlikeness of God possesses an infinitely greater power of appeal than any other element of the Christian Gospel. To Christianity as a system and a rival religion I have often found strong antagonism, for Jesus Christ as Teacher, Friend and Saviour, I have found with rare exceptions, nothing but cordial regard and even adoring reverence. (ibid., p. 7).

5. Ideas of 'gathering up', 'putting together', 'summing up', which arose from the Pauline verse which speaks of God's intention 'to sum up all things in Christ' (Eph.1.10) are found relatively infrequently in the Edinburgh responses. Only C.F. Andrews, the true disciple of B.F. Westcott, made a major point of the *Christus Consummator* theme when he wrote of his understanding of the incarnation as extending 'in wider and wider reaches of humanity, till all is summed up in Christ Himself' (123, p. 17). Other missionaries who used the idea did not quite attain this vision. Colin Campbell Brown, the English Presbyterian who had affirmed that 'Confucius was sent of God', was equally clear that the ideals of Confucius awaited completion: 'in Christ all is gathered up and rendered effective. Out of Christ all fails' (48, p. 7). R.S. Fyffe in Mandalay declared that 'the claim of Christ is supreme, and all the treasures that can be gathered from other systems must be laid at his feet' (158, p. 13). Stanley P. Smith (Independent, Tsechowfu) had a clear statement of the goal of mission based on Ephesians 1.10.[190] 'God has', Smith asserted,

> 'made known unto us the mystery of His will' that he will finally 'head up all things in Christ', reconcile the universe to Himself and become as Father – 'everything in everybody' – *panta en pasi*, Eph. 1.9; Col. 1.20; I Cor. 15.28 (95, p. 10).

Yet, however few the explicit references to the thought of Ephesians 1.10, there were many suggestions in the correspondence that there would be some kind of consummation for the world of religions. Such proposals were influenced by a reading of the previous verses in Ephesians, where it is said that the 'mystery of God's will and purpose', long undisclosed, had now become an 'open secret' because of Jesus Christ. In such a context other references by the missionaries, whether to Logos Christology, or to 'unbroken evolution' upwards to Christianity as the perfect religion, or to 'fulfilment' of the *praeparationes evangelicae*, all move toward the vision of the summing up of all things in the 'fullness of Christ'.

This is the other major theme in the Pauline writings: the idea of the 'measure of the stature of the fullness of Christ' (Eph.4.13). This 'fullness' (*Pleroma*) always points to the future, representing an as yet attainable ideal. In the Edinburgh responses a sense of this is to be found in a marked awareness that Christians were still *in via* and had *yet* to discover the fullness of the meaning of Christ for the world. Such dynamic conceptions we have already seen at work in Timothy Richard, Arthur Lloyd and C.F. Andrews.

But others shared similar inklings, even if they did not give so full an expression of them. George Lefroy, the Anglican Bishop of Lahore, wrote 'not merely of the points of contact (with the Truth which we can find in their systems), but of the substantial contributions which the peoples, and in a certain sense I believe we may say the Faiths, which are outside of Christ, can bring into the life of the Body when they are brought into the City of God' (190, p. 11).[191] Lefroy admitted that this was not so much an argument to be presented to non-Christians (although he thought there might be ways in which it could be so used, if handled properly) but rather one which had to do with the 'motive and incentive for Mission work' (ibid., p. 11). Lefroy owed this thinking to B.F. Westcott.

Some Minority Positions

Thus far we have been able to indicate the generous positions represented in the Edinburgh responses. But there were other voices. These gave expression to views abandoned by the greater number of the respondents or set out ideas so idiosyncratic that they have long since been discounted. But a thorough analysis of the Edinburgh response must indicate that these views existed in 1910.

Distortion of original revelation

The most widely held of such views was that which recognized an 'original revelation' still embedded in non-Christian religion despite all the vicissitudes of humanity since the fall of Adam and Eve and their ejection from the Garden of Eden. This position was explicitly stated by an American Baptist missionary, W.B. Boggs, working in the Madras Presidency.[192] For him 'points of contact' between Hinduism and Christianity ('unquestioning belief in the supernatural'; the immanence of God, the Hindu triad of Brahma, Vishnu and Siva; Hindu ideas of incarnation; and the 'great fundamental idea of sacrifice') were 'distant echoes of primal truths, which have come down from the far-past ages when the human race knew God, and have survived the universal apostasy (*sic*) of the race' (129, pp. 5-6). Another missionary in India, William Bonnar, asserted of Hinduism that it was 'a corruption of God's truth which was originally given to man, and which had become distorted and discoloured through the corroding and disintegrating influences of the stratum in which it had lain so long embedded' (130, p. 15).[193] In China, the theological teacher Courtenay H. Fenn saw the 'elements of truth' in Confucianism as evidence of 'the common origin of all in God's earliest revelations of Himself and of His will to man' (53, p. 6). The single representative of missionary work in South America, Barbrooke Grubb of the Paraguayan Chaco Mission, disclosed similar understandings of primal revelation when he wrote about his missionary methodology: 'The missionary should try and impress on the people that the Christian religion is not the faith of a higher, more civilized nation, but that it is the gradual development of a pure

faith held in the beginning of the ages by the ancestors of the human race...'
(316, p. 7).

Albertus Kruyt, a Dutch Reformed missionary in the Celebes (Sulawesi),
struck the same note as Grubb when he tackled question 5.[194] Kruyt's statement here helps us to compare 'continental' with Anglo-American thinking.
'The missionary', he wrote 'ought not to consider the heathen religion as an
inspiration of the devil and to condemn, in accordance with it, all utterances
of heathenism' which he said was a 'point of view, often taken by
Missionaries of former days'. Such religion ought rather to be considered as
'a deviation, an alienation of the true knowledge of God' (334a, p. 6).

Kruyt spoke of the content of his own preaching: 'I have preached to the
people, that we have come to bring them the true religion of their ancestors;
not anything new, but something very old. God has always been the same,
but men have fallen off from Him.' Kruyt tells us, too, that it is 'a principal
thing to convince the people that God is universal, that He is the God of
their ancestors, who are also our ancestors' (ibid.).

This sense that the good and true in other religions has endured from pri-
mordial time is to be found frequently in reflections sent in by Lutherans. It
is clearly apparent in the reply of F.H. Hahn of the Gossner Mission in
Bengal. In replying to question 5, Hahn recommended that the Christian
preacher

> should closely study the religion of the people among whom he labours
> and try to find out the sparks of truth which he must expect to meet,
> because even to the heathen God has revealed himself in some way;
> besides many of the nations of the earth possess something of the original
> revelation brought down from the dawn of history to the present time
> through oral traditions (169, p. 5).

Some of the missionaries put the 'groping in the dark' imagery into the
context of 'original revelation', for why else would any person set out on 'the
long search' for God Hahn wrote with some passion that 'the preacher
should understand that he has to do with fellow men who are groping in the
dark after the light, who are waiting in the dim light of stars for the rising of
the sun, who are struggling to get out of the mire and to set their foot on a
rock' (169, p. 5). The consequence of this is a missionary method which gently leads the other person 'on to the full truth as it is in Jesus, bearing up
patiently with their errors, exposing them principally by putting the full revelation before them, not by vehemently denouncing them...' (ibid.). But of
course this is not dialogical in the fullest sense, for Hahn has no thought that
there may be something to be learnt as well as taught. It remains essentially a
negative judgment upon the faith of other people.

F.W. Steinthal also used an older and more traditional theology to speak of the created order and of its values. Thus he wrote of the 'old religion' that 'it is the expression of the highest and divinest in the people's life, the remnant of God's image, the search for the living God' (234, p. 16). Steinthal affirmed that

> below the strange forms and hardly intelligible language lies life, the spiritual life of human souls, needing God, seeking God, laying hold of God, as far as they have found Him. Often the life is all but dead, more often it is crippled and deformed, sick unto death; yet it is life (ibid.).

Not to begin to understand this, wrote Steinthal, was to fail to understand Hinduism at all and to miss 'the essential connection with the people's religious life' (ibid.).

Imperfect response to general revelation

The missionary respondent who demonstrated himself to be the most hostile to what he perceived as the new 'eirenic' attitude towards other religions was Arthur Evans Moule, Archdeacon of Ningpo.[195] The most positive reflection to which he could commit himself concerning Chinese religion was only: 'I have, sometimes, thought that Taoism, Confucianism and Buddhism, in this order, may be regarded as faint adumbrations in the minds of the Chinese of the idea and desire for the Way, the Truth and the Life' (82, p. 5). But this had not much to do with the term 'eirenic attitude' by 'many modern theorists'. This, said Moule, meant 'the complementary recognition of false and idolatrous creeds as forerunners or companions of the Faith, or as auxiliary helpers' (ibid.). He told the Edinburgh Commissioners that he failed to see why 'missionaries or Christian apologists' should begin to 'laud and recognise' these religions as 'forerunners and companions of the Faith' just at the point in history 'when with the lips of conscience and with the illumination of science and higher education, the natives (*sic*) themselves are beginning to be ashamed of their idols and superstitions' (ibid.). This is the clearest statement of the 'older view' in the Edinburgh responses.[196] In principle Chinese religion was only a human affair, full of superstitious inventions of which the newly enlightened mind can only be ashamed, and with at most merely 'faint adumbrations' of a desire for something better.

The human search for God

Other missionaries spoke of human struggles and strivings on the basis of Paul's Areopagitica address, with its reference to searching after an 'Unknown God' (Acts 17.23).

John L. Dearing from the American Baptist Missionary Union in Yokohama, wrote that the fundamental idea behind the old faith in Japan was 'a reaching out of the ancients after that which is spiritual and better' (8, p. 2). Agnes de Selincourt (Zenana Bible and Medical Society, Allahabad) affirmed that the task of the missionary was to show that 'Christ perfectly meets the needs towards the satisfaction of which other religions are but imperfect gropings' (224, p. 5).

Many others saw Paul's attitude on the Areopagus as their model for missionary activity. The search for an 'Unknown God' followed by the announcement of the 'True God' by the Christian preacher seemed to be the clearest model for missionary work. To be sure Paul himself was being as gentle and as conciliatory in Athens as he possibly could.[197] The modern missionary had to be just as delicate. Paul Bergen describing methods in China, wrote that: 'preaching of a denunciatory or controversial character, is rarer than in earlier years, the rule now being to start from common ground, whenever possible, thus following the example of the great Apostle in Athens' (43, p. 5). Donald MacGillivray of the CLS in Shanghai insisted that Christian preaching must avoid 'the iconoclastic attitude, and present the *light*, which will naturally drive out the darkness', and affirmed that 'Paul on Mars Hill is generally copied by enlightened workers' (77, p. 3, emphasis his).[198]

From Japan Imbrie and Ibuka noted that when 'Paul stood on Mars Hill he said to the Athenians, "as certain even of your own poets have said". He willingly recognized the truth that men feel after God and that they find something of him.' Therefore they recommended that the 'Christian preacher in Japan should take the same attitude towards its non-Christian religions; and with the same willingness' (17 and 19, p. 6).

From India came testimonies from two missionaries from the Basel Society, Samuel Ambat and Friedrich Braun. Although the first of these was mainly concerned with tribal peoples, and the second with lower caste Hindus, they shared the same point of view. Ambat wrote that 'just as St Paul amongst the Athenians has acknowledged that which was good in their past and present religious life and thereby has roused their conscience and prepared them to receive the highest truth and reality... So we also should treat our Hindu and Mohammedan brethren pointing to what is real religious life and truth in Hinduim and Islam ...' (122, p. 16); and Braun stated that by 'acknowledging the good in the religion of the people and using it for his purpose' the missionary will follow the example 'of the Apostle Paul on the Areopag (*sic*)' (130a, p. 2).[199]

Missionaries working among Muslims also found 'the unknown God' concept helpful. One of these was Franklin Hoskins in Beirut, who thought that 'a willingness to recognise and emphasise every point of contact and likeness' in Islam represented Paul's saying, 'whom therefore ye ignorantly worship, him declare I unto you' (265a, p. 10). George Swan in Cairo wrote,

> It is then because I believe that the *Zikr* is the altar to the Unknown God of Islam, that I would earnestly appeal to the Conference to initiate some research work with regard to it, to the end that the average missionary to the Mohammedans may have some concise information in his hands and thereby intelligently may be able to say to the Mohammedans, 'Whom therefore ye ignorantly worship, Him declare I unto you' (275, pp. 3-4).[200]

The special case of Islam

Hoskins and Swan were unusual in that they could conceive of their work among Muslims as dealing with human searching for God. For most missionaries working among Muslims, Islam was a system hostile to the gospel message. The God that Muslims worshipped could not be an 'unknown God' in the sense that Paul used the word at Athens. On the contrary, if the Qur'anic testimony were to be taken seriously, God was more perfectly revealed in Islam than in the Bible. Islamic claims were in direct conflict with all that Christianity wished to affirm of itself. None of the categories – the *paidagogos*, or 'schoolmaster to Christ', the *praeparatio evangelica*, 'fulfilment', 'distortion of original revelation', 'imperfect response to general revelation', 'human striving after an unknown deity' – fitted the Muslim religious situation. And yet, with the exceptions of Robert Sterling in Jerusalem ('the whole system of Islam is founded on a lie, and is built up by a whole series of lies', 274, p. 9);[201] Miller and Alvarez in Nigeria ('the blatant and inaccurate plagiarism of the Koran', 300, p. 7);[202] and J. Verhoeven in West Java ('the Allah of Islam is an idol, a false god, a despot above all despots', 340a, p. 2, and 'Islam is a lie from the evil one', ibid., p. 3.),[203] very few of the missionaries responding to the questionnaire from the Islamic context could bring themselves to denounce it as satanic.

But if Islam did not arise as the work of the Devil or as pure imposture, what place could it have within the missionaries' theology of religion? Temple Gairdner spelt out the problem for the Edinburgh Commissioners. 'I have', he wrote, 'tried to show in *The Reproach of Islam*, Chapter VIII... why it is difficult to look at Islam as modern missionary thought is trying to look at Buddhism and other Eastern paths, namely as a *praeparatio evangelii* (263, p. 5). Gairdner put the issues thus:

> It cannot be treated like any other, for it is more difficult to concede to it what is gladly conceded to other religions that appeared before Christ, that they are in some sort prepared and prepare a way for Him. How can that which denies the whole essential and particular content of his message be

said to prepare for Him, or be half-way house to His Kingdom? For that is what Islam does. Other religions know nothing of Christianity: one and all they came before it and speak of it neither good nor evil. But the whole theory of Islam is that it, the latest-sent of all religions, does not so much *abrogate* Christianity with its Book, as specifically and categorically deny both as wilful corruption and lies. Point by point, each truth of Christianity, steeped through and through with the tenderness of the love of God, is negated with abhorrence by Islam; – the Fatherhood of God; the Sonship and Incarnation of Jesus Christ; the Divinity of the Holy Ghost; the death of Christ and all that it means, whether ethically – of love, infinite tenderness, infinite self-sacrifice; or spiritually – of sin condemned, and sin forgiven; the Resurrection of Christ on the third day; His glorification with the Father with the glory which He had with Him before the world was – each several truth of these truths is a blasphemy in the eyes of every Moslem, a lie which Islam came expressly to blast, taught by a Book which the Koran came expressly to replace.[204]

In his Edinburgh response, Gairdner expressed grave hesitation about any suggestion that 'the Muslim belief in one God' or 'their belief in Jesus' might be called a *praeparatio* (see 263, p. 7). This inability to speak theologically about Islam had led in Gairdner's experience to a plain impasse: 'In our public preaching, we simply ignore Islam, Mohammed and the Koran' (263, p. 6). This statement was borne out by the veteran Herman N. Barnum.[205] Fifty-one years of service in Turkey-in-Asia led him to tell the Edinburgh Commissioners that the claims of Christianity could 'be presented without attacking Islam or the character of its Founder. Controversy generally begets hostility' (258, p. 5). This was, however, as much a non-dialogical position as those of denunciation and attack, since it no more took the Muslim seriously as a religious person within a great tradition of faith than they did.

Other missionaries, however, did try to deal with the faith of Muslim people expressed in Muslim practices. The range of material treated in this way was remarkable. It included Samuel Zwemer's testimony about *Ramadan*, 'Fasting is observed, I believe, very often with a real sense of communion and fellowship with God' (283, p. 2). Zwemer asserted that Christians hold 'great fundamental truths... in connection with Mohammedans' and that we should admit 'the excellencies of doctrine and life in Mohammedanism' (ibid.). John Cameron Young, of the Keith Falconer Mission in Aden, was able to affirm 'earnest faith and hearty belief in the observance of all the rites and ceremonies' (282, p. 2), and that there are Muslims who 'genuinely prize the privilege of prostrating themselves before God as a real religious help and consolation' (ibid., p. 3). Samuel G. Wilson, in Tabris, said that 'we should show our appreciation of the good points of Islam in our dealings with the inquirer' (342, p. 7).[206] Among these good points Wilson listed 'Its teaching and practice of reverence to God, of resignation and submission to His will, its prohibition of wine-drinking.' These things he said 'should be commended' (ibid.). There was also the view of Wilson's fellow American Presbyterian, Andrew Watson in Cairo, who spoke of the undisputed truth in Islam, especially in 'the doctrines of the unity and spirituality of God, Inspiration, the Decrees, the Resurrection, and the General Judgment' (280, p. 6).

For most respondents it was in just these elements of 'genuine faith' and 'undisputed truths' that the problem concerning Islam lay. None expressed this better than Andrew Watson:

> It seems to me that there is just enough of undisputed truth in Islam, to fortify the Moslem against the attacks of Christians and to make him satisfied with his own faith, which affords him so much opportunity to gratify human pride and passion (ibid., pp. 6-7).

We should note that Watson is using the expression 'attacks' in this context to describe conventional missionary encounters. He himself repudiated whatever was implied by this expression, for he wrote: 'Never can any good be done by epithets of detraction and abuse, or by the use of irony and mockery in discussing the faith of others, especially the religion of Islam' (ibid., pp. 5-6).

The only way forward appeared to be by 'displacement'. The hold of Islam on individual Muslims had to be replaced by a new understanding of God, revealed in Jesus Christ. Islam itself could not function as a tutor – *paidagogos* – towards this new understanding, so that the only position that could be adopted in relation to the Muslim's faith was that of discontinuity. The theorist-practitioner who helped the Edinburgh Commissioners most at this point was William Shedd from Persia.

Displacement and discontinuity: the case of Islam

William Shedd was among the most percipient of the Edinburgh respondents. His formulations were frequently used by Alfred Garvie in the section on Islam in *The Missionary Message*. In his Edinburgh response, Shedd spoke of his search for a *via media* between denunciation of Islam as a 'gentile Judaism' or degraded form of Christianity' and the increasingly widespread suggestions that Islam had a role to play alongside Christianity.[207] His answer to question 6 dealt with 'points of contact' and 'preparations' for Christianity. There were, he thought, three main points of contact to be found. These lay in (1) Islamic monotheism ('Christians may rightly take their place beside Moslems as believers in the Unity', (272, p. 17); (2) belief in divine revelation on the part of Muslims ('The acceptance of the Old Testament prophets, the peculiar honour paid to Our Lord, and the acceptance of the

Sacred Books of the Jews and Christians are very important preparatory elements, in spite of many qualifications and denials' (ibid., p. 18); (3) the
Muslim emphasis on the cardinal virtues, Islamic teaching of the direct
accountability of human beings to God for their deeds, and the noble equality of all people in the sight of God (ibid., pp. 18-9). In the Persian Shi'ite
context, Shedd also saw a fourth point of contact in the 'attempt to supply
the idea of an Incarnation' (ibid., p. 19) in the concept of the Imamat and the
veneration paid to the Sheikhs, pirs and other religious leaders. In the fifth
place he called 'the attempt to found a doctrine of the atonement in the sufferings of the Imams... the great hope of multitudes'. 'However crude, it is a
real preparation for the truth' (ibid.) He concluded this list of 'preparatory'
elements with a reference to the religious vocabulary of the Arabic language
('full, flexible and precise') and in ideas and forms of worship, especially in
the use of preaching in the mosques (ibid., p. 20).

This is far from being hostile to, or derogatory of Islam. Yet Shedd
doubted whether any of these elements of Islamic faith could be seen as
helps towards Christian faith. He wrote:

> It may be remarked of almost all of the above that they often seem to be
> hindrances rather than preparations, and one often longs to find minds
> without these ideas rather than to find minds filled with apparently similar
> but really perverted beliefs as compared to those of Christianity (ibid.).

He asserted the importance of the vital distinction between the attitude to
be adopted towards Muslim people themselves and the true inwardness of
Christian understanding:

> while there is danger of exaggerating differences and creating them where
> none exist; there is quite as much danger of ignoring real differences
> because they are hidden by superficial resemblances. The most profound
> and significant differences are not always the most obvious and assent does
> not always imply real acceptance or even apprehension (ibid., p. 14).

Shedd made two other points of great importance. The first lay in the
necessity of being able to recognize and then to distinguish between the popular faith and the essential elements of Islam: 'It is also important by sympathy and tact to learn the view-point of both the history of the religion and
its actual present form' (ibid.). Shedd insisted that the missionaries were not
dealing with abstractions: 'we meet Moslems and not Islam' (ibid., p. 15).
'The individuals we meet are permeated with the characteristic ideas of
Islam... They also have the ideas that permeate society as to shrines, ill-luck
and good-luck... They probably belong to various sects with different tenets
(ibid., p. 18).

Shedd's second general point concerns the still unfinished task of rightly estimating the 'Christian' significance of Muhammad. He had been involved in discussions about whether Islam 'in its origins was a sincere attempt to meet religious needs or rather the scheme of an ambitious man to advance his own power' (ibid., p. 15). Shedd called this a 'highly interesting historical question', but suggests that in controversy the missionary needed to deal with the inadequacy of the religion 'as a whole and on specific teachings rather than to impugn the motives of the founder or of his followers' (ibid.). Shedd touched upon the 'broader question as to the place of the faiths of the world, in God's self-revelation and in His redemption of the world' (ibid.). Once again he allowed the question to be of the deepest historical and philosophical interest but insisted that 'there is a possibility of exaggerating its immediate practical importance. I am sure that we are justified in assuming that the spiritual needs of those we meet have not been filled and that the Gospel is offered to them in order to fill these needs' (ibid., p. 16).

As a working missionary, Shedd felt that he had to 'distrust a priori judgments based on theological theory' and 'to give the religious leaders and religious systems every right to a fair hearing'. But, he added straightaway, 'fairness implies a willingness to condemn as well as to commend' (ibid.).

Not as a matter of theory but as a belief strengthened by increasing acquaintance with Islam and its offshoots in Persia, I am convinced that they are all powerless to enable men to live holy lives, or to satisfy the needs of the soul, or to give society the new life required for the reconstruction of out-worn civilizations. Personally I find in this conviction of the inadequacy of Islam and of the barriers actually placed by it on individual and national progress a powerful motive for missionary work for Moslems (ibid., pp. 16-17).

Others among Shedd's colleagues, like H.H. Jessup of the American Presbyterian Mission in Beirut, had moved in the same direction.[208] Writing specifically of Muslims, Jessup told the Commissioners that we should 'admit the truth we hold in common with them'. But he went on to make this intriguing comment: 'It was long supposed that Islam was in some sense a preparation for Christianity, a kind of quarantine of the nations previously pagan and idolatrous, through which they would the more readily pass on to Christianity' (266, p. 3).[209] Jessup repudiated any such idea of Islam as a *praeparatio evangelii*.

Shi'ite Islam was problematical for other missionaries besides Shedd. Walter Rice, of the CMS in Isfahan, showed himself in his response to have been deeply affected by living among Shi'ites.[210] Rice provided for the Commissioners a specially written paper on the Christian approach to the Shi'ite Muslim and concluded his scrutiny of the elements of Shi'ite Islam:

But I cannot regard these things as a valuable preparation for Christianity.
They make the idea familiar, they testify to the heart's needs; but inasmuch
as they claim to satisfy them in certain ways, which are national popular,
oriental and easy for them to assimilate, I doubt whether they make believers in them any more willing to substitute our teaching for their own (270,
p. 21, emphasis his).

Rice's colleague in the same station was the prolific author and scholar,
W. St Clair Tisdall, who was equally emphatic about the need for 'displace-
ment'.[211] However many truths Islam may contain bound up within its errors,
'Mohammedanism' he wrote, 'cannot be said to be a preparation' (271, p. 4).
Although Tisdall was already a writer with a considerable reputation in the
field of Christianity and the other religions, he is noticeably under used by
Garvie and Cairns in the compilation of the section on Islam of *The
Missionary Message*. This was due, perhaps, to Tisdall's central metaphor for
understanding Islam: 'The missionary gladly recognises the truths that he
finds hidden and buried under masses of error... He endeavours to cleanse
the jewel from the mire into which it has fallen' (ibid., pp. 3-4). In this view
Tisdall was in line with other CMS colleagues in the Muslim world. For
example, T. Alvarez and W. Miller in Northern Nigeria stated that Islam
could easily lead to superstition and credulity. For them it was 'safer to build
on a new foundation... without attempting to drag failing similarities "and
points of contact" into the arena' (300, p. 9). Likewise the veteran antagonist
of Islam in Jerusalem, Robert Sterling, declared that 'the preacher to the
Mohammedan has of necessity a unique position; he must pull down before
he can build up' (274, p. 9).

Discontinuity with other religious traditions

Despite the preponderance of ideas of completion and fulfilment in the
replies of correspondents dealing with other religions there were some who
forthrightly protested against the use of points of contact on which to build
the faith of new churches.

From Japan, the Commissioners received the opinion of Gideon Draper of
the Methodist Episcopal Church, who declared that 'There can be no successful compromise with any system of error' (9, p. 3), and 'we cannot build
upon Buddhism and Shinto. We must supplant them' (ibid.). Although as we
have seen Imbrie and Ibuka espoused the missionary policy which Paul used
on the Hill of Mars, they were more at home with the idea that the Japanese
gods were 'all purely subjective creations of the mind, as subjective as the
angels of Gnosticism... Amida is only a *cry* for light; Christ *is* the Light of
the world' (17/19, p. 10, emphasis theirs). Of a different outlook from that
of Arthur Lloyd, they insisted that;

If there are those who hope to discover in Shintoism or Buddhism much that is comparable with what is found in Judaism as points of contact with or as preparation for, Christianity, they will be disappointed; and if there are any who think to find in the non-Christian religions of the world great truths which will complement Christianity, they will not find them in Japan (ibid., p. 9).

After twenty-eight years service in China, Bishop F.R. Graves of the Protestant Episcopal Church had concluded that 'too much is often hoped for from the study of non-Christian religious systems. As a matter of experience one finds that the people rarely understand what they believe or why' (61, p. 5). Graves told the Commissioners that to claim either Confucianism or Buddhism as 'a preparation for Christianity, if we mean a preparation divinely designed is questionable. As it appears to me Christianity goes behind both of them, and appeals to the higher nature of men rather than builds upon any foundation they have prepared' (ibid., p. 6).

The Scottish missionary in Manchuria, James Inglis, was familiar with scholarly literature on Chinese culture and religion, had studied *The Sacred Books of the East* closely, and revealed in his answers wide knowledge of other scholarly literature on Chinese culture and religion.[212] For Inglis the contrast was marked between the popular religion surrounding him, which he saw as formal and superstitious, and the higher values of Buddhism, Confucianism and Taoism: 'Buddhism having got into a backwater', much of its teaching was of 'antiquarian interest rather than of practical moment' (66, p. 8). In the Tao Teh King, Inglis wrote, 'one may see the points of contact with theism on the speculative side. This book is, however, so obscure, and so neglected even by the Taoist priesthood, that its philosophy cannot be considered as of any great help in preparation for Christianity' (ibid., p. 6). Confucian classics were helpful to Christian apologists when they could point out that 'the early Chinese knew only one Ruler on high, that polytheism is a degeneration not countenanced by the ancient sages, and that image worship has only prevailed since the first century of our era' (ibid.). Inglis thought that 'the history of the Chinese religion points everywhere to degeneration' (ibid., p. 9). Arguing against evolutionist and progressivist notions, he wrote:

Compare the elevated tone of the early Mahayana Buddhism of the Tao Teh King with the present degradation; the clear objective faith of the early books with the silence of Confucius and the agnosticism of his modern followers. Why do we assume that religion must develop from below upward? Why must the religion of the savage be thought the most primitive? (ibid., pp. 9-10).

The Basel missionary A. Schosser also repudiated the evolutionist position, despite being in basic agreement with the change of missionary methods within the Great Century. 'Forty and fifty years ago', he wrote, 'there was the danger of taking too antagonistic an attitude'. Nevertheless, Schosser insisted that

> at the present time there is decidedly the danger of compromise. Many, especially English and American missionaries, are taking it as a matter of course that the theory of evolution holds good for the religious development of mankind, and they consider the heathen world as the minor child, and not as the lost son, who has to turn from these vain things to the living God (223, p. 3).

Schosser pleaded that no concession to Hinduism should be made at 'the expense of truth as it is in Christ Jesus' and suggested that any such conceding would 'not only not draw people to Christ', but would 'also weaken our position, and to some extent at least, deprive us of the right of our existence out here' (ibid., p. 3). Schosser's feeling that the English and Americans had accepted the theory of evolution too easily represented the mainstream of European thinking at Edinburgh.

One impressive and far reaching response which dealt with the issue of evolution in relation to the theology of religion comes from a missionary who was classified as working among 'Animistic' religions. This was the Australian Anglican Copland King at work in the Diocese of New Guinea, who stated firmly that there was 'much to be said for the old system of indiscriminate disapproval. It is understood by the convert' (328, p. 8). The implication that his colleagues were no longer applying the system of indiscriminate disapproval to even 'Animistic' religions is clear. King referred to the 'glamour' of the old beliefs. If the missionary, he wrote, 'is too sympathetic the convert will consider there is no need for him to resign or fight against what exercises such a hold on his teacher' (ibid., p. 7).

Such perceptions called forth what was virtually an essay on the missionary theology of religion as his answer to question 6. King dealt sharply with the evolutionist position that 'it took several thousand years for the progression of the True religion out of the shadows of myth to the light of Revelation' (ibid., p. 10). Such a sentiment might suggest animist mythologies could be used as 'a foundation on which to base the teaching of the truths about God' (ibid.). The myths would then be used as an introduction to Christianity. But why, asked King, 'the work having been once done, and the true Religion revealed, should it be necessary to start from another set of myths and do the work over again?' He thought it 'unreasonable' to attempt to evolve Christianity from 'the Animistic myths of our savages' (ibid.).

Then King turned to 'the other theory' that there was 'an original revelation to Mankind, but that whereas in Israel it was developed, in other countries it remained practically unused, and often lost' (ibid.). According to this theory animism had taken the place of original revelation. Myths and observances of the tribal people were then worked out, and rites invented according to the requirements of the myths. Some of these ideas were, King agreed, 'lofty and educative' (ibid., p. 11). He listed the conceptions of sacrifice, belief in the unseen world, and retribution or reward in the future life according to what has been deserved in this. But King criticized all three conceptions, pointing out on the one hand that of them none was strictly analogous to Christian ideas and, on the other, that all of them were intrinsically connected with false mythic frameworks. 'The myth on which the rite is founded', he wrote, 'is shadowy. The observance has outlasted the creed' (ibid.). 'I think', he concluded, 'it is dangerous to speak of the Animistic Religion as being a preparation for the true' (ibid.). Despite all his reservations about these religious traditions, King had a high regard for the mental and spiritual attitudes of the people of New Guinea. 'The mental attitude is a different matter', he wrote, and the Pacific Islander was a person of genuine faith in 'the Unseen World, in beings more powerful than himself who can influence his life, and in the recognition of those beings'. It is, King said, 'our duty to make use of his mental and spiritual attitude, while not accepting the faith on which it is based' (ibid., p. 12.).

Copland King reinforced his argument against working with the grain of 'evolution' in alluding to the advantage, as he perceived it, of working among people who were not touched by any of the great world religious traditions. It had not been progress, he declared, when tribal peoples accepted Hinduism, Buddhism or Islam. That had been 'advance up a dead lane, a blind alley' (ibid., p. 13). Those groups which had moved in that direction had put themselves in a more difficult position for the reception of the true religion. King considered this view to be identical with another Edinburgh correspondent, George Whitehead, of the SPG in Burma. In an article in *The East and the West* in 1908, Whitehead had written:

> The conversion of the Buddhists, Hindus and Mohammedans may well be the work of centuries, as was the conversion of the Hellenic world; the conversion of the hill tribes of India and Burma, or their absorption into one of those great faiths, will be the work of this or the next generation (ibid., pp. 13-14).[213]

To sit back and to just allow the quiet evolution of Hinduism or Buddhism into Christianity was for respondents like Draper, Graves, Inglis, Schosser and King a snare and a delusion.

The fallacy of verbal similarity

Other missionaries repudiated the theorizing about 'points of contact' for another reason. They suggested that such notions usually were based upon merely superficial resemblances. The need to recognize 'discontinuity' often implied displacement rather than fulfilment.

From China, the independent missionary Stanley Smith insisted that the Gospel was *sui generis* and that 'compromise and fusion with other religions should be wholly avoided' (95, p. 7). He made the point that the missionary should be 'on his guard against reading Christian ideas into Chinese terminology, in which, originally, the Chinese thought underlying those terms was very different, and even opposite in meaning to the Christian idea'. Chinese understandings of sin and holiness, for example, 'differ radically from Christian definitions' (ibid.).

A similar point was made by Arnold Foster. The Christian teacher needed to guard 'against allowing identity *of language or of expression* used by Christianity on the one hand, and by the ethnic religions on the other, to veil the essential difference of thought which the same words may cover in these differing systems of religion' (54, p. 9, emphasis his). Foster reminded the Commissioners of J.B. Lightfoot's discussion of the relation of St Paul to Seneca in his *Commentary on Philippians*. But Foster, the pupil of F.D. Maurice, could conceive of the alternative danger, where 'identity or similarity of religious conception between Christianity and the ethnic religions' might be 'disregarded simply because differently *expressed*' (ibid., emphasis his).

The two Scotsmen Morrison and Hogg explicitly declared themselves against 'fulfilment' conceptions. A.G. Hogg had serious difficulties with the 'fulfilment' ideology in John Nicol Farquhar's work.[214] In his Edinburgh reply he wrote:

> Outside of the region of vague abstractions what does it mean? Christian doctrines are not the fulfilment of Hindu doctrines, nor Christian rites of Hindu rites. Christian ideals of practice do not uniformly commend themselves to Hindus as better than their own, and if it be alleged that the Christian's religious fruition is a deeper satisfaction of his religious yearning than the Hindu finds in his own experience of religious fruition, the assertion is one incapable of proof or disproof (176, pp. 13-14).

Christianity was, Hogg believed, the solution of a religious problem which typical Hindus did not feel but which, under favourable conditions, they 'could be made to feel' (ibid., p. 15). In his view, there was little to be gained from treating Hinduism as though it were an immature form of Christianity.

John Morrison, the Principal of the Church of Scotland College in Calcutta, criticized the terms in which question 6 had been formulated: 'This conception of presenting Christian truth as the consummation of Hinduism or of certain elements in Hinduism seems to me to belong to a past generation in Bengal' (206, pp. 3-4).[215] Morrison then referred to 'a recent writer in South India' (he meant Slater) as writing a 'great deal' from 'the same standpoint' (ibid., p. 4), and then commented: 'It seems to me strengthening to converts to see that their old Hinduism has been pointing out the way, but to Hindus that treatment of Hinduism seems to bring Hinduism no nearer to Christianity than it brings Christianity nearer to Hinduism' (ibid., p. 4).

Indifference and hostility to other religious traditions

There was a small number of Commission IV respondents (they can be counted on the fingers of one hand) who showed themselves to be entirely hostile to the whole thrust of the questionnaire. We tell their stories for the sake of accuracy and completeness.

There was the case of E.C. Fry in Japan who had a real difficulty in responding to the questionnaire in any way at all.[216] He wrote: '*Here let me put in an objection to being regarded as an expert in any of the matters dealt with in this entire list of questions.* (I have been in Japan 15 years but really know very little about the other religions here – less than I ought to know, and much of that at second hand)' (11, p. 1, emphasis his). As a result of this attitude he offered the Commissioners comments like: 'The formal and the genuine seem to be pretty thoroughly mixed. That is the vague impression made on me by what I have noticed' (ibid.). The reason why he knew so little after fifteen years in Japan is shown from this non-dialogical prescription. The missionary, Fry wrote, 'should avoid fraternizing with other religions and their advocates, for that is to fraternize with their errors as well as their truths, at least it would be so understood by most people around him' (ibid., p. 2). No one else so categorically rejected the idea of meeting on the same level people of another faith-commitment.

The language of inflexible erudition and combativeness is found in the remarks of William Hooper, a CMS veteran missionary in North India.[217] Hooper wrote to the Commissioners of the 'vast inferiority' of Hinduism and Islam, and of his own determined opposition to Pantheism' (178, p. 7).

The long-serving Southern Baptist missionary R.H. Graves told the Commissioners that the worship of the Chinese was 'prompted by fear' and was an 'attempt to avert evil' (61a, p. 1).[218] Of the faith of the people he asserted : 'Like in all heathen mythologies there is nothing consistent in the belief of the Chinese. The same man will assert that the spirit ceases with breath and yet worship the spirits of his ancestors as still existent. If you point out the inconsistancy of the two, he will only say "this is our Chinese belief"' (ibid.,

p. 3). Consequently Graves had no room for appreciation, and in answer to question 5 Graves could only speak of 'pity' for their beliefs, however splendid their other virtues might be:

> We should pity them as those who from their ancestors have gone astray from God, and view them as men for whom Christ has died, and look upon them as a future valuable asset for the Kingdom of God and as possible efficient instruments for His service (ibid., p. 2).

Just as patronizing was the reply of the Anglican Metropolitan Bishop in Calcutta, R.S. Copleston, a former Oxford don, who talked generalities.[219] 'The essence of what I have to say', he wrote, 'is, that the chief hindrance to the acceptance of Christianity is everywhere the same, namely – "the corruption that is in the world through lust"' (135, p. 5). He did allow that some of 'the various so-called religions' could be helps, as he called them, in the acceptance of Christianity, 'so far as they tend to reveal or to heal that corruption; hindrances, so far as they are a screen, more or less consciously held up, between the human conscience and the demands of the Truth (ibid., p. 5). Copleston appears not to have had any Hindu friends even after thirty years in India and had no helpful comments to make on the theology of religion.

Changes in Missionary Attitudes

An awareness of the great changes in missionary motivation during this period pervades the Responses, together with a defensiveness about the distance that separated the newer from the older positions. Clearly some respondents felt anxious lest they had betrayed their honoured predecessors. One way of dealing with this anxiety was to deny that there had been such a change.

Thus, James Beattie in Amoy wrote in answer to question 5, 'We are largely giving up the sledge hammer condemnation style of preaching, if indeed such an attitude ever existed to any great extent.' On the whole he thought 'the missionary attitude has been persuasive rather than needlessly aggressive' (42, p.7). Similarly W. St Clair Tisdall, in wanting to urge, despite his reservations about Islam, that other religions should not be condemned altogether, added in parenthesis 'but this no missionary does' (271, p. 3).

On the other hand, some wanted to clear the ground by stating firmly that their fathers and mothers had been wrong. The Baptist missionary, W.R. James in Calcutta declared that in the past there had been too much 'denunciation of other faiths' and that a 'more excellent way is the rule today' (183, p. 12). The Danish Lutheran Steinthal expressed a similar view: 'Earlier generations of missionaries have undoubtedly had a tendency to deal with

Hinduism as a conglomeration of devilish falsehood and ridiculous ceremonies, and though much rarer now, it has not disappeared, especially
among the Indian evangelists' (224, pp. 16-17). The Chinese YMCA leader
C.T. Wang had people like Moule and Graves in his mind when he wrote:
'Two or three decades ago the attitude of most missionaries was that
Christianity alone was the true religion while all others were false. The latter
must be displaced by the former.' Wang continued, 'This is of course wrong
all together' (104, pp. 4- 5). The 'of course' carries its own significance.

For James Bashford, Methodist Bishop in Peking and former President of
Ohio Wesleyan University, the old missionary attitudes had to be repudiated
because they were harmful. He expressed the conviction in his response that
'missionaries could have done far better work' had they been 'more familiar
with the results of modern science, and had their minds been more open to
scientific teaching'. 'Upon the whole we are in more danger of blundering
from extreme conservation than through too great liberalism' (41, p. 2).

Bashford's contemporary in China, Paul Kranz, had experienced difficulties with the German missionary society under whose auspices he had come
to China on this point. By 1910 he had severed his connection with it,
becoming an independent missionary precisely because of the theological
conflict he had with the Board of the Rheinische Mission. In his response he
called the Commissioners' attention to the 'intense discussions' going on in
China. He instanced the findings of the Shanghai Conference of 1907, and
especially the remarks of the American Presbyterian, D.Z. Sheffield: 'The
truths of Confucianism, if rightly presented, will be made stepping stones to
the higher truths of Christianity, but if ignored or treated with disregard,
will be changed into barriers against the progress of Christianity among the
people.'[220] As Kranz told the Commissioners: '*This is the key to the whole
missionary problem in the East*' (ibid., p. 6, emphasis his). He went on to
take the debate into other areas. 'The same principle should be applied to
Mohammedanism. I have written at the time of the Cairo Conference an
explicit letter on this to Dr Zwemer, but he has not acknowledged it. Dr
Lepsius in a conversation approved of it' (ibid., p. 6, emphasis his). Kranz's
frequent underlining in the original indicated the intensity of his feeling.

Some who welcomed the new methods and attitudes voiced their suspicion
that perhaps they were in danger of going too far in the opposite direction.
Thus F.W. Steinthal saw dangers in the newer missiology, because there
were 'few older highly experienced missionaries' who, in his view, had been
led too far through their studies of Hinduism 'in the direction of compromise
perhaps without realising the dangerous consequences' (224, p. 37).
Presumably T.E. Slater, R.A. Hume and Bernard Lucas were among them.
Steinthal pleaded for 'a strong and clearly defined exposition of the doctrines
of revelation' (ibid., p. 38).

Likewise, the CMS missionary, Herbert M. Weitbrecht in Simla, qualified his approval of the contemporary approaches of fellow-missionaries in India.[221] 'I have no doubt that the duty of finding some soul of goodness in things evil will be dwelt upon by most of the replies' (249, p. 6). Though he 'fully' agreed with this approach he wanted to 'emphasise the fact that the need of a suitable polemic still exists... It is a poor kindness on the part of the surgeon to deal tenderly with gangrenes which threaten the life of his patient' (ibid.) In connection with this view we note that Weitbrecht appears to be among the earliest to have used the term 'syncretism' as a missiological pejorative:

> There is a great deal of unsound syncretism among Non-Christians, and some among Christians. The false or distorted conception of God, the moral defects which disqualify a religious teacher from the office of Saviour, the flaws in Non-Christian Scriptures, these and kindred things need to be pointed out clearly, yet charitably. But the methods of polemic need to be carefully adapted to modern knowledge and conditions, and the missionary needs to be carefully trained to use polemic effectively yet charitably (ibid., pp. 6–7).

Working in an Islamic context, George Swan of the General Mission in Cairo, distinguished between 'the attitude of the Missionary who admits of no truth outside of Christianity and who dogmatically deprecates everything in the religion of the people among whom he is working', and 'the attitude of the man who looks on Christianity as only one of the many phases of God's dealings with the nations, but withal believing that the best of these phases is Christianity' (275, p. 11). He believed there must be a 'happy mean' between these two attitudes. Swan was an engaging and modest person. Cheerfully splitting his infinitive, he wrote, 'To exactly point out the happy mean... is quite beyond my powers' (ibid., pp. 11–12). But he did suggest that justice, courtesy and love were the essentials for a proper 'attitude'. Under these controls, Swan wrote:

> there will be ample scope for all temperaments and dispositions that are under the control of the Spirit of God. Some will be as the fiery torch, revealing error of doctrine and wrong-doing of life, others with a Divine winsomeness wooing the soul from the coldness of a system into the warmth of the Divine love as revealed in the Lord Jesus Christ (ibid., p. 13).

The Re-shaping of Christian Theology through Missionary Experience

As they sought a new approach to the religions of other men and women, five aspects of Christian theology came to dominate the missionaries' thinking. These centred in the fatherhood of God, of the Trinity, the teaching concerning the Kingdom of God, in the personality and character of Jesus, and the reality of 'new life in Christ'.

The doctrine of God as father

The missionary in the Muslim world who revealed himself as most sympathetic towards Islam was George E. White of the American Board in Marsovan, Turkey.[222] When answering question 5, White declared that the Christian preacher must 'recognise that Mohammedanism contains much truth' (281, p. 5). He had many 'dervish friends' with whom he was in dialogue (he calls it 'conversation'). It is hardly surprising to find that he stressed the fatherhood of God in his answer to question 10. This, he wrote, is the 'central Christian doctrine', and for the Islamic world, the one thing lacking: 'God for them is an absolute sovereign, and among all his "ninety nine beautiful attributes" there is no "God is Love"' (ibid., p. 7). Few nineteenth-century theologians were more convinced of this sense of God's 'fatherliness' than the Congregationalists in the line of Bushnell and Fairbairn. White was however speaking not just as a Congregationalist, but as a missionary: 'My growing sense of God as Father as the critical Christian doctrine has received renewed emphasis by observing how much Mahommedans need and lack this truth' (ibid., p. 8).

There appear in the responses many first stirrings of the importance for missiology of 'theocentricity' rather than 'christocentricity', the sense that God rather than Jesus was the One to whom worship and witness must be given. John van Ess from the Reformed Church in America, who had had seven years' experience in Turkish Arabia when he filled in the Edinburgh questionnaire, represented this point of view.[223] He clearly enjoyed his life among Muslim people: 'I find in Turkey that when a missionary has gained a reputation for sociability he is practically overrun with visitors' (277, p. 1). Such visitors van Ess found 'affable, intelligent and not at all fanatical'. He wrote of his experience in this part of the Muslim world: 'The Oriental is primarily a religious being. *Allah* is to him *first* and *last* and *all the content* of his daily life' (ibid., p. 4, emphasis his). As a result of his continual contacts with Islamic 'centredness' upon God, van Ess now found himself thinking in a new way: 'though in America I held to theocentric theology in theory... it was in practice christocentric. Now I think theocentric theology to be a vital, soul-saving system' (ibid., pp. 4-5). Van Ess insisted that Christ was 'still the same precious Saviour from sin'. But this Christ was becoming increasingly the teacher of 'righteousness and truth', 'walking by my side and showing me ever higher and greater visions of God'. Therefore, van Ess concluded, 'I find the Gospel ever fuller of just these elements [of righteousness and truth] which appeal especially to the Semitic mind, and find ready and intelligent audience' (ibid., p. 5).

The Doctrine of the Trinity

The Doctrine of God, Father, Son and Holy Spirit, receives two kinds of treatment in the responses. On the one hand there were those whose thought is too Greek and too metaphysical to make any sense in their mission fields. For example, the vigorous Baptist missionary W.R. James of Calcutta felt that 'It was a sorry day for the cause of Christ when the word Trinity was coined. There is not the slightest need for it' (183, p. 7). In writing thus, James had not become a Unitarian, but was concerned rather about the metaphysical freight which, in his view, weighed down the gospel simplicities. His views had other exponents in China and Japan, India and Africa.

In Japan the theological educator, George W. Rowland of the American Board, confided to the Commissioners in answer to question 10 that his opinions had changed 'very decidedly':

> The dogmas of the theologians as such have now little place in my thinking and less in my teaching, and the most important and vital elements in the Christian Gospel seem to me to be few in number and simple in fact. Peter's confession, 'Thou art the Christ, the son of the living God' for faith; and the young lawyer's summary, 'Thou shalt love the Lord thy God and the Neighbour as thyself' seem to me to comprise the vital and the important (34, p. 3).[224]

Another American scholar, George F. Herrick in Constantinople, expressed the widespread unease of missionaries among Muslims about the traditional formulation of the church: I am not as sure as I once was that the divines of the fourth century put Greek compound words to effective and fruitful use in their attempt to define Christ's theanthropic person' (264, p. 10). Johannes Lepsius, writing as a respondent rather than as a Commissioner, put it positively: 'the language and spirit of Holy Scripture appeal directly to the Oriental mind if he is spared the abstract conceptions of Christian dogma' (347, p. 8). T.E. Slater told the Commissioners of the harm done to the understanding of the Gospel by 'severe dogmatic statements, which have a mediaeval rather than a modern derivation, especially those bearing on human destiny, which, though made in all good faith, cannot possible come as "good news" to the nations' (229, p. 23).

Many others may well have agreed wholeheartedly with Rowland, Herrick, Lepsius and Slater, if question 10 had addressed only the effective presentation of the gospel message. But somewhere they needed also to tell Cairns and his colleagues that they had themselves gained a renewed understanding of the Trinitarian God as a result of their missionary activity. For them the question was not so much of the words and the concepts to use, the 'how?' of missionary work, but rather of the aims and basis of it all, the 'why?' questions: why was there mission at all, and what kind of mission were they caught up in by the Triune God These were the theologians who most impressed the compilers of *The Missionary Message*, as we can tell from the heavy pencil scoring in many of the typescripts and the frequent extended quotations in the text.

For example, both Temple Gairdner in Cairo, and Samuel Zwemer in Bahrein, affirmed that the very essence of the difference between Muslim and Christian was the Trinitarian understanding of God. Zwemer put it thus: 'I am more than ever convinced that the heart of Christianity is the doctrine of the Trinity and of the Atonement' (283, p. 10). Gairdner also made a great impression on Alfred Garvie, who wrote the Islam section in *The Missionary Message*. Gairdner was convinced both that the doctrine of the Trinity summed up the whole gospel, and that this doctrine had to be presented in an ethical and spiritual, rather than a metaphysical form. In his own words:

I see more clearly however, that the Holy Ghost *must* be represented always, as in vital and essential connection with the Incarnate One; that He must not be preached as simply another Person of the Trinity; of the Spirit of God (simply) 'Proceeding from the Father'; but that the *spirit* if not the letter of the *Filioque* version must be ever and always preached; and the truth upheld by lip and life, that to us at least, dispensationally, the Spirit of God is the SPIRIT OF JESUS (263, p. 12, emphasis his).

From India came a chorus of voices stressing the importance of Trinitarian doctrine. One of these stands for many others. The theological teacher in South India, W.H. Campbell, wrote, to the great approval of David Cairns:

There are some of the doctrines of Christianity which at one time seemed to render faith more difficult, which practical experience has placed in an altogether new light. The most notable is the doctrine of the Trinity. In view of the notable failure of Indian monistic thought to retain the idea of the divine Personality, or even to retain an idea of God with any positive content, this doctrine is seen to be not merely an aid to, but a necessity of faith (133, p. 13).

The Kingdom of God

'At the present time when the whole country is ringing with renaissance,' George Douglas wrote from Manchuria, 'old Chinese texts concerning the "renovation of the people" are being revived with a new meaning' (43, p. 13). This fact, Douglas told the Commissioners, 'affords us a great opportunity for preaching re-creation in Christ as alone the hope of the individual and of the nation.' There was no doubt, Douglas insisted, 'that the whole body of the people is very much moved as to the future of the nation and they listen with marked respect to Christ's teaching on the Kingdom of God' (ibid.). In this way Douglas set the scene for his own exposition of the place of the Kingdom of God in missionary preaching.

In his testimony to the Commissioners about the Kingdom of God, Douglas held together 'otherworldly' or spiritual concerns for regeneration and the hope of eternal life, and a strong sense of 'kingdom growth' or 'extension' in this world. He wrote on the one hand, 'I am not aware that I have altered in my belief that religion is nothing if it is not personal, and that we must one by one enter by regeneration into the Kingdom of God' (ibid., p. 19). But, on the other hand, he was able to set out another vision of Christ's Kingdom teaching. In this he pleaded for 'a change of conception on the part of the Church as to its missionary call', and hoped that this would be 'the principal aim of the coming Conference'. Missionary work had to be more than an 'enterprise' and be recognized as 'woven into the very texture of Christianity'. 'It is time now that the Church as a whole conceived that for this she exists, and that a Christian life which does not concentrate upon the extension of the Kingdom of God is a contradiction. "Seek ye first the Kingdom of God"' (ibid.).

Douglas affirmed the passing away of older, more individualistic motives for mission, for 'the Kingdom of God', which '"cometh not with observation"', is, he said, 'much wider than the visible church' (ibid.). The 'older missionary appeal', he wrote, 'founded upon compassion for the millions hurrying to eternity was too limited in its outlook'. But now, just as 'the day of the proof-text has gone for our theology, so must the individualist motive give place to Christ's concentration upon the idea of the Kingdom of God (ibid., pp. 19-20).

For, as Douglas declared, Christ is

still working towards its consummation through us the members of His Body slow though we be to respond to His touch. I have learned a deeper respect for the non-Christian faiths and for those who sincerely hold them. They have in a very real sense prepared the way of the Lord. And at the same time my faith has been greatly strengthened in the uniqueness and universality of Jesus, – '*God manifest in the flesh*' – and in His power to save unintermittantly put forth (ibid., p. 20).

The personality of Jesus

We have already become aware of the deep sense of the presence of the risen Christ in testimonies already given by men like John van Ess and Temple Gairdner. One woman who clearly rediscovered the Jesus of the Gospels through her missionary work was Anna Smith of the CMS. She wrote full replies to the questionnaire which were used in *The Missionary Message* both by Garvie in the section on Islam and by Robinson in the section on Hinduism. She had been moved, as we have already seen, by the strength of the faith of the Muslim women among whom she had worked, seeing 'genuine resignation to the will of God', and 'patience in suffering' so that she had felt that 'God had revealed to them something of his love' (231, p. 1). The existence of Islam therefore challenged Christians, she thought, to reflect anew about the nature of inspiration and revelation, the power of the Holy Spirit and the Person and work of Jesus Christ. 'These', she wrote, 'are the vital elements in our Gospel, but we must not cling blindly to the old forms in which they have been expressed – we must go behind the words to the Spirit of God to teach us their meaning afresh' (ibid., p. 5). 'Higher Criticism' was, for Anna Smith, potentially a medium for new insight in Christian-Muslim relations. 'We should not be afraid of meeting them with the argument that our view of inspiration in the Revelation which God has given us, is not the same as theirs, that we care not whether the actual words are always the same' (ibid.). Rather, it is the Person of Jesus that is to be pointed to, whose words 'are spirit and they are life' (ibid.). Consequently, Smith had rethought her whole position on the Atonement and on what she calls 'the mechanical theory, which was taught to me when I was a child – that the death of Christ our Lord outweighing in value that of sinners was accepted instead of theirs' (ibid., p. 7). Such teaching she repudiated as having no power with Muslims: 'They doubt the justice of the transaction as people in England do now' (ibid.). Yet Smith, as a missionary to Muslims, was groping for a better way of understanding the work of Christ and its place in Trinitarian thinking: 'my work among them has made me realize more than ever that the death of Christ, His atoning sacrifice is the very centre of our creed, and with His resurrection the source of a new life' (ibid.).

After thirty years' experience among the Shi'ite Muslims, Samuel Wilson also recorded a shift of emphasis:

The Book, the Church, the sacraments, the means of grace receive less attention. The living Christ, the divine Saviour, and our personal relation to Him is the great theme. Christ 'the incarnate Logos' who was manifest in divine signs wrought by His own power, is still 'ever present' in the power of the Holy Spirit 'author of spiritual life and power to man, the always abiding illuminator, guide and counsellor, whose presence with every believer makes unnecessary any human Imam, Sheikh or Pir' (342, p. 17).

Both Smith's and Wilson's statements are unusual among missionaries in the Islamic world, but many others realized that the work among Muslims could not go forward simply through claims, and counter-claims, about doctrine and ethics but rather through the offer of a personal relationship to the living Christ.

Christianity as new life

We have seen much evidence of the Edinburgh correspondents' sense that the Divine Spirit was, as Slater wrote (229, p. 54), 'everywhere present'. To this conviction must always be added the sense that the older faiths could achieve realization of all their values and aspirations in Christ as the '*Fulfiller*'. But these two perceptions were linked with a further set of insights. The expected 'fulfilment' would not be realized within the forms of Christianity prevailing in 1910. Instead we sense among the respondents inklings and glimmers of a great hope that a new form of Christian faith would arise. The denominations and creeds of 1910 must be replaced by new forms which should be marked by an intensity of 'philosophical thought and Christian love'. The treasures of the Eastern religions would be part of that transformation. Missionaries with this vision also believed that the spirituality of the East would ensure that this new Christianity would become an expression of 'life', rather than intellectual assent to creeds or conformity to ritual practice.

Many Edinburgh responses tried to articulate these new thoughts and perceptions. They may be open to charges of simplicism and naiveté and of being starry eyed, yet what they were longing for is merely faith and worship that should be 'in spirit and in truth'. 'Has your experience in missionary labour', asked the Commissioners in question 10, 'altered either in form or substance your impression as to what constitutes the most important and vital elements in the Christian Gospel?' This question was taken by many to be an opportunity to spell out their personal visions for a transformed Christianity.

Like his fellow member of the Persian Mission of the American Presbyterians, Samuel Wilson, William Shedd was impressed by the 'wonderful vitality' of Muslim faith in Shi'ite Persia. He told the Commissioners that the Shi'ite faith in the *Imamat*, 'in some sense a divine presence among men, is of very real power' (272, p. 3), and that 'Another belief of very strong power is the faith in the saving virtue of sufferings, especially the sufferings of the

Imams' (ibid.). Shedd described Shi'ite Islam as 'a living faith' and as 'a genuine faith in one living God, who has a real relation to men and human affairs' (ibid., p. 1) despite the reservations we have seen about the possibility of Christians building on this faith. He reported his impressions like this:

> I think that I have learned to look at Christianity more than ever as a Gospel, a glad message from God to men, promising salvation, and more than that the power of God, which can enable men to live holy lives in the midst of evil. That is, Christianity is not a code of ethics, a social theory, a system of philosophy or a theology, although each of them must result from the working of Christianity... In this Christianity differs radically from the religions of Persia (ibid., p. 29).

As an early and devoted ecumenist, Shedd added to these words, 'The importance of particular systems of theology, such as Calvinism, either as the basis of denominational differences or as the medium for the impartation of the sum of necessary truth, has become very slight' (ibid., pp. 30-31). Shedd was not among those who believed that renewal of understanding of the gospel would result from encountering Eastern thought. Nevertheless he thought that 'Christians of the West can learn lessons in religion from the non-Christians of the East'. Shedd was convinced that in 'spiritual things' the unity of the race was 'so profound and real that the need is not so much for a new conception of the Gospel for the East as the presentation to the East by minds full of sympathy for the East of the great truths that have brought blessing to the West' (ibid., pp. 25-26). The implication of all this he put into a significant formula. 'Systems of theology made in the West are not adapted to the East but the great truths that underlie those systems are as cogent in the East as in the West' (ibid., p. 26).[225]

The American Methodist in Japan, Gideon Draper, made similar points from the Japanese context:

> I have deeply felt the unimportance to the Japanese of so much of that upon which the churches at home insist; and I have come to feel more definitely that salvation is not through church ordinances or organizations nor by man-made creeds but in the life, death and resurrection of our Divine-human Lord alone (9, p. 6).

Because for him, Christ was 'the great center of all thought and teaching', Draper was sure that the questions which divide the Christian Church are human in their origin and hence very secondary' (ibid.).

From India F.W. Steinthal wrote vividly of his theological shift, almost in Maurician terms: 'God's revelation in Christ is essentially life, not knowledge, and His salvation is not primarily a new view of life but a new life, not

a judicial rearrangement of the relation between God and man, but an actually restored fellowship with God' (234, p. 40).[226] This was, Steinthal went on
to stress, 'the essential characteristic of the Christian faith in distinction from
all other religions; this constitutes the unique personality, the unique message and the unique life work of Jesus Christ'. When new Christians set 'the
life of Jesus Christ at the centre, every element of the Christian faith gets its
true light and relative importance' (ibid.).

Such views had immediate consequences, especially with regard to the
form of the Indian church. Life so many of his colleagues, Steinthal was vigorously opposed to the planting of denominational structures, believing that
any success in the mass movements had been merely sociological: 'That it
has been possible to introduce the denominational systems in so wholesale a
manner as the case has been in India can to my mind only be explained by
the fact that the church has been reared so largely on uncultured ground;
among the educated classes it would have been and is impossible' (ibid., pp.
38-39).

New and indigenous forms of Christianity must therefore arise. Steinthal
told the Commissioners that he did not see 'any other way of preparing an
indigenous Indian Christianity and theology than by clearing the ground, laying down the true foundation and leaving it to themselves to build up the
superstructure' (ibid., p. 41).[227]

The Baptist scholar George Howells at Serampore also had a vision to
share. Writing in answer to question 10, his words to sum up the vision of
many others that new life would come through Christ Himself:

> My experience in India has made me realise very deeply that the one vital
> element in the Christian Gospel is Christ Himself. Our philosophical theo-
> ries and our theological dogmas can be very largely paralleled in
> Hinduism, but Christ cannot in any real or vital sense. I have unceasingly
> felt that my concern as a Christian missionary is not with Christianity as a
> religious system, but with the presentation of the Personality of Christ as
> the Supreme Revelation of the redeeming love of God. This is the one
> Gospel that India needs (179, p. 11).

He added, 'I am far from thinking a theological system useless, but I feel
strongly that no attempt should be made to impose on Eastern Christianity
any theological system worked out by Western theologians' (ibid., pp. 11-12).
Howells echoed Westcott: 'Eastern theology will in my judgment be more on
the lines of the Gospel of John than the Epistle to the Romans' (ibid., p.
12).[228]

Neither church and denominational structures nor theological systems
could or would remain unchanged as a result of the encounter with the great
world religions. To the missionaries of Edinburgh 1910 this was no bad

news. On the contrary, they saw it opening the way to the new life of the *Christus Consummator*.

The Conclusions of Commission IV

The Missionary Message in Relation to Non-Christian Religions in its final form was presented to the WMC on 18 June. Both the morning and afternoon sessions had been set aside for discussion of its main themes. The Standing Orders of the WMC provided for 'a period not exceeding forty-five minutes in all' to be at the disposal of the Commission presenting each Report, and for the remainder of the time to be reserved for delegates to speak.[229] To make best use of the time three strategies were adopted. The 'Business Committee' was assigned the duty of preparing an agenda in the light of recommendations from the Commission. Those intending to participate had to indicate what issues they wanted to speak about by 2 p.m. on the previous day. The time allotted to each speaker would be no more than seven minutes. Since in the general design of the Conference there were to be no resolutions and no voting, the Business Committee had no need to provide time for debate on specific issues. Accordingly speakers were expected to 'direct their remarks to the large questions related to the subject under review'.[230]

With these rules in place, David Cairns inaugurated the day's discussions on *The Missionary Message*.[231] These centred in turn upon animistic religions, the religions of China, the religions of Japan, and, in the afternoon, Islam and Hinduism. Among those listed as taking part in these discussion include Robert A. Hume, John Peter Jones, Henry T. Hodgkin, Arthur Smith, J. A. Lepsius, S. M. Zwemer, W. H. Temple Gairdner and John Morrison.[232]

In his introductory address Cairns made the point that all the evidence upon which he and his colleagues had based their Report ought to be printed in full. One reason to have taken this step lay in the extreme difficulty of covering every point. Already the group dealing with Hinduism had received suggestions that they had not dealt adequately with popular religion in India. A second reason for printing the whole lot lay in the need, as Cairns saw it, to 'bring to light the latent elements in the Gospel'.[233] Speaking to the assembly, Cairns said that the evidence had impressed the Commission 'in the profoundest way', that 'the whole position of affairs abroad is at the present moment one of extraordinary opportunity and extraordinary peril', and that

inevitably we were set considering not only what spiritual resources there might be in the present position of the Christian Church, but what resources might be latent in the Christian Gospel for the meeting of that emergency and that peril.[234].

Cairns stressed that the evidence presented to all eight Commissions offered the opportunity of 'looking into the great workshop of history'.

> We discern the forces at work which make nations and which make religions. We see the clash of the great historic religions; we see the forming of a new world. Something very vast, something very formidable, something very full of promise and wonder is there, if we have eyes to see it. But inevitably the question arises, Whether the Church has within itself, resident within it, the forces to meet this great emergency? Is it equal to its providential calling?[235]

Cairns thought this was the great *theological* calling of the church, which should lead to a broadening and deepening of its conceptions of the Living God.

> For us this can only mean a new discovery of God in Christ. It is this motive which has set us on our quest, this search for the hidden riches of God in him. We are persuaded that in the religions of the world we have the utterance of human need, and that the answer to that long need and prayer of humanity is found in the Lord Jesus Christ and His Spirit.[236]

With this guidance offered by Cairns himself about the most important issues arising out of his Commission's work, we turn to the section entitled 'General Conclusions' in *The Missionary Message*. These may be analysed as follows: 1. The Christian attitude towards other religions; 2. Training for a different approach; 3. The Renewal of the Churches' Theology; 4. The urgent need for the study of religion in theological education; and, 5. An incipient theology of dialogue.

The Christian attitude towards other religions

If Cairns was right and Christianity needed help to expand its horizons, a start had to be made in recognizing that other religious paths had to be able to be laid under tribute. This would only be possible if older and more exclusive attitudes were fully abandoned. Happily Cairns was in the position to declare that the 'practically universal testimony' of the Christian missionary community was that the attitude towards the other religious traditions of the world 'should be one of true understanding and, as far as possible, of sympathy'.[237] Cairns fully acknowledged that there would be elements in other religions which 'lie outside the possibility of sympathy' and that in some forms of religion the evil was appalling. But nothing, he felt, was more remarkable in the whole of his evidence than the 'agreement that the true method' of assessing other forms of faith and belief 'is that of knowledge and charity'. Other religions had 'nobler elements' and some of them in their 'higher forms' plainly manifested 'the working of the Spirit of God'.[238]

Training for a different approach

'On all hands the merely iconoclastic attitude is condemned as radically unwise and unjust,' Cairns wrote.[239] Consequently a new missiology was called for which would 'seek for the nobler elements in the non-Christian religions and use them as steps to higher things,' and recognize that even less noble aspects revealed fundamental needs of the human soul. Speaking on behalf of all his fellow Commissioners, Cairns asserted that this insight could be and ought to be made prescriptive for missionary methods. Polemical combativeness had come to the end of its useful life.

This in its turn would require a different attitude in theological training centres, as Cairns hinted in the following sentences:

... provision should made in our colleges for the training of missionaries in the art of teaching. The ordinary training in homiletics seems hardly suffi- cient for the peculiar conditions under which the missionary must labour. The teaching function is different from that of moving an audience which has already been instructed in the elements of Christian truth. An expert who has studied the entire correspondence has expressed the conviction that the errors which in past times have hindered the presentation of Christian truth would in large measure have been avoided had missionaries been trained in the art of teaching – an art which has as one of its first principles, the finding of the true point of contact with the hearer.[240]

Sadly, Cairns had to admit that there was little chance of this happening, because theological courses had been 'planned on another system', but he nevertheless thought his suggestion 'well worthy of consideration'.[241]

The renewal of the churches' theology

We have seen the extraordinary impression made on Cairns and his fellow Commissioners by the missionaries' desire for new forms of Christian faith adequate to meet the situations of their mission fields. As he wrote in *The Missionary Message*, 'What is needed is a living faith, and a living faith demands a living theology.' [242] Cairns himself was in no doubt 'that each of the great world fields has its own contribution to make to the great world problem, its own suggestion to the Church at home'.[243]

It would take us too far afield to do more than hint at all that Cairns meant by this. His material about the lessons to be learned from primal and traditional religion in the section on 'animistic religion' is still very relevant, as for example when Cairns asks if 'the working compromise between science and faith' inherited from 'the apologists of the eighteenth century' allows enough room for the full religious conception of the world which lies at the heart of Christianity but which is to be rediscovered through contact with primal cultures. It was, perhaps, in the discussion of Islam that Cairns became most prophetic of a new vision.

> Islam is something grander than the religion of scribe and Pharisee and dreamer of Apocalypse. That religion could never have laid hold on so vast a variety of human beings and types of social and national life as have been won by Islam. Mohammed is a far greater figure than any Rabbi; more noble in his attainment and more tragic in his partial failure than any Rabbi, except Judaism's greatest son. So if in some things he sinks below the level of the Rabbis, in others he far transcends them in his profound sense of the splendour and power of God and the impassioned poetry of his utterances about Him.[244]

Yet Cairns recognized that even this analogy did not do justice to Islam, for it taught 'the compassion and mercy of Allah for weak and sinful men' and he suggested that there was some validity in the plea that Islam was legalism 'only when the poetry goes out of it'.[245] Remarkably (this was still 1910), Cairns was able to put forward the idea that it was because of the 'larger and more spiritual element in Mohammed' that Islam has nurtured 'noble types of character, spirits purer than the Prophet's own, and that religious movements have arisen within it and come out from it, of a humaner ethos and a purer piety'.[246] Given all that, Cairns believed profoundly that Christian theologians should turn their attention to the issues raised by Islam:

> It will be strange, therefore, if the conflict between the living forces of Islam and the living forces of Christianity has not something to teach us about the inner meaning of the New Testament, and if that in turn has not something to teach as to the secret of success in that conflict.[247]

As a result of his reading the Responses Cairns was clear that the Muslim understanding of God did not attain the Christian sense of 'Fatherhood'. 'Yet', wrote Cairns:

> He is at least a real power, the only real power in the world. There is a simplicity and grandeur in the Moslem conception of God, His unity, His omnipotence, and His absolute sovereignty which we must recognise. Admitting the truth of all that has been said by the critics of Islam as to the defects of this idea, its inhumanity, its sterility, its negation of human

personality, still the question suggests itself: Have we in our modern theology and religion sufficiently recognised what Islam stands for, – the unity
and sovereignty of God?[248]

Like his master Maurice before him, Cairns was able to raise seriously the
question whether Muslims might not need to preach to Christians. Could it
be the case that 'in its profound sense of the sovereignty of God', Islam
might cherish something 'which is eternal, which is vital to Christianity, and
which, it may be, is obscured in our modern versions of it?'[249]

But it was the Indian religious traditions which Cairns found 'by far the
richest of all in suggestion' for the renewal of Christian theology.[250] The closest parallel he could think of to the opportunities presented by the encounter
of Western and Eastern thought was the time of the Alexandrian fathers.[251]
Despite all that was said in criticism of Hinduism and its practices, there was
nothing in all the responses, Cairns thought, more remarkable than the missionaries' 'generous and profound appreciation of all that in it which is true
and eternal'.[252]

Cairns believed that a number of issues were raised by Indian thought for
the church. Some turned upon the nature of the Kingdom of God itself.
India's conception of 'the redemption of the world through realisation of
unity with the supreme Being', Cairns believed to be the 'very core of Hindu
religion and philosophy'.[253] How did Christian faith compare with these
ancient Hindu perceptions? Rather badly, Cairns suggested, for much in
Western Christianity tended to see redemption as just inward deliverance
from the power of sin. Encounter with Indian thought might suggest to
Christians that they must give further consideration to the idea that salvation
must include 'ultimate deliverance from everything that cripples and
depresses the entire life of man'.[254] In common with his great friend, the
Madras professor A.G. Hogg, Cairns believed profoundly in the 'radical
supernaturalism' of the Kingdom of God and its consequent 'redemption
from the evil world'.[255] At this point, Cairns wrote, 'Indian thought has
something to teach our current conceptions of Christianity'.[256]

Like Maurice again, Cairns certainly thought that Hindus had something
to preach to the West. To be sure there were grave difficulties with the common Hindu thought that the world is mere illusion, but Cairns asked
whether there was not

...deep truth in the Hindu conviction of the nothingness of the world in
comparison with God. If we must choose, it is better to believe that God
is all and the world nothing, than to believe that the world is all and
God nothing, which is a view widely prevailing to-day in Christian lands.
No Christian holds the latter view in either theory or practice. Yet have

not both our Christian theory and practice become deeply tinged with the prevailing naturalism of the West?[257]

One last example of what the West might learn from the East comes from Cairns' reflections on the difference between Christian and Hindu mysticism. Writing of India's search for God, Cairns suggested that what Easterners sought was 'participation in the very life of the Eternal, above the flux and reflux of the world of illusion, in the passionless calm of Brahma'.[258] Cairns thought it doubtful whether Westerners had fully realized 'the immeasurable value of the idea of the Holy Spirit' in this context, and in particular of the Holy Spirit in the light 'which India casts on the inner nature of the religious aspiration of man'.[259]

> Much labour has been expended in discussion on the place of the Spirit in the life of God. But we still wait for any thorough understanding of the place of the Spirit in the life of man. We have an abundance of popular devotional literature on the subject, a great mass of unassorted and dimly understood psychological data, and the most recent research in New Testament thought has yielded also much that is of the greatest moment which has not as yet been assimilated by theology.[260]

In this situation Cairns was clear that much help could be gained through careful comparing and contrasting of the two ways of understanding spiritual reality. Indeed he spent the next twelve pages exploring the possibilities opened up for the renewal of Christian thinking. For our purposes it is sufficient to note that the challenges and opportunities for Christian theology that arose from the missionary encounter with other religion had been decisively recognized. Whether any of them could be taken up by those without missionary experience remained to be seen.

The urgent need for the study of religion in theological education

The only way those without first-hand experience of meeting people of other faiths could be introduced to the issues raised by the missionary respondents was the study of comparative religion. Cairns was convinced from his reading of the responses that every person intending to be a missionary should have a 'thorough and sympathetic knowledge' of the religious traditions of humankind. He wrote:

> Many of our correspondents speak feelingly of the incalculable harm which has been done in the past by the want of this; of the harm which has been done even by faithful and devoted men who, in this respect, were imperfectly equipped; the wholly unnecessary alienation and misunder-

standing which have thereby been created and to-day form a barrier to the progress of the Gospel.[261]

The inevitable conclusion that should be drawn, Cairns thought, was that 'provision should be made for thorough teaching in Comparative Religion in all our colleges and training institutes'.[262] This suggestion, it must be noted, was intended to apply to all students for Christian ministry, whether they were missionary candidates or not. Cairns was very firm about that. 'We do not in any way', he wrote, 'suggest the institution of separate curricula for the home and foreign ministry':

> We submit that the whole course of the enquiry is against such isolation, that either field yields invaluable results for the other. We trust that the evidence which we have submitted substantiates the conclusion that it is in truth impossible adequately to teach either theology or apologetics without provision for instruction in the nature and history of the religions of the world, for these reveal the elemental and eternal need of man to which the Gospel is the Divine answer. The absolute religion can only be fully understood in the light of the imperfect religions, if religion is a practical matter at all, and theology other than a mere abstract science.[263]

As such the new science of the comparative study of religion was not an enemy of the Church, even though many were using it in a 'negative interest with a view to proving that Christianity is only one among other religions'. On the contrary, the Commissioners were 'persuaded that its results lead to precisely opposite conclusions, and that rightly used they will fling abounding light on the undeveloped elements in the Christian religion'.[264]

An incipient theology of dialogue

Cairns called attention to the fact that along with the 'generous recognition of all that is true and good' in the other religious traditions there was a 'universal and emphatic witness to the absoluteness of the Christian faith'.[265] 'Superficial criticism', he wrote, 'might say that these two attitudes are incompatible, that if Christianity alone is true and final, then all other religions must be false, and as falsehood, they should be denounced as such.'[266] But denunciation was the very last thing from the minds of the Commissioners, as they reported on the evidence. To be sure in the claim to finality and absoluteness there was no sense of Christianity's being one religion among others. On the contrary, there was a strong sense that the other great religious traditions of the world would be taken up into Christianity. But it had to be recognized that dialogical attitudes are not dependent upon an *a priori* assent to religious pluralism. Cairns' manifest conviction that there was so much to learn from the encounter with the other religious traditions was also a perfectly proper basis for interfaith dialogue. This position was to be described later in the century as 'dialogue into truth', where all parties recognize that they still have much to learn from each other, and that because of dialogue their understandings of their own traditions will be altered and transformed. In fact Cairns' last words spoke of the 'inward transformations' that had taken place in the minds of the missionaries as a result of what we would now call inter-faith dialogue.[267] Such 'softening of wrong antagonisms' marched side by side with 'the centralising and deepening of faith in the Lord Jesus Christ' and with 'the growth of the spirit of love' towards Christian and non-Christian alike. 'Justice, courtesy, and love' are the key concepts for the kind of encounter with the world religious traditions that Cairns had in mind.

5

The Reception of *The Missionary Message*:
Two Theologians and a Postscript

In the contemporary Ecumenical Movement it has become customary to speak of 'reception' as the necessary consequence of, and follow-up to, any major Conference findings. How, for example, the decisions taken by the Faith and Order Conference at Lima have been 'received' by the churches was a major subject on the agenda of the most recent Faith and Order Conference in Santiago of Compostella in 1993. For this reason, this book does not finish with the 'findings' of the WMC, but with two theologians of the period who represent all those who warmly appreciated and gave a ready 'reception' to *The Missionary Message in Relation to Non-Christian Religions*. Of these the first was W.H. Temple Gairdner, a CMS missionary in Egypt and scholar of Islam, and the other a Methodist Manchester University professor and scholar of Zoroastrianism, James Hope Moulton. More than any others these two men played the role of advocates of the Commission's recommendations in relation to other faith traditions. By his journalistic skills Gairdner reached a new audience with his astonishing reportage of the WMC, completed only weeks after the closing ceremonies in Edinburgh and rushed into print just two months later. As a passionate missionary his personal authority was immense, and he put his own style of evangelical imprimatur upon the WMC views of other religions both in what he wrote and through his practice. The gentle and saintly James Hope Moulton, world class scholar in two distinct fields, added his seal of approval first through an influential series of lectures and then through a journey to India to put the Edinburgh message to the test.

W.H. Temple Gairdner: The Advocate of Edinburgh

William Henry Temple Gairdner (1873-1928) was born in Ardrossan in Ayrshire. His Scottish father was a professor of Medicine at Glasgow University, and his mother came from Norwich in England. While the family home remained in Ardrossan, Gairdner was educated at an English public school and at Trinity College, Oxford, where he was a contemporary of J.H. Oldham. He chose to be ordained in the Church of England, and after working with the British Colleges Christian Union, he entered upon service with the CMS in Egypt. Gifted as an artist and as a musician, as a linguist and a writer, as a scholar and a poet, he deeply impressed his contemporaries, and their unstinted appreciation comes through in an uncritical biography, *Temple Gairdner of Cairo* (1929), prepared immediately after his death in 1928 by his colleague Constance Padwick of the CMS Egyptian Mission.[1] Two years later, his wife Margaret Dundas Gairdner published a selection of his correspondence and other writings under the title *W.H.T.G. to His Friends* (1930).[2] This little volume was widely used as a source of spiritual reading in the thirties, especially by the British Broadcasting Corporation.[3] For all that, Gairdner comes to our attention now as a forerunner of today's interfaith understanding, particularly in relation to Islam.

Gairdner was also the great publicist of the World Missionary Conference, and filtered its findings through his own capacious intelligence. He stands now as the first of two post-Edinburgh witnesses to justice, courtesy and love for two reasons. First, there is the material in his vivid book of the Conference, *Edinburgh 1910* (in North America, *Echoes from Edinburgh 1910*).[4] Second, we have in Gairdner's writings in these years the record of his own changes in attitude. It is possible to see him moving missionary confrontation to a position resembling modern interfaith dialogue.[5]

Gairdner as the interpreter of Edinburgh

One of the urgent matters before the Edinburgh Preparation Committee was to publicize its findings. To whom could a task of such importance be entrusted? And who could write so fast that a book could be produced within six weeks or so of the end of the Conference? Joseph Oldham knew that the man for the job was his old Oxford room mate and colleague in the Christian Union, Temple Gairdner.[6] But fellow Preparation Committee members were also aware of Gairdner as a rising star, for he had recently distinguished himself at the Pan-Anglican Congress in London.[7] There he had made speeches on Muslim questions and on the relation of the Anglican Communion to the Eastern churches.

After the Pan-Anglican Congress, Gairdner had taken himself away to a house in Croydon. There he wrote two books in four months. The first was a tribute to a friend and colleague in Cairo: *D.M. Thornton: A Study in Missionary Ideals and Methods* (1909).[8] At the same time Gairdner wrote the largest part of a textbook for the United Missionary Educational Council, which was called originally *The Reproach of Islam* (1909).[9] Oldham had observed this literary activity and was aware of its result in these two lucid and influential books. He had no difficulty in getting the work assigned to Gairdner, who thus became a key figure for the whole Edinburgh experience.

Gairdner attended every session of the WMC from 13-23 June, giving close attention both to what was being said and to the manner in which it was said. Immediately afterwards he read through the piles of documents; he was ready to begin writing on 6 July. By 7 September the last proof had been read.[10] David Cairns was astonished at this achievement, and wrote to Gairdner:

> The way in which you have mastered the immense material and cast it into swift and telling narrative – which is never dull and sometimes rises into pages which are most striking and even brilliant – is quite extraordinary – particularly good is the unity which you have given to the whole – but the great thing is that you have grasped the lesson of the whole and bring it home to the imagination of the slowest.[11]

The Missionary Message *through Gairdner's eyes*

Gairdner was well aware of his responsibility. He wrote at the time to John Mott: 'Have you reflected that in this book, I, and I only, have the chance of *co-ordinating* the massed information and suggestions of that Conference, and giving to the world what I feel to be its most important themes?'[12] It was with this sense of responsibility that Gairdner singled out for greatest emphasis the Report of Commission IV. He wrote of this: 'By common consent the Report now laid on the table and presented by the Chairman of the Commission, Professor D.S. Cairns, was one of the most remarkable, perhaps the most remarkable of a great series.'[13]

But, to be sure, Gairdner was as much speaking on his own behalf as summing up the Edinburgh findings. His own supreme interest was in the relation of the Christian message to non-Christian religions. Acknowledging gladly that the Commission 'had been presented with the results of years of thought, lavished by the deepest thinkers in the field upon the work of their lives', Gairdner offered his own interpretation of the structure of the Report. He saw this rising to a climax in the last section which discusses 'the religion of Christ – as it was (and is) in Him; as it has been actually realised; *and as it might be*, if the Church responds to the Macedonian call of today'.[14]

But first Gairdner dealt with the older views of the non-Christian religions which held that they 'were perfect specimens of absolute error, masterpieces of hell's invention, which Christianity was simply called to oppose, uproot and destroy'.[15] Gairdner suggested that this view was not so much wrong as 'simply the exaggeration of one extreme aspect of a wide question'. He described the alternative and, as he understood it, prevalent conception within *The Missionary Message* which appeared to him to demonstrate

... a general consensus that, representing as they do so many attempted solutions of life's problem, they must be approached with very real sympathy and respect; that they must be *studied*, if only to bring the evangelist into touch with the minds of his hearers. More than that, the conviction has grown that their 'confused cloud-world' will be found to be 'shot through and through with the broken lights of a hidden sun'. And, these things being true, another conviction has dawned: – Christianity, the religion of the Light of the World, can ignore no lights however 'broken' – it must take them all into account, absorb them all into its central glow.[16]

This, however, could not be a restatement of triumphalism on the part of Christians. On the contrary the church was as much to be renewed as any of the other religious traditions through its mission in the world:

... since the Church of Christ is itself partially involved in mists of unbelief, failing aspiration, imperfect realisation, this quest of hers among the non-Christian religions, this discovery of their 'broken lights' may be to her the discovery of facets of her own truth, forgotten or half forgotten – perhaps even never perceived at all save by the most prophetic of her sons.[17]

Thus 'by going into all the world', Gairdner suggested, 'Christ's Church may recover all the light that is in Christ'. Only then would the Church 'become like her Head', the Light of the World.[18]

Gairdner's next pages describe in some detail what there was to be learnt from other religious traditions, including traditional religion (the then so-called 'animism'). These pages reflect the spirit of F.D. Maurice in the nature of the questions Gairdner either raises himself or strongly emphasizes from within the pages of *The Missionary Message*. Thus 'animists', and not only Hindus, preach to Englishmen about the reality of God. The questions which face China about naturalism and closed systems face Westerners also. The failure of the gospel to make progress in industrial Japan lay as much in its failure 'to dominate the life of our western civilization', as Galen Fisher had suggested in *The Missionary Message*. Aware like Maurice and Westcott of the spiritual crisis in the West, Gairdner suggested like them that 'the missionary enterprise may *compel* the Church to seek and find God, and in so doing solve her own social question also'.[19]

On the fundamental questions of the relation of non-Christian to Christian faith Gairdner had much to highlight. On the one hand there was Hinduism with its profound challenge to any understanding of the physical universe as 'closed system'. Hindu philosophy, Gairdner thought, constituted 'a hint, a challenge, an inspiration to Christian thought – not indeed to deny reality to that universe, but to assert that it is only real *because* there is One who is

Spirit transcending it, containing it, and not contained by it'.[20] On the other hand there was Islam, 'the great antagonist', which had 'actually within the Christian era erected under the very eyes of an impotent Christendom a new theology and a new social system'.[21] Like Maurice before him, Gairdner could attribute the 'marvellous record' of Islam 'through thirteen centuries' only to 'its living faith in a personal God'.[22]

The publication of *The Missionary Message* had become, in Gairdner's view, the moment for the Christian church when the scientific study of religion, hitherto often either 'an instrument of religious scepticism or equally sterile religious universalism' could 'be recognised as a marvellous instrument for the recovery of the full content of the faith of Christ'.[23]

'The full content of the faith of Christ' was exactly what was needed in 1910. As has frequently been said in the preceding pages the first decade of this century was not one of complacency for those Christians who could read the signs of the times. Gairdner referred to 'the enormous crisis' of our day in which the church 'defenceless as a new-planted slip, is face to face with the World'.[24] By this imagery Gairdner meant that:

> Once more the World, nay, Nature, the Universe itself, smashed ruthlessly into the conventionalised theology of Christendom: it needs no seer standing on the shore of any Patmos to see The Beast rising from the world-tide and presenting once more the immemorial alternative, 'Naturism, or, Deeper into God!' The spectacle of the East, with half a worldful of men, suddenly drawn into the full current of world-thought is one scene in the vision of the modern Apocalypse. The spectacle of the West rapidly surrendering to a radically atheist philosophy of Nature is the other.[25]

Gairdner's diagnosis was accurate and the convulsions of our century with their attendant loss of God need no detailing. But here the 'theology of religion', marginalized by the academies, was placed as the *sine qua non* of the renewal of the church. 'May it not', Gairdner wrote of the Christian community, 'in substituting for her conventional ideas a theology that shall once more pervade all life, bring in the East and bring back the West to the fold of the bosom of God?'[26] In this spirit he could endorse the closing sentence of *The Missionary Message*: 'Once again the Church is facing its duty, and therefore once more the ancient guiding fires begin to burn and shine.'[27]

Happily this ballooning late Edwardian rhetoric was anchored in Gairdner's own life and work, and we may take as a further commentary on *The Missionary Message* the attitude change discernible between Gairdner's thinking in *The Rebuke of Islam*, written in 1908, and his seminal article 'The Vital Forces of Christianity and Islam' which appeared in the first issue of the *International Review of Missions* in 1913.

The Reproach of Islam

By 1909, as we have seen, Gairdner felt able to publish two sizable books, the one about the missionary methods of D.M. Thornton and the other his textbook about missionary work among Muslims entitled *The Reproach of Islam*. But almost as soon as the latter book was in the bookstores Temple Gairdner realized that he had blundered. He wrote that it was with 'pain that the author found, when too late, that an undesigned *double entente* lurked in the original title'.[28] For Gairdner had not meant by 'reproach' anything else than that Islam had to be understood as a 'perpetual reminder to Christendom of the latter's failure truly to represent her Lord. For if she had done so, Mohammed would have been a Christian. And the world by this time had been won for Christ.'[29] The biblical sense of 'reproach' as 'something so unspeakably vile that its very existence is a shame' had passed Gairdner by.[30] He was glad to redress the balance by republishing it eventually as *The Rebuke of Islam*. But by the time he did this, he had changed some of his ideas about the way in which Islam should be approached.

From 1909 onwards the Church Missionary Society saw in Temple Gairdner its own ready-made guide and adviser in things Arabic and Islamic. Characteristically he protested against being cast as 'an authority without authority', for he knew that he had never made any sustained and scholarly study of Islam.[31] His objection was noted and the CMS gave Gairdner the opportunity for a study year to take place immediately after he completed *Edinburgh 1910*. Now he had the opportunity to study Islam in some depth with the help of such scholars as Duncan Black Macdonald in Hartford, Connecticut and Ignaz Goldziher in Budapest.[32]

Constance Padwick has recorded one glimpse of how these scholarly encounters enabled Gairdner to transcend his missionary mode in encountering Muslims after these studies. It comes from a letter written in Aleppo as Gairdner returned home to Cairo. In it he described his success at getting a 'fresh insight into Oriental and especially Islamic life and thought, unencumbered by recognition as a missionary':

I managed to enter on relations of great intimacy and cordiality with the sheikhs there, sitting with them long hours in the college-mosque, fez-cap on head, and minus shoes on feet, conversing on questions congenial to men with the typical education of Islam. In this way I could enter more deeply into the Moslem mind and thought than I had ever been able to do before.[33]

The experience of this kind of encounter enabled Gairdner as missionary to find more doors opened to him elsewhere. Here for example is his description of a visit in the Sudan:

A *zikr* (mystic worship) of special solemnity and with a specially full attendance – a 'command' *zikr*, so to speak – was arranged for Dr W. and myself on the occasion of my visit. Chairs were placed for us, with the leading members of the family, in the midst; and the senior, a venerable old Sudanese, representing the Grand Master of the Order, who was away from Omdurman explained things to us as they proceeded. He told us that we were the first Europeans who had ever seen certain parts of this *zikr*. At the end he made a speech to the whole company of devotees, saying what a pleasure it had been to them to show a *zikr* to those who had studied Sûfism and were able to enter into the meaning of what they saw; and making various other kind remarks. To this we replied in Arabic, there in the midst, addressing the whole of that throng of Sudanese devotees... .[34]

The point Gairdner wanted to emphasize was what he called 'the singular nature of the friendly connexion between our Mission and that powerful and influential Order and its "Lodge" in Omdurman'. It was 'a connection which is not only personal but *spiritual*. Government officials, even respected ones, are not admitted to these *zikrs*, nor are they saluted with the special salute which implies spiritual affinity, as our workers are.'[35]

Such experiences of a 'new relationship' lay behind Temple Gairdner's seminal article in the *International Review of Missions*.[36] In it he addressed the question of the 'vital forces' in Islam as well as Christianity. Published in 1913 it brings us close to the cut-off point for this book.

Gairdner saw Islam's 'vital forces' as three-fold: its doctrine of God; its attitude to Muhammad; and its prayer-life, both 'the canonical *salat*' and the 'uncanonical *dhikr*'. Each of these had its consequence in a pattern of dialogue.

Dialogue into truth – the nature of God

It was necessary, Gairdner believed, to 'strip the Mohammedan doctrine of all that is admittedly of purely theoretical interest' in order to discover what was 'of living significance to Muslims'. This lay in their conviction that 'Allah *is*, that He is more than a principle or an "influence not themselves", that He is a personal force, and that He has a definite relation to the world'.[37]

Though the length to which they have pushed Deism might seem to imply a hopelessly remote Deity, their conception of the unmitigated omnipotence of Allah brings Him virtually near – for man is in every way surrounded by, nay, himself exists through the immediate working of Allah's will and power.[38]

This view was in line with Gairdner's earlier comment on *The Missionary Message* about 'the living faith in a personal God' among Muslims. Here 'Islam teaches us to emphasize, to realize afresh, in some cases, perhaps even to re-discover'.[39] The immediate rediscovery that Gairdner urged upon the church was a new emphasis on 'the Unity of God':

> until the divine Unity has been grasped and re-emphasized, the enriching effect, the real value of the revelation of Father, Son and Spirit, cannot be felt. To find love and social life, and relations of reciprocal joy in the very heart of Godhead is surely to be for ever assured of the *Personality* of God.[40]

Christians still had to sort out for themselves some of the falsehood about God which they came near to uttering. 'Some presentations of the Atonement', he wrote, 'were distressingly suggestive of tritheism, even to the extent of asserting the existence of differences of ethical character within the Godhead...'[41] These ought to be buried, as should any other notion of God which suggested 'mere barren sovereignty, loveless and unloved'. Rid of such notions about God, Christians would be better placed to speak with Muslims of the love and holiness of the God and Father of the Lord Jesus Christ.[42]

Dialogue into truth – Jesus and Muhammad

Alongside the 'vital force' of the doctrine of God in Islam, Gairdner placed the 'Moslem's devotion to his Prophet, his admiration and personal love for him'. These were 'intense realities' in the Muslim world.[43] Gairdner has a fine description of these realities as they affected the life of the individual Muslim:

> He believes that the Prophet suffered and sacrificed in loyalty to his mission. Sometimes he throws over theological or philosophical proofs of the Truth of Islam and simply points to 'the fact of Mohammed'. He feels a personal relationship to him; he is conscious of a personal gratitude for the ineffable services he rendered.[44]

In laying so much stress upon the inescapability of Muhammad as the uniquely beloved figure in Christian-Muslim understanding, Gairdner was absolutely correct. He was equally right in pointing to the central paradox here, when he wrote that 'Islam, the very religion which arose to protest against the excessive esteeming of any man, ended by binding itself, hand and foot, to one man's dictation in all the concerns of both public and private life'.[45] In 1913 Gairdner expressed a hope that this, in his view, mistaken devotion was beginning to come undone, and that some Muslims were beginning to be dissatisfied with the moral ideal presented by Muhammad's moral character. Such people were distressed by the stories in the Tradition which showed that 'he often rose no higher than current Arab ideal and current Arab practice'.[46] 'As incidents in the life of an Arab conqueror,' Gairdner wrote, 'the tales of raiding, private assassinations and public executions, perpetual enlargements of the harem, and so forth, might be historically explicable and therefore pardonable; but it is another matter that they should be taken as a setting forth of the moral ideal for all time.'[47] Gairdner cited a young Muslim of this critical tendency as saying to him that the important thing was to accept the Qur'an, that it was no part of the mission of the prophet to give a moral ideal. The cry was 'Accept the *Koran*, and let Jesus, if you like, be better than Mohammed!'[48]

But here lay the problem for Christians. The Jesus of the Gospels was unknown to Muslims, and the instinctive aversion and antipathy of Islam toward Christianity as a system ensured that the question which had been closed through Muhammed's teaching in the seventh century could not be re-opened. As Gairdner sorrowfully recorded in 1913: 'There are no signs of a more sympathetic study or understanding of our faith. Deliberate ignorance or contemptuous knowledge is still the rule.'[49]

The one mitigating factor, however, after all the work of the Great Century, lay in 'the fact that modern missions have at least made Moslems respect some Christians, and in them recognize, however unwillingly, the fruits of faith and love'.[50] Upon this 'fact' Gairdner proposed to build. For this reason the word which stands out on page 55 in his article is 'friend'. In working out a way of speaking of Jesus in the midst of the prejudices and misunderstandings in Islamic theology, Gairdner wrote this fertile sentence: 'Yet these represent his honest, his earnest attempt, and the Christian cannot but begin on that understanding, and then try to show his friend feature after feature, lovely and glorious, of the true portrait.'[51]

Dialogue with the saints of Islam

Gairdner was able to distinguish between outward forms and inward religion as he discussed the 'vital force' of Islamic prayer. In his *IRM* article, Gairdner wrote that 'what strikes the superficial observer as of enormous importance, often expresses formal allegiance rather than religious life'.[52] Emotion and feeling entered into the 'less statutory services' and in these teachers like Al-Ghazzali found a 'road to God'.[53] 'Mohammedan mysticism' had opened a door to the world of religious emotion. For Gairdner this was then the place to begin the profoundest dialogue, because, as he was to write a little later, 'the Mohammedan Wali at his best is wonderfully like his Christian brother Saint'.[54] Therefore the task of the church was obvious: 'Let Christian Sufism appeal to the heart of the Sufism of Islam.'[55]

Gairdner's lasting contribution

Gairdner on many occasions came close to despair because of what passed in his own day for the communication of the gospel among Muslims. Once he compared the usual missionary approach to a man from China 'expounding with Chinese accent in indifferent English the doctrines of Taoism, from the exclusive point of view of the people of Shen-si, to an audience of British Britons at Hyde Park Corner!'[56] Courtesy and love make dialogue into truth possible, but the need to sit where others sit, to speak their language properly, and to know, with a knowledge that comes only by listening, what their longings and aspirations are, is a way of doing justice.[57] Modern Christians need to catch up with their best role-models from among those who have sought to understand other religious paths and aspirations from 'within'. In this company Temple Gairdner holds a remarkable place.

James Hope Moulton: Pioneer and Witness

James Hope Moulton (1863-1917) straddled three worlds: those of New Testament philology, of the comparative study of religion, and of the Christian missionary movement.[58] He has also a serious claim to be included among the most outstanding of the forerunners of present-day interfaith dialogue, as we shall see later. But he is treated now chiefly as a post-Edinburgh exponent of the new and generous Christian theology of religion which emerged from the WMC in 1910.

Moulton was a significant figure among the great Methodist scholar-theologians at the beginning of this century.[59] He had distinguished himself at Cambridge as a classicist of the first rank, and was the first Methodist ever to be appointed as a Fellow of a Cambridge college, having been elected at King's College in 1888.[60] One of his senior colleagues at King's was B.F. Westcott, who was a 'Professorial Fellow'. Another close friend in Cambridge was the anthropologist J.G. Frazer (1854-1925). In 1902 he went from Cambridge to teach in the Wesleyan College at Didsbury in Manchester, and later (in 1908) became also the Greenwood Professor of Hellenistic Greek and Indo-European Philology in the Victoria University of Manchester. Here he prepared standard works on Greek linguistics and philology.[61] These studies had led him, most significantly, into pioneering studies on Zoroastrianism, notably *Early Zoroastrianism* (1913), the Hibbert Lectures for 1912, and *The Treasure of the Magi* (1917).[62]

Wesleyan Methodism's chief intellectual forum at the turn of the century was the Fernley Lectures, which were given annually at the Wesleyan Conference.[63] For 1913, the year of the centenary of the formation of the Wesleyan Methodist Missionary Society, the Fernley Trustees selected

Moulton as a man who could give some world-wide perspective on the challenges to Christian mission.[64] Fully aware of his task to give a centenary reflection on the world mission of the church, Moulton chose as his subject *Religions and Religion: A Study of the Science of Religion, Pure and Applied.* The key word here is 'applied', and we shall see his theology of religion become a theology of mission. After 1910 *The Missionary Message* shaped his thinking and writing, and he constantly referred not only to *The Missionary Message* itself but also to his friend David Cairns.

Moulton's missionary interests

James Hope Moulton came from a family which had produced one of the great Wesleyan missionaries. His uncle, James Egan Moulton, had been a pioneer missionary in the Friendly Islands and Moulton described his lasting influence:

> ... I recall that I am a missionary's nephew, and seek an inspiration for my work in the memory of a long life spent in the South Sea Isles, of great and varied abilities lavished in pastoral and educational labour, in massive translation work, in the anxieties of a native church guided through slow but fruitful development, and upheld and encouraged through a savage persecution. How can I, with these memories write with cold impartiality, as if these men had wasted their gifts on a meddlesome effort to disturb the simple savage in his hold on the religion that is good enough for him, and especially adapted to his nature.[65]

Other missionaries who inspired Moulton were David Hill (the friend of Timothy Richard), and Sidney Rupert Hodge who had worked in China, and F.W. Kellett, who had died in India in 1904.[66] His brother, W.F. Moulton, recalled that on one visit to the family home in Cambridge, David Hill spent much time with James Hope Moulton in discussing whether he should become a missionary.[67]

Moulton's view of scientific impartiality

When Moulton found himself, at rather short notice, having to write enthusiastically on behalf of Christian missionary work, he had been engrossed in the preparation of his 1912 Hibbert Lectures on *Early Zoroastrianism*. The tension between objective study and missionary conviction produced in his own mind, Moulton described vividly.

> Fresh from an effort to delineate with scientific impartiality, and with real warmth of appreciation, the religion preached by a prophet outside Israel,

I turn now to a duty in which impartiality, as pure science understands it, can have no place. [68]

Moulton felt first of all that it was his duty to declare his position that Christianity was the 'one perfect religion'. However little temptation he had 'to become an advocate, sternly impeaching other religions' (for he knew 'too well' where he had learnt a profound sympathy for all 'humanity's groping after the divine'), he wrote that he would not 'pretend to think that these are anything but broken lights of Him who came to bring the dawning of the perfect day'.[69] But at the same time Moulton said he had no intention of indulging 'a lofty scorn for "superstition"', a word which, he said tartly, he reserved 'for degenerate and degrading conceptions obstinately maintained by those who know better'.[70] Rather he wanted to 'miss nothing of the spiritual illumination that shines in many dark places, for I am sure that the first great Christian missionary was right when he declared that God had never left Himself without witness'.[71]

Moulton's reflections on the study of comparative religion

Perhaps because of his profound understanding of evolution in terms of language (he had contributed much original research in the study of the Indo-European languages) Moulton had no difficulty at all in using the framework of evolution as a fundamental category for his dealing with the world religious traditions.[72] Rejecting 'special creations' in the natural world (including the field of linguistic development, which he knew most about), he did not expect there to be any other aspect of human experience which would be cut off from the operation of a single divine law.[73] On the contrary, he enquired, 'Is it not reasonable to expect that if evolution is a good enough method for God to employ everywhere else, it will be good enough for Him in the crown of all his work?' Answering his own question, Moulton affirmed,

> We need not categorically deny that what men call the miraculous has ever entered into the history of revelation. But we are free to believe that the evolutionary mode has been the normal. And we believe this because we have come to understand evolution in a theistic light. All things have reached their present condition by evolutionary process; but God has been as vitally present throughout that process as He was in the framing of the evolutionary law.[74]

By so wholehearted an acceptance of the idea of evolution Moulton stepped straight into the controversies of his own time, claiming the work of E.B. Tylor and J.G. Frazer for a Christian understanding of the development of religion. He was at pains to show how the 'natural' is 'supernatural'. 'We cannot be afraid of the Reign of Law when once we come to realize that it is *His* Law', he wrote, emphasizing the personal pronoun.[75] But like his contemporary the missionary scholar, Robert A. Hume, Moulton knew the phenomena of 'degeneration and decay' and never thought there was a natural evolution moving inexorably upwards.[76]

Moulton and special revelation

But so naturalistic an interpretation of religious development obviously threatened the uniqueness of the biblical revelation. Moulton thought the gift that Israel had brought to the world was unique, and he described it as 'the most wonderful and fruitful growth in all the long history of religion'.[77] Nevertheless it was within the natural order that revelation had taken place, since what he called 'the manifest principle of God's providence' had to apply to every department of religion. It just so happened that the 'genius of Israel was supremely adapted for the place of missionary of religion to mankind', just as it had so happened that the genius of the Greeks and the Romans had given humanity philosophy, science, literature and law. In this sense it was unique, but this understanding of uniqueness did not deny that God could work through other peoples. Moulton wrote rather eloquently,

> It is no part of our case to assert that Israel had a monopoly of this great gift. Socrates, Gautama the Buddha, Confucius, Zarathushtra, even Mohammed, though one gives him the name rather less readily, are prophets by every title that the Science of Religion or true Christian insight can recognise; and the 'goodly fellowship' has its members, famous or obscure, in every land and every time.[78]

Moulton made a distinction between this 'company of prophets' among the nations and those within Israel mainly because in Israel there was an almost unbroken succession of those who penetrated into 'the most vital truths of religion'. Writing as the world expert on Zoroastrianism of his day, Moulton declared that 'Parsism, with a doctrine of God purer than any Gentile faith possessed, might have become a world-religion if only Iran had produced men worthy to follow and extend the work of Zarathushtra'.[79] Interestingly, he compared this with the case of Islam, where Islam had become a world religion, 'because it has had a succession of true prophets, many of them of higher character than the founder himself, though behind him in genius, and to us mostly unknown'.[80]

This pattern of prophethood was to be contrasted with the situation in India. Despite all its manifold gifts and achievements in spiritual understanding, India had no prophetic succession, bringing 'religion into indissoluble union with conduct'. In this lack lay the solution to the problem India presented, as the 'land of profoundest thinkers, aesthetic devotees, dreamers and mystics without number'.[81] If one were to ask why India did not compete with Israel in the supply of prophets who could have taught the whole world, Moulton thought the answer should be along these lines:

> India has always been far more religious than Greece or any Western nation: religion with her has taken up a larger arc of the periphery of life, and she has pursued it with incomparable earnestness. Her time is not yet, but it is coming. Israel was free from philosophy and mere intellectualism on the one side, from dreamy mysticism and profitless asceticism on the other.[82]

Moulton affirmed values in other forms of faith as he traced humankind's spiritual development. If the 'comparative religionist' then exclaimed, 'this is evolution' Moulton was not, he said, minded to dissent. He could still cry, 'this is the finger of God'.[83] As a student of comparative religion, Moulton confidently expected development in all the world's religious traditions. As he said of India, 'her time is not yet, but it is coming'.[84]

Moulton's theology of mission

In chapter III of *Religions and Religion*, Moulton assumed fully his role as a Christian thinker and addressed the theology of mission. His approach here is distinctive not least because of his fearless welcome of 'syncretism'.[85] First he sought to make it clear to his Methodist audience that Christianity had always borrowed from other faith traditions. As the great philologist of the New Testament of his day, he could take it for granted that the Christianity of the first century had absorbed much else beside language from Greek and Roman sources.[86] Alien ideas and concepts, he said, had always been 'baptised into Christ', and had become 'a not unworthy part of our Christian inheritance'. More than that, the power to live with what a later scholar has called 'faithful syncretism', Moulton saw as proof of the power of Christianity.[87] As he wrote,

> when once a sure foundation had been laid... stones from widely distant quarries could be brought and fitted into a superstructure which must shelter the whole world. Professor Gunkel is quite justified in his claim that a syncretic origin is entirely in keeping with the universal destiny of Christianity, whether or not we accept or deny the particular instances for which he makes the claim.[88]

Moulton then moved to the judgment of a contemporary anthropologist, E.B. Tylor, author of *Primitive Culture*, in what he called Tylor's 'weighty words'.

In *Primitive Culture*, Tylor had written that the 'thoughts and principles of modern Christianity' were 'attached to intellectual clues which run back through far pre-Christian ages to the very origin of human civilisation, perhaps of even human existence'.[89]

But that did not mean that everything had to be made welcome in the church's life and worship. Here the missiological issues of 'accommodation' and 'adaptation' surfaced. In Moulton's own words:

> Now one of the most urgent problems of our modern missionary policy is that of the limits of accommodation. How far may the long-established customs or beliefs be let alone when suited with an adequate Christian interpretation? The study of history, in the new light of Comparative Religion, will be a good preparation for framing our reply.[90]

After some incisive pages on the experience of both Western and Eastern churches (with Christmas replacing the 'feast of the Unconquered Sun' at the time of the winter solstice; Lent replacing a pre-Christian period of abstinence which was aimed at giving strength to the new crops; and the cult of the Mother and Child replacing Demeter and Persephone in Mediterranean lands), Moulton concluded that the net result of the experience of Christendom did not encourage anything beyond a most cautious use of accommodation as a deliberate policy. He saw the error to lie in too eager a desire to make converts. Little or no attention was paid to what is in the hearts and minds of the people who are pressed into mass baptisms. In its long history, wrote Moulton, 'the church has not been very careful as to the character of her members on trial, whether individuals or ideas. She has baptized new converts in droves with only perfunctory questions. And in her eagerness to win men to membership, she has practised accommodation on a very large scale indeed.'[91] Contemporary theory and practice of dialogue is as concerned as Moulton that the differences in the speech of other women and men about their religious paths should be heard, and that no one should move inadvertently into syncretisms which are ultimately other than 'faithful'. Though he could not have used the terminology of dialogue, Moulton would have concurred with its essential aims.

A missionary theology of religion

After this cautionary discussion, Moulton turned specifically to a post-Edinburgh theology of religion. Again it is best if he is allowed to speak for himself:

> We turn to the question of modern non-Christian religions, their strong and weak points, and their relation to the missionary message. In this part

of my subject, I need not say, the ground has been occupied already, and in the most authoritative way. The Report of Commission IV of the Edinburgh Conference, embodying the experience of a host of missionaries as studied by men exceptionally qualified for their task, makes it sheer presumption for any one man to trespass on the theme, especially without access to that unique collection of first-hand evidence upon which Professor Cairns and his colleagues based their masterly survey.[92]

He intended therefore to take what he called 'the Edinburgh Classic' for granted in his reflections on the subject, for he had been 'powerfully impressed' by the 'tolerance, the modernity, and the open-mindedness' of the missionaries whose experiences were distilled in *The Missionary Message*.

> We in our armchairs at home need not indite any lectures to our brethren on the supreme importance of sympathy and knowledge of the religions of the people they evangelise. They can preach better sermons than we on the pregnant saying of the Master, 'I came not to destroy but to fulfil.'[93]

Moulton found great joy in all because the days were over (as far as Edinburgh was concerned) when missionaries went forth deliberately in order to 'drag men out of their systems of unredeemed darkness and error'.[94] Missionaries had made it clear that they no longer felt it as part of their duty to destroy other religions 'root and branch as works of the devil'.[95] Such attitudes, Moulton told his audience of Wesleyan Methodists, had passed away.

> In every part of the field the most typical missionaries are seen to be bending their whole force of brain and heart to the great task of acquiring a sympathetic understanding of their people's thoughts. They are busy with the heaps on their threshing floor, not to estimate with scorn the mass of chaff good for nothing but the fire, but to pick out scattered grains of seed-corn that may grow in their Master's field.[96]

Quoting from W.T. Balmer in Sierra Leone and Sidney Gulick in Japan (words already highlighted in this present work), Moulton was sure that their 'sympathetic attitude' was that of the missionary body as a whole.[97]

But true to his own discussion of 'degeneration', Moulton went on immediately to say that he did not intend to suggest that missionaries were blind to the darker sides of Hinduism and other religions. Moulton instanced the words of the Methodist missionary C.H. Monahan from Mysore at the WMC, who had expressed fear lest 'the ugly aspects of Hinduism should be forgotten in the endeavour to bring out its better features'. 'Mr Monaghan shows himself entirely with the Commission in their recognition of what is good, and they wholly endorse his warning against a possible misinterpretation of Christian tolerance.'[98] Moulton went on to quote some remarks from a personal letter that he had received from another Wesleyan Methodist missionary in India, William Goudie. 'He is very much afraid lest the new attitude should be supposed to involve too high an estimate of the elements of truth to be found in non-Christian systems, by which we may often read into them by mistaken explanation of acts only outwardly capable of the higher meaning.'[99]

Encounter with other faith changes Christians' conception of Christianity

Moulton had absorbed from his reading of *The Missionary Message* two other sets of insights. These had to do with the effects the encounter of the world's religions would have upon Christian doctrine, and upon the exegesis of the Bible. First there was the area of theological refinement and recovery. There was, for example, the doctrinal work that the church had to do over again, as *The Missionary Message* had itself suggested.[100] 'Practical contact with other religions', wrote Moulton, 'may sometimes indeed shake doctrines on which the Church has set her seal at one time or another; but when the Christian goes back to his authentic documents they find they are not there.'[101]

> Each several field of non-Christian religion can supply much-needed correctives of our popular Christian doctrine. The missionary takes with him the crude Western setting of New Testament truths, and is soon forced to reconsider his theology. He finds the doctrine of the Trinity a grievous stumbling-block to the Moslems. He tries to explain it, and realises that the doctrine elaborately worked out by the Greek theologians, so to express monotheism in its most absolute form, has been developed into practical Tritheism in the religious language of a race unaccustomed to fine distinctions and minutely exact statement. No wonder if he demands as an imperative necessity a re-statement of Trinitarian doctrine, which shall emphasise the Unity of God and define the meaning of 'Son' as applied to Christ, so that we may in coming back to the New Testament escape a reproach cast at us by the thoughtful Moslem.[102]

Moulton gave other examples of this process. One came from his own field of expertise in dealing with the central question of Zoroastrianism, i.e. the origin and nature of evil. In Zarathushtra's teaching, Moulton suggested, Christians may find 'the problem of evil seriously faced and solved' on lines which 'only popular misunderstanding removes very far from those of the New Testament':[103]

> Christian theology has not a little to learn on this subject by careful comparison with the thoughts of a profound religious genius, living perhaps

nearly a millennium before the coming of Christ. On the combination of
monotheism with the idea of a plurality of hypostases within the Godhead,
and on the postulates of ethical immortality, Zarathushtra's teaching is full
of suggestiveness.[104]

A fresh reading of the New Testament

The second aspect of theological renewal and recovery was in biblical exegesis and interpretation. Moulton had some forceful remarks to make on the
way in which too many Christians in his own day were bothered by biblical
criticism and research, known then as the 'Higher Criticism'. Moulton was
impressed by the presence of question 9 in the Commissioners' questionnaire, and thought that the responses as he saw them in *The Missionary
Message* indicated 'most remarkable tranquillity in the missionary mind as to
subjects which greatly disturb good Christians at home'.[105] As a New Testament professor at this period, Moulton was endlessly engaged in controversy
about biblical inspiration, and it was with obvious pleasure therefore that he
quoted David B. Schneder:

> Just an honest and impartial presentation of the truth, with emphasis on
> the positive, saving the elements of the gospel, is what is needed. When
> this course is pursued there is nothing to fear from the Higher Criticism –
> at least if it be not of the extreme type. The kernel of the Gospel is what
> touches the Japanese, and they do not care about secondary questions.[106]

'Surely', wrote Moulton, 'this missionary (who would neither 'keep back
the results of criticism' nor 'flaunt them before the people') gives the right
message to the Church everywhere.'[107] To his Methodist audience he offered
these comments:

> Need I point out how completely in harmony this conclusion is with the
> whole genius of our Methodist missionary work at home and abroad
> throughout these hundred years? We have always stood for the living
> experience of Christ as the supreme element in religion. We have shared
> the general 'shaking' in our views of the Bible, and even in our formulated
> Christology. We have been, and still are, deeply divided in these important
> matters... Yet in all alike our salvation as a Church is still, as it has ever
> been, that we instinctively make personal experience the indispensable
> evidence of the Faith.[108]

Reviewing briefly the Methodist succession, from John Wesley to Hugh
Price Hughes, Moulton thought that Methodists should be the last people to
'turn craven at the signs of the times' and to be prepared to 'commit the

Gospel to a blind defiance of knowledge'.[109] Biblical and theological knowledge, he said, moved 'from one stage of development to another, and we are never at one stay'. What mattered for the future was 'the sense of the presence of Christ the Saviour'.[110] At this point Moulton showed himself to be a 'theologian of faith' like John Wesley before him (and Wilfred Cantwell Smith after him).[111] Moulton was never interested in faith as intellectual assent. For him, as for Wesley and the whole Methodist tradition, faith was commitment to live in love and hope, and, as such, 'a means to an end', not an end in itself.

> Throughout the New Testament – though the fact has been in all ages grievously overlooked by too narrow a view of the place of faith in Christian theology – the right relation of the human soul to God is exclusively regarded as a means to an end... The one purpose of the New Testament, then, is to bring us to the knowledge of God as he is, by the only way that can bring it to us in its perfection. Jesus Christ enables us to see the Father and realise His love for us; and he who surrenders himself to the gracious influence perfectly is compelled by the mightiest power yet seen on earth to love his neighbour as himself.[112]

In so writing, Moulton was in full accord with what David Cairns had seen to be the most important matter to have arisen from the Edinburgh responses. In his Address presenting *The Missionary Message* to the World Missionary Conference Cairns had spoken of the need to search for 'the reserves of spiritual energy' which remain unappropriated in the Christian tradition.[113] Moulton interpreted these new energies as springing up in the future, for God, as he wrote, 'will assuredly not be content to repeat Himself. He has no duplicates to give'.[114] Consequently the most important chapter in *Religions and Religion* is entitled 'The Christ Who is To Be'.

Exhilaration and confidence

In this chapter Moulton was writing for the last time with 'the innocence of Western Man' in 1913. A year later and the beginning of the First World War would have made it impossible for him to exude the optimism which pervades the last pages of *Religion and Religions*. But in the three years immediately following the Edinburgh Conference, Moulton shared its sense of exhilaration and confidence that renewal was on the way for the church.[115] *The Missionary Message* demonstrated conclusively for him that a new age was dawning. He saw everywhere in the Report 'welcome indications that the facing of the non-Christian world is beginning to burst some bonds that held the Church fast'. No doubt, Moulton felt, for the time being denominationalism would remain, but a new ideal had been set before the Christian church at Edinburgh, and because of Edinburgh. 'The missionary who has imagination and faith... learns to transcend all sectional limitations,' Moulton wrote.[116] 'He loves his own church and strives to make her ever worthier of his love, but she does not become the jealous rival of other communions.' Alongside ecumenical renewal in the West, Moulton also believed that the new churches of the world should be allowed to make Christian faith their own and to express their faith without the overbearing presence of the past.

> Teaching men this personal loyalty to a Living Saviour, known to us in His present significance by our records of what He was in His human life... we shall show them, how to observe all that He commanded us. This supreme task achieved, we can afford to leave the Church in each mission-field to organise itself according to its native temperament.[117]

But more than anything else Moulton wanted justice to prevail among peoples and nations. His theology of religion was a theology of mission in which Christians must look for the 'enthronement of righteousness' as the fit climax of New Testament Scripture.[118] This, and nothing else, was the supreme purpose and meaning of the existence of religion. As almost the last words of *Religions and Religion*, Moulton set down this credo:

> We have seen how through the many myriad years Man has groped after God, never deserted by Him who only would not make the finding easy because the seeking was to be blessed. We found religion, even its rudimentary stages, the providential guardian of all man's earliest strivings after social righteousness. We found new evidence of the witness borne to God by earnest and high-souled men of every tribe and kindred and tongue.[119]

All the evidence he has brought to bear in *Religions and Religion* made Moulton conclude the long march of religion had eventually found a 'consummation in the coming of Him who shall gather from all the scattered limbs of Truth'.[120] The Christ who is to be, Moulton declared will 'bring together every joint and member, and shall mould them into an immortal feature of loveliness and perfection', and in that union humankind would 'find strength to resist every form of evil' and the crown would be 'set upon the whole creation of God'.[121]

No armchair expert in dialogue

Moulton referred frequently to his 'impertinence' in handling missionary problems, alluding to his lack of first hand knowledge. But Moulton was abundantly qualified as a practitioner of inter-religious relationships. Real meetings with Parsis took place even while he was pursuing his academic studies of Zoroastrianism. In *Religions and Religion*, Moulton reproduced some of the material which had been originally used in talking with the London Zoroastrian community.[122] In this very early example of interfaith dialogue in Britain, discussion took place on the possibility of Christians and Zoroastrians praying the same prayer, and Moulton told his audience that he reflected 'with satisfaction that the prayer "Let the good kingdom come" will equally well go into your sacred language and mine – in the words of the Gathas and those of the Lord's Prayer'.[123] Moulton could always find common ground 'with the best and purest of the non-Christian faiths'.

In this way Moulton could express an idea (sometime before 1912) which was not to become familiar until much later in the twentieth century, saying to his audience,

> were I to venture to preach to Parsis, I would urge them to be better Parsis – to learn more and more of the essence of their great Prophet's teaching, and believe more fervently and to put into action more continually the doctrine of God and man which he set forth nearly three thousand years ago. I cannot think of a single doctrine that has any claim to originate from Zarathushtra which I should press a Parsi congregation to abandon.[124]

These are astonishing words from a Methodist preacher of this period. On the basis of such an acceptance of the greatness in Zoroastrianism, Moulton could challenge his Parsi audience in friendly and courteous phraseology about whether they were doing enough to bring about *Frashokereti*, the 'regeneration not only of India, but of the world', to which their Prophet bade them look forward. History, he told them, 'leads us to expect great things from a people so enlightened and public spirited as yours'.[125]

But Moulton also put into practice that later 'principle of dialogue' which speaks of its becoming the 'medium of authentic witness'. He did not expect Parsis to ask him to minimize any of the claims of Christianity. Rather he asked them to recognize his own feeling 'that a Christian student of Parsism must always carry at the back of his mind his Master's words 'I came not to destroy but to fulfil'. Reminding the Parsis that Zarathushtra had taught that his work should be completed by the coming of other *Saoshyants*, Moulton wrote, 'And we say that the *Saoshyant* has come and you were the first to greet Him.'[126] He continued:

> Am I suggesting to you an apostasy – am I urging you to become worse Parsis or better, when I plead that you should recognise the Prophet of Nazareth now as you did then and help him to destroy the works of Ahriman in preparation for that final renovation of the Wise Lord's world?

We claim that no one nation can fully interpret our Christ, or grasp fully the religion which will one day dominate the world. We look for the help of the Moslem, the Buddhist and the Confucian, to bring their several treasures to the feet of the coming Lord of men. And when the dream is realised, surely no gold shall shine so richly, no frankincense smell so sweet as that which shall be brought into his presence by those who follow the saintly Sage of Iran and the heroic Pilgrim Fathers who brought his sacred fire from Persia to Bombay.[127]

Here properly, we must finish our study of James Hope Moulton, and indeed our study of the themes which have occupied this whole book. Moulton's work continued after 1914, nevertheless, for in 1915 he accepted the invitation of the YMCA in India to visit Bombay and other Parsi centres. The story of this journey I tell elsewhere.[128] But it is appropriate to say to things about Moulton's last contribution to 'justice, courtesy and love' in interfaith relationships. When he arrived in Bombay he received a hero's welcome from the Zoroastrian community, who later took it upon themselves to publish his lectures and addresses to them.[129] In India Moulton wore himself out, travelling sixteen thousand miles in seventeen months. On the journey home, his ship was torpedoed in the Mediterranean. Even though he was totally exhausted, he insisted on taking his turn at the oars of the life boat. He died and was buried at sea. Like Charles Cuthbert Hall before him, he had given himself so fully to his new task that he laid down his life as a result. By his death as well as his life, James Hope Moulton symbolizes the beginning of new relationship of justice and courtesy and love on the part of Christians towards men and women of different faith commitments.

The End of a Beginning: A Postscript

Unfortunately, the generous and sympathetic appreciations of other religions which we have found not only in Gairdner and Moulton but in in so many other theologians and missionaries, were a short lived phenomenon in terms of the broad sweep of the last two centuries. Though the tradition was carried on by a number of distinguished missionaries in the 1920s and 1930s (as I hope to show in a sequel to this present work), by 1914 other forces were at work which virtually ensured that no significant advance could be made on what we may call the 'Edinburgh position'. Certainly no progress was made at either of the two Conferences of the International Missionary Council between 1910 and the outbreak of the Second World War. Neither the meeting at Jerusalem in 1928 nor the assembly at Tambaram in 1938 was able to engage in serious reflection on the significance for God's purposes in the presence of other religious traditions in the world. The 'theology of religion' had become negative, and from the point of view of the Christian church, self-serving. No one expressed the change of emphasis at Jerusalem in 1928 more clearly than Robert Speer (who had been the Vice Chairman of Commission IV at Edinburgh):

At Edinburgh the first business was the report on carrying the Gospel to the world, and it consisted of a survey of the fields still to be occupied. The matter of the message was relegated to the fourth place. At this Conference it was now in the foreground. The topic at Edinburgh was the missionary message in relation to the non-Christian religions. At Jerusalem there were two noticeable changes. It was the Christian message that was being discussed in relation to non-Christian systems. Another significant change was that a new word had been inserted. It was the Christian life and message that was being discussed in relation to the non-Christian systems. The word 'life' was significant and its warrant and meaning demanded reflection.[130]

At both Jerusalem and Tambaram, therefore, the focus of concern was upon the nature of the Christian message itself, as can be seen in the title of Hendrik Kraemer's magisterial preparatory volume for Tambaram, *The Christian Message in a Non-Christian World*. For whatever reason, the Christian movement had lost some of its nerve and had turned inwards. Little room was left for the contemplation of other religions as having any part to play in God's purposes. This is reflected in the official Statement of the International Missionary Council in 1928, entitled 'The Christian Message'. Of the sixteen pages this Statement takes up in *The Christian Life and Message*, only three or four have direct reference to the 'non-Christian systems'. The Statement reflects very little of either the Conference preparatory papers or the intense discussion which went on in Jerusalem.[131] It is clear that deep differences of opinion among the missionaries and theologians there made it impossible to produce anything other than vague assertions about the other religions.[132] They had perforce to limit themselves to making affirmations only about the Christian faith.[133] The Jerusalem Meeting did go so far as to suggest that 'followers of non Christian religions' could, in a crisis, be called upon 'to co-operate with us against all the evils of secularism', but in the end of the day it is apparent that the other 'religious systems' were irrelevant to its essential message. There was not a trace of the sense, which was so manifest at Edinburgh, and in the work of Gairdner and Moulton, that there could be a life-giving encounter with other forms of faith and spirituality which might help Christians to do their theology better.

Even more sterile, from this point of view, were the results of the Tambaram Conference ten years later. This too was concerned more about the nature of the Christian message itself than with other religions and religious paths. In Tambaram the Christian message had to be spelt out against the background of the 'new Paganisms' in their fascist, nationalist, communist and scientific-materialist forms. It is not surprising, therefore, that the emphasis should have been upon 'The Authority of the Faith', with little room left for doubt and self-questioning.[134] Kraemer caught the prevalent mood:

> The Christian Church, religiously speaking, in the West as well as in the East, is standing in a pagan, non-Christian world, and has again to consider the whole world its mission field, not in the rhetorical but in the literal sense of the word.[135]

All forms of idealism and liberalism (together with their always attendant possibility of 'syncretism') were vehemently to be opposed by Kraemer's 'biblical realism', in which the 'self-revelation of Christ the Crucified' was at the same time 'an act of divine salvation and divine judgment'.[136] The 'Findings' of Tambaram are redolent with this sense of unique salvation and ultimate judgment, as for example in this passage:

> There are many non-Christian religions that claim the allegiance of large multitudes. We see and readily recognize that in them are to be found values of deep religious experiences and great moral achievements. Yet we are bold enough to call men out from them to the feet of Jesus Christ. We do because we believe that in him alone is the full salvation which man needs. Mankind has seen nothing to be compared with the redeeming love of God in the life and death and resurrection of Christ.[137]

To be sure this kind of faith sustained vast numbers of European Christians in their confrontation with the gross syncretism of 'German Christianity', the neo-paganism of National Socialism, the 'blood and soil' ideology of fascism, and the materialism of Leninist-Marxism. There is no wonder that the First Assembly of the World Council of Churches in Amsterdam, together with succeeding Assemblies at Evanston and New Delhi found no room on their agendas for the concerns of Edinburgh 1910.

In New Delhi in 1961, however, the International Missionary Council merged with the WCC and became its Division of World Mission and Evangelism. Just faintly, the relationships with people of other faiths which we call 'dialogical' began to be explored once again.[138] By the early 1970's the DWME had taken the first steps towards setting up a Sub Unit on 'Dialogue with People of Living Faiths and Ideologies' and the theological questions raised at Edinburgh were again on the agenda. But as we have continually implied, the inheritance was very nearly lost. Certainly a young missionary in training in the period 1957-62 never heard any mention of it, and was nurtured on the missiology of Hendrik Kraemer and the theology of Karl Barth.

Ahead of its time

The Sri Lankan theologian and church leader, Wesley Ariarajah, in a fine survey of Protestant Ecumenical thought since 1910, has said that the thinking of *The Missionary Message in Relation to the Non-Christian Religions* was, in many ways, 'ahead of its time'.[139] As we draw to a close, we want to apply Ariarajah's judgment and the reasons lying behind it to most of the missionaries and theologians we have discussed in this work.

Ariarajah attributes the remarkable achievement of the Edinburgh Report to three causes. First there was the refusal on the part of Cairns and his colleagues to become defensive about the presence of the other religions in the world. The immediate consequence of this was an unwillingness to engage in mere polemic, or to seek to marginalize other religious experiences. The Report did not describe other religions, Ariarajah writes, as 'primitive', 'preparatory', 'natural', or 'human'. On the contrary, he discerns in it a serious effort to listen to and learn about other faith traditions and to deal with them theologically.

Second, there was, in Ariarajah's view, no attempt to judge the other religions on the basis of their unacceptable manifestations or practices in social life, even though such manifestations and practices were taken seriously and criticized. 'We see a willingness to examine other faiths at their best and as they receive expression in the life of the true believers in those faiths.'[140] The third reason lay, he suggests, in the genuine attempt in the Edinburgh documents to understand other religious traditions in their own terms, in order to grasp 'the meaning behind the formulations and the spiritual search that had produced them'.[141] In this way the doctrinal formulations and belief systems were not always immediately ruled out as hostile to, or incompatible with the message of the gospel.

In a similar vein, Jan van Lin, the Dutch missiologist, has written of the Edinburgh period as a time when (at least among the Anglo-Saxons), 'the manifestation of God's spirit in other religions' was accepted and 'the good and true elements' in the non-Christian religions were seen as signs of 'God's revealing activity'.[142] Certainly, as van Lin goes on to stress, such views were held in conjunction with a sense that other religion was to be fulfilled and completed in Christ, and that no provision for syncretism or pluralism should be made.[143] Neverthless the Holy Spirit is present in the world of religions, and God the Father is not far from any human creature.

We have seen numerous statements of these positions: in the writings of the five theologians whose work lay behind much of the missionaries' thinking; in the eight missionary theologians to whom we paid close attention; in the one hundred and eight responses to the Edinburgh questionnaire; in the Report of the Commission (and especially as it was summed up by David Cairns), and in the attitudes and actions of Temple Gairdner and Hope Moulton, the two representative voices which provided the epilogue to this work. Ariarajah suggested in his book that the discussion of the theology of religion should be picked up from where it was left in 1910. If we have the will, we have the resources, and, I suggest, we have also the inspiration in those who first saw a vision of 'justice, courtesy and love'.

Notes

Details of the works cited are given in the bibliography.

1 The Early Theology of Religion in the Modern Period

1. David Bosch in *Transforming Mission: Paradigm Shifts in Theology of Mission* (1991) applies the concept of the 'paradigm shift', which he adapts from Thomas Kuhn, to discuss six shifts in missiological thinking. When the accumulation of more and more evidence requires a change in basic perception, 'a paradigm shift' occurs. None of the six movements or 'transformations' of mission Bosch deals with have to do directly with Christian attitudes towards other religions. His otherwise excellent work is seriously deficient in its treatment of other religions from a missiological perspective.

2. The 'Great Century' refers to Kenneth Scott Latourette's title for volumes IV-VI of his seven-volume work, *A History of the Expansion of Christianity*, (1938-47). Individual volumes of Latourette's *History*, used below, are cited by their own titles.

3. There are some fine studies of what scholars in the universities of Europe and North America were beginning to think about other religions in the earlier part of our period, notably David Pailin, *Attitudes to Other Religions: Comparative Religion in Seventeenth and Eighteenth Century Britain* (1984) and Peter Harrison, *'Religion' and the Religions in the English Enlightenment* (1990). Only specialized studies have dealt with missionaries as for example: J.J.E. van Lin, *Protestantse Theologie der Godsdiensten van Edinburgh naar Tambaram 1910-1938* (1974); Eric J. Sharpe, *Not to Destroy But to Fulfil: The Contribution of J.N. Farquhar to Protestant Missionary Thought in India before 1914* (1965) and *Faith Meets Faith: Some Christian Attitudes to Hinduism in the Nineteenth and Twentieth Centuries* (1977), S. Wesley Ariarajah, *Hindus and Christians: A Century of Protestant Ecumenical Thought* (1991).

4. I have been concerned mainly with the missionaries' responses to official questionnaires, in particular that sent out by Commission IV of the World Missionary Conference, see pp.191ff, and with their published works, much of which is not easily accessible. Most of this literature remains virgin territory for the researcher. How much greater is the work still to be done by using their writings in the archives of their missionary boards. Cf., my indebtedness to the researches of B.S.Stanley on Timothy Richard, see pp.341ff.

5. There have been many attempts to answer the question, why did the Protestants wake up to their missionary obligations only in about 1800. Gustav Warneck (1834-1910), the founder of modern Protestant missiology, found no reference in either Luther or Calvin to the idea of missions 'in the sense in which we understand them today'. This fact Warneck ascribed to 'fundamental theological views', see his *Outline of a History of Protestant Missions from the Reformation to the Present Time* (1906), pp.8-20. Luther believed that Christianity had already fulfilled its universal calling to

be the religion of the whole world, and that no further action therefore needed to take place. 'The spiritual Jerusalem which is the kingdom of Christ, must be extended by the Gospel throughout the whole world. That has already come to pass. The Gospel has been preached, and upon it the kingdom of Heaven has been firmly established in all places under heaven, so that it now reaches and abides to the end of the world, and in it we, by the mercy and compassion of God, are citizens', cited without reference by Warneck in op. cit., pp 12-3. Calvin taught that the apostolate was a *munus extraordinarium* and as such has not been perpetuated. In words which Carey would have eventually to challenge, Calvin insisted that 'we are taught that the kingdom of Christ is neither to be advanced or maintained by the industry of men, but is the work of God alone, *docemur, non hominum industria, vel promoveri vel fulciri Christi regnum, sed hoc unius Dei esse opus*', see Warneck, op. cit., p.19. In any case the fragmentation of the Protestant churches meant an obsession with ecclesiology. Which was the true church? Descriptions of the nature of the church became self-serving and inward looking. There was little sense of any 'kingdom' beyond the four walls of the sacred places of each denomination, Cf., the *Augsburg Confession* (1530): the church is 'the assembly of saints in which the gospel is taught purely and the sacraments are ministered rightly'. Succeeding ecclesiologies built upon this, and thus localized rather than universalized the presence of Christ and his kingdom. Cf. A.V.G. Allen's comments on why there was no mission in the Reformation period, p.88. For a brief indication of the Reformers' views on other religions see Cracknell, *Towards a New Relationship: Christian and People of Other Faith* (1986), pp.9ff.

6. For the most stimulating treatment of American protestant thought and overseas mission in the nineteenth century, see William R.Hutchison, *Errand to the World* (1987).

7. For reasons indicated in the Introduction there will be few references in this work to Roman Catholic missionary activity, except where it directly impinged on Protestant work. But it is useful to set out some key dates for the purpose of comparison. In 1493 Pope Alexander VI laid on the Spanish king the injunction 'to bring to Christian faith' peoples in his new possession. In another Bull he recognized the rights of the King of Portugal, and laid upon the Portuguese Crown the responsibility to find and support missionaries, and at a later date to establish and maintain bishoprics. The next most important event was the foundation of the Jesuits in 1534, and the recognition of the Order in the Bull *Regimini Militantis* in 1540. Francis Xavier (1506-52), the most famous of the early Roman Catholic missionaries, was a Jesuit. Matteo Ricci (1552-1610), the next most famous, began his work in China in 1582. Franciscans and Dominicans were also involved in missionary activity. In 1622 Rome acted to bring much diverse work under central control by the establishment of the Sacred Congregation for the Propagation of the Faith.

8. The history of the oldest British missionary society is told in detail by H.P. Thompson, *Into All Lands: The History of the Society for the Propagation of the Gospel in Foreign Parts 1701-1750* (1951). The second oldest, celebrating its bicentennial anniversary in 1992, has a fine new history by Brian Stanley, *The History of the Baptist Missionary Society 1792-1992*, (1992). Eugene Stock's four volume *The History of the Church Missionary Society: Its Environment, its Men and its Work*, first three volumes (1899) and the Supplementary Volume (1916) has not been superseded. The

LMS has a more recent history by Norman Goodall, *A History of the London Missionary Society 1895-1945* (1954). Elizabeth Hewat deals with Scotland in one volume, *Vision and Achievement 1796-1956. A History of the Foreign Missions of the Churches united in the Church of Scotland* (1960). *The History of the Wesleyan Missionary Society*, was treated by G.G. Findlay and W.W. Holdsworth in five vols. (1921-4). In the USA there is a dearth of scholarly missionary society histories. Notable exceptions are Wade Crawford Barclay, *History of Methodist Missions*, 3 vols (1949-1957), F.F. Goodsell, *You Shall Be My Witnesses* (1959), Baker J.Cauthen and others, *Advance: A History of Southern Baptist Foreign Missions* (1970).

9. See W.Canton, *The History of the British and Foreign Bible Society*, 5 vols. (1904-1910) and Henry Otis Dwight, *The Centennial History of the American Bible Society* (1916).

10. Cf. the following foundation dates: 1796, The Society for Bettering the Condition of the Poor; 1799, The Religious Tract Society; 1802, The Society for the Suppression of Vice; 1803, The Sunday School Union; 1804, The British and Foreign Bible Society; 1807, The African Institution (succeeding the Sierra Leone Society); 1808, The Royal Lancastrian Society (later the British and Foreign Schools Society); and 1809, The National Society for the Education of the Poor according to the Principles of the Established Church; and in the USA, 1813, The Connecticut Morals Society. On the 'Voluntary Way to Christian Civilization' see Robert T. Handy, op. cit., pp.37-47 and Sidney E. Mead, *The Lively Experiment: The Shaping of Christianity in North America* (1963), especially ch. 8.

11. For the period before Carey see S.C.Neill, *A History of Christian Missions* (1964), J. van den Berg, *Constrained by Jesus' Love: An Inquiry into the Motives of the Missionary Awakening in Great Britain in the Period between 1698 and 1815* (1956); D.Bosch, op. cit., pp.239ff.; J.Verkuyl, *Inleiding in de Nieuwere Zendingswetanschap* (1976), pp.34ff., ET: *Contemporary Missiology: An Introduction* (1978), pp.18-25; Ernest A.Payne, *The Church Awakes: The Story of the Modern Missionary Movement* (1942), and also his *The Growth of the World Church: The story of the Modern Missionary Movement* (1955).

12. On Pietism see Bosch, op. cit., pp.252 ff., Warneck, op. cit., pp.53-73 and Ernest Stoefler, *The Rise of Evangelical Pietism* (1965), Cf. Gerhard Rosenkranz, *Die Christliche Mission: Geschichte und Theologie* (1977), and on Moravianism and Zinzendorf, see A.J. Lewis., *Zinzendorf the Ecumenical Pioneer* (1962).

13. There are two full studies of Classic Puritan missiology in Sidney H. Rooy, *The Theology of Missions in the Puritan Tradition* (1965), J.A. de Jong, *As the Waters cover the Sea: Millennial Expectations in the rise of Anglo-American Missions 1640-1810*, (1970) To these may be added R.Pierce Beaver, *Pioneers in Mission: A Source Book on the Rise of American Missions to the Heathen* (1966).

14. On the early Anglican societies see Thompson, op. cit., pp.3-106; William Kellaway, *The New England Company 1649-1776: Missionary Society to the American Indians* (1961). The early missionary thinking of John Wesley is treated by Martin Schmidt in *The Young Wesley: Missionary and Theologian of Missions* (1958), ET of *Der junge Wesley als Heidenmissionar und Missionstheologe* (1955), which also deals with Wesley's missionary adventure in Georgia. Schmidt makes a strong case for the presence of a distinctive missionary theology in Wesley: 'He was possessed by the missionary ideal in a manner rare in the whole history of the Church', p.18. 'For Wesley,

the point at issue was the primal meaning of the Evangel – which discloses itself only in a primal situation, the heathen situation in fact... John Wesley made early Christianity mean the same as primitive Christianity; and primitive Christianity meant preaching to the heathen', p.22. This would be a proper understanding of Wesley's words, often quoted out of their context: 'My chief hope, to which others are subordinate, is the hope of saving my own soul', Letter to Dr John Burton, 10 October 1735 cited in Schmidt, ibid., p.24. The immediately following words are 'I hope to learn the true sense of the Gospel by preaching it to the heathen', and he contrasts the 'simplicity' of the Indians with 'the luxurious, sensual, covetous ambitious expounders' who 'soften unpleasant truths' in order to reconcile earthly mindedness and faith. As Schmidt suggests, perhaps Wesley saw in 'the missionary will and the missionary success of his day, a judgement upon the deism and atheism of Europe'. Schmidt discerned also another feature in Wesley's missionary thinking. Wesley's sense of call to Georgia was determined by the fact that he was not to go alone, 'but was definitely to take two or three of his comrades with him. Thus the intensive educating of one another, which in many ways recalls the Greek monasticism of the early church under the impress of Basil the Great, could be continued and further intensified. Behind the acceptance there was not only a wish to retain a practice which had become dear to him, but also an essentially Christian consciousness that a mission is not the act of an individual but the work of a community', ibid., p.20. Wesley was of course deeply committed to reviving what he conceived to be the spiritual patterns of the early church; see Ted A. Campbell, *John Wesley and Christian Antiquity: Religious Vision and Cultural Change* (1991). A vivid and stimulating account of Methodism's turn-about in taking up overseas missions vigorously in quite different patterns after Wesley's death is to be found in Bernard Semmel, *The Methodist Revolution* (1974) pp.157-69.

15. To be sure there was already much interaction and mutual influence between the representatives of these movements, and the streams intermingled long before the beginning of the great century. August Francke corresponded with Cotton Mather, and Jonathan Edwards was Mather's cousin. David Brainerd lived the ideals of John Eliot and Thomas Mayhew, and was a friend of Increase Mather. The Pietist and Moravian influence on John Wesley was unmistakable, and Susannah Wesley read to him the stories of Ziegenbalg and Plutschau in the Epworth Rectory. John Wesley had himself been a missionary associated with the SPG. He was also the colleague of George Whitefield in the Oxford 'Holy Club' and worked with him until 1741. Whitefield became part of the American Awakening and a friend of Jonathan Edwards. Edwards' writings influenced John Wesley, who in his later life talked with Charles Simeon and corresponded with Melvill Horne, and so on. But for purposes of analysis these streams and currents may be distinguished. They each have distinctive marks, each of which determined specific attitudes within the missionaries of the Great Century towards the religions of the non-Christian world.

16. The Book of Revelation pictures the defeat of Satan as occurring in two stages before the end of the world. Before his final destruction in the 'lake of fire' (Rev. 20.10) he would be 'bound' in a bottomless pit so that he should no longer 'deceive the nations' until a thousand years had been ended (Rev. 20.1-3). At this point Christ would begin a thousand year reign over the earth with 'the saints' who would come back to life in the 'first resurrection' (20.4). How this should be interpreted is moot.

Those expositors who see this happening in some more or less literal and materialistic form after the *parousia* or 'second coming' are to be differentiated from those who interpret the thousand years as a symbol of 'the age of the Church'. These then understand the *parousia* as ushering in immediately the final judgment and the 'new heaven and the new earth' (Rev.21.1). This view is known as 'a-millennialism'. The third position interprets all the apocalyptic images of the Book of Revelation as symbolic of God's working in history, and does not look for the *parousia* until after the millennium, hence they are called 'post-millennialists'.

17. See J.F.C Harrison, *The Second Coming: Popular Millenarianism 1780-1850* (1979).

18. As in William Wordsworth's lines in *The Prelude*, Book XI, lines 108-9, reprinted separately as 'The French Revolution as it Appeared to Enthusiasts':

Bliss was it in that dawn to be alive

But to be young was very heaven.

19. I owe much of my interpretation of millennialism in the seventeenth and eighteenth centuries to Ernest Lee Tuveson, *Redeemer Nation: The Idea of America's Millennial Role* (1968). I also follow Tuveson in finding the terms 'premillennialist' (for those in the eighteenth and nineteenth centuries expecting the speedy literal and physical return of Jesus Christ), and 'postmillennialist' for those espousing a more gradualist, progressive understanding of the reign of Christ on earth, too limited for interpreting the thought of this period. For the first group Tuveson uses the term 'millenarian', for the second 'millennialist'. Tuveson's usage is followed throughout this book.

20. Clark H.Pinnock in *A Wideness in God's Mercy: The Finality of Jesus Christ in a World of Religions* (1992) has recently pointed to the features in Augustine's thinking which 'led him inexorably to a pessimism of salvation', p.37. He quotes from Augustine's *The City of God*, ch.21, para.12, 'Many more are left under punishment than are delivered from it, in order that it may thus be shown what was due for all', op. cit., p.38. Pinnock writes further: 'With Augustine a new and severe paradigm in theology was born, a package of dismal beliefs which would eat its way into the consciousness of the Western churches and erode the positive biblical spirit in their thinking', ibid., p.39.

21. *The City of God*, 15.1, translation by Henry Bettenson in the Penguin edition (1972), p.595. Cf. also 14.28, 15.21, 12.28, 10.32, 14.26.

22. In *The City of God*, 20.7 Augustine calls notions of an earthly 'sabbath' with the saints rising again for a thousand year reign 'fables' that can 'be believed only by carnal men' exceeding all the bounds of credibility (*credulitatis*). Augustine's views prevailed for more than a thousand years and yet suddenly with Edwards and millennialism it all changed. Cf. T.F.Glasson, *His Appearing and His Kingdom* (1953), for a general historical survey of Christian thinking about the future. Tuveson comments on this: 'It has not been generally realized that some version of the 'millennialist' position has probably been predominant among English-speaking Protestants since the later seventeenth century'; see op. cit., pp.34ff. Cf. Tuveson's further judgment, 'It is a curious fact that those who, like Edwards, restored the spirit of Augustine's doctrine of original sin were the ones who reversed his doctrine of history', op. cit., p.28. A recent treatment of Calvin's thinking bears this judgment out. Calvin, it suggests,

demonstrates a 'philosophy of church history rather than an eschatological interpretation of the end', H. Quistorp, *Calvin's Doctrine of the Last Things* (1955), p.144.

23. For Milton as theologian see Dennis Danielson, 'The Fall of Man and Milton's Theodicy' in Dennis Danielson (ed.), *The Cambridge Companion to Milton* (1989), and for Milton and contemporary thought, B.Rajan, *Paradise Lost and the Seventeenth Century Reader* (1947), pp.78 ff.

24. *Paradise Lost*, Oxford Authors Edition (1991), book XII, lines 508ff.

25. On Baxter as a 'rational' thinker see Geoffrey Nuttall, *Richard Baxter* (1965) who speaks of him as 'having a modern man's pride in his modernity', p.126. For Baxter as a missionary thinker see Sidney Rooy, op. cit., pp 66-155. Baxter's (and Milton's) contemporary John Bunyan (1628-88) appears to have held a similar view to Baxter concerning a this-worldly kingdom; see his *The Holy City: or New Jerusalem*: '...a great harvest of sinners shall be gathered by the grace of the Gospel... the scriptures go with open arms toward the latter end of the world, even as if they would grasp and compass about almost all people then upon the face of the whole earth with the grace and mercy of God. "The earth", saith God, "shall be full of the knowledge of the glory of the Lord, as the waters cover the sea"', in T.F. Glasson, op. cit., pp.163. Glasson thinks that this was probably the first extended description of a 'Christian world' in the English language, ibid.

26. J.A.de Jong gives an example of Baxter's consistent opposition to what he called the 'fantastical' in his refutation of Thomas Beverley, author of *The Prophetical History of the Reformation* (1689), who set the date of the Rapture as 27 August, 1697, op. cit., p.82.

27. Quoted in Tuveson, op. cit., p.36.

28. On Cotton Mather see Rooy, op. cit., pp.242-284, de Jong, op. cit., pp.91 ff., and Raymond J.Cunningham's edition of the *Magnalia Christi Americana, or the Ecclesiastical History of New England* (1970).

29. *Magnalia*, Book VII, in Cunningham, op. cit., p.143.

30. *Magnalia*, Book I, in ibid., p.18.

31. As quoted by de Jong, *op.cit*, p.91.

32. For discussion of the events and their meanings see Darrett B. Rutman (ed.), *The Great Awakening: Event and Exegesis* (1970). For documentation se Alan Heimert and Perry Miller (eds.) *The Great Awakening: Documents Illustrating the Crisis and its Consequences* (1967).

33. *Some Thoughts Concerning the Revival* (1742) in *The Great Awakening*, edited by C.C.Goen, (1972), Vol.4 of the Yale edition of the *Works of Jonathan Edwards*, p.353. For the other texts of Jonathan Edwards' works used here see *Works of Jonathan Edwards: Apocalyptic Writings* edited by Stephen J. Stein (1977), Vol.5 of the Yale edition; and *The History of the Work of Redemption* (1989), edited by John F.Wilson, Vol.9 of the Yale edition. For a detailed study of the importance of Edwards for the American missionary awakening by Charles L.Chaney, *The Birth of American Missions* (1976), pp.65-74.

34. *Some Thoughts Concerning the Revival*, Yale edition, Vol.4., p.353.

35. *The History of the Work of Redemption*, Yale edition, Vol.9., pp.482-4.

36. *Some Thoughts Concerning the Revival*, Yale edition, Vol.4. pp. 324. Cf. this passage: 'And 'tis worthy to be noted that America was discovered about the time of the Reformation, or but little before: which Reformation was the first thing that God

did towards the glorious renovation of the world, after it had sunk into the depths of darkness and ruin under the great anti-Christian apostasy. So that as soon as this new world is (as it were) created, and stands forth in view, God presently goes about doing some great thing to make way for the introduction of the church's latter-day glory, that is to have its first seat in, and is to take its rise from that new world', ibid., p.325.

37. Cf. art., 'Eschatology in American Missions' in Hermelink and Margull (eds.), *Basileia* (1959) p.67.

38. The further words of the title. For the text of the *Humble Attempt* see Vol.5 of the Yale edition of Edwards' works, pp.308-346.

39. Ibid., pp.312 ff.

40. Cf. R.P.Beaver, art. cit., pp.67ff. David Bosch comments, 'In a remarkable way millennial convictions were not just a *summons* to conversion activity; missionary work itself became a sure sign of the dawn of the millennium', op. cit., pp.313-5.

41. *Letters on Missions addressed to the Protestant Ministers of the British Churches* (1794), p.20 in the 1834 edition. Melvill Horne is usually neglected in studies of the rise of modern missions. There are no references to him in Neill, op. cit., in Bosch, op. cit. or in Verkuyl, *Contemporary Missiology* (1978), and he has no entry in the *Concise Dictionary of the Christian World Mission* (1970).

42. *An Humble Enquiry into the Obligation of Christians to use Means for the Conversion of the Heathen* (1792), Facsimile edition (1961), pp.78-9.

43. Ibid., p.68. Note, however, Stephen Neill's view that Carey's mind was 'entirely free from the eschatological speculations of the pietists. Christ, he held, has a kingdom that is to be proclaimed in its power to the ends of the earth; it is the duty of all Christians to engage in the proclamation of this kingdom, whether the time allotted by God for this purpose be long or short', op. cit., p.262.

44. Ibid., p.12.

45. Quoted by van den Berg, op. cit., p.162.

46. S.Wilberforce (ed.), *Journals and Letters of Henry Martyn 1781-1812*, Vol.I, p.272.

47. *Sermons Preached in London* (1798), quoted by van den Berg, op. cit., p.161.

48. Three years previously Bogue had been awarded a DD by Yale College, a fact which establishes the close connection between the English and American Congregationalists, and their shared concern with the Millennium. Like Hopkins, see below, Bogue thought it inappropriate to say when the Millennium would begin.

49. Quoted in Stuart Piggin, *Making Evangelical Missionaries 1789-1858: The Social Background, Motives and Training of British Protestant Missionaries to India* (1984), pp.142-3.

50. *The Form of Agreement respecting the great Principles upon which the Brethren of the Mission at Serampore think it their Duty to act in the work of Instructing the Heathen, agreed upon at a Meeting of the Brethren at Serampore, On Monday October 5th, 1805*, Appendix A in A.H.Oussoren, *William Carey, especially his Missionary Principles* (1945), p.275. Cf. the report of the Serampore trio to the BMS Home Committee: 'We live in eventful and amazing times and ought to expect much from that God, who in his millennial glory appears to be coming very near to us', November 1808 in Piggin, op. cit., p.142.

51. For some critical comments on Samuel Hopkins' 'unfortunately persisting influence' see R.P.Beaver, art. cit., pp.67ff. See further on Hopkins and the rise of

missionary societies in America, Chaney, op. cit., pp.74ff. Chaney gives further examples of millennialist sermons, pp.269-80.

52. *Treatise on the Millennium* (1793), p.81. Note William Ellery Channing's comment on Hopkins: 'The millennium was his chosen ground. If any subject of thought possessed him above all others, I suppose it to have been this. The millennium was more than a belief to him. It had the freshness of visible things. He was at home in it... While to the multitude he seemed a hard, dry theologian, feeding upon the thorns of controversy, he was living in a world of imagination, feeding on visions of a holiness and a happiness which are to make earth all but heaven', quoted by H.Richard Niebuhr, *The Kingdom of God in America* (1937), pp.143-4.

53. See Tuveson, op. cit., p.41.

54. Beaver, op. cit., p.67.

55. *Extracts from the Minutes of the General Assembly, of the Presbyterian Church, in the United States of America*, 1815, pp.237-8, quoted in Robert T. Handy, *A Christian America: Protestant Hopes and Historical Realities*, second edition (1984), p.40.

56. Niebuhr, op. cit., pp.144-6.

57. See eg., p. 128.

58. Reprinted in *Missionary Sermons: A Selection from the Discourses delivered on behalf of the Baptist Missionary Society on various occasions* (1924), pp.47-62.

59. Ibid., p.62. Note here also the very late use of Archbishop Ussher's chronology.

60. Arthur Campbell Ainger (1841-1919) spent most of his life as a schoolmaster. This hymn was composed at Eton College in 1894 and was entitled 'Missions'. Ainger was using Habbakuk 2.14 for his theme, and doubtless thought that he was writing a hymn which expressed exactly the sentiments of the best Anglican missionaries of his day.

61. For illuminating studies of the phenomenon of millenarianism see Ernest R.Sandeen, *The Roots of Fundamentalism: British and American Millenarianism 1800-1930* (1970), and George M.Marsden, *Fundamentalism and American Culture: The Shaping of Twentieth Century Evangelicalism 1870-1925* (1980), together with Timothy Weber, *Living in the Shadow of the Second Coming: American Premillennialism 1875-1925* (1979).

62. For examples of the choice of date see note 68 below.

63. Sandeen, op. cit., p.13.

64. Cf. Bosch, op. cit., p.318. Note there his quotation from D.L.Moody: 'I look upon this world as a wrecked vessel. God has given me a lifeboat and said to me, "Moody, save all you can."' Cf. Marsden, op. cit., pp.72ff. and 93ff.

65. Cf. 'Meanwhile multitudes of heathen were daily going down into the everlasting torments of hell. Their salvation became doubly urgent in view of the imminent advent of the millennium, and the old compassion for the heathen now took a somewhat sentimental turn, became the all important motive in missionary vocation and support, and took precedence over glory to God, love of Christ, and obedience to the Great Commission', Beaver, art. cit., p.69.

66. Edward Irving (1792-1834) was the unintentional founder of the Catholic Apostolic Church in 1832. C.F.Andrews' parents were fully committed members of this Church in Birmingham, see below, p.174. Irving remained a minister of the Church of Scotland until 1833. For Irving see David Allen, art., 'A Belated Bouquet: A Tribute to Edward Irving (1792-1834)' in *The Expository Times*, Vol.103, No.11,

pp.328ff., who portrays Irving at the height of his popularity, when Coleridge, Bentham, Carlyle, Canning and Lord Liverpool were among his hearers: 'Sabbath by sabbath, with total disregard for the "house rules" of polite society, he denounced the materialism spawned by the new industrial age'. Sandeen writes, 'If early nineteenth century millenarianism had produced a hero he would have been Edward Irving', op. cit., p.14. For the importance of Irving to missionary theology see my commentary on Maurice above, pp.35-37, and cf. note 103 on p.342.

67. John Nelson Darby (1800-1882), an Irishman and a graduate in Law of Trinity College, Dublin, was the founder of the Plymouth Brethren movement which, like the Catholic Apostolic Church, was a withdrawal from the Church of England. Darby was part of a devout Evangelical circle in Oxford from 1827 onwards and worked out his doctrine during the 1830s, see Sandeen, op. cit., pp.29ff. At a conference in 1833 Darby attacked the apostasy of the churches and taught for the first time his doctrine of the 'secret rapture' of the true church. This is essentially the theology of 'dispensationalism': 'Christ's coming was expected to precede the Last Judgement by a period of a thousand years, therefore the gathered church must keep the faith in withdrawal from the world'. Note that this was politically reactionary: 'Catholic emancipation, the Reform Bill, democracy, industrialization, the millenarian opposed them all, but with a sense of resignation born of the knowledge that the world must grow more evil day by day', Sandeen, op. cit., p.41.

68. William Miller (1782-1849) was a layman of Baptist background in New York state, with no formal theological training. In 1831 Miller began predicting the parousia, when Christ would return and the wicked be judged and when the world would be cleansed by fire. Within a short period up to 100,000 people joined the Millerite movement, see W.R.Cross, *The Burned-over District* (1950), pp.288-321. Miller's first choice of the date of the Advent was 21 Marcht 1843, and his next alternative, 22 October 1844. For a graphic account of the effects of the 'first disappointment' and the 'Great Disappointment' of 22 October 1844 on the Temperance Reformer Gerrit Smith see John Kobler, *Ardent Spirits* (1973), pp.105ff.

69. Sandeen, op. cit., p.81.

70. Quoted in Sandeen, op. cit., p.95.

71. See Dana L. Robert, '"The Crisis of Missions": Premillennial Mission Theory and the Origins of Independent Evangelical Missions' in Joel A. Carpenter and Wilbert R. Shenk (eds), *Earthen Vessels: American Evangelicals and Foreign Missions* (1990). There is a hagiographical study of Pierson by his son D.L. Pierson, *Arthur T. Pierson: A Spiritual Warrior, Mighty in the Scriptures, and a Leader of the Modern Missionary Crusade* (1912).

72. Pierson was the star speaker at both the Mount Hermon meeting in 1886 and at Liverpool in 1896. His addresses at Liverpool, of which one had as its text Matt. 24.14b, recorded in the conference volume, *Make Jesus King* (1896), had the double theme of 'the evangelization of the world in this generation', see pp.22f., 178 ff., and the urgency of proclaiming this message to 'a dying world', see pp.21, 25, and 261. Pierson's emphasis is in marked contrast to other speakers who were present as the new generation of leaders, among them Sherwood Eddy, F.W.S. O'Neill, Donald Fraser, Agnes de Selincourt and many others, who were to be experienced missionaries by the time of the Edinburgh WMC in 1910. They dreamt rather of 'a time when not merely at a Conference, but in a life of spiritual, moral and social confederacy we

shall be united, when all "the kingdom of this world is become the kingdom of our Lord and of his Christ'", op. cit., p.110.

73. Cf. Dana L.Robert, art. cit., p.29.

74. This body was founded in 1878 as the East London Institute for Home and Foreign Missions by H. Grattan Guinness, a leading member of the Mildmay Park Conferences, see Sandeen, op. cit., p.147.

75. Founded originally as both the Christian Alliance ('a brotherhood of acquaintance, love and prayer' for work in the USA) and as the International Missionary Alliance in 1887 by A.B. Simpson, originally a Presbyterian minister, the two bodies merged in 1897. Its programme is avowedly millenarian: 'It does not look toward world conversion as a goal but rather toward reaching the whole world with the witness of the gospel and calling out from every nation, tribe and tongue "a people for His name"', *Encyclopaedia of Modern Christian Missions* (1967), p.134, col.2.

76. TEAM, as it is now known, was founded by Fredrik Fransen, a convert of Dwight L. Moody, as the Scandinavian Alliance Mission of North America. Its missionaries were originally of Scandinavian background and their theology was millenarian.

77. Bosch, op. cit., p.317.

78. Ibid.

79. For Kellogg as a millenarian see Sandeen, op. cit., pp.153ff.

80. *The Light of Asia and the Light of the World*, pp. xii–xiii.

81. *The Crisis of Missions* (1886), pp.293-4. Pierson refused an invitation to the World Parliament of Religions in Chicago in 1893. His son wrote, 'while he honoured many of the men who were behind the movement, he replied in no uncertain negative to their invitation to take part in a Parliament which he believed would give the enemies of God the opportunity to blaspheme', op. cit., p.303.

82. See Cracknell, *Towards a New Relationship: Christians and People of Other Faith* (1986), pp.10ff.

83. On Mather see Rooy, op. cit., pp.242-285, J.A. de Jong, op. cit., pp.99- 105.

84. For Francke see Gary R. Sattler, *God's Glory, Neighbor's Good: A Brief Introduction to the Life and Writings of August Hermann Francke* (1982) and for Mather's correspondence with Francke, see de Jong, op. cit., pp.102ff.

85. See Mather's thinking as analysed by de Jong, op. cit., pp 86ff.

86. See R.P.Beaver, art. cit., p.63.

87. *Miscellaneous Observations*, esp. ch.7 'The Insufficiency of Reason as a Substitute for Revelation', cited by Rooy, op. cit., p.299.

88. *History of the Work of Redemption*, cited by Rooy, op. cit., p.300.

89. Among these 'false religions' were both Judaism and Islam, see Rooy, ibid., p.301. Jonathan Edward's view of Muhammad is characteristic of the period: 'When he was about forty years of age, he began to give forth that he was the great prophet of God and was to worshipped as the head next under God. [He] published his Alkoran which he pretended that he had received from the Angel Gabriel, and being a subtile crafty man... he gained a number to be his followers and set up for their prince, and propagates (*sic*) his religion by the sword, and made it meritorious of paradise to fight for him', *History of the Work of Redemption*, Yale Edition, Vol. 9 p.382.

90. *History of the Work of Redemption*, op. cit., p.471. Cf. Rooy, op. cit., p.306.

91. For the origins of the SPG and the SPCK in Pietism and the Age of Reason see J. van den Berg, op. cit., pp.42ff. (Van den Berg quotes Patrick Gordon, one of the foundational thinkers for the SPG, 'it is far more honourable to overcome the paganism in one than to destroy a thousand pagans') and H.P. Thompson, *Into All Lands* (1951), pp.4-5, ('the eighteenth century became an age of philanthropy on a new scale').

92. See the full biography by H.P.Thompson, *Thomas Bray* (1954).

93. C.H.Robinson, *History of Christian Missions* (1915), but cf. the first Annual Sermon in 1702: SPG missionaries were to 'settle the state of religion as well as may be among our own people there, which by all accounts we have, very much wants their Pious care; and then to proceed in the very best Methods they can towards the Conversion of the Natives... who may by this be converted from that state of Barbarism and Idolatry in which they now live, and be brought into the Sheepfold of our Blessed Saviour', Thompson, *Into All Lands*, pp.20-1.

94. The instructions of the Society to its Missionaries appended to its 1706 report, quoted by Margaret Dewey, *The Messengers*, (1975), p.17 and Thompson, op. cit., p.27.

95. Quoted by Dewey, op. cit., p.29.

96. For Robert Boyle see William Kellaway, *The New England Company 1649-1776: Missionary Society to the American Indians* (1961), pp.47-9.

97. Book Six of Grotius' *De Veritate Religionae Christiana* is, in the translator John Clarke's words, a 'confutation of Mahometanism' which shows that there are 'many absurd things in the Mohametan books'. One of those who urged upon Boyle the funding of this translation was Richard Baxter, see Rooy, op. cit., p.69.

98. F.D Maurice was eventually to give a series of Boyle's Lectures in 1846, see pp.39-60.

99. See A.F. Walls, 'A Christian Experiment: The Early Sierra Leone Colony' in G.J. Cuming (ed.), *The Mission of the Church and the Propagation of the Faith* (1970). Anglican circles like these maintained throughout the Great Century a conception of the missionary task which differed from those of the revivalists and millennialists, see Anthony Grant's Bampton Lectures for 1843, *The Past and the Prospective Extension of the Gospel by Missions to the Heathen* (1844), *passim*. In the eighteenth and early nineteenth centuries 'charity', 'practical Christianity', 'benevolence' and 'compassion' were watchwords. The terminology changed later in the century as ever more money went into schools and colleges, hospitals and clinics, and other social projects, but the dominating concern was to raise the standards of life for people overseas. If there was one text that these Anglicans used more than any other it was 'I am come that they may have life, and have it abundantly', John 10.10. See, e.g., R.H. Malden's *Foreign Missions: Being a Study of Some Principles and Methods in the Expansion of the Christian Church* (1910), 'The Gospel is life, and life without growth is inconceivable', p.19. This was matched by long-term views of 'inevitable progress' for humanity, Cf. Bishop H.H. Montgomery's 'Introduction' to *Mankind and the Church* (1907): 'I dream of the new song, the new heaven and the new earth to be realized when humanity is Christian', p.xliv. Cf. also the views of the English Anglican Bishop Westcott in *The Gospel of Life*, pp.70ff. above and the American Episcopal theologian A.V.G. Allen, on pp.94-95 above.

100. For the particular influence Melvill Horne had on the founding of the LMS, see the 'Introduction' to the *Sermons Preached in London at the Formation of the Missionary Society* (1795), pp.xviiff.

101. *Letters on Mission*, 1834 edition, pp.74-5, emphases his.

102. For the medieval and early modern stereotypes of Islam see Norman Daniel, *Islam and the West: The Making of an Image* (1960, second edition, 1993). For the breaking down of these stereotypes in our period see Clinton Bennett, *Victorian Images of Islam* (1993).

103. Charles Wesley's hymn 'Sun of Unclouded Righteousness' appeared in the 1758 collection, *Hymns of Intercession for all Mankind*, entitled 'For the Turks', and is reprinted in G. Osborn (ed.), *The Poetical Works of John and Charles Wesley* (1868-72). It was included in the 1780 *Collection of Hymns for the People Called Methodists* as No. 431, with the title 'for the Mohammetans' added for the 1781 edition. It kept its place in the 1831 Wesleyan Hymn book but was dropped in 1876. I am grateful alike to S.T. Kimbrough, Jr. and to Martin Wellings and Edward Houghton for this information. The verses are cited by authors as different as C.H. Robinson, *The Interpretation of the Character of Christ* (1911), pp.98-9 and H.G. Woods, *Frederick Denison Maurice* (1950), p.78.

104. Shrubsole's hymn is quoted in full by Ernest Payne, *The Church Awakes: the Story of the Modern Missionary Movement* (1942), pp.76-7.

105. See David Pailin, *Attitudes to Other Religions: Comparative Religion in Seventeenth and Eighteenth Century Britain* (1984) and Cf. Peter Harrison, *'Religion' and the Religions in the English Enlightenment* (1990).

106. Quoted in Piggin, op. cit., p.118, emphasis in original quotation.

107. Quoted in Piggin, ibid., p.84.

108. Quoted in R.P. Beaver (ed.), *To Advance the Gospel: Selections from the Writings of Rufus Anderson* (1967), p.102.

109. George Burder 'Jonah's Mission to Nineveh', in *Sermons Preached in London at the Formation of the Missionary Society* (1795), p.31. Part of this sermon may be found in Pailin, op. cit., pp.281-4.

110. *Sermons*, p.32.

111. For those who are not familiar with the intricacies of the argument between Calvinism and Arminianism which now occupy us, Alan P.F. Sell has a clear and often exciting account in his *The Great Debate: Calvinism, Arminianism and Salvation* (1982); other useful studies include A. Dakin, *Calvinism* (1940), Wilhelm Niesel, *The Theology of Calvin* (1956), and Heinrich Quistorp, *Calvin's Doctrine of the Last Things* (1955).

112. Wilfred Cantwell Smith has an important discussion of how the Latin title, *Christianae Religionis Instituto* of Calvin's great work (1536) should be translated: 'The matters set forth in Calvin's *magnum opus* – a pattern of doctrines, Church practices, interpretations of Scripture and of the Lord's supper, etc. – are not themselves *religio*. They are rather, things that he hoped would institute or induce in people or guide them to or instruct them in a personal, dynamic, and worshipful 'recognition' of God to which he gave that name (*Christiana religio*)', *The Meaning and End of Religion* (1978), pp.37ff.

113. The profundity of Calvin's 'religion' and his doctrine of God may be sensed in these words: 'our feeling of ignorance, vanity, want, weakness, in short, depravity

and corruption, reminds us that in the Lord, and in none but He, dwell the true light of wisdom, solid virtue, exuberant goodness', *Institutes of the Christian Religion*, I,i,1, in Henry Beveridge's translation (my edition 1962), p.38. Cf. the comment of A.M. Fairbairn: 'The strength of Calvinism lay in the place and pre-eminence it gave to God: it magnified Him; humbled man before His awful majesty, yet lifted man in the very degree that it humbled him, *The Place of Christ in Modern Theology* (1894), p.149.

114. *Institutes of the Christian Religion*, Beveridge translation, vol. 2, p.202.

115. '...God by his eternal and immutable counsel determined once for all those it was his good pleasure one day to admit to salvation, and those whom on the other hand it was his good pleasure to doom to destruction. We maintain that this counsel, as regards the elect is founded on his free mercy, without any respect to human worth, while those he dooms to destruction are excluded from access to life by a just and blameless, but at the same time incomprehensible judgment.' *Institutes*, III, xxi,7, op. cit., pp.210-1.

116. Calvin taught that in Scripture the full truth had been revealed, to the end that humankind might 'thereby learn to worship Him with integrity of heart and unfeigned obedience, and also to depend entirely on his goodness', *Institutes*, I,x,2. Cf. the *Shorter Catechism*, answer to question two: 'The Word of God which is contained in the Scriptures of the Old and New Testaments, is the only rule to direct us how we may glorify and enjoy him'.

117. Developed Calvinist scholasticism can be found in the 'high Calvinism' and 'supralapsarianism' of Theodore Beza (1519-1605). Beza taught that God had chosen the elect before the Fall, indeed before the Creation. It was against such teaching that Jacobus Arminius (1560-1609) protested.

118. The expression 'wooden and rigid' comes from the Dutch Reformed scholar David Bosch, op. cit., p.285.

119. See Peter Toon, *The Emergence of Hyper-Calvinism* (1967). Toon borrows the phrase 'no offers of grace' from the Cambridge Presbyterian preacher and theologian Joseph Hussey (1660-1726), who published *God's Operations of Grace but No Offers of His Grace* in 1706. Hussey believed that 'Offers rob the Gospel of its properties, privileges and glory', see Toon, p.82, who in a definition of hyper-Calvinism later in his book speaks of its 'notion that grace must only be offered to those for whom it was intended', p.145.

120. For a valiant attempt to make sense of the Confession for mainstream Christians today see Jack Rogers, *Presbyterian Creeds: A Guide to the Book of Confessions* (1985).

121. See A.W. Harrison, *The Beginnings of Arminianism to the Synod of Dort* (1926) and *Arminianism* (1937). The term 'Evangelical Arminianism' denotes the form which the doctrine took in the teaching of John Wesley, John Fletcher, Thomas Jackson, Richard Watson and other Methodist theologians, with its twin emphases on justification by faith and on Christ's free offer of salvation to all. But in the controversies of the eighteenth and nineteenth century, as Robert C. Whittemore has well said about the term 'Arminian', 'In the lexicon of high Calvinist orthodoxy, the sense is always derogatory, intentionally demeaning and insulting', *The Transformation of New England Theology* (1987), p.167.

122. *The Westminster Confession of Faith*, chap.III, para.iii.

123. Ibid., para.v.

124. Ibid., para.vii.

125. Ibid., chap. X, para.iv.

126. The concepts of 'fewness' and 'restrictedness' here I owe to Clark H.Pinnock, op. cit.

127. Van den Berg, op. cit., p.73. Cf. the Diary of John Ryland: 'When I first entered upon the ministry, though I ventured to say as much to sinners as my views on the subject would allow, yet I was shackled by adherence to a supposed systematic consistency, and carefully avoided inviting sinners to come to Christ for salvation.' cited by B.J. Griffiths in the BMS commemoration volume for the *Ter-Jubilee Celebrations 1942-4* (1945), p.36.

128. See van den Berg, op. cit., pp.71 and 117, citing G. Laws, *Andrew Fuller, Pastor, Theologian, Ropeholder* (1942) a book which I have not been able to see, and Toon, op. cit., pp.149-51.

129. See Ernest Payne, 'Introduction' to the 1961 Facsimile Edition of the *Humble Enquiry*, p.iii.

130. For a full discussion of the *Enquiry* see Payne, *The Church Awakes* (1942), pp.65ff.

131. On the Reformers' understanding of mission to the world as already having taken place see note 5 above.

132. *Enquiry*, 1961 Facsimile edition, pp.8-9.

133. The story of David Brainerd was told in Jonathan Edwards' *An Account of the Life of the Late Reverend Mr David Brainerd* (1749). This often reprinted book achieved two goals. By his evangelistic work among the Indians in Pennsylvania and New Jersey, David Brainerd (1718-47) had illustrated perfectly what Jonathan Edwards meant by 'distinguishing marks of a work of the Spirit of God in the soul'. The publication of his 'Life' also kept the missionary ideals of Brainerd, John Eliot and other early missionaries like Thomas Mayhew alive, and inspired many people to follow their example. The *Account of the Life of David Brainerd* was widely read: as well as William Carey, John Wesley and Henry Martyn testified to the influence it had had upon them.

134. Carey's sense of the discovery of the world was matched by his rediscovery of the Prophetic Books of the Old Testament which he read in Hebrew. In Nottingham in May 1792 Carey preached on Isaiah 54 and told his congregation, the Northampton Baptist Association: 'Get up. Find larger canvas, stouter and taller poles, stronger tent-pegs. Catch wider visions. Dare bolder programmes. Dwell in an ampler world', for 'Thy Maker is Thy Husband. He is the Lord of all the earth', S.P. Carey, *William Carey* (1923), p.83.

135. See A.L. Drummond and J. Bulloch, *The Scottish Church 1688-1843: The Age of the Moderates* (1973), pp.218-9

136. *The Extent of the Propitiation: or The question, for whom did Christ die? Answered* (1847), quoted by Cheyne, *The Transforming of the Kirk* (1983), pp.63-4.

137. Ibid., but we must be aware that some missionaries thought it possible to do this. John Cockin wrote a reply to the Wesleyan Methodist Thomas Jackson who had alleged the contrary. 'We' (i.e. Calvinists), Cockin said, 'make the decree of election as extensive as actual salvation' and 'therefore in our plan the multitude of the redeemed is as great as yours, but our peculiarity is to ascribe their final happiness to

discriminatory mercy and special grace', *A Valedictory Letter to the Rev. T. Jackson, Containing a Reply to his Remarks in His Second Letter* (1815), quoted by Bernard Semmel, *The Methodist Revolution* (1974), p.152. Nevertheless Cockin was unusual in not moving with the LMS and Congregationalist stream. Ralph Wardlaw's *Extent of the Atonement* (1830) argued that the Atonement was sufficient for all, even if it could only become efficient in the case of those elected. By 1842 John Kirk was contending in *The Way of Life Made Plain* that Jesus Christ died for every one and that 'the saved are those who yield to him', see W.B.Selbie, *Congregationalism* (1934), pp.168-9.

138. A.L. Drummond and J. Bulloch comment on the foundation of the Evangelical Union: 'There had been a revolt against Calvinism in what had been its strongest citadel' (i.e., the Secession Kirk), op. cit., p.219.

139. See pp.73ff. and 167.

140. David W. Simon (1830-1909), Principal of the Congregational Theological Hall, Edinburgh, spoke in 1891 of the 'changing evangelical consciousness': 'The positive result has been to substitute a "Christocentric system" for "theocentric Calvinism", or to speak more exactly, to replace the latter "with its two co-ordinate foci, the Divinity and Atonement of Christ" by the former – with its "foci of the fatherhood of God and the living Personality of Jesus", from an address 'The Present Direction of Theological Thought in the Congregational Churches', at the first International Congregational Council London 1891, quoted by F.J. Powicke, *David Worthington Simon* (1912), p.167.

141. See Colin Brown, *Jesus in European Protestant Thought 1778-1860* (1985) and Daniel L. Pals, *Victorian "Lives" of Jesus* (1982).

142. Following on from the work of F.C. Baur and the Tübingen School, the 'Kingdom of God' was the main theme in theologians like Albrecht Ritschl (1822-89), and Julius Kaftan (1848-1926); see W. R. Hogg, 'The Rise of Protestant Missionary Concern 1517-1914' in G. Anderson, (ed.), *The Theology of the Christian Mission* (1961), pp.108-9. A. M. Fairbairn, see pp.71-81, was among the chief of those responsible for making the Kingdom of God central to British theology. His student Alfred E. Garvie, who was to write the Islam section of the Commission IV report, see below, p.190, published the first scholarly exposition of Ritschl in 1899 (*The Ritschlian Theology: Critical and Constructive*). In the last part of the Great Century the ideas of these German teachers were mediated by two American systematic theologies, those of W. Newton Clarke, *An Outline of Christian Theology* (1898) and W. Adams Brown, *Christian Theology in Outline* (1906) both of who were enthusiasts for overseas missions as 'kingdom bringing'. Among the missionary respondents to Edinburgh 1910, A. G. Hogg of Madras was particularly influenced by the teachings of Julius Kaftan., see pp.185ff., and cf. his extremely influential *Christ's Message of the Kingdom* (1912).

143. See below for their various applications of the new understanding of the place and personality of Jesus Christ and his teaching of the Kingdom of God, among the theologians A.M. Fairbairn, pp.73ff., A.V.G. Allen, pp.87ff., C.C. Hall, pp.96ff., and notably among the missionaries, Timothy Richard, pp.122ff., and Bernard Lucas, pp.166ff.

144. The most recent study of Erskine is Marian Foster, *Representation and Substitution in the Theology of Thomas Erskine of Linlathen*, Unpublished Ph.D. thesis, London University, 1992. For Campbell see George M. Tuttle, *So Rich a Soil* (1986).

145. See the comments of L. E. Elliott-Binns, *English Thought 1860-1900: The Theological Aspect* (1956), p.248, where he says that the whole idea of substitution is not possible in the sphere of moral and spiritual relationships. p.248.

146. For Maurice on Election see above, pp.38ff.

147. Barbara Cross, *Horace Bushnell: Minister to a Changing America* (1958) told of his link with Maurice: 'Bushnell could find in Maurice's books, with which he had stocked his library, the central figure of a suffering God in a condemned world', p.141.

148. For Bushnell's debt to Coleridge's *Aids to Reflection*, see Cross, op. cit., p.21ff.

149. See Stephen Prickett, *Romanticism and Religion* (1976) for many insights into the role played by the romantic movement for people like Bushnell.

150. Cf. Bushnell's extended comment: 'On the whole this matter of a contrived compensation to justice, which so many take for a gospel, appears to me to contain about the worst reflection upon God's justice that could be stated, without some great offence against reverence; for in whatever manner the compensation, or judicial satisfaction, is conceived to be made, in the suffering of Christ, we shall find everything pushed off the basis of truth. The justice satisfied is satisfied with injustice! the forgiveness prepared is forgiveness on the score of pay! the judgment-day award disclaims the fact of forgiveness after payment is made, and even refuses to be satisfied, taking payment again! What meantime has become of the penalties threatened, and where is the truth of the law? The penalties threatened, as against wrongdoers, are not to be executed upon them, because they have been executed on a right-doer! viz., Christ. And it is only in some logically formal, theologically fictitious, sense, that they are executed even on Him.' *The Vicarious Sacrifice* (new edition 1880), p.240.

151. Cross, however, finds no connection between Bushnell and Lessing, but rather stresses the growth of religious experience growing in the child in the home, as represented by the popular *Letters of Pestalozzi on the Education of Infancy*, see op. cit., pp.63ff. Cf. Hutchison, *The Modernist Impulse in American Protestantism* (1976), pp. 43-8.

152. See *Christian Nurture* where Bushnell refers to 'the grand idea that has taken possession of the churches of our times'. Bushnell recorded that 'they have taken hold of the promise... of a time when the reign of Christ shall be universal, extending to all nations and peoples'. p.125. But Bushnell wanted to show that 'conversion over to the church is not the only way of increase' but that also God has 'ordained a law of population' by which there shall be 'increase from within', ibid., p.126. This he saw as a 'scheme of organic unity', ibid., p.127, and 'habit or process of culture', ibid., p.131. Bushnell had also a vision of a this-worldly kingdom: 'The sacred writings show the fact of celestial institutions finally created on earth, which is fitly called the Kingdom of God, because it shows Him reigning as a Regenerator and Restorer of the Broken Order of the world', *The Character of Jesus*, as quoted by W. Wilson Cash, *The Missionary Church* (1939), p.14.

153. *The Vicarious Sacrifice* (1880), p.35.

154. Ibid., pp.35-6.

155. Robert Rainy (1826-1906), Principal of New College, Edinburgh from 1874-1906 as quoted by Cheyne, op. cit., p.76. These words are particularly significant because they emanate from an essentially conservative thinker, cf. the words of his first biographer, Robert Mackintosh, 'Dr Rainy remained personally an old-fashioned Christian, at home in the old interpretation of the old or timeless truths of the gospel', *Principal Rainy: A Biographical Study* (1907), p.38.

156. See Andrew L. Drummond and James Bulloch, *The Church in Late Victorian Scotland 1874-1900* (1978), pp.29ff, 263ff., and 292ff.

157. The full text of the 1879 Declaratory Act is in Drummond and Bulloch, op. cit., p.36.

158. W.B. Selbie, *The Life of Andrew Martin Fairbairn* (1914), p.75.

159. Drummond and Bulloch, op. cit., p.216. According to these authors Alexander Whyte, a popular preacher of that generation, 'frequently gave copies of Hodge's *Systematic Theology* to Free Church ministers but students now resented having to use Hodge', ibid. One of the Scottish theological students in the 'eighties was David Cairns. In his *Memoir*, he wrote 'I *hated* Charles Hodge, with his hard dogmatism...', emphasis his, p.87, cf. pp.188-89 above.

160. This is the subtitle of his excellent survey, *The Transforming of the Kirk*, (1983). Chapter three in this work deals brilliantly with what Cheyne calls 'The Confessional Revolution'. For two other perspectives see Lefferts A. Loetscher, *The Broadening Church: A Study of Theological Issues in the Presbyterian Church* (1954); Rolf Sjolinder, *Presbyterian Reunion in Scotland: Its Background and its Development, 1907-1921* (1962) and Ian Hamilton, *The Erosion of Calvinist Orthodoxy: Seceders and Subscription in Scottish Presbyterianism* (1990).

161. Strictly speaking the College of New Jersey became Princeton University. The Seminary proper was founded in 1812.

162. See M. Noll, *History of Christianity in the United States and Canada* (1992), pp.233-7.

163. Cf. Winthrop S. Hudson and John Corrigan: '...Charles Hodge became the great theologian of Old School Presbyterianism. He had been appointed to a professorship at Princeton in 1822 and remained there for 50 years, sharing in the training of over 3,000 ministers and contributing more than any other single person to the shaping of American Presbyterianism... His great monument and source of much of his later influence was his three volume *Systematic Theology*, explicitly designed as a defensive rampart against all doctrinal aberrations', *Religion in America* (fifth edition, 1992), pp.161-2. See also the introduction to the recent abridged edition of Hodge's *Systematic Theology*, (1988) by Edward N. Gross.

164. *Systematic Theology* (1878), Vol.2, pp. 670-1.

165. Ibid. pp. 676-7. Hodge continued, 'This Paul says even of the light of nature. The heathen are without excuse for their idolatry, because the eternal power and Godhead of the divine Being are revealed to them in his works', p.676. I have it on the authority of O. G. Myklebust, *The Study of Missions in Theological Education* (1955), p.150, note 14, that Charles Hodge never once referred to overseas missions in the *Systematic Theology*.

166. Hodge gained the evidence for his views of Hinduism from much the same selection of books which Maurice used for *The Religions of the World*, see note 58 on p.312. To these were added Max Müller, *A History of Ancient Sanskrit Literature, as*

far as it illustrates the Primitive Religion of the Brahmans and Alexander Duff, *India and Indian Missions.*

167. Hodge, op. cit., Vol. 1, pp.311-4. Pantheism 'as the most portentous error' was discussed on p.309.

168. Ibid., pp.317-318.

169. For the development of the Princeton theology and Warfield's role in it see Noll, op. cit., pp.371ff., Sandeen, op. cit., pp.114ff.

170. With his colleague A.A. Hodge, Charles Hodge's son, Warfield wrote in 1881, 'the scriptures not only contain, but ARE THE WORD OF GOD, and hence... all their elements and all their affirmations are absolutely errorless, and binding the faith and obedience of all men', quoted in Noll, op. cit., p.371, the emphasis is in the original quotation.

171. *Studies in Theology* (1932), p.650.

172. Ibid.

173. When anti-modernism broke out in 1910 with the beginning of the publication of *The Fundamentals*, Warfield was much involved. See W.R. Hutchison, *The Modernist Impulse*, pp.196ff, where he refers to Warfield's 'inspired obstinacy', and to the prevalent theological *machismo*, 'a virile contempt for all weak, spineless, compromising systems of quasi belief', prevalent at Princeton. See also George Marsden, *Fundamentalism and American Culture* (1980).

174. See W. J. Schmidt and E. Ouellette, *What Kind of Man: the Life of Henry Smith Lieper* (1986). Lieper was to become an ABCFM missionary in China and eventually Associate General Secretary of the newly formed WCC in 1948, as well as leading missionary administrator in the USA. Lieper described his interview for the Presbyterian ordination in 1914: 'I found some difficulty! They wanted more convictions about the Devil and Hell than I could present', p.45. Lieper became a Congregationalist almost on the spot.

175. One of these was G. S. Eddy, later to become an Edinburgh respondent. Eddy recalled studying with Warfield whom he described as 'a razor-edged fundamentalist theologian' at Princeton in 1894. He and some colleagues felt Princeton to be so unendurable that they transferred to Union Seminary in New York, see his autobiography *A Pilgrimage of Ideas: or the Re- education of Sherwood Eddy* (1935), pp.38-9. In fact Warfield appears to have got under Eddy's skin. In *Pathfinders of the World Missionary Crusade* (1945), Sherwood Eddy discussed the missionary methods of Timothy Richard, remarking that Richard was 'not like my old theological professor who would calmly consign ninety per cent of humanity to an endless burning hell and then go home to toast his feet by the fire and then enjoy an untroubled sleep', p.183. It is clear from Eddy's personal recollections in *Pathfinders* that he did not feel himself alone among SVM missionaries in repudiating the 'horrible doctrine' which suggested that they were called to preach the gospel as a testimony against 'the heathen'. On Eddy's considered views of Timothy Richard's new missionary methods, see *Pathfinders*, p.184; on Eddy's own 'revivalist' sense of seeking the lost, see p.31 above.

176. There is a vast range of literature dealing with Revivalism as an aspect of Evangelicalism (it is not a synonym). The best guide to this is Leonard I. Sweet's 'bibliographical' essay in the volume which he edited entitled *The Evangelical Tradition in America* (1984). He persuades me that a sharp and clear distinction has to be made between 'revivalism' and 'evangelicalism', not least on the ground that 'evan-

gelicals' as such were not, and are not, 'empty-headed country bumpkins', see pp. 26ff. But they were certainly anti-intellectual. Works used in my assessment of 'revivalism' include Timothy L. Smith, *Revivalism and Social Reform: American Protestantism on the Eve of the Civil War*, New York, Abingdon Press 1957, William G. McLoughlin, *Revivals, Awakenings and Reform: An Essay on Religion and Social Change in America 1607-1977* (1978), and David W. Dayton and Robert K. Johnson (eds.), *The Varieties of American Evangelicalism* (1991). Cf. the useful source book edited by W.G. McLoughlin, *The American Evangelicals 1800-1900: An Anthology* (1976). For a vivid personal assessment see David W. Dayton, *Rediscovering an Evangelical Heritage* (1976, second edition 1988).

177. D. L. Moody's return from Britain in 1873 marked the beginning of his inestimable influence on American college students in the following years. In July 1886 there took place the great Mount Hermon student conference when the Student Volunteer Movement was first thought of and a hundred young men 'signified their willingness and desire, God permitting, to become foreign missionaries'. Among them was John R. Mott. In 1888 the Student Volunteer Movement was formally established at Northfield, Massachussetts with Mott as its first chairman. Its British counterpart was the Student Volunteer Missionary Union founded in 1892. See Sherwood Eddy, *Pathfinders of the World Missionary Crusade*, pp. 43-45. For a fine biography and assessment of Moody's developed 'revivalism' which so much appealed to college students, see James F. Findlay, *Dwight L. Moody* (1969), esp. chap.7, 'The Theology of a Popular Preacher', pp.227-261, and chap.9, 'New Approaches to Evangelism', pp.309-338. An older work which is still authoritative on the Student Volunteer Missionary Union is C. P. Shedd, *Two Centuries of Student Christian Movements* (1934).

178. For the work of the Halle Pietists see G. Warneck, op. cit., chap.3., and a convenient anthology in the 'Classics of Western Spirituality' series, Peter C. Erb (ed.), *Pietists: Selected Writings* (1983). Cf. also F. Ernest Stoeffler's *The Rise of Evangelical Pietism* (1965) and *Continental Pietism and Early Evangelical Christianity* (1976).

179. Spener also rediscovered the Great Commission (Matt.28. 19-20). An obligation, he taught, 'rests on the whole church to have care as to how the Gospel shall be preached to the whole world, and thus may be continually carried to places whither it has not yet come, and to this end no diligence, no labour, or cost be spared in such work on behalf of the poor heathen or unbelievers'. That no thought had been given to this was not just 'the fault of kings and princes as the earthly heads of the church', but rather was 'evidence how little the honour of Christ and humanity concerns us', see Warneck, op. cit., pp.39-40.

180. Studies of Zinzendorf in English are still few. See A.J. Lewis, *Zinzendorf The Ecumenical Pioneer* (1962) which is still the best available. A shorter account is H. J. Margull, 'The Awakening of Christian Missions' in the WSCF volume: *History's Lessons for Tomorrow's Mission* (1960), pp.137-48.

181. 'Seelen fur das Lamm zu werben' in the original German, see Warneck, op. cit., p.66. Cf. Zinzendorf's statement: 'To seek for souls, souls, in order that Jesus may love them and that His kingdom may be inhabited, that is my work', see Lewis, op. cit., p.12.

182. The reference is to the story of the Ethiopian eunuch, the servant of Candace, Queen of Ethiopia.

183. To gauge the importance of this it is worth reflecting upon the work of John Eliot (1604-90) in the Massachusetts Bay Colony. He established fourteen 'Praying Towns' among the Indians. In these settlements the entire daily life of the community was organised according to guidelines he thought he could read in Exodus 18. By the time of his death in 1690 there were twenty-four Indian preachers and a community of perhaps 3,600 Christian Indians. Eliot once wrote, 'That which I aimed at was to declare and deliver unto them the law of God... (Galatians 3.19), to convince, bridle, restrain and civilise them...' 'To civilise' as a dominant missionary motive could be said to have begun its long career among Protestants at this point. For Eliot's theological principles see Rooy, op. cit., pp.160ff.

184. The references here may be found in J. C. Hoekendijk, *Kerk en Volk in de Duitse Zendingswetanschap* (1962), pp.43ff.

185. For the Moravian influence on Methodism, see Henry D. Rack, *Reasonable Enthusiast* (1989), pp.162ff. and 184ff; and, more detailed, Richard Heitzenrater, *Mirror and Memory: Reflections on Early Methodism* (1989), pp.118ff, 124ff and 129ff.

186. Some historians have gone so far as to call the nineteenth century 'The Methodist Century', see chap.7 of Hudson and Corrigan, op. cit., esp., pp.172-4.

187. See note 119 above. That Methodists, at least originally, never thought 'hell-fire' a dominant motive or theme is shown by the Minutes of the Wesleyan Conference of 1746:

'Q. What inconvenience is there in speaking much of the wrath of God and little of the love of God?

A. It generally hardens them that believe not, and discourages them that do.'

188. J. van den Berg, op. cit., pp.156ff. See also the *Collection of Hymns for the Use of the People called Methodists* (1876 edition) No. 526. Charles Wesley wrote:

Not in the tombs we pine to dwell
Not in the dark monastic cell
By vows and grates confined
Freely to all ourselves we give
Constrained by Jesu's love to live
The servants of mankind.

189. These are called in order by van den Berg, 'political', 'humanitarian-cultural', 'ascetic', 'the motive of debt', 'romantic', 'theocentric', 'ecclesiological', 'eschatological', and 'obedience to the 'Great Commission', see op. cit. pp.144-65.

190. 'A History of Foreign Mission Theory in America' in *American Missions in Bicentennial Perspective* (1977), p.71.

191. See H. Richard Niebuhr, *The Kingdom of God in America* (1937), p.126.

192. 'Practically the Awakening stimulated very great interest in, and reading of, the Scriptures while insisting upon the personal experience of the truth taught in the scriptures', ibid., p.109.

193. For an assessment of Wesleyan heart religion see Kenneth Cracknell, 'What is Faith?', *Epworth Review*, Vol. 15, No.1, January 1988, pp.65-73.

194. See among many others, Bernard Weisberger, *They Gathered at the River: The Story of the Great Revivalists and their impact upon Religion in America*, (1958); Charles A. Johnson. *The Frontier Camp Meeting: Religion's Harvest Time* (1955); Whitney R. Cross, *The Burned Over District: The Social and Intellectual History of Enthusiastic Religion in Western New York, 1800-1850* (1950).

195. Note that the use of the term 'Evangelical' to define a limited segment of the Protestant world, i.e., as having a specific reference to those who hold that the essence of Christian faith 'consists in the doctrine of salvation by faith in the atoning death of Christ, and deny the saving efficacy of either good works or the sacraments', became widespread only at this period. The OED's earliest reference to this use is to 1792. The term 'evangelist' and the widespread use of the related word 'evangelism' are of even later date. Bernard A. Weisberger quotes the following passage: 'We have no doubt that Mr. Finney is essentially right in his notions of revivals, technically speaking. They belong to no particular set of opinions, but to a system of operations set in motion by human contrivance. Consequently, the most modern and approved practice has been to make use of particular persons, who have acquired practical skill in the art of bringing about an excitement, on the principle, we suppose, of the perfection in art, which is compassed by division of labor, and of a particular adaptation to a particular branch of professional work', op. cit., p.158. Weisberger thinks that the designation of 'particular persons as 'Evangelists' with a professional or semi-professional order or class dates from about 1851. Much about Revivalism as it practised even today is owed to Charles Grandison Finney (1792-1875), its first great theorist; see his *Lectures on Revivals of Religion* (1835). For a stimulating treatment of Finney's thinking, see David L. Weddle: *The Law as Gospel: Theology and Reform in the Theology of Charles J. Finney* (1985) and see also D. W. Dayton, op. cit., pp.137ff.

196. *Evangelism in the Wesleyan Spirit* (1971), p.60.

197. Ibid.

198. Weisberger, op. cit., p. 27.

199. Ibid.

200. Outler, op. cit., p.61.

201. Ibid., pp.61-2.

202. *Sacred Songs and Solos: Twelve Hundred Pieces*, compiled under the direction of Ira D. Sankey, No.814.

203. See the *Collection of Hymns for the Use of the People called Methodists* (1876 edition) No.579. This hymn is also in Sankey's *Sacred Songs and Solos: Twelve Hundred Pieces* at No.815 but without this verse. Perhaps it was too dismal for D.L. Moody and Ira Sankey.

204. Eddy gives a first hand account of this powerful interchange between the non-intellectual D.L. Moody and the student classes in *Pathfinders in the Modern Missionary Crusade* (1945), pp.40-3. Clifton Jackson Phillips offers a critical overview in 'Changing Attitudes in the Student Volunteer Movement of Great Britain and North America 1886-1928', in Torben Christensen and William R. Hutchison (eds.), *Missionary Ideologies in the Imperialist Era, 1880-1920* (1984). Robert Wilder, John R.Mott and Robert Speer were all caught up in the Student Volunteer Movement.

205. Eddy, *Pilgrimage of Ideas* (1935), p.7.

206. See Handy, op. cit., p.110, Noll, op. cit., p.98, and Cross, op. cit., pp.64-5.

207. I owe the reference to Isaac Taylor to Stuart Piggin, op. cit., pp. 67ff.

208. *The Natural History of Enthusiasm* (1823), p.79.

209. Ibid., p.80.

210. Ibid.

211. See Noll, op. cit., pp. 235-6. Noll comments that Hodge meant by this remark that Princeton 'intended to pass on Reformed faith as it had been defined in the sixteenth and seventeenth centuries'.

212. For the state of theological education in the early and mid-nineteenth century see E.A. Payne, 'The Development of Nonconformist Theological Education in the Nineteenth Century, with special reference to Regent's Park College', in E.A. Payne (ed.) *Studies in History and Religion* (1942), pp.229-53, where Payne speaks of 'competent, if cautious, instruction' as the prevailing mode. William Hale White (1831-1913) described the ethos of New College, London *circa* 1850 in his novel *The Autobiography of Mark Rutherford*. In Scotland, Robert Flint (1838-1910), from 1876 Professor of Divinity at New College, Edinburgh, described the products of the training given in the theological halls as 'strong-minded, logical sharp men... but rigid and one-sided. Their ground is narrow, their thoughts all run in beaten tracks', quoted in Andrew L. Drummond and James Bulloch, *The Church in Victorian Scotland 1843-1874* (1975), p.295.

213. See F.J. Powicke, op. cit., p.33, who is quoting Dr John Brown who had been a classmate of David W. Simon. Brown went on to say 'I happen to know that his studies in comparative religion began about that time with Maurice's *Religions of the World*'. Quite certainly this work would not have been on the Lancashire College syllabus in between 1851 and 1854.

214. Piggin, op. cit., p.248. Robert Mackintosh, Rainy's biographer had stronger words for it in 1907. He called it an 'absurdly confident dogmatism', p.37.

215. Cf. Brooke Foss Westcott at the age of 22 speaking of the 'fear and doubt which oppress his heart', which he calls 'Dark doubt and unbelief', A. Westcott, *Life and Letters of Brooke Foss Westcott* (1903), vol.1, p.90.

216. Piggin, op cit., p.249.

217. This passage, 1 Cor 2.1 ff., was customarily expounded in Evangelical circles as a repudiation of philosophical studies and of the attempt to win intellectuals to Christ by intellectual means. This was based on an expository tradition represented by Sir William Ramsay in *St Paul the Traveller and Roman Citizen*, see Cracknell, *Towards a New Relationship*, pp.30ff., and note 11 on p.171.

218. Piggin, op. cit., pp.249-50.

219. See above, p.16.

220. Cracknell, op. cit., p.21.

221. Ibid., p.22.

222. Piggin, op. cit., p.248.

223. See J. Guinness Rogers, *Christ for the World: Sermons in Connection with the Centenary of the L.M.S.* (1894), p.56.

224. Ibid.

2 Five Theologians and World Religions

1. Maurice's reputation as a theologian is discussed almost conventionally in every book about him: see H.G. Wood, *Frederick Denison Maurice* (1950), pp. 1ff., A.M. Ramsey, *F.D. Maurice and the Conflicts of Modern Theology* (1951), pp. 9-25, Alec Vidler, *F.D. Maurice and Company* (1966), pp. 15ff., Torben Christensen, *The Divine Order: A Study in F.D. Maurice's Theology* (1973), pp. 19ff. Frank Maudlin McClain in *Maurice, Man and Moralist* (1972) is an exception to this rule. In her fine study,

Frederick Denison Maurice: Rebellious Conformist (1971), Olive Brose judges accurately when she writes that Maurice is 'generally acknowledged as one of the greatest and most original thinkers the Church of England has managed to produce' (p. xii). Brose accurately describes the polarities in Maurice: 'truly radical faith which could rank with that of a Luther, a Kierkegaard, and a Barth, and even a Bonhoeffer' and a 'truly monumental conservatism which saw the hoary institutions of the family, the nation, and the church as divine', op. cit., p. xv. For a striking, but little known, testimony to Maurice's greatness see Ellen Flesseman-van Leer, *Grace Abounding: a Comparison of Frederick Denison Maurice and Karl Barth* (1968). Another Dutch testimony to Maurice's power can be found in Hendrik Berkhof's *Two Hundred Years of Theology* (1989). Berkhof speaks of Maurice's 'original and individual mind', and, like Flessemann-van Leer, sees him as a forerunner of Karl Barth, op. cit., p. 87. Studies of Maurice's indebtedness to his teachers are also many and varied. For the Unitarian influence of his father, Michael Maurice, there is H.G. Wood, op. cit., pp. 25-29 and David Young *Maurice and Unitarianism* (1992); for some seminal comments on how this Unitarian universalism was related to the Calvinism of his mother, Priscilla Hurry Maurice, see A.V.G. Allen, art. 'Frederick Denison Maurice' in F.W. Farrar and others, *Prophets of the Christian Faith* (1897); for the Platonizing influence of Julius Hare, see Vidler, op. cit., pp. 221-41 and Stephen Prickett, *Romanticism and Religion* (1972); for the influence of Samuel Taylor Coleridge see C.R. Sanders, *Coleridge and the Broad Church Movement* (1942); for Edward Irving see Brose, op. cit., pp. 36-42; for Thomas Erskine of Linlathen see Torben Christensen, *Origin and History of Christian Socialism 1848-54* (1962), Vidler, op. cit., pp. 241-249, and Olive Brose, op. cit., pp. 42-51. The relationship between Maurice and John McLeod Campbell has also been given attention by G.M. Tuttle, *So Rich a Soil: John McLeod Campbell on Christian Atonement* (1986), pp. 7off.

2. John F. Porter and William F. Wolf, *Toward the Recovery of Unity: the Thought of Frederick Denison Maurice* (1964), pp. 3ff. These authors attribute Maurice's abiding influence to an extraordinary sensitivity to 'the unbelief that lay hidden beneath the conventional religion and popular theologies of his day, and that had even insinuated itself into theological method', p. 4. Cf. the judgment of W.R. Hutchison. '... the prevailing mood of Maurice's thought was affirmative, catholic, expansive. Preceding conceptions of the creation, of predestination, of Christ's work of justification, of the meaning in the creeds, of miracles, had all been not so much wrong, in his view, as small and cramping', in *The Modernist Impulse in American Protestantism* (1976), p. 81.

3. See pp.110ff. for T.E. Slater in *The Philosophy of Missions*, and pp.164ff. for Bernard Lucas in *The Empire of Christ*.

4. See above, pp.16ff.

5. *The Kingdom of Christ* was published in the form we have it now in 1842, as *The Kingdom of Christ: or Hints Respecting the Principles, Ordinances and Constitution of the Catholic Church in Letters to a Member of the Society of Friends*, 2nd edn, revised and altered, 2 volumes. Quotations here are from the 1959 reprint, cited as *Kingdom*.

6. For the connection between Maurice and Stephenson, see Frank Maudin McClain, op. cit., McClain has written that 'Maurice's debt to Julius Hare, to Coleridge, to Erskine of Linlathen, even to Edward Irving, has been systematically explored. There has never been, however, a thorough investigation into Maurice's association with the Millenarian rector of Lympsham, one of the most important

determinative influences on Maurice's thought', op. cit., p. 54. He owed this way of thinking to Edward Irving and Thomas Erskine, as well as J.A. Stephenson. Cf. 'I remember thirty-two years ago, being led by a book of Mr Irving's to feel that the basis of human experience and faith must be in theology, or the revelation of God; that human experience and faith can never be its basis', see Brose, op. cit., p. 40, quoting *Tracts for Priests and People, No. XIV*. In *The Brazen Serpent*, Erskine had said that a man may be surrounded by light and yet be in darkness by shutting his eyes, but the act of opening his eyes gave no light unless there was actually some light there. 'The light of forgiving love, Erskine said, was the very life of God made intelligible and visible; it became light and shone on every man. Thus the light of God really was given *to* every man, but did not become life *in* the man until he saw the light.', Brose, ibid., p. 51.

7. *Kingdom*, Vol. 2, p. 270. See also Ernest Lee Tuveson on Maurice in relation to the old Augustinian theology: 'Maurice, then, sees the Christian horizon as having expanded to include the whole of society; like the millennialists generally, he feels that the greatest progress in these stirring times has been the exposure of the Augustinian idea of the City of God', *Redeemer Nation*, p. 75. See above, pp. 4-6.

8. *Kingdom*, Vol. 2, p. 271.

9. Ibid.

10. Ibid.

11. Ibid.

12. Ibid.

13. *Life*, Vol. 2, p. 243.

14. *Kingdom*, Vol. 2, p. 269.

15. *Life*, Vol. 2, p. 244.

16. *Kingdom*, Vol. 2, p. 1.

17. The subtitle of *The Kingdom of Christ*.

18. *Kingdom*, Vol. 2, p. 332.

19. Ibid.

20. *Kingdom*, Vol. 1, p. 55, Cf. 'The Divine Word had been speaking to the conscience and reason of men in all ages', ibid., p. 59. Maurice has sometimes been accused of being more a Platonist than a Christian, but see the accurate judgment of Ellen Flesseman-Van Leer, 'Maurice regularly uses the terms '*Logos*', 'Word' or 'Eternal Son'. These were no philosophical concepts for him; they received their context very concretely from Jesus. If that is forgotten, Maurice will mistakenly be considered a Platonist in the guise of a Christian, instead of a Christian who often makes use of Platonist terminology', op. cit., p. 2.

21. *Kingdom*, Vol. 1, p. 50. Cf. 'That Jesus Christ is the revelation of the Creator means that in him the intention of God is to be seen when he created the world. Jesus Christ on earth reveals 'the will and the mind that had been creating and ruling all things', *Gospel of St. John*, p. 264. 'So Christ is not only the Head of a new humanity; he has changed the moral situation for all men', Flesseman-Van Leer, op. cit., p. 38.

22. Ibid.

23. *Sermons Preached at Lincoln's Inn*, (1892 edition), Vol. 4, p. 9.

24. Porter and Wolf, op. cit., p. 13.

25. *Life*, Vol. 2, p. 19, cf. Flesseman-Van Leer: 'Repeatedly Maurice uses such terms as "vindication", "restitution", "re-establishment", when speaking of the work of Christ. For "if Jesus was the word made flesh, if the order of the world was established by Him, then His acts on earth would be done for the purpose of vindicating this order"', *Gospel of St John*, p. 64. To express this in theological terms: only in re-creation can it be seen what creation is, i.e. creation has to be re-interpreted by re-creation, and the link which connects the two is Christ's atonement and reconciliation', op. cit., pp. 12-3.

26. See above, pp. 7ff. For similar processes at work in the case of Andrew Fuller and William Carey, and of James Morison and the establishment of the Evangelical Union, see above, pp. 22ff.

27. Cited in Flessman-van Leer, op. cit., p. 40. Emphasis in original.

28. All quotations from *The Religions of the World* are from the Sixth edition, 1886. The first edition was published by J.W. Parker, London, 1847. Hereafter cited as *Religions*.

29. *Religions*, p.1. For Robert Boyle as a missionary thinker, see above, pp. 16-17.

30. Ibid.

31. This was much like the dilemma which faced Karl Barth when he was asked to give the Gifford Lectures. These are supposed to be about 'Natural Theology', but Barth was an opponent of natural theology, consequently *The Knowledge of God and the Service of God*, (1938) carries a similar kind of argumentation. Trust terms failed, not for the first or the last time, to match the intention of the lecturer and needed imaginative reinterpretation.

32. *Religions*, p. 7.

33. Ibid.

34. *Life*, Vol. 1, p. 430. Porter and Wolf comment, 'Scholarly recognition came to him in 1845 with his appointment by the Archbishop of York and the Bishop of London to the Boyle Lectureship. The lectures developed in *The Religions of the World*, a pioneer work in the field which enjoyed immense popularity. So much more is now known about the world's religions, and Maurice so frequently employs an inadmissible style of asserting what the Buddhist or the Hindu "will have thought" (Leslie Stephen calls this tense "the conjectural preterite" in Maurice), that little attention is paid to this book today', op. cit., p. 10. They add, 'It has, however a surprising relevance the recent debate by William Ernest Hocking, Hendrik Kraemer, and Arnold Toynbee on the Christian attitude toward the world's religions'. Cf. the judgment of A.C. Bouquet: 'Maurice may be said to have originated a new kind of approach, and perhaps to have laid the foundations for a new study of the religions of the world, for he made use of the latest and most scholarly information available in his own day, and brought to bear upon his subject the freshness and originality of his own mind', *Christian Faith and Non-Christian Religion* (1958), p. 340. The one writer who has given attention to *The Religions of the World*, in a general survey of Maurice's work, is H.G. Woods, who writes that his task 'is to discover the element of truth in other religions, to show how Christianity, rightly understood, can do justice to them, to admit that in actual fact Christianity has needed the corrective contained in the insights of other faiths, to suggest that Christianity, again rightly understood, can supply what is lacking in other faiths. Throughout he has in mind the theory that the religions of the world are but so many products of man's wishful thinking, and also

that kind of speculation which blurs all distinctions between them and so misses their true significance', op. cit., pp. 77-8.

35. *Religions*, p. 7.
36. See above, pp. 17.
37. *Religions*, p. 8.
38. Ibid.
39. Ibid.
40. Ibid., pp. 8-9.
41. Ibid., p. 9.
42. Ibid.
43. Cf. Charles Wesley's verses quoted above, pp. 17-18.
44. See Clinton Bennett, *Victorian Views of Islam* (1993).
45. For a recent study of Carlyle's attitude to Muhammad and Islam see Ruth Roberts, *Thomas Carlyle and Comparative Religion* (1988), pp. 87-101, and cf. Clinton Bennett, op. cit., pp. 10 and 52-4.
46. *Religions*, p. 21.
47. Ibid.
48. Ibid., p. 22.
49. Ibid., p. 23.
50. Ibid.
51. Ibid., p. 24.
52. Ibid., pp. 24-25.
53. Ibid., p. 26.
54. Ibid.
55. Ibid., p. 33.
56. Ibid.
57. Maurice used very much the same range of material as Charles Hodge for his understanding of Hinduism, but with entirely different results. See above, pp. 303ff.
58. Maurice acknowledges his dependence upon both the British and German scholars. William Jones (1746-1794) was Judge of the Supreme Court in Fort William, Calcutta, as well as a linguist (he had studied Arabic, Persian, Turkish and other languages at Oxford). He was the first to translate the Laws of Manu (the *Manavadharmasastra*). He founded The Asiatic Society of Bengal in 1784. *Asiatick Researches*, its journal, was well known to Maurice, and indeed he counsels reading it, *Religions*, p. xiv. For a sample of Jones' views on the authenticity of the Hindu religious quest, see David Pailin's *Attitudes to Other Religions: Comparative Religion in Seventeenth and Eighteenth Century Britain* (1984), pp. 252. As a student of philology, Jones was among the first to gain a clear conception of an Indo-European family of languages. There is a study of Jones and his contribution in Garland Cannon, *Oriental Jones: A Biography of Sir William Jones (1746-1794)* (1964). Henry Thomas Colebrooke was another resident in Bengal, 'who owed much to the fact that he followed rather than preceded Sir William Jones'. He wrote on Hindu law, philosophy, literature and mathematics, chiefly in the series *Asiatick Researches*. He produced a Sanskrit Grammar in 1808, which was published by the Serampore missionaries, and a translation of the *Sankhya Kariaka*, in 1837. Maurice could well have known his *Essays on the Religion and Philosophy of the Hindoos*. Horace Hayman Wilson, was the first Boden Professor of Sanskrit in the University of Oxford. Wilson had gone as an

assistant surgeon to India in the service of the East India Company. He had returned to India in 1832 and died in 1860. His works were eventually collected as *Essays and Lectures chiefly on the Religion of the Hindus* and published in two volumes in 1862. He was the first translator of the *Vishnu Purana*. It was possible for Maurice to have known his *History of British India* and his translation of the *Kalindasa*. In addition Maurice was able to obtain works by German scholars: Friedrich August Rosen published two Latin versions of the Rig Vedas: *Rigvedae Specimen* (1830) and *Rigveda-Sanhita: Liber Primus, Sanscrite et Latine* (1838). Maurice also referred in his Preface to both Hegel and Schlegel who, he wrote, 'have enabled me to feel the connection between the thoughts of other periods and countries and those which characterise our own times', *Religions*, preface, p. xviii. G.W.F. Hegel's *Philosophy of History* did not appear in English until 1858. The German version had appeared in 1817, and had seen the world religions as rungs on a ladder, culminating in Christianity as the religion of the Spirit. Maurice may also have known the *Vorlesung uber die Philosophie der Religion*, published in Berlin in 1832. Friedrich von Schlegel's *Über die Sprache und die Weisheit der Indier* had been published in 1808. Eric J. Sharpe calls it a 'confused work but one in which a real intellectual relationship between Europe and India was mooted and a second Renaissance prophesied', *Comparative Religion: a History*, p. 22.

59. There is a fascinating reference to Max Müller in the preface to *The Religions of the World*: 'I understand that a young German now in London, whose knowledge of Sanskrit is profound, and his industry *plus quam Germanica*, has it in contemplation to publish and translate all the Vedas'. *Religions*, p. xv. Monier Williams, who became the Boden Professor of Sanskrit in Oxford in 1861 was not known to Maurice.

60. *Religions*, p. 52.

61. Ibid.

62. Ibid. p. 53.

63. Ibid., p. 55. Cf. Maurice's further statement that the Hindu is 'right in his belief, that the wisdom of which he sees the image and reflection must speak and declare it self to him; that he cannot always be left to grope his way amidst the shadows which it casts in his own mind, or in the world around him', ibid., p. 48.

64. Ibid., p. 65.

65. Ibid.

66. Ibid.

67. Maurice's knowledge of Buddhism was, he said, the result of trying to get a sense of a 'history in process' rather than as a 'system at rest', *Religions*, p. xix. He had therefore eschewed the reading of 'digests', preferring narrative from 'intelligent observers who saw it in motion and described its different appearance'. These accounts are chiefly to be found in the *Transactions* of the Royal Asiatic Society and in *Asiatic Researches*. Maurice, however, did allow that he had read the article on Buddhism in *The Penny Cyclopaedia*. Cf. H.G. Wood's comments on Maurice's idea of the universality of the longed-for Saviour: how much more he would have been helped in his argument if he had known the distinction between Buddhism in Ceylon, Siam, Burma, and Buddhism in North Eastern Asia, i.e., between the Hinayana and the Mahayana', op. cit., p. 92. In 1845, Ceylon (Sri Lanka) was the only British possession in which Buddhism was the religion of the majority of the people, and the form of Buddhism there was *Theravada* rather than *Mahayana*. In the introductory

remarks to his third lecture, Maurice dealt with Buddhism as though it were still trying to answer the riddle of the Sphinx and as though it had not come to 'enlightenment' and the solution of the problem of suffering. Maurice appears to have heard of
neither 'The Four Noble Truths' nor 'The Noble Eight-fold Path'.

68. *Religions*, pp. 66–7.

69. Ibid., p. 94.

70. Ibid., p. 84.

71. Ibid., p. 197.

72. Ibid., pp. 197–8.

73. Ibid., p.202. Maurice is referring to the Mahayanan ideal of the *boddhisattva*,
opposed to the *arhat* of Theravada doctrine. The *arhat* seeks release from the painful
rounds of rebirth for himself alone. The *bodhisattva* is an individual who throws himself back time and again into the raging seas of *samsara* in order to help others. We
may note also Maurice's understanding of Tibetan Buddhism: 'In some person or
other the spirit of Buddha dwells; he is meant to be the head of the universe; to him
all owe homage'. Maurice thought that Tibet must have been 'the centre and proper
home of the religion', ibid., p. 82.

74. At this point in his lectures Maurice was torn between leaving all he had to say
under the headings 'The Mahometan, The Hindoo and The Buddhist', and his
intense awareness of the diversity of humankind. As a historian he knew that diversity
extended into the past; the Greeks, Romans, Egyptians, Persians, and the Old Norse
people had all had religious traditions of profound interest. Also it would have been
be a matter of great 'practical ignorance' to have tried to put all 'religious apprehensions' under the headings of the three great types he had already discussed. In any
case the feelings and apprehensions which belong to actual human beings 'will not
bear to be so treated', *Religions*, p. 96. Maurice's great aphorism, about 'A man will
not really be intelligible to you if, instead of listening and sympathizing with him, you
determine to classify him', quoted in the main text follows these words. Nevertheless
the attempt to work out a typology of religions had its own value. For Maurice it had
been of great importance to have 'patiently studied and livingly realised the characteristics of these widespread beliefs', found in Islam, Hinduism and Buddhism. Only so
would he have not been 'hopelessly puzzled' by the diversity of human religious
activity, and its manifold forms of belief. But he thought it important to reflect upon
the 'defunct systems', which had 'yielded to the might of the Crescent or the Cross'.
Yet for Maurice they were only defunct in one sense, because 'they had that in them
which is not dead and cannot die; that which is exerting an influence on the mind and
education of Christendom to the present day', *Religions*, p. 97.

75. Ibid., , pp. 1, 2.

76. Ibid., p. 248.

77. Ibid., p. 91.

78. Ibid., p. 239.

79. Ibid.

80. Ibid.

81. Ibid., p. 240.

82. Cf. Maurice's own description of the world of religions if his theology of unity
does not hold: 'To look out upon the world, and see a valley covered with the dry
bones of several systems, to hear them clashing together as if they might be joined to

each other, and then to be told, "It is all in vain; there is no voice which can bid the breath enter these bones; perhaps it might have come from Christians, but it does not; they too occupy part of this valley; they have become dry bones, very dry indeed; clashing always, never uniting" – such an announcement as this... must be a very mournful one', ibid., pp. 240-1.

83. Ibid., p. 244.

84. Ibid., p. 245.

85. Ibid., p. 240.

86. Ibid.

87. Ibid.

88. Ibid., p. 244.

89. Maurice could use the concept of the Devil when he wanted to, see Christensen, *The Divine Order*, pp. 118. Hort, shrewdly, wrote to Maurice that he had found 'no distinct recognition of the devil's personality' in his books. Maurice replied, *inter alia*, that he agreed with Charles Kingsley who had said, 'the devil is shamming dead, but that he was never busier than now'. Maurice did not want to deny that there was an 'evil will' which tempted him, 'If he is an evil will, he must I think be a person'. But Maurice admitted, 'I need scarcely say that I do not mean by this acknowledgement of an evil *spirit* that I acknowledge a *material* devil', see *Life*, Volume 2, p. 21. But the reality of evil lay in the human heart: 'I said that men found continually that the further they went down into themselves, the more there was of corruption, and darkness, and evil, till at last they suppose the very root of their being was nothing else. St Paul had gone down into these depths, he had found this rottenness; in himself he says he found only that. But he discovered there was a root below himself, a true divine root, for himself and for every man. He found that each man, when he tries to contemplate himself apart from Christ, is that evil creature in whom no good dwells. But no man, so he teaches, has a right to contemplate himself apart from Christ; God does not so contemplate him. He was formed from the first in the Divine Word; in Him he lives and moves and has his being still', *Sermons Preached in Lincoln's Inn Chapel*, Vol. 1, pp. 97-86. In the light of this the doctrine of the Devil functions against 'total depravity': as Christian faith confesses 'an Evil Spirit whose assaults are directed against the Will in Man, it forbids us ever to look upon any disease of our nature as the ultimate cause of our transgression. The horrible notion, which has haunted moralists, divines and practical men, that pravity is the law of our being, and not the perpetual tendency to struggle against the law of our being, it discards and anathematises', *Theological Essays*, p. 12.

90. See above, p. 38. Cf. 'There was no flaw in creation before man fell, there is no flaw in it since man fell. That fall had actually no power to subvert it, or derange it. That fall was precisely the refusal of a man to recognise his own glorious place *in* this order... but the eternal order goes on asserting itself, – calmly, uninterruptedly. God treats man according to the law which He laid down for him on the creation day', *Patriarchs and Lawgivers*, p. 140. Compare this with some words written in 1858: 'I feel very strongly that the ascension of our Lord into the heavens, and the glorification of our nature in Him, with the corresponding truth that the Church exists to witness of Him, not only as her Head, but as the Head of every man, will be the battle-cry that will rally Protestants and Romanists, hungry seekers after wisdom, lonely tatterdemalions without bread, about the one standard; and that opposition to this

proclamation, a resolute clinging to the Fall as determining man's condition, a practical acknowledging of the Devil, as arbiter of it, with the characteristic of the opposing host, gathered also from all sects, schools, churches', Letter to Miss Williams Wynn, in *Life*, Vol. 2, p. 317.

91. See *The Kingdom of Heaven*, p. xvi, cf. p. 157. Maurice always resisted any idea that the world was created in Adam. We are 'not to think that world was created in Adam, or stood in his obedience; for the Scriptures of the New Testament, illustrating those of the Old, teach us that it stood and remains in the obedience of God's well-beloved Son; the real image of the Father, the real bond of human society and of the whole universe, who was to be manifested in the fulness of time, as that which He had always been; who was to exhibit in the sorrow, tears and death of a man, the full grace and truth of which all men, so far as they had trusted in God, had exhibited some tokens and reflections', *Patriarchs and Lawgivers*, p. 66.

92. *The Kingdom of Heaven*, pp. 160.

93. *Religions*, p. 192.

94. Ibid., p. 193. 'By seeing man as existing solely in his relation to God as "image", Maurice eliminated all question of inherent righteousness or inherent evil. If man's redemption consisted in partaking of a righteousness not his own, as the reformers had asserted, so his creation itself "stood" in a righteousness not his own, as did the creation of the entire universe. "Christ in every man" was a statement about Grace.' Brose, op. cit., p. 72. Here is Maurice reflecting on the constitutive element of the 'image': '"God"', it is said, '"was in Christ reconciling the world to Himself." "It pleased God," says St. Paul, "to reveal His Son in *me*, that I might preach Him among the Gentiles." Was man, then, according to his original constitution related to Christ? Was the restoration of the world to God, the relation of it to its proper condition in the well-beloved Son? Was that Son really in St Paul of Tarsus, and did he only become Paul the converted when that Son was *revealed* in him? Could he preach to the Gentiles, who were bowing down to gods of wood and stone, Christ is in you?', *The Doctrine of Sacrifice*, pp. xx-xxi.

95. *Religions*, p. 193.

96. The Christian socialist J.M. Ludlow reproached Maurice in 1852 for using the expression 'An Order, and Beauty and a Power' accusing him of Platonizing the Gospel and for being too interested in abstractions. This enabled Maurice to respond saying that 'society was not to be anew by arrangements of ours', but could only be regenerated by 'finding the law and ground of its order and harmony' which is all that Maurice meant by the Kingdom of Heaven. 'The Kingdom of Heaven is for me the great practical existing reality which is to renew the earth and make it a habitation for blessed spirits instead of for demons'. *Life*, Vol. 2, p. 137.

97. *Religions*, p. 148.

98. Ibid.

99. *Religions*, p. 149.

100. In one of his rare allusions to a missionary contemporary, Maurice referred to one of the LMS pioneers, Walter Medhurst. 'Mr Medhurst, the author of an interesting book on China, the result of his own observations, expresses his wonder and even indignation, that Confucius, having dwelt so beautifully on the rights and duties of a father, should not have carried up his thoughts to the great Father of all',

Religions, pp. 91-2. The book Maurice had discovered was *China: Its State and Prospects with Special Reference to the Spread of the Gospel* (1842).

101. *Religions*, p. 210.

102. Ibid.

103. Ibid., p. 198.

104. Ibid., p. 199.

105. Ibid.

106. Heading to page 199.

107. *Religions*, p. 199.

108. Ibid.

109. Ibid., p. 200.

110. Ibid., p. 201.

111. Ibid.

112. On the fulfilment concept, see pp. 171ff.

113. Maurice's thought here matches that of A.G. Hogg much later, see below, p. 240.

114. *Religions*, p. 181.

115. Ibid., pp. 181-2.

116. Ibid., p. 186.

117. Ibid.

118. Ibid.

119. For A.M. Fairbairn's impressions of the British rule in India, see 78-79, and for C.F. Andrews' protest against its distortions, cf. p. 179.

120. *Religions*, p. 153.

121. Ibid., p. 215.

122. Ibid., p. 211.

123. Cf. 'There cannot be a more undoubted prophecy than that the Gospel, if it be a human system, must perish as all systems are perishing', *Religions*, p. 238.

124. *Religions*, p. 159.

125. Ibid., pp. 182-3.

126. Ibid., p. 211.

127. Ibid., pp. 211-12.

128. Ibid., p. 212.

129. Ibid.

130. Page headings, p. 229, p. 237, and p. 211.

131. See the discussion of Augustinian theology on pp. 7ff. above.

132. *Religions*, p. 229.

133. Ibid.

134. Ibid.

135. Ibid., p. 238.

136. Ibid., p. 241.

137. Ibid.

138. Ibid.

139. Ibid., p. 243.

140. Ibid., p. 245.

141. Cf. Cracknell, op. cit., p. 114, the reference is to the WCC guidelines 1979 para. 20: "Dialogue should proceed in terms of people of other faiths rather than impersonal theoretical systems".

142. *Religions*, p. 96. See also Cracknell op. cit., p. 115, and note 11 on p. 186.

143. Maurice's interest in missionary activity can be illustrated from his letter to Mrs Colenso in Natal in August, 1856, 'But all you are doing for the Caffre children and for the Zulu's and for your own, is really fulfilling, in the best and simplest way, that duty which comes to us with so many complications – the deliverance from the yoke of a tyrant, by telling them of their true King. It seems to me that all civilization and all Christianity had that same foundation, as if devil worship was the common enemy which both in their different ways had to struggle with', *Life*, Volume 2, p. 296. There is one almost unknown work by Maurice, *The Ground and Object of Hope for Mankind* (1868), a series of University Sermons preached in Cambridge in 1867, when he was Professor of Moral Philosophy. (It does not appear to have been read very much, in Cambridge at least: the volume belonging to the Divinity School Library, used by the present writer, had to have its pages cut in 1990). The first sermon is entitled 'The Hope of the Missionary', and in view of the ideas of Grubb and Hahn (see below pp. 227f.), is worth quoting. 'Saul of Tarsus must have been equipped in the school of Gamaliel with weapons for overthrowing all different forms of idolatry. When he entered into the actual fight he found use for them. He exposed no fable. He ridiculed no tradition. He only induced any one to cast away his torch by bidding them go forth into the sunlight', op. cit., pp. 13-4. It would be interesting to know who was in Maurice's congregation on that Sunday morning in November 1867, for he argues on the basis of this insight that the missionary's business was in no circumstance to 'debate and refute' but to be witnesses of the 'unchangeable God', ibid., p. 25. One future LMS missionary in the congregation could have been Arnold Foster, see p. 217.

144. *Religions*, p. 154.

145. Ibid.

146. The maieutic approach has been popularised by Arnulf Camps, see his *Partners in Dialogue* (1983): 'The word "maieutic" comes from Greek, and it originally meant "to serve as a midwife"... the new world and the new human being must be born out of two profound encounters'. The first is with Christ, but the second is 'with the deepest inspiration which lies buried in those religions and world views, but which has sometimes been obscured by centuries long developments'. Camps says that Christians must help others in this process, but that the process is achieved only through dialogue, op. cit., p. 155.

147. Cf. Wilhelm Andersen writing in Gerald Anderson (ed.), *The Theology of the Christian Mission*, (1961): 'The basic and decisive recognition for a theology of missions consists in this: *Mission has its source in the Triune God*, p.301. Andersen goes on to quote the Willingen statement on the 'Missionary Calling of God': Out of the depths of his love for us, the Father has sent forth his own beloved Son to reconcile all things to himself, that we and all men might, through the Spirit be made one with the Father in that perfect love which is the very nature of God'. Cf. Georg Vicedom's introduction to the theology of mission entitled *Missio Dei*, (1958). and see the remark of J.C. Hoekendijk, 'Every-church centred theory of mission is bound to go astray

because it revolves around an illegitimate centre', art. 'The Church in Missionary Thinking', in *IRM*, Vol. 42 (1952), p. 332.

148. *Religions*, p. 160.

149. Ibid., p. 24.

150. Ibid., p. 161.

151. Ibid., p. 220.

152. Ibid., p. 220-221.

153. Matthew 5.17 became the central text for missionaries in the second half of the Great Century. See pp. 219ff.

154. *Religions*, p. 171.

155. Ibid., p. 172.

156. See pp. 115ff., 139ff. and 170ff.

157. *The Life and Letters of Brooke Foss Westcott*, by his son Arthur Westcott, 2 vols. (1903), (hereafter cited as *Life and Letters*), Vol. 2, p. 410.

158. *The Gospel of Life* (1892) was subtitled 'Thoughts Introductory to the Study of Christian Doctrine'. Chapter 5 dealt with 'The Religions of China', 'The Religions of India' and with Buddhism and Zoroastrianism. In some sixty pages Westcott outlined the ground work of a theology of religion. This was the first time a systematic treatment of Christian theology had suggested 'The value of the prae-Christian Book-religions to the Christian student', i.e. the heading to pages 122-3 of *The Gospel of Life*.

159. Westcott shared with Maurice a profound sense that Christ is related by the Incarnation with every human being. *The Gospel of Life* has two texts in Greek on its title page: 'I am the Way, the Truth and the Life', (John 14.6) and 'In whom we live and move and have our being', (Acts 17.28), both of which were beloved of Maurice. Westcott strongest words on this are, 'By taking humanity into Himself, He has revealed the permanence of human individuality and being', *Commentary on the Gospel of St John* (1882), p. 168. Westcott refused to be a disciple of Maurice, as his biographer, Joseph Clayton, noted: 'he deliberately declined reading the works of F.D. Maurice on the ground that his own development might be more independent; and though Westcott's thought is distinctly Maurician, it is not learnt from Maurice', *Bishop Westcott* (1906), p. 24. Nevertheless, Westcott had imbibed a great deal from Maurice: he described Maurice's *Social Morality* as 'one of my few favourite books', *Life and Letters*, Vol. 2, p. 160. There is also Westcott's striking comment in a letter of 28th March, 1884: 'For the last week I have spent my leisure in Maurice's *Life*. I never knew before how deep my sympathy is with his most characteristic thoughts. It is most refreshing to read such a book – such a life', *Life and Letters*, Vol. 2, p. 37.

160. 'I trust my earnestness for higher objects has not grown colder. My faith is still wavering. I cannot determine how much we *must* believe; how much in fact is necessarily required of a member of the Church', *Life and Letters*, Vol. 1, p. 46. Doubt is also expressed in a rather trite set of verses, but it is felt as a moral failing rather than serious *Anfechtung*, see *Life and Letters*, Vol. 1, p. 905, but cf. note 215 on p. 308 above.

161. Cf. his correspondence with Hort, Lightfoot and J.F. Wickenden, at the time of the *Essays and Reviews* (1860) controversy, in *Life and Letters*, Vol. 1, pp. 213-5.

162. For Alexandrian Platonism see C. Bigg's Bampton Lectures for 1886, *The Christian Platonists of Alexandria*, second edition, 1913. Strictly speaking this was

Middle Platonism; see S.R.C. Lilla, *Clement of Alexandria: A Study in Christian Platonism and Gnosticism* (1971), pp. 3ff, and E.F. Osborn, *The Philosophy of Clement of Alexandria* (1957), *passim*.

163. He had already published seven books and articles on the Bible, including *The Bible in the Church* (1866). While he was prepared to publish material on the Bible in the form of treatises, Westcott's doctrinal work was often done through the medium of sermons and addresses. Peter Hinchliff has recently commented that 'Both Westcott and Lightfoot preferred to use popular lectures or sermons as a vehicle for their theological ideas. It may be unkind to suggest that they chose this way of presenting their ideas because they could not then be expected to present their argument rigorously and in detail, but it does seem, sometimes that they deliberately avoided engaging in discussion of historically difficult theological issues', *God and History* (1992), p. 95. *The Gospel of Life* is an exception to this stricture.

164. *The Gospel of the Resurrection* (1866), p. 113; cf. Westcott's interpretation of Christianity itself as 'eternal in its essence, as well as universal in its application. It was itself beyond time, though it was wrought out in time', ibid., p. 53.

165. *The Gospel According to St John* (1882), p. 202.

166. See, for example, the responses of C.F. Andrews on pp. 178f., and of Westcott's son George H. Westcott on p. 217.

167. Cf. Letter to J.F. Wickenden, *Life and Letters*, Vol. 1, p. 215.

168. *Christus Consummator* (1886), p. 12.

169. For Maurice's use of the word 'fulfil', see above, p. 48.

170. Westcott was as certain as Maurice about the absolute priority of the Creation over the Fall for doctrinal construction, cf. 'the ultimate cause of the defectiveness of the modern teaching on the Person of Christ' is 'most plainly shewn in the prevalent opinion as to the ground of the Incarnation. The Incarnation is commonly made to depend upon the fall, *Christus Consummator* p. 104. That this is a consistent theme in Westcott's writings is shown by the following passage from his earliest theological work, *The Gospel of the Resurrection* (1866): 'the Apostles... expressly caution us against thinking that the Incarnation of the Word was in any way an afterthought consequent upon the Fall, and not already included in the Creation', p. 52. Westcott continued, 'The Fall necessarily modified the circumstances of the Incarnation, but the true conception of the World and of Humanity becomes first possible when they are thus regarded in their essential relation to the Word, the Son', pp. 52-3.

171. *Christus Consummator*, p. 104. Cf. 'Man did not lose the image of God by the fall. His essential nature still remained capable of union with God, but it was burdened and hampered', ibid. p. 118.

172. Ibid., p. 106.

173. Ibid., pp. 106-111.

174. Ibid., p. 111, emphasis Westcott's.

175. Ibid. p. 11.

176. Ibid., pp. 11-2, emphasis Westcott's.

177. Ibid., p. 22.

178. Ibid. When he wrote *Christus Consummator* Westcott's mind was primarily on the challenge of contemporary natural sciences, but he had already begun to study *The Sacred Books of the East*. He referred for example to the 'Announcement of Thang, in the *Shu king*, where an early Chinese king said to his people, "When guilt

is found any where in you who occupy the myriad regions, let it rest upon me the One man"; and faithful to his prayer said again, when a human victim was demanded to avert a drought, "If a man must be a victim, I will be he?"', p. 123. This Chinese classic is to be found in Vol. 3 in *The Sacred Books of the East: The Texts of Confucianism*, translated by James Legge. It is also an early example of a Western theologian being able to affirm that stories of 'uncalculating self-devotion... brighten the annals of every people', p. 122. To understand why, in his words, 'the human instinct has always rejoiced' in such stories is the task of the theologian confronted with the phenomena of human religion.'

179. *Christus Consummator*, p. 77.

180. *The Gospel of Life* had two editions, in 1892 and 1895. Westcott said they represented twenty years of lecturing in Cambridge. One indication of the toil represented here is to be found in the widely used (in its time) *The Cambridge Companion to the Bible* (1905) where there is an 'Appendix on Sacred Books of Other Faiths' by B.F. Westcott, pp. 39-55.

181. *The Gospel of Life*, p. 99.

182. Ibid.

183. *Gospel of Life*, p. 100. Cf. 'No one language exhausts man's capacity for defining, combining, subordinating objects of thought, but all languages together give a lively and rich picture of his certain and yet gradual advance in innumerable different paths towards the fulness of intellectual development. So too it is with the many faiths and observances which men have spontaneously adopted. These in due measure reveal something of his religious powers and needs', ibid., pp. 100-1.

184. *Gospel of Life*, p. 101.

185. See ch.5 of *The Gospel of Life* for Westcott's own views.

186. For Westcott's debt to Müller see *Gospel of Life*, p. 103, note 1. Westcott had clearly studied Müller's *Introduction to the Study of Religion* (1873) and the volumes entitled *Chips from a German Workshop* (vols. 1-2, 1867, Volume 3, 1870, and Volume 4, 1875).

187. *The Sacred Books of the East*, translated by various scholars, and edited by F. Max Müller, was published by the Clarendon Press between the years 1879 and 1894 in forty nine volumes. Wilfred Cantwell Smith has recently reminded us that in Müller's original intention the Old and New Testaments were to have been part of the series. This plan had been resisted by E.B. Pusey as a delegate to the University Press in Oxford, see W.C. Smith, *What is Scripture?* (1993), p. 244, note 4.

188. *Gospel of Life*, p. 113. Cf. 'It will be enough for the student to compare the Jewish people before and after the captivity to understand what they owe to Persian influence. Idolatry, which had been their besetting sin in earlier years disappeared. At the same time fuller visions of the unseen world were opened before them. The kingdom became a church: an ecclesiastical system was consolidated: teachers stood by the side of priests: prayer assumed a new importance in worship: the bond of society was felt more and more to be spiritual and not only local', ibid.

189. *Gospel of Life*, pp. 113-4. Cf. 'The conquests of Alexander and the consequent increase and wider extension of the Jews "of the Dispersion" served to deepen this feeling of the potential universality of the Jewish revelation in its final completeness. Alexandria was added as a third centre of the faith to Jerusalem and Babylon'. In particular, the 'Greek language was slowly adapted to the more exact and complete

expression of the conception which the Hebrew could only convey in a colossal outline', ibid. p. 113.

190. *Gospel of Life*, p. 114.

191. Ibid., p. 114-5.

192. Ibid., p. 115.

193. Ibid.

194. Ibid., pp. 115-6.

195. For recent treatment of Justin and Clement as missionary thinkers within the second century context see two studies by Eric F. Osborn, *The Philosophy of Clement of Alexandria* (1957) and *Justin Martyr* (1973). Another study, by the African theologian, Kwame Bediako, *Theology and Identity: The impact of Christian thought in the second century and modern Africa* (1992), demonstrates the abiding importance of these two figures for the mission of the Church.

196. *Gospel of Life*, p. 116.

197. Ibid. The material from Justin which Westcott had in mind comes from the *Second Apology*. 2.18, 2.13; and cf. 1 *Apol* 46, 44; and again 1 *Apol*, 1.5, 2.10.

198. Ibid., pp. 117-9. Westcott's references are to the *Stromateis*. 1.87, 1.57, cf. 1.18, 28, 6.28, 42, 167,1.99, 6.44.

199. Ibid., p. 121.

200. Ibid., pp. 121-2.

201. Ibid., p. 122.

202. Ibid.

203. Ibid., p. 123.

204. Ibid., p. 141.

205. Ibid., p. 142.

206. Ibid.

207. Ibid.

208. On the influence of Westcott at the WMC see pp. 220, 225.

209. *Leaders of the English Church 1828-1944* (1971), p. 213.

210. The expression is to found in Westcott's letter to J.L. Davies, 8th August, 1900. About his hopes for the work in India of his son Basil, Westcott wrote: '... I looked forward confidently to the time when he would be a Hindoo to Hindoos', *Life and Letters*, Vol. 2, p. 321.

211. For the beginnings of Cambridge University work in India see *The Story of the Delhi Mission* (second edition 1917), pp. 24-5. For Thomas Valpy French's missionary vision see Daniel O'Connor, *Gospel, Raj and Swaraj* (1990), pp. 7ff.

212. *Life and Letters*, Vol. 1, p. 383.

213. The story of the death of Basil Westcott is in *Life and Letters*, Vol. 2, pp. 319-25. For Andrews' reaction see p. 175.

214. For Westcott's constant involvement with Indian missionary work see *Life and Letters*, Vol. 1, p. 384.

215. The first of these, preached in St Paul's Cathedral on May 28th, 1895, was based on the text 'unto us was the grace given to preach unto the nations the unsearchable riches of Christ', Eph.3.8. The second has a complementary text, from Colossians 2, 2-3, 'that they may know the mystery of God, even Christ, in Whom are all the treasure of wisdom and knowledge hidden' and was preached in St Bride's Church, London on April 29th, 1895.

216. In 'The Call of the English Church', Westcott called England 'the mother and mistress of nations', *Christian Aspects of Life*, p. 144, and spoke in 'Missions as the Revelation of the Mystery of God' of the 'consciousness of social and intellectual superiority with which we are filled', ibid., p. 175.

217. Ibid., p. 144.

218. Ibid., p. 145.

219. Ibid., p. 148.

220. Ibid.

221. Ibid., p. 149. Cf. my own exposition of Revelation 21 which derives much from Westcott, though not consciously, in *Towards a New Relationship* (1986), pp. 51ff.

222. Ibid., p. 144. Cf. Westcott's well-known suggestion that the greatest commentary on the Fourth Gospel would come from India was referred to in a speech by C.F. Andrews quoted in B. Chaturvedi and Marjorie Sykes, *Charles Freer Andrews: A Narrative*, (1949), p. 18: 'one of his great hopes was that Indian thinkers would be able to interpret fully the Gospel of John', p. 18. But I have not located it in any writings of Westcott's available to me. Perhaps it is oral tradition.

223. *Christian Aspects*, p. 153.

224. See above, p. 13.

225. *Christian Aspects*, p. 164.

226. Ibid., p. 165.

227. Ibid., p. 166, cf. the lapidary sentence on p. 176: 'Sympathy was the mind of Christ; and sympathy is the soul of missions.'

228. Ibid.

229. Ibid., p. 167.

230. *Missio Dei*, as a missiological concept was not widely used until after the Second World War, cf. note 147, on p. 318.

231. *Christian Aspects*, p. 169.

232. Westcott wrote of the Gospel as a 'disclosure of human and Divine relationships': 'we set forth... Christ Himself, in his self-sacrificing love, "as the image of the invisible God through Whom it was the good pleasure of the Father to reconcile all things to Himself"... Of this Gospel there is no anticipation in the noblest utterances of prae-Christian Gentile teachers, though their speculations and their hope cannot find satisfaction without it. And we must not scruple to insist on the novelty of our message', *Christian Aspects*, p. 171.

233. Ibid., p. 170.

234. Ibid., p. 177.

235. Ibid.

236. Ibid., p. 183.

237. Ibid.

238. Ibid.

239. The standard biography of Fairbairn is *The Life of Andrew Martin Fairbairn* by W.B. Selbie (1914). It has the merit of much extensive quotation from Fairbairn's own letters, diaries and journals. A brief treatment of the main themes of Fairbairn's theology may be found on pp. 126-30 of Eric J. Sharpe, *Not to Destroy But to Fulfil: The Contribution of J.N. Farquhar to Protestant Missionary Thought in India before 1914* (1965). For a full bibliography of Fairbairn's writing to 1909, see *Mansfield*

College Essays: Presented to the Reverend Andrew Martin Fairbairn on the Occasion of his Seventieth Birthday, with a Bibliography (1909), pp. 367-356.

240. Selbie, op. cit., p. 353.

241. Ibid., pp. 352-3.

242. Ibid., p. 353.

243. For the origins of the Evangelical Union see above, pp. 21-22. The Evangelical Union held in general to a modified Calvinism, with the exception of its view on the Atonement. This could be summed up in the 'Three Universalities': 1. The love of God the Father in the gift and sacrifice of Jesus, to all men everywhere without distinction, exception, or respect of persons; 2. The love of God the Son in the gift and sacrifice of Himself, as a true propitiation for the sins of the world, and 3. The love of God the Holy Spirit in his present and continuing work of applying to the souls of all men the provisions of divine grace, Selbie, op. cit., p. 8.

244. Selbie, op. cit., p. 35.

245. For I.A. Dorner see standard histories of nineteenth-century thought, notably, Clause Welch, *Protestant Thought in the Nineteenth Century: Volume 1, 1799-1870* (1972), p. 273, For Schleiermacher see above, pp. 90ff.

246. Selbie, op. cit., p. 41.

247. Ibid., pp. 50-1; the article appeared in the *Contemporary Review*, Vol. 6, 1871, pp. 416-442

248. John Muir was Professor of Sanskrit in the University of Edinburgh. In another article in the *Contemporary Review*, 'Religion in India', see below, p. 327, note 278. Fairbairn wrote of Muir as having been the one from whom he had 'learned to know the Hindus, their literature and religion' and noted Muir's 'love of freedom of thought and inquiry', as well as his 'pure and disinterested interest in humanity' which served for Fairbairn as an example during his own travels in India, pp. 761-2. Sir William Muir, his brother, was famous for his early investigations of the life of Muhammed and of the rise of Islam.

249. See notes 186 and 187 above.

250. Selbie, op. cit., p. 51.

251. A.E. Garvie commented on Fairbairn's preaching in Aberdeen: 'He was also a pioneer in recognizing the importance of the study of the religions of the world, and drew to his Sunday evening lectures in Aberdeen the professors and students of the University. One of the deacons in his church poured out the vials of his wrath on the young minister for this departure from the simple Gospel; he quite quietly asked him to seek God's blessing on this utterance, and closed the strained silence with the benediction', *Memories and Meanings of My Life* (1938), p. 89.

252. See above, pp. 167-83.

253. Between the years 1878-1882 Fairbairn was invited to give the Muir Lectures in the Science of Religion in Edinburgh University. This particular lectureship had been founded by Dr John Muir as one of many benefactions to the University of Edinburgh. Fairbairn took the opportunity of gathering up the results of his study of the religions of the world and the lectures he gave then would no doubt have formed the substantial part of the book on Comparative Religion which he had always wanted to write. Selbie tells us that they comprised a survey and comparison of all the great religions of the world outside Christianity and that Fairbairn made the account of them as complete as the materials then available would allow. Selbie tells us further

that the tone of the lectures indicated that Fairbairn 'never fell into the error of interpreting the higher religions by the lower and that in them he never lost sight of the fact that the study of Comparative Religion had a positive apologetic value of its own', Selbie, op. cit., p. 121.

254. Selbie, op. cit., pp. 61 and 103.

255. These were 'The Idea of God' (the article from the *Contemporary Review*, noted above), 'Theism and Scientific Speculation', 'The Belief in Immortality', and 'The Place of the Indo-European and Semitic Races in History', cf. Selbie. op. cit., pp. 76ff. Fairbairn spoke of his considerable hesitation in re-issuing the articles, and indicated that 'they were and still are intended to be "studies" preliminary to what should be at once a philosophy and a history of religion', *Studies in the Philosophy of Religion and History* (1871) (cited as *Studies*), p. iii.

256. *Studies*, p.13

257. Ibid., p. 72.

258. Ibid.

259. Ibid., emphasis his.

260. Selbie wrote in 1914 that 'The science of Comparative Religion and even the historical study of religion, was then in its infancy, and Fairbairn was among the first in this country to use the work of men like Muir, Tiele, Max Muller, and Chantepie de la Saussaye, and to show its intimate bearing on theological and religious conceptions', Selbie, op. cit., p. 351.

261. See pp. 253 above.

262. Selbie, op. cit., pp. 83-4.

263. For a discussion of the founding of Mansfield College as within an intellectual tradition identified as the '"New Evangelicalism" of R.W. Dale see Mark D. Johnson, *The Dissolution of Dissent, 1850-1918* (1987); cf. Johnson's article 'The Crisis of Faith and Social Christianity" in Richard J. Helmstadter and Bernard Lightman, *Victorian Faith in Crisis: Essays on Continuity and Change in Nineteenth Century Religious Belief* (1990), pp. 357.ff.

264. Among those students at Mansfield were one of the future Edinburgh Commissioners, Alfred Garvie, and his biographer, W.B. Selbie. Garvie was the first British scholar to write on Ritschl, and Selbie the first to write on Schleiermacher. See notes 360-63 on pp. 330-31 below. For Garvie as a Commissioner at the WMC see p. 190. Selbie lists these and other scholars trained by Fairbairn on page 90 of the *Life*. It could be shown that each of them was aware of the importance of the study of comparative religion for whichever specialist area of Christian theology he later adopted.

265. Selbie, op. cit., p. 89.

266. Selbie, op. cit., p. 184.

267. Selbie, op. cit., p. 174. For Legge's life see H.E. Legge, *James Legge: Missionary and Scholar* (1905). In Hong Kong from 1843-1873 Legge produced an edition of the Chinese classics in eight large volumes, each consisting of Chinese text, English translation, critical and exegetical notes, and copious introductory material. This extraordinary accomplishment formed the basis of six volumes of the *Sacred Books of the East*. Legge wrote many other books and articles on China, among them *The Notions of the Chinese concerning God and Spirits* (1852), *Confucianism in Relation to Christianity* (1877), and *The Religions of China. Confucianism and Taoism Described*

and Compared with Christianity (1880). As Professor of Chinese in Oxford he was a staunch supporter of Fairbairn's work at Mansfield College. After his death Legge was depicted in the stained glass windows of Mansfield College Chapel alongside David Livingstone.

268. H.E. Legge, op. cit., p. 231. Legge and Fairbairn are even buried close to each other in Wolvercote cemetery, with Aberdeen granite reminding any passers-by of their Scottish origins.

269. To this change Legge had contributed more than any other mid-great century missionary. First because he reacted against 'inflexible erudition' and its associated 'combative mentality': 'One is often grieved to read the incautious assertions of writers who think that apart from our Christian scriptures there are no lessons for men about their duties, and that heathendom has in consequence never been anything but a slough of immoral filth and outrageous crime. Such writers betray their ignorance of the systems and peoples about which they affirm such things, and their ignorance also of the sacred volume which they wish to exalt. Their advocacy is damaging rather than beneficial to Christianity,' *Christianity and Confucianism Compared* (1887), p. 23. Second, Legge advised listening rather than preaching; study rather than talkativeness: 'Let missionaries', he said, 'go about their work everywhere – and I believe they can do so more easily in China than in other mission fields – in the spirit of Christ, without striving, or crying, with meekness and lowliness of heart', all the time labouring to master the Chinese classics, for only then would missionaries in China come 'fully to understand the work they have to do; and the more they avoid driving their carriages rudely over the Master's grave, the more likely they are soon to see Jesus enthroned in His room in the hearts of the people', from an address given in Oxford, and quoted by H.E. Legge, op. cit., pp. 37-8.

270. In the wake of the Chicago Parliament of Religions in 1893, Mrs Caroline E. Haskell, of Michigan City, Indiana, who had already founded the Haskell Museum of Oriental Research in Chicago, endowed a number of lectureships in comparative religion. She offered the University of Chicago twenty thousand dollars to fund a lectureship in the 'Relations of Christianity to other Religions' in which 'in a friendly, temperate and conciliatory way, and in the fraternal spirit which pervaded the Parliament of Religions, the great questions of the truths of Christianity, its harmonies with the truths of other religions, its rightful claims and the best methods of setting them forth, should be presented to the scholarly and thoughtful people of India'. J.H. Barrows, her own minister in Michigan City, gave the first series entitled 'Christianity, the World Religion', and Fairbairn the second series entitled 'Religion and the Philosophy of Religion'. The third and fourth series were given by Charles Cuthbert Hall, see above, pp. 96ff. They were known as the Barrows Lectures in memory of the first lecturer.

271. Selbie, op. cit., p. 351. For a missionary view of the impression Fairbairn made in Calcutta, Madras, Bombay, Lahore, Poona, Delhi, Benares, Allahabad, and Lucknow, see Frank Lenwood, *Mansfield Essays* (1909), who describes them as 'those lectures to educated Indians which embodied so much of Dr Fairbairn's deepest thought and [which] left so grateful a memory behind them in many of the great cities of Hindustan', p. 307.

272. Selbie, op. cit., p. 359.

273. Selbie, op. cit., pp. 358-9.

274. The phraseology is that of Martin Buber.

275. Cf. the title of C.F. Andrews' book, see 177.

276. Selbie, op. cit., p. 358.

277. Selbie, ibid., p. 349.

278. 'Religion in India', *The Contemporary Review*, Vol. 50 (June 1899), pp. 761-781, and 'Race and Religion in India', in Vol. 51 (August 1899), pp. 153-173.

279. 'Race and Religion in India', in op. cit., p. 173.

280. *The Philosophy of the Christian Religion*, pp. vii-viii.

281. Ibid., p. vii.

282. Ibid., p. ix.

283. Ibid.

284. Ibid.

285. Ibid., pp. 186-288. In Chapter 6, Fairbairn deals with the origins of religion in general and in Chapter 7 with the origins of the historical religions. Chapter 8 discusses what he called the 'founded religions and their founders'.

286. Selbie, op. cit., pp. 365-366.

287. Ibid., p. 365.

288. Ibid., p. 366.

289. Ibid.

290. Ibid.

291. Ibid.

292. Ibid.

293. Cf. Wilfred Cantwell Smith, *Belief and History* (1977), *Faith and Belief* (1979) and *Towards a World Theology* (1981).

294. Selbie, op. cit., p. 366.

295. For Allen, see Charles L. Slattery, *Alexander Viets Griswold Allen, 1841-1908* (1911). There are also relevant chapters in a brochure from the EDS, *Faith and Freedom: A Study of Theological Education in the Episcopal Theological School* (1967). See also an earlier brochure also in the EDS archives: *The Episcopal Theological School 1867-1943*, by James Arthur Muller, published by the ETS (1943), pp. 98ff.

296. Westcott and Fairbairn were fully aware of spiritual kinship with Allen. Cf. "'Tell Dr Allen," said Westcott to visiting Massachusetts dignitary Endicott Peabody, "....That I warmly welcome his effort to put the emphasis on Greek Theology'", Slattery, op. cit., p. 99. For Fairbairn's approval of Allen, see a review in *The Spectator*, 11 January, 1890.

297. *The Continuity of Christian Thought: A Study of Modern Theology in the Light of its History*, was first published in 1884, but all quotations below are taken from the second edition (1895), cited as *Continuity*.

298. *Life and Writings of Jonathan Edwards* (1889); *Christian Institutions*, (1897); *Life and Letters of Phillips Brooks* (1900), together with a shortened version, *Phillips Brooks 1835-1893: Memories of his life with extracts from his letters and notebooks* (1907); *Freedom in the Church; or the Doctrine of Christ 'as the Lord hath Commanded, and as the Church hath received the Same according to the Commandments of God'* (1907).

299. See above, pp. 94-95.

300. See a full account of this 'reconstruction' between the ages of nineteen and twenty one in Slattery, op. cit., pp. 30-33. Slattery wrote that Allen was 'beginning to

find a master second only to Coleridge in Frederick Dennison Maurice, who was helping him to become constructive', p. 32.

301. Although this is the first time that the name of Frederick Robertson of Brighton has occurred in these pages, he should not be neglected as a preacher and teacher who did much to change the spiritual atmosphere of the nineteenth century; see Hansley Hanson, *Robertson of Brighton, 1816-1853* (1916).

302. Slattery, op. cit., p. 56. Slattery recorded that 'Those who did not like the School were prone to say that it was tainted with Harvard Unitarianism.'

303. H.S. Nash, of the Class of 1881 and L. Stoddard, of the Class of 1871, in ibid., pp. 98-99.

304. That he taught his students the same methodology we know from some lecture notes which still exist in the archives of the Episcopal Divinity School: 'What does it mean is the fundamental question of Church History. What if some supposed history be proved a myth? The question remains, what is the meaning? Maurice too much inclined to ask "Is it true?" We must know what it means before we can say much as to its truth'. Notes taken by F.L. Palmer, in a set of Kreutz's *Church History* during 1890.

305. Mulford was the author of two books which had Christian-political themes: *The Nation* and *The Republic of God*. Both these books were much influenced by Maurice whom Mulford had known personally in England.

306. 'Elisha Mulford – a Memorial Sermon', in the archives of the EDS, Cambridge, MA.

307. Ibid.

308. *Continuity*, p.1.

309. Ibid., p. 2.

310. Ibid.

311. Allen used the primary sources and nineteenth-century church historians. He acknowledges his debt to Giesiler, Neander, Dorner, Ritschl, Baur and Bunsen, and less frequently to others like Pressense, Renan and Milman.

312. *Continuity*, p.18.

313. *Logic and Life, with other sermons*, p. vii, quoted in *Continuity*, pp. 18-9.

314. *Continuity*, p. 20.

315. Allen has six chapters on these themes within a total of 438 pages. These chapters include a survey of the Greek and Latin theology; two chapters on the theology of the Middle Ages and the Reformation, and two chapters dealing with the conflicts of theology with rationalism and 'the renaissance of theology in the nineteenth century'.

316. See p. 178.

317. *Continuity*, p. 29.

318. Ibid.

319. Ibid.

320. Ibid., p. 30.

321. Ibid., pp. 34-5.

322. It will not be forgotten that Plotinus (204-270 CE) was an Egyptian and studied in Alexandria.

323. *Continuity*, p. 35.

324. Cf. the studies of this period already alluded to, by E.F. Osborn and Kwame Bediako, note 195 on p. 322 above.

325. As for example the material on the *Paidagogos*, concerning the education of the human race into the Truth by the indwelling *Logos*. But Allen himself reminded us that F.D. Maurice had already pointed many people in Clement's direction: 'He seems to me that one of the old Fathers whom we should have reverenced most as a teacher and loved as a friend,' Maurice had written in his *Ecclesiastical History of the First and Second Centuries*, p. 239, quoted by Allen on p. 70.

326. *Continuity*, p. 39.

327. Ibid.

328. Ibid., p. 40.

329. Ibid., p. 46.

330. Ibid., p. 47.

331. Ibid.

332. See p. 156 above.

333. *Continuity*, p. 47.

334. Cf. 'If in any respect in his view of the Incarnation, Athanasius advances upon the teaching of his predecessors, it is in the more emphatic assertion of the solidarity of the human race in Christ. Christ is the Head and representative of all mankind, and through His organic relationship with humanity, all that He was, all that he did, belongs to the race of man. From him mankind inherits a glory and distinction which all its members share; from him a Spirit flows for upon all anointing them as with a precious ointment; or, in other words, humanity has been actually redeemed in Christ,' ibid., p. 82.

335. Ibid., pp. 92–93.

336. This was the title given to two articles Allen wrote for the *Princeton Review*, November 1882, and January 1883.

337. As a sample of what Allen was describing and rejecting, see his interpretation of Calvin: 'In no Latin writer is found such a determined purpose to reject the immanence of Deity and assert His transcendence and His isolation from the world. In his conception of God, as absolute arbitrary will, he surpasses Duns Scotus; he rivals Mohammedanism by a doctrine of decrees that subdues the creature into fatalistic submission to necessity. The separation between God and humanity is emphasised as it has never been before, for Calvin insists, dogmatically and formally, upon that which had been to a large extent, hitherto, an unconscious though controlling sentiment,' *Continuity*, p. 302. In a similar way Allen had described Luther as 'but the child of the ages preceding; the protestant revolution was the natural and orderly sequence of a long concourse of preparation', ibid., p. 271. Whatever his greatness in other ways, Luther remained a Latin theologian.

338. *Continuity*, p. 39, *Fide Christianae Expositio*, op. cit., iv. 65. Cited by Allen on p. 291. Luther said to Zwingli after discussions on the eucharist, 'Ihr habt einen andern Geist dann wir', see *Continuity*, p. 392. For Zwingli, see Peter Stephens, *Zwingli: An Introduction to his Thought* (1972).

339. Zwingli, Allen thought, had no need to confine the Real Presence to the sacrament for this beneficent presence was everywhere in the world and its secret shrine was in every faithful heart. On the other hand Luther could not begin in the terms of

his Latinate theology 'formally to recognise the immanence of the essential Christ', *Continuity*, p. 292.

340. Allen's view here is exemplified in the following sentences: 'The principle that in the moral consciousness lies the foundation of truth', as set forth by the Cambridge Platonists, Archbishop Tillotson and the Deists, had an 'inevitable tendency... to bring back the belief, which underlay the ancient Greek theology, that God and humanity were connected by an organic tie, that God indwelt in his creation, that the revelation through the reason or the moral nature was the manifestation of present Deity', ibid., p. 362.

341. Ibid., p. 370.

342. A good anthology of the Protestant mystics referred to here is that edited by Ann Fremantle, *The Protestant Mystics* (1964).

343. See above, p. 2 and note 5 on p. 287.

344. *Continuity*, pp. 315-16.

345. See above, pp. 250f.

346. *Continuity*, p. 22.

347. Allen allowed no eulogy of Calvinism at any point. He saw it only as an incubus upon humanity, ibid., p. 339. Witness this striking sentence: 'The service which it rendered cannot be traced altogether to its theology as its inspiring source; the evil which it has done is all its own', ibid., p. 338. It must be remembered that Allen himself had fought his way out of Calvinism, see above, pp. 81-82.

348. *Continuity*, p. 374.

349. Ibid., p. 375, emphasis mine.

350. See above, pp. 30ff.

351. See, for example, Jonathan Edwards, *Treatise on the Religious Affections* (1746).

352. *Continuity*, p. 377.

353. Ibid., p. 378.

354. Ibid., p. 379.

355. For the 'Methodist Century' in America, see note 186 on p. 306.

356. Cf. Albert Outler's masterly introduction to his selection of Wesley's writings, *John Wesley* (1972).

357. *Continuity*, p. 380.

358. Ibid. Allen immediately added the rider: 'At the same time its defect was its want of intellectual tone and a more ethical aim. For the lack of these it failed to retain its grasp upon the advancing life of Christendom.'

359. Ibid., pp. 378, 381.

360. Schleiermacher's fame in the English speaking world is a reflex of the need to understand Karl Barth. Readers of this work who are not theologians are invited to compare this passage from Oman's translation of the fifth Speech with the Barthian position that 'religion is the affair of godless people': 'I invite you to study every faith possessed by man, every religion that has a name and character. Though it may long ago have degenerated into a long series of empty customs, into a system of abstract ideas and theories, will you not, when you examine the original elements at source, find that this dead dross was once the outpourings of the inner fire? Is there not in all religions more or less of the true nature of religion, as I have presented it to you? Must not therefore each religion be one of the special forms which mankind, in some

region of the earth and some stage of development has to accept?' *On Religion: Speeches to its Cultured Despisers* (1958), p. 216.

361. Allen alluded to this in *Continuity*, pp. 399-400, and p. 407, where Allen wrote that for many, Schleiermacher's teaching will seem 'a source only of confusion and disintegration' and that 'such a Deity as Schleiermacher worshipped' would be to them 'no God at all'.

362. Note should however be taken of John Oman's remarks in the Preface to his 1893 translation of the *Reden*: 'Though this work, so far as I know, is translated for the first time, it does not now begin to enter into English thought. Traces of the movement at least, of which it is the most characteristic product, may be found in our philosophy, our history and our literature', op. cit., p. xxi.

363. W.B. Selbie, *Schleiermacher, A Critical and Historical Study* (1913).

364. *Continuity*, p. 381.

365. Ibid., p. 382.

366. Ibid. We shall see this image appear many times before it was used in *The Missionary Message*. Here we note its use in as early as 1884.

367. Ibid., p. 384.

368. Ibid., p. 385.

369. Ibid., p. 387.

370. Ibid., p. 386.

371. Ibid., p. 387, and see above, pp. 7ff. and pp. 41-42.

372. Ibid.

373. Ibid., p. 388.

374. Ibid., p. 389.

375. Ibid.

376. Ibid., p. 391.

377. Ibid.

378. Slattery gives full accounts of how *Continuity*, was received, op. cit., pp. 100-13. According to Slattery, most of the reviews appeared in 1886 and were both long and respectful. But note the perceptive remarks of William R. Hutchison: 'The responses to Allen's *Continuity of Christian Thought* and Munger's *Freedom and Faith* show such an alteration in tone that one is prompted to return to Gladden's gathering-storm imagery, and just at this point to picture woodland animals suddenly on the alert. From here on, reviewers increasingly object in principle to the New Theology, and express apprehensiveness about the future. In place of basically indulgent critics one begins to meet basically querulous ones', *The Modernist Impulse in American Protestantism*, p. 107. Hutchison gives the example of A.A. Hodge, Charles Hodge's son, who asserted in *The Presbyterian Review* that the Augustinian-Calvinist mode of religious thought was superior to those emanating from the 'dormitories of the East', and of the conservative Congregational journal *Bibliotheca Sacra* which found Allen's work promotive of pantheism and 'radically vicious', op. cit., pp. 107-8. But one positive anecdote is sufficient to show the fame of the book in its own period. The Archbishop of Canterbury, Randall Davidson, was visiting the ETS in 1904. In the robing room of the chapel of the school the members of the ETS faculty were being presented by Bishop Lawrence to Archbishop Davidson, and he made his formal bow to each of them. 'As Dr Allen moved away to put on his surplice, Bishop Laurence said "That is Dr Allen who wrote *The Continuity of Christian Thought*." "Is

that Allen of *Continuity*?" the Archbishop said and went instantly over to him and shook hands with him.' Slattery adds 'It was a symbolic act of English appreciation of an American contribution to theology', op. cit., pp. 112-3.

379. He saw this as a parallel to what was taking place in Germany. Allen knew only too well of the reactions that the Romantic movement caused, particularly among the ecclesiastics. He found no kind word to say about Tractarianism, which he saw as a return to Latinate theology. He wrote of it that 'the object of the movement known as Tractarianism, Newman confesses in his apologia, was to "hold back the aggressive force of the human intellect". In order to overcome liberalism he set himself to restore the idea of the Church as it had appeared in the Latin Fathers', *Continuity*, p. 410. There is a striking footnote to this which reads 'A glance at the "Tracts for the Times" is sufficient to show that it was the Latin Fathers almost exclusively who received attention from the Tractarian School'.

380. But see note 1 on p. 308.

381. *Continuity*, first edition, p. viii.

382. Ibid., second edition, p. iii.

383. As well as reflecting a fundamentally Maurician theology, *The Continuity of Christian Thought* frequently invoked Maurice directly to support Allen's positions with regard to nineteenth-century controversies. Maurice was called as a witness against the Tractarian revival of Latin theology. 'It might have been said of Dr Pusey's great contemporary, the late Mr Maurice, that he was only asserting another phase of belief among those catholic Fathers whom the Tractarians neglected, when he proclaimed that God had never ceased to make a communication to men; that now, as always, he revealed Himself by the law of His being, in the reason, the conscience, the experience of humanity. To neither Pusey nor Keble was it given to read this law of the divine life, in the order of nature or in the courses of history', ibid., p. 414. This sentiment was but part of Allen's attack on the 'skepticism', which he, like Maurice, detected as lurking behind Augustinian and Calvinistic theologies. The disowning of reason, and the seeking of refuge in remote or obscure principles of external authority imply deep unbelief. Allen saw this in the controversy between Mansell and Maurice in the eighteen sixties over the former's book, *The Limits of Religious Thought* (1859): 'The controversy which took place between him and Mr Maurice in which the latter called attention to the question, "What is Revelation", is perhaps the most significant one in the whole history of the Church since Athanasius took up to resist the Aryans on a similar, if not the same identical issue', ibid., pp. 422-3. In Allen's view this whole matter turned upon the question as to whether God had actually spoken to humankind. Allen quoted from the recently published *Life of Maurice* (1884): '... We start from exactly opposite points; we, naturally, from that which is above us and speaks to us; they, naturally, from that which is within them and which seeks for some object above itself... I am most anxious to assert the worth of our English position, to prove that Truth must look down upon us, if we would look up to it; that Truth must be a person seeking us, if we are to seek Him', ibid., p. 433. But, Allen said, this distinction marked the difference between Schleiermacher and Hegel. Allen in bringing together the thought of Maurice and Schleiermacher believed that 'Christian Theology has regained at last the point where it was left by the master minds of the ancient Church', ibid., pp. 437-8. For Allen Latin theology

had to be to abandoned as a mere 'parenthesis in the larger record of the life of Christendom', ibid., p. 438.

384. These articles on 'the prophets of the church', which included Clement of Alexandria, and Horace Bushnell, as well Augustine, Martin Luther and Jonathan Edwards, were published as *Prophets of the Christian Faith* in 1897.

385. Art. 'Frederick Denison Maurice' in *Prophets of the Christian Faith* (1897), pp. 214-5.

386. Ibid., pp. 215-6.

387. *Continuity*, p. 438. Note at this point Allen's ecclesiology. Like many of his Anglican fellows, he saw a vital role for the church in the education of humanity. This is the reason why the institution exists, as 'essential to the well-being of an external society which proposes to itself no less an end than the conversion of the world to Christ'. Schleiermacher asserted the importance of the church 'as vitally related to the well-being of man', and attached to it 'the highest significance making it essential to the realization of human redemption: Salvation, instead of being exclusively an individual process, is accomplished only through the fellowship of the church. The principle of association enters into the religion of Christ as a necessary factor. The Spirit which saves men is a Spirit of Holy Fellowship seeking to unite them more closely together. It is a Spirit of Love and not of selfishness or division. Man is most highly exalted and honoured by his membership in a common humanity, of which Christ is the head. It is in his relationship to the race of mankind that he has been redeemed. In the church, as the congregation of faithful men, there is the conscious knowledge of the work of Christ; it is the pledge of a regenerated society to be realised in the future, the picture and the model after which is slowly fashioning itself the Kingdom of God in the world', *Continuity*, pp. 396-7.

388. Ibid.

389. A detailed biography of Hall was written by his son Basil Douglas Hall some fifty-seven years after his father's death. *The Life of Charles Cuthbert Hall: 'One Among a Thousand'* (1965) is a mine of information about late Victorian America, as it based on 'hosts of personal letters, scrapbooks, diaries, clippings and other papers' in a 'family archive', p. 5. There are also tributes from Harry Emerson Fosdick and Henry Sloane Coffin. Many other papers are in the Union Theological Seminary Library.

390. *History of Union Theological Seminary in New York* (1976), pp. 102-118, and 114-117. The Union Seminary portrait of Hall is reproduced on p. 103.

391. Handy, op. cit., p. 102, and B.D. Hall, op. cit., pp. 256 and 261. Cf. on the influence of Hall upon Henry Sloane Coffin, 'Whatever may have been the initial attraction the two men were drawn to each other at once, and a friendship developed which grew steadily in warmth and strength until Dr Hall's untimely death in 1908. It was to Dr Hall that Coffin turned with the request that he preach his ordination sermon... it was Dr Hall who laid the cornerstone of the new church in Coffin's first pastorate', see Morgan Phelps Noyes, *Henry Sloane Coffin: The Man and His Ministry* (1964), p. 63.

392. See above, pp. 25-26. Another of Briggs' colleagues at Union was the church historian Philip Schaff who affirmed at the Parliament of Religions at Chicago in 1893: 'Our theological Systems are but dim rays of the sun of truth which illuminates

the universe.' Both Schaff and Briggs were friends of Hall and he strongly supported their positions. See Handy, op. cit., pp. 71–93.

393. Charles A. Briggs was fully supported by the Union Faculty and Board of Directors. Hall had become a Director of Union in 1883 and was therefore a signatory to this statement: 'We know Dr Briggs to be an earnest Christian, a devout student of the Bible, an indefatigable teacher and worker, and one who holds the standards of the church with an intelligence based on an exhaustive study of their history and literature', Handy, op. cit., p. 76. B.D. Hall records a diary entry by his father, saying C.A. Briggs 'is the noblest man I know in the ministry', op. cit., p. 118.

394. The Carew Lectures for 1895 at Hartford Theological Seminary.

395. These phrases come from Harry Emerson Fosdick, who wrote in his autobiography *The Living of these Days* (SCM Press 1957): 'Under the stimulus of the president, Charles Cuthbert Hall, Christianity was made vivid to us, both as a profound personal experience and as an affair of world-wide concern', p. 77.

396. *Qualifications for Ministerial Power*, p. 229.

397. See note 270 on p. 326.

398. B.D. Hall offers many hints why Cuthbert Hall was chosen for this task. Barrows himself was a friend of Hall's and had given the Morse Lectures at Union in 1898 with the title of 'The Christian Conquest of Asia', op. cit., p. 148. Hall was well known in University of Chicago circles, having given the Convocation Address in 1898, ibid., p. 153. Hall was also a friend of A.M. Fairbairn, and B.D. Hall gives an eyewitness account of a visit to Scotland in August 1899. There, in the village of Kincraig, undisturbed by the threat of a violent storm, Fairbairn and Hall were 'deep in the problems of Brahmanism', ibid., p. 165. Later Fairbairn was to entertain Hall in Oxford and to introduce him to the Bodleian Library, where Hall's first series of Barrows Lectures were mainly written, ibid., p. 177. If Fairbairn forms a link with the past, we should note the connection with the future made through Hall's employment of Robert Ernest Hume as his secretary for the first Indian trip. R.E. Hume had already obtained his Ph.D. at Union, and was soon to gain fame through his translation of the *Thirteen Principal Upanishads*. Hume was the son of Robert A. Hume of the Maratha mission, see above pp. 132–143. B.D. Hall recalled that Robert A. Hume joined the Hall family in Scotland that summer, ibid., p. 179.

399. One leading Episcopalian missionary, Bishop Charles H. Brent of the Philippines, was asked to contribute the memorial standing at the beginning of *Christ and the Eastern Soul*. Brent wrote, 'The God-designed oneness of the human race was to him no idle theory or doubtful speculation; it was a guiding principle for practical activity through a lifetime. With the courage of deathless conviction, he chose the widest chasm that breaks the unity of mankind and divides the world into two sharply contrasted sections of East and West, upon which to spend the constructive force of his manhood at its zenith, laying down his life for his espoused cause as willingly and as truly as a Livingstone or a Patteson,' p. xix.

400. *Christ and the Eastern Soul*, p. 4.

401. Ibid., p. 75.

402. Cf. Cuthbert Hall's account: 'when all was over I could hardly make my way to the carriage. The street was crowded with men young and old, who laid their hands on me in blessing. Garlands and a large basket of flowers were given me... I

had almost lived with the Bengalis, morning, noon, and night. I understood them, they understood me,' B.D. Hall, op. cit., p. 226.

403. *Christ and the Eastern Soul*, p. 75.

404. B.D. Hall, op. cit., pp. 182-195, 216-230.

405. Ibid., p. 183.

406. Ibid., p. 222.

407. Ibid., pp. 226-7.

408. Ibid., p. 225.

409. Ibid., p. 194.

410. There were exceptions. After the lectures at Bishop's College, Calcutta, the wife of a C.M.S. missionary denounced Hindu and Muslim thought as wholly 'the lie of Satan,' and added 'How can you say that they have any truth? They are altogether vile and their thoughts are of the devil'. Cuthbert Hall recorded in his *Journal* that 'the thermometer dropped by several degrees,' ibid., p. 224.

411. Ibid., p. 3.

412. The last of these works was produced after Hall's death in March 1908. They were all published in Britain as well as America, and the two series of Burrows lectures were published also in India and Sri Lanka, the second series under the title of 'The Witness of the Oriental Soul to Christ'. In addition, *Christian Belief interpreted by Christian Experience* was published in Japan by the Methodist Publishing House, Tokyo in 1903.

413. See note 144 on p. 302.

414. The nearest Hall got to Maurice was in meeting Charles Kingsley, who befriended Hall when he was a young American student in London 1874-5. Cf. the long quotation from Kingsley in *Christ and the Eastern Soul*, pp. 47-8. Hall was present at Kingsley's funeral in January 1875. Incidentally, Max Müller was also at this funeral; cf. B.D. Hall, op. cit., pp. 38-40. Hall would have known the broad sweep of Maurice's thought through such writings as Tulloch's *Movements of Religious Thought in the Nineteenth Century*, which he does use; see *Universal Elements*, p. 232.

415. *Christ and the Eastern Soul*, p. 50.

416. *Universal Elements*, p. 231.

417. Ibid., p. 232.

418. Ibid., p. 233.

419. He uses the Fourth Edition of *Letters of Erskine*, 1884.

420. Ibid., p. 401, and in *Universal Elements*, p. 241.

421. Ibid., p. 404, in *The Universal Elements*, p. 243.

422. Cf. Hall in *Christ and the Human Race*, 'Little was known of the East. Its religions were assumed to be wholly vile and foolish, unworthy of serious consideration – the vagaries of backward and inferior races... The religious assumption was that the East must depend upon the West for salvation, and that salvation could be received only by entire renunciation of its own religious inheritances. At that time, Oriental studies being yet in their infancy, it had scarcely occurred to Occidental Christians that the viewless spirit of God had also been preparing a way in the Oriental consciousness, whereby ultimately to express truths as yet largely unrealized in Anglo-Saxon religious experience,' pp. x-xi.

423. See above, pp. 20ff., 25ff.

424. *Universal Elements*, p. 12.

425. Ibid. The date of the *Westminster Confession* is usually given as 1646.

426. Ibid., p. 252.

427. Ibid., p. 253.

428. Ibid., p. 15. Cf. Bishop Brent, 'The road to Christianity for the adherents of great pre-Christian religions is not through the laborious route of Old Testament thought, but through their own beliefs straight into the gospel. I once suggested to an eminent scientist and mystic that it might be well for Christian hands to bind up representative Oriental scriptures with the New Testament. He replied that the association of the Jewish scriptures with the Christian writings had not been a converting factor among the Jews. That is true. But it has had the effect of giving to the world the real wealth of the Old Testament; and the wealth of the Oriental religious mind will come to us only when its product is studied appreciatively in the light of the gospel,' *Christ and the Eastern Soul* p. xxi. Cf. 'Touched by Christianity the ideals and religions of the Orient are a contribution to the Kingdom of God; unconverted and unfulfilled they are a menace to the very life of Christianity,' ibid., p. xxiv.

429. Ibid., p. 218.

430. C.Bigg, *The Christian Platonists of Alexandria* (1886).

431. But note that this is not the kind of 'immanentism' which believed it could go through nature to God. Cf. Hall in *Christ and the Human Race*: 'So long as we look upon the Incarnation Idea as a breach of the natural order, as the breaking into the world of a God who ordinarily lives apart in the inscrutable solitudes of infinity, so long will the Incarnation of Jesus Christ present to many minds aspects of unreality which invalidate his claim to be the Redeemer and the Light of the world,' p. 59.

432. For the rise of the 'theological universities' see Handy, op. cit., p. 108. George William Knox, a former Presbyterian missionary in Japan, was appointed as the Professor of the Philosophy and History of Religion in 1907. Five years later his professorial chair was endowed in the name of Marcellus Hartley. Robert Ernest Hume, the son of R.A. Hume (see note 398 above), was appointed to Union to teach Indian religions in that chair in 1912.

433. *Universal Elements*, p. 194.

434. Ibid., p. 195.

435. Ibid.

436. Ibid., p. 272.

437. See Handy, op. cit., p. 125, for the founding of the Religious Education Association, and Hall's part in this.

438. *Christ and the Eastern Soul*, pp. 101-2.

439. Ibid., p. xix.

440. Ibid., p. 21.

441. Ibid., p. 118.

442. Ibid., p. 21.

443. Ibid., p. 31.

444. Ibid., pp. 51-2.

445. Ibid., p. 31.

446. See Handy, op. cit., p. 116, cf. B.D. Hall, op. cit., pp. 237ff.

447. *Christ and the Eastern Soul*, p. 208.

3 *Eight Missionaries and their Theology of Religion*

1. Its full title is *The Higher Hinduism in Relation to Christianity: Certain Aspects of Hindu Thought from a Christian Standpoint* (1902), cited hereafter as *The Higher Hinduism*. His other works include: *The Philosophy of Missions: A Present-Day Plea* (1882), cited hereafter as *Philosophy*; *Studies in the Upanishads* (1897); *Transmigration and Karma,* (1898) and *Missions and Sociology* (1908).

2. So much so, that the work had little or no impact upon his contemporaries as far as one can judge by the non-existence of reviews or citations. Some of the work did appear, however, in *The Christian World*, and its influence would have been widely diffused.

3. For J.H. Barrows see above p. 326.

4. Preface to *The Higher Hinduism*, p. vi.

5. J. Sibree, *London Missionary Society: A Register of Missionaries, Deputations, etc., from 1796 to 1923* (1923), see entry for 'Slater'.

6. For Slater's own discussion of this kind of educational work see 'The Attitude of Educated Hindus towards Christianity' in *The East and the West*, Vol.III (1905),pp. 254-63.

7. E.J. Sharpe, *Not to Destroy but to Fulfil* (1965), p. 95.

8. This was the second Decennial Missionary Conference in India and represented most of the major Protestant missions.

9. The LMS experiments in higher education are discussed in Goodall, *History of the London Missionary Society 1895-1945* (1954), pp. 40ff., but note the quotation from Slater on p. 26. For a dissenting voice raised against this far reaching educational policy in Indian missions see Henry Whitehead, note 183 on p. 389 below.

10. *God Revealed*, p. iii, quoted from Sharpe, op. cit., emphasis his, p. 98.

11. *God Revealed*, p. 2. in ibid.

12. *God Revealed*, p. 8. in ibid.

13. Sharpe, op. cit., p. 99.

14. Monier Monier Williams was the author of *Indian Wisdom* (1875) and *Hinduism* (1877) as well as other works published after *The Philosophy of Missions*. Though strictly an 'Orientalist', Monier Williams was well-known among evangelical missionaries because of his inaugural lecture at Oxford, entitled, 'The Study of Sanskrit in Relation to Missionary Work In India', 19 April, 1861.

15. Quoted from Sharpe, op. cit., p. 101.

16. *The Philosophy of Missions*, pp. 2-3: 'It does not lie as a burden upon the conscience of the church, which the members as body are prepared to bear', he lamented, ibid., p. 3.

17. Ibid., p.6, emphasis his.

18. Ibid.

19. Ibid., p. 10, emphasis his.

20. Ibid., p. 11.

21. Ibid., p. 16.

22. Ibid.

23. Ibid.

24. Ibid., p. 16-17.

25. Ibid., p. 17.

26. See above, pp. 4-11.

27. *Philosophy*, p. 18.

28. Ibid., pp. 25-6.

29. Ibid., p. 26, emphasis his.

30. Though there were exceptions to this stricture. Slater specifically mentions and quotes extensively speeches and sermons of Raleigh, R.W. Dale and Griffith John, ibid., footnotes pp. 26-30.

31. Ibid., p. 31.

32. For Maurice's modified millennialism and doctrine of universal restoration, see above, pp. 36ff.

33. Ibid., p. 37. For Bushnell, see above, pp. 23-24.

34. For Lessing, see also above, p. 126. Slater's reference is to the *Education of the Human Race*, third edition, p. 75, see ibid. p. 38, footnote. Slater was to focus increasingly upon the education of humanity, see his last book: 'Faith in humanity is the inspiration of modern missions', *Missions and Sociology*, p. 65, and 'This is the gospel of spiritual renewal and social redemption which the present generation has to give to the world', ibid.

35. *Philosophy*, p. 38.

36. Ibid.

37. See above pp. 11-14.

38. *Philosophy*, p 41.

39. Ibid., p. 46. Slater's texts in support of this position were: John 12.32, John 5.17, John 11.4, Rev. 11.15, Acts 3.21, Col. 1.20, Rev. 5.13, Eph. 4.6, I Cor. 11.13, and I Tim. 2.4.

40. No studies are available of how and why Congregationalists became so keen to adopt Maurice's theology, but cf. David Simon, above, p. 32 and note 213 on p. 308.

41. *Philosophy*, pp. 47-8, emphasis his. The phrases in quotations marks in the passage are from Maurice, *The Religions of the World*.

42. *The Religions of the World*, fourth edition, pp. 243-244.

43. *Philosophy*, p. 46. Cf. *Mission and Sociology*, ch. 1.

44. *Philosophy*, p. 47. Arnold Foster, another Congregationalist disciple of F.D. Maurice and Slater's LMS colleague in China, had a striking comment of the alternative methods of mission: 'What of the men sent out by us? Years ago a young missionary called upon me to ask my advice. "I want you to advise me as to the best way of getting out the largest numbers of workers in the shortest possible time." I replied, "I am afraid that I so entirely disbelieve in your plan that I cannot make any suggestion on the subject." Who that had studied the methods of Christ would have thought that worthy representatives of His Gospel, with its perpetual call for sacrifice, self-surrender and thoughtful knowledge, could be turned out as fast as there was money to pay them their wages and to rent or build buildings for them to occupy'. Foster added of this type of young mission, 'and there are many of them in China' – I regard them and all their works as among the greatest obstacles that the Kingdom of God has to face,' *Memoirs* (1921), p. 103. For Foster as an Edinburgh Respondent, see above, pp. 217ff.

45. *Philosophy*, pp. 90-1, footnote, emphasis his.

46. Ibid.

47. Ibid.

48. Ibid., p. 112.

49. Ibid., p. 113.

50. Ibid.

51. Ibid., pp. 113-4.

52. Ibid., p. 114. Slater is quoting *The Natural and the Supernatural*, ch. xiii.

53. Ibid.

54. As we have seen, Neander, as a disciple of Schleiermacher, was influential upon the way in which A.V.G. Allen taught church history in Cambridge, Mass., cf. note 311 on p. 328.

55. *Church History*, vol. I, p. 240, quoted in ibid., p. 114.

56. See above, pp. 90ff.

57. *Philosophy*, p. 125, emphasis his.

58. Ibid., p. 125-6, emphases his.

59. Ibid., p. 126.

60. For Coxe see Sandeen, op. cit., p. 44.

61. *Philosophy*, p. 118.

62. Ibid.

63. *The Higher Hinduism*, p.2. Unlike *The Philosophy of Missions*, this work received appreciative critical attention, see e.g. the review in *The East and the West* (possibly by its editor C.H. Robinson), which spoke of its 'great value for the Sanskrit scholar, the student of philosophy and religion, and not least for the thoughtful Christian reader', vol. 1, pp. 113ff. But the anonymous reviewer did confess to 'some alarm' as he read the title of the book: 'In its pages we expected to meet a Hinduism created by a Western and Christian mind, and our pleasure was the greater as we discovered and welcomed an unbiased, scholarly and masterly examination of the whole Hindu philosophical and religious system,' ibid.

64. In *The Philosophy of Missions* in 1882, Slater had welcomed the growth of the science of Comparative Religion and had referred frequently to A.M. Fairbairn, cf. 'Professor Fairbairn in the Muir Lectures on the Science of Religion... said that no religion was an accident, each had a rational cause; no religion walked with aimless feet; each had a place to fill, and a work to do in the system that was being slowly built up by myriad independent yet co-ordinate hands into what might be called the history of man in time,' p. 116. Slater also appreciated the views of E.B. Tylor, the anthropologist, who had written, 'No religion of mankind lies in utter isolation from the rest; and the thoughts and principles of modern Christianity are attached to intellectual clues which run back through far pre-Christian ages to the very origin of human civilisation, perhaps, even, of human existence,' *Primitive Culture*, vol. I, p. 381, quoted by Slater, ibid. Cf. his later testimony: 'The science of Comparative Religion has given a new life to Christianity. We now see that no religion lies in utter isolation from the rest, and that if Christianity is historical, it cannot stand alone in the midst of history, but has its place in the continuity of history. And we find that a stream of Divine inspiration – a connecting current – has been flowing unbroken through the plains of history: that God has "never left himself without witness" among the nations; that he has always had vital relations with the spirits of men; and that there is good in all religions because of the abiding presence of God in His world. All the spiritual truths that have been venerated for ages in other faiths, and that have given them their persistence to the present day – for no great religion was

ever based on falsehood – *we claim for the spiritual and eternal Christ*, "the Light which lighteth every man as he cometh into the world", *Edin.Response*, 229, pp. 52-3, emphasis his. For an explanation of the method of reference to the replies to the Edinburgh Conference questionnaire (cited as *Edin. Response*), see p. 193 above.

65. *The Higher Hinduism*, p. 290.

66. *The Higher Hinduism*, p. 291 Cf. Slater later on C.C. Hall, 'It was Dr Hall's conviction that India's '"great pantheistic inheritance", which we are sometimes apt to depreciate and deplore, qualified India in an exceptional degree to apprehend and interpret the deeper mysteries of the Christian faith as they gather round the *Person and Consciousness of Christ*; that the day was coming when India, so far from being repelled by the *Divinity* of Christ, would become the great exponent of it, recovering its meaning for the world,' *Edin.Response*, 229, p. 239, emphasis his.

67. *The Higher Hinduism*, p. 291.

68. Ibid.

69. Ibid. This passage was used by J.P. Jones. See note 326 below.

70. Ibid.

71. Ibid.

72. *Edin. Response*, 229. This was quite the longest of the replies and covered ninety pages of double spaced quarto typescript together with a further thirty three pages of 'continuation papers' in which Slater addressed interfaith issues.

73. *Edin. Response*, 229, p. 3.

74. Ibid., p. 74.

75. Ibid., p. 75.

76. Ibid., 229, continuation papers, p. 20, emphasis his.

77. In presenting this view to the Edinburgh commissioners Slater was relying on A.V.G. Allen. The selection of material very closely resembles that of Allen. For a summary of this issue see Cracknell, *Towards a New Relationship* (1986), pp. 100-2. A.V.G. Allen had discussed this matter in full see *Continuity*, pp. 38-7 and above, pp. 85-86. Slater was reflecting such discussion when he wrote: 'In the second century, the Person of Christ exercised a deep influence on the Oriental mind. He was regarded as the Logos of the Infinite – who speaks in Nature and in the heart of man, and who reveals in sacrifice the very heart of God. And there is little doubt that it will be in this direction that the highest Hindu minds will turn.' *Edin. Response*, 229, p. 74. Slater also recorded the frequent objection of Indian intellectuals, '"If Christ is the true and only Saviour of mankind, and faith in him is necessary to salvation, why did He not appear in the world before; and why did He not make Himself manifest to the world generally?"' Clement of Alexandria answered this question as it might have been put to him in the second century AD, by suggesting that the Word was in the world before Jesus Christ walked on earth, and that it was through this Word that Greek philosophy was a fragment of eternal truth from the theology of the ever living Word. Expressing the continuity of the Christian revelation with the rest of human experience, Justin wrote: "Christ is the first-begotten of God... the Word in whom the whole human race shares." Clement followed this through when he said that the person who "brings together the separate fragments and makes them one, will... contemplate the perfect Word, the Truth".' *Edin. Response*, 229, continuation papers p. 20.

78. *Edin. Response* 229, continuation papers, pp. 20-1. Notice the ease with which Slater used concepts like 'fulfiller' and 'fulness' with their implicit evolutionary framework, and how he linked these with 'Comparative Religion'.

79. *Edin. Response*, 229, continuation papers, p. 3. Slater's suggestion that there was a movement from impersonal to personal belongs in the context of late Victorian theology. For the importance of J.R. Illingworth in his own time see Thomas A. Langford, *The Search for Foundations* (1969), pp. 190ff. Illingworth in his widely read *Personality Human and Divine* (1895) had written that 'the derivation of the personal from the impersonal would appear to have been a gradual process. And even when we reach the climax of ancient civilization, in Greece and Rome, there is no adequate sense either in theory or practice of human personality as such.' Illingworth's book was influential and we may take it that Slater had read it or at least extended reviews of it. Certainly he took Illingworth's argument on board and showed the Edinburgh commissioners how it could be used effectively in India.

80. Ibid.

81. *Edin. Response*, 229, p. 59.

82. Ibid., emphasis his.

83. Ibid., emphasis his.

84. Ibid., p. 68, emphasis his.

85. The concluding words of *The Higher Hinduism*, emphasis his, p. 291. This was genuinely unpatronizing, cf. his remarks about the 'many superior minds and kindly hearts and noble souls to be met within Hinduism and Buddhism and Islam and other faiths', in his last work, *Missions and Sociology*, p. 15.

86. Brian Stanley, *The History of the Baptist Missionary Society 1792-1892* (1992), p.181.

87. W.E. Soothill, *Timothy Richard of China* (1924), p.324, cf. the portrait in Richard, *Forty Five Years in China: Reminiscences*, facing p.332. Soothill's volume is often largely a paraphrase of Richard's own reminiscences, but he did have access to Mary Richard's diaries and some later papers. Soothill, who later became Professor of Chinese in Oxford, was an eyewitness of much of Richard's public activity after 1901, having been at Shanxi University, first as a teacher and then as its second President. Richard's memories, like those of St Paul and many others, need to be handled with caution when they deal with historical events, but this book is more concerned with Richard's attitudes in his later years when such events have become pert of his personal 'myth'. His reminiscences are cited as *Forty Five Years*. Richard had earlier attempted an autobiographical sketch in *Conversion by the Million* (1907), cited as *Conversion*.

88. Soothill, op. cit., p. 326.

89. For Richard as a Baptist Missionary see Stanley, op. cit., pp. 180-96, 200-3, 205-6, 231, 303-7; as a famine administrator, see Paul Richard Bohr, *Famine in China and the Missionary; Timothy Richard as Relief Administrator and Advocate of National Reform* (1972). For background to Richard's theories see Ralph Covell, *Confucius, the Buddha, and Christ: A History of the Gospel in Chinese* (1986), pp.125-8.

90. Soothill, op. cit., p.18.

91. Rowland Williams was Professor of Hebrew at St David's College, Lampeter from 1850-1864. In 1860 he contributed an essay on biblical criticism to *Essays and Reviews*, and was prosecuted for heresy by the Bishop of Salisbury. He also wrote *Christianity and Hinduism* (1856). Lampeter, by one of the ironies of history, is today

a centre for interfaith dialogue because of the coming of Muslim scholars to the Faculty of Theology and Religious Studies of the University of Wales.

92. The dates given to this Revival are 1858-60. Richard was baptized in a flooded river, by a rather too total immersion, in 1858, aged 12, see *Conversion*, p. 79.

93. Stanley, op. cit., p. 180, footnote 18.

94. *Forty Five Years*, p. 26. For Bushnell's ideas see above, pp. 23-24.

95. Ibid., p. 35.

96. Ibid., p. 146. On funeral and ancestral rites and the controversies surrounding them among Protestant missionaries, see Covell, op. cit., p. 117-121. See Richard's defence of W.A.P. Martin at the 1877 General Missionary Conference, as described by Covell, p.120.

97. *Forty Five Years*, pp. 48-9

98. Ibid., p. 49. For Richard's view that many Nestorians had joined a secret society known as the 'Jin Dan Jiao', see Covell, op. cit., pp. 24ff.

99. *Forty Five Years*, p. 48.

100. Ibid., p. 49. Richard's reply to the Commissioners of the WMC in 1909 indicated his feelings at this period of his career. He described briefly the result of his earliest attempts at evangelism, added, 'after finding that the theology that I was taught at home did not win converts, I read Chinese religious books to find what the people were seeking after and re-read the New Testament to find out what was the message of our Lord Jesus Christ and the New Testament to the human race', *Edin. Response*, 92, p. 13.

101. *Forty Five Years*, pp. 145-6. For David Hill, see Soothill, op. cit., p. 113. Richard believed that God's Kingdom 'will necessarily contain all that is good in the Kingdoms of this world and something more. It will not allow a submerged tenth to be oppressed as at present by diabolical armaments, land-laws and trusts... It is a kingdom of the poor and needy even in this world', *Conversion*, p. 100. Richard repeated this view in 1909: 'What also strongly appeals to the poor and the oppressed is the coming of the Lord's anointed to reign and break oppression and rule in equity and deliver the submerged tenth from the corrupt governments of non-Christian nations and from the tyrannical governments of Christendom which overawe the poor with their terrible armaments', *Edin. Response*, 92, p. 16. For the movements taking place in Europe associated with the names of Ritschl and Kaftan, see above, pp. 123, 301.

102. *Forty Five Years*, p. 146.

103. In 1824 Edward Irving had preached a sermon on Matt.10.11., entitled 'Missionaries after the Apostolic School', to the LMS London Meeting, where it had dismayed many of his hearers. in 1887 Richard reprinted it and sent it to leading missionaries in China, India and Japan, see Soothill, op. cit., pp.77-9. For Irving, see note 66 on p. 294 above.

104. Richard was particularly impressed by the anthology of popular Confucianism and Taoism known as the 'Record of Devout Faith', transliterated by Richard as *King Shin Lu*, as well as the 'chief book of the Buddhists, the 'Diamond Classic'. A Chinese friend had given him the latter: 'a beautiful little copy in two volumes all written by hand,' *Forty Five Years*, p. 86. He did not discover the Lotus Sutra until 1884, see above, p. 123.

105. See Covell, op. cit., pp. 85ff.

106. *Forty Five Years*, p. 86.

107. Ibid., p. 195. *The Awakening of Faith* or Lotus Sutra is discussed above, pp. 157, 160. For a fuller description of David Hill's reaction see *Higher Buddhism*, p. 45.

108. The former Miss Mary Martin. See Stanley, op. cit., pp. 189-90 for a description of Richard's relations with the BMS Committee while he was on leave.

109. *Forty Five Years*, p. 204.

110. Ibid., p. 205.

111. Stanley, op. cit., p. 190.

112. Ibid., pp. 190-1. Cf. Soothill's judgment of Richard as a pioneering Baptist missionary: 'He was the real founder of the mission in Shantung and sole founder of that mission in Shansi. His methods were adopted and developed by his colleagues in Shantung and the mission has been a great success. Unwisely his inexperienced colleagues in Shansi virtually drove him from their midst, otherwise there is every reason to believe that Shansi would have become one of the most remarkable Baptist mission fields in the world,' Soothill, op. cit., pp. 171-2. The American historian of Christian missions, Kenneth Scott Latourette, himself a Baptist, is even more emphatic in naming Timothy Richard as 'the real founder of the English Baptist mission in China', *Christianity in a Revolutionary Age*, Vol. 3, p. 44.

113. Stanley, op. cit., p. 190

114. Soothill, op. cit., p. 159. Mary Richard was a formidable missionary in her own right having gone to China with the United Presbyterian mission before she married Richard, see *Forty Five Years*, pp. 320-22. She agreed entirely with her husband's views as a few paragraphs from her tract written in Chinese, *A Conversation between Two Chinamen* (1893) indicate: 'Christian' is talking to 'Non-Christian' who has met a Christian preacher of the old type: 'What further did this Chinese preacher say was important in the Christian religion?' 'Non-Christian' – , 'He said that I must feel and see that I was a criminal who had broken all the laws of God and man before God could forgive me and receive me as his child...' 'Christian' – 'Strange, again my teacher only tried to shew me that as I acknowledge that the food I ate was from God I had been very ungrateful in not rendering Him worship and thanks and service all my life. True, since I have known God as revealed in the life and death of Jesus Christ, I see many other sins in my heart and life than ingratitude, and sincerely wish to be purified from all that is displeasing to my Heavenly Father.' 'Non-Christian' – 'Heavenly Father, that is a beautiful name! It was not once mentioned by the preacher in our conversation. He seemed to speak of God as angry with but the few who had accepted a certain set of truths that had not come to our country until a few years ago, and that all our sages are suffering punishment now because they did not know and believe these truths. Could anything be more absurd?' 'Christian' – 'That man must have been imperfectly taught. My teacher spoke with the greatest reverence and respect of Confucius, Mencius and Lao-tze, and said they were sent by God to teach and prepare the way for the higher teaching of Jesus Christ. He said too that were Confucius living now he would accept Christianity if it were offered to him, as those who know and appreciate what is good are always ready to accept anything higher and better when they see it.' English version in *Conversion*, pp. 51-3.

115. Cf. Stanley, op. cit., p. 192

116. Legge confirmed the accuracy of the translation of the *Order of Study* and commented that while Richard's proposals for national reform were 'utter dreams and foolish fancies', there was 'little evidence in the submitted writings of theological

error, principally because there was so little that was theological in them', Stanley, op. cit., p. 193.

117. Ibid., p. 194.

118. E.W. Price Evans, *Timothy Richard* (1945), p.107. Richard's wrote sharply about this situation: 'I was... driven to look for help and funds elsewhere, or assent to the assumption that the opinion of one of fifteen years experience in China was of no more value than that of the latest newcomer, and that the ministers at home know the needs of China better than the missionaries themselves', *Conversion*, p. 91.

119. *Forty Five Years*, p. 215.

120. See Stanley, op. cit., p. 195.

121. The SDK, Guano Xuechi in Chinese, had been formed in 1887. See Leslie Marchant, *British Protestant Christian Evangelists and the 1898 Reform Movement in China*, (1977), pp. 10-1 for an account of its founding.

122. In 1889, Alexander Williamson had begun publication of the *Wan Kuo Kung Pao* or International Review, commonly known in English as *The Review of the Times*. In due course this was to be edited by Young C. Allen of the American Methodist Episcopal Church South. Soothill says from his first hand knowledge, 'No magazine ever published in China had so far reaching an influence as this during the editorship of Dr Allen', Soothill, op. cit., p.173. Along with Williamson and Allen there must also be mentioned the name of Ernst Faber who was a missionary of the Rheinische Missionary Society. The correspondence from China at the time of the Edinburgh Conference is full of references to Faber, see note 168 on p. 387.

123. Soothill, op. cit., p. 174.

124. Brian Stanley records the rehabilitation of Richard in the eyes of the BMS by the year 1907. One of the members of the BMS deputation wrote of the 'prophetic insight of this man of God, whose one aim is to glorify Jesus Christ'. The BMS committee agreed to provide an office manager for two years in order that Richard could have a 'roving commission to take whatever opportunity he wished to advance the Kingdom of God in China'. Stanley writes that after the 'years of hesitation with which the Society had greeted Richard's plans this was a strange conversion', op. cit., pp. 203-4.

125. There is a full account of Richard's work with the SDK/CLS. in H.R. Williamson, *British Baptists in China* (1957), pp. 252-7.

126. Stanley, op. cit., p. 303. Timothy Richard gets barely a page in Varg's *Missionaries Chinese and Diplomats: the American Protestant Missionary Movement in China 1890-1952* (1958), for the obvious reason that Richard was not American. But it is interesting that Varg does single him out for a supercilious comment. Varg writes: 'Several high officials were active in the Reform Movement and one of them, Wang T'ung-Ho, asked Richard to outline a program. Richard's recommendations offer remarkable testimony to the typical westerner's faith in the universality of his own political ideals and the notion that there was nothing wrong with China that good upright westernness could not cure. There were to be two foreign advisers to the Emperor, a Cabinet of eight, of whom half were to be foreigners, reform of the currency system, building of railways and opening of factories, establishment of a Board of Education to introduce modern schools and colleges, a modern army and navy, and a press guided by foreign journalists'. In the last of these ideas Varg plainly misrepresents Richard, who did not speak of guidance but rather of the assistance of

experienced foreign journalists. Incidentally Varg is in error about two other points within the same account: Richard was not English and Liang Ch'i-cha'o had been Richard's secretary prior to 1894 and did not become Richard's secretary during the Reform Movement.

127. Soothill, op. cit., pp. 232-243. Cf. Leslie Marchant, op. cit., p. 17. Richard published at the CLS a series of works with such titles as *Reform* (in Chinese), *Social Evolution* (in Chinese), *The Right Principles of Universal Progress* (in Chinese), *Prospectus of a Society Aiding China to Fall in with the Right Principles of Social Progress* (in English), and *The World: its Fall and its Redemption.*

128. Soothill, op. cit., pp. 244-270.

129. *Report* of SDK, 1891, quoted in Soothill, op. cit., p. 174.

130. See *Forty Five Years*, pp. 218ff. for his reminiscences of working with the CLS and *Conversion by the Million, passim.*

131. Cf. 'I asked the Revd J. Lambert Rees, BSc, of the London Mission to translate Lessing's remarkable essay on "The Education of the Human Race" and I left him my Chinese writer, Mr Ts'ai. one of the best in China to assist him'. Richard neither tells us why he thought it remarkable, nor indicates what made it important to have it in Chinese. He was extremely contented with the outcome. He had it printed as one of the CLS publications and 'sent a copy to Viceroy Chang Chi-tung'. The Viceroy was 'so pleased that he sent another donation of a thousand taels for the Society asking that a history of the whole world should be brought out'. Richard promptly arranged for Rees to be set aside to write an original work in Chinese in ancient and modern history of the world which was duly published in three volumes in 1910. Richard records 'Chang Chi-tung was delighted... evidently his intense prejudice against Christianity was passing away, *Forty-Five Years*, p. 228.

132. *Conversion*, pp. 108-9. Richard argued in these volumes that Christian literature was the weakest link in the church's chain in China. It was the cheapest agent as it was the most far reaching, but missionaries were so occupied with local affairs, and missionary secretaries with administration, that the national was subordinated to the individual. Dealing with individuals, important as that was, would never achieve the 'christianizing of China, or India, or the world'. Conversion by the million was what the Kingdom of God required.

133. Ibid.

134. Richard's translations of *The Awakening of Faith* and the *Essence of the Lotus Scripture* were published in Britain as *The New Testament of Higher Buddhism* (cited as *Higher Buddhism*). In addition, Richard also published a long, complicated translation of a work which he entitled *A Mission to Heaven. Being a Chinese Epic and Allegory, by Ch'iu Ch'ang Ch'un AD 1208-1288*, in 1913, and *An Epistle to All Buddhists*, in 1916. Soothill, writing as Professor of Chinese in Oxford University, noted, 'looked on as mere translation, Richard's version of *The Awakening of Faith* is open to criticism. Looked on as expressing the Mahayana's mind, it has a value of its own. I cannot endorse his interpretation in detail, but there are many Chinese and Japanese Buddhists who would agree with his point of view', op. cit., p. 317.

135. 'Higher Buddhism' translates a Chinese term for Mahayana Buddhism and was not used in imitation of T.E. Slater. Cf. Richard: 'The Old Buddhism was atheistic, the New is theistic; the Old Buddhism trusted in salvation by one's own efforts (Karma); the New trusted in the help of God as well; the Old Buddhism believed in

retirement from this evil world, the New believed in living in the world and saving others as the highest virtue; the Old Buddhism believed in countless transmigrations before the many could be delivered; the New believed in passing into Paradise at once without any rounds of transmigration,' *Higher Buddhism*, p. 48.

136. The Lotus Scripture belonged to the Tendai or Tien Tai school and the Awakening of Faith, in Chinese *Qi Xin Lun* to the Pure Land school, see Covell, op. cit., p. 125-8. Covell briefly comments that 'Richard's vision was too radical to be implemented in any practical sense' though it did help to motivate K.L. Reichelt, see ibid., p. 128.

137. Avalokitesvara is also known as Padmapani, 'the Lord who has seen', and functions in various ways within Mahayana Buddhism.

138. In 1907 Richard discovered the very similar view of the *Saddharma Pundarika* adopted by Arthur Lloyd, see note 375 on p. 358. Richard visited Lloyd him in Japan in 1908, *Forty Five Years*, pp. 335-8. Through Lloyd, Richard met Mrs E.A. Gordon, who annotated his translation in *The New Testament of Higher Buddhism*, and visited the Buddhist college in Koyasan, where he lectured to the faculty and students of the Buddhist college and had discussions also with the Abbot. Because of this meeting a monk from that community, named Iwashashi, came to Shanghai and stayed two months with Richard. Richard's views of Buddhism were based upon wider experience than that of Chinese Buddhism only. For Lloyd, see pp. 151-61.

139. See above, p. 123.

140. *Forty Five Years*, p. 334.

141. Ibid., p. 335.

142. But note Soothill's judgment on his work: 'Richard made no pretence to understand Sanskrit or Pali, but he was able to enter the mind of Chinese interpreters of the religion. In this respect he is the advocate, if not the discoverer of a new mode of regarding Mahayanism, and of a new interpretation which in principle is more faithful to the form of Buddhism to be found in China than the old methods of dependence upon Sanskrit or Pali records', op. cit., p.317

143. *Higher Buddhism*, p. 4.

144. Ibid., p. 6.

145. Ibid., p. 7.

146. Ibid., p. 9.

147. Ibid., p. 33.

148. Ibid., p. 34.

149. Ibid., p. 36.

150. Ibid., p. 131

151. Ibid.

152. Ibid., p. 133, emphasis his. Cf. 'In view of the fuller knowledge of God's Providence and inspiration of the East which we now possess, Christian theology needs revising to make the Gospel universally acceptable, and the out of date and out of place creeds should be dropped just as the NT dropped the sacrifices of the OT and just as modern science dropped its ancient science of astrology and geomancy. We simply recognize that God spoke at sundry times and in divers manners. We lose nothing, but gain immensely by following the latest revelations of God to man,' *Edin.Response*, 92, p. 16.

153. *Higher Buddhism*, pp. 134-5. Cf. 'True Christianity alone, not the Greek form, not the Roman form, nor the Protestant form, can win the head and heart and conscience of all religions and races and tongues, and make them willing to unite in one Universal Kingdom of God, so as to include the best from all to shine forth in a greater glory of religion than was ever known before', *Edin.Response*, 92, p. 9.

154. *Higher Buddhism*, p. 135.

155. Ibid.

156. Cf. Soothill, op. cit., pp. 33-2.

157. *Conversion*, p. 99.

158. Ibid., pp. 99. In *Forty Five Years* Richard recorded examples of their 'enlightened views', p. 357, their 'charity to the poor', p. 358, and their 'spiritual devotion', p. 361.

159. *Forty Five Years*, p. 323. Soothill writes of both Richard and Jones: 'Such a fine conception was possible only to men of great soul and equal faith. The ordinary Christian is afraid that co-operation with other religions will endanger his own, and always has one hand out to support the Ark of the Covenant... he hardly realises that it is impossible for it to fall over', Soothill p. 283. E.W. Price Evans thought a defensive word on behalf of Richard had to be spoken in 1945: 'It was a daring thing to do but it was done not out of feebleness but out of firmness of religious conviction see *Timothy Richard* (1945), p. 140. Soothill was conscious of another charge laid against Richard: 'there are some who assume from the broadminded attitude that Richard was nebulous in his religious ideas. Such was far from being the case'. Soothill instances a sharp interchange with Mrs Besant in New York in 1897. In a letter to his wife, Richard wrote: 'I told her that we were missionaries in the chief land of the Buddhists as they did not remove the causes of suffering in China. These causes were poverty, imperfect social conditions... ignorance and devilry... I wanted to indicate to her that there is a better way than Theosophy (which is Buddhism) and that way lay in the right understanding of the Kingdom of Heaven,' op. cit., p. 313.

160. Soothill, op. cit., p. 284.

161. Ibid., pp. 283-4.

162. Soothill, op. cit., p. 307, cf. *Forty Five Years*, p. 354. Gilbert Reid was an American Presbyterian missionary working among the Chinese literati.

163. Soothill, ibid.

164. *Forty Five Years*, p. 355.

165. Soothill, op. cit., p. 308.

166. *Forty Five Years*, p. 355.

167. Ibid.

168. Ibid.

169. *Edin.Response*, 92, p. 9. Richard sent the two volumes of *Conversion by the Million* with his response to Edinburgh.

170. Ibid. p. 13. Cf. 'Ancient and medieval views of astrology have given way to superior knowledge of modern times which we call science. But ancient and medieval views of inspiration and revelation have not given way to superior knowledge of religion,' ibid., p.4.

171. Ibid., p. 13.

172. Ibid., p. 3, cf. *The Missionary Message*, p. 44.

173. Ibid., p. 13.

174. Ibid., p. 13-4

175. Ibid., p. 9.

176. Ibid. p. 16-7.

177. Soothill, op. cit., p. 326.

178. Cf. Gerald H. Anderson, art. 'Robert Allen Hume' in the forthcoming *Biographical Dictionary of the Christian Mission*. See also Hume's *Edinburgh Response*, 180, p. 1.

179. *Hume, Missions from the Modern View*, p. 7. (Hereafter cited as *Missions*.)

180. Ibid.

181. Henry Churchill King, the President of Oberlin College wrote the preface to *An Interpretation of India's Religious History*, pp.5-7. (Cited as *Interpretation*.) King was a leading liberal theologian of the period, see W.R.Hutchison, *The Modernist Impulse in American Protestantism* (1976), pp. 152ff.

182. See Anderson, art. cit.

183. Narayan Vaman Tilak (1869-1919) was extremely well-known in the first two decades of the twentieth century as a writer, lecturer and writer of Christian hymns. Most of the lyrics in the Maratha hymn book are his. See his autobiographical writings, *I Follow After* (ET, 1950) and *From Brahma to Christ* (1956). Tilak was the mentor and friend of another Edinburgh respondent, Nicol Macnicol. Hume has an account of Narayan Vaman Tilak's conversion on pp. 6-7 of his *Edinburgh Response*. By 1910 Tilak was a teacher in the Ahmednagar Theological Seminary. In describing the obstacles that had first prevented this gifted Brahman scholar from becoming a Christian, Hume describes first of all Tilak's search for an universal religion which would unite his beloved India: 'The conviction that Christ alone can elevate and unify the life of his countrymen was the supreme motive in his becoming a disciple of Christ'. To men such as Tilak few things awoke such opposition to Christianity, Hume declared, 'as the preaching of the so-called "good news"', which left the impression that God had a different feeling for ' Christians and non-Christians'. The latter, unable to confess Jesus Christ as the only Saviour, are lost, and this 'fate applies to the myriads who have never heard of and will never hear of God', ibid., p. 11.

184. See e.g. his *Edin. Response*, 180, p. 1. Having been born in India, with Marathi as a second mother tongue helped.

185. For R.E. Hume, see note 432 on p. 336.

186. *Missions*, p. 5.

187. Ibid., p. 2.

188. Ibid., p. 3.

189. Cf. 'When the Lord Jesus says, "I am the way, the truth, and the life; no man cometh unto the Father but by Me", He means that He is and shows the way of God *to* men, even before He is, and shows, men's way to God. And by revealing God as the Father He teaches that God is ready not only for the future to do His utmost for every human child, but also that in the past He has done His workable best for all men,' *Interpretation*, p. 22, emphasis his.

190. *Missions*, p. 31.

191. Ibid. pp. 17-18.

192. *Interpretation*, p. 17.

193. Ibid. p. 24. The echo of Horace Bushnell here is clear, see above, p. 24, and cf. 'Where the Christ has revealed God's real attitude toward His human children, men have begun to understand that the fundamental relation between God and His children is one in which He... is suffering because His children are ignorant of and estranged from Him', and 'And nowadays I suppose the understanding to be very common that the suffering of Christ expresses God's eternal sorrow for sin, and the profound truth that He must always suffer, when for any reason His human children fail to live up to right relations with Himself, and that the sufferings of Christ as expressing the sorrow of God are the way by which sinners are brought into reconciliation with their Heavenly Father, because through the sufferings of Christ as a revelation of God's suffering there awakens in the sinner's heart a sense of his own wrongdoing, and a repentance and a desire to sin no more,' *Missions*, pp. 164-5.

194. *Interpretation*, p. 25. and p. 207

195. Hume had been involved in the so-called Andover Controversy during his first furlough at home in the USA, 1885-87, for which, see Hutchison, op. cit., pp. 77ff.

196. *Interpretation*, p.25

197. Ibid.

198. *Missions*, p. 199.

199. Ibid., pp. 199-200.

200. Ibid., p. 200, cf. Wilfred Cantwell Smith, *Towards a World Theology* (1981), p. 171: 'If it had turned out that God does not care about other men and women, or was stumped and had thought up no way to save them, then that would have proven our Christian understanding of God to have been wrong. For a century or so recently, much of the Church seemed to take this line; and a good many members decided that the Christian teaching must be wrong, and left.'

201. *Missions*, p. 50.

202. Ibid., p. 51.

203. Ibid.

204. *Interpretation*, pp. 53-4.

205. Ibid., p. 56.

206. Ibid., p. 60.

207. Ibid., pp. 70-1.

208. Ibid., p. 81.

209. Ibid., p. 94.

210. Ibid., pp. 76-7, cf. p. 84.

211. Robert Hume told the Commissioners that he thought the missionary ought '*to seek not to conquer* that religion, *but by leavening* the thought and the life of the people with the truth and power of Christ', *Edin.Response*, 180, p.8, emphasis his. This Hume saw as being 'in accordance with Christ's attitude to the older dispensation, to fulfil, i.e. to fill fuller, the best phases of what the people now accept' (ibid., p.8). These "phases" were (1) Belief in the superiority of the invisible and spiritual over the material, (the widespread doctrine of illusion denies the reality of the visible); (2) That man is ignorant, and weak, and tempted, and in a sense sinful; (3) That his greatest need and blessing is a vision of the divine ONE; (4) That to help men the divine One assumes incarnations, (5) That liberation from the imperfect and from sin is obtainable, etc. Hume commented: 'While these doctrines are associated with vari-

ous defects and errors, they are a preparation for the fuller, simpler truths of Christianity, and for Jesus Christ as Saviour', ibid., p. 9.

212. *Interpretation*, pp.83-4.

213. *Missions*, p.84.

214. *Interpretation*, p.28. Cf. Hume's reflection on his experience with missionaries of 'narrower persuasions'. He pictured their state of mind using the parable of the wheat and tares: 'to Christ's disciples the mystery lay not in the growth of the wheat, but of the tares. In the history of non-Christian religions, to many Christians, the mystery has been in the growth of the wheat, not of the tares, which were easily supposed to be all, or nearly all, the crop in those religions, and which were considered due to the evil one'. Hume suggested that the unmistakable evidence of 'wheat' growing in the field of non-Christian faiths' had given some Christians have a genuine problem as to whom the 'wheat is to be credited'. They had not 'not been accustomed to look for wheat in the non-Christian religions' and when it is found they can 'hardly credit it to God', ibid. Cf. Hume's use of the parable of the wheat and the tares with that of Arthur Lloyd, see pp. 155ff.

215. *Interpretation*, p.25.

216. Ibid., p.17.

217. *Missions*, p.13.

218. *Interpretation*, p.24.

219. *Missions*, p.53.

220. *Interpretation*, p. 5.

221. Ibid., p.166.

222. Ibid., p.168.

223. Ibid., p.177.

224. Ibid.

225. *Missions*, p.50.

226. Ibid., p. 85.

227. *Interpretation*, p.147.

228. Cf. 'The spiritual interpreter of the past must see and confess that many another religious leader in many lands has been the unconscious, but anointed, instrument of God to help the world sooner or later to the one Christlike God, the Father of the spirits of all men', *Interpretation*, p.22.

229. Ibid., p.190.

230. Ibid., p. 26.

231. Ibid., p. 27.

232. *Interpretation*, p.186.

233. Cf. 'But on our assumption that the living God has always been seeking His Indian children, and that they have ever been groping after Him, we may be sure that for the majority of Indians this cold, pantheistic abstraction was not the essence of religious thought and life', ibid., p.48.

234. Ibid., p.49.

235. Ibid., p.88. Hume added the qualification 'even though the alleged incarnations of Vishnu are inadequate and even grotesque specimens of what would seem worthy incarnations of the divine', ibid.

236. Ibid., p.207.

237. Ibid., p. 14.

238. Ibid., p. 192

239. *Missions*, p. 241

240. Ibid.

241. See pp. 161–67.

242. *Missions*, pp. 88ff.

243. *Interpretation*, pp. 218–9.

244. Ibid., p. 195.

245. Ibid., p. 197.

246. Ibid., p. 201.

247. Ibid., p. 202.

248. Cf. Farquhar, pp. 169ff.

249. *Interpretation*, p.52.

250. Ibid., p. 206.

251. Ibid., p. 109.

252. Ibid., pp. 214–5.

253. *Missions*, p. 215. The question of the 'essence' of Christianity was very important at this period, see the title of William Adams Brown's very influential book, *The Essence of Christianity* (1902).

254. *Missions*, p. 215.

255. Ibid., p. 214.

256. Ibid., p. 212.

257. Ibid.

258. *Interpretation*, p. 210. Hume took a less superficial view than some of the significance of caste, and pleaded that though it was 'not uncommon to consider the caste system as wholly a device of the devil, it can be shown that, in this institution too, can be seen the hand of God. Few institutions which have very wide acceptance and long life in a large community are wholly bad', ibid., pp.134–5. Hume saw the familiar pattern of progress and decay in the caste system, but nevertheless expressed a conviction that transformation, or fulfilment could take place even with caste. He wrote that 'when the Spirit of Christ transforms the institution, its better elements will be not destroyed, but fulfilled. In social institutions, as well as in religious thought and practice, the Christ lives not to destroy, but to fulfil', ibid., p. 135.

259. *Interpretation*, p. 211.

260. Cf. 'But there is no proper distinction between true and false religions. A more proper term would be less perfect and more perfect religions. Every religion has something of truth in it, because it recognizes the existence of God, the fact of His relation to men, and of His activity toward them, and the importance of men's relations to God being made right. Yet every religion is still imperfect. According to the definition of religion just given, even the Christian religion has not yet attained to full-orbed apprehension of all spiritual things in their right proportions,' *Missions*, p.13. Equally, 'Paul did not think of some religions as false and of one as true. He thought of God as trying to enlighten all men, and of all men as straining to see God, but of most men as having a veil over their spiritual vision which prevents them from adequately seeing God,' *Interpretation*, p.189.

261. Cf. 'Moreover, from my own missionary experience I can assure you that whereas a statement by a Christian missionary that the Christian religion is absolutely the best religion in the world, strikes the cultivated non-Christian as offensive and as

claiming too much, presenting that same religion as better than those which have been followed by non-Christians hitherto receives a more ready and respectful acceptance than any other way of teaching the helpfulness of the Lord Jesus Christ,' *Missions*, pp. 40-41.

262. *Missions*, p. 198.

263. Ibid., p. 192.

264. *Interpretation*, p. 21.

265. *Edin.Response*, 180, p. 15.

266. Ibid. Hume thought that the earlier strains of his missionary career had disappeared, and he now worked with a 'certain contentment', 'because now I better realize that the Holy Spirit is preparing them then to receive, and me then to give, His message, and that He will do what He can in the following-up of that message', ibid., p.16.

267. Ibid.

268. See pp. 219ff.

269. *India's Problem: Krishna or Christ*, (1903), cited as *India's Problem*; *India: Its Life and Thought* (1908), cited as *India*; *The Modern Missionary Challenge: A Study of the Present Day World Missionary Enterprise, Its Problems and Results* (1910), cited as *Challenge*. Jones' two most significant articles are 'Hindu Religious Ideas as they Affect the Progress of Christianity in India', *The East and the West*, Vol. II, (1904), pp. 164-175, cited as 'Hindu Religious Ideals', and 'The Modern Missionary Outlook', in *The Harvard Theological Review*, January 1915, cited as 'Outlook'. How acceptable Jones' change of views was to his contemporaries may be judged by the fact that he was appointed as Professor in the Kennedy School of Missions, Hartford, Connecticut, in 1914.

270. *India's Problem*, p.216. Cf. 'We no longer believe as our fathers did that all faiths which did not find their origin in our sacred Scriptures are the offspring of the evil one and are his mighty agencies in debasing untold millions and in consigning a moiety of our race to eternal perdition,' *Challenge*, p.54.

271. *India's Problem*, p.216. For the wider American audience Jones was even more clear about this change: there. he said, was a vast gap between 'the Carey of a generation ago and his great-grandson who is a missionary in North India today. In devotion and zeal for the Master, they are all one; but in their conception of Christianity, of Hinduism, and of the missionary motive, they are much wider apart than many imagine,' *India*, pp. 422-3.

272. Cf. *India's Problem*, p.71

273. p.216. Cf. He 'who is to become a missionary in India' must study Sanskrit...' too much emphasis cannot be placed on this science [the Comparative Study of Religion] as an aid to the modern missionary,' *India's Problem*, p.209. In 1910 Jones wrote that 'We live under the growing light and effulgence of this modern science which compares intelligently, and classifies wisely, the faiths of the world. It not only analyzes and classifies the many ethnic and non- Christian religions; it also dignifies them by ascribing to them a message and a mission in the religious progress of our race...It shows everyone of those religions to be in possession of teachings worthy to be conserved and utilized, as well as of others which should be discarded and overthrown,' *Challenge*, pp. 54-5.

274. *India's Problem*, pp.216-7.

275. See his article 'Hindu Religious Ideas as they Affect the Progress of Christianity in India', in *The East and the West*, Vol. 2 (1904), pp. 164-175.

276. *India's Problem*, p.54.

277. Ibid., p.58.

278. *India*, p.338. His chapter on 'Christ and Buddhism' is excellent and makes up some of the deficiencies in the treatment of Buddhism in *The Missionary Message* (1910), see p. 198.

279. *India*, p.341. Jones cited the words of the French Indologist A. Barth: 'The religion of India has not only given birth to Buddhism and produced, to its own credit, a code of precepts which is not inferior to any other but in the poetry which they have inspired there is at times a delicacy and bloom of moral sentiment which the western world has never seen outside of Christianity,' *The Religion of India*, p. 288, in *India's Problem*, p. 76.

280. *India's Problem*, p. 71.

281. Ibid.

282. Ibid.

283. Ibid.

284. Ibid.

285. Ibid.

286. Ibid.

287. Ibid. But in his article 'Hindu Religious Ideals' two years later Jones was rather more insistent on the differences between Hinduism and Christianity and this raises a doubt about his full commitment to 'points of contact'. Cf. his quotation of the earlier Indian missionary, John Robson: 'While no religion has done more to overthrow other religions than Christianity, no religious teacher has said less against other religions than Christ. We have from him only one short saying condemning the Gentiles' aim in life, but not even one reflecting on the gods they believed in, or the worship they paid them. Was not this because he came not to destroy but to fulfil', *Hinduism and Christianity* (1893) quoted in *India's Problem*, p.72.

288. Ibid., pp.72-3.

289. Ibid., p. 73.

290. Ibid., pp. 73-4.

291. Ibid., pp. 74-5

292. Ibid., p.75.

293. Ibid., p.76.

294. Ibid.

295. Ibid. Jones quoted Monier Williams at this point, suggesting that Vaishnavism was the only Hindu system which was 'worthy of being called a religion'.

296. Ibid.

297. Ibid., p.77. Jones wrote 'I believe, with not a few illustrious scholars, that this doctrine traces its origin to Christianity.' For the contrary point of view see Robert A. Hume, p.136.

298. Ibid.

299. Jones wrote very ably of Indian philosophy and theology, and the section on pp.80-113 would still stand up as an excellent brief introduction to the 'comparatives' of Christianity and Hinduism.

300. Ibid., p.112.

301. Ibid.

302. Ibid., p.109.

303. Ibid., p.108. In his answer to question 6 of the Edinburgh questionnaire, Jones spoke of 'these days of sympathy and appreciation', affirming the concept of 'points of contact', *Edin.Response*, 184, p.12 where he referred the commissioners to *India's Problem*. In 1909 he was still emphasizing the points made in this earlier work: Hinduism was a 'spiritual religion', with its doctrine of faith (*Bhakti*) ('salvation by faith in Hinduism is kindred to that in Christianity', *Edin.Response*, 184, p.13); its doctrine of *Karma* ('Justice is the very essence of Karma. At this point Hinduism and Christianity are fundamentally one, though the divergence in the interpretation in this doctrine is equally basal', ibid., p.14); its eschatological teaching which Jones stated had 'deep kinship' with Christian doctrine: 'there is no faith upon earth that teaches the doctrine of the immortality of the soul with so much of sincerity and power as the Hindu faith', ibid.

304. *India's Problem*, p.108. We note here the twinning of the concepts of fulfilment in 'and broken lights'. These were to become central images for the World Missionary Conference.

305. Ibid., p.130.

306. Ibid., p.137.

307. Ibid.

308. Ibid.

309. Ibid.

310. Ibid., p.139: the full sentence reads: 'We have been strong and continue strong in that aspect of our faith which we associate with the words 'assertion' and 'attack'.

311. Ibid., and see also his 1904 article 'Hindu Religious Ideals': '...I am inclined to believe that we of the West have few things of greater importance and of deeper religious significance to learn from the East than the appreciation of such graces of life as patience and endurance under evil,' p.171, and again 'For let it not be forgotten that the Hindu regards what we call our foibles of petulance, arrogance and intolerance, with the same disapprobation and disgust as we do their more frequent violation of the seventh, eighth and ninth commands of the Decalogue. And who is to decide as to which catalogue is the worse and the more heinous in the sight of God', ibid.

312. *India's Problem*, p.141.

313. Ibid.

314. Ibid., p.140.

315. Ibid., p.141. Cf. Charles Hodge's view of pantheism set out in his *Systematic Theology*, above p.26, and note 167 on p.304. To the Edinburgh Commissioners Jones wrote 'Hinduism has doubtless many good points. The Christian preacher should be as familiar with its good points as he is with its bad ones. He should be able to disentangle the good from the evil. He should be competent to take a doctrine which is evil and to discover in it those elements of good which has given it perpetuity through these many centuries. Even pantheism, though it has wrought more evil for India perhaps than any other of her doctrines, is only an over-emphasis upon the immanence of God. It has within it, despite all the error which has characterized it, an element of truth which must be conserved and emphasized by the Christian teacher,' *Edin.Response*, 184, pp.10-1.

316. *India's Problem*, p.141.

317. Ibid.

318. Ibid., p.142.

319. Ibid.

320. 'Hindu Religious Ideals', p. 175.

321. *India's Problem*, p. 142.

322. *India*, ch.XIV, pp. 412-443.

323. Ibid., p.444.

324. *India's Problem*, p.142.

325. Jones owed the distinction which he made in *India's Problem*, p.356, between 'substantival' and 'Adjectival' Christianity to Kali Charran Bannerjee, see *Challenge*, pp.861ff.

326. *India*, p.425. In *India's Problem*, Jones quotes from *The Higher Hinduism in Relation to Christianity*, p.291: 'The West has to learn from the East and the East from the West. The questions raised by the Vedanta will have to pass into Christianity if the best minds of India are to embrace it; the Church of the "farthest East" will doubtless contribute something to the thought of Christendom of the science of the soul, and of the omni-penetrativeness and immanence of the Deity', p.357. Slater's book had been published only after Jones' MS had been completed.

327. *India's Problem*, pp.356-7. Cf. 'The religious forms of life and thought which we of the West have inherited and in whose environment we have grown up, we have come to identify with the *essence* of our religion; and it seems all but impossible for us to think of a Christianity apart from these outward forms. I believe there is to be a rude awakening for our children if not for ourselves in this matter,' *India*, p.425.

328. *Edin.Response*, 184, p.11.

329. *Edin.Response*, 184, pp.11-2.

330. is not mentioned by either the most recent authorities, like Richard H. Drummond, *A History of Christianity in Japan* (1971), or by earlier writers like Charles W.Iglehart, *A Century of Protestant Christianity in Japan* (1959), but see Notto Thelle's appreciative comments in *Buddhism and Christianity in Japan: From Conflict to Dialogue 1854-1899* (1989), pp. 256-7, even though Lloyd mainly falls outside his period.

331. The two books of lasting missiological interest are *The Wheat among the Tares: Studies of Buddhism in Japan* (1908), hereafter cited as *Wheat*, and *The Creed of Half Japan: Sketches of Japanese Buddhism* (1912), hereafter cited as *Creed*.

332. Cf. the Japanese scholar of religion, Masaharu Anesaki, a professor at Tokyo University who refers to Honen, *Catechism in Twelve Articles*, and writes, 'The translations are from Arthur Lloyd's pen. Though the translator has lost somewhat the simple purity of the original, the author keeps his wording here in memory of his lamented friend', *History of Japanese Religion* (1930). *The Creed of Half Japan* was recommended for reading by the Buddhist Society of London as late as 1956; see *Buddhist Students' Manual* (1956), p.267.

333. *Every-day Japan: Written after Twenty-five years' Residence and Work in the Country* was published simultaneously in Britain and America in 1909. It had a second 'popular' edition in 1911. In his introduction Count Tadasu Hayashi, Japanese Ambassador in London, called the book 'one of the most useful contributions we have had to our stock of information', p.xvi.

334. This was *The Gold Demon* by Koyo Ozaki, 'Rewritten in English', by Arthur and Mary Lloyd, and published in Tokyo by Seibundo in 1906.

335. See *inter alia*, 'Gnosticism in Japan', in *The East and the West*, vol.8, 1910, pp.160-174, and 'The Prince of Parthia', in *The East and the West*, vol.9, 1911, pp.293-301.

336. *The Praises of Amida; Seven Buddhist Sermons Translated from the Japanese of Tada Kanai*, were published by The Kyobunkwan, in Tokyo 1907: Notto Telle also lists two earlier works published in Tokyo to which I have not had access: *The Higher Buddhism in the Light of the Nicene Creed* (1893) and *Buddhist Meditations from the Japanese: with an Introductory Chapter on Modern Japanese Buddhism* (1905).

337. See note 138 on p.346.

338. Charles Robinson, an Edinburgh commissioner as well as editor of *The East and the West* and author of *A History of Christian Missions* (1915) recognized the importance of Lloyd's work. There are two brief expositions of Lloyd's theories in his *History*, pp.161ff, and 219ff.

339. See the records of the Pan-Anglican Congress, vols IV and V.

340. One exception to this judgment is Hakan Eillert's thesis *Boundlessness: Studies in Karl Ludvig Reichelt's Missionary Thinking with Special Regard to the Buddhist-Christian Encounter* published as 'Studia Missionalia Upsaliensis XXIV' (1974), pp. 30-33.

341. *Classified Digest of the S.P.G. Records 1701-1872,*(1873) pp.720-1, 922; H.P. Thompson, *Into All Lands* (1951), p.455.

342. Lloyd had been asked to reply to the questionnaire by the Bishop of Tokyo, *Edin.Response*, 28a, p.1.

343. *Wheat*, p.34.

344. *Edin.Response*, 28a, p.1.

345. Drummond, op. cit., pp.144ff.

346. Ibid., pp.168-9. Cf. C.H. Robinson, 'A special characteristic of the work done by Christian missionaries in Japan up to about 1888 was the successful appeal to men of culture and education', op. cit., p.228.

347. Thompson, op. cit., p.455.

348. *Edin.Response*, 28a, p.1.

349. *The Missionary Message* (1910), pp.118-19.

350. Cf. *Edin.Response*, 28a, p.1.

351. For Andrews, see p.178.

352. *Edin.Response*, 28a, p.91.

353. 'My book is not what I intended it to be. I had a much larger work, embodying the result of many years of study, actually in the press a few weeks ago, when an unfortunate fire in the printing office in Yokohama destroyed it all, and left me with only a few ashes,' *Wheat*, p.v.

354. Ibid.

355. Ibid.

356. Drummond, op. cit., p.213, and on the anti-intellectualism which could be aroused by revivalism, see above, pp.27-31.

357. *A Century of Protestant Christianity in Japan*, pp.112-4, cited in Drummond, op. cit., p.213.

358. *Wheat*, p.12.

359. Ibid., p.15.

360. A review by Nelson Bitton of *The Wheat and the Tares* in the *Chinese Recorder* for April 1909 pleaded that it was not 'fair to dismiss a book like this with the statement that the author is non-Christian since he is attempting to dethrone Christ by bringing him to the level of Sakyamuni or exalting Sakyamuni to the unique position of the historic Christ. It is neither a true nor a worthy criticism.' But clearly such views were to be found among Lloyd's contemporaries.

361. *Wheat*, p.15.

362. Ibid., p.16.

363. Ibid.

364. Ibid.

365. See above, p.157.

366. For an account of the attempts to give the new study a neutral ideology which would have been available to Lloyd see Louis Henry Jordan, *Comparative Religion: Its Genesis and Growth* (1905), *passim*.

367. *Wheat*, p.17.

368. Ibid.

369. Ibid.

370. Ibid.

371. Ibid., p.18.

372. Ibid., p.14. The *Sukhavati* is the 'Pure Land' or 'Western Paradise' of the Jodo and Shinshu sects. Its glories are described in the two *Sukhavati Vyuha Sutras* in the *SBE*, vol.49. The *Saddharma Pundarika* was written in India probably in the second century CE, and is translated as *The Lotus of the True Law*, in the *SBE*, vol.21, by H. Kern in 1884, and from the Chinese text as the *Lotus of the Wonderful Law* by W.E. Soothill in 1930. Cf. Richard's views of this material above, p.127-28.

373. *Edin.Response*, 28a, p.10. Lloyd knew of five sects of Amida-Buddha devotees in his own day, one a sub-sect of Tendai, *Wheat*, pp. 56-7. The two largest were the Jodo, founded by Genku or Honen Shonin (1133-1211) in 1190, and the Shinshu, founded by Shinran (1173) in 1224. 'These have appealed to Buddhist history and tradition, have boldly claimed to represent the true teaching of Sakyamuni in his later years, and have gathered three-quarters of Japanese Buddhists into their folds,' *Wheat*, p.16, pp. 57-8.

374. Ibid., p.5. In the *Wheat* Amida's vow was described by Lloyd like this: 'The Shinshu or Jodo sects select one special Being, Amitabha, the Buddha of Infinite Life and Light, whose home they place in the country to the West of India, in the "Western Paradise". Infinite ages ago this Amitabha was monk of the Name of Hozo. Hozo was filled with compassion for the miseries of his fellow-men, whose fruitless efforts after salvation were truly pitiable to see. He therefore set himself to obtain the Power requisite for so great an undertaking, and for a long series of lives accumulated merit until he reached the stage of a Boddhisattva, who at his death would be entitled to pass into Nirvana. But here he stopped. He looked back upon the world, saw his fellow-creatures in their hopeless misery, thought of all the long and arduous way by which he had climbed, and made a vow that unless he could discover some simpler and easier way of salvation he would not accept the rest of Nirvana to which his own merits entitled him. In accordance with this vow he recommenced his austerities and penances and at last succeeded in founding a Paradise into which all might enter,

without labour or toil, who had faith to believe what Amitabha had done for them, and to call upon his Name. This is Amitabha's Western Paradise or Pure Land,' *Wheat*, p.70.

375. *Edin.Response*, 28a, p.10. Cf. 'I have spoken of Christianity and Mahayana as two parallel faiths, originating in the same fruitful sixth century before Christ, with the Hebrew prophets of the Captivity, with the Indian reformer in the valley of the Ganges. I have spoken of them again as each experiencing a new revival and expansion, at a period fraught with the greatest issues for the human race, the period when the Buddhist said that "the Buddha had appeared again in the lifetime of As'vaghosha", and the Christian turned to worship at the cradle in Bethlehem. I have shown Buddhism working its way through the Agnosticism of Sakyamuni, the Polytheism of the "Expansion", the Henotheism of the Amidist, to the Mandala, the *pleroma*, which comprises in itself all things divine. I have shown Christ, in Whom the whole *pleroma* of the Godhead dwells in human form. It is hard to resist the conclusion that the two – the Eternal Sakyamuni and the Eternal Christ – are meant to represent the same person, and that the last phase of the Mahayana received its developing impulse from the manifestation of Christ to the Gentiles,' *Wheat*, pp.9-10. We may however see a contradiction here, for if Lloyd's conclusions were to be correct as a historical reconstruction, then there would be a sufficient explanation for the resemblance of Mahayana Buddhism to Christianity without having to invoke a doctrine of 'God's universal revelation'.

376. *Edin.Response*, 28a, p.8. Cf. Lloyd's judgment in the *Creed*: 'To grasp the salvation wrought out for man by Amida... nothing is needed but faith – no works of the Law, no austerities, penances, or devotions, no resolutions of amendment, no futile strivings, nothing but Faith.' This he immediately went on to say was not an 'immoral doctrine', for 'faith brings salvation, the realization of salvation arouses the gratitude of the heart' and then begets good deeds 'through the new life imparted to the soul finds its expression', p. 268.

377. *Creed*, pp. 266-7. In the footnote on p.266 Lloyd refers for the information behind this judgment to two partners in his own interfaith work, Tada Kanae (Kanai), see note 339 above, and Dr Anesaki, see note 334 above.

378. *Edin.Response*, 38a, p.8.

379. *The Missionary Message* (1910), p.118.

380. *Wheat*, pp.10-1.

381. *Creed*, p.385. The very last page of the book has Lloyd's rendering of 1 Cor.13. 'Charity never faileth; but, whether there be prophecies, they shall fail; whether there be tongues they shall cease; whether there be knowledge, *gnosis, bodhi*, it shall vanish away', p.386.

382. Ibid., p.385.

383. *Edin.Response*, 28a, p.9.

384. Ibid.

385. Ibid.

386. Ibid.

387. *Wheat*, p.xii.

388. The texts Lloyd used can be found in the *SBE* edition of the *Saddharma Pundarika* (1884), p.17 and p.73.

389. *Wheat*, p.94.

390. Ibid., p. 95.

391. Ibid.

392. The quotation here is from C.F. d'Arcy, the Edinburgh Commissioner responsible for the Japanese section of *The Missionary Message* (1910), p.118. Lloyd is mentioned by name twice as many times as any other missionary in this section.

393. Thelle, op. cit., p.257.

394. This dictum was first used of T.E. Slater by E.J. Sharpe. As in the case of Slater the chief reason for Lucas's 'burying' is the supersession of its thought by J.N. Farquhar's *The Crown of Hinduism* (1913). But like Slater, Lucas worked long before Farquhar at 'crowning' and 'fulfilling' as basic images for the relationship between Hinduism and Christianity. Another reason may have been the triumphalism, as it has been perceived, of the title of the most important of the three books, *The Empire of Christ* (1908).

395. All three works were published by Macmillan, who were also the publishers of all the works of F.D. Maurice and B.F. Westcott. Lucas also wrote devotional works like *Conversations with Christ* (1905) and *The Fifth Gospel* (1907).

396. For some limited biographical information, J. Sibree, *London Missionary Society: A Register of Missionaries, Deputations, etc., from 1796 to 1923*. A somewhat ironic fact in view of Lucas' wrestlings with the concept of 'empire' was that he received the rare distinction for a missionary, of the Membership of the Order of the British Empire (MBE) for his services to India during the 1914-18 war.

397. *Our Task in India* (1914), p.16 (cited as *Task*). But Lucas did not feel his motivation had altered: 'It is of supreme importance that we should recognise that the missionary motive abides the same under the newer as under the older thought. That motive was found neither in the faith which crystallised in a creed, nor in the hope which narrowed itself into the effort to save the remnant of those who believed, but in the love of Christ which constrained...', *The Empire of Christ*, p.27 (cited as *Empire*).

398. For Slater's methods among English-speaking Hindus, see above, p.109.

399. M.M. Thomas, *The Acknowledged Christ of the Indian Renaissance* (1969). p.325, cf. Norman Goodall, *A History of the London Missionary Society 1895-1945* (1954), pp.66ff. Lucas drafted the Bangalore United Theological College Constitution, as well as its Memorandum and Articles of Association.

400. *Twenty Five Years of LMS Work* (1923), p.168. James sensed that Lucas would represent a problem for historians: 'Whether he is to rank with the most brilliant missionary names is yet to be seen, but that he will be the more honoured the more his work is understood I have no doubt,' ibid., p.167.

401. Ibid.

402. Ibid.

403. *Empire*, p.21

404. Ibid., p. 16.

405. Ibid., p. 17.

406. Ibid.

407. Ibid., p.15

408. Ibid.

409. Ibid.

410. Ibid., pp. 15-6.

411. Ibid., p. 18.

412. Ibid.

413. Ibid., p.16.

414. Ibid.

415. Ibid., p.20 When Lucas wrote to the Edinburgh Commissioners in 1909 he emphasized that missionary practice and missionary theology were intertwined. If Christian understanding assumed that other religions are the 'inventions of the devil', then only points of opposition would be found. In his own day, Lucas wrote that missionaries holding this view were in a decreasing minority. But he acknowledged that there were 'numbers of such minds still' and advised that 'they should be counselled to avoid all hostility, and, if they cannot sympathise with the religious ideas of the people, at least to refrain from criticising them and misrepresenting them'. If, on the other hand, the Christian missionary 'believes that religion, wherever found, is the evidence of the working of the Divine Spirit, then he will see on all sides the working of the one and the self-same spirit', *Edin.Response*, 126, pp.8–9. Lucas told the Commissioners that this was particularly true in 'obscure and unknown writings, found in all the vernaculars', which showed a prophetic rather than a priestly cast of mind. He believed that 'they invariably touch religious reality, and their ministry has been of incalculable benefit to the Hindu religious nature'. Lucas affirmed that 'in their writings the missionary finds abundant evidence of the Divine Spirit's working', ibid., p.11.

416. Ibid., p.33

417. Ibid., p. 6.

418. Ibid., p. 20.

419. Ibid., p. 21.

420. Writing of a 'ministry to religious need, rather than of combating of religious error', Lucas said latter belongs to 'proselytism', the former to 'the ministry which Evangelism regards as the supreme work of the missionary'. 'In the region of what is called Higher Hinduism, Professor Hogg's book *Karma and Redemption* with its intensely sympathetic treatment of Hindu religious thought and sentiment, is an excellent illustration of the method of Evangelism,' *Task*, p.88.

421. *Christ for India* (1910), p.vi. Richter's *A History of Missions in India* was cited for stressing that the 'intellectual struggle' rather than the 'increase of the number of mission stations' is the 'main thing in India'. Hall was quoted as asking 'Shall the Oriental Consciousness place its sublime qualities at the service of Jesus Christ, and become unto the twentieth century what she was unto the first, a Prophet of the Highest?', *Christ and the Eastern Soul* (1909), p.207.

422. *Empire*, p.4.

423. Ibid., p.85.

424. For Westcott's use of 'solidarity' see above, p.67. Lucas uses the term in *Christ for India*, where he defines humanity as 'not a mere aggregate of individuals but a body of innumerable members, with a life which circulates through all its parts', p.27.

425. Ibid., p.5.

426. Ibid., p.6. See ch.9 of *Christ for India* for Lucas's presentation of the concept of salvation for a Hindu readership.

427. Ibid., p.31.

428. Ibid.

429. Ibid., p.32. Note the conflation of two different texts: John 3.16 and John 10.10.

430. Ibid., p. 99.

431. Ibid. Bernard Lucas' Edinburgh response contained a statement about the new theology he had come to hold. He told the Commissioners of his conviction that 'the essence of the Christian Gospel is not dogma and theology, but a distinct and unique spirit. I must not be misunderstood in this matter by being supposed to mean that dogmatic theology is either unimportant or unconnected with this spirit. The missionary who has no definite theology will soon cease to be a missionary. Experience however has taught me that you can replace Hindu error by Christian truth, without thereby replacing the Hindu by the Christian spirit'. As a result he had come to put 'far more emphasis on the propagation of the Christian spirit.' 'We shall have', he concluded, 'to give our strength in the future to the propagation of the Christian spirit in the assurance that the spirit will construct its creed', *Edin.Response*, 126, pp. 14-5. Most of these words are quoted in *The Missionary Message* (1910), p. 208, where they are attributed to a 'missionary in South India'.

432. Ibid.

433. See *Christ for India*, pp. viii–ix.

434. *Empire*, pp. 71-2.

435. *Christ for India*, pp. 404.

436. Ibid.

437. Ibid., pp. 405-6.

438. Ibid., p. 406.

439. *Empire*, p. 37.

440. Ibid., p. 36.

441. Ibid., p. 20.

442. There is an extensive study of Farquhar by Eric J. Sharpe, *Not to Destroy But to Fulfil: The Contribution of J.N. Farquhar to Missionary Thought in India before 1914* (1965). More easily available is Sharpe's own summary of Farquhar in *Faith Meets Faith* (1977), pp. 19-3.

443. See such works as E.C. Dewick, *The Christian Attitude to Other Religions*, (1953), p. 49, Alan Race, *Christians and Religious Pluralism* (1983), pp. 57ff., Gavin D'Costa, *Theology and Religious Pluralism: The Challenge of Other Religions*, (1986), p. 7. All refer to *The Crown of Hinduism*, (1913) with the result that many more people have quoted the title than have read the book.

444. For the Evangelical Union see pp. 22, 73f.

445. Quoted in Sharpe, *Not to Destroy*, p. 116.

446. For Fairbairn in Aberdeen see above, p. 74 and note 251 on p. 324.

447. See above, p. 20.

448. See Sharpe, *Not to Destroy*, pp. 122ff.

449. There is a letter in the LMS archives in which Fairbairn commends Farquhar saying, *inter alia*, 'when Mansfield was founded he was one of our most constant friends'; see *Not to Destroy*, p. 127.

450. The YMCA of this period was evangelical and revivalist, having leaders like Robert P. Wilder and John R. Mott. These men thought 'strategically' about the need for Christian literature and the necessity of dealing with Asian intellectuals, cf. C. Howard Hopkins, *John R. Mott 1855-1965: A Biography* (1979). There are several

references in Hopkins' work to Farquhar, but see notably pp.264ff. where Hopkins writes, 'To Mott's delight, he accepted an offer to become educational or literature secretary for India, '"a great accession to our force". His book, *The Crown of Hinduism*, would be a major contribution to the dialogue with Hindus and a force in the changing attitude of Christians to other religions.'

451. *Gita and Gospel* (1903), *The Crown of Hinduism* (1913), *A Primer of Hinduism* (Indian edition 1911, second edition 1914), *Modern Religious Movements in India* (1915), *An Outline of the Religious Literature of India* (1920).

452. 'In India alone, important works produced by missionaries as a result of Farquhar's initiative included Nicol Macnicol, *Indian Theism* (1915) and *Psalms of Maratha Saints* (1920); Margaret Stevenson, *The Heart of Jainism* (1915) and *The Rites of the Twice Born* (1920); J.M. McPhail, *Asoka* (1917); H.A. Popley, *The Music of India* (1921) and H. Whitehead, *The Village Gods of India* (1916), Sharpe, *Comparative Religion: A History* (1975), p. 154.

453. Speech by the Diwan of Mysore, December 1907, archives of the YMCA Historical Library, quoted by Sharpe, *Not to Destroy*, p. 241.

454. 'The Greatness of Hinduism' was the title of this article in *The Contemporary Review*, in June 1910. It was followed by one called 'The Crown of Hinduism' in the following issue (July 1910).

455. Cf. his important speech to the Calcutta Missionary Conference in 1905 printed as 'The Missionary study of Hinduism' in *The Harvest Field*, Vol.xvi (1905), discussed in Sharpe, *Not to Destroy*, pp. 206ff.

456. Quoted from the *Inquirer*, Vol. V., p. 1 (September 1903) by Sharpe, *Not to Destroy*, pp. 189-90. Sharpe comments that this 'is essentially an evolutionist position'.

457. Ibid.

458. Ibid.

459. See above, p.33. The only crisis of faith that Sharpe has been able to trace in Farquhar was to probably to do with science and religion, see *Not to Destroy*, p. 119. Note also Fairbairn's formative influence in overcoming these doubts through suggesting that 'evolution was a highly significant hypothesis which would be of value in gaining a better understanding of the universe', ibid., p. 29.

460. *Contemporary Review*, XCVIII:12 (June 1910), p. 67.

461. Ibid., p. 68.

462. Ibid.

463. *The Crown of Hinduism* (1913), pp. 457-8. Dewick, Race and D'Costa, see note 443 above, all in their own ways misquote the passage.

464. *The Missionary Message* (1910), p. 181.

465. Eric Sharpe has a valuable discussion of 'fulfilment' theology in the last chapter of *Not to Destroy*, pp. 329-360. Among the possibilities canvassed there are the understanding that Hinduism is 'fulfilled' when it is replaced by Christianity in some form which has Sanskritic elements and aspects; or that the 'truths' in Hinduism are 'fulfilled' by appearing in a higher form in a Christian guise; or that Christ 'fulfils' the 'quests' of Hinduism by proving an answer to its questions, a resolution to its problems and a goal for its religious strivings. Sharpe concludes that there is is little real ambiguity in Farquhar's own use of the term, 'provided that we keep in mind its various facets, and particular the cardinal point that fulfilment invoved replacement

and took place in the active exercise of the human will in passing from one religion to another, in which the needs in expressed in the former could be fully satisfied,' ibid, p. 358.

466. *Edin. Response*, 154, p. 13.

467. Ibid.

468. Ibid.

469. Ibid.

470. Ibid., pp. 13-4.

471. Ibid., p. 16.

472. Ibid., p. 17.

473. Ibid., p. 19.

474. Ibid., p. 20.

475. Ibid., p. 23.

476. Ibid.

477. Ibid., p. 24.

478. Ibid., p. 32.

479. Ibid.

480. Ibid., p. 21.

481. Ibid, pp. 37-8.

482. 'Field Training for Missionaries' in *The East and the West*, Vol. 8, (1910), pp. 316-25.

483. Ibid., p. 319.

484. Ibid., pp. 319-20.

485. Ibid., p. 321.

486. There are several good biographies of Andrews. The two best are Benarsidas Chaturvedi and Marjorie Sykes, *Charles Freer Andrews: A Narrative* (1949), and Hugh Tinker, *Ordeal of Love: C.F. Andrews and India* (1979). But of the greatest value to the study of Andrews' life and work up to 1914 is Daniel O'Connor, *Gospel, Raj and Swaraj: The Missionary Years of C.F. Andrews 1904-1914* (1990), cited as *Gospel, Raj*. Andrews's best-seller, *What I Owe To Christ* (1932) is an unscientific autobiography, cited as *What I Owe*.

487. Chaturvedi and Sykes, op. cit., p. 37.

488. Andrews' first article in C.H. Robinson's new journal *The East and the West* appeared in October 1905 and was highly 'pro-Indian'. It dealt with 'The Effect of The Japanese Victories upon India', Vol. 2. (1905), pp. 361-372. A series of articles followed 'The Situation in the East', October 1907, 'Race within the Christian Church', July 1910, 'The Indian Missionary Ideal', January 1911, and 'The King's Announcement at Delhi', July 1912. In addition Andrews wrote copiously for the Indian press, see the full bibliography provided by O'Connor in *Gospel, Raj*, pp.314-319.

489. For the literature concerning Gandhi and Andrews, see *Gospel, Raj*, pp.244ff.

490. Chaturvedi and Sykes called C.F. Andrews ' the rebel devotee' and Hugh Tinker described him as a 'gentle, humble but ferocious seer activist', quoted in *Gospel, Raj*, p.2.

491. *The Missionary Message* (1910), pp.160-2, 4-5, 178, 189, 203, and 208-210. Louise Creighton quotes in her turn long passages from Andrews as used in *The Missionary Message* in her report in the *Church Quarterly Review*, Vol. LXXI, (Oct. 1910), p. 68.

492. and Sykes, op. cit., pp.3ff. 6., and *What I Owe*, p.35.

493. See notes 210, 213 and 222 on pp.322-23 for these connections.

494. As is often the case with such organizations as CICCU the enthusiasm was better than the doctrine. Andrews remembered that 'It was a great inner strength to me to share their ardour', and I attended their prayer meetings regularly', *What I Owe*, p.113.

495. Ibid.

496. Chaturvedi and Sykes, op. cit., p. 16. For a detailed account of the Cambridge intellectual milieu in which Andrews formed his earliest views of other religious traditions, see O'Connor, *Gospel, Raj*, p. 16; and for the particular influence of E.C. Browne, see Chaturvedi and Sykes, op. cit., p. 16.

497. Westcott's social theory also engaged Andrews, leading him to write a prize essay on 'The Relation of Christianity between Capital and Labour'. This was published in 1895. Andrews wrote there from direct experience of the Christian Social Union as well as from conversations during vacations with Bishop Westcott, see Chaturvedi and Sykes, op. cit., 17ff.

498. Ibid., p. 18, and cf. esp. Westcott's address, 'The Universities in Relation to Mission Work' in *The Religious Office of the Universities* (1873).

499. On Basil Westcott's death see above, p.68.

500. For Westcott's vision of an Alexandria on the Jumna see above, pp.ooff. For the Cambridge Mission to Delhi see *Gospel, Raj*, pp.6-14.

501. S.S. Allnutt, the first Head of the Cambridge Mission, had designed the College buildings in Moghul style in defiance of conservative missionary feeling, in order to symbolize appreciation of Indian tradition, life and thought, see Chaturvedi and Sykes, op. cit., p. 37. There is a fine description of the buildings in *The Story of the Delhi Mission* (1917), pp. 62ff. They were erected in 1890-91.

502. Cf. 'Many have wondered how I came to qualify to understand the people of India, and to be understood by them. The answer is quite simple and the secret is easily told. Such a close friend as Susil Rudra is very rarely given in this life to any man. He received me first for Basil's sake and then for my own. We became life-long companions,' *What I Owe*, p.159. Rudra's father Pyare Mohan Rudra, had been influenced into Christian faith by Alexander Duff in Calcutta. But, says Andrews, 'had remained a Hindu in outward things, while his inner life was more and more transformed by Christ. It was the attitude towards the great inheritance of Hindu religion which his son faithfully kept,' ibid. See also *Gospel, Raj*, p. 44.

503. The modernizing Islamic movement led by Sir Syed Amir Khan (1817- 98) had two great representatives in Delhi, Nazir Ahmad (c.1832-1912) and Zaka Ullah (1832-1910). For a fine sketch of their relationships with Andrews see O'Connor, *Gospel, Raj*, pp. 215ff.

504. Cf. 'He was a Sikh Sadar, the President of the Regency Council of Patiala, whom I learnt to revere for his goodness in a similar manner. Whenever I went to see him, we spoke together about the deep things of religion, not in any spirit of controversy, but as lovers of God', *What I Owe*, p. 164.

505. *Zaka Ullah of Delhi* (1929) p. 149.

506. Quoted in Chaturvedi and Sykes, op. cit., p. 40. and O'Connor, *Gospel, Raj*, p. 225.

507. See *Gospel, Raj*, p. 224.

508. *North India* (1908), p. 224.

509. Ibid., p. 223.

510. Ibid., p. 224.

511. Ibid.

512. Ibid., p. 225.

513. Ibid., p.226.

514. *The Renaissance in India: Its Missionary Aspect* (1912), p. 163, cited as *Renaissance*.

515. Ibid., p. 164.

516. Ibid., p. 252.

517. Cf. *North India*, pp. 226-7.

518. *Renaissance*, p. 25.

519. *Gospel, Raj*, pp. 213-263.

520. I hope to take up the story of Andrews' theological pilgrimage from 1914 to 1940 in a sequel to this present work.

521. C.H. Robinson of the SPG, see p.90.

522. *Edin.Response*, 123, pp.17-8. Andrews also repudiated the idea of a 'salvation history': 'not a single scheme or plan of salvation dominates my thoughts as in the past... but a redemption, a reconstruction, and consecration of all life, of society as well as the individual', ibid., p. 19.

523. 'I am more attracted today by Illingworth and Moberly than by Dale, more by S. Athanasius than S. Augustine', *Edin.Response*, 123, p. 18. Illingworth's books *Personality Human and Divine* and *Divine Immanence*, had been published in 1891 and 1898, and Moberley's *Atonement and Personality*, in 1901.

524. *Edin.Response*, 123, p. 21, cf. *The Missionary Message*, p. 210, and Louise Creighton, op. cit..

525. *Edin.Response*, 123, p. 18.

526. *Edin.Response*, 123, p. 21. Cf. 'I should not condemn any one who said he did not *wish* to define his belief in the Divinity of Christ, but who could from his heart say with the Apostle Thomas, "My Lord and my God", or with Simon Peter, "Lord, to whom else should we go, for Thou hast the words of eternal life". I should not condemn any one who could not hold as an article of faith the Virgin Birth, but who could make the above confession of Simon Peter and Thomas. I would not condemn a doubt as to the "objectivity" of the Resurrection of Christ, if the fact of the Living Christ were granted and His Living Presence were a daily experience,' ibid.

527. *Edin.Response*, No.123, pp. 11-2.

528. Ibid., p. 12.

529. Ibid.

530. Ibid., pp. 15-6. It followed that Andrews now laid 'stress on the ethical following of Christ and the practice of the Christ-life, as the supreme criterion', with its attendant demands for a new ethical shape to the community of Christ, with 'racial unity and brotherhood on terms of equality and freedom' as its hallmarks. 'And this root principle of Christianity now dominates my ideas of Human Society, past present and future,' ibid., pp. 21-2.

531. Ibid. p. 22.

532. On 'Andrewsism' see *Gospel, Raj*, pp.256ff. O'Connor reports the visit of Nathaniel Micklem to India on behalf of the SCM, who was struck by the 'unspeakable vileness and degradation of heathenism' and was emphatic that Andrews' views did not represent Hinduism as 'Hinduism appeared to most of the missionaries working there'; see *Gospel, Raj*, pp. 215, and 264, note 11.

533. C f. Lloyd, pp.154ff. above.

534. *Gospel, Raj*, p. 4. Cf. a later sentence on the same page; 'I hope also that a fuller understanding of him in his own times will underline his continuing significance as he moves ahead of us on roads we have not yet had the courage to tread.'

4 *The Theology of Religion at the World Missionary Conference 1910*

1. The best survey of these is by William Richey Hogg, *Ecumenical Foundations* (1952).

2. *Report* of the Conference of Missions held at Liverpool 1860, p. 321, quoted Hogg, op. cit., p. 40.

3. Among those inspired and enthused by the *Report* of this Conference was David Cairns, see above, p. 188.

4. Hogg, op. cit., pp. 44-5.

5. Op. cit., p. 45.

6. Gorge Robson, 'History of the Conference' in *History, Records and Addresses*, Vol. 9 of the WMC Reports, p. 5.

7. Ibid., p. 6.

8. Ibid.

9. On the watchword or slogan 'The evangelization of the world in this generation' see above pp. 11-14. J.R. Mott had given the slogan currency through his book *The Evangelization of the World in this Generation* (1900, revised in 1902).

10. For Mott see the extended work by C. Howard Hopkins, *John R. Mott 1865-1955, A Biography* (1979) and note also that the earlier work by Basil Matthews, *John R. Mott: World Citizen* (1934) is still of great value since it uses many personal conversations and interviews with Mott. Mott was the master strategist and publicist of the Protestant missionary movement for fifty years, see his own story in *Five Decades and a Forward View* (1939). In many ways Mott's was the creative mind behind the WMC as well as its leading committee man and master of ceremonies. Were this a different book attention would have to paid to his synthesis of a transformed millennialism together with his faith in 'providential achievements of modern science and technology' and an evangelical, Pietist understanding of the salvation wrought in Christ. By astonishing dexterity he managed to hold together conservatives and liberals within a single vision of the Kingdom of God.

11. *The Decisive Hour of Christian Missions* (1910), pp. 2-3.

12. Ibid., p. 29.

13. Ibid., p. 31.

14. Ibid., p. 32.

15. Ibid., p. 35.

16. Ibid., pp. 44-5.

17. Ibid., p. 46.

18. Ibid., p. 47.

19. Ibid., p. 48.

20. Cf. ibid., pp. 51ff. 'The textbooks in these modern schools are indifferent, if not actually hostile to religion. The men educated in these Government schools under non-Christian or hostile influence thus drift into agnosticism and materialism, and become a great menace to the Church,' pp. 53-4.

21. Ibid., p. 57.

22. Ibid., p. 66.

23. Ibid., p. 60.

24. In 1907 Mott had arranged a small conference of national YMCA secretaries in conjunction with the 1907 Tokyo WSCF Conference. J.N. Farquhar was present along with other Edinburgh respondents like G.S. Eddy and G.M. Fisher. Eric Sharpe tells us that the minutes of this conference have been lost but nevertheless it is known that that Mott sketched out there a programme of 'mission-study' which fell into six categories. These were: 1. the study of mission fields; 2. the study of non-Christian races; 3. the study of the great non-Christian religions 'including a comparison of these with one another and with Christianity and an examination of the best methods of presenting Christianity to the people of these faiths'; 4. the history of overseas missions, and 5. home missions, and finally; 6. the study of the Biblical basis of missions. Sharpe comments on this in relation to J.N. Farquhar: 'The launching of this scheme does not necessarily mean that Mott explicitly advocated at this stage the production of large scale works on the relation of Christianity to the non-Christian religions, but that he provided a further impetus for the starting of such work in India seems clear,' Sharpe, *Not to Destroy* (1965), p.235.

25. Hogg, op. cit., p. 109. Hogg comments that there was in 1952 no major biography of Oldham, and forty years later that gaps remains. A vivid sketch of Oldham can be found in Sherwood Eddy's *Pathfinders of the World Missionary Crusade* (1945), pp. 277-86.

26. W.H.T. Gairdner, *Edinburgh 1910* (1910), p. 65. In the USA this book was published under the title *Echoes from Edinburgh* (1910).

27. George Robson in op. cit., pp. 9-10. Oldham and Mott were already known to each other, for they had first met in 1891 when Oldham was sent to Oxford station to meet the young American evangelist coming, on his first visit to the city, to conduct a mission, see Hopkins, op. cit., p. 345. They had been in correspondence over the 'watchword' as early as February 1904, see the Archives of the Day Missions Library. Oldham wrote then: 'I cannot thank you enough for your address at the Edinburgh Conference on the Watchword as a spiritual force. That together with the article by Mr Cairns, have given me quite a new conception of the demands and the glory of the Kingdom of God.' As early as 1904 the three names associated with Commission IV had come together. Oldham's letter raised with Mott the question of responsibility for 'evangelization'. If evangelization in this generation meant only ensuring that every person in the world had been given the opportunity to hear the gospel, that raised grave difficulties in Oldham's mind. For him evangelization meant 'bringing the Gospel within the region not merely of the intellect, but of the heart and feelings'. This was especially true of the mission field: 'when we take into account the difficulties of language, the difference in modes of thought, and most of all, the prejudice which steels the heart of the native against the missionary, we must confess that mere verbal preaching of the Gospel is very far from adequate evangelization', Mott archive, Day Missions Library, letter dated Feb. 2nd, 1904. The Edinburgh

Conference referred to by Oldham was on the recruitment of candidates for the ministry; see Hopkins, ibid., p. 28.

28. Ibid., p. 10.

29. Some insight into the way in which Oldham worked can be gained from the correspondence between Mott and Oldham with regard to the formation of Commission I, 'Carrying the Gospel to All the Non-Christian world' in the archives of the Missionary Research Library, Union Theological Seminary, and available in photocopied form in the Day Missions Library at Yale. See also Hopkins, op. cit., pp. 347ff.

30. Art., 'The World Missionary Conference' in *The East and the West*, Vol.VI (1908), p.373.

31. Cairns had, as a young man recovering from illness, visited Cairo in 1893, and had stayed on a station of the American United Presbyterian Mission in Egypt, meeting people who were later to be respondents to the Edinburgh questionnaire, e.g. Andrew Watson, see below, pp. 233. In his autobiography, Cairns describes the missionaries in Egypt as a fine upstanding body of men and women, 'though straitened in their theology', *David Cairns: An Autobiography* (1950), p. 95. Cairns was clearly much impressed by what he saw of practical missionary work at that time.

32. *David Cairns: An Autobiography* (1950), p. 151. Cairns came from a family of Seceder and United Presbyterian ministers. His father was a minister and his uncle was John Cairns, Principal of the UP Theological Hall. 'I was never really influenced theologically by my father's preaching, which was on the same lines as my uncle's. His influence, which I now see to have been very deep, was one of character or outlook. No one who knew him could fail to be impressed by his own humility before God, his deep sense of reverence for holy things and of the profound difference between right and wrong and the seriousness of life. I wanted to believe as he believed, and wrestled with the old Calvinism and its solutions of the problems of the world and of human life. But it was in vain. It seemed to me to make God unjust and something in me rose up in inextinguishable protest against it. From that moment, I now see, I broke clear of the Seceder theology and Calvinism, and even from the final authority of St Paul,' ibid., p. 85.

33. Ibid., pp. 167-8.

34. See note 144 on p. 302. Cairns had other masters who helped bring him to faith. On his way to Egypt in 1883, in the midst of spiritual as well as physical exhaustion, he had picked up 'two books by Dr Newman Smythe... called *The Religious Feeling* and *Old Faiths in a New Light*... The former of the two books being largely influenced by Schleiermacher and the latter by Bushnell'. Cairns continues 'Neither book can now be called classical as sermons nor as Apologetics... but they remain in my memory as books which made a deeper mark in my mind than many books which are famous. They fitted into something that was beginning to live and grow in my mind at that time,' ibid., p. 91.

35. Ibid., p. 121. The last phrase echoes the teaching of W. Herrmann in Marburg. A generation later than David Cairns, Karl Barth also studied at Marburg under Herrmann. Cairns recorded his debt to Hermann, pp. 131ff. Looking back over his long life Cairns described his feelings at the end of his theological studies in words which contain a phrase of great significance. Jesus 'reveals the Father by being the absolute perfect Son', ibid., p. 122.

36. Ibid., emphases his.

37. Cairns recorded his debt to Henry Drummond, ibid., pp. 112ff.

38. Ibid., p. 49.

39. Ibid. Cf. this passage from his *Autobiography* which shows why he could so readily fall in with the suggestion that he might be the Chairman of Commission IV: 'Just about this time, when I was feeling about for something that would enable me to feel that the apparently insuperable difficulties of transforming the world of human society from that which it was to that which it ought to be, I fell in with the big ten-volume of the Great Missionary Conference of 1888, that is to say five years before the period of which I am writing. Here I had, for the first time, a panorama of what Christian missions were doing in every great mission field of the world,' ibid., p. 150.

40. Ibid.

41. Cairns remembered him as a 'grave and meagre young man', ibid., p. 170. Oldham told Cairns that the whole lecture on this occasion 'was really an expression of the characteristic ideals of the Student Christian Movement' and asked if Cairns would be willing to contribute to a volume that the Student Christian Movement was just about to publish. A further consequence was that Cairns began while still a Scots Parish Minister to speak at Student Christian Movement southern conferences held in those days, under canvas, at Cornishead Priory and later at Baslow and Swanwick. Cairns also recalled another figure listening to him during these meetings of the Student Christian Movement. This was Tissington Tatlow, the General Secretary of the Student Christian Movement. 'I remember his eager, watchful face at a meeting which I addressed in one of the tents on "Science and Providence"... I suspect that he was then taking stock of me, but of the meeting I remember little else'. 'Taken stock of' Cairns certainly was, and Tissington Tatlow could have seconded Oldham's suggestion that Cairns became Chairman of the Commission at the Oxford meeting. Tissington Tatlow was a member of the International Committee by virtue of his General Secretaryship of the Student Christian Movement.

42. Tissington Tatlow's extraordinary achievement in getting the Church of England to support the WMC is one of the great stories of the Ecumenical Movement, see W.R. Hogg, op. cit., pp. 111ff. Here we need only record the contribution he made to Commission IV through selecting Cairns as its Chairman.

43. For Cairns' constant repudiation of Augustinian pessimism see D.M. Baillie's *'Memoir'* introducing the *Autobiography*, pp. 9-21, and especially Baillie's ref. to Cairns' article, 'Victory in this World' *IRM*, (1942). For Cairns' views on Hodge and Patton and other Princeton Calvinists see note 159 on p. 303, and op. cit., pp. 87-8.

44. See D.M. Baillie in op. cit., p. 23.

45. For the process see Robson in *History, Records and Addresses*, Vol. 9 of the WMC Reports, pp. 10-11.

46. Glover had been part of the Deputation to China which had helped resolve the crisis in which Timothy Richard was involved, see above, pp. 123-25.

47. Robert Elliott Speer (1867-1957) was one of the founding spirits within the SVMU, acting as its travelling secretary in 1889-90. He was just in his second year at Princeton Seminary when he was called by the Presbyterian Board of Foreign Missions to be one of its secretaries. From 1891 to 1937 this was his sole occupation. Eddy felt that Speer would have made a great lawyer for he was brilliant in debate.

Notes to page 190

For many first hand recollections of Speer, see Eddy, op. cit., pp. 259-70. Speer was never primarily a theologian, however, and Eddy speaks of his 'deep grained conservatism and his yet deeper reserve', Speer made no significant contribution to *The Missionary Message* being content with his role of advocate for its findings, see his, *The Finality of Jesus Christ* (1933). There is a biography, W.R. Wheeler, *A Man Sent from God: A Biography of R.E. Speer* (1956).

48. A.B. Leonard (1837-1916) had been the Corresponding Secretary (i.e. the chief executive) of the ME Board since 1888 and had by 1910 visited twenty-five countries on five missionary tours. He retired in 1912 and died in 1915. There is an autobiography, *The Stone of Help* (1915).

49. Edgar Young Mullins was a well-known author in his day, having been teaching at the Southern Baptist Seminary in Louisville since 1899. For some details of his distinction as a Baptist theologian see William A. Mueller, *A History of the Southern Baptist Theological Seminary, 1859-1959* (1959) who also indicates Mullins' missionary interests (he had wanted to became a missionary in Brazil). He was the author of a fine systematic theology, *The Christian Religion in its Doctrinal Expression*, which owed much to the 'personalism' of the Boston philosopher Borden Parker Bowne. Mullins espoused also 'progressive revelation', referring to 'the divine pedagogy in the training of a race', op. cit., p. 147, which enabled him to speak of Christianity as 'the goal and crown of the other religions'. 'It is foolish', he wrote, 'to argue against Christianity because it contains all the fine elements of the ethnic faiths, as if it were derived from them. Its greatness appears in part, from the fact that it presents in synthetic unity all the elements of true religion', ibid., p. 103. Mullins specifically repudiated both Arminianism and Calvinism as systems or schools: 'we are learning to discard both names and to adhere more closely than either to the Scriptures, while retaining the truth in both systems', ibid., p. vii.

50. Wilhelm Dilger, of the Basel Mission in India from 1880 to 1907, was asked to respond to the WMC questionnaire and did so (at no. 147), but he is not mentioned in the list of respondents. In his response he warned against the danger of 'mystical monism' creeping into the consciousness of the Indian church' (147 p. 5). But he was also an exponent of 'points of contact', see pp. 6-7. He was sympathetic in his response to the main concerns of Commission IV, where he argued for the training of both missionaries and Indian preachers in 'higher criticism, modern science, and comparative religion', ibid. p. 10, and for the 'idea of the Kingdom of God' as the counterpart of the Hindu *moksha*. As a result of his experience in India, Dilger wrote that 'every Christian doctrine has received a fresh and more practical significance by this re-arrangement of my views. If comparative religion is studied on these lines, I am firmly convinced it will mean no loss but an immense gain to Christian theology,' ibid., p. 11. Dilger's widely influential essay in German-speaking countries, *Die Erlösung der Menschen nach Hinduismus und Christenthum* (1902) was not translated into English until 1908 *Salvation in Hinduism and Christianity: A Comparison and a Contrast*. Published only in Mangalore it was not available to Commissioners generally. Wesley House, Cambridge, possesses one of the few surviving copies.

51. Jan Willem Gunning (1862-1923) had been Director of the Nederlandsche Zendinggenootschap since 1897. In 1900-1 he made a memorable journey to the Dutch East Indies along with C. W. Th. Baron van Boetzelaar van Dubbeldam and

N. Adriani, of which there is a vivid impression in Rita Smith Kipp, *The Early Years of a Dutch Colonial Mission: the Karo Field* (1990), pp.18off.

52. There was also a response from J.A. Lepsius, see no. 347, but it differs from all the others in being a summary of the view of the missionaries from the German Oriental Mission. As such it is of less value than the personal statements.

53. W.P. Paterson (1860-1939) succeeded Robert Flint as Professor in Edinburgh University in 1903, and remained in that post until 1934, becoming Moderator of the General Assembly of the Church of Scotland in 1919. Paterson's immediate reputation before the WMC was based upon his Baird Lectures, *The Rule of Faith*, in which he had set out the proposition that 'we have to approach theology with an intense realisation that our primary datum is a religion, which as such undertakes to produce practical results, and that our primary certitude is that the Christian religion is an effective instrument for grappling with the heavy spiritual tasks which it undertakes to accomplish', op. cit., fourth edition, 1932, p. 27. Therefore, Paterson wrote, 'Christianity is most fitly compared to the medical art which addresses itself to the remedy of evils and the assurance of well-being in an analogous sphere,' ibid. Such views commended Paterson to Cairns, and related very well to the views of J. Warneck, see following note. At the WMC itself Paterson was chosen to give a public address on 'Christianity, the Final and Universal Religion, I. As Redemption' in which he drew heavily upon the missionary responses. Paterson was later to publish two related volumes, *The Nature of Religion* (1925) and *Conversion* (1939).

54. Johannes Warneck (1867-1944) worked among the Batak people of Sumatra from 1892-1906, and was appointed to the home staff of his Society in 1908. His account of this period of his life is in *Die Lebenskrafte des Evangeliums* (1908), English version, *The Living forces of the Gospel*, and American version, *The Living Christ and a Dying Heathenism* (1909). In this work Warneck suggested that 'animist' peoples grasp the message of Christ's domination over the spirit world before they understand the message of sin and grace. See *The Concise Dictionary of the Christian World Mission*, pp. 644-5.

55. Like Timothy Richard, George Owen was Welsh-speaking. He was born in Pembroke in 1843. Arriving in China in 1865 he began his work there in the period when that city was recovering from the aftermath of the Taiping rebellion. The sufferings of the people at that period had a lasting effect upon him. His mastery of the Mandarin dialect was exceptional: 'it is said that a short-sighted Chinese listener to his preaching refused to believe that the speaker was not Chinese', Goodall, *History of the LMS* (1954), p. 154. He died in 1914.

56. A Dubliner, C.F. d'Arcy (1859-1937) eventually became Archbishop of Armagh and Primate of all Ireland. The formative moment of his interest in overseas mission and particularly of the work of the church in Japan was the 'Pan Anglican Congress' in 1908, the reports from which are frequently quoted in his *Missionary Message* section on 'Japanese Religions'; see d'Arcy's autobiography, *The Adventures of a Bishop* (1934), pp.163ff. Concerning the WMC he wrote: 'Long preparation had been made for this event. Many months before I had been invited to become a member of one of the commissions which had been instructed to deal thoroughly with the immense amount of material which had been supplied by selected missionaries, possessed of expert knowledge and long experience, on every important question arising out of their work. The commission on which I served had to deal with a question which

was, to me, of extraordinary interest: "The Missionary Message in Relation to Non-Christian Religions." Already at the time I had been giving some attention to the religions and philosophies of the East, especially to those of China and Japan. I had read the works of competent scholars on Buddhism and Confucianism, and found these studies profoundly interesting. When therefore it appeared that I was to be a member of a group appointed to examine the reports on the religions of the East, I was strongly attracted. But the mass of the material was so great that this group had to be divided into sections, and even some of these sections had to be again divided.' In the event it turned out that d'Arcy was to be the only member of the sub-group on Japan, cf. *The Missionary Message*, p. 3, and d'Arcy recalled his embarrassment: 'I made frantic efforts to get some expert on Japan associated with me but to no effect. When however the material with which I had to deal came into my hands, I found it so rich that I realised at once that my sole duty was to sift it, arrange the resulting product and present it as simply and clearly as possible for the benefit of the English reader. Twenty-eight separate reports came into my hands. They took the form of replies to a very thorough and systematic set of queries, with added comments and illustrations. These correspondents belonged to nine distinct missionary organisations. They varied in fullness and value, but on the whole I was deeply impressed by their thoroughness and by their ability and intellectual honesty,' op. cit., p. 170. Particularly impressive in d'Arcy's eyes was Arthur Lloyd, see ibid. where he writes, 'The spirit, the insight, and the breadth of view of Dr Lloyd were admirable and inspiring,' and cf. above, pp.152ff. D'Arcy remained deeply interested in other religious traditions. In 1916 he was asked to review N. Macnicol's first large book, *Indian Theism* for the *IRM*. As much in description of himself as of Macnicol, d'Arcy wrote, 'His sympathy is unfailing. Even when confronted with those forms of Indian thought which seem most alien, in relation to the Christian point of view, he can still detect those elements of truth which are never withheld from the sincere seeker after God,' *IRM*, Vol. 5 (1916), p. 149.

57. Garvie was born in Glasgow in 1861. After studying with Fairbairn in Oxford he worked as a minister in Scotland, and then became a theological educator in 1900, becoming Principal of New College, Edinburgh in 1907. His own memory of Edinburgh reads, 'I have deeply regretted that I was not present at the epoch-making missionary conference in 1910. I was on the commission which prepared the report on the religions of the world under the presidency of the Rev. Dr. David Cairns, whose friendship I have since enjoyed and prized. I was associated with Dr. Simon, a German missionary in one of the Dutch possessions in Asia in writing the report on Islam,' *Memories and Meanings* (1938), pp. 151-2. Garvie was to remain interested in this area for the rest of his ministry. Cf. his remarks in the *IRM* in 1916: 'It was a common assumption that men for the foreign ministry need not be so capable or so well educated as for the home ministry... The heathen to whom the Gospel was to be preached were regarded as ignorant degraded savages, and it was thought that a less educated and less intellectual man could better deal with them. Both views are false,' art. 'The Education of Missionaries', *IRM*, Vol. 5 (1916), pp.127ff. . His own textbook on this subject, *Tutors Unto Christ: An Introduction to the Study of Religions* (1920) falls outside the scope of this book, but is replete with echoes of *The Missionary Message*.

58. Like Warneck, Simon had served among the Batak peoples in Sumatra. Shortly after Edinburgh Gottfried Simon published his *Islam und Christenthum im Kampf um die Eroberung der Animistischen Welt* in Berlin in 1910. His views in this work were summarized in an article, '*The Vital Forces of Christianity and Islam:-3*, in *IRM*, Vol.I (1913), pp. 452-473. Later this and the first two articles in the series, by W.A. Shedd and W.H.T. Gairdner were brought together in one volume: *The Vital Forces of Christianity and Islam* (1915).

59. C.H. Robinson (1861-1925) deserves a full study in his own right. There is a biography by Florence Robinson, *Charles H. Robinson: A Record of Travel and Work* (1928), and in its 'Foreword' the then Archbishop of Canterbury, Randall Davidson, calls Robinson 'one of the few really great men whom I have known', p. vii. As a traveller he had visited Armenia on behalf of the Archbishop of Canterbury, and had been the first European to cross the great Hausa district north of Nigeria. As a linguist he compiled the grammar and dictionary of the Hausa language and translated St John's Gospel into that language. As a scholar he produced many works on the history of Christian missions including *The Conversion of Europe* (1918) and lives of Otto of Pomerania and Anskar. His *History of Christian Missions* (1915) remains an excellent reference work and has been used many times in the writing of the present work. But as a missionary thinker and theologian he was outstanding, and here his major achievement was in his editing of *The East and The West* from its inception in 1902 to its demise in 1925. This was a scholarly and ecumenical journal with a high standard of commissioned articles, with regular editorial comment and excellent book reviews, many of which Robinson wrote himself. One important missiological work from the W.M.C period was *The Interpretation of the Character of Christ to Non-Christian Races: An Apology for Christian Missions* (1911), in which Robinson draws on the thinking of F.D. Maurice (on Islam) and Cuthbert Hall (on Hindu thought), as well as from numerous Edinburgh respondents who had either contributed to *The East and the West*, or were known to him through other writings, e.g., J.P. Jones, C.F. Andrews, G.H. Westcott, Arthur Lloyd, W.E.S. Holland, Timothy Richard, Charles Lefroy, and the Indian Christian John Lazarus. This immensely rich work anticipated many of the conclusions of the *The Missionary Message*. In February 1910, Robinson wrote these words: '...the work of the Christian missionary, if he is to follow the lines laid down by the founder of Christianity, must be constructive and not destructive. Christ is, we believe, the Sun of Righteousness, but in order to prepare for His complete manifestation we have not got to extinguish the stars which have helped to illumine the darkness of the non-Christian world and guide seekers after truth in their search for God,' op. cit., p. viii.

60. The printed and unbound Minutes of the preparatory committees are in the Missionary Research Library, Union Theological Seminary and in the Day Missions Library, Yale Divinity School, with another in the archives of the Council of Churches of Britain and Ireland (formerly the Edinburgh House archives).

61. *The Missionary Message*, p. 1.

62. Ibid.

63. Ibid.

64. Though neither the formulation of the questionnaire nor the selection of the missionaries who were to receive it was done by the whole group, see the implications of d'Arcy's description of receiving the Japanese responses in note 56 above. Since

there are no other records we can only surmise from their personal qualities why they were chosen. Hence the importance of the notes on each respondent, see below, pp. 376ff.

65. *The Missionary Message*, p. 2.

66. A copy can be found in the archives of the WMC in the Missionary Research Library, New York.

67. With the advent of the photocopying machine other full sets have been made. Known to me are the sets in the libraries of the Centre for the Study of Christianity in the Non-Christian World at New College, Edinburgh, and at Wesley House, Cambridge.

68. The last set was especially commissioned by Robert Speer and is different therefore in its typing from all the others. A letter explaining the circumstance of this still exists. Dated 26 September 1912, it was addressed to William Adams Brown, the Professor of Systematic Theology at Union Seminary. The letter offered the collection to the Seminary Library. Through the judgment of the Faculty of the Seminary, probably led by W.W. Rockwell, the Professor for World Christianity, the whole collection was put into an archive at Union. Speer wrote, 'The letters differ very much in quality and it may be that you will want to have them weeded out before binding and placing in the Library the part of the material which is of permanent value. Some of the letters, also, are a little incoherent, either in their translation or because their writers were unfamiliar with English. In copying them we have been obliged to follow the original sent to us by the Commission and the Secretary of the Conference.' Happily they were not weeded out and the whole collection appears to be intact in five volumes.

69. Missionaries were not often taken seriously in the thinking and planning of the Home Boards which habitually thought they knew better than the people on the field. See the characteristic behaviour of 'The Committee' of the BMS in 1888-1891 towards Timothy Richard, as described by Brian Stanley, *The History of the Baptist Missionary Society 1792-1992* , pp. 192-96, to which we have alluded above, p. 125.

70. Cf. the reasons for the calling of the most recent WCC Commission on World Mission and Evangelism Consultation in Baar, Switzerland, September 1993. A full report is in *Current Dialogue* No.26 (June 1994), pp. 1-68.

71. See Clark H. Pinnock, *A Wideness in God's Mercy: The Finality of Jesus Christ in a World of Religions* (1992) for the best attempt to tackle these issues by an evangelical theologian. Pinnock lists other evangelical scholars on both sides of the debate on p. 12 of this work, commenting that the 'harshness characteristic of the relationship between Protestant theology with the other religions historically has not lessened but is actually growing in some quarters'. For an annotated bibliography for the debate in the world Christian community, Roman Catholic, and Orthodox as well as Protestant, see Kenneth Cracknell, 'Interfaith Dialogue and the Theology of Religion: A Selective Bibliography for Ministerial Formation', in *Current Dialogue*, No. 17 (December 1989). Note also Gerald Anderson's bibliography, 'Christian Mission and Religious Pluralism: A Selected Bibliography of 175 Books in English, 1970-1990' in *Mission in the Nineteen 90's* (1991).

72. *The Missionary Message*, p. 273.

73. Ibid., p. 3.

74. Robert Speer thought that this was the case, cf. his letter to Union Theological Seminary referred to in note 67 above: 'Possibly it was the amount of editing that the letters would require before the could be printed that led the Continuation Committee to advise against the publication of the whole material, but there was so much of value in it that it took a long time before the Continuation Committee could bring itself to decide not to issue the whole body of letters.'

75. For detailed studies of the theological forces at work within the IMC and its conferences, see: Tomas Shivute, *The Theology of Mission and Evangelism in the International Missionary Council from Edinburgh to New Delhi* (1980); J.J.E. van Lin, *Protestantse theologie der godsdiensten: van Edinburgh naar Tambaram 1910-1938* (1974); Gerard Vallée, *Mouvement Oecumenique et Réligions non Chretiennes: un débat oecumenique sur la rencontre interreligieuse de Tambaram à Uppsala (1938-1968)* (1975) and S. Wesley Ariarajah, *Hindus and Christians: A Century of Protestant Ecumenical Thought* (1991) For a brief commentary based on these works see Kenneth Cracknell, 'The Theology of Religion in the IMC and the WCC, 1910-1989', in *Current Dialogue*, No.19, January 1991.

76. Evaluations of the *The Missionary Message* have been uniform, in terms of their high praise, from the very beginning. Robert Hume described it at the WMC itself as 'pulsating with life', see the report of discussions in *The Missionary Message*, p. 321. Temple Gairdner called it a masterpiece op. cit., p. 135; Hogg called it a 'sterling report' and said that 'its stimulus encouraged missionary training in comparative religion probably more than had any previous work', op. cit., p. 127. G.H. Anderson wrote in 1961 of the 'continuing worth' of the Report, *Theology of the Christian Mission*, p. 5, note 6. Cairns himself has had an equally good press: a recent evaluation of the *The Missionary Message* describes him as 'a man of exceptional scholarship, combined with a rare ability to listen and learn, and an attitude of sympathy', Wesley Ariarajah, op. cit., p. 29.

77. This was noted by some of the respondents, e.g., John Morrison, see his response on pp. 240f.

78. In his introduction to *The Theology of the Christian Mission* (1961), Gerald H. Anderson writes that at Edinburgh the major question put to the missionary enterprise was simply 'How Missions?', p.5. 'Edinburgh', he says, 'was primarily concerned with strategy, and most participants seemed to take it for granted that the Great Commission of Christ (Mt.28:19) was the only basis needed for the missionary enterprise', ibid, p.6. Analysing the main thrusts of succeeding missionary conferences, Jerusalem 1928, Tambaram 1938, and Whitby 1947, Anderson does not find the question of what the Christian mission is, surfacing until Willingen in 1952, with the most radical question 'what is the Christian mission?' put at the Ghana IMC Assembly in 1957-8. Anderson states that that judgment 'does not minimise either the historical significance of Commission IV at Edinburgh nor the continuing worth of its report on "The Missionary Message in Relation to Non-Christian Religions"', ibid., p.6, note 6. Perhaps one consequence of the present work might be be to call in question Anderson's premise. Even if the question addressed to them was simply, 'How Missions?' there is much evidence in these pages that many missionaries knew that much deeper issues were involved.

79. See above, pp. 182-85.

80. Cf. the discussion of Christian theology in the *The Missionary Message*, pp.259-67.

81. Ibid., p.171 emphasis his.

82. Ibid., p.94.

83. Ibid., p.52 but compare A.E. Moule and R.H. Graves, pp.229, 241 below.

84. Ibid., p.20.

85. Ibid., p.139.

86. There is no need to labour this point. Missionaries of this period were ill-equipped to do more than speak of African worship in terms of 'Fetishism'. Cf. the reading list for missionary candidates in *Religions of the Mission Fields as viewed by Protestant Missionaries*, published by the Student Volunteer Missionary Union in 1905, which includes titles like A. Bastian, *Der Fetisch an der Kuste Guineas* (1884); F. Schultze, *Der Fetischismus* (1871) and, by an Edinburgh respondent, R.H. Nassau, *Fetishism in West Africa* (1904). In addition the compiler suggested looking in Encyclopaedias under three headings, 'Fetishism', 'Animism' and 'Africa', and suggests himself the articles or chapters on Fetishism in F.B. Jevons, *Introduction to the Study of Religion* (1902), F. Ratzel, *The History of Mankind* (1898), and E.B. Tylor, *Primitive Culture* (1891). Other texts mentioned have titles such as *Among the Wild Ngoni*, *Sketches from the Dark Continent*, and *Die Religion der afrikanischen Naturvolker*. With these limited resources it is little wonder the author of the article wrote that the African 'lacks knowledge of a Creator' and has 'no name for Him', p.6.; that 'there is no knowledge of His attributes', p.7., and 'His only inheritance is hopeless darkness', p.14. Nevertheless the compiler thought that the African had a religious nature, 'a capacity for comprehending religion', p.15: 'This capacity for better things and his religious nature constitute for him what we may term his religion. He has no other worthy of the name', p.15. In the light of these remarks the comments of Balmer and Nassau and other African missionaries quoted are the more remarkable.

87. Samuel Ambat was working with the Basel German Evangelical Missionary Society in Nettur, Tellicherry, Malabar, the most southerly part of the Basel Mission field. The work in Tellicherry had begun in 1839.

88. T. Grahame Bailey, a missionary of the Church of Scotland in the Punjab from 1894, was a specialist in North Indian languages. See his article, 'Should languages be studied at home or in the mission field?' in *IRM*, Vol.II, 1913, pp.554-566.

89. William T. Balmer was sent to Sierra Leone in 1901 to serve as the first principal of 'Richmond College', the Wesleyan Theological College for Native Ministers in Freetown, from where he wrote his response. In 1909, he was seconded to the Gold Coast District of the Wesleyan Methodist Church for two years, returning to Sierra Leone in 1914. On Balmer's 'genius' for African education, see Findlay and Holdsworth, *History of the Wesleyan Methodist Missionary Society*, Vol.IV., pp.114ff.

90. J.M. Bannerjea, M.A., B.L., was Pleader and Vice President in the Metropolitan Institution in Calcutta, and a second generation Christian.

91. James Whitford Bashford (1848-1919) was the Bishop of the American Methodist Episcopal Church in Peking. He had arrived in China at the age of fifty-five, having been President of Ohio Wesleyan University from 1889-1904. He wrote many books about China, of which the most important was *China: an Interpretation*, published in 1916 and enlarged and revised in 1919. See Latourette *History of*

Christian Missions in China (1929), p. 577, and Neill, Anderson and Goodwin, *Concise Dictionary of the Christian World Mission*, (1970), pp. 53-4. There is a biography of Bashford entitled *James W.Bashford: Pastor, Educator Bishop*, published in 1922 but I have not been able to see this work.

92. James Beattie was, from 1908, the second Principal of the Amoy Theological College, where he worked alongside American Dutch Reformed and London Missionary Society personnel, including another Edinburgh respondent, F.P. Joseland. Beattie had a considerable reputation as a spiritual teacher and theological educator. J.H. Oldham's brother Harry was also a missionary of the English Presbyterian Church in Amoy, and was to become Beattie's successor in 1913. See references in Band, *Working His Purpose Out* (1947).

93. Mrs (Dr) Ferguson Davie was a medical missionary in north India. Her husband, C.J. Ferguson Davie, became Bishop of Singapore. Her response is full of stories about dialogue, including one whose climax was the cry of angry villagers to her husband and the local Maulvie: 'we have come to hear a controversy between you two upholders of different religions and you waste your time talking of the crops' (155, p.25).

94. Jerome Dean Davis (1838-1910) was among the second group of ABCFM missionaries to Japan, arriving in 1872. He was a colleague of D.C. Greene in pioneering Christian days schooling in Japan, cf. Strong, The *Story of the American Board* (1910), pp.269, 273). With J.H. Neesima he founded the Doshisha College, see *IRM*, Vol.6, 1917, p.614. and wrote a very gracious tribute to his colleague, *A Maker of New Japan: the Revd Joseph Hardy Neesima* (1905) He was an exponent of modern religious movements in Japan. See for example his article on 'Yabutsu Sekken' in *The Advance*' 11 March 1897. Davis is among the small group of respondents who actually attended the WMC. There is a biography by his son, J. Merle Davis, *Davis: Soldier-Missionary* (1917).

95. John Lincoln Dearing (1858-1916), was a frequent writer on Japanese subjects and editor of the annual volumes, *The Christian Movement in Japan*. See Robinson, *History of Christian Missions* (1915), p. 232.

96. The Principal of the Lady Muir Memorial Training School, Allahabad, when she wrote her response, Agnes de Selincourt returned to the UK because of ill-health and eventually became Principal of Westfield College in the University of London. She was one of the first ever women members of the CMS Foreign Committee; see Stock, *History of the CMS*, Vol.4 (1916), p. 439. A statement of her central concerns can be found in 'The Place of Women in the National Movements of the East' in *IRM*, Vol.I, 1912., pp.98-107. Her Edinburgh response contains moving material about her friendship with a Sufi professor of Arabic (see 224, p.3).

97. Courtenay H. Fenn was Dean and Professor of Systematic Theology in the Union Seminary in Peking. He had been a missionary since 1893.

98. Alexander Gordon Fraser had served for four years with the CMS in Uganda as a schoolmaster, 1900-4, before becoming the Principal of Trinity College, Kandy. At the time of responding he was a lay missionary, though he was later ordained, see Stock, op. cit., p.262.

99. Joshua Crowe Garritt was known as the editor of *Jubilee Papers of the Central China Presbyterian Mission, 1844-1894, comprising Historical Sketches of the Mission Stations at Ningpo, Shanghai, Hangchow, Soochow, and Nanking*, Shanghai, 1895.

100. Frederick Rogers Graves (1858-1940) had been the Protestant Episcopal Bishop of the Missionary district of Shanghai since 1893, having come to China in 1881. For his general position see articles in the PECUSA monthly, *The Spirit of Missions*.

101. Daniel Crosby Greene (1843-1913) was the first ABCFM missionary to set foot in Japan, in 1869. His work extended through Kobe, Osaka and Kyoto. He began a boys school at Kobe in 1872 and eventually formed part of the team which translated the New Testament into Japanese (1880); see Strong op. cit., pp. 265ff. He received the Third Order of the Rising Sun from the Emperor in May 1913 for 'valuable services in promoting international relations between Japan and America, and in introducing a knowledge of Japan to other countries'. Greene died in September, 1913; see Goodsell *You Shall be My Witnesses* (1959), p. 402.

102. A missionary since 1883, H.G. Grey had just returned to England after serving at St John's College, Lahore and acting as Secretary of the Punjab Mission of the CMS when he wrote his response. He became Principal of Wycliffe Hall, Oxford in 1909.

103. Henry Gulliford was appointed a missionary of the Wesleyan Methodists in Mysore in 1878. Much of his work had been in education, but by 1910 he had become what the WMMS called a 'Literature Missionary'. He was member of the National Missionary Council of India.

104. Ferdinand Hahn worked within the Gossner Mission, from 1868-76 as a theological teacher in Chota Nagpur, 1887-1901 among a hill tribe known as the Kurukh or Oraons (Hahn was the first to master their language), and last in the Parulia Leprosy asylum, at this time the largest in India. Hahn had been awarded the Gold Medal of the Kaisar-i-Hind Order; see J. Richter, *History of Missions in India* (1908), pp. 239, 302.

105. William Harris was Principal of The Prince Royal's College in Chieng Mai, but had worked 'among all classes, Siamese officials, local (Laos) princes, Chinese traders, priests and people' (332, p. 1).

106. R.H.A. Haslam was from Toronto and worked for the CMS until the transfer of the Kangra District to the newly formed Missionary Society of the Anglican Church of Canada in 1902.

107. Headland had an outstanding ministry in the court circles in Peking. This he achieved through the medical knowledge of his wife, who was the Empress's personal physician. He wrote numerous books, including *Court life in China: The* Capital, its Officials, its People (1909) and *China's New Day: A Study of Events that have led to its Coming* (1912). His knowledge of Chinese folk lore is reflected in his charming little book, *Chinese Mother Goose Rhymes* (1902).

108. G.F. Herrick was at Bible House, Constantinople when he replied. In 1912 he published *Christian and Mohammedan: A Plea for Bridging the Chasm*. About Herrick and this book the anonymous reviewer in *IRM*, Vol.I, 1912, p. 533, wrote: 'Dr Herrick is intensely and humanly sympathetic with Moslems as they are and carefully avoids all crusading hysterics. He sees the futility of mere controversy and of such sensational phrases as "the evangelization of the world in this generation". Being instinct with the love that beareth all things, believeth all things, hopeth all things and which never faileth, his ideal of the courtesy, patience and brotherliness which the missionary should possess could not easily be bettered.'

109. W.E.S. Holland had been Warden of the Oxford and Cambridge Hostel in Allahabad since 1900; see Stock, op. cit., p. 227. For some of his previous writings about Hinduism, see Sharpe, *Not to Destroy* (1965), p. 23. Eugene Stock had a clear desire to highlight the abuses and degradation in other religious systems and therefore was delighted to quote some hostile comments by Holland about sadhus at the *mela* in Allahabad in 1906 in op. cit., pp. 148-9. Nevertheless Stock described Holland as one whose 'whole temperament is to seek for whatever is good in Hinduism'.

110. Franklin E. Hoskins worked in the Syria Mission of the Board of Foreign Missions of the Presbyterian Church of the USA. He had been a missionary for twenty-six years.

111. Frank P. Joseland had been working with the LMS in the Fukien province since 1888. This was the scene of the most rapid progress in any of the LMS's seven areas of influence. There was also close co-operation with the two other missions at work in this territory, namely the English Presbyterians and the American Reformed (formerly the Dutch Reformed Church of America). These had joint enterprises in education and theological training, and Joseland was much involved in teaching. Goodall, however, asserts that 'his most characteristic role was that of a district missionary'; see Goodall, op. cit., p. 164.

112. F. Kingsbury was, despite his English name, a former Hindu, a pastor in the South India United Church at Pasumalai.

113. John Lazarus described himself as a Christian of the sixth generation, with forty-four years of service. He was the Editor of *The Christian Patriot*, and a Fellow of Madras University.

114. Duncan Leith was a missionary of the WMMS in Madras, appointed in 1901. Particularly interested in social affairs, he established the Kellett Institute in Triplicane. He eventually became a Madras City Councillor and, at the height of his powers, drowned while swimming off the Madras coast; see Ranson, *A Missionary Pilgrimage*, (1988), pp. 48-9.

115. P.J. Maclagan went to Swatow as a missionary of the Presbyterian Church of England in 1888. In Swatow his work was mainly in translation and literature, and teaching in the Swatow theological college. He became secretary of the Home Board in 1914. He was, as a considerable scholar in Chinese religion holding a D.Phil. of Edinburgh University (1897), capable of taking on and worsting H.A.Giles, see his review of the latter's *Confucianism and its Rivals* in *IRM*, Vol.V, 1916, pp. 315-7. For his own writings see 'The Position and the Prospects of Confucianism in China' in *IRM*, Vol.III, 1914, pp. 225-242 and *Chinese Religious Ideas* (1926). See Band, op. cit., pp. 337-8, and 570.

116. In 1905, having already worked for six years in South India, James Mathers was appointed by the LMS to continue the pattern of work (i.e., Christian advocacy among caste Hindus) established by T.E. Slater in Bangalore. He did this 'ably and faithfully' until 1910 when he accepted an appointment with the YMCA in Bangalore. See Goodall, *History of the LMS* (1964), p. 65. Mathers was originally an Irish Presbyterian.

117. D.A. Murray was a professor on the faculty of the Osaka theological school of the USA Presbyterian West Japan mission. He added to his testimony: 'A missionary should be a person of true courtesy, and it is as uncourteous (*sic*) to ridicule his clothes or the furniture in his house' (32, p. 6).

118. Pandita Ramabai (1858-1922) was the leading Christian woman Sanskritist of her day. Converted through Nehemiah Goreh she came into contact with the Wantage sisters in England and was baptized in 1883. With the help of Western friends the 'Mukti' (Deliverance) mission for young widows and orphan girls was started in Bombay, later moving to Kedgaon, near Pune, from where the Pandita wrote her response. For an admirable brief summary of her life and achievement see Stephen Neill in the *Concise Dictionary of the Christian World Mission*, pp. 505-6 and a life by Nicol Macnicol, *Pandita Ramabai* (1926).

119. David B. Schneder was a missionary of the Board of Foreign Missions of the Reformed Church in America, and thus a member of the United Church of Christ in Japan. See Stephen W. Ryder, *A Historical Sourcebook of the Japan Mission of the RCA (1859-1930)* (1935).

120. Arthur H. Smith arrived in China in 1872. He had become well-known as an interpreter of the Chinese people in the early 1890s through a series of newspaper articles originally prepared for the *North China Daily News* in Shanghai. These were republished in 1890 and widely circulated. The Fleming H.Revell Company of New York produced a number of editions of these essays entitled *Chinese Characteristics* from 1894 onwards. Smith himself calls these essays 'mere outline sketches in charcoal of some features of the Chinese people, as they have been seen by one observer'. By the time of his Edinburgh response he had served thirty-five years in China, ten in Tientsin and twenty-five in Shangtung. As well as *Chinese Characteristics*, his writings included *China in Convulsion*, 2 Vols (1901), *Rex Christus: An Outline Study of China* (1903), and *The Uplift of China* (1908). Smith has attracted the attention of the secular historian Charles Hayford. See Hayford's essay on Smith's *Chinese Characteristics*, entitled 'Chinese and American Characteristics' in Barnett and Fairbank (eds) *Christianity in China* (1985). Hayford concludes on p.174: 'The book stands as a morally earnest examination of the problem of "modernizing" Chinese life without losing its moral center... Smith did not spare effort or attention in his attempt to see China whole or real. The attempt is not successful because Smith lacked self-consciousness and the sense, which perhaps only historical experience could give, of irony and ambiguity.' Smith left a sketch for an autobiography in his article 'A Chapter of Experience in China' in *IRM*, Vol. 5, 1916, pp. 372-5.

121. Joshua Vale arrived in China in December 1887. He had perhaps come to the attention of the Commissioners through his paper 'The Unreached Reading Classes' in the *Report* of the West China Conference, pp. 271 ff. There he had written, 'There are large numbers of devout men and woman in West China who take their religion seriously' (103, p. 1). He was the author of *Chinese Superstitions*, second edition London, 1906, first published by the Methodist Publishing House in Shanghai in 1904.

122. W. Gilbert Walshe served for ten years in the CMS Chekiang Mission before becoming secretary of the C.L.S. of China in 1909 succeeding Timothy Richard. He was the editor of *China: the Quarterly Record of the Christian Literature Society of China*. By 1910 he was well known as a translator into Chinese of works of secular interest, as for example a life of Queen Victoria, and also church history and Biblical subjects, see Stock, op. cit., p. 323.

123. The son of a CMS Pastor in Ningpo, C.T. Wang (Wang Cheng-Ting) was to become a prominent lay leader of the Chinese church as well as a well-known Chinese

statesman of the period. He wrote his response to the Commissioners while studying at Yale. For a sharp statement of his views about the inner dialogue with China see his article, 'The Importance of Making Christianity Indigenous' in *IRM*, Vol.5, 1916, pp.75-86. Wang was to become National Secretary of the YMCA in China in 1915. He was later (circa 1920 onwards) to have an important role in Chinese politics and diplomacy, representing China in the Paris Peace Conference. He became successively Minister of Justice, Minister of Foreign Affairs and Acting Premier, see Latourette *History of Christian Missions in China* (1929), p. 835.

124. Andrew Watson ministered within the American United Presbyterian Mission in Egypt, an evangelical church of over 10,000 communicants, virtually all former Copts. Watson wrote 'We do not claim our mission is especially for the followers of Mohammed' (280, p. 1). He was a conservative theologian, writing in response to question 9, 'A person with advanced ideas on higher criticism had better not come to the Mission Field, for belief in the practical inerrancy of God's word is the chief weapon of success' (ibid., p. 8.).

125. George Whitehead served in Burma from 1888 to 1921, leading the SPG Mission among the Chin people. His major literary achievement was a *Life of Christ* in Burmese. He had come to attention because of a particularly impressive article in *The East and the West* on the Chin tribes people; see the quotation from it by Copland King in the main text, p. 239, and note 213 below.

126. Samuel Marinus Zwemer (1867-1952) was born in Vriesland, Michigan. In 1890 he set out for Arabia as a member of a pioneer band of missionaries. Their work was adopted by the Reformed Church in America. Eventually he became Professor of Christian Mission at Princeton. In the Edinburgh period he was over-optimistic even by the standards of his contemporaries in his repeatedly stated belief that Islam was a 'dying religion'. See for example H.U. Weitbrecht's courteous review of Zwemer's 1916 volume *The Disintegration of Islam*, in *IRM*, Vol. 6, 1917, p. 473, 'With all respect to the wide range of information and the vivid gift of portrayal which we find in this volume, we feel the conclusion may be somewhat too sweeping'. There is a good biography of Zwemer by J.C. Wilson, *Apostle to Islam* (1952).

127. *Guidelines on Dialogue* (1979), part. II, para. 22.

128. Wilfred Barbrooke Grubb of the South American Missionary Society pioneered work in the Paraguayan Chaco from 1889 onwards, and was later to establish (in 1914) the first mission in the Argentine Chaco. There is a full biography by R.J. Hunt, *The Livingstone of South America* (1932). Note its subtitle, 'The Life and Adventures of W. Barbrooke Grubb among the wild tribes of the Gran Chaco in Paraguay, Bolivia, Argentina, the Falkland Islands and Tierra del Fueguo'. Little of the theology that Grubb set out in his Edinburgh response comes through Hunt's pages, where he is portrayed as an explorer and pioneer, the bearer of a 'romantic name', see p. 311.

129. Robinson was Missionary Bishop of the Methodist Episcopal Church for South Asia, with his headquarters at Bombay. His area covered Central, Southern and Western India. He had been in India since 1874 and Bishop since 1904. For his work see M.H. Harper, *The Methodist Episcopal Church in India* (1936), p. 182.

130. Robert Hamill Nassau, a medical doctor, was a member of the American Presbyterian Mission in Equatorial West Africa from July 1861 to December 1907. Retired by the time he wrote his response, Nassau was living in Germantown,

Pennsylvania. For Nassau's work and connection with Albert Schweitzer, see C.P. Groves, *The Planting of Christianity in Africa*, Vol. I, 1954, p. 242, and Vol. II, 1958, p. 480. Nassau was the author of *Fetichism in West Africa* (1904).

131. George A. Lefroy, Bishop of Lahore since November 1899. Having arrived in India in 1879, he became head of the Cambridge Delhi Mission from 1882; see Thompson, 1951, *Into all the World*, p. 366. In 1913 he became Metropolitan of India and Bishop of Calcutta succeeding R.S. Copleston. For an evangelical appreciation of his work and that of the Cambridge Delhi Mission see Stock, op. cit., pp. 214-4, and for his connections with C.F. Andrews, particularly as they made common cause against British racialism, see O'Connor, *Gospel, Raj and Swaraj* (1990), pp. 74-9.

132. V.S. Azariah, a young man in Anglican orders and a delegate from South India working for the YMCA, complained boldly but courteously about the lack of a proper 'co-operation between foreign and native workers' in the Indian church. Indian Christians were already wanting missionaries to be friends, not benefactors. During an evening address, Azariah implored the Conference to act in these terms: 'Through all the ages to come the Indian Church will rise up in gratitude to attest the heroism and self-denying labours of the missionary body. You have given your goods to feed the poor. You have given your bodies to be burned. We also ask for love. Give us FRIENDS.' An eyewitness, H.L. Houlder, describing this occasion fifty years later, recalled the sentence 'too often you promise us thrones in heaven, but will not offer us chairs in your sitting rooms'. Writing immediately after the event, W.H.T. Gairdner reported that Azaraiah's speech was not received altogether appreciatively: 'an electric silence, broken now by a sort of subterraneous rumbling of dissent, or startled by thunderish claps of applause, is the least comfortable of all atmospheres to speak in, and demanded all the evident courage of the man to speak in it'. Many of the Edinburgh respondents would have been among those applauding Azariah. For the full text of V.S. Azariah's address, 'The Problem of Co-Operation between Foreign and Native Workers', see *History Records and Addresses*, WMC, Vol. IX, pp. 306-315; Gairdner's reportage in *Edinburgh 1910*, (1910), pp. 109-111; H.L. Houlder's memories are in an unpublished typescript, '"Edinburgh 1910" Reminiscences of the World Missionary Conference Held in Edinburgh 1910' in my own possession. Houlder, who had recently graduated from Oxford, was a steward at Edinburgh.

133. G.P. Taylor, a missionary of the Presbyterian Church of Ireland, was to become Principal of Stevenson College, Ahmedabad.

134. John Wherry, a DD of Princeton Seminary, was a member of the Presbyterian Church of the USA Mission in Peking where he served from 1864 until his death in 1918, see Brown, op. cit., p. 285.

135. John Cameron Young was a minister of the United Free Church of Scotland and a member of its 'Keith Falconer Mission' in Aden.

136. Sidney Lewis Gulick (1860-1945) was a member of one of the great missionary families of the American Board, see Strong, op. cit., *passim*. He had been in Japan since 1887 and became a professor in the Doshisha College and a lecturer at the Imperial University in Tokyo. His special sphere was the production of theological literature in both English and Japanese, though the only work which still deserves attention is his missionary theorizing, as for example in *The Growth of the Kingdom of God* (1897), his writing on Japanese culture, like *Evolution of the Japanese: Social and*

Psychic (1903), and a series of books beginning in 1905 and ending in 1935 designed to instigate American-Japanese political dialogue. See, for examples, *The White Peril in the Far East: An Interpretation of the Significance of the Russo-Japanese War* (1905) and *Towards Understanding Japan: Constructive Proposals for Removing the Menace of War* (1935). Gulick was particularly interested in the incipient Japanese inter-religious dialogue represented by the 'Conference of the Three Religions' held in February 1912, see *IRM*, Vol. II, 1913, p. 693, and by the newly formed academic group 'The Association Concordia' (Ki-itsu Kyokwai) see *IRM*, Vol. II, 1913, pp. 802- 3. Gulick was strongly dependent on Fairbairn, Cf. 'One further characteristic of the new movement is the modern reconstructions of theology, giving Christ a more conspicuous position if not always the pivotal place... Not infrequently do we hear now of "Christocentric theology". One of the most widely read of recent theological works is that entitled *The Place of Christ in Modern Theology*...' (*The Growth of the Kingdom of God*, p. 194). Immediately before this passage Gulick had written: 'It is no longer common to dwell at length on the wrath of God against the sinner, and the awful doom that awaits the unrepentant unbeliever who dies in his sin. Rather it is common to dwell on the love and the mercy of the Father, and on the matchless sympathy of Jesus. The sinner is to be attracted home by love, rather than driven into the fold by fear', ibid., p. 193.

137. Elwood Morris Wherry was the author of several works which were well used in this period. They were *The Comprehensive Commentary on the Quran* (1885), *The Muslim Controversy* (1905), and *Islam and Christianity in India and the Far East*, which were lectures he gave at Princeton in 1906-7. In the last of these works, Wherry has a valuable appendix on what he calls 'Controversy with Moslems: Its place and message', pp. 220-229. While these are not exactly 'guidelines and dialogue', Wherry insists upon justice ('In public debate it is all-important to give one's opponent full opportunity to express his views'), courtesy ('A controversial writer should be respectful in language and address... Quite a large proportion of the books and tracts written on the Moslem controversy need to be thoroughly revised in this respect and some of them should be suppressed'), and love ('The wonderful words of Paul, recorded in his First Epistle to the Corinthians, ought to constitute the motto of him who would enter the field of religious controversy'). It is notable that Wherry throughout speaks in terms of having many Muslims as his personal friends, see especially p. 224. He was among the first to be clear that 'The God of Islam is undoubtedly the only true God, inasmuch as He is represented as a personal God, the Creator and preserver of all things, as a prayer hearing God, and as possessing many other characteristics of the God of the Bible', ibid.

138. Campbell Moody (1865-1940) was a graduate of Glasgow University with a particular interest in church history, see Band, op. cit., p. 129. He became a missionary of the English Presbyterians in Formosa (Taiwan) in 1895 and was noted for his itinerant evangelistic methods, see Band, ibid., p. 136, and Latourette, *A History of Christian Missions in China*, pp. 683-4, where he summarizes Moody's reflections on mission among the Chinese contained in his three books, *The Heathen Heart* (1907), *The Saints of Formosa* (1911), and *The Mind of the Early Converts* (1920).

139. W.A. Shedd (1865-1918) had become a member of the American Presbyterian Mission in Persia in 1892. He later wrote: 'What is the reality in our relations as missionaries with men of other religions? The question is easily answered if one's con-

ception of the work is merely to make a proclamation of the Gospel, to sow the seed without thought as to the ground into which it falls. As soon, however as one honestly seeks to discuss spiritual problems with Mohammedans the problem becomes more complex'; from an article, 'Moslems and Christians in Western Persia', *IRM*, Vol. 6, 1917, pp. 99-112. An admiring biography was produced by Mary Lewis Shedd, *The Measure of a Man: William Ambrose Shedd* (1922).

140. WCC *Guidelines*, part II, para. 17.

141. There is an appreciation, including biographical material, of this respondent entitled *Cornaby of Hanyang: A Great Souled Missionary*, by Coulson Kernahan (1923). William Arthur Cornaby (1860-1920) was born in Sydenham, South London, and his early days are well described in Kernahan, pp. 28 ff. His first career was in chemistry but in 1883 he was a candidate for the Methodist Ministry and entered Richmond College, London University. In September 1885 he sailed for China. His colleagues then were Arnold Foster and Griffith John, when he was learning Chinese in Hankow. Cornaby was a person of wide interests and an engaging wit (on the lines of Jerome K. Jerome) and his writings show a deep and sympathetic understanding of central China, as e.g., in *A String of Chinese Peach Stones* (1895) and *China under the Searchlight* (1901). At this period he became heavily influenced by Timothy Richard. The biographical memoir, *Cornaby of Hanyang* records: 'Because of his wide knowledge of Chinese literature, and his skill in writing Chinese, Cornaby was appointed to take up literary work in Shanghai under the Christian Literature Society for China of which Dr. Timothy Richard was secretary and chairman. With such a colleague Mr. Cornaby could not but be happy. A genial, kindly soul, a keen and appreciative scholar, with the widest of human sympathy, Dr. Richard was best fitted to draw out and make best use of the talented scholar who had come to his aid, and whom he fully appreciated. At his home Mr Cornaby was ever welcome, and many happy hours were spent there,' Kernahan, op. cit., pp. 72-3. Cornaby refers to two works of his own, *In Touch with Reality* (n.d.s.) and *China Under the Searchlight* (1902). How far he himself succeeded in his self-appointed task may be evaluated by looking at his article, 'God (China)' in Hastings' *Encyclopaedia of Religion and Ethics*, to which he referred the Edinburgh Commissioners.

142. WCC *Guidelines*, part II, para. 19.

143. Cf. Jones' remarks on pp. 146ff.

144. Murdoch Mackenzie was replying from Chang Ta Fu, Honan, North China, a missionary of the Canadian Presbyterian Church with some twenty years' experience. For the record, we should note that though he had in fact been favourably disposed to Chinese religions ('No one could be more disposed to hope for meeting many good things among such systems of thought as China possesses than I was on coming out' (78, p. 3), by and large he had been disappointed: 'As a matter of fact the non-Christian systems furnish but little of which we can make a practical use in our work' (ibid, p. 13).

145. Op. cit., part III, para. 4.

146. An American Methodist minister, J.H. Messmore had contributed two works towards understanding India, *Land of Regrets* (1905), and a biography of an American Methodist Bishop in India: *The Life of E.W. Parker* (1903). He was a frequent contributor to the Methodist Episcopal magazine for India, *The Indian Witness*, and other publications of the ME mission. In one of these he had suggested in 1907 that the

great watchword of his period was not going to work out: 'We sympathize with those whose watchword is the evangelization of India in this generation; yet we know that such a triumph is impossible'; see M.H. Harper, op. cit., p. 28.

147. For Hogg in relation to Farquhar, see Eric Sharpe, *Not to Destroy*, pp. 288-294 and *Faith Meets Faith*, pp. 37-44, and in relation to Kraemer, see Wesley Ariarajah, *Hindus and Christians* (1991), pp. 75-7. I hope to offer a full study of Hogg in a sequel to this book.

148. WCC *Guidelines*, part 1, para. 19.

149. Gideon Draper was a long-serving missionary of the Methodist Episcopal Church, and wrote to the Commissioners from the context of his new work in Yokohama.

150. Copland King had arrived in New Guinea in 1891, a member of the first 'English Mission' party to this island.

151. Henry Woods, who worked in Hwaianfu in the Khangsu Province. was one of the few respondents from the Southern Presbyterian Mission in the Edinburgh material. He was also one of the most conservative, keywords in his response being 'heathen' and 'idolatry'. Higher criticism he associated with 'infidel literature'. Nevertheless, his considered judgment on Chinese religion shows that he had been in some kind of dialogue. 'The more closely and sympathetically one studies the religious beliefs and the Confucian classics which have dominated Chinese thought for 25 centuries, the more one is led to adore the infinite wisdom of God in the Scriptures, and the excellency of the Gospel of Christ...' (113, p. 13).

152. For Kajinosuke Ibuka and William Imbrie, see Arthur Judson Brown, *One Hundred Years*, pp. 699-700. Imbrie served as a Presbyterian missionary in Japan from 1875 until his death in 1922.

153. See on the later movements Kenneth Cracknell, 'The Theology of Religion in the International Missionary Council and the World Council of Churches' in *Current Dialogue*, No. 19, December 1991, and Wesley Ariarajah, *Hindus and Christians: A Century of Protestant Religious Thought* (1991).

154. A. Duncan Dixey was a member of the Baluchi mission in the Diocese of Lahore. Eugene Stock records: 'Mr Dixey has done very important work by his itinerations in the semi-independent territory of the Khan of Kalat'; see Stock, op. cit., p. 213. Dixey was a frequent contributor to the *CMS Intelligencer* and the *CMS Review*.

155. W.R. James had been appointed by the BMS to Mudaripore, in 1878. He wrote to the Commissioners in 1909 from Simla, but stressed 'I am really located in Calcutta.' He was an excellent speaker of Bengali.

156. See above, p. 203.

157. Joseph Taylor (1857-1927) was an English Quaker born in Sunderland. Taylor worked in the Nerbudda Valley, where the Friends' Foreign Mission Association had settled in 1876. For some details about his later work in Calcutta and his links with C.F. Andrews; see John Ormerod Greenwood, *Quaker Encounters*, Vol. 3, *Whispers of Truth* (1978), pp. 333, 369. His reply to question 5 read: 'sympathetic... It is very essential that the people should feel that the preacher really loves them, and is seeking their welfare; and is not simply engaged in a proselytising exercise' (237, pp. 7-8).

158. The reference here is to the well-known image of Klaus Klostermaier, in *Hindu and Christian in Vrindaban* (1969), the title of ch. 4. The contrast is with doing

theology at seventy degrees: 'They have an easy time, the 70° theologians. They settle down in some library and find enough books there by means of which it can be proved that the non-Christian religions are the normal way of salvation for the non-Christian, that each one finds God even without mission – that one should not disturb the conscience of a non- Christian. In Europe's libraries no goats die of heatstroke, there are no vultures and no dogs eating the goats', pp. 47-48.

159. J.R. Illingworth's phrases come from his chapter 'The Incarnation and Development' in Charles Gore (ed.), *Lux Mundi*, eighth edition, 1890, p. 181. The full sentence reads: 'Organisms, nations, languages, institutions, customs, creeds, have all come to be regarded in the light of their development, and we feel that to understand what a thing really is, we must examine how it came to be. Evolution is in the air; a "Partibus temporis"; a necessary consequence of our wider field of comparison'. For the importance of Illingworth see Thomas A. Langford, *In Search of Foundations: English Theology 1900-1920* (1969), pp. 190 ff. Illingworth's thought was adopted and adapted by Charles Cuthbert Hall, see above, pp. 101-2. In turn, Hall was quoted by Slater in his Edinburgh response. 'It was', wrote Slater, 'Dr. Hall's conviction that India's "great pantheistic inheritance", which we are sometimes apt to depreciate and deplore, qualified India in an exceptional degree to apprehend and interpret the deeper mysteries of the Christian faith as they gather round the *Person and Consciousness of Christ*; that the day was coming when India, so far from being repelled by the *Divinity* of Christ, would become the great exponent of it, recovering its meaning for the world' (239, p. 74, emphasis his).

160. W.H. Campbell (1859-1910), who had died just before the Conference took place, had been intensely involved in the establishment of what was to become the United Theological College in Bangalore. He had been designated as its first principal; see Goodall, op. cit., p. 66. An Ulsterman, he had arrived in India in 1884. His previous experience had been gained in Telegu village work, and in training catechists at Gooty, and he had published in Telegu a number of theological works which were regarded as of outstanding quality. He was also asked by the Madras government to revise the existing Telegu dictionary and grammar; see Goodall, ibid, p. 56.

161. C.H. Basil Wood, in 1909 a CMS worker, had been in Japan for eighteen years but was an SPG Missionary for his first five year term of service.

162. Gulick had also written a book, entitled *The Evolution of the Japanese: Social and Psychic* (1903). This was a thorough-going evolutionist work, based, he wrote, 'on the principles of social science'. From the point of view of later dialogue theorizing, the book points to 'dialogue in community'. Gulick wrote that in writing this book 'his ruling motive is profound love for the Japanese people', and the pages which follow manifest all his concerns, see note 136 above.

163. Arnold Foster (1846-1919) was educated at Mill Hill School and St John's College, Cambridge. He went to China in 1871 with the LMS, and served in Hanyang, Hankow and Wuchang. 'The range and depth of Arnold Foster's influence in China during nearly forty years can scarcely be exaggerated. His name was one which, thirty years after his death, continued to be spoken with peculiar warmth and intimacy and with growing appreciation of his qualities,' Goodall, op. cit., p. 165, cf. Latourette, op. cit., p. 364, and *Arnold Foster: Memoir, Selected Writings etc.*(1921). In the last of these, a contemporary of Foster's at Cambridge (1866-71), H. Arnold Thomas recalled: 'The great Cambridge scholars and theologians, especially, I think,

Dr. Westcott, had a very warm place in his regard, and to the end of his life he was in the habit of commending them to all young students. And he had a great love for Frederick Maurice, who was at that time lecturing in Cambridge.' Foster's diary entry for 21 July 21 1871, reads: 'Said Good-bye to dear old Cambridge – saw Mr Maurice for the last time', *Memoir*, pp. 9, 17. A later note in Foster's diary listed all the teachers who moulded his thinking. This includes the names of McLeod Campbell and Thomas Erskine, ibid., p. 49.

164. Shortly after writing his response Steinthal was appointed Principal of the Danish Mission Theological School in Santalia. That he went on thinking about truth and dialogue can be seen in an article entitled 'Lectures to Educated Indians' in the *Harvest Field*, April 1912.

165. This was not always obvious because of the use of circumlocutions to describe Steinthal like 'a worker among educated Hindus in Calcutta'.

166. Colin Campbell Brown, an English Presbyterian missionary in Swatow from 1893-1913, was a Chinese scholar from Oxford, having studied under Professor James Legge; see Band, op. cit., p. 302. He was a particularly gifted writer. By the time he responded to the Commissioners he was well known for a volume of stories, *China in Legend and Story* (1908) about the lives of individual Chinese people in the city of Chuanchow and the hilly countryside of southern Fukien. Brown believed that the people of the Middle Kingdom would make a specific contribution to Christian understanding and would reveal afresh 'the possibilities latent in Christianity'; see p. 251. Another book with the same themes is *A Chinese St Francis: or the Life of Brother Mao* (1912). Brown also wrote two commentaries in Chinese (on Amos and Philippians) and founded the Bible school in Chuan-chow; see Band, ibid., p. 403.

167. Henry T. Hodgkin, M.D. (1877-1933) was to become one of the most noted of all Quaker missionaries. He began his career as medical missionary but was soon involved in literature and administrative work. In 1915 he wrote a study guide on medical missions, *The Way of the Good Physician*. There is a biography by H.G. Wood, *Henry T. Hodgkin: A Memoir* (1937). See also ch. 4, 'The Friends Mission in West China', in J.E. Greenwood, op. cit.

168. Paul Kranz had come to China in 1892 to assist Ernst Faber. They were agents of 'The General Evangelical Protestant Missionary Society' whose headquarters were in Weimar. The aims of this Society were to present the Gospel undenominationally to the educated classes, 'building upon elements of truth already prevalent' among non-Christian peoples. See Latourette, op. cit., p. 398, and Warneck, *History of Protestant Missions*, p. 126. Kranz wrote a study of Faber which had been published in 1912. He also contributed other studies in German, notably *Die Welterlösungsreligion ist die Vollendung des Konfucianismus* (1899) but alas I have had no access to these works.

169. Murray has one of the most gracious tributes to Japanese religions to be found anywhere in the responses: '...there are many excellencies in these religions. If Christianity were unknown one might take the highest purest elements in them and have one of the best systems of teaching available. If it were not so they would never have gained hold on such large numbers of people' (32, p. 6).

170. G.H. Westcott was one of the five sons B.F. Westcott gave to India. He became Bishop of Lucknow in 1910. The extended quotation he gave came from the pen of another member of the brotherhood, A. Crosthwaite.

171. Edwin Greaves was a powerful figure among the LMS missionaries in the north of India. He served for a total of thirty nine years (1881-1920) and was widely respected as a scholar of Hindi, having published by the time he wrote his response such works as *Notes on the Grammar of the Ramayon of Tulsidas* (1895) and a *Grammar of Modern Hindi* (1896). Later he was to write *A Sketch of Hindi Literature* (1918), see Goodall; op. cit., p. 31.

172. Sherwood Eddy (1871-56) wrote a detailed and fascinating autobiography entitled *A Pilgrimage of Ideas: or the Re-education of Sherwood Eddy* (1935), which carries an account of his early missionary enthusiasm, see above, p. 31. Like many others Eddy fell immediately in love with India when he arrived there in September 1896: 'I found the people of India most attractive – intelligent, courteous, loveable, excelling in the passive virtues in the South, while warlike tribes and traditions were found in the North. The people were deeply religious with an affinity for the spiritual, in contrast to the Far East where the background is prevailingly concrete and often materialistic', ibid., p. 83. Eddy was a close friend of V.S. Azariah, the first Indian Anglican bishop; see ibid., pp. 96-7.

173. At the time of writing his response, Paul Bergen was working among college students in Weihsien, North China. He had already made a contribution to interfaith understanding in China: *The Sages of Shantung: Confucius and Mencius*, published by the CLS, in Shanghai. Bergen lists 'the doctrines most genuinely accepted and of most pronounced effect upon the spiritual and social life of the people': '(a) the Life, Character, and Teachings of Confucius. (b) the Doctrine of Amitya Buddha and the Western Heaven. (c) The Compassion and Self-abnegating love of Kwanyin. (d) A general belief in and reverence for Tienlaoyeh, a somewhat vague but popular term for the Creator. The Classic designation is Shangti. (e) Strictly local divinities are worshipped in the hour of stress with some sincerity. (f) The mass of the people believe in the Life to come, and in the doctrines of everlasting rewards and penalties. These last named doctrines are modified somewhat by an ill-defined acceptance of the theory of Metempsychosis. (g) In China there are several hundred Sects, each having its peculiarities. Some are political, some half political and half religious, and others purely religious. They are all really or nominally secret. In the gatherings of those which are religious, doing good by means of the different forms of social service is emphasized; spiritual life is cultivated through fasting, prayers, meditation, pilgrimages and vows. The people in these sects are more religious than the generality, and commonly hold to a mixture of the teachings of the Three Churches (Confucius, Bhudd. (*sic*) Taoism). (h) Ancestral worship is probably regarded by the Chinese as the holiest of their religious duties. It is universally practised, and makes the deepest impression. The neglect of it is to the Chinese a base and ungrateful omission. (i) Generally speaking, the ethical teachings of religion are valued more highly than doctrines, liturgies or ceremonial usages. And here again doctrine is thought to be of less importance than conformity to social religious rites' (43, p. 2).

174. In his *Memoir*, Arnold Foster makes three distinctions in his theory of the Logos. There are three degrees of light to be found among men – but each comes from the same source – the Light that lighteneth every man as he cometh into the world. The light in each case, however, shines with varying degrees of brightness. To suppose that the light which exists in one heathen nation is either the same in every other heathen nation, or that in the same nation it shines with equal brilliancy in each

individual heart is, of course, untrue. But in general terms the light of the Gentile nations is of the same character. The Light of Israel is the light of a chosen people – a people endowed with special mental and moral characteristics, a people chosen to witness to a living and righteous God Who made all men and can speak to men so that His voice can be recognized. The Light which comes from Christ is final, it contains in itself the germ of all that God has to reveal to men; op cit., p.136.

175. Nicol Macnicol was a missionary of the UFCS in Poona where he had established the *Indian Interpreter*. Eric Sharpe records Macnicol's initial statement of policy: 'The attitude of this paper will be one of sympathy with all that is worthy in the religions of India and the aspirations of the Indian people as pointing to and finding their fulfilment in Christ', *Not to Destroy*, p. 238. Macnicol's first large work was *Indian Theism* (1915) which was favourably reviewed by C.F. d'Arcy in *IRM*, Vol. 5, (1916). Macnicol was later to publish much on this tradition.

176. On the Logos in the thinking of the theologians and missionaries already treated, see above, pp. 48ff., 65ff., 84ff., 118., etc.

177. Anna M. L. Smith was in England serving as the Candidates Secretary of the Church of England Zenana Missionary Society. when she wrote her response. She had previously served with the CZMS in Bangalore, South India.

178. *The Missionary Message*, p. 176.

179. 'The Law hath been our tutor to bring us unto Christ, that we might be justified by faith', Galatians 3. 24-7 (RV). The *paidagogos* was the guide or protector of the child in ward until he came of age, and Paul used this imagery of the old Jewish religion, the *nomos* or 'law'.

180. The concept of the *praeparatio evangelica*, comes ultimately from the first church historian Eusebius in the fourth century: for an illuminating discussion see Robert M. Grant, 'Civilization as a Preparation for Christianity in the thought of Eusebius', in Church and George (eds), *Continuity and Discontinuity in Church History* (1979), pp. 62-70.

181. The RSV renders Ephesians 1.10 as 'Unite all things in Christ', but compare the RV which has 'unto a dispensation of the fullness of the times, to sum up all things in Christ'. 'United in Christ' is an attempt to translate the Greek verb *anakephalaioo*, here in its middle form, *anakephalaiosasthai*. Other possible translations could be 'gather into one', 'present as a whole', 'put all things under one head' or 'sum up all things' (as in the RV), these last two being renderings of the Latin *consummatus, consummator* theme, which we have seen fully developed by Brooke Foss Westcott; see above, pp. 62ff.

182. The controlling Biblical image in the Epistle to the Hebrews is: 'the law has but a shadow (*skia*) of the good things to come, not the true form (*eikona*) of these realities', Hebrews 10.1, RSV, cf. 'the law having a shadow of the good things to come, not the very image of the things', RV.

183. Henry Whitehead (b. 1853), brother of the philosopher and mathematician Alfred North Whitehead, was consecrated Bishop of Madras in 1899, having been, since 1889, head of the Oxford Mission in Calcutta and Principal of Bishop's College, Calcutta. Whitehead's particular love, however, was for the rural work at Barisal at the centre of the Ganges Delta, see Longridge, *History of the Oxford Mission to Calcutta* (1910), p. 156. Whitehead published a celebrated small booklet, *The Village Gods of South India* (1916) which was later revised with the help of V.S. Azariah.

184. R.S. Fyffe was leader of the Winchester Brotherhood, founded in Mandalay in 1905, when he responded to the Commissioners. Shortly afterwards he was appointed Anglican Bishop of Rangoon, serving for the next eighteen years, see Thompson, op. cit., pp. 638-9.

185. George Douglas was a missionary of the United Free Church of Scotland in Liaoyang. This mission field had been established through the work of Dr. John Ross of the United Presbyterian Church. From 1874 the Irish Presbyterians had come to the aid of the Scottish neighbours. Douglas was therefore a colleague of F.W.S. O'Neill, whom I hope to discuss in a sequel to this book.

186. O.J. Grainger was Principal of the Christian Bible College in Jubbulpore in the Central Provinces, having had experience in villages and educational institutions. He was a missionary of the Foreign Christian Missionary Society, which was founded in 1875 and merged into the United Christian Missionary Society. The Disciples had been working in India since 1882. See for Grainger's work, Archibald McLean, *The History of the Foreign Missionary Society* (1919).

187. For hints of this see the discussion of Farquhar in note 465 on p. 362.

188. That Ibuka and Imbrie do not share this opinion is evident from their later comment: 'The most that can be said of the elements in Shintoism and Buddhism that represent points of contact with Christianity is that they are tapers flickering in the night and in the wind' (17/19, pp. 9-10).

189. George Howells had begun in 1906 a series of articles entitled 'Short Papers on Non-Christian Religions' in which it was stressed that the missionary is compelled by loyalty to Christ to recognize truth wherever it may be found. He wrote: 'Our aim should be not to destroy, but to preserve everything that is consistent with the essentials of the Christian faith', *Missionary Herald*, IX NS (1906), p. 16; see Sharpe, *Not to Destroy*, pp. 237-8. In 1910, he told the Commissioners that he had written a thesis on the *Bhagavadgita* and the New Testament, but had not published it because he regarded it, 'in its present form, as incomplete, and so liable to be misunderstood'. Perhaps some of this work was incorporated in his later publication of the Angus Lectures 1910-1913, entitled: *The Soul of India: An Introduction to the Study of Hinduism, in its Historical Setting and Development, and in its Internal and Historical Relations to Christianity*, (1913), see Book III, chapter II, 'An Essay on the Common Elements of the Bhagavad Gita and the New Testament'.

190. Stanley P. Smith was one of the Cambridge Seven, along with D.E. Hoste, W.W. Cassels, C.T. Studd, Montagu Beauchamp and Cecil and Arthur Polhill-Turner. They all served with the China Inland Mission from 1884 onwards. He wrote an account of the Boxer troubles, *China from Within* (1910). For Smith see Latourette, op. cit., pp. 391 and 601, Pollock, *The Cambridge Seven*, pp. 71-89.

191. Lefroy told the Commissioners that this had been the theme of the Ramsden Sermon which he had preached before the University of Cambridge in 1904. I have not been able to trace this in Cambridge.

192. W.B. Boggs had worked in Ramapatam in the Nellore District of the Madras Presidency for the Baptist Missionary Union. He had left India in February 1907. Boggs may be counted among those who pleaded for a courteous approach to the Indian people if not to their religion. His answers to question 5 began with the words, 'Certainly not the attitude of antagonism and attack'. A few sentences later he wrote: 'While there should never be anything like heartless ridicule of the religion of the

people, or angry attack, there should be no shrinking from the full exposure of the utter absurdity of idolatry. Even this can be done kindly. There is nothing in manners which Hindus esteem so highly as courtesy' (129, p. 4).

193. William Bonnar wrote out of more than thirty years' experience in Rajputana. No indication is given in his response of the missionary agency for which he worked. Perhaps he was an Independent. His reply demonstrates close contact with all kinds of Hindus. There is a reference to a thirty-year long friendship with a Brahmin, whose remains Bonnar followed to the burning-ghat: 'As I watched the flames rise over the bier I wondered if ever again I should embrace him. I had no assurance although he seemed to have hope. According to human standards his was a comparatively beautiful life, yet he was an idol worshipper...' (130, p. 4). Bonnar entered a strong *caveat* about the irreligious lives, together with their pride and arrogance, of the British in India as a hindrance to the progress of the gospel. This, he saw, as having an effect on the attitude of many missionaries in India. 'During the time of his noviciate, while he is studying the language, the young missionary unconsciously imbibes more or less of the spirit of the English in India, a spirit of superior excellence and general aloofness, and this usually clings to him ever after, and gives a hard tone and colour to all his intercourse with the people.' William Bonnar judged that few missionaries ever entered into 'true fellowship with the people' (130, p. 7). This was for Bonnar a defect of love as well as of courtesy.

194. A missionary of the Nederlandsche Zendelings genootschap in Kuku, Central Celebes, where in 1910 no single conversion had taken place (334a, p. 10), Albertus C. Kruyt was to become well-known in the English-speaking missionary world through an article in the *IRM*, Vol. 4, No. 13, Jan. 1915, pp. 81-95, entitled 'The Presentation of Christianity to Primitive Peoples'.

195. Arthur Evans Moule arrived in China in 1861 shortly before the T'aip'ing Rebellion, and left in 1909. Moule's autobiography, *Half a Century in China: Recollections and Observations* (1911), written from the Shropshire rectory of Burwarton, where Moule was parish priest even at the age of seventy-five, has an illuminating chapter on 'The Missionary in China, and the presentation of his Message'. Moule was clearly a person of extreme courtesy and his exposition of missionary activity is in terms of St Paul in Athens. Resistance to the gospel he interpreted as 'foolishness to the Greeks', see pp. 262-263. 'I was once reading and speaking far into the night in a house in a country village. The schoolmaster and reading men of the village were there, with a number of husbandmen. They listened well, and reasoned keenly and fairly. Then as I drew to my climax, and held up the Cross of Christ, the offence of the Cross broke out with its ancient virulence. They frowned, and moved uneasily, and would listen no more. Ethics and science and philosophy, even western discoveries yes! But atonement and the doctrine of one dying for those who themselves deserved to die – no! they did not care to hear of this. It was late, too; at some convenient season they would hear me again of this matter,' (op. cit., p. 263). On the beginning of CMS work in China, see Latourette op. cit., p. 370, and Stock, op. cit., p. 317. Moule's earliest work *Four Hundred Millions* (1871) betrays ambivalence to what he had found in China during his first ten years there. He wrote of the contrast between Ningpo at night and London, to London's disadvantage. 'Let China have full praise for the outward appearance of morality, and if her religions have tended to promote this virtuous exterior let full merit be given to them,' *Four Hundred*, p. 5.

392   Notes to pages 229 to 231

Moule centred his attack upon what he calls a 'mental immorality'. 'People who think that religion is about virtue', he opined 'forget or deny that the first three commandments are pre-eminently moral laws, and that to worship false deities, or to make and reverence idols, is a most immoral act, staining and ruining the character of the most punctilious observer of the last six commandments,' ibid., p. 4. His call to his fellow Westerners was therefore pitched like this: 'Think of China, her vast and wide-spreading provinces, her enormous population, her decent exterior, her high-toned moral code, her unreligiousness, her atheistic religions, her gods many and lords many, her alienation from the life of God, her well-nigh smothered belief in the existence of the Most High, her hopeless deaths, her dreary hereafter, her sons and daughters in solemn despair passing into eternity; and shall we not love her, weep for her, plead for her, pray for her, more heartily and more earnestly, than we have ever done before,' ibid., pp. 399-400.

196. Moule held an anti-evolutionary theory of religion: 'When the Chinese throw their images into the canals to make room for the schoolmaster, why should we find some niche for them in mistaken theories of the history and evolution of religion' (82, p. 5). His answer to the question concerning 'higher criticism' was intemperate in its language, which includes such words as 'crudest and most audacious assumptions' of modernist 'professors from England', who run the risk of 'not only overthrowing the faith of many, but covering themselves and the creed they so feebly advocate with ridicule', *Four Hundred*, p. 121.

197. See for a brief account of the exegetical problems surrounding Acts 17, Cracknell, *Towards a New Relationship*, pp. 30ff. and the literature cited there.

198. Donald MacGillivray was a missionary of the Canadian Presbyterian Church, working for the Christian Literature Society of Shanghai. His major and still indispensable work was *A Century of Protestant Missions in China (1807-1907)* (1907).

199. Frederick Braun (he anglicized his Christian name for the Commissioners) was working in Byapur in Southern Mahratta. He wrote 'I have had most to do with the Lingayats, a Reform Sect of the Siva faith' (130a, p. 1).

200. George Swan served the Egypt General Mission, (later the Middle East General Mission), which was founded in 1897 in Belfast. Swan wrote about his work in a small volume, *Lacked Ye Anything?* published by the Egypt General Mission. I have been unable to find a copy of this book.

201. For an opinion of the medical work engaged upon by Robert Sterling see Stock, op. cit., pp. 126-7. His missionary preaching was described with approval by Rice, *Crusaders of the Twentieth Century* (1910), p. 25: 'He plainly and fearlessly sets forth Jesus as the divine Son of God and shows them the fallacies of their own creed.'

202. T.E. Alvarez and W.R. Miller were partners in Hausaland in Northern Nigeria. Stock described Alvarez as 'an intrepid pioneer in the hinterland' of Sierra Leone before taking up his work as the CMS Secretary in Northern Nigeria in 1901, op. cit., pp. 61-2, 77. W.R. Miller had been a member of the first CMS party to go to the Hausa States in 1900, and served as a CMS missionary from 1900-35. Though trained as a medical practitioner his gifts were primarily linguistic. He was responsible for the completion of the Hausa translation of the Bible. A full account of his work and views is in his *Reflections of a Pioneer* (1936).

203. The Nederlandsche Zendings-Vereniging for which J. Verhoeven worked in West Java was one of the most conservative Dutch groups, having broken away from

the Dutch Hervormde Kerk missionary body in 1858. Verhoeven had first arrived in Java in 1875. His thirty-three years in Java had been spent in finding and understanding 'the poor souls withering away in the darkness' and in 'preaching the "full counsel of God" to them' (340a, p. 6).

204. *The Missionary Message*, pp. 311-2.

205. Herman N. Barnum is referred to by William Strong as 'quiet but masterly' in the work at Harpoot, *The Story of the American Board* (1910), p. 220. He played a leading role in rehabilitation after the Armenian massacres (1895-6), and was accused by the Turkish government of 'sedition' (ibid., p. 398).

206. Samuel Graham Wilson was for thirty-two years a missionary of the American Presbyterian Church in Northern Persia. One of his earliest literary works was *Persian Life and Customs* (1899). He was later to publish a work refuting the claims of Bahai'ism, see *Bahaism and its Claims* (1915). H.U. Weitbrecht reviewed it in *IRM*, Vol. 5, 1916, pp. 672-4, and wrote, 'One could wish that the presentation was less exclusively polemical and more constructive. Bahaism is an effort, if sometime a perverse one, towards freedom and light; and the Christian messenger has to ask not only what are the errors to be removed, but how may the needs which it represents to be met?'

207. The first of these expressions was used by Robert Sterling in Jerusalem, Cf. 'The Muslim of today is the counterpart of the Pharisee of old: he believes that his good deeds can earn for him a title to Eternal Salvation' (274, p.1). For the second 'degraded form of Christianity' see Franklin Hoskins, 265a, p. 12.

208. Henry Harris Jessup (1832-1912) was the author of *The Mohammedan Missionary Problem* (1879), *The Setting of the Crescent and the Rising of the Cross* (1899), *Fifty Three Years in Syria* (1910) and a number of other works. The anonymous reviewer of the last named work in *IRM*, Vol. I, 1912, p. 532 points to the great lesson of Jessup's long service: the missionary 'should have fallen in love with his people and taken them for better and for worse'.

209. Jessup's suggestion that it was a kind of quarantine that pagan tribes had to pass through on their way to Christianity is unusual and unfamiliar to the present writer.

210. Walter Ayscliffe Rice, sometime Scholar of Christ's College, Cambridge, served from 1888 with the CMS Punjab Mission in Peshawar, and had then transferred to the Persia Mission in 1894. He had arrived in Shiraz in 1899. His attitudes are fully set out in a book called, somewhat alarmingly (but see the quotation from Raymond Lull below), *Crusaders of the Twentieth Century: or the Christian Mission and the Muslim* (1910). This volume, running to 561 pages, Rice published himself, though it was distributed by the CMS. Rice declared in his preface: 'A mastery of the ordinary lines of controversy should certainly be part of a missionary's equipment, whether for defence or for demonstrating the weakness of the opposite side. If we have this weapon at our command and can deftly use it, the less occasion shall we usually have for employing it and the sooner we shall be able to lay it aside' (ibid., p. xlii). Rice's understanding of mission is not dialogical. His book is, however, a mine of information, based as it is upon copious notetaking over twenty years. Rice continually urges tact and courtesy and quotes Raymond Lull: 'I see many knights cross the sea to Muslim lands; they think they shall conquer by force of arms. It appears to me that victory can be won in no other way than Thou, O Lord Christ, with Thy

Apostles, did seek to win it, with love and prayer, by shedding of tears and blood, by self-sacrifice, by spiritual and not by carnal weapons; see Rice, ibid., p. 44.

211. W. St. Clair Tisdall was, according to Stock, 'a distinguished alumnus of the University of New Zealand', op. cit., p. 537, and had followed Bishop Stuart of Waiapu to the Persia Mission of the CMS. Tisdall had a range of publications to his name and was a well-known speaker at such gatherings as the Pan Anglican Congress in 1908. He also gave lectures on the James Long Foundation, ibid., p. 509. His writings include: *The Sources of Islam: A Persian Treatise*, translated and abridged by Sir William Muir (1901), 'Islam in Persia' in Zwemer, Wherry, and Barton (eds), *The Mohammedan World of Today* (1906), *The Religion of the Crescent*, third edition revised (1910), and *Christianity and Other Faiths* (1912).

212. James W. Inglis had come to Manchuria in 1891 as a missionary of the UFCS. He was appointed Principal of the Theological Hall at Mukden in 1910. In his article 'The Christian Element in Chinese Buddhism' in *IRM*, Vol. 5, 1916, pp. 587ff., Inglis is tougher minded than Arthur Lloyd about the possibility of Gnostic influences on Amida-Buddhism, but postulates a close connection between the Nestorians in Christian and the Mahayanist Zendo (Chinese, Shan-Tao). His conclusion, however, is this: The ancient vow of Amida 'is absolutely unrelated to space and time; it is but a myth. That there is mercy in the heavens is the natural hope of every man; it is but a pathetic dream until we know that the heavens have spoken and declared that mercy in the Word made flesh', ibid., p.ooo.

213. See his article 'The Chins of Burma' in *The East and the West*, Vol. VI (1908), pp. 361-85.

214. See above, pp. 170-71.

215. What John Morrison meant by this was more fully explained at the WMC itself. There he made a strong speech insisting that while the missionary had to know the mind of the people to whom he was going, it was not his task to teach them about their own religion: 'I fear, Mr Chairman, a missionary going as a comparative theologian.' Citing his own experience, he continued, 'although I had drawn up the points I had found to appeal to the Hindus, I found it unnecessary to repeat them'. An effective presentation of the Gospel, he thought, did not have to take account of the existing framework of belief, in his words: 'When we seek for the aspect of the Christian message which will appeal most to the Hindus or to any people, we must be clear that we know the distinctive message of Christianity to our own souls'. He suggested that if that were done then 'we can put it in terms which can be understood by anyone unfamiliar with our Christian thought and Christian terms'. He concluded that 'the appeal in South Africa, the appeal in Japan, the appeal in China, the appeal even to Moslems is much the same as the effective appeal to the modernised Hindu people,' *The Missionary Message*, pp.312-3.

216. I can discover nothing at all about this missionary.

217. Eugene Stock wrote in 1916, 'Dr Hooper, who joined the mission fifty-three years ago, still lives in the hills, at Mussoorie, diligent as ever in literary work,' op. cit., p. 223. William Hooper was a specialist in Hindi. His 'controversialist' volume of apologetic, *Christian Doctrine in Contrast with Hinduism and Islam*, was published in Madras in 1896. This work was still prescribed reading in the Theological College in Lahore when C.F. Andrews made proposals for reforming theological education in India; see O'Connor, *Gospel, Raj and Swaraj*, p. 195.

218. Roswell Hobart Graves (1833-1912) had been in China since 1856, engaged upon extensive literary work. The Edinburgh Commissioners might have known his work *Forty Years in China: or China in Transition* (1845). For Graves, see Latourette, op. cit., p. 25.

219. Reginald Stephen Copleston, Bishop of Calcutta and Metropolitan of India, 1902-1913. Previously he had been Bishop of Colombo from 1875-1902. Coplestone had been a 'brilliant young Oxford don of decidedly high church views' (see M.E. Gibbs, *The Anglican Church in India 1600-1970*, p. 262) when he was consecrated Bishop of Colombo at the age of thirty. For some autobiographical comments see his article 'The Approach of the Young Missionary to Buddhists and Hindus' in *IRM*, Vol. 5, 1917. While Copleston was against the language of aggression ('It is quite possible we overdo the language of warfare') the missionary was in the business of 'establishing the Truth' however gently this was done ('It is better to cherish the seed of health than to attack the symptoms of the disease'); see op. cit., Vol. 6, 1917, p. 516. Copleston was for neither dialogue nor 'points of contact' (see his review of K.J. Saunders' *The Story of Buddhism*); 'when some word or act of Gautama is shown to be like a word or act of Christ, it would be well to take care that the reader is reminded that even identical words or acts have an infinitely deeper significance when they come from Him who is not only truly Man but the Eternal God', *IRM* Vol. 6, 1917, p. 187.

220. See Sheffield's speech 'The Chinese Ministry' in the *Records of the China Centenary Conference* (1907), pp.34-52. The words quoted by Kranz are on p.43.

221. Herbert Udny Weitbrecht, was of German background, his father John James Weitbrecht having served with the CMS from 1830-1852. H.U.Weitbrecht had studied in Berlin and served the CMS in the Punjab and the Sindh missions for more than thirty four years. An expert in Urdu, he was deeply committed to the Urdu translation of the New Testament. He was a Fellow of the Punjab University. On his return to Britain he became the first Secretary of the Missionary Education Council.

222. George E. White is not mentioned in the standard histories of the American Board. From his response, however, he is clearly an interesting character and more work could be done on him, as indeed on the whole of the ABCFM in Turkey at this period.

223. John van Ess had been appointed to Busrah (Basra) in Turkish Arabia or Mesopotamia (Iraq) in 1902. His work was chiefly among the Turkish military, and his response includes a testimony from a Turkish officer converted to Christianity in 1899.

224. George W. Rowland was singled out by d'Arcy as 'going much further than others' in this respect in *The Missionary Message*, p.117.

225. Shedd's response was subjected to very heavy underlining by David Cairns.

226. There can be no way of telling whether or not Steinthal ever read Maurice, but his expression 'an actually restored fellowship with God' is purely Maurician.

227. Cf. Bernard Lucas' vision of 'foundation laying', see above, p. 162.

228. Cf. Westcott's hopes, see note 222 on p. 223.

229. *Conference Daily Paper*, No. 1, p. 7. A bound copy of these papers is in the archives of the CCBI, Interchurch House, London.

230. Ibid., p. 8.

231. *History and Records of the Conference*, vol. IX of *The World Missionary Conference 1910*, pp. 86ff.

232. Summaries of their speeches can be found in 'Presentation and Discussion of the Report' in *The Missionary Message in Relation to Non-Christian Religions*, WMC vol. IV, pp. 291-p. 396.

233. Ibid., p. 293.

234. Ibid.

235. Ibid., p. 294.

236. Ibid.

237. Ibid., p. 267.

238. Ibid.

239. Ibid.

240. Ibid., p. 270.

241. Ibid.

242. Ibid., p. 218.

243. Ibid.

244. Ibid., p. 238.

245. Ibid.

246. Ibid., pp. 238-9.

247. Ibid., p. 239.

248. Ibid., p. 241.

249. Ibid.

250. Ibid., p. 244.

251. Ibid., p. 245.

252. Ibid., p. 246.

253. Ibid., p. 250.

254. Ibid.

255. Cairns referred in a footnote (p. 251) to work contributed by Hogg in the *Madras Christian College Magazine*, 1909., which suggested that Jesus viewed his Kingdom as 'essentially redemption from the evil world by means of union with God' and that therefore that Kingdom was in its very essence supernatural.

256. *The Missionary Message*, p. 250.

257. Ibid., pp. 252-3.

258. Ibid., p. 255.

259. Ibid.

260. Ibid.

261. Ibid., p. 269.

262. Ibid.

263. Ibid., pp. 270-71.

264. Ibid., p. 273.

265. Ibid., p. 268.

266. Ibid.

267. Ibid., p. 274.

5 *The Reception of The Missionary Message: Two Theologians and a Postscript*

1. Constance Padwick's *Temple Gairdner of Cairo* sold thirteen thousand copies in its first two years, and had a second revised edition in 1930. This work has not been

superseded but a new volume on Gairdner is much needed. We look forward to the publication of Michael Shelley's doctoral thesis at Birmingham, 1987, which examines the changing patterns in Gairdner's thinking. There is a valuable sketch of Gairdner in G.S. Eddy's *Pathfinders of the World Crusade* (1954), pp. 247-251.

2. Its full title is *W.H.T.G. to His Friends: Some Letters and Informal Writings of Canon W.H. Temple Gairdner of Cairo 1873-1928* (1930).

3. Cf. Eddy, op. cit., p.250: 'Gairdner's published letters are used by the British Broadcasting Corporation in their radio religious services as among the finest pieces of Christian literature of the last fifty years.'

4. *Edinburgh 1910* had two editions within four months.

5. The most significant of Gairdner's writings about Islam from this period are *D.M. Thornton: A Study in Missionary Ideals and Method* (1909), *The Reproach of Islam* (1909), and his important article 'The Vital Forces of Christianity and Islam' published in the *IRM*, Vol. 1, 1913, pp. 44-61. The ideas there reappeared after the war in *The Rebuke of Islam. Being the Fifth Edition, rewritten and revised of The Reproach of Islam* (1920).

6. For these and other links see Padwick, op. cit., pp. 36, 43, and 57.

7. The Pan-Anglican Congress took place in July 1908. In a paper on 'The Moslem Question', Gairdner asked 'Who shall gauge the debt we shall have yet to confess to Islam if that great antagonist prove finally to have compelled us to explore unknown depths of the revelation of the Triune God?', quoted in Padwick, op. cit., pp. 179-80.

8. Padwick says that Gairdner wrote this book with 'nearly incredible swiftness', for the scheme of it had lived in his mind since Thornton's death in 1906, op. cit. p. 181 . Like Gairdner, Thornton was a missionary among Muslims and must count as a forerunner in dialogue. Gairdner's comments on Thornton's visionary hopes and grand strategies for the whole Muslim world described his own views. David Cairns also considered Thornton to be one of the greatest of missionaries to the Muslim world: 'In Egypt he left a beloved name... His high sense of the universality of Christ, the brotherhood of man, the sacred missionary duty of being at one with the people to which he had come, went very far to modify the inveterate Anglo-Saxonism of his natural man; or at any rate threw into relief the reality of the love that inspired it... The broad impression remains of a man who understood Egypt and the Egyptians, and was the true friend of the people, sharing in the sympathy which comes of a fundamental love for men, and that sympathetic study of the manners, habits, thoughts and aspirations of the people that is born of love.'

9. For detailed comment on this work, see below, pp. 266ff. Meanwhile note Gairdner's main thrust: 'If Islam's forces are indeed nature, the world and the flesh, then Islam has left to us only one weapon, in taking away all others, – it has abandoned us to the Sword of *the Spirit*... The Spirit of Jesus is the only asset of the Church,' emphasis Gairdner's. Padwick comments, 'That final sentence gives us the motive and key-note of his life work.'

10. Padwick describes this process: 'Once at least he read seventeen hours in a day, and that in seaside lodgings in and out of the room where he sat with his piled up papers. The chapters were sent to the Printer, generally in the small hours, with the ink scarcely dry, and by September the 7th the last proof was read', op. cit. pp. 199-200.

11. Ibid., p. 200.

12. Ibid.

13. *Edinburgh 1910*, pp. 134.

14. Ibid., pp. 135-6, emphasis his.

15. Ibid., p. 137.

16. Ibid., emphasis his.

17. Ibid., p. 38.

18. Ibid.

19. Ibid., pp. 141-7.

20. Ibid., p. 148, emphasis his.

21. Ibid., p. 147.

22. Ibid., p. 148. Gairdner had read *The Religions of the World*. See *The Reproach of Islam* (1909), p. 134; cf. *The Rebuke of Islam* (1920), p.104.

23. Ibid., p. 149.

24. Ibid., p. 151.

25. Ibid., p. 152.

26. Ibid., p. 153.

27. Ibid., cf. *The Missionary Message*, p. 274.

28. *The Rebuke of Islam*, p. iii.

29. Ibid.

30. The allusion is to the Hebrew term *cherpah*, as in Jer. 29.18, cf. Jer. 44.12., 49.13 and Ezek. 5.14-5.

31. Padwick, op. cit., p. 196. From Clinton Bennett's researches it is apparent that Gairdner had no high opinion of other missionary experts' grasp of Islamic scholarship. Cf. the reply of Duncan Black Macdonald to Gairdner in 1910: 'You are a missionary, look around you and see where are the other missionaries in your position. You know what to think of Zwemer's knowledge and reading. With St Clair Tisdall it is not much better. Canon Sell made a good beginning in his day but he had not the books or the patience and he never really got into the light, and who else is there in the second or third rank?', quoted in Bennett, *Victorian Images of Islam* (1992), p. 146.

32. The first three months were spent in Potsdam to learn German, then four months in Hartford in order to study Muslim theological Arabic and the Arabic theological literature together; then back to Europe to visit the Hamburg Institute to study Arabic phonetics with Carl Meinhof, and lastly to go to Budapest in order to study with Goldziher. With the last of these Gairdner entered into Christian-Jewish dialogue. 'The Goldzihers he wrote, 'are a pair of Hebrew Angels. Their generosity and friendship are simply *absolute*... These are Jews of the stamp of the Greatest of the Sons of Israel; and in His day would have recognised and received Him. I am at every turn trying to learn Goldziher's attitude and method and grasp his grasp so to speak...', Padwick, op. cit., p. 212. The academic publications that resulted are not great, for Gairdner was always deprived of his dream of becoming a full-time 'research missionary' by the exigencies of the 1914-18 War. For a bibliography of Gairdner's articles and booklets on Islamic theology, see Padwick, op. cit. pp. 328-329.

33. Padwick, op. cit., pp. 213-4.

34. *W.H.T.G. to His Friends*, pp. 4-5.

35. Ibid., p. 5.

36. The article 'The Vital Forces of Christianity and Islam' became part of a volume of the same name to which G. Simon, W.A. Shedd and others also contributed.

37. 'The Vital Forces', p. 46.

38. Ibid., pp. 46-7.

39. Ibid., p. 58.

40. Ibid.

41. Ibid.

42. Ibid., p. 59. Cf. this dictum: Islam '... by its uncompromising insistence on the Unity, helps us to find the love and the action of God at the beginning, middle and end of the entire redemptive work, both for the race and the individual', ibid.

43. Ibid., p. 47.

44. Ibid.

45. Ibid., pp. 47-8.

46. Ibid., p. 49.

47. Ibid., pp. 49-50.

48. Ibid., p. 50.

49. Ibid., p. 51.

50. Ibid. Cf. Gairdner's view that 'this would justify missions to Islam even if they did not produce a single convert', ibid.

51. Ibid., p. 55.

52. Ibid., p. 46.

53. Gairdner had hoped to make Al Ghazzali his specialist subject, see his article 'Al Ghazzali's al Anwar and the Ghazzali Problem' in *Der Islam*, Strasbourg, 1914, and later the small volume, *Al Ghazzali's Mushkat al Anwar (The Niche for Lights)*; a translation with Introduction, published by the Royal Asiatic Society in 1924.

54. *The Rebuke of Islam*, p. 58.

55. 'Vital Forces', p. 59.

56. *The Rebuke of Islam*, p. 205.

57. There is an extended description of this way of dialogical sharing in what Gairdner terms 'a history of a soul' in *The Rebuke of Islam*, pp. 205-10, which contains the words: 'I was treating the missionaries with hatred and insult, but the missionaries never ceased to treat me with courtesy and even with love,' p.208.

58. There is a memoir of J.H. Moulton by his brother, W. Fiddian Moulton, simply entitled *James Hope Moulton* (1919), and a centenary tribute edited by H.K. Moulton also called *James Hope Moulton* (1963). There is a good, if brief assessment of his work as a scholar and teacher by Gordon Wakefield, 'Ministerial training: James Hope Moulton (1863-1917)' in *The Epworth Review*, Vol. 15, No. 1, Jan.1988, pp. 45-51. Also there are recollections of his life and work in other places, e.g. in *The Story of Our Colleges 1835-1914: A Centenary Record of Ministerial Training in the Methodist Church* (1935), p. 64, where W. Bardley Brash records the story of D.S. Cairns visiting Didsbury College in Manchester and remarking that 'there was something unique in the fact that one man could be a specialist of international fame in two subjects', i.e. Hellenistic Greek and Zoroastrianism.

59. Moulton belonged within the elite of the scholar theologians of the Wesleyan Methodist Church, his father William, having been the first headmaster of the Leys School in Cambridge, and one of the Revisers of the New Testament in 1881. He had also been responsible, with A.S. Geden, for the New Testament *Concordance* which bears their name.

60. He had graduated at King's earlier but was unable to proceed to the BA and MA degrees.

61. Of these the most notable is his five-volume *Grammar of New Testament Greek* (1906 onwards), but he also produced a well-known work on papyrology, *From Egyptian Rubbish Heaps* (1916) and with George Milligan of Aberdeen, the *Vocabulary of New Testament Greek*, of which only two parts had been completed by the time of his death in 1917.

62. Moulton's main contribution in *Early Zoroastrianism* was to insist upon Zoroaster's monotheism, ascribing the radical dualism which characterizes later Zoroastrianism from the later Avesta onwards to the Median Magi. He also defended the historicity of Zarathushtra's person as portrayed in the *Gathas* and claimed these texts for a very early date. To support these views, Moulton offered his own translation of the *Gathas*. Despite the many other theories and suggestions made since *Early Zoroastrianism*, Moulton's view still prevails. For example, R.C. Zahner wrote in 1961 that it was the Median Magi who 'presented so curious and distorted an image of the Prophet Zoroaster to the West'. Certainly Moulton's ideas were promulgated in the standard text books on the comparative study of religion in the next generations. From R.E. Hume, *The World's Living Religions* (1924), through A.C. Bouquet, *Comparative Religion* (1942), D.W. Gundry (*Religions* (1958) and Geoffrey Parrinder (*The World's Living Religions* (1964), Moulton has exercised his great influence on the understanding of Zoroastrianism in the West. Critical comments have largely arisen because of Moulton's (as some have seen it) over-enthusiastic admiration for early Zoroastrianism. Two examples must suffice. R.E. Hume, the Comparative Religion Professor at Union Seminary, New York, doubted very early whether Moulton's translation of *spenta mainyu* as 'Holy Spirit' did not connote 'to most English readers more than was intended by Zoroaster'. A second example comes from R.C. Zaehner in a discussion of the Magi in his last book, *The Dawn and Twilight of Zoroastrianism* (1961): 'For Moulton,' he wrote, 'whose zeal for the prophet burned a little too brightly, the Magi were the villains of the piece and were not allowed to belong to either the Aryan or Semitic race, so repulsive did their particular doctrines appear to him to be', p.161. After his Hibbert Lectures, Moulton completed two other works, both published after his death, *The Teaching of Zarathushtra: Eight Lectures and Addresses delivered to Parsis in Bombay* (1917) and *The Treasure of the Magi: A Study of Modern Zoroastrianism* (1917).

63. The Fernley Lectures had been founded in 1869 by a Manchester businessman of that name, in order to give scope to Methodist scholarship.

64. A Methodist missionary scholar, W.H. Findlay from India, was the original choice, but had fallen ill. Hence the rather hurried preparation of the 1913 Fernley lectures to which Moulton alludes on p. vii.

65. *Religions and Religion: A Study of the Science of Religion, Pure and Applied* (hereafter cited as *Religions*) was produced in time for the 1913 Conference by the Wesleyan Methodist Publishing House. Moulton wrote about *The Missionary Message*, 'I cannot resist the temptation to express my very strong wish that the Continuation Committee could devise means for publishing this evidence, or at least a very large selection from it. It is obvious from the Report that it would make a volume of immense value', *Religions*, p. 90.

66. Of these three F.W. Kellett (1862-1904) deserves special notice; see Sharpe, *Not to Destroy* (1965), pp.105ff. Moulton would presumably have read Kellett's pamphlet, *Christ the Fulfiller of Hinduism* (1896).

67. *James Hope Moulton* (1919), p. 35.

68. *Religions*, p. viii.

69. Ibid., p. viii-ix. Note here the 'broken lights' phraseology taken directly from the Report of Commission IV.

70. *Religions*, p. ix.

71. Ibid.

72. Compare the analysis of the part played by the concept of evolution in the Edinburgh Responses and in *The Missionary Message*, see above pp. 168ff., 213ff.

73. *Religions*, p. 51.

74. Ibid. Cf. the doctrinal issue that Moulton saw as undergirding this point: 'Not by objective, external authoritative voices, compelling an unintelligent assent, will He speak to those whom He created in His own image. He attains His supreme object when, after age-long processes have developed matter and force, conscious, minds and will, He has worked His will in the only way worthy of it', ibid.

75. *Religions*, p. 58.

76. For Hume, see above, pp. 137ff. Moulton wrote that we must always allow for 'the degeneration that comes from mere slackness. It is incomparably easier to say prayers than to pray, to perform rites than to love mercy and walk humbly with God. And so there is a force ever dragging men back to those "beggarly alphabets" of religion, necessary enough when they were just learning to read God's lesson, but childish in later days', *Religions*, p. 114. For one example of degeneration see Moulton's treatment of 'the loss of God' in traditional or 'animistic' religions on pp. 56-7, which cites material from *The Missionary Message*, p. 25.

77. *Religions*, p. 60.

78. Ibid., p. 61.

79. Ibid.

80. Ibid.

81. Ibid., p. 63.

82. Ibid.

83. Ibid., p. 62.

84. Ibid.

85. For the word 'syncretism' as a term of abuse. see above, p. 244. Only recently have there been attempts to rehabilitate it, see Stanley Samartha, *One Christ, Many Religions* (1992) and Victor Hayes, art. 'Faithful Syncretism' in Norman C. Habel (ed.), *Religion and Multiculturalism in Australia* (1992), pp. 56-78.

86. When Moulton was writing, S.A. Cook's *Zeus* had just appeared, and he registered his impression of the lasting power of Pheidias' image of Olympian Zeus on Christianity in these startling words, 'The Zeus begins to reappear, though with a new name. It is the name of Christ,' *Religions*, p. 81.

87. Hayes, op. cit.

88. *Religions*, p. 84. Moulton is referring to the German professor H. Gunkel's work on the New Testament in 1903, *Zum Religionsgeschichtliche Verständnis des Neuen Testaments*, which he discussed on pp. 30ff. of *Religion*s.

89. *Religions,* p. 85. Cf. 'Our study of Comparative Religion has made us thankful for the truth understood by those who have not received the Gospel, and has removed the reproach which narrower views of God brought upon religion. He has not left Himself without witness anywhere, nor allowed a small proportion of His children to monopolise the life-giving knowledge of Himself. But the more carefully and sympathetically we study other religions, the more clearly does it appear that Christ completes and crowns them all', ibid.

90. Ibid., pp. 85-6.

91. Ibid., p. 85.

92. Ibid., p. 90.

93. Ibid., p. 91

94. Ibid.

95. There were other related matters on which Moulton expressed himself, e.g., the salvation of other people, of any religion or of no religion, was not to be doubted: 'We feel quite sure that God will act justly and lovingly towards those who are kept from the knowledge of His highest truth by no fault of their own', ibid., p. 125. Moulton thought the criterion for this was ethical: 'Not only men who never heard the Gospel, but men who have heard it and in perfect honesty rejected it, will have their place in the vaster energies of the next world determined by their treatment of their brethren here', ibid., p. 127. As a NT scholar Moulton knew that against this position would be advanced texts like Mark 16.16 ('he that disbelieveth shall be condemned') and John 3.31 ('he that believeth not the Son shall not see life, but the wrath of God abideth upon him'). Therefore he particularly discussed the verb *apeithein,* concluding that the NT knew 'nothing of punishment to fall upon men for intellectual belief honestly held', ibid., p. 125. He then gave a brief exegetical study of Matt.25, stressing the surprise on the part of the 'righteous' in the parable, and the 'clear law laid down that men are to be judged by God according to their behaviour to their fellow men'. This pattern of exegesis, familiar enough to us, Moulton saw as opening a 'stupendous field of discovery' for the world, ibid., p. 127.

96. *Religions,* pp. 91-2. Attentive readers will draw their own conclusions if I say that nothing of this was brought to my attention during my own training and preparation as a missionary in 1961.

97. Ibid., pp. 92-3. Balmer's words are quoted on p. 199 above and Gulick's on p. 221.

98. Ibid. Monahan took part in the Edinburgh debates and is quoted at length in the 'Concluding Note' in *The Missionary Message,* p. 277.

99. Ibid. William Goudie's words in his letter to Moulton are worth recording: 'Christianity conquers through its difference from, and not through its approximations to, all other forms of faith. Its first grip on the mind and heart of the new convert is almost invariably through some point of contrast, and its first impact on his own faith is nearly always destructive. The first effect of Christianity on the Hindu systems must be to disintegrate. The constructive and inclusive process will come later; the experienced Christian will look back and see that though the sun has risen in him but lately, the stars of God have shone all through the long night; he will be ready to cry "Lo God was with me all the time, and I knew it not"; it is only in the light of the Christian faith that the fragments of truth in the other systems can be discovered, valued and placed in the final system,' in *Religions,* pp. 93-4.

100. *The Missionary Message*, pp. 292-4.

101. Ibid., p. 97.

102. Ibid., pp. 99-100.

103. Ibid., pp. 101-2.

104. Ibid., p. 102.

105. *Religions*, p. 154.

106. Ibid., p. 155; the quotation from David B. Schneder, was used by C.F. d'Arcy, *The Missionary Message*, p. 115. For Schneder see above, p. 204.

107. Ibid.

108. Ibid.

109. Ibid., p. 156.

110. Ibid.

111. See K. Cracknell, 'What is Faith?' in *The Epworth Review*, Vol. 15, No. 1, Jan. 1988, pp. 65-73.

112. *Religions*, p. 128.

113. Ibid.

114. Ibid.

115. There are occasional hints in the text that German imperialism was beginning to be felt as a threat.

116. Ibid., p. 154.

117. Ibid., p. 153; cf. 'If means of grace, ecclesiastical attachment, subsidiary doctrines of our creed, help us towards a more vital realisation of Christ, and of God through Him, they will be of service towards the ultimate end of religion; but if they draw off our attention towards themselves, they weaken the ethical energy of the Faith. It does matter, therefore what we believe, and even what form of Christianity we accept; for we need in our human weakness the most living force we can command to make us what we ought to be,' ibid., p. 130. The alternative was difficult to contemplate: 'We must not and dare not bewilder the non-Christian world with the spectacle of acute divisions. Our brethren who cannot bring themselves to tolerate a doctrine or Church Order widely different from their own, yet equally held "in Christ" must ask themselves whether, after all, such forms are not preferable to paganism,' ibid., p. 151.

118. Ibid., p. 211.

119. Ibid., p. 211-2.

120. Ibid., p. 211.

121. Ibid.

122. Ibid., p. 94.

123. Ibid.

124. Ibid., p. 95.

125. Ibid.

126. Ibid.

127. Ibid., pp. 95-6. Note here the dialogue exponent's ability to use the language of his hearers in fresh contexts. 'Wise Lord' is the exact translation of *Ormazd* or *Ahura Mazda*.

128. In an art. 'The contribution of J.H. Moulton' in *Methodist Contributions to the Study of Religions*, a volume of essays to be published in 1994 by Westminster College, Oxford.

129. See the chapter entitled 'India' in *James Hope Moulton* (1919), pp. 133-200. The lectures were published as *The Teaching of Zarathushtra: Eight Lectures and Addresses delivered to Parsis in Bombay* in Bombay in 1917. In Bombay he received a hero's welcome from the Zoroastrian community, who later took it upon themselves to publish his eight lectures and addresses both in English and in Gujarati. W.F. Moulton has some interesting comments about his brother's actual experience of being drawn into party controversies on matters which divided the 100,000 strong Parsi community in Bombay: 'When he arrived there was waiting for him an invitation to address the Iranian Association, which represented what may be called the Radical wing, and which is therefore an object of suspicion to the orthodox and to the Conservative wing. Dr Modi had told him that already some of those advanced men had been appealing to the authority of the Western scholar in support of these contentions...,' op. cit., p. 188. Wisely Moulton talked to the orthodox first, who then published his lectures in English. Copies of these still survive, and have their own enormous charm and significance as examples of 'truth tell' by a member of one religious tradition about another. In his prefatory remarks to *The Teaching of Zarathushtra*, Moulton thanked his 'friends Mr. H.J. Bhabha and Mr. P.A. Wadia for the unfailing kindness in making the publication possible, and Dr. Daji for undertaking the companion volume in a language unhappily unknown to me....' Moulton also commented on the 'large and attentive audiences of Parsis he had met with everywhere, in Karachi, Hyderabad, Ootacamund, Rajkot, Ahmadabad, and Poona was well as in Bombay. He sent this book out with the words "I feel I am talking to friends..."', pp. i-ii. It was not only the Zoroastrian community which was impressed by Moulton's knowledge of Sanskrit and Indian religion. His brother records that the Hindu College at Veranasi made a tentative approach at this time to see if Moulton would think of becoming its Principal; see op. cit., pp. 157-162.

130. 'Minute of Discussions' in *The Christian Life and Message in relation to Non-Christian Systems* (1928), p. 343.

131. These papers were produced by Nicol Macnicol (Hinduism), Leighton Stuart and Willard Lyon (Confucianism); K.J. Saunders and A.K. Reischauer (Buddhism), and W.H. Temple Gairdner and W.A. Eddy (Islam).

132. E.g., the sentence which begins, 'thus, merely to give illustrations, and making no attempt to estimate the spiritual value of other religions to their adherents...' on p. 491.

133. For a brief discussion of the way this Conference went see K. Cracknell, 'The Theology of Religion in the International Missionary Council and the World Council of Churches 1910-1939' in *Current Dialogue*, No. 19, Jan. 1991, pp. 32-43

134. *The Authority of the Faith* (1939) was the title of the relevant volume of the records of the International Missionary Council Meeting at Tambaram, Madras, 12-19 December 1938.

135. *The Christian Message in a Non-Christian World* (1938), pp. 16-7.

136. Ibid., p. 71.

137. 'Findings' in *The Authority of the Faith*, p. 200.

138. See Cracknell, art. cit., p. 8.

139. In *Hindus and Christians: A Century of Protestant Ecumenical Thought* (1991), p. 28.

140. Ibid., p. 29.

141. Ibid., p. 30.

142. *Protestanse theologie der godsdiensten; van Edinburgh naar Tambaram (1910-1938)*, p. 374., cf. p. 32, where van Lin speaks of 'een houding van sympathie en erkenning ten aanzien van de andere godsdiensten...' The reason for this is that 'God is ook in de niet-christelijke godsdiensten werkzaam geweest, wat zich uitdrukt in de elementen van waarheid en goedheid die daar kunnen worden gevonden,' ibid.

143. 'Wel kan men vastsstellen, dat en vanuit Continentale en vanuit Angelsaksiche zendingkringen uitdrukkelijk tegen neigingen tot syncretisme is gewaarschuwd. De uniciteit van het Christendom mag niet worden losgelaten,' van Lin, ibid., p. 35.

Bibliography

Addison, James Thayer, *The Christian Approach to the Moslem: A Historical Study*, New York, Columbia University Press 1942.

— *The Episcopal Church in the United States*, New York, Charles Scribner's Sons 1951.

Adriani, N., 'Moslem Advance in Malaysia' in Wherry, E.M., Zwemer, S.M., and Mylrea, C.G. (eds), *Islam and Missions. Being Papers read at the Second Missionary Conference on Behalf of the Mohammedan World at Lucknow, January 23-28, 1911*, New York, Fleming Revell Co. 1911.

Ahlstrom, Sydney E., *The American Protestant Encounter with World Religions*, Beloit, WI, Beloit College 1962.

— *A Religious History of the American People*, New Haven, Yale University Press 1972.

Ahlstrom, Sidney R., '*Annuit Coeptis*: America as the Elect Nation, the Rise and Decline of a Patriotic Tradition', in Church, R. Forrester, and George, Timothy, (eds), *Continuity and Discontinuity in Church History*, Leiden, E.J. Brill 1979.

Albers, C., Jr., and Verhoeven, J., Sr., 'Islam in Java', in Zwemer, S.M., Wherry, E.M., and Barton, James L. (eds), *The Mohammedan World of Today. Being Papers read at the First Missionary Conference on Behalf of the Mohommedan World held at Cairo, April 4-9th, 1906*, New York, Fleming H. Revell Co. 1906.

Alphonse, Martin Paul, *The Gospel and Hindu 'Bhakti': Indian Christian Responses from 1900 to 1985 – A Study in Contextual Communication*, unpublished thesis, Fuller Theological Seminary 1990.

Alden, E.K., *Missionary Motives*, Boston, American Board of Commissioners for Foreign Missions 1890.

Allen, Alexander V.G., *Life and Writings of Jonathan Edwards*, Edinburgh, T. and T. Clark 1889.

— *The Continuity of Christian Thought: A Study of Modern Theology in the Light of its History*, second edition, London, Ward, Lock and Bowden 1895.

— 'Frederick Denison Maurice' in *Prophets of the Christian Faith*, London, James Clarke 1897.

— *Christian Institutions*, Edinburgh, T. and T. Clark 1897.

— *Life and Letters of Phillips Brooks*, New York, E.P. Dutton 1900.

— *Phillips Brooks 1835-1893: Memories of his life with extracts from his letters and notebooks*, New York, E.P. Dutton 1907.

— *Freedom in the Church; or the Doctrine of Christ 'as the Lord hath Commanded, and as the Church hath received the Same according to the Commandments of God'*, New York, Macmillan 1907.

Allen, David, 'A Tribute to Edward Irving (1792-1834)' in *The Expository Times*, August 1992, Vol. 103, No.11.

Allen, Roland, *Missionary Methods: St Paul's or Ours*, London, Robert Scott 1912.

Allin, Thomas, *Race and Religion: Hellenistic Theology – Its Place in Christian Thought*, London, James Clarke 1899.

Anderson, Gerald H. (ed), *The Theology of the Christian Mission*, London, SCM Press 1961.

Anderson, Gerald H., Phillips, James M., and Coote, Robert T. (eds), *Mission in the Nineteen 90's*, New Haven, Overseas Study Centre 1991.

Anderson, Rufus, *Foreign Missions: Their Relations and Claims*, New York, Charles Scribner 1869.

Andrews, C.F., 'The Effect of the Japanese Victories upon India' in *The East and the West*, Vol. III, (1905), pp. 361-363.

— 'The Situation in the East' in *The East and The West*, Vol. V (1907), pp. 419-429.

— *North India*, London, A.R.Mowbray 1908.

— 'Race within the Christian Church' in *The East and The West*, Vol. VIII (1910), pp. 251-263.

— 'The Indian Missionary Ideal' in *The East and The West*, Vol. IX (1911), pp. 45-51.

— 'The King's Visit to Delhi' in *The East and The West*, Vol.X (1912), pp. 275-282.

— *The Renaissance in India: Its Missionary Aspect*, London, Church Missionary Society 1912.

— *Zuka Ullah of Delhi*, Cambridge, W.Heffer & Sons Ltd. 1929.

— *What I Owe to Christ*, London, Hodder and Stoughton 1932.

— *Christ in the Silence*, London, Hodder and Stoughton 1933.

— *Sadhu Sundar Singh: A Personal Memoir*, London, Hodder and Stoughton 1934.

— *India and Britain: A Moral Challenge*, London, Student Christian Movement Press 1935.

— *The Sermon on the Mount*, with a foreword by Rabindranath Tagore, London, George Allen and Unwin 1942.

Anesati, Maseharu, *History of Japanese Religion*, London, Kegan Paul, Trench, Trubner 1930.

Anonymous:

Biblical and Theological Studies, by members of the Faculty of Princeton Theological Seminary, Published in Commemoration of the One Hundredth Anniversary of the Founding of the Seminary, New York, Charles Scribner's Sons 1912.

The Cambridge Companion to the Bible, Cambridge, Cambridge University Press 1905. Appendix on 'Sacred Books of Other Faiths' by B.F. Westcott, pp.39-55.

Conferences of Christian Workers among Moslems 1924: A brief account of the Conferences together with their findings and lists of members, New York, International Missionary Council 1924.

The Fundamentals: A Testimony to the Truth, Chicago, Testimony Publishing Co. 1910-1915.

History's Lessons for Tomorrow's Mission: Milestones in the History of Missionary Thinking, Geneva, World's Student Christian Federation, n.d.s., probably 1960.

Mansfield College Essays: Presented to the Reverend Andrew Martin Fairbairn on the Occasion of his Seventieth Birthday, with a Bibliography, London, Hodder and Stoughton 1909.

Missionary sermons: A Selection from the Discourses delivered on behalf of the Baptist Missionary Society on various occasions, London, Carey Press 1924.

Present Day Tracts on the Non Christian Religions of the World, London, Religious Tract Society 1887.

Records of the General Conference of the Protestant Missionaries of China, May 7-20, 1890, Shanghai, American Presbyterian Mission Press 1890.

Religions of the World as Viewed by Protestant Missionaries, New York, Student Volunteer Movement for Foreign Missions 1905.

The Story of the Delhi Mission, London, SPG, second edition 1917.

Ter-Jubilee Celebrations 1942-4, London, Baptist Missionary Society 1945.

The Vital Forces of Islam and Christianity; Six Studies by Missionaries to Moslems, with an introduction by the Rev. S.M.Zwemer, and a concluding study by Professor Duncan B.Macdonald, London, Oxford University Press 1915.

Ariarajah, S.Wesley, *Hindus and Christians: A Century of Protestant Ecumenical Thought*, Amsterdam, Editions Rodopi, and Grand Rapids, Eerdmans 1991.

Augustine, *The City of God*, translated by Henry Bettenson, Penguin Edition, Harmondsworth, Penguin Books 1972.

Austin, Alvyn J., *Saving China: Canadian Missionaries in the Middle Kingdom 1888-1959*, Toronto, University of Toronto Press 1986.

Awdry, W., 'The Contribution of the Church of Japan to the Body of Christ' in Montgomery, H.H., *Mankind and the Church: being an Attempt to Estimate the Contribution of Great Races to the Fulness of the Church of God by Seven Bishops*, London, Longmans, Green, and Co. 1907.

Band, Edward, Working *His Purpose Out: The History of the English Presbyterian Mission 1847-1947*, London, Presbyterian Church of England Publishing Office 1947.

Banks, John S., *The Tendencies of Modern Theology*, London, Charles H.Kelly 1897.

Barclay, Wade Crawford, *History of Methodist Missions*, New York, Board of Missions of the Methodist Church, 3 vols. 1949-1957.

Barnett, Susan Wilson and Fairbank, John King (eds), *Christianity in China: Early Protestant Writings*, Cambridge, Harvard University Press 1985.

Bartlett, Samuel C., *Historical Sketches of the Missions of the American Board*, Boston 1876, Arno Press Reprint 1976.

Barrows, John Henry, (ed.), *The World's Parliament of Religions*, two vols., Chicago, The Parliament Publishing Co. 1893.

— *Christianity the World Religion: Lectures delivered in India and Japan*, Chicago, A.C.McClury 1897.

— *The Christian Conquest of Asia: Studies and Personal Observations of Oriental Religions*, New York, Charles Scribner 1899.

Barth, A., *The Religions of India*, London, Kegan Paul, Trench, Trubner, third edition 1891.

Barton, James L., *Human Progress through Missions*, New York, Fleming H.Revell Co. 1912.

Bashford, James W., *The Chinese Church*, New York, Board of Foreign Missions of the Methodist Episcopal Church 1907.

— *China and Methodism*, New York, Board of Foreign Missions of the Methodist Episcopal Church 1907.

— *God's Missionary Plan for the World*, New York, Eaton and Mains 1907.

— *China: an Interpretation*, New York, Abingdon Press 1916.

Bates, M. Searle, 'The Theology of American Missionaries in China, 1900- 1950' in Fairbank, John K. (ed.), *The Missionary Enterprise in China and America*, Cambridge, Harvard University Press 1974.

— *Gleanings from the Manuscripts: The Protestant Endeavour in Chinese Society 1890-1950*, New York, National Council of Churches of Christ 1984.

Beaver, R.Pearce, 'Eschatology in American Missions' in Hermelink, J. and Margul, H.J., (eds) *Basileia: Walter Freytag zum 60 Geburtstag*, Stuttgart, Evang. Missionsverlag 1959.

— *Ecumenical Beginnings in Protestant World Mission: A History of Comity*, New York, Nelson 1962.

— *Pioneers in Mission: The Early Missionary Ordination Sermons, Charges and Instructions. A Source Book on the Rise of American Missions to the Heathen*, Grand Rapids, Eerdmans 1966.

— *To Advance the Gospel: Selections from the Writings of Rufus Anderson*, Grand Rapids, Eerdmans 1967.

— 'Missionary Motivation through Three Centuries' in Brauer, Jerald C. (ed.), *Reinterpretation in American Church History*, Chicago, University of Chicago Press 1968.

— (ed.) *American Missions in Bicentennial Perspective*, South Pasadena CA, William Carey Library 1977.

Bediako, Kwame, *Theology and Identity: The impact of Christian thought in the second century and modern Africa*, Oxford, Regnum Books 1992.

Bennett, Adrian A., *Missionary Journalist in China: Young J.Allen and his Magazines, 1880-1883*, Athens GA, University of Georgia Press 1983.

Bennett, Clinton, *Victorian Images of Islam*, London, Grey Seal Books 1992.

Berkhof, Hendrikus, *Two Hundred Years of Theology: Report of a Personal Journey*, Grand Rapids, Eerdmans 1989.

Bigg, Charles, *The Christian Platonists of Alexandria*, Oxford, Clarendon Press, reprinted with some additions and corrections 1913. (Originally published in 1886.)

Bishop, Arthur Stanley (ed.), *Ceylon Buddhism, being the Collected Works of Daniel John Gogerly*, Colombo, The Wesleyan Methodist Bookroom, and London, Kegan Paul, Trench, Trubner 1908.

— *The World's Altar Stairs, Introductory Studies in the Religions of the World*, London, Robert Culley 1910.

Bitton, Nelson, *The Regeneration of New China*, London, London Missionary Society, n.d.s.

Blunt, John Henry, *A Christian View of Christian History: From Apostolic to Mediaeval Times*, London, Rivingtons 1866.

Bohr, Paul Richard, *Famine in China and the Missionary: Timothy Richard as Relief Administrator and Advocate of National Reform, 1876-84*, Cambridge, Harvard East Asian Monographs, Harvard University Press 1972.

Bosch, David J., *Witness to the World: Christian Mission in Theological Perspective*, London, Marshall Morgan, and Atlanta, John Knox Press 1980.

— *Transforming Mission: Paradigm Shifts in Theology of Mission*, Maryknoll, Orbis Books 1991.

Bouquet, A.C., *Comparative Religion*, Harmondsworth, Penguin Books 1942.

— *The Christian Faith and Non-Christian Religions*, London, Nisbet 1958.

Bowden, Henry Warner, 'An Overview of Cultural Factors in the American Protestant Missionary Enterprise' in Beaver, R.Pierce (ed.), *American Missions in Bicentennial Perspective*, South Pasadena , William Carey Library 1977.

Bowne, Borden Parker, *Theism*, New York, American Book Co. 1902.

— *Studies in Christianity*, Boston, Houghton Mifflin Co. 1909.

Boyce, Mary, *Zoroastrians: their Religious Beliefs and Practices*, London, Routledge and Kegan Paul 1979.

Boyd, Robin H.S., *India and the Latin Captivity of the Church: the Cultural Context of the Gospel*, Cambridge, Cambridge University Press 1974.

— *An Introduction to Indian Christian Theology*, Madras, CLS of India, second edition 1975.

Brace, C.Loring, *The Unknown God, or Inspiration among Pre-Christian Races*, London, Hodder and Stoughton 1890.

Brash, W.Bardsley, *The Story of our Colleges: A Centenary Record of Ministerial Training in the Methodist Church*, London, Epworth Press 1935.

Bratton, Theodore DuBose, *An Apostle of Reality: The Life and Thought of the Reverend William Porcher DuBose*, London, Longmans, Green and Co. 1936.

Brauer, Jerald C. (ed.), *Reinterpretation in American Church History*, Chicago and London, University of Chicago Press 1968.

Brent, Charles H., *Adventure for God*, London, Longmans, Green 1905.

Brose, Olive J., *Frederick Denison Maurice: Rebellious Conformist*, Athens OH, Ohio University Press 1971.

Brown, Arthur J., *The Foreign Missionary: The Incarnation of a World Movement*, New York, Fleming H.Revell 1907.

—— *The Why and How of Foreign Missions*, Cincinnati, The Foreign Christian Missionary Society 1908.

—— *One Hundred Years: A History of the Foreign Missionary Work of the Presbyterian Church in the USA With Some Account of Countries, Peoples and Problems of Modern Missions*, New York, Fleming H.Revell 1937.

Brown, Colin, *Jesus in European Protestant Thought 1778–1860*, Grand Rapids, Baker Book House 1985.

Brown, C. Campbell, *China in Legend and Story*, Edinburgh, Oliphant, Anderson and Farrier 1908.

— *A Chinese St Francis: or the Life of Brother Mao*, London, Hodder and Stoughton, n.d.s. (1912).

Brown, William Adams, *The Essence of Christianity: A Study in the History of Definition*, New York, Charles Scribner's Sons 1902.

— *Christian Theology in Outline*, New York, Charles Scribner's Sons 1906.

— *The Christian Hope: A Study in the Doctrine of Immortality*, London, Duckworth 1912.

— *A Teacher and His Times: A Story of Two Worlds*, New York, Charles Scribner's Sons 1940.

Bruce, Alexander Balmain, *Apologetics, or Christianity Defensively Stated*, Edinburgh, T. and T. Clark 1892.

Buchanan, Claudius, *The Star in the East*, a sermon preached in the Parish Church of St James, Bristol on February 26, 1809, London, Longman and Hurst and Co. 1809.

Burke, James, *My Father in China*, New York, Farrar and Rinehart 1942.

Burton, John Wear, *Modern Missions in the South Pacific*, London, Livingstone Press 1949.

Bushnell Horace, *Christ and His Salvation: in sermons variously related thereto*, New York, Scribner 1864.

— *God in Christ*, Hartford CT, Brown and Parsons 1949.

— *Christian Nurture*, New York, Charles Scribner 1861.

— *Forgiveness and Law: Grounded in Principles interpreted by Human Analogies*, London, Hodder and Stoughton 1874.

— *Nature and the Supernatural as Together Constituting the One System of God*, New York, Charles Scribner 1858.

— *Vicarious Sacrifice: Grounded in Principles of Universal Obligation*, New Edition, London, Richard D. Dickinson, 1880 (first published in 1866).

Cairns, David S., *Christianity in the Modern World*, London, Hodder and Stoughton, n.d.s, probably 1906.

— art. 'Christian Missions and International Peace' in *The International Review of Missions*, 1913, Vol. 1, pp. 193-201.

— *The Reasonableness of the Christian Faith*, London, Hodder and Stoughton 1919.

— *Life and Times of Alexander Robertson MacEwen*, London, Hodder and Stoughton 1925.

— *The Riddle of the World*, London, Student Christian Movement Press 1937.

— *David Cairns: An Autobiography, Some Recollections of a Long Life and Selected Letters*, edited by his Son and Daughter with a Memoir by Professor D.M.Baillie, London, SCM Press 1950.

— *A System of Christian Doctrine*, At his request compiled and set in order by his son David Cairns, Edinburgh, St Andrew Press 1979.

Calvin, John, *Institutes of the Christian Religion*, translated by Henry Beveridge, two vols, London, John Clarke 1962.

Campbell, John MacLeod, *The Nature of the Atonement and its Relation to the Remission of Sins and Eternal Life*, first published in 1856, fourth Edition with a new introduction by Edgar P.Dickie, London, James Clarke 1959.

— *Reminiscences and Reflections: Referring to his Early Ministry in the Parish of Row 1825-31*, London, Macmillan 1873.

Campbell, R.J., *A Spiritual Pilgrimage*, London, Williams and Norgate 1916.

Campbell, Ted A., *John Wesley and Christian Antiquity: Religious Vision and Cultural Change* Nashville, Kingswood Books 1991.

Campbell, W.H., art. 'Mass Movements in the Mission Field' in *The East and the West*, Vol. IV (1906), pp. 9-26.

Canton, W., *The Story of the Bible Society*, London, John Murray 1904.

— *The History of the British and Foreign Bible Society*, five vols, London, John Murray 1904-1910.

Carpenter, J. Estlin, *Buddhism and Christianity: A Contrast and a Parallel*, London, Hodder and Stoughton 1923.

Carpenter, Joel A., and Shenk, Wilbert R. (eds), *Earthen Vessels: American Evangelicals and Foreign Missions, 1880-1980*, Grand Rapids, Eerdmans 1990.

Carey, S.Pearce, *William Carey*, London, Carey Press, eighth edition 1934.

Carey, William, *A Humble Enquiry into the Obligations of Christians to Use Means for the conversion of the Heathens*, Facsimile edition, with an Introduction by Ernest A. Payne, London, Carey Kingsgate Press 1961.

— *Form of Agreement respecting the great Principles upon which the Brethren of the Mission at Serampore think it their Duty to act in the work of Instructing the Heathen, agreed upon at a Meeting of the Brethren at Serampore, On Monday October 5th, 1805*, Appendix A in A.H. Oussoren, *William Carey, especially his Missionary Principles*, Leiden 1945.

Cary, Otis, *A History of Christianity in Japan: Roman Catholic, Greek Orthodox and Protestant Missions*, New York, Fleming H. Revell Co. 1909.

Carver, William O., *Missions in the Plan of the Ages*, New York, Fleming H. Revell Co. 1909.

— *Missions and Modern Thought*, New York, Macmillan 1910.

Cash, W. Wilson, *The Missionary Church: A Study in the Contribution of Modern Missions to Oecumenical Christianity*, London, Church Missionary Society 1939.

Cauthen, Baker J. and Others, *Advance: A History of Southern Baptist Missions*, Nashville, Boardman Press 1970.

Cavert, Samuel McCrea and Van Dusen, Henry Pitney (eds), *The Church through Half a Century*, New York, Charles Scribner's Sons 1936.

Chaney, Charles L., *The Birth of Missions in America*, South Passadena, William Carey Library 1976.

Chaturvedi, Bernarsidas and Sykes, Marjorie, *Charles Freer Andrews: A Narrative*, London, George Allen and Unwin 1947.

Chaudhury, P.C.Roy, *C.F.Andrews: His Life and Times*, Bombay, Samaiya Publications 1971.

Cheyne, A.C., *The Transforming of the Kirk: Victorian Scotland's Religious Revolution*, Edinburgh, St Andrew Press 1983.

Chorley, E. Clowes, *Men and Movements in American Episcopal Church*, New York, Charles Scribner's Sons 1946.

Christensen, Torben, *Origin and History of Christian Socialism 1848-54*, Åarhus, Universitetsforlaget 1962.

— *The Divine Order: A Study in F.D.Maurices's Theology*, Leiden, E.J. Brill 1973.

Christensen, Torben and Hutchinson, William R. (eds), *Missionary Ideologies in the Imperialist Era, 1880-1920*, Åarhus, Aros Publishing 1984.

Church, R. Forrester, and George, Timothy (ed.), *Continuity and Discontinuity in Church History*, Leiden, E.J. Brill 1979.

Clarke, William Newton, *An Outline of Christian Theology*, New York, Charles Scribner's Sons 1898.

— *A Study of Christian Missions*, New York, Charles Scribner's Sons, and London, James Clarke 1900.

— *Sixty Years with the Bible: A Record of Experience*, New York, Charles Scribner's Sons 1912.

Clayton, Joseph, *Bishop Westcott*, London, A.R.Mowbray 1906.

Clebsch, William A., *American Religious Thought: A History*, Chicago and London, University of Chicago 1973.

Coffin, Henry Sloane, *A Half Century of Union Theological Seminary 1896- 1945: An Informal History*, New York, Charles Scribner's Sons 1954.

Cornaby, William Arthur, *A String of Chinese Peach-Stones*, London, Charles H. Kelly,1895.
— *China under the Searchlight*, London, T. Fisher Unwin 1901.
Covell, Ralph R., *W. R. Martin, Pioneer of Progress in China*, Washington DC, Christian University Press 1978.
— *Confucius, the Buddha and Christ: A History of the Gospel in Chinese*, Maryknoll, Orbis Books 1986.
Cox, Jeffrey, 'C.F. Andrews and the Failure of the Modern Missionary Movement' in MEWS, Stuart (ed.), *Modern Religious Rebels*, London, Epworth Press 1993.
Cracknell, Kenneth R., *Towards a New Relationship: Christians and People of Other Faith*, London, Epworth Press 1986.
— 'What is Faith?' in *Epworth Review*, Vol. 15, No.1, (January 1988), pp.65-73.
— 'Interfaith Dialogue and the Theology of Religion: A Selective Biography for Ministerial Formation' in *Current Dialogue*, No.17 (December 1989).
— 'The Theology of Religion in the International Missionary Council and the World Council of Churches' in *Current Dialogue*, No. 19 (January 1991), pp. 3-17.
— *Protestant Evangelism or Catholic Evangelization?: A Study on Methodist Approaches*, Keswick, Methodist Sacramental Fellowship 1992.
Creighton, Louise, 'The Meeting of the Continuation Committee of the World Missionary Conference' in *The International Review of Missions* 1913, Vol. 2, pp. 118-125.
Cross, Barbara M., *Horace Bushnell, Minister to a Changing America*, Chicago, Chicago University Press 1958.
Cross, Whitney R., *The Burned-over District: The Social and Intellectual History of Enthusiastic Religion in Western New York, 1800-1850*, Ithaca NY, Cornell University Press 1950.
Cuming, G.J., (ed.), *The Mission of the Church and the Propagation of the Faith*, Cambridge. Cambridge University Press 1970.

Dakin, A., *Calvinism*, London, Duckworth 1940.
Daniel, Norman, *Islam and the West: the Making of an Image*, second edition, Oxford, Oneworld Publications 1993 (first edition 1960).
Danielson, Dennis, (ed.), *The Cambridge Companion to Milton*, Cambridge, Cambridge University Press 1989.
d'Arcy, Charles Frederick, *The Adventures of a Bishop: A Phase of Irish Life – A Personal and Historical Narrative*, London, Hodder and Stoughton 1934.
— *Idealism and Theology: A Study of Presuppositions*, The Donnelan Lectures, delivered before the University of Dublin, 1897-8, London, Hodder and Stoughton, n.d.s.
Datta, Surendra Kumar, *The Desire of India*, London, Young Peoples' Missionary Movement 1908.
Davids, T.W. Rhys, *Buddhism: Being a Sketch of the Life and Teachings of Gautama, the Buddha*, London, SPCK 1878.
Davis, Jerome Dean, *A Maker of New Japan, Rev. Joseph Hardy Neesima*, New York, Fleming H. Revell Co. 1905.
Davis, John Merle, *Davis: Soldier: Missionary: a biography of Rev. Jerome Davis, D.D.: lieutenant colonel of volunteers and for thirty-nine years a missionary of the*

American Board of the Commissioners for Foreign Missions in Japan, Boston, Pilgrim Press 1916.

Dayton, David W., *Discovering an Evangelical Heritage*, Peabody, MA., Hendrickson 1976.

— *Theological Roots of Pentecostalism*, Peabody, MA., Hendrickson, 1987.

Dayton, David W., and Johnston, Robert K. *Varieties of American Evangelicalism*, Knoxville, University of Tennessee Press 1991.

Dearing, John L. (ed.), *The Christian Movement in Japan: Tenth Annual Issue*, Yokohama, The Conference of Federated Missions 1912.

Deforest, Charlotte B., *The Evolution of a Missionary: A Biography of John Hyde DeForest*, New York, Fleming H. Revell Co. 1914.

De Groot, J.J.M., *The Religion of the Chinese*, New York, Macmillan Co. 1910.

De Jong, J.A. *As the Waters Cover the Sea: Millennial Expectations in the Rise of Anglo-American Missions 1640-1810*, Kampen, J.H.Kok 1970.

Dennis, James A., *Foreign Missions after a Century*, New York, Fleming H.Revell Co. 1893.

— *The Message of Christianity to other Religions*, New York, Fleming H.Revell Co. 1893.

— *Christian Missions and Social Progress: A Sociological Study of Foreign Missions*, 3 vols, New York, Fleming H. Revell Co. 1897-1906.

De Sélincourt, Agnes, "The Place of Women in the Modern National Movements of the East" in *The International Review of Missions*, 1913, Vol. 1, pp. 98-107.

Deussen, Paul, *The Philosophy of the Upanishads*, Edinburgh, T. and T. Clark 1906.

Dewey, Margaret, *The Messengers: A concise history of the United Society for the Propagation of the Gospel*, London and Oxford, Mowbrays 1975.

Dhahmaraj, J.S. 'Serampore Missions and Colonial Connections', in *Indian Church History Review*, June 1992, pp. 21-35.

Dickie, James, *Fifty Years of British Theology: A Personal Retrospect*, Edinburgh, T. and T. Clark 1937.

Dilger, Wilhelm, *Salvation in Hinduism and Christianity: A Comparison and a Contrast*, Mangalore, Basel Mission Book and Tract Repository 1908

Dixey, A. Duncan, 'Islam in Baluchistan' in Zwemer, S.M., Wherry, E.M. and Barton, James L. (eds), *The Mohammedan World of Today. Being Papers read at the First Missionary Conference on Behalf of the Mohommedan World held at Cairo April 4-9th, 1906*, New York, Fleming H. Revell Co. 1906.

Dods, Marcus, *Mohammed, Buddha and Christ: Four Lectures on Natural and Revealed Religion*, London, Hodder and Stoughton 1878.

Drummond, Andrew L., and Bulloch, James, *The Scottish Church 1688-1843: The Age of the Moderates*, Edinburgh, St Andrew Press 1973.

— *The Church in Victorian Scotland 1843-1874*, Edinburgh, St Andrew Press 1975.

— *The Church in Late Victorian Scotland 1874-1900*, Edinburgh, St Andrew Press 1978.

Drummond, Richard H., *A History of Christianity in Japan*, Grand Rapids, Eerdmans 1971.

Duchesne-Guillemin, *The Western Response to Zoroaster*, Oxford, Clarendon Press 1956.

Dwight, Henry Otis, *The Centennial History of the American Bible Society*, New York Macmillan, 1916.

Edkins, Joseph, *Chinese Buddhism*, London, Kegan Paul, Trench, Trubner Co. 1893.
— *The Early Spread of Religious Ideas, especially in the Far East*, London, The Religious Tract Society 1893.
Eddy, George Sherwood, *The New Era in Asia*, Edinburgh, Oliphant, Anderson and Ferrier 1914.
— *A Pilgrimage of Ideas: or the Re-education of Sherwood Eddy*, London, George Allen and Unwin 1935.
— *Pathfinders of the World Missionary Crusade*, New York and Nashville, Abingdon-Cokesbury Press 1945.
— *Eighty Adventurous Years: An Autobiography*, New York, Harper 1955.
Eddy, W.K., 'Islam in Syria and Palestine' in Zwemer, S.M., Wherry, E.M., and Barton, James L. (eds), *The Mohammedan World of Today, Being Papers read at the First Missionary Conference on Behalf of the Mohommedan World held at Cairo April 4-9th, 1906,*, New York, Fleming H. Revell Co. 1906.
Edwards, Jonathan, *Treatise on Religious Affections* (The Works of Jonathan Edwards, Vol. 2), edited by John E.Smith, New Haven, Yale University Press 1959.
— *The Great Awakening* (The Works of Jonathan Edwards, Vol. 4) edited by C.C. Goen, New Haven, Yale University Press 1972.
— *Apocalyptic Writings* (The Works of Jonathan Edwards, Vol. 5), edited by Stephen J.Stein, New Haven, Yale University Press 1977.
— *A History of the Work of Redemption* (The Works of Jonathan Edwards, Vol. 9), edited by John F.Wilson, New Haven, Yale University Press 1989.
Eilert, Håkan, *Boundlessness: Studies in Karl Ludvig Reichelt's Missionary Thinking with Special Regard to the Buddhist-Christian Encounter*, Ringkbing, Aros, 1974 (Studia Missionalia Upsaliensia XXIV).
Elliott-Binns, L.E., *Religion in the Victorian Era*, London, Lutterworth Press, second edition 1946.
— *English Thought, 1860-1900: The Theological Aspect*, London, Longmans, Green 1956.
Elsbree Oliver Wendell, *The Rise of the Protestant Missionary Spirit in America 1790-1815*, Williamsport, PA, Williamsport Printing and Binding Company 1928.
Erb, Peter C., *Pietists: Selected Writings*, London, SPCK 1983.
Erskine Thomas, *The Brazen Serpent; or Life Coming through Death*, Edinburgh, Waugh and Innes, second edition 1831.
— *Letters of Thomas Erskine of Linlathen*, edited by William Hanna, 2 vols, Edinburgh, David Douglas 1877.

Fairbairn, A.M., *Studies in the Philosophy of Religion and History*, London, Strahan and Co. 1876.
— *The City of God; a Series of Discussions in Religion*, London, Hodder and Stoughton 1883.
— 'The Influence of the Study of Other Religions on Christian Theology' in Webster, Eugene C. (ed.), *Volume of Proceedings of the Second International Congregational Council*, Boston, Press of Samuel Usher 1900, pp. 111-7.

— 'Some Thoughts on Modern Hinduism' in *The Proceedings of the Society of Historical Theology*, 1898-89, pp. 50-55.

— *The Place of Christ in Modern Theology*, London, Hodder and Stoughton 1893 (thirteenth edition 1907).

— *Religion in History and in Modern Life, Together with an Essay on the Church and the Working Classes*, London, Hodder and Stoughton 1893 (fourth edition 1903).

— 'Religion in India' in *The Contemporary Review*, Vol. LXXV, June 1899, pp.761-81.

— 'Race and Religion in India', in *The Contemporary Review*, Vol. LXXVI, August 1899, pp.153-73.

— *Catholicism: Roman and Anglican*, London, Hodder and Stoughton 1899.

— *The Philosophy of the Christian Religion*, London, Hodder and Stoughton 1902.

— *Religion in History and in Modern Life, Together with an Essay on the Church and the Working Classes*, London, Hodder and Stoughton 1903.

— *Studies in Religion and Theology: the Church in Idea and in History*, London, Hodder and Stoughton 1910.

Fairbank, John K. (ed.), *The Missionary Enterprise in China and America*, Cambridge, Harvard University Press 1974.

Fairbank John K., 'Introduction: The Many Faces of Protestant Missions in China and the United States' in Fairbank, John K. (ed.), *The Missionary Enterprise in China and America*, Cambridge, Harvard University Press 1974.

Fairbank, John, and Barnett, S.W. (eds), *Christianity in China: Early Protestant Writings*, Cambridge, Harvard University Press 1985.

Farquhar, J.N., *Gita and Gospel* Madras, Christian Literature Society 1903,

— 'Is Christianity the Only True Religion' in the *Inquirer*, Vol. V, no.1, September 1903.

— 'The Missionary Study of Hinduism', in *The Harvest Field*, Vol. XVI, no.5, May 1905.

— 'The Greatness of Hinduism' in *The Contemporary Review*, Vol. XCVII, 1910, pp. 647-682.

— 'The Crown of Hinduism' in *The Contemporary Review*, Vol. XCVIII, 1910, pp. 74-87

— *The Crown of Hinduism*, London, Oxford University Press 1913.

— *A Primer of Hinduism*, Oxford University Press, second edition 1914 (first published in India in 1911).

— *Modern Religious Movements in India*, London, Macmillan 1924, (first published in New York in 1915).

— *An Outline of the Religious Literature of India*, London, Oxford University Press 1920.

Findlay, James F., *Dwight L. Moody: American Evangelist 1837-1899* , Chicago, University of Chicago Press 1969.

Findlay, George G. and Findlay, Mary Grace, *Wesley's World Parish: A Sketch of the Hundred Years Work of the Wesleyan Methodist Missionary Society*, London, Hodder and Stoughton 1913.

Findlay, G.G., and Holdsworth, W.W., *The History of the Wesleyan Missionary Society*, 5 vols, London, Epworth Press 1921-4.

Finney, Charles Grandison, *Lectures on Revivals of Religion* (ed. William G. McLoughlin), Cambridge, Belknap Press of Harvard University Press 1960 (first published in 1835).

Fisher, Galen M., 'Annual Review of Religious Literature' in Dearing, John L. (ed.), *The Christian Movement in Japan: Tenth Annual Issue*, Yokohama, The Conference of Federated Missions 1912.

Flesseman-Van Leer, Ellen, *Grace Abounding: A Comparison of Frederick Denison Maurice and Karl Barth, The F.D. Maurice Lectures given in King's College, London in 1968*, London, King's College 1968.

Forman, Charles W., 'A History of Foreign Mission theory in America' in Beaver, R.Pierce (ed.) *American Missions in Bicentennial Perspective*, South Pasadena, William Carey Library 1977.

Forrester, Duncan B., *Caste and Christianity: Attitudes and Policies on Caste of Anglo-Saxon Protestant Missions in India*, London, Curzon Press 1980.

Forsythe, Sydney A., *An American Missionary Community in China, 1895-1905*, Cambridge, Harvard University Press 1971

Fosdick, Harry Emerson, *The Living of These Days: An Autobiography*, London, SCM Press 1957.

Foster, Arnold (ed.), *Christian Progress in China: Gleanings from the Writings and Speeches of Many Workers*, London, London Missionary Society 1889.

— *Arnold Foster: Memoir, Selected Writings etc.*, London, London Missionary Society 1921.

Foster, George B., *The Finality of the Christian Religion*, Chicago, University of Chicago Press 1906.

Fraser, Agnes R., *Donald Fraser of Livingstonia*, London, Hodder and Stoughton 1934.

Fraser, Brian J., 'For the Uplift of the World: The Mission Thought of James A. Macdonald 1890s-1915' in Moir John S. and McIntire, C.T. (eds), *Canadian Protestant and Catholic Missions, 1820s-1960s: Historical Essays in Honour of John Webster Grant*, New York and Bern, Peter Lang Inc. 1987.

Fraser, Donald, *Winning a Primitive People*, London, Seely 1912.

Fremantle, Ann Jackson (ed.), *The Protestant Mystics*, London, Weidenfield and Nicholson 1964.

Fulton, Austin, *Through Earthquake, Wind and Fire: Church and Mission in Manchuria 1867-1972*, Edinburgh, St Andrew's Press 1967.

Gairdner, W.H.T., *D.M.Thornton: A Study in Missionary Ideals and Methods*, London, Hodder and Stoughton 1909.

— *The Reproach of Islam*, second edition revised, London, Young Peoples' Missionary Movement 1909.

— *The Muslim Idea of God*, Madras, The Christian Literature Society 1909.

— *Edinburgh 1910: An Account and Interpretation of the World Missionary Conference*, Edinburgh, Oliphant, Anderson and Ferrier 1910 (North American edition, *Echoes from Edinburgh*, New York, Fleming H. Revell Co. 1910).

— 'Islam Under Christian Rule' in Wherry, E.M., Zwemer, S.M. and Mylrea, C.G. (eds), *Islam and Missions. Being Papers read at the Second Missionary Conference on*

Behalf of the Mohammedan World at Lucknow, January 23-28, 1911, New York, Fleming H. Revell Co. 1911.

— 'The Vital Forces of Christianity and Islam' in *The International Review of Missions*, 1913, Vol. 1 , pp.44-61, reprinted as the 'First Study' in *The Vital Forces of Islam and Christianity; Six Studies by Missionaries to Moslems*, with an introduction by the Rev. S.M.Zwemer, and a concluding study by Professor Duncan B.Macdonald, London, Oxford University Press 1915, pp.11-44.

— *The Rebuke of Islam. Being the Fifth Edition, rewritten and revised of The Reproach of Islam*, London, The United Council for Missionary Education 1920.

— *W.H.T.G. to His Friends: Some Letters and Informal Writings of Canon W.H.Temple Gairdner of Cairo 1873-1928*, edited by M.D. Gairdner, London, SPCK 1930.

Gardner, C.E., *Life of Father Goreh*, London, Longmans, Green 1900.

Garritt J.C. (ed.), *Jubilee Papers of the Central China Presbyterian Mission, 1844-1894, comprising Historical Sketches of the Mission Stations at Ningpo, Shanghai, Hangchow, Soochow, and Nanking*, Shanghai 1895.

Garvie, Alfred E., *The Ritschlian Theology, Critical and Constructive: An Exposition and an Estimate*, Edinburgh, T. and T. Clark 1899.

— *Studies in the Inner Life of Jesus*, London, Hodder and Stoughton 1907.

— 'The Christian Challenge to the Other Faiths' in *The International Review of Missions*, 1913, Vol. I, pp.659-673.

— 'Christianity and other Religions' in the *Homiletic Review*, June 1913.

— *The Missionary Obligation in the Light of Modern Thought*, London, Hodder and Stoughton 1914.

— *Tutors unto Christ: Introduction to the Study of Religions*, London, Oxford University Press 1920.

— *Revelation though History and Experience: A Study of the Historical Basis of the Revelation of the Godhead*, London, Ivor Nicholson and Watson 1934.

— *Memories and Meanings of My Life*, London, George Allen and Unwin 1938.

Geden, Alfred S., *Studies in Comparative Religion*, London, Charles H.Kelly 1898.

— *Studies in Eastern Religions*, London, Charles H.Kelly, 1900.

— *Comparative Religion*, London, SPCK 1917.

Gibson, J.Campbell, *Mission Problems and Mission Methods in South China*, Edinburgh, Oliphant, Anderson and Ferrier 1902.

Glasson, T.F., *His Appearing and His Kingdom*, London, Epworth Press 1953.

Gogerly, Daniel John, *Ceylon Buddhism, being the Collected Works of Daniel John Gogerly*, edited by Arthur Stanley Bishop, Colombo, The Wesleyan Methodist Bookroom, and London, Kegan Paul, Trench, Trubner 1908.

Goel, Sita Ram, *History of Hindu-Christian Encounters*, New Delhi, Voice of India 1989.

Goddard, Burton L., *The Encyclopaedia of Modern Christian Missions*, London and Camden, NJ 1967

Goldsmith, M.G., 'Islam in South India' in Zwemer, S.M., Wherry, E.M. and Barton, James L. (eds), *The Mohammedan World of Today, Being Papers read at the First Missionary Conference on Behalf of the Mohommedan World held at Cairo April 4-9th, 1906*, New York, Fleming H. Revell Co. 1906.

Goodall, Norman, *A History of the London Missionary Society 1895-1945*, London, Oxford University Press 1964.

Goodsell, Fred Field, *You Shall Be My Witnesses*, Boston, American Board of Commissioners for Foreign Missions 1959.

— *They Lived their Faith; an Almanac of Faith, Hope and Love*, Boston, American Board of Commissioners for Foreign Missions 1960.

Gordon, George Angier, *The Gospel for Humanity: Annual Sermon before the American Board of Commissioners for Foreign Missions*, Boston, American Board of Commissioners for Foreign Missions 1895.

— *My Education and My Religion; An Autobiography*, Boston, Houghton, Miflin Co 1925.

Gore, Charles (ed.), *Lux Mundi: A Series of Studies in the Religion of the Incarnation*, London, John Murray, fifth edition 1890.

Goreh, Nehemiah Nilakantha Sastri, *A Mirror of the Hindu Philosophical Systems*, translated from the original Hindi, by Fitz-Edward Hall, third edition, Madras, Christian Literature Society for India 1911.

Grant, Anthony, *The Past and the Prospective Extension of the Gospel by Missions to the Heathen*, Bampton Lectures for 1843, London 1844.

Grant, George M., *The Religions of the World*, London, A. and C. Black 1885.

Grant, Robert M., 'Civilization as Preparation for Christianity in the Thought of Eusebius' in Church, R. Forrester, and George, Timothy (ed.), *Continuity and Discontinuity in Church History*, Leiden, E.J. Brill 1979.

Graves, F.R., 'Chinese Christianity and the Chinese National Character' in *The East and the West*, Vol. IV (1906), pp. 373-382.

Graves, R.H., *Forty Years in China: or, China in Transition*, Baltimore, R.H. Woodward Co. 1895.

Greaves, Edwin, 'India for the Christian Church' in *The East and the West*, Vol. VIII (1910), pp. 42-48.

Green, F.Pratt, *Methodism and the Mountain Summit a Survey of Methodist World Missions*, London, Cargate Press 1931.

Greenwood, John Ormerod, *Quaker Encounters*, Vol. 3: 'Whispers of Truth', York, William Sessions 1978.

Greschat, H.J. and Jungrithmayr, H., (eds) *Wort und Religion: Kalima na Dini*, Stuttgart, Evangelischer Missionsverlag 1969.

Griffiths, B.J., 'The Tradition of Great Things', in *The Commemoration Vol. of the Ter-Jubilee Celebrations of the BMS* London, BMS 1945.

Grotius, Hugo, *The Truth of the Christian Religion*, translated by John Clarke, Oxford, printed by W. Baxter for Law and Whittaker 1818.

Guelzo, Allen C., *Edwards on the Will: A Century of American Theological Debate*, uncorrected proof, Middletown CT, Wesleyan University Press 1989.

Gulick, Sidney Lewis, *The Growth of the Kingdom of God*, London, Religious Tract Society 1897.

— *Evolution of the Japanese: Social and Psychic*, New York, Fleming H. Revell Co. 1903.

— *The White Peril in the Far East: An Interpretation of the Significance of the Russo-Japanese War*, New York, Fleming H. Revell Co. 1905.

— *Towards Understanding Japan: Constructive Proposals for Removing the Menace of War*, New York, Macmillan 1935.

Gulick, Sidney L., and Edward L., *Outline Studies of the Growth of the Kingdom of God*, Boston, The Pilgrim Press 1910.

Gulliford, Henry, 'Christian Literature as a mission agency in India' in *The East and the West*, Vol.VII (1909), pp. 147-152

Habel, Norman (ed.), *Religion and Multiculturalism in Australia: Essays in Honour of Victor Hayes*, Adelaide, AASR 1992.

Hall, Basil Douglas, *The Life of Charles Cuthbert Hall: 'One Among a Thousand'*, New York, Carlton 1965.

Hall, Charles Cuthbert, *Qualifications for Ministerial Power*, The Carew Lectures for 1895, Hartford, Hartford Seminary Press 1895.

— *Christian Belief Interpreted by Christian Experience: lectures delivered in India, Ceylon, and Japan on the Barrows Foundation*, The Barrows Lectures 1902-1903, Chicago, University of Chicago Press 1905.

— *The Universal Elements in the Christian Religion: An Attempt to Interpret Religious Conditions*, The Cole Lectures for 1905, New York, Fleming H.Revell Co. 1905.

— *Christ and the Human Race; or, The Attitude of Jesus Christ to Foreign Races and Religions*, The William Belden Noble Lectures for 1906, Boston and New York, Houghton, Mifflin and Co. 1906.

— *Christ and the Eastern Soul: The Witness of the Oriental Consciousness to Jesus Christ*, The Barrows Lectures 1906-7, Chicago, University of Chicago Press 1909.

Hamilton, Ian, *The Erosion of Calvinist Orthodoxy: Seceders and Subscription in Scottish Presbyterianism*, Edinburgh, Rutherford House Books 1990.

Handy, Robert T., *A Christian America: Protestant Hopes and Historical Realities*, second edition, revised and enlarged, New York and Oxford, Oxford University Press 1984.

— *A History of the Churches in the United States and Canada*, Oxford, Clarendon Press 1976.

— 'Wilderness Experiences of Religion in America' in Church, R. Forrester, and George, Timothy (eds), *Continuity and Discontinuity in Church History*, Leiden, E.J. Brill 1979.

— *A History of Union Theological Seminary in New York*, New York, Columbia University Press 1987.

Hardwick, Charles, *Christ and Other Masters: An Historical Inquiry into some of the Chief Parallelisms and Contrasts between Christianity and the Religious Systems of the Ancient World*, London, Macmillan, fourth edition 1874.

Harper, Marvin Henry, *The Methodist Episcopal Church in India*, Lucknow, Lucknow Publishing House 1936.

Harountunian, Joseph, *Piety versus Moralism: the Passing of New England Theology*, New York, Henry Holt 1932.

Harris, John, *The Great Commission: or, The Christian Church Constituted and Charged to Convey the Gospel to the World*, Boston, Gould, Kendall and Lincoln 1842.

Harris, J.C., *Couriers of Christ: Pioneers of the London Missionary Society*, London, Livingstone Press 1931.

Harrison A.W., *The Beginnings of Arminianism to the Synod of Dort*, London, University of London Press 1926.

—— *Arminianism*, London, Duckworth 1937

Harrison, J.F.C., *The Second Coming: Popular Millenarianism 1780-1850*, London, Routledge and Kegan Paul 1979.

Harrison, Peter, *'Religion' and the Religions in the English Enlightenment*, Cambridge, Cambridge University Press 1990.

Hastings, James (ed.), *Encyclopaedia of Religion and Ethics*, 13 vols, Edinburgh, T. and T.Clark 1908-21.

Hayes, Victor, 'Faithful Synoretism' in Habel, Norman (ed.), *Religion and Multiculturalism in Australia: Essays in Honour of Victor Hayes*, Adelaide, AASR 1992.

Hayford, Charles W., 'Chinese and American Characteristics: Arthur H. Smith and His China Book' in Barnett, Susan Wilson and Fairbank, John K. (eds), *Christianity in China: Early Protestant Writings*, Cambridge, Harvard University Press 1985.

Headland, Isaac Taylor, *Chinese Mother Goose Rhymes*, New York, Fleming H.Revell Co. 1900.

— *Chinese Heroes*, New York, Eaton and Mains 1902.

— *Court Life In China: The Capital, Its Officials, Its People*, New York, Fleming H. Revell Co. 1909.

— *Christ's New Day: A Study of Events that have led to its Coming*, West Medford MA, Central Committee on the Study of Missions 1912.

— *Some By-Products of Missions*, Cincinnati, Jennings and Graham 1912.

Heimert, Alan, and Miller, Perry, (eds), *The Great Awakening: Documents Illustrating the Crisis and its Consequences*, Indianapolis, Bobbs-Merrill 1967.

Helmstadter, Richard J, and Lightman, Bernard (eds), *Victorian Faith in Crisis: Essays on Continuity and Change in Nineteenth Century Religious Belief*, London, Macmillan 1990.

Heitzenrater, Richard P., *Mirror and Memory: Reflections on Early Methodism*, Nashville, Kingswood Books 1989.

Henson, Hensley, *Robertson of Brighton 1816-1853*, London, Smith, Elder 1916.

Herrick, George F., *Christian and Mohammedan: A Plea for Bridging the Chasm*, New York, Fleming H. Revell Co. 1912.

Herron, George D., *The Larger Christ*, Chicago, Fleming H. Revell 1891.

Hewat, E.G.K., *Vision and Achievement 1796-1956. A History of the Foreign Missions of the Churches united in the Church of Scotland*, London, Nelson 1960.

Hewitt, Gordon, *The Problems of Success: A History of the Church Missionary Society*, London, SCM Press 1971.

Hoare, J.C., 'The Contribution of the Church in China to the Body of Christ' in Montgomery, H.H. (ed.), *Mankind and the Church: being an Attempt to Estimate the Contribution of Great Races to the Fulness of the Church of God by Seven Bishops*, London, Longmans, Green, and Co. 1907.

Hocking, W.E., *Re-Thinking Missions, A Layman's Enquiry after One Hundred Years*, New York, Harper 1932.

Hodge, Charles, *Systematic Theology*, New York, Charles Scribner, London, Nelson 1878, (first edition 1871-2).

— *Systematic Theology*, abridged edition, Edward N.Gross (ed.), Grand Rapids, Baker Book House 1988.

Hodgkin, Henry T., 'The Missionary Motive and the Present World Situation' in Paton, W. (ed.), *The Missionary Motive*, London, Student Christian Movement 1913.
— *The Missionary Spirit and the Present Opportunity*, London, published by Headley Brothers for the Woodbrook Extension Centre 1916.
— *Britain and China: A Psycho-Political Study*, London, Journal of the British Institute of International Affairs 1925.
Hoekendijk, J.C., *Kerk en Volk in de Duitse Zendingswetanschap*, Amsterdam, Drukkerij Kampert en Helm, n.d.s., probably 1962.
Hogg, A.G., 'Christianity as Emancipation from this World' in *Madras Christian College Magazine*, Vol. ix, no.1-2, July-August 1909.
— 'A New Year Message from India' in *World Missionary Conference Monthly News Sheet*, January 1910.
— *Karma and Redemption: An Essay toward the Interpretation of Hinduism and the Restatement of Christianity*, Madras, Christian Literature Society for India, second edition 1910.
— 'The presentation of Christ to the Hindu' in *The East and the West*, Vol.VIII (1910), pp. 264-287.
— *Christ's Message of the Kingdom: A Course of Study for Private Students and for Bible Circles*, Edinburgh, T. and T. Clark 1912.
— *Redemption from this World or the Supernatural in Christianity*, Edinburgh, T. and T. Clark 1924.
— *The Christian Message to the Hindu*, London, SCM Press 1947.
Hogg, William Ritchey, *Ecumenical Foundations: A History of the International Missionary Council and its Nineteenth Century Background*, New York, Harper 1952.
— 'The Rise of Protestant Missionary Concern 1517-1914' in Anderson, Gerald H. (ed.), *The Theology of the Christian Mission*, London, SCM Press 1961.
Holland, W. E. S., 'Indian versus Western virtues' in *The East and the West*, Vol. VII (1909), pp. 306-316.
Hollister, John N., *The Century of the Methodist Church in Southern Asia*, Lucknow, India, Lucknow Publishing House 1956.
Hood, George A., *Mission Accomplished? The English Presbyterian Mission in Lingtung, South China*, Frankfurt, Peter Lang Verlag 1986.
— *Neither a Bang nor a Whimper: The End of a Missionary Era in China*, Singapore, The Presbyterian Church in Singapore 1991.
Hopkins, C.H., *The Rise of the Social Gospel in American Protestantism 1865-1915*, New Haven, Yale University Press 1940.
— *John R.Mott 1865-1955: A Biography*, Grand Rapids, Eerdmans 1979.
Hopkins, Edward Washburn, *The Religions of India*, London, Edward Arnold 1896.
Hopkins, Samuel, *Treatise on the Millennium*, Boston, printed by Isaiah Thomas and Ebenezer Andrews 1793.
Horne, Melvill, *Letters on Missions: Addressed to the Ministers of the Protestant Churches*, London, L.B. Seely, 1824, (first edition 1794).
Houlder, H.F., '"Edinburgh, 1910", Reminiscences of the World Missionary Conference held in Edinburgh in 1910', cyclostyled typescript in the possession of K. Cracknell.

Howells, George, *The Soul of India: An Introduction to the Study of Hinduism, in its Historical Setting and Development, and in its Internal and Historical Relations to Christianity*, London, James W. Clarke and The Kingsgate Press 1913.

Hoyland, John S., *C.F.Andrews: Minister of Reconciliation*, London, Allenson and Co. 1940.

— *The Man India Loved: C.F. Andrews*, London, Lutterworth Press 1944.

Hudson, Winthrop S., *American Protestantism*, Chicago, University of Chicago Press 1961.

— and Corrigan, John, *Religion in America: An Historical Account of the Development of American Religious Life*, New York, Macmillan, fifth edition 1992.

Hume, Robert A., *Missions from the Modern View*, New York, Fleming H. Revell Co. 1905.

— *An Interpretation of India's Religious History*, New York, Fleming H. Revell Co. 1911.

Hume, Robert E., *The World's Living Religions*, New York, Charles Scribner's 1959.

Hunt, R.J., *The Livingstone of South America: The Life and Adventures of W. Barbrooke Grubb among the wild tribes of the Gran Chaco in Paraguay, Bolivia, Argentina, the Falkland Islands and Tierra del Fuego*, London, Seeley Service and Co 1932.

Hunt, William Remphry, *Heathenism under the Searchlight: The Call of the Far East*, London, Morgan and Scott, n.d.s.

Hutchinson, William R., *American Protestant Thought: The Liberal Era*, New York, Harper and Row 1968.

— 'Modernism and Missions: The Liberal Search for an Exportable Christianity, 1875-1935' in Fairbank, John K. (ed.), *The Missionary Enterprise in China and America*, Cambridge, Harvard University Press 1974.

— *The Modernist Impulse in American Protestantism*, Cambridge, Harvard University Press 1976.

— 'American Missionary Ideologies: "Activism" as Theory, Practice and Stereotype' in Church, R. Forrester, and George, Timothy, (eds) *Continuity and Discontinuity in Church History* , Leiden, E.J. Brill 1979.

— 'A Moral Equivalent for Imperialism: Americans and the Promotion of "Christian Civilization", 1890-1910' in Christensen, Torben and Hutchinson, William R., (eds), *Missionary Ideologies in the Imperialist Era, 1880-1920*, Aarhus, Aros Publishing 1982.

— *Errand to the World: American Protestant Thought and Foreign Missions*, Chicago, University of Chicago Press 1987.

— 'Americans in World Mission: Revision and Realignment' in David W.Lotz, (ed.), *Altered Landscapes: Christianity in America 1935-1985*, Grand Rapids, Eerdmans 1989.

Hyatt, Irwin T., *Our Ordered Lives Confess: Three Nineteenth Century American Missionaries in East Shantung*, Cambridge, Harvard University Press 1976.

Illingworth, J.R., *Personality Human and Divine*, Bampton Lectures for 1894, London, Macmillan 1895.

Imbrie, William, 'Nihon Kirisuto Kyokwai', in *Proceeding of the General Conference of Protestant Missionaries in Japan (1900)*, Tokyo, Methodist Publishing House 1901.

424   *Justice, Courtesy and Love*

Jathanna, Origen Vasantha, *The Decisiveness of the Christ-Event and the Universality of Christianity in a World of Religious Plurality, with special reference to Hendrik Kraemer and Alfred George Hogg as well as to William Ernest Hocking and Pandipeddi Chenchiah*, Berne, Peter Lang Inc. 1984.

Jessup, H.H., 'Introductory Paper' in Zwemer, S.M., Wherry, E.M., and Barton, James L. (eds), *The Mohammedan World of Today, Being Papers read at the First Missionary Conference on Behalf of the Mohommedan World held at Cairo April 4-9th, 1906*, New York, Fleming H. Revell Co. 1906.

Johnson, Charles A., *The Frontier Camp Meeting: Religion's Harvest Time*, Dallas TX, Southern Methodist University Press 1955.

Jones, John P., *India's Problem: Krishna or Christ*, New York, Fleming H. Revell Co. 1903.

— 'Hindu Religious Ideas as they Affect the Progress of Christianity in India' in *The East and the West*, Vol.II (1904), pp.164-175.

— *India: Its Life and Thought*, New York, The Macmillan Company 1908.

— *The Modern Missionary Challenge: A Study of the Present Day World Missionary Enterprise, Its Problems and Results*, New York, Fleming H. Revell Co. 1910.

— 'The Modern Missionary Outlook' in *The Harvard Theological Review*, January 1915.

Jordan, Lewis Henry, *Comparative Religion: Its Genesis and Growth*, Edinburgh, T. and T. Clark 1905.

Kellaway, William, *The New England Company 1649-1776: Missionary Society to the American Indians*, London, Longmans 1961.

Kellogg, Samuel H., *The Light of Asia and the Light of the World, a comparison of the Legend, the Doctrine, and the Ethics of the Buddha, with the Story, the Doctrines and the Ethics of Christ*, London, Macmillan 1885.

— *A Handbook of Comparative Religion*, Philadelphia, Westminster Press 1899.

Kernahan, Coulson, *Cornaby of Hanyang: A Great Souled Missionary, An Appreciation, with Biographical Chapters by Mrs W.A. Cornaby, B.A.*, London, Epworth Press 1923.

King, Copland, 'Some Notes on New Guinea' in *The East and the West*, Vol. III (1905), pp. 68-80.

King, Henry Churchill, *Reconstruction in Theology*, New York, Macmillan 1901.

Kipp, Rita Smith, *The Early Years of a Dutch Colonial Mission: the Karo Field*, Ann Arbor, University of Michigan Press 1990.

Kirschenmann, Frederick, 'Horace Bushnell: Cells or Crustacea' in Brauer, Jerald C. (ed.), *Reinterpretation in American Church History*, Chicago and London, University of Chicago Press 1968.

Klostermaier, Klaus, *Hindu and Christian in Vrindaban*, London, SCM Press 1969.

Kobler, John, *Ardent Spirits: The Rise and Fall of Prohibition*, London, Michael Joseph 1973.

Kraemer, H., *The Christian Message in a Non-Christian World*, London, Edinburgh House Press 1938.

Kruyt, Albertus C., 'The Presentation of the Gospel to Primitive Peoples' in *International Review of Mission*, Vol. 5, No. 13, Jan. 1915, pp. 81-95.

Laird, M.A., *Missionaries and Education in Bengal 1793-1837*, Oxford, Clarendon Press 1972.

Langford, Thomas A., *In Search of Foundations: English Theology 1900-1920*, Nashville, Abingdon Press 1969.

Larsen, E. John, 'Islam in Bokhara and Chinese Turkestan' in Zwemer, S.M., Wherry, E.M. and Barton, James L. (eds), *The Mohammedan World of Today. Being Papers read at the First Missionary Conference on Behalf of the Mohommedan World held at Cairo April 4-9th, 1906*, New York, Fleming H. Revell Co. 1906.

Latourette, Kenneth Scott, *History of Christian Missions in China*, London, SPCK and New York, Macmillan 1929.

— *A History of the Expansion of Christianity*, 7 vols, New York, Harper, 1938-47.

— *Christianity in a Revolutionary Age*, 5 vols, New York, Harper 1958-62.

Lau, Tze-Yui, *James Legge (1815-1897) and Chinese Culture: A Missiological Study in Scholarship, Translation and Evangelization* , unpublished Ph.D thesis, New College, University of Edinburgh 1994.

Lefroy, G.A., 'Mohammedan Races: their Contributions to the Body of Christ' in Montgomery, H.H. (ed.), *Mankind and the Church: being an Attempt to Estimate the Contribution of Great Races to the Fulness of the Church of God by Seven Bishops*, London, Longmans, Green, and Co. 1907.

Legge, Helen Edith, *James Legge: Missionary and Scholar*, London, Religious Tract Society 1905.

Legge, James, *The Notions of the Chinese concerning God and Spirits*, Hong Kong, printed at the 'Hong Kong Register' Office 1852.

— *The Religions of China. Confucianism and Taoism Described and Compared with Christianity*, London, Hodder and Stoughton 1880.

— 'Christianity and Confucianism Compared in their Teaching of the Whole Duty of Man' in *Present Day Tracts on the Non Christian Religions of the World*, London, Religious Tract Society 1887.

Lenwood, Frank, 'The New Apologetic in India' in *Mansfield College Essays: Presented to the Reverend Andrew Martin Fairbairn on the Occasion of his Seventieth Birthday, with a Bibliography*, London, Hodder and Stoughton 1909.

Leonard, A.B., *The Stone of Help*, New York and Cincinnatti, The Methodist Book Concern 1915.

Leonard, Jane Kate, 'W. H. Medhurst: Rewriting the Missionary Message' in Barnett, Susan Wilson and Fairbank, John K. (eds), *Christianity in China: Early Protestant Writings*, Cambridge, Harvard University Press 1985.

Lewis, A.J., *Zinzendorf the Ecumenical Pioneer*, London, SCM Press 1962.

Lidgett, John Scott, *The Victorian Transformation of Theology*, London, Epworth Press 1934.

Lilla, Salvatore R.C., *Clement of Alexandria: A Study in Christian Platonism and Gnosticism*, London, Oxford University Press 1971.

Liu, Kwang-Ching (ed.), *American Missionaries in China: Papers from Harvard Seminars*, Cambridge, Harvest East Asian Monographs, Harvard University Press 1966.

Lloyd, Arthur, *The Higher Buddhism in the light of the Nicene Creed*, printed at the Tokyo Tsukjii type founding 1893.

— *The Praises of Amida; Seven Buddhist Sermons Translated from the Japanese of Tada Kanai*, Tokyo, Kyobunkwan 1907.

— *The Wheat among the Tares: Studies of Buddhism in Japan*, London, Macmillan 1908.

— *Every-day Japan: Written after Twenty-five years' Residence and Work in the Country*, London, Cassell and Co. 1909.

— 'Gnosticism in Japan' in *The East and the West*, Vol. VIII (1910), pp.160-174.

— *Shinran and His Work: Studies in Shinsu Theology*, Tokyo, Kyobunkwan 1910.

— 'The Prince of Parthia' in *The East and the West*, Vol. IX (1911), pp.293-301.

— *The Creed of Half Japan; Historical Sketches of Japanese Buddhism*, London, Smith, Elder and Co. 1911.

Lloyd, Arthur and Mary von Fallot, *The Gold Demon by Koyo Ozaki. Rewritten in English*, Tokyo, Seibundo 1906.

Loetscher, Lefferts A., *The Broadening Church: A Study of Theological Issues in the Presbyterian Church*, Philadelphia, University of Pennsylvania Press 1954.

Longridge, George A., *History of the Oxford Mission to Calcutta*, second edition, revised and abridged by W.H. Hutton, Oxford, Mowbray 1910.

Lotz, David W. (ed.), *Altered Landscapes: Christianity in America 1935-1985*, Grand Rapids, Eerdmans 1989.

Lotz, Denton, *'The Evangelization of the World in this Generation': the Resurgence of a Missionary Idea among Conservative Evangelicals*, Hamburg 1970.

Lucas, Bernard, *Conversations with Christ: a Biographical Study*, London, Macmillan 1905.

— *The Empire of Christ: Being a Study of the Missionary Enterprise in the Light of Modern Religious Thought*, London, Macmillan 1908.

— *Christ for India: Being a Presentation of the Christian Message to the Religious Thought of India*, London, Macmillan 1910.

— *Our Task in India: Shall We Proselytise Hindus or Evangelise India?*, London, Macmillan 1914.

Lutz, Jessie Gregory (ed.), *Christian Missions in China: Evangelists of What?*, Boston, D.C.Heath 1965.

— *China and the Christian Colleges 1850-1950*, Ithaca NY, Cornell University Press 1971.

— 'Karl F. Gutzlaff: Missionary Entrepreneur' in Barnett, Susan Wilson and Fairbank, John K. (eds), *Christianity in China: Early Protestant Writings*, Cambridge, Harvard University Press 1985.

McClain, Frank Maudlin, *Maurice, Man and Moralist*, London, SPCK 1972.

MacCulloch, J.A., *Comparative Theology*, London, Methuen 1902.

MacGillivray, D. (ed.), *A Century of Protestant Missions in China (1807- 1907), being the Centenary Conference Historical Vol.*, Shanghai, American Presbyterian Mission Press 1907.

— 'The need of more and better Christian literature in China' in *The East and the West*, Vol. IX (1911), pp. 402-207.

MacGowan, John, *Christ or Confucius, Which?, or, The Story of the Amoy Mission*, London, London Missionary Society 1889.

Mackenzie, Murdoch, *Twenty Five Years in Honan*, Toronto, Board of Foreign Mission, Presbyterian Church in Canada 1913.

Mackenzie, W. Douglas, *Christianity and the Progress of Man as Illustrated by Modern Missions*, Chicago, Fleming H. Revell Co. 1897.

Mackintosh, Robert, *Principal Rainy: A Biographical Study*, London, Andrew Melrose 1907.

Maclagan, P.J., 'Confucian Idealism' in *The East and the West*, Vol. VII (1909), pp. 453-463.

— *Chinese Religious Ideas: A Christian Valuation*, London, Student Christian Movement 1926.

McLoughlin, William G., *Revivals, Awakenings, and Reform: An Essay on Religion and Social Change in America, 1607-1977*, Chicago, University of Chicago Press 1978.

— *The American Evangelicals 1800-1900: An Anthology*, Gloucester, Mass, Peter Smith 1976.

Macnicol, Nichol, *Indian Theism*, London, Oxford University Press 1915.

Malden, R.H., *Foreign Missions: Being a Study of Some Principles and Methods in the Expansion of the Christian Church*, London, Longmans 1910.

Marchant, Leslie R., *British Protestant Christian Evangelists and the 1898 Reform Movement*, Perth, Occasional Paper No. 1, University of Western Australia Centre for East Asia Studies, October 1975.

— *The Harrowing of Hell in China: A Synoptic Study of the Role of Christian Evangelists in The Opening of Hunan Province*, Perth, Occasional Paper No.3, University of Western Australia Centre for East Asia Studies, December 1977.

Marsden, George M., *Fundamentalism and American Culture: The Shaping of Twentieth Century Evangelicalism*, New York, Oxford University Press 1980.

Martin, William A.P., *The Chinese, Their Education, Philosophy and Letters*, New York, Harper and Brothers 1881.

Marty, Martin E., *Pilgrims in their Own Land: 500 Years of Religion in America*, New York, Viking Penguin 1985.

— *Modern American Religion: the Irony of It All 1893-1919*, Chicago and London, University of Chicago Press 1986.

Marty, Martin E., and Greenspahn, Frederick E. (eds), *Pushing the Faith: Proselytism and Civility in a Pluralistic World*, New York, Crossroad Publishing Co. 1988.

Mather, Cotton, *Magnalia Christi Americana, or The Ecclesiastical History of New England*, edited and abridged by Raymond J.Cunningham, New York, Frederick Ungar Publishing 1970.

Matthews, Basil, *John R. Mott: World Citizen*, London, Student Christian Movement Press 1934.

Maurice, Frederick, *The Life of Frederick Denison Maurice Chiefly told in his own Letters*, 2 vols, London, Macmillan, Vol. I, 1883, Vol. II, 1884.

Maurice, Frederick Denison, *The Kingdom of Christ: or, Hints Respecting the Principles, Ordinances and Constitution of the Catholic Church in Letters to a Member of the Society of Friends*, London, Rivington 1842, the second and revised edition of *The Kingdom of Christ: or, Hints to a Quaker on the Principles, Ordinances and Constitution of the Catholic Church. In Letters to a Member of the Society of Friends*, London, Darton and Clark 1838. The 1842 edition was reprinted in two volumes by SCM Press in 1958 and by James Clarke in 1959.

— *The Religions of the World and their Relations to Christianity*, London, Macmillan 1847 (sixth edition 1886; first published in 1846).

— *The Patriarchs and Lawgivers of the Old Testament*, London, Macmillan 1851.

— *Theological Essays*, London, Macmillan 1853 (fifth edition 1891).

— *Sermons on the Sabbath Day on the Character of the Warrior and on the Interpretation of History*, Cambridge, Macmillan 1853.

— *The Doctrine of Sacrifice deduced from the Scriptures*, London, Macmillan 1854.

— *What is Revelation: a Series of Sermons on the Epiphany, to which are added Letters to a Student of Theology on the Bampton Lectures of Mr Mansel*, Cambridge, Macmillan 1859.

— *Dialogues Between a Clergyman and a Layman on Family Worship*, London, Macmillan, 1862.

— *Lectures on the Apocalypse*, London, Macmillan 1861.

— *The Kingdom of Heaven: A Course of Lectures on the Gospel of St Luke*, London, Macmillan 1864.

— *The Ground and Object of Hope for Mankind; Four Sermons Preached before the University of Cambridge* in November 1867, London, Macmillan 1868.

— *The Prayer Book and the Lord's Prayer*, London, Macmillan 1880.

Mead, Sidney E., *The Lively Experiment; The Shaping of Christianity in America*, New York, Harper and Row paperback 1976 (first published in 1963).

Medhurst, Walter Henry, *China: Its State and Prospects, with special reference to the Spread of the Gospel*, London, J. Snow 1838.

— *An Inquiry into the Proper Mode of Rendering the Word God in Translating the Sacred Scriptures into the Chinese Language*, Shanghai, printed at the Mission Press 1848.

Messmore, T. H., *The Land of Regrets*, Lucknow, Methodist Publishing House 1905.

— *Life of Edwin Wallace Parker: Missionary Bishop of Southern Asia*, New York, Eaton and Mains 1903.

Mews, Stuart (ed.), *Modern Religious Rebels*, London, Epworth Press 1993.

Michie, Alexander, *Missionaries in China*, London, Edward Stanford 1891.

Milton, John, *Collected Poetical Works*, Oxford Authors Series, London, Oxford University Press 1991.

Mitchell, J. Murray, *The Zend-Avesta and the Religion of the Parsis*, first published in *Present Day Tracts on the Non Christian Religions of the World*, London, Religious Tract Society 1887.

— *The Hindu Religion: A Sketch and a Contrast*, n.d.s.., reprinted in *Present Day Tracts on the Non Christian Religions of the World*, London, Religious Tract Society 1887.

— *Christianity and Ancient Paganism*, n.d.s., reprinted in *Present Day Tracts on the Non Christian Religions of the World*, London, Religious Tract Society 1887.

Moir, John S. and McIntire, C.T. (eds), *Canadian Protestant and Catholic Missions, 1820s–1960s: Historical essays in Honour of John Webster Grant*, New York and Bern, Peter Lang Inc. 1987.

Monier Williams, Monier, *Hinduism*, London, SPCK, ninth edition 1889.

Montgomery, H.H. (ed.), *Mankind and the Church: being an Attempt to Estimate the Contribution of Great Races to the Fulness of the Church of God by Seven Bishops*, London, Longmans, Green, and Co. 1907.

— 'Introduction: the Church of the Far West' in Montgomery, H.H., *Mankind and the Church: being an Attempt to Estimate the Contribution of Great Races to the Fulness of the Church of God by Seven Bishops*, London, Longmans Green, and Co. 1907.

Moody, Campbell N., *The Heathen Heart*, Edinburgh, Oliphant, Anderson, and Ferrier 1907.

— *The Saints of Formosa; Life and Worship in a Chinese Church*, Edinburgh, Oliphant, Anderson and Ferrier 1912.

— 'The Western Form of Christianity' in *The East and the West*, Vol. XI (1913), pp.121-148.

— *The Childhood of the Church*, London, George Allen and Unwin 1938.

Moscrop, Thomas, *The Kingdom Without Frontiers*, London, Robert Culley 1910.

Mott, John R., *The Evangelization of the World in this Generation*, New York, Student Volunteer Movement for Foreign Missions and London, Student Volunteer Missionary Union 1900.

— 'A World Missionary Conference' in *The East and the West*, Vol. VI (1908), pp. 368-85.

— *The Decisive Hour of Christian Missions*, New York, Student Volunteer Movement and London, Church Missionary Society, Student Volunteer Missionary Union and other missionary societies, 1910.

— *Five Decades and a Forward View*, New York, Harpers 1939.

Moule, Arthur Evans, *Four Hundred Millions: Chapters on China and the Chinese*, London, Seely Jackson, and Halliday 1871.

— *Half a Century in China: Recollections and Observations*, London, Hodder and Stoughton 1911.

Moulton, James Hope, 'Parseeism and Christianity' in *The East and the West*, Vol. V (1907), pp. 410-418.

— *Early Zoroastrianism*, Lectures delivered at Oxford and in London February to May, 1912 (The Hibbert Lectures for 1912), London, Williams and Norgate 1913.

— *Religions and Religion; A Study of the Science of Religion, Pure and Applied*, London, Charles H. Kelly 1913.

— 'The Parsis in India' in *The East and the West*, Vol. XIV (1916), pp. 266-277.

— *The Teaching of Zarathushtra: Eight Lectures and Addresses Delivered to Parsis in Bombay*, second edition, published by Pestonji Ardeshir Wadia, M.A., Hormazd Villa, Malabar Hill, Bombay 1917.

— *The Treasure of the Magi; A Study of Modern Zoroastrianism*, London, Oxford University Press 1917.

— 'The Word and the World' in *The International Review of Missions*, 1913, Vol. 2, pp. 83-95.

Moulton, W.F., *James Hope Moulton, by His Brother*, London, Epworth Press 1919.

Müller, F. Max (ed.), *The Sacred Books of the East*, 49 vols, Oxford, Oxford University Press 1879-1904.

Mueller, William A., *A History of the Southern Baptist Theological Seminary*, Nashville, Boardman Press 1959.

Muir, William, *Mohomet and Islam: A Sketch of the Prophet's Life from Original Sources and a Brief Outline of His Religion*, third edition, revised, London, Religious Tract Society 1895.

— *The Rise and Decline of Islam*, first published in *Present Day Tracts on the Non Christian Religions of the World*, London, Religious Tract Society 1887.

Munger, Theodore H., *Horace Bushnell, Preacher and Theologian*, London, James Clarke 1899.

Myklebust, O.G., *The Study of Missions in Theological Education*, 2 vols, Oslo, Egede Institutet 1955.

Mylne, L.G., *Missions to Hindus*, London, Longmans, Green, and Co. 1906.

— '"The Hidden Riches of Secret Places": The Possible Service of Hinduism to the Collective Thought of the Church' in Montgomery, H.H., (ed.), *Mankind and the Church: being an Attempt to Estimate the Contribution of Great Races to the Fulness of the Church of God by Seven Bishops*, London, Longmans, Green, and Co. 1907.

Nassau, Robert Hamill, *Fetichism in Africa; forty years' observation of native customs and superstitions*, New York, Charles Scribner's Sons and London, Duckworth 1904.

Naylor, Wilson S., *Daybreak in the Dark Continent*, New York, Laymen's Missionary Movement 1905.

Neill, Stephen, *The Christian Society*, London, Nisbet 1952.

— *A History of Christian Missions*, Harmondsworth, Penguin Books 1964.

— 'The Missionary Contribution to Ethology', in Greschat, H. J. and Jungraithmayr, H. (eds), *Wort und Religion: Kalima na Dini*, Stuttgart, Evangelischer Missionsverlag 1969.

— *A History of Christianity in India 1707-1858*, Cambridge, Cambridge University Press 1985.

Niebuhr, H. Richard, *The Kingdom of God in America*, New York, Harper and Row 1937.

Niesel, Wilhelm, *The Theology of Calvin*, London, Lutterworth Press 1956.

Noll, Mark A., *The History of Christianity in the United States and Canada*, Grand Rapids, Eerdmans 1992.

Norwood, Frederick A., *The Story of American Methodism*, Nashville, Abingdon 1974.

Noyes, Morgan Phelps, *Henry Sloane Coffin: The Man and His Ministry*, New York, Charles Scribner's Sons 1964.

Nuttall, E., 'The Special Influence which the African or Negro Race may Exercise on the Future Developments of Christianity' in Montgomery, H.H. (ed.), *Mankind and the Church: being an Attempt to Estimate the Contribution of Great Races to the Fulness of the Church of God by Seven Bishops*, London, Longmans, Green, and Co. 1907.

Nuttall, Geoffrey F., *Richard Baxter*, London, Nelson 1965.

Oldham, J.H., 'The Will of Christ regarding the Evangelisation of the World' in Paton, W. (ed.), *The Missionary Motive*, London, Student Christian Movement 1913.

— 'The World Missionary Conference' in *The East and the West*, Vol VII (1909), pp. 409-420.

Ohlinger, Franklin, 'How Far Should Christians be Required to Abandon Native Customs?', speech to the 1890 Missionary Conference in Shanghai, reprinted in

Lutz, Jessie Gregory (ed.), *Christian Missions in China: Evangelists of What?*, Boston, D.C.Heath 1965.

O'Connor, Daniel, *The Testimony of C.F. Andrews*, Madras, CLS 1974.

— *Gospel, Raj and Swaraj: The Missionary Years of C.F Andrews 1904-14*, Frankfurt am Main, Peter Lang Verlag 1990.

O'Neill, F.W.S. (ed.), *Dr. Isabel Mitchell of Manchuria*, London, James Clarke, second edition 1913.

— *The Call of the East: Sketches from the History of the Irish Mission to Manchuria, 1869-1919*, London, James Clarke 1919.

— *The Quest for God in China*, London, George Allen and Unwin 1925.

Osborn, Eric F., *The Philosophy of Clement of Alexandria*, Cambridge, Cambridge University Press 1957.

— *Justin Martyr*, Tubingen, J.C.B.Mohr (Paul Siebeck) 1973.

Oussoren, A.H., *William Carey, especially his Missionary Principles*, Leiden, no publisher indicated, 1945.

Outler, Albert (ed.), *John Wesley*, New York, Oxford University Press 1964.

— *Evangelism in the Wesleyan Spirit*, Nashville, Tidings 1971.

Padwick, Constance E., *Temple Gairdner of Cairo*, London, SPCK 1929.

Pailin, David A., *Attitudes to Other Religions: Comparative Religion in seventeenth and eighteenth century Britain*, Manchester, Manchester University Press 1984.

Pals, Daniel L., *The Victorian 'Lives' of Jesus*, San Antonio, Texas, Trinity University Press 1982.

Parrinder, Geoffrey, *The World's Living Religions*, London, Pan Books 1964.

Paterson, W.P., *The Rule of Faith, Being the Baird Lecture for 1905*, London, Hodder and Stoughton 1912.

— *The Nature of Religion: Gifford Lectures of 1924 and 1925*, London, Hodder and Stoughton 1928.

— *Conversion*, London, Hodder and Stoughton 1939.

Pathak, Sushil Madhava, *American Missionaries and Hinduism: A Study of their Contacts from 1813 to 1910*, Delhi, Munshiram Manoharlal 1967.

Paton, W. (ed.), *The Missionary Motive*, London, Student Christian Movement 1913.

Payne, Ernest A., *The Church Awakes: The Story of the Modern Missionary Movement*, London, Cargate Press 1942.

— 'The Development of Nonconformist Theological Education in the Nineteenth Century, with special reference to Regent's Park College' in E.A. Payne (ed.), *Studies in History and Religion*, London, Lutterworth Press 1942.

— *The Growth of the World Church: The story of the Modern Missionary Movement*, London, Macmillan 1955.

Philip, Robert, *The Life and Opinions of the Rev. William Milne, D.D.: Missionary to China*, London, John Snow 1840.

Phillips, Godfrey E., *The Outcastes' Hope*, London, Baptist Missionary Society 1912.

Phillips, Clifton Jackson, *Protestant America and the Pagan World: The First Half Century of the American Board of Commissioners for Foreign Missions*, Cambridge, Harvard University Press 1969.

Pierson, Arthur T., *The Crisis of Missions: or, the Voice out of the Cloud*, New York, Fleming H. Revell Co., 1886.

— *The Divine Enterprise of Missions*, New York, Baker and Taylor 1891.

— *The New Acts of the Apostles: or the Marvels of Modern Missions*, London, Nisbet 1898.

— *The Modern Missionary Century: Viewed as a Cycle of Divine Working*, New York, Fleming H. Revell Co. 1901.

Pierson, Delavan Leonard, *Arthur T.Pierson: A Spiritual Warrior, Mighty in the Scriptures, and a Leader of the Modern Missionary Crusade*, New York, Fleming H.Revell Co. 1912.

Piggin, Stuart, *Making Evangelical Missionaries 1789-1858: The Social Background, Motives and Training of British Protestant Missionaries to India*, Abingdon, Sutton Courtenay Press 1984.

Pinnock, Clark H., *A Wideness in God's Mercy: The Finality of Jesus Christ in a World of Religions*, Grand Rapids , Zondervan 1992.

Popkin, Richard H. (ed.), *Millenarianism and Messianism in English Literature and Thought 1650-1800*, Leiden, E.J. Brill 1988.

Porter, John F. and Wolf, William J., *Toward the Recovery of Unity: The Thought of Frederick Denison Maurice*, edited from his letters, with an introduction, New York, The Seabury Press 1968.

Powicke, Frederick J., *David Worthington Simon*, London, Hodder and Stoughton 1912.

Price, Lynne, *Interfaith Encounter and Dialogue: A Methodist Pilgrimage*, Frankfurt Am Main, Peter Lang Verlag 1989.

Price Evans, E.W., *Timothy Richard: A Narrative of Christian Enterprise and Statesmanship in China*, London, Carey Press 1945.

Prickett, Stephen, *Romanticism and Religion*, Cambridge, Cambridge University Press 1976.

Quistorp, H., *Calvin's Doctrine of the Last Things*, London, Lutterworth Press 1955

Rack, Henry D., *Reasonable Enthusiast: John Wesley and the Rise of Methodism*, London, Epworth Press 1989; second edition London, Epworth Press and Nashville Abingdon Press 1992.

Rajan, B., *Paradise Lost and the Seventeenth Century Reader*, London, Chatto and Windus 1947.

Ranson, Charles W., A Missionary Pilgrimage, Grand Rapids, Eerdmans 1988.

Reardon, Bernard M.G., *Religious Thought in the Victorian Age: A Survey from Coleridge to Gore*, London, Longmans 1980.

Reckett, Maurice B., *Maurice to Temple: A Century of the Social Movement in the Church of England*, London, Faber 1947.

Reynolds, Henry Robert, *Buddhism: A Comparison and a Contrast between Buddhism and Christianity*, reprinted in *Present Day Tracts on the Non Christian Religions of the World*, London, Religious Tract Society 1887.

Rice, W.A., *Crusaders of the Twentieth Century: or The Christian Mission and the Muslim, An Introduction to Work among Muhammedans*, published by the Author, Supplied by the Church Missionary Society, London 1910.

Richard, Timothy, *Conversion by the Million*, Shanghai, Christian Literature Society Book Depot 1907.

— *The New Testament of Higher Buddhism*, Edinburgh, T. and T. Clark 1910.

— *A Mission to Heaven. Being a Chinese Epic and Allegory, by Ch'iu Ch'ang Ch'un A.D. 1208-1288*, Shanghai, Christian Literature Society Book Depot 1913.

— *An Epistle to All Buddhists*, Shanghai, Christian Literature Society Book Depot 1916.

— *Forty Five Years in China: Reminiscences*, London, T. Fisher Unwin 1916.

Richardson, R.D., *Causes of the Present Conflict of Ideals in the Church of England*, London, John Murray 1927.

Richter, Julius, *A History of Missions in India*, Edinburgh, Oliphant Anderson and Ferrier 1908.

Robert, Dana L., '"The Crisis of Missions": Premillennial Mission Theory and the Origins of Independent Evangelical Missions' in Carpenter, Joel A., and Shenk, Wilbert R (eds), *Earthen Vessels: American Evangelicals and Foreign Missions, 1880-1980*, Grand Rapids, Eerdmans 1990.

Robinson, Charles H., *The Interpretation of the Character of Christ to Non- Christian Races: An Apology for Christian Missions*, London, Longmans, Green and Co. 1911.

— *Our Bounden Duty*, London, Longmans, Green and Co 1912.

— *History of Christian Missions*, Edinburgh, T. and T. Clark 1915.

Robinson, Florence, *Charles H. Robinson: A Record of Travel and Work*, London, SPG 1928.

Robson, John, *Hinduism and its Relations to Christianity* Edinburgh, Oliphant, Anderson and Ferrier 1893.

Rogers, Jack, *Presbyterian Creeds: A Guide to the Book of Confessions*, Philadelphia, Westminster Press 1985.

Rogers, J. Guinness, *Christ for the World: Sermons in Connection with the Centenary of the LMS*, London, Congregational Union 1894.

Rooy, Sidney H., *The Theology of Missions in the Puritan Tradition*, Delft, W.D. Meinema 1965.

Rouse, Ruth, 'The Missionary Motive in Protestant Missions during the last two centuries' in Paton, W. (ed.), *The Missionary Motive*, London, Student Christian Movement 1913.

Rouse, Ruth, and Neill, Stephen Charles (eds), *A History of the Ecumenical Movement 1517-1948*, London, SPCK 1954.

Rose, Ruth, *The World Student Christian Federation*, London, SCM Press 1948.

Rosenkranz, Gerhard, 'China und der Westen in der 2.Halfte des 19. und am Anfang des 20. Jahrhunderts' in Greschat, H.J. and Jungrithmayr, H., *Wort und Religion: Kalima na Dini*, Stuttgart, Evangelischer Missionsverlag 1969.

— *Die Christliche Mission: Geschichte und Theologie*, Munich, Chr.Kaiser Verlag 1977.

Rutman, Darrett B. (ed.), *The Great Awakening: Event and Exegesis*, New York, London, Sydney, and Toronto, John Wiley and Sons, Inc. 1970.

Sackett, F. Colyer, *Vision and Venture: Fifty Years in Hyderabad*, London, Cargate Press 1930.

Samartha, Stanley J., *One Christ, Many Religions*, Maryknoll NY, Orbis Books 1992.

Sampson, R.V., 'The Limits of Religious Thought: The Theological Controversy' in Appleman, Madden and Wolfe (eds), *1859: Entering an Age of Crisis*, Bloomington IN, Indiana University Press 1959.

Sandeen, Ernest R., *The Roots of Fundamentalism: British and American Millenarianism 1800-1930*, Chicago, University of Chicago Press 1970.

Satter, Gary, R., *God's Glory, Neighbor's Good: A Brief Introduction to the Life and Writings of August Hermann Francke* Chicago, Covenant Press 1982.

Schmidt, Martin, *The Young Wesley: Missionary and Theologian of Missions*, London, Epworth Press 1958.

Schmidt, William J. and Ouellette, Edward, *What Kind of Man: the Life of Henry Lieper Smith*, New York, Friendship Press 1986.

Schneder, D.B., 'Christian Education' in Dearing, John. L. (ed.), *The Christian Movement in Japan: Tenth Annual Issue*, Yokohama, The Conference of Federated Missions 1912.

Sedding, E.D., *Godfrey Callaway: Missionary in Kaffraria 1892-1942, His Life and Writings*, London, SPCK 1945.

Selbie, W.B., *The Life of Andrew Martin Fairbairn: First Principal of Mansfield College, Oxford*, London, Hodder and Stoughton 1914.

— *Congregationalism*, London, Methuen 1927.

Sell, Alan, 'An Englishman, an Irishman and a Scotsman' in *The Scottish Journal of Theology*, Vol. 38 (1985), pp.41-83.

— *The Great Debate: Calvinism, Arminianism and Salvation*, Grand Rapids MI, Baker Book House 1983

— *Aspects of Christian Integrity*, Louisville, Westminster/John Knox Press 1990.

Semmel, Bernard, *The Methodist Revolution*, London, Heinemann 1974.

Sharpe, Eric J., *Not to Destroy But to Fulfil: The Contribution of J. N. Farquhar to Protestant Missionary Thought in India before 1914*, Uppsala, Gleerup 1965.

— *The Theology of A.G.Hogg*, Madras, CLS 1974.

— *Comparative Religion: A History*, London, Duckworth 1975.

— *Faith Meets Faith: Some Christian Attitude to Hinduism in the Nineteenth and Twentieth Centuries*, London, SCM Press 1977.

— *The Universal Gita: Western Images of the Bhagavadgita*, London, Duckworth 1985.

Sharrock, John A., *Hinduism Ancient and Modern viewed in the light of the Incarnation*, London, Society for the Propagation of the Gospel in Foreign Parts 1913.

Shedd, Clarence P., *Two Centuries of Christian Student Movements*, New York, Association Press 1934.

Shedd, Mary Lewis, *The Measure of a Man: the Life of William Ambrose Shedd, Missionary to Persia*, New York, George H.Doran Co. 1922.

Shelley, Michael Thomas, *The Life and Thought of W.H.T. Gairdner 1873-1928: A Critical Evaluation of A Scholar Missionary to Islam*, Unpublished Ph.D. thesis, University of Birmingham 1988.

Shedd, William Ambrose, *Islam and the Oriental Churches: their Historical Relations*, New York, Young People's Missionary Movement 1908.

— 'The religious outlook in Persia, a coming crisis for Islam' in *The East and the West*, Vol VII (1909), pp. 257-266.

— 'The Vital Forces of Christianity and Islam – II' in *The International Review of Missions'*, 1913, Vol. 1, pp.279-293., reprinted in 'The Vital Forces of Christianity and Islam' in *The Vital Forces of Islam and Christianity; Six Studies by Missionaries to Moslems*,with an introduction by the Rev. S.M. Zwemer, and a concluding study by Professor Duncan B.Macdonald, London, Oxford University Press 1915.

Shivute, Tomas, *The Theology of Mission and Evangelism in the International Missionary Council from Edinburgh to New Delhi*, Helsinki, Missiologian Ekumeniikan Seura R.Y. 1980.

Simon, G.K., *Progress and Arrest of Islam in Sumatra*, London, New York, Marshall Brothers 1912.

— 'Pan-Islamism in Malaysia' in Wherry, E.M., Zwemer, S.M. and Mylrea, C.G. (eds), *Islam and Missions: Being Papers read at the Second Missionary Conference on Behalf of the Mohammedan World at Lucknow, January 23-28, 1911*, New York, Fleming H. Revell Co. 1911.

—— 'The Vital Forces of Christianity and Islam' in *The Vital Forces of Islam and Christianity; Six Studies by Missionaries to Moslems*, with an introduction by the Rev. S.M. Zwemer, and a concluding study by Professor Duncan B. Macdonald, London, Oxford University Press 1915.

Sjolinder, Rolf, *Presbyterian Reunion in Scotland: Its Background and its Development, 1907-1921* , Edinburgh, T. and T. Clark 1962.

Slater, T.E., *The Philosophy of Missions: A Present-Day Plea*, London, James Clarke 1882.

— *Studies in the Upanishads*, London and Madras, Christian Literature Society for India 1897.

— *Transmigration and Karma*, London and Madras, Christian Literature Society for India 1898.

— *The Higher Hinduism in Relation to Christianity: Certain Aspects of Hindu Thought from a Christian Standpoint*, London, Elliott Stock 1902.

— 'The Attitude of Educated Hindus to Christianity' in *The East and the West*, Vol. I (1903), pp. 254-53.

— *Missions and Sociology*, London, Elliott Stock 1908.

Slattery, Charles Lewis, *Alexander Viets Griswold Allen, 1841-1908*, London, Longmans, Green 1911.

Smith, Arthur Henderson, *Chinese Characteristics*, London, Kegan Paul, Trench Trubner 1892, New York, Fleming H. Revell Co., second edition, revised, with illustrations, 1894.

— *China in Convulsion*, 2 vols, Edinburgh, Oliphant, Anderson and Ferrier 1901, reprinted (facsimile) Shannon, Irish University Press 1972.

— *Rex Christus: An Outline Study of China*, New York, Macmillan 1903.

— *The Uplift of China*, London, Young People's Missionary Movement 1907.

Smith, H. Shelton (ed.), *Horace Bushnell*, New York, Oxford University Press 1965.

Smith, Stanley, *China from Within*, London, Marshall Brothers 1901.

— 'Chinese Philosophy and the truth as it is Jesus' in *The East and the West*, Vol. XI (1913), pp. 413-438 .

Smith, Timothy L., *Revivalism and Social Reform: American Protestantism on the Eve of the Civil War*, Nashville, Abingdon Press 1957.

Smith, Wilfred Cantwell, *Belief and History*, The Richard Lectures for 1974-1975, Charlottesville , Univerisity of Virginia Press 1977.
— *Faith and Belief*, Princeton, Princeton University Press 1979.
— *The Meaning and End of Religion*, London, SPCK 1978 (first published in 1962).
— *Towards a World Theology: Faith and the Comparative History of Religion*, London, Macmillan 1981.
— *What is Scripture?; A Comparative Approach*, London, SCM Press and Minneapolis, Fortress Press 1993.
Smyth, Newman, *The Religious Feelings*, New York, Charles Scribner's Sons 1877.
— *Old Faiths in New Light*, London, Ward, Lock and Co. and New York, Charles Scribner's Sons 1879.
— *The Orthodox Theology of Today*, New York, Charles Scribner's Sons 1881.
Soothill, W.E., *A Mission in China*, Edinburgh and London, Oliphant, Anderson and Ferrier 1907.
— *The Analects of Confucius: a new translation*, Edinburgh, Oliphant, Anderson, and Ferrier 1911.
— *Timothy Richard of China*, London, Seely, Service and Co. 1924.
— *China and the West: A Sketch of their Intercourse*, London, Oxford University Press 1925.
— *The Lotus of the Wonderful Law, or The Lotus Gospel: Saddharma Pundarika Sutra Miao-Fa Lien Hua ching*, Oxford, The Clarendon Press 1930.
Speer, Robert E., *Presbyterian Foreign Missions: An Account of the Foreign Missions of the Presbyterian Church in the USA*, New York, Fleming H. Revell Co. 1901.
— *Missionary Principles and Practice: A Discussion of Christian Missions and of Some Criticisms upon Them*, New York, Fleming H. Revell Co. 1902.
— *Christianity and the Nations*, New York, Fleming H. Revell Co. 1910.
— *The Finality of Christ*, New York, Fleming H. Revell Co. 1933.
— *The Light of the World: A Brief Comparative Study of Christianity and Non-Christian Religions*, West Medford, MA, The Central Committee on the United Study of Missions 1911.
— *The Gospel and the New World*, New York, Fleming H. Revell Co. 1919.
— *George Bowen of Bombay: A Memoir*, published privately, New York, The Missionary Review of the World 1938.
Stanley, Brian, *The Bible and the Flag: Protestant missions and British imperialism in the nineteenth and twentieth centuries*, Leicester, Apollos 1990.
— *The History of the Baptist Missionary Society 1792-1992*, Edinburgh, T. and T. Clark 1992.
Stobart, J.W.H., *Islam and its Founder*, London, SPCK 1876.
Stock, Eugene, *The History of the Church Missionary Society: Its Environment, its Men and its Work*, 3 vols, London, Church Missionary Society 1899.
— *The History of the Church Missionary Society: Supplementary Vol., The Fourth*, London, Church Missionary Society 1916.
Stoeffler, F. Ernest, *The Rise of Evangelical Pietism*, Leiden, E.J. Brill 1971.
Strong, Augustus Hopkins, *A Tour of the Missions: Observations and Conclusions*, Philadelphia, The Griffith and Rowland Press 1917.
Strong, Josiah, *Our Country: Its Possible Future and Its Present Crisis*, New York, Baker and Taylor 1885.

Strong, Thomas B., A *Manual of Theology*, London, A. & C. Black, second edition 1913.

Strong, William E., *The Story of the American Board: An Account of the First Hundred Years of the American Board of Commissioners for Foreign Missions*, Boston, The Pilgrim Press 1910.

Swan, George, 'The Mystical Life in Modern Islam' in John R. Mott (ed.), *The Moslem World of To-day*, London, Hodder and Stoughton 1925.

Sweet, Leonard I. (ed.), *The Evangelical Tradition in America*, Macon, GA, Mercer University Press 1984.

Taylor, Isaac, *The Natural History of Enthusiasm*, London, Holdsworth and Ball 1829.

Thangaraj, M. Thomas, 'Toward a Dialogical Theology of Mission' in Sheila Greeve Devaney (ed.), *Theology at the End of Modernity: Essays in Honour of Gordon D. Kaufman*, Philadelphia , Trinity Press International 1991.

Thelle, Notto R., *Buddhism and Christianity in Japan: From Conflict to Dialogue 1854–1899*, Honolulu, University of Hawaii Press 1987.

Thomas, M.M., *The Acknowledged Christ of the Indian Renaissance*, London, SCM Press 1969.

Thomas, Owen C. (ed.), *Attitudes Toward other Religions: Some Christian Interpretations*, London, SCM Press and New York, Harper 1969.

Thompson, David M., 'F.D. Maurice: Rebel Conservative' in Mews, Stuart (ed.), *Modern Religious Rebels*, London, Epworth Press 1993.

Thompson, Edgar W., *The Word of the Cross to Hindus*, London, Epworth Press 1933.

Thompson, Henry Paget, *Into All Lands: The History of the Society for the Propagation of the Gospel in Foreign Parts 1701–1750*, London, SPCK 1951.

— *Thomas Bray*, London, SPCK 1954.

Thompson, R.Wardlaw, *Griffith John: the Story of Fifty Years in China*, London, Religious Tract Society 1906.

Tiele, C.P., *Outlines of the History of Religion to the Spread of the Universal Religions*, sixth edition, London, Kegan Paul, Trench, Truber and Co. 1896.

Tinker, Hugh, *The Ordeal of Love: C.F.Andrews and India*, Delhi, Oxford University Press 1979.

Tisdall, W. St Clair, *The Sources of Islam: A Persian Treatise*, translated and abridged by Sir William Muir, Edinburgh, T. and T. Clark 1901.

— 'Islam in Persia' in Zwemer, S.M., Wherry E.M. and Barton, J.L. (eds), *The Mohammedan World of Today*, New York, Fleming H. Revell Co. 1906.

— *The Religion of the Crescent*, London, SPCK, third edition revised 1910.

— *Christianity and Other Faiths*, London, SPCK 1912.

Toon, Peter, *The Emergence of Hyper-Calvinism in English Nonconformity 1689–1765*, London, The Olive Tree 1967.

Trager, Helen G., *Burma through Alien Eyes: Missionary Views of the Burmese in the Nineteenth Century*, London, Asian Publishing House 1966.

Tucker, Henry St George, *The History of the Episcopal Church in Japan*, New York, Charles Scribner's Sons 1938.

Turner J.G., *The Pioneer Missionary: The Life of the Revd Nathaniel Turner*, London, Wesleyan Conference Office 1872.

Tuveson, Ernest Lee, *Redeemer Nation: The Idea of America's Millennial Role*, Chicago, University of Chicago Press 1968.

Vallée, Gerard, *Mouvement Oecuménique et Religions non-Chrétiennes: un débat oecuménique sur la recontre interreligieuse de Tambaram à Uppsala (1938-1968)*, Tournai, Desclée et Cie. 1975.

Varg, Paul A., *Missionaries, Chinese and Diplomats: The American Protestant Missionary Movement in China, 1890-1952*, Princeton, Princeton University Press 1958.

— 'The Missionary Response to the Nationalist Revolution' in Fairbank, John K. (ed.), *The Missionary Enterprise in China and America*, Cambridge, Harvard University Press 1974.

Van Den Berg, Johannes, *Constrained by Jesus' Love: An Inquiry into the Motives of the Missionary Awakening in Great Britain in the Period between 1698 and 1815*, Kampen, J.H. Kok 1956.

Van Lin, J.J.E., *Protestantse Theologie der Godsdiensten van Edinburgh naar Tambaram 1910-1938*, Assen, Van Gorcum and Comp, B.V. 1974.

Vaughan, James, *The Trident, the Crescent and the Cross: A View of the Religious History of India during the Hindu, Buddhist and Christian Periods*, London, Longmans Green and Co. 1876.

Veitch, Robert, *The Christian of Today: A Brief Description of his Thought and Life*, London, James Clarke 1909.

Verkuyl, J., *Inleiding in de Nieuwere Zendingswetanschap*, Kampen, J.H. Kok 1976;. ET *Contemporary Missiology: An Introduction*, Grand Rapids, Eerdmans 1978.

Verkuyl, J., *Gedenken and Verwachten*, Kampen, J. H. Kok 1983.

Verstraelen, F.J. (ed.), *Oecumenische Inleiding in de Missiologie, Teksten en Conteksten van het Wereld-Christendom*, Kampen, J. H. Kok 1988.

Vidler, A.R., *The Theology of F.D. Maurice*, London, SCM Press 1948.

— *F.D. Maurice and Company*, London, SCM Press 1966.

— *The Church in an Age of Revolution: 1789 to the Present Day*, Harmondsworth, Penguin 1969.

Wacker, Grant, 'Second Thoughts on the Great Commission: Liberal Protestants and Foreign Missions 1890-1940' in Carpenter, Joel A., and Shenk, Wilbert R. (eds), *Earthen Vessels: American Evangelicals and Foreign Missions, 1880-1980*, Grand Rapids, Eerdmans 1990.

Wadsworth, Kenneth W., *Yorkshire United Independent College: Two Hundred Years of Training for the Christian Ministry by the Congregational Churches of Yorkshire*, London, Independent Press 1954.

Walls, Andrew F., 'A Christian Experiment: the Early Sierra Leone Colony' in Cuming, G.J. (ed.), *The Mission of the Church and the Propagation of the Faith*, Cambridge, Cambridge University Press 1970.

— 'The American Dimension in the History of the Missionary Movement' in Carpenter, Joel A., and Shenk, Wilbert R (eds), *Earthen Vessels: American Evangelicals and Foreign Missions, 1880-1980*, Grand Rapids, Eerdmans 1990.

Walshe, W. Gilbert, 'Islam in China' in Zwemer, S.M., Wherry, E.M. and Barton, James L. (eds), *The Mohammedan World of Today*, New York, Fleming H. Revell Co. 1906.

— 'Buddhism *versus* Christianity: a challenge' in *The East and the West*, Vol. IV (1906), pp. 70-81.

Ward, W.R., *The Protestant Evangelical Awakening*, Cambridge, Cambridge University Press 1992.

Wardlaw Ralph, *The Contemplation of Heathen Idolatry an Excitement to Missionary Zeal*, London, The Missionary Society 1818.

— *Systematic Theology*, Edinburgh, A. and C. Black 1856-1857.

Warneck, Gustav, *Outline of a History of Protestant Missions from the Reformation to the Present Time: A Contribution to Church History*, translated by Thomas Smith, Edinburgh, James Gemmell 1884.

— *Modern Missions and Culture: Their Mutual Relations*, translated by Thomas Smith, Edinburgh, James Gemmell, second edition 1888.

Warneck, Johannes, *The Living Forces of the Gospel: Experiences of a Missionary in Animistic Heathendom*, translated by Neil Buchanan from the third German edition, Edinburgh, Oliphant Anderson and Farrier 1909 (American edition, *The Living Christ and a Dying Heathendom*, 1909).

Watson, Andrew, *The American Mission in Egypt*, New York, United Presbyterian Board of Publications 1898, second edition 1904.

— 'Islam in Egypt' in Zwemer, S.M., Wherry, E.M. and Barton, James L. (eds), *The Mohammedan World of Today*, New York, Fleming H. Revell Co. 1906.

Watson, Charles R., 'Statistical and Comparative Survey of Islam in Africa' in Zwemer, S.M., Wherry E.M., and Barton, James L. (eds), *The Mohammedan World of Today*, New York, Fleming H. Revell Co. 1906.

Weber, Hans-Reudi, *Asia and the Ecumenical Movement 1895-1961*, London, SCM Press 1966.

Weber, Timothy P., *Living in the Shadow of the Second Coming: American Premillenarianism 1875-1925*, New York, Oxford University Press 1979.

Weddle, David L. *The Law as Gospel: Theology and Reform in the Theology of Charles F.Finney*, New York, Peter Lang 1985.

Wehrle, Edmund S., *Britain, China, and the Anti-missionary Riots 1891-1900*, Minneapolis, University of Minnesota Press 1966.

Weisberger, Bernard A., *They Gathered at the River: The Story of the Great Revivalists and their impact upon Religion in America*, Boston and Toronto, Little, Brown and Company 1958.

Weitbrecht, H.U., 'The New Islam in India' in Zwemer, S.M., Wherry E.M. and Barton, James L. (eds), *The Mohammedan World of Today*, New York, Fleming H. Revell Co. 1906.

— 'Reform Movements in India' in Wherry, E.M., Zwemer, S.M. and Mylrea, C.G. (eds), *Islam and Missions. Being Papers read at the Second Missionary Conference on Behalf of the Mohammedan World at Lucknow, January 23-28, 1911*, New York, Fleming H. Revell Co. 1911.

Welbon, Guy Richard, *The Buddhist Nirvana and its Western Interpreters*, Chicago, University of Chicago Press 1968.

Welch, Claude, *Protestant Thought in the Nineteenth Century: Vol.1, 1799-1870* and *Vol. 2, 1870-1914*, New Haven, Yale University Press 1972 and 1985.

Westcott, Arthur, *Life and Letters of Brooke Foss Westcott*, 2 vols, London, Macmillan 1903.

Westcott, Brooke Foss, *The Gospel of the Resurrection: Thoughts on its Relation to Reason and History*, London, Macmillan 1966.

— *On Some Points in the Religious Office of the Universities*, London, Macmillan 1873.
— 'Origen and the Beginnings of Christian Philosophy' in *Contemporary Review*, May 1879.
— *The Revelation of the Risen Lord*, London, Macmillan 1881.
— *Commentary on the Gospel According to St John*, London, Macmillan 1887.
— *Christus Consummator: Some Aspects of the Work and Person of Christ in Relation to Modern Thought*, London, Macmillan 1886.
— *Social Aspects of Christianity*, London, Macmillan 1887.
— *The Gospel of Life: Thoughts Introductory to the Study of Christian Doctrine*, first edition 1892, second edition, London, Macmillan 1895.
— *Christian Aspects of Life*, London, Macmillan 1897.
— *Lessons from Work*, London, Macmillan 1901.
— *Words of Faith and Hope*, London, Macmillan 1902.
Westcott, G.H., *Kabir and the Kabir Panth*, Cawnpore, Christ Church Mission Press 1907.
Wheeler, W.R., *A Man Sent from God: A Biography of R.E. Speer*, New York 1956.
Wherry, Elwood Morris, 'Islam in North India' in Zwemer, S.M., Wherry E.M. and Barton, James L. (eds), *The Mohammedan World of Today*, New York, Fleming H. Revell Co. 1906.
— *Islam and Christianity in India and the Far East*, New York, Fleming H. Revell Co. 1907.
Wherry, E.M., Zwemer, S.M., and Mylrea, C.G. (eds), *Islam and Missions. Being Papers read at the Second Missionary Conference on Behalf of the Mohammedan World at Lucknow, January 23-28, 1911*, New York, Fleming H. Revell Co. 1911.
Wherry, John, 'Historical Summary of the Different Versions of the Scriptures' in *Records of the General Conference of the Protestant Missionaries of China, May 7-20, 1890*, Shanghai, American Presbyterian Mission Press 1890.
Whitehead, George, 'The Chins of Burma' in *The East and the West*, Vol. VI (1908), pp. 361-85.
Whitehead, Henry, 'The Future of Indian Christianity' in *The East and the West*, Vol. III (1905), pp. 9-21.
— *The Village Gods of India*, London, Oxford University Press and Calcutta, The Association Press 1916.
Whittemore, Robert C., *The Transformation of New England Theology*, New York, Peter Lang 1987.
Whyte, Bob, *Unfinished Encounter: China and Christianity*, London, Collins Fount Paperbacks 1988.
Wilberforce, Samuel (ed.), *The Journals and Letters of Henry Martyn 1781-1812*, 2 vols, London, R.B. Seeley and W. Burnside 1837.
Williamson, Henry R., *British Baptists in China 1845-1952*, London, Carey Kingsgate Press 1957.
Wilson, Horace Hayman, *Essays and Lectures chiefly on the Religion of the Hindus*, collected and edited by Dr Reinhold Rost in 2 vols, London, Trubner 1862.
Wilson, Samuel Graham, *Persian Life and Customs*, New York, Fleming H. Revell Co. 1899.
— *Modern Movements Among Muslims*, New York, Fleming H. Revell Co. 1916.
Winston, W.R., *Four Years in Upper Burma* London, C.H.Kelly 1892.

Wolf, William J., 'Frederick Denison Maurice' in WOLF, William J. (ed), *The Spirit of Anglicanism*, Wilton CT, Morehouse-Barlow 1979.

Wood, Herbert G., *Henry T. Hodgkin: A Memoir*, London, Student Christian Movement Press 1937.

— *Frederick Denison Maurice*, Cambridge, Cambridge University Press 1950.

World Missionary Conference, 1910, *Report of Commission I, Carrying the Gospel to all the Non Christian World*, published for the World Missionary Conference by Oliphant, Anderson and Ferrier, Edinburgh and London 1910.

World Missionary Conference, 1910, *Report of Commission II, The Church in the Mission Field*, published for the World Missionary Conference by Oliphant, Anderson and Ferrier, Edinburgh and London 1910.

World Missionary Conference, 1910, *Report of Commission IV, The Missionary Message in Relation to Non-Christian Religions*, published for the World Missionary Conference by Oliphant, Anderson and Ferrier, Edinburgh and London 1910.

World Missionary Conference, 1910, *Report of Commission V, The Preparation of Missionaries*, published for the World Missionary Conference by Oliphant, Anderson and Ferrier, Edinburgh and London 1910.

World Missionary Conference, 1910, *The History and Records of the Conference, together with Addresses Delivered at the Evening Meetings*, published for the World Missionary Conference by Oliphant, Anderson and Ferrier, Edinburgh and London 1910.

World Missionary Conference, 1910, *Monthly News Sheet, October 1909–May 1910*, published by the World Missionary Conference Office, Edinburgh.

World Missionary Conference, 1910, *Official Handbook*, published by the World Missionary Conference Office, Edinburgh.

Yates, T.E., 'Edinburgh Revisited' in *The Churchman*, Vol. 94, No. 2, 1980, pp. 145–155.

Young, David, *F.D. Maurice and Unitarianism*, Oxford, Clarendon Press 1992.

Young, George A., *The Living Christ in Modern China*, London, Carey Kingsgate Press 1947.

Young, J.C., 'Islam in Arabia' in Zwemer, S.M., Wherry E.M. and Barton, James L. (eds), *The Mohammedan World of Today*, New York, Fleming H. Revell Co. 1906.

Zaehner, R.C., *The Dawn and Twilight of Zoroastrianism*, London, Weidenfield and Nicolson 1961.

Zwemer, Samuel M., *The Moslem Doctrine of God*, Boston, New York, American Tract Society 1905.

— 'Political Changes in Arabia' in Wherry, E.M., Zwemer, S.M., and Mylrea, C.G. (eds), *Islam and Missions. Being Papers read at the Second Missionary Conference on Behalf of the Mohammedan World at Lucknow, January 23–28, 1911*, New York, Fleming H. Revell Co. 1911.

— *The Origin of Religion*, London, Marshall Morgan and Scott 1935.

Zwemer, S.M., Wherry, E.M., and Barton, James L. (eds), *The Mohammedan World of Today, Being Papers read at the First Missionary Conference on Behalf of the Mohammedan World held at Cairo, April 4–9th, 1906*, New York, Fleming H. Revell Co. 1906.

Index